RESURRECTING
JESUS

RESURRECTING

JESUS

THE EARLIEST CHRISTIAN TRADITION
AND ITS INTERPRETERS

DALE C. ALLISON JR.

t&t clark

NEW YORK • LONDON

T & T Clark International, Madison Square Park, 15 East 26th Street, New York, NY 10010

T & T Clark International, The Tower Building, 11 York Road, London SE1 7NX

T & T Clark International is a Continuum imprint.

Cover design: Brenda Klinger

Library of Congress Cataloging-in-Publication Data

Allison, Dale C.
  Resurrecting Jesus : the earliest Christian tradition and its interpreters / Dale Allison.
      p. cm.
  Includes bibliographical references and indexes.
  ISBN 0-567-02900-X (hardcover) – ISBN 0-567-02910-7 (pbk.)
      1. Jesus Christ – History of doctrines – Early church, ca. 30–60. 2. Jesus Christ – Historicity. I. Title.
  BT198.A45 2005
  232.9′08 – dc22

                                                                    2005008016

Printed in the United States of America

05   06   07   08   09   10   10   9   8   7   6   5   4   3   2   1

CONTENTS

For Mike Neth
θεραπεία ζωῆς φιλία

PREFACE

I NEVER INTENDED to write this book, by which I mean yet another book on Jesus; but since the publication of *Jesus of Nazareth: Millenarian Prophet* (1998), and largely because of it, I have repeatedly been asked to write and lecture further on the subject. Having often obliged, I now find that I have in hand more than enough material for a second collection — whence this volume. Insofar as *Resurrecting Jesus* repeatedly concerns itself with matters central to its predecessor, it serves as a sort of sequel. It allows me to clarify, qualify, and expand upon things said earlier. This volume is also, like its predecessor, a collection of fragments, for I have, regarding Jesus, no "theory of everything."

The first chapter is a new edition of "The Secularizing of Jesus," which Richard Vinson solicited for an issue of *Perspectives in Religious Studies* dedicated to the historical Jesus. It first appeared there (*PRSt* 27, no. 1 [2000]: 135–51) and reappears here with only modest reworking.

Chapter 3, "The Problem of Gehenna," with its attendant excursus on Shelley, grew out of an invitation to address the Historical Jesus Section of the Society of Biblical Literature Annual Meeting in Toronto in November of 2002. I should like to thank the convener, Mark Allan Powell, as well as Richard Horsley, with whom I shared the platform, for an enjoyable session. In its present form the chapter was also usefully discussed at the Catholic Biblical Association's annual meeting in Halifax, Nova Scotia (August 2004). I am grateful to Rick Murphy and Greg Sterling for asking me to join their continuing seminar on the historical Jesus. A much-abbreviated version of the first section of the chapter is printed in "Jesus and Gehenna," in *Testimony and Interpretation: Early Christology in Its Judeo-Hellenistic Milieu. Studies in Honour of Petr Pokorný* (ed. Jiří Mrázek and Jan Roskovec; London: T & T Clark, 2004), 114–24.

Chapter 4, "Apocalyptic, Polemic, Apologetic," is a revised and much-expanded version of a lecture delivered at a symposium on "Apocalypticism, Anti-Semitism and the Historical Jesus: Subtexts in Criticism," which the University of Toronto hosted in March of 2003.

My thanks go to John Kloppenborg, who organized the symposium and invited me, as well as the other participants — Bill Arnal, Paula Fredriksen, Amy-Jill Levine, John Marshall, and Bob Miller — for a pleasant and profitable day. The much-shorter, original lecture can be found in *Apocalypticism, Anti-Semitism and the Historical Jesus: Subtexts in Criticism* (ed. John S. Kloppenborg; London: T & T Clark, 2004), 98–110. Like the first chapter, this one features cannibalistic scholarship: it is not exegetical or reconstructive but rather sustains itself by digesting the work of others.

"Torah, Urzeit, Endzeit," chapter 5, had its beginnings in a lecture for the Annual Symposium on Exegetical Theology, Concordia Seminary, Fort Wayne, Indiana (January 2001). Appreciation goes to Charles Gieschen for the invitation and to the school for its hospitality. The original lecture appears as "Jesus and the Torah," in *The Law in Holy Scripture* (ed. Charles A. Gieschen; St. Louis: Concordia, 2004), 75–95. The present chapter 5, however, represents a thorough rewrite that has become twice as long as that earlier attempt to sort and refine my conflicting thoughts on Jesus and the Torah.

The final and much the longest chapter, "Resurrecting Jesus," and its two accompanying excursuses have not heretofore seen the light of day. I composed them as the basis for the Zarley Lectures at North Park University, Chicago, Illinois (November 2003). Scot McKnight of North Park and the sponsor of the annual lectureship, Kermit Zarley, warmly welcomed me and saw to it that I had a thoroughly delightful time. One might imagine that the topic of Jesus' resurrection, of perennial interest and incessant discussion, has been exhausted, so that there is nothing new or interesting left to say. I hope, however, that I have brought enough new material to bear on the issues so as to fortify against the fatigue that so often comes from reading academic essays on issues long and thoroughly debated.

The only chapter that reflects nothing save my own interest is the second, "The Problem of Audience." I wrote it because, following 9/11, my wife did not want me to fly from Pittsburgh to Denver for the annual Society of Biblical Literature Meeting in 2001, and I had to find something to do on a couple of very long train rides. It has not been published before.

In addition to those named in the previous paragraphs, I am indebted to my wife, Kristine Allison; my colleague, John Burgess; my former teacher, the late W. D. Davies; and my friends Tim Crosby, Chris Kettler, Joel Marcus, and Mike Neth — all of whom read various portions of the manuscript. I am also beholden to my secretary, Kathy Anderson, for her help every day with a thousand things; to Anita Johnson and the staff of the Barbour Library at Pittsburgh Theological Seminary for their assistance in obtaining through interlibrary loan numerous books and articles, many hard to obtain; to my childhood friend, Bob Harrington, for so many conversations over the years on so many topics that I no longer know which ideas were originally mine and which his; and to Jeff Gibson, who invited me to lead an online discussion of earlier versions of chapters 1–3 for X-Talk, March 25–April 5, 2003. Responding to multiple questions every day was hard work, but the result has been, if I may say so, a better book.

As I write, it is Easter Sunday. This morning the pastor asked us to imagine the Easter story without the resurrection. Suppose, he said, that the gardener — in response to Mary Magdalene's despondent remark, "They have taken away my Lord, and I do not know where they have laid him" — told the woman exactly where the body now lay, and that she, retrieving it, dragged it back to its proper resting place. The pastor's point, I take it, was that whereas we could tow a dead Jesus wherever we will, a resurrected Jesus may resist us, for he is not passive but active and so lives beyond our control: he must be encountered, not directed. Although my first thought was of Achilles dragging Hector before the walls of Troy, soon enough I began to think about this book and to wonder to what extent I am dragging texts this way and that before the walls of the guild, dragging texts that, because dead, cannot go where they wish but must instead suffer to go wherever I lead them. I have no answer, except to confess that, despite my best efforts and intentions, I am sure that I have done violence — how often I do not know — to the texts and to the history behind them. My sincere hope, however, is that, like Jesus in this morning's sermon, the texts are not really dead, that they yet speak, and that sometimes I have indeed heard what they, and those responsible for them, may still wish to say.

DALE C. ALLISON JR.
April 11, 2004

ONE

SECULARIZING JESUS

It's one thing not to see the forest for the trees, but then to go on to deny the reality of the forest is a more serious matter.
— Paul Weiss

Writing bad history is pretty easy.
— J. H. Hexter

A DEFECTIVE TYPOLOGY

Modern times have, according to the current wisdom, witnessed three quests for the historical Jesus.[1] The first was the German endeavor of the nineteenth century, which Albert Schweitzer so ingeniously and memorably reported.[2] The second was the "new quest." Inaugurated by Ernst Käsemann's famous 1953 lecture in Marburg,[3] it was carried on by some of Rudolf Bultmann's students and admirers, who went a different direction than did the great scholar. The so-called "third quest," christened

---

1. Cf. Marcus J. Borg, *Jesus in Contemporary Scholarship* (Valley Forge, PA: Trinity, 1994), ix ("a third quest is underway"); C. E. Braaten, "Jesus and the Church: An Essay on Ecclesial Hermeneutics," *ExAud* 10 (1994): 59–71; Luke Timothy Johnson, *The Real Jesus: The Misguided Quest for the Historical Jesus and the Truth of the Traditional Gospels* (San Francisco: Harper Collins, 1996), 4; Gerd Theissen and Annette Merz, *The Historical Jesus: A Comprehensive Guide* (Minneapolis: Fortress, 1998), 10–11; David Wenham, *Paul: Follower of Jesus or Founder of Christianity?* (Grand Rapids: Eerdmans, 1995), 17, 21; etc. The terminology has become so widespread that some current catalogues of seminaries and graduate schools of religion describe courses on the historical Jesus in terms of the three quests.

2. Albert Schweitzer, *The Quest of the Historical Jesus* (Minneapolis: Fortress, 2001 [ET of *Geschichte der Leben-Jesu-Forschung*, 1906, 1913, 1950]).

3. ET, "The Problem of the Historical Jesus," in Ernst Käsemann, *Essays on New Testament Themes* (SBT 41; London: SCM, 1964), 15–47.

such by Tom Wright,[4] is the name many now bestow upon the labors of the present moment.[5]

It is unfortunate that this oft-repeated, neat triadic division of an important area of research has now established itself in surveys and textbooks, for in its simplicity it is simplistic: it obscures far more than it illumines.[6] One fundamental failing is that the scheme dismisses with silence the period between the "first quest" and the "new quest." The inescapable implication is that nothing much, or nothing much of importance, was then going on. Some chroniclers of Jesus research have even affirmed, to my incredulity, that the interval in question can indeed be called the period of "no quest."[7] One avows that, between 1906 and 1953, the acids of form criticism, a new theology that isolated faith from history, and a growing awareness that Christians typically look down the well of history only to see their own reflected faces — all conspired to create "a period where the general optimism of discovering a relevant historical Jesus behind the portraits of the Gospels, an optimism which fueled the 'Old Quest,' was lost."[8] In line with this, Tom Wright says that during the first half of our century there was a "moratorium" upon questing for Jesus.[9]

---

4. See Stephen Neil and N. T. Wright, *The Interpretation of the New Testament 1861–1986* (New York: Oxford, 1988), 397–98, as well as Wright's article, "Jesus, Quest for the Historical," in *ABD* 3:796–802.

5. For Wright himself, however, the "new quest" continues beside the "third quest"; see "Jesus, Quest for the Historical." According to him, the works of the Jesus Seminar, Burton Mack, and F. Gerald Downing, although they appeared after the publication of books that Wright assigns to the third quest, really belong to the new quest. Contrast Johnson, *The Real Jesus*, 4, who in contradiction to Wright declares: "The Jesus Seminar thinks of itself as the vanguard of the 'Third Quest.'"

6. After publishing an earlier edition of this chapter, I was gratified to run across the similar doubts of Stanley E. Porter, *The Criteria for Authenticity in Historical-Jesus Research: Previous Discussion and New Proposals* (JSNTSup 191; Sheffield: Sheffield Academic Press, 2000), 28–59; Graham Stanton, *The Gospels and Jesus* (2nd ed.; Oxford: Oxford University Press, 2002), 165; and Walter Weaver, *The Historical Jesus in the Twentieth Century, 1900–1950* (Harrisburg, PA: Trinity, 1999), xi–xii.

7. John Reumann, "Jesus and Christology," in *The New Testament and Its Modern Interpreters* (ed. Eldon Jay Epp and George W. MacRae; Philadelphia: Fortress, 1989), 502. Reumann, who finds "no quest" misleading (see 504), implies that it was commonly used in the 1950s and 1960s.

8. Gregory A. Boyd, *Cynic Sage or Son of God?* (Wheaton: Victor, 1995), 37–40. Already W. Barnes Tatum, *In Quest of Jesus: A Guidebook* (Atlanta: John Knox, 1982), 71–74, uses "no quest" for the period 1906–53. On 78, however, he deconstructs his own category: "Not all scholars suspended the effort to rediscover the Jesus of history. An interest in Jesus as a historical figure continued without interruption, especially within British and American scholarship." See further his discussion of A. M. Hunter, T. W. Manson, Vincent Taylor, C. H. Dodd, and Shirley Jackson Case on 85–89.

9. N. T. Wright, "Jesus, Quest for the Historical," 798; he does, however, refer to "some writers" who ignored the moratorium and names T. W. Manson. Cf. his statement in Stephen

This is just not true.[10] Anyone can properly assess this claim by walking into a decent theological library and looking at the shelves. If one accepts the testimony of one's own eyeballs, and if the expectation is that, after Schweitzer and before Käsemann, times were dull, and New Testament scholars had given up questing for Jesus, one will be dumbfounded. As a sample of what one might find in such a library, I subjoin at the end of this essay a list of some of the relevant books that appeared between 1906 and 1953. With the understandable exception of a couple of years during World War I (1914, 1915), only one year (1919) did not, according to my cursory researches, witness a new book on Jesus by an academic. Moreover, few of the names on my list will be unfamiliar to anyone who has done serious work on the New Testament, so it was scarcely only marginal scholars who were engaged in the quest for Jesus: we are not talking about second-stringers on the sidelines of New Testament studies. It was, on the contrary, not only a rather large but more importantly a fairly august body of scholars that was unaware of the supposed moratorium upon questing for Jesus.

The inevitable inference from my list of titles, that questing for Jesus was alive and well in the decades after Schweitzer, is more than confirmed by the hundreds upon hundreds of articles then written on the historical Jesus[11] as well as by the surveys of research that come from that time. In 1925 Shirley Jackson Case remarked that "writers upon the life of Jesus who have taken up seriously the task of carrying forward the work of historical criticism, in its application to the study of the life of Jesus, have performed some significant tasks during the past quarter century."[12] A decade later E. F. Scott could write, "Nothing is more remarkable in the literature of our time than the endless procession

---

Neil and Tom Wright, *Interpretation of the New Testament*, 380: "Actual historical enquiry after Jesus has not reached an impasse: it could not have, since until a few years ago it had hardly started."

10. Cf. Porter, *Criteria*, 36–47, and Reumann, "Jesus and Christology," 504. According to Werner Georg Kümmel, *Dreißig Jahre Jesusforschung (1950–1980)* (ed. Helmut Merklein; BBB 60; Bonn: P. Hanstein, 1985), 1, although "Jesusforschung in German Protestant theology strongly retreated after the end of WWI, of course it in no way was completely given up."

11. For the journals see Bruce M. Metzger, *Index to Periodical Literature on Christ and the Gospels* (NTTS 6; Leiden: Brill, 1966).

12. Shirley Jackson Case, "The Life of Jesus during the Last Quarter-Century," *JR* 5 (1925): 568. He was referring primarily to attempts to understand Jesus in the light of source criticism, that is, the priority of Mark and the existence of Q. On 575 he writes: "Historical inquiry still has much to do upon the subject of the life and teaching of Jesus."

of Lives of Jesus." He was not just offering a generalization about popular books: "All the time it [our critical picture of Jesus] is taking more
definite shape. Each of these writers [Joseph Klausner, J. Warschauer,
Shirley Jackson Case, Rudolf Bultmann, B. W. Bacon], and the list might
be greatly extended, has brought at least one aspect of the history into
fuller relief. All the discussion...is clearly the way towards something
like a true judgment."[13] C. C. McCown spoke in 1940 of "evidence
of progress" in connection with the study of the historical Jesus in the
period since Schweitzer, and he was optimistic about its continuation:
"The new critical techniques and the new philosophical points of view
which now prevail provide new means for solving the [old] problems in
their new forms. Progress is possible."[14] Two years later D. T. Rowlinson wrote about "The Continuing Quest of the Historical Jesus" and
how it had been "carried forward in recent years."[15] And in 1950 A. M.
Hunter published *The Work and Words of Jesus*,[16] a popular digest of
the allegedly nonexistent quest.

SOURCES OF CONFUSION

In view of the manifest facts, what has nurtured our ignorance of the
past and led to the injudicious generalization, now so often voiced, that
the period after Bultmann was devoid of any quest, or at least little
concerned with such? Beyond the unfortunate fact that too many now
neglect to read old books because they evidently imagine that new books
have rendered them obsolete, two factors especially suggest themselves.
One is that, largely because of source criticism, and to a lesser extent
because of form criticism, even conservative English scholarship came to

---

13. E. F. Scott, "Recent Lives of Jesus," *HTR* 27 (1934): 1, 2.

14. Chester Carlton McCown, *The Search for the Real Jesus: A Century of Historical
Study* (New York: C. Scribner's Sons, 1940), 281–84, 287.

15. D. T. Rowlinson, "The Continuing Quest of the Historical Jesus," in *New Testament
Studies: Critical Essays in New Testament Interpretation, with Special Reference to the Meaning
and Words of Jesus* (ed. Edwin Prince Booth; New York: Abingdon-Cokesbury, 1942), 42–69,
esp. 43.

16. A. M. Hunter, *The Work and Words of Jesus* (Philadelphia: Westminster, 1950). On
14 Hunter expressed his own confidence about the direction of research: "The problems are
not all solved, but many of them are; and the scholarship of the last two or three decades, by its
patient research on many aspects of Christ's Life and Teaching, has gradually been accumulating
materials for a worthier and truer portrait."

the conclusion that "a biography of Jesus cannot be provided."[17] Thus, at midcentury A. M. Hunter thought that one of the chief features of books on Jesus over the previous fifty years was that they had largely ceased to aspire to be biographies in any traditional sense.[18] Perhaps some have misunderstood the circumstance that academics quit writing biographies of Jesus to mean that they had given up writing about his words and deeds. But the one thing is not the other. The dearth of traditional lives, the abandoning of the Markan framework, and the refusal to map the development of Jesus' self-consciousness cannot be equated with an eclipse of studies on the historical Jesus. The first half of our century was, then, not the period of "no quest" but of "no biography."[19]

Another factor, and probably the weightier one behind the erroneous judgment that there was a period without questing, is that so many now, regardless of their own theological stance, see the past through Bultmannian eyes. This is a mistake, although it is understandable. Rudolf Bultmann must be reckoned the foremost New Testament scholar of his century. At no time, however, were he and his students the only players in the theological game, even in Germany, and it took several decades before the majority of those abroad began to feel the full impact of his skeptical form-critical investigations.[20] Before the 1950s many serious researches in the English-speaking world still regarded form criticism as a "tempest in a teapot."[21] Beyond that, it was only in the late 1950s that Bultmann's theological views began to net numerous converts outside his

---

17. Edwyn Hoskyns and Noel Davey, *The Riddle of the New Testament* (London: Faber & Faber, 1931), 171.

18. A. M. Hunter, "The Life of Christ in the Twentieth Century," *ExpTim* 61 (1950): 235. Cf. Vincent Taylor, "Is It Possible to Write a Life of Christ?" *ExpTim* 52 (1941): 60: "The veritable spate of attempts to delineate the Life of Jesus has given place to a slow trickle." In an article with the same title in *ExpTim* 53 (1942): 248–51, T. W. Manson argues that we cannot produce a biography of Jesus, not even a complete narrative of the ministry, only "some kind of outline of the events that led up to the Cross" (251).

19. So rightly John Reumann, "Lives of Jesus during the Great Quest for the Historical Jesus," *Indian Journal of Theology* 23 (1974): 33–59.

20. For English resistance see esp. Vincent Taylor, "Is It Possible to Write a Life of Christ?" 59–62.

21. D. T. Rowlinson, "The Continuing Quest of the Historical Jesus," 61, quoting Mary Ely Lyman. English-speaking presentations of form criticism generally eschewed what they saw as the unnecessary "skepticism" of German practitioners. See, e.g., Burton Scott Easton, *The Gospel before the Gospels* (New York: C. Scribner's Sons, 1928); Frederick C. Grant, *The Growth of the Gospels* (Nashville: Abingdon, 1933); Donald W. Riddle, *The Gospels: Their Origin and Growth* (Chicago: University of Chicago Press, 1939); Vincent Taylor, *The Formation of the Gospel Tradition* (London: Macmillan, 1933). The skepticism famously expressed by R. H. Lightfoot in *History and Interpretation in the Gospels* (New York: Harper & Row, n.d. [1935]) was exceptional.

own country.[22] Hugh Anderson could still write, in 1964, "The big guns of the new theological movement on the Continent certainly caused no immediate tottering at the foundations of British historical-critical scholarship. It would be safe to say that there has been hardly less distrust among British than among American scholars in these last forty years toward the 'crisis theology' or the 'theology of the Word.' "[23]

In 1959 W. D. Davies entitled his inaugural lecture at Union Theological Seminary in New York "A Quest to Be Resumed in New Testament Studies."[24] The subject was the historical Jesus. By that time a significant number of Anglo-American scholars had indeed begun to notice that the quest had been or was being given up in certain important quarters: skepticism was settling in everywhere. Timidity in reconstructing the life and teachings of Jesus was, however, a quite recent development. As the late Professor Davies once told me, no one in Britain or America would have delivered a lecture with a title like his, which implied that the quest had been interrupted, in 1920 or 1930 or 1940 or even 1950. Only after midcentury did the sort of confidence in the Jesus tradition that T. W. Manson and Vincent Taylor enjoyed begin to look uncritical to just about everybody everywhere. Only in the 1950s did English-speaking scholars come to appreciate fully that the Gospels reflect above all the manifold interests of early Christians, and that those interests were far removed from those of modern historians. Concurrent with this realization, and spurred on by the growing influence of Paul Tillich and translations of the writings of Bultmann and Karl Barth, doubt as to the theological relevance of the historical Jesus began to assail many. It is no coincidence that Martin Kähler's *Der sogennante historische Jesus und der geschichtliche, biblische Christus* — the original German edition

---

22. Allan Barr, "Bultmann's Estimate of Jesus," *SJT* 7 (1954): 337–52, is in part a straightforward presentation of what Bultmann thought, the assumption being that mid-1950s readers of the *Scottish Journal of Theology* still had no clear idea on the subject. One should remember that *Kerygma and Myth: A Theological Debate*, with Bultmann's essay, "New Testament and Mythology," was translated into English only in 1953 (London: SPCK), and that *The History of the Synoptic Tradition* (New York: Harper & Row, 1963) did not show up in English until ten years later. The work of Martin Dibelius, *From Tradition to Gospel* (London: Ivor Nicholson & Watson, 1934), had appeared much earlier in English, but it was not so skeptical, and it had no sharp theological edge.

23. Hugh Anderson, *Jesus and Christian Origins: A Commentary on Modern Viewpoints* (New York: Oxford University Press, 1964), 78.

24. W. D. Davies, *Christian Origins and Judaism* (London: Darton, Longman & Todd, 1962), 1–17.

was first published in the nineteenth century — found no English translator until the 1960s.[25] And yet, by then, by the time the influence of the
old British-anchored conservatism was waning, the so-called new quest
had already roused itself, so there was never a period of "no quest."

All this was at one time not esoteric knowledge. In 1959, James M.
Robinson began his book, *A New Quest of the Historical Jesus*, by
referring to the obvious, to "the relatively untroubled and uninterrupted quest of the historical Jesus going on in French and Anglo-Saxon
scholarship."[26] As Robinson knew, the quest had been discontinued in
Bultmannian quarters, not elsewhere.[27] So the "new quest" that he hailed
was quite self-consciously a specifically post-Bultmannian undertaking,
constructed upon "a critical restudy of the Bultmannian position by his
leading pupils."[28] Some retrospects, however, now often leave the mistaken impression that the evolution of the Bultmannian school — which
was a thoroughly German Protestant phenomenon that interacted hardly
at all with Catholics or even with Protestants who did not write in German — can be equated with the course of New Testament studies after
World War I. Such revisionist history has led the unwary astray, to the
defective inference that since the old quest ended with Schweitzer and
the "new quest" started with Käsemann, in between no one could have
been searching for the historical Jesus.

Perhaps some are enamored of the current typology because, despite the post-Schweitzerian labors outside of Bultmann's circle, they
condescendingly presume that nothing of lasting value or interest was
produced. Robinson for one eschewed the "relatively untroubled and
uninterrupted quest of the historical Jesus" in France and the English-
speaking world, as well as the products of the old-style German questers

---

25. Martin Kähler, *The So-Called Historical Jesus and the Historic, Biblical Christ* (Philadelphia: Fortress, 1964). In the preface to this edition Paul Tillich remarks on the "Kähler
revival that is taking place." The book was reissued in Germany in 1953; before then, it had
gathered little attention.

26. James M. Robinson, *A New Quest of the Historical Jesus* (SBT 25; London: SCM,
1959), 9. On the French quest through Maurice Goguel, see Jean G. H. Hoffmann, *Les vies de
Jésus et le Jésus de l'histoire* (ASNU 17; Paris: Messageries Evangeliques, 1947).

27. Cf. Otto A. Piper, "Das Problem des Lebens Jesu seit Schweitzer," in *Verbum Dei
manet in Aeternum: Eine Festschrift für Prof. D. Otto Schmitz* (ed. Werner Foerster; Witten:
Luther, 1953), 73, where Piper remarks on the great disparity between the number of German
books on Jesus and those written in English.

28. Robinson, *New Quest*, 12. Others have given "new quest" a much broader sense,
so that it includes all the critical study of Jesus after Käsemann's lecture. This only confuses
matters.

such as Joachim Jeremias and Ethelbert Stauffer. For Robinson, the important studies had not and were not going to come from anywhere but dialogue with Bultmann. A similar sort of judgment is, even if unintended, seemingly implicit in the current typology of the quest, according to which there was, despite the plethora of literature, no real quest for fifty years.

But maybe Robinson was wrong and had things backward, and I at least am tempted to think of the current typology as a miscarriage of scholarship and an expression of ingratitude. For if anything failed it was the so-called "new quest." Despite being the middle member of the current typology, its productivity, comparatively speaking, was short-lived and hardly far-reaching.[29] Non-Bultmannian circles, by contrast, had produced, before Käsemann's oft-cited lecture, at least four crucial works of enduring value — Jeremias's *Die Gleichnisse Jesu*, his *Die Abendmahlsworte Jesu*, Dodd's *The Parables of the Kingdom*, and T. W. Manson's *The Sayings of Jesus*.[30] Manson's book still "is consulted regularly for its commentary value"[31] — a rare feat for a volume written over fifty years ago. As for the contributions of Jeremias and Dodd on the parables, they remain as important as anything else on the same subject that has since come along. Norman Perrin had it right when he observed, of Jeremias's *The Parables of Jesus*, "Today it is the essential starting point for parable research. It represents a watershed in the development of the discussion, taking up into itself...the work of the two most important previous contributors, Adolf Jülicher and C. H. Dodd."[32] This sentence, written in 1975, has not been undone by a quarter century of further study. One could equally say that Jeremias's

---

29. Perhaps its greatest legacy is its emphasis that Jesus' conduct was the context for his speech: this redressed an earlier imbalance, an almost exclusive focus on Jesus' words. See esp. Ernst Fuchs, *Studies of the Historical Jesus* (SBT 42; London: SCM, 1964). Particularly important to subsequent discussion has been the significance of Jesus' table fellowship.

30. Joachim Jeremias *Die Gleichnisse Jesu* (Zurich: Zwingli, 1947); ET, *The Parables of Jesus* (3rd ed.; New York: C. Scribner's Sons, 1972), follows the text of the 8th German edition (1970); idem, *Die Abendmahlsworte Jesu* (2nd ed.; Göttingen: Vandenhoeck & Ruprecht, 1949); ET, *The Eucharistic Words of Jesus* (London: SCM, 1966), is based upon the 3rd German edition (1960); C. H. Dodd, *The Parables of the Kingdom* (rev. ed.; New York: C. Scribner's Sons, 1961); T. W. Manson, *The Sayings of Jesus* (London: SCM, 1949).

31. Alan Kirk, *The Composition of the Sayings Source: Genre, Synchrony, and Wisdom Redaction in Q* (NovTSup 91; Leiden: Brill, 1998), 11n47.

32. Norman Perrin, *Jesus and the Language of the Kingdom: Symbol and Metaphor in New Testament Interpretation* (Philadelphia: Fortress, 1976), 92. Although some classify Perrin himself as a new quester, a careful reading of his work shows the dominating influence and discussion partner to be, despite much disagreement, Jeremias.

work on the Last Supper took up into itself the important contributions that came before it, and that it has become foundational for all subsequent studies of its subject, even for those featuring quite different conclusions.

There is more to my argument, I should like to emphasize, than just getting our own history down right and recognizing, out of courtesy and for the sake of humility, our debt to predecessors, whom we should hold in higher esteem.[33] Those who fail to honor their elders and to learn the exegetical past condemn themselves to repeating that past, to needlessly recapitulating older debates unknowingly.[34] Many now suffer from exegetical amnesia, so that without embarrassment they stake out old claims as though they were new. If, moreover, we can cast aside the strange notion that New Testament scholarship must, like the hard sciences, ever progress onward and upward, then there is no reason to doubt that some of the older books about Jesus might get us as close or closer to the truth than some of the more recent ones. The passing of time does not always and everywhere carry us closer to the truth.

CHARACTERIZING MORE RECENT WORK

If the typology I am criticizing falsely characterizes the first half of the twentieth century and has misled people into believing that during that time scholars did not produce instructive literature on Jesus, it also distorts the facts for the period between 1950 and 1980, the latter being the date one chronicler offers for the approximate birth date of the so-called third quest.[35] This is the period in which the "new quest" of Bultmann's students is located. But much else — I would say much else of more

---

33. Although we should also not pretend that some not meriting our esteem were questing for Jesus. There was, e.g., an Aryan quest for the historical Jesus, carried on by supporters of the Nazis, such as Georg Bertram, Walter Grundmann, and Rudolf Meyer. See Marshall D. Johnson, "Power Politics and New Testament Scholarship in the National Socialist Period," *JES* 23 (1986): 1–24; Paul M. Head, "The Nazi Quest for an Aryan Jesus," *Journal for the Study of the Historical Jesus [JSHJ]* 2 (2002): 55–89.

34. For some illustrations of the phenomenon, see my article, "Forgetting the Past," *Downside Review* 120 (2002): 255–70. Appropriately enough, my complaint itself should occasion déjà vu; already Schweitzer wrote that most writers on Jesus "have no suspicion that they are merely repeating an experiment which has often been made before" (*Quest*, 10).

35. See James H. Charlesworth, "Christian Origins and Jesus Research," in *Jesus' Jewishness: Exploring Jesus' Place in Early Judaism* (ed. J. H. Charlesworth; New York: Crossroad, 1991), 78: "Jesus research" — Charlesworth's name for what has gone on since the waning of the "new quest" — "commenced around 1980."

importance — must also be located here.[36] Concurrent with and more or less independent of the much ballyhooed but disappointing new quest, and before 1980, publishers distributed the books in the second list subjoined to this chapter (which, like the first list, makes no pretense to being exhaustive). The 1950s, 1960s, and 1970s also saw, outside the circle of Bultmann, the publication of important New Testament Christologies that had much to say about Jesus — those of Oscar Cullmann (1957), Ferdinand Hahn (1963), and R. H. Fuller (1965) were perhaps the most prominent — as well as three significant German theologies of the New Testament that open with substantial accounts of the historical Jesus — those of Werner Kümmel (1969), Leonard Goppelt (1975), and Jeremias (1971, unfinished).[37] And then there were the articles that, as a glance at the appropriate volumes of *Elenchus* reveals, were not lacking. Writing in 1973, Gustav Aulén observed: "Literature on Jesus is now experiencing prosperity."[38] That was over thirty years ago, before many now tell us the supposed third quest started. Aulén was correct.[39] So one wonders why 1980 marks some sort of watershed, and why so much of the literature I have cited should be excluded from the standard typology and so undeservedly shoved into oblivion. In my judgment, what merits oblivion is rather the typology itself.

What supposedly sets the so-called third quest apart from previous quests or from pre-1980 work?[40] Although several traits have been

---

36. Unless one just puts everything between 1953 and 1980 under the rubric, "new quest." But that is to throw away the original definition.

37. Oscar Cullmann, *Die Christologie des Neuen Testaments* (Tübingen: Mohr Siebeck, 1957); ET, *The Christology of the New Testament* (rev. ed.; NTL; Philadelphia: Westminster, 1959); Ferdinand Hahn, *Christologische Hoheitstitel: Ihre Geschichte im frühen Christentum* (FRLANT 83; Göttingen: Vandenhoeck & Ruprecht, 1963); ET (in shortened form), *The Titles of Jesus in Christology: Their History in Early Christianity* (New York: World, 1969); R. H. Fuller, *The Foundations of New Testament Christology* (New York: Scribner, 1965); Werner Kümmel, *Die Theologie des Neuen Testaments* (Göttingen: Vandenhoeck & Ruprecht, 1973); ET, *The Theology of the New Testament* (Nashville: Abingdon, 1973); Leonard Goppelt, *Theologie des Neuen Testaments* (Göttingen: Vandenhoeck & Ruprecht, 1975); ET, *Theology of the New Testament*, vol. 1, *The Ministry of Jesus in Its Theological Significance* (Grand Rapids: Eerdmans, 1981); Joachim Jeremias, *Neutestamentliche Theologie*, vol. 1, *Die Verkündigung Jesu* (Gütersloh: Gerd Mohn, 1971); ET, *New Testament Theology: The Proclamation of Jesus* (New York: C. Scribner's Sons, 1971).

38. Gustav Aulén, *Jesus in Contemporary Historical Research* (ET of 2nd Swedish edition, 1974; Philadelphia: Fortress, 1976), 21. Also see the surveys in Kümmel, *Dreißig Jahre Jesusforschung.*

39. See further Etienne Trocmé, *Jesus as Seen by His Contemporaries* (Philadelphia: Westminster, 1973), 1–13.

40. With what follows cf. Porter, *Criteria*, 51–55, who rightly rejects the notion that recent work marks a new epoch in research.

nominated, none much helps us with this question. The attention to extracanonical sources — so important for some current questers — is sometimes said to stamp the "third quest." But many questers nowadays, including E. P. Sanders and John Meier, stick pretty much to the canonical sources.[41] And in any case the discussion and evaluation of traditions about Jesus in extrabiblical materials is scarcely a post new quest phenomenon.[42] The discovery of the Nag Hammadi documents, including the *Gospel of Thomas*, has certainly much enlarged our interest in the noncanonical sources for Jesus, but such interest was hardly born around 1980.[43]

The struggle against apocalyptic eschatology — against the belief that Jesus thought the eschatological consummation to be at hand, a struggle that characterizes the work of John Dominic Crossan, Marcus Borg, and Burton Mack — might also be thought a singular feature of the current discussion.[44] But this too is nothing new under the sun. Crossan and the others have just taken the baton from earlier scholars such as C. H. Dodd, T. Francis Glasson, and John A. T. Robinson, and it is not obvious that the former have had more influence in our day than the latter had in theirs.[45]

Nor can one find anything much original in the way of method. Tom Wright has indeed urged on the contrary that the third quest sets itself apart by an emphasis upon Jesus' Jewish context and Jewish character.[46] Certainly great attention is being paid to Jesus' place within Judaism. But this emphasis is part and parcel of a much larger tendency to attempt to interpret all of earliest Christianity as a Jewish phenomenon.[47] Thus

---

41. E. P. Sanders, *Jesus and Judaism* (Philadelphia: Fortress, 1985); John Meier, *A Marginal Jew*, 3 vols. (New York: Doubleday, 1991–2001).

42. See Alfred Resch, *Agrapha: Aussercanonische Evangelienfragmente* (Leipzig: J. C. Hinrichs, 1889); James H. Ropes, *Die Sprüche Jesu, die in den kanonischen Evangelien nicht überliefert sind* (Leipzig: J. C. Hinrichs, 1896); E. Klostermann, *Apocrypha II: Evangelien* (Bonn: Marcus & Weber, 1929); J. Jeremias, *Unbekannte Jesuworte* (Gütersloh: Mohn, 1948).

43. For some of the literature on *Thomas* published before 1980 see Craig A. Evans, *Life of Jesus Research: An Annotated Bibliography* (rev. ed.; NTTS 24; Leiden: Brill, 1996), 260–70.

44. So Marcus Borg, *Jesus in Contemporary Scholarship*, 7–9.

45. Dodd, *Parables*; T. Francis Glasson, *His Appearing and His Kingdom: The Christian Hope in the Light of Its History* (London: Epworth, 1953); *Jesus and the End of the World* (Glasgow: Saint Andrew, 1980); John A. T. Robinson, *Jesus and His Coming: The Emergence of a Doctrine* (New York: Abingdon, 1957). See further my comments in *The Apocalyptic Jesus: A Debate* (ed. Robert J. Miller; Santa Rosa, CA: Polebridge, 2001), 113–14.

46. Wright, "Jesus, Quest for the Historical," 800.

47. See W. D. Davies, *Christian Engagements with Judaism* (Valley Forge, PA: Trinity, 1999), 1–12.

present scholarship also highlights Paul's Jewish context and character. In addition, the focus upon Jesus the Jew marks not a novel movement but only an intensification of a line of investigation that we can trace back ultimately to the likes of John Lightfoot (1602–75) and Johann Salomo Semler (1725–91), as well as to some of the deistic critics of Christianity, such as Lord Bolingbroke.[48] Their orientation was then carried forward by Jewish and Christian scholars such as Adolf Schlatter (1852–1938), Gustav Dalman (1855–1941), Joseph Klausner (1874–1958), and Joachim Jeremias (1900–1982). They were all, in one way or another, trying to find Jesus by looking for Judaism.[49] Having abandoned many of the old stereotypes, we may now regard their use of Jewish sources as less sophisticated than our own; and Christian scholars may further — with the guilt of the Holocaust hanging over our heads and the modern spirit of relativism urging us not to reckon our religion better than any another — see more continuity with Judaism, whereas our predecessors saw less. Yet we are not walking down some new, hitherto-undiscovered path but rather just going further down the old one.[50]

Birger Pearson has suggested that the alleged third quest is "distinguishable from the first two quests in claiming to lack *any* theological agenda."[51] One can concur that Ed Sanders does not wear his theo-

---

48. See, e.g., *The Works of the Late Right Honourable Henry St. John, Lord Viscount Bolingbroke* (London: D. Mallet, 1754), 4:305: "Christ himself was, in outward appearance, a Jew. He ordered his disciples, and the crowds that followed him, to observe and do whatever the scribes and Pharisees, who sat in the chair of Moses, should direct. He only warned them against the examples that these men gave, who did not practise what they taught.... He was a better Jew than they, and he exhorted others to be the same. It is true that he commissioned his apostles to teach and baptize all nations, when he gave them his last instructions. But he meaned no more, perhaps, by all nations, than the Jews dispersed into all nations, since he had before that time forbid them to go into the ways of the Gentiles, and into the cities of the Samaritans."

49. One can without difficulty find pleas in the older literature for putting Jesus in his Jewish context; see, e.g., McCown, *Search for the Real Jesus*, 124–43. Albert Schweitzer himself, we should recall, reconstructed his own Jesus by reading him within the context of Jewish apocalyptic expectation.

50. Upon which many Jewish scholars in addition to Klausner have also traveled. See the helpful overview of Donald Hagner, *The Jewish Reclamation of Jesus* (Grand Rapids: Zondervan, 1984).

51. Birger Pearson, "The Gospel according to the Jesus Seminar," *Religion* 25 (1995): 320; online: http://id-www.ucsb.edu/fscf/library/pearson/seminar/home.html. Cf. the more nuanced statements of Craig Evans, *Jesus and His Contemporaries: Comparative Studies* (AGJU 25; Leiden: Brill, 1995), 10–12; and Jörg Frey, "Der historische Jesus und der Christus der Evangelien," in *Der historische Jesus: Tendenzen und Perspektiven der gegenwärtigen Forschung* (ed. Jens Schröter and Ralph Brucker; Berlin: de Gruyter, 2002), 287–88. Closer to the truth is

logical convictions, whatever they may or may not be, on his sleeve, and that John Meier has been trying to write about Jesus with minimal interference from his Catholic convictions. And yet it is at the same time true that neither scholar is in this respect obviously representative. Marcus Borg and Tom Wright, for example, are forthright about their theological interests, which largely drive their projects, as they freely acknowledge.[52] And surely no one would contend that those who do write with significant theological interest are thereby excluded from the purported "third quest." It is, furthermore, evident that some we might think of as having no theological agenda are partly motivated by an animus against traditional Christian doctrine, which is in reality just another sort of theological agenda.[53] The trite truth is that none of us is without philosophical bias or theological interest when we sit down to study Christian origins, so the alleged lack thereof seems a dubious criterion for classifying scholars who quest for Jesus.[54]

One is not even sure that the volume of production of the so-called third quest, a circumstance so much remarked upon, means much. There just happen to be, for reasons that have nothing to do with historical Jesus research, more New Testament scholars and publishers of what those scholars produce than in the past. This is why books on Paul have also multiplied of late. So too have books on Hebrews, and even books on James and Jude, not to mention *Festschriften*. The guild is much larger than in the past, more young scholars are seeking tenure in a publish-or-perish academy than in the past, and there are many more publishers and journals — including now *The Journal for the Study of the Historical Jesus* — than in the past, so there are naturally more books and articles on Jesus, as on everything else, than in the past.[55] No surprise there.

Tom Holmén, "A Theologically Disinterested Quest? On the Origins of the 'Third Quest' for the Historical Jesus," *ST* 55 (2000): 175–97.

52. Marcus Borg, *Jesus: A New Vision: Spirit, Culture, and the Life of Discipleship* (San Francisco: Harper, 1987); N. T. Wright, *Jesus and the Victory of God* (Minneapolis: Fortress, 1996).

53. See, e.g., Robert W. Funk, *Honest to Jesus: Jesus for a New Millennium* (San Francisco: HarperSanFrancisco, 1996). Cf. the comments of Frey, "Historische Jesus," 288–89.

54. One difference from the past may be that discussions of how theology and history are related to each other are less common than they once were. Still, some so-called third questers, such as Tom, are much concerned with this problem.

55. Charlesworth, "Christian Origins and Jesus Research," 82–83, does not mention this crucial factor when trying to explain the recent "explosion of interest" in the historical Jesus. If volume of publication is our criterion, then there has been an explosion of interest in just about every subject under the sun — Shakespeare, true crime, angels, barbed wire collecting, whatever. One should keep in mind how the attendance, number of lecturers, and quantity of

Maybe the major difference between what is going on now and what went on earlier is that today, for whatever reason, some of the books about Jesus have garnered unexpected publicity. Maybe the quest has changed less than its marketing.

I am no antagonist of innovation, but I do not wish to trumpet it where it does not exist. The assertion that we have recently embarked upon a third quest may be partly due, one suspects, to chronological snobbery, to the ever-present temptation, instinctive in a technologically driven world, where new is always improved, to flatter ourselves and bestow upon our own age exaggerated significance, to imagine the contemporary to be of more moment than it is. Is it not a jolly good thing to believe that the promise of past scholarly endeavors has been realized today in our own work? John Dominic Crossan, observing that "in Indo-European folklore, the third quest is always the successful one," thinks its transfer to Jesus research implies that our day is witnessing "the final and victorious" quest, "as in all good fairy-stories."[56] We are the champions.

We often cannot read our place in history very well, and out of vanity we may be tempted to enlarge and isolate that place and so misinterpret its meaning. A friend recently sent me an article explaining how science and religion are finally finding common ground. I read an article much like it the year before, and another the year before that; and if the truth be known, the public has been treated to the same fare every year for the past one hundred. In like manner, there is less new about the current quest than its promoters seem willing to concede: all the excitement is overdone. It is refreshing that John Riches, whose work Wright slots into the third quest, characterizes himself as addressing the issues of Reimarus.[57] There is something to be said for Colin Brown's analysis: "Plus ça change, plus c'est la même chose. For connections between current research and what has gone before appear to continue without interruption."[58] It would be a wholesome antidote to our self-aggrandizement if more of us would dust off some of the old books and

publishers at the annual meetings of the Society of Biblical Literature have mushroomed over the last three decades. Talking to someone who attended SBL meetings in 1965 is revelatory.

56. John Dominic Crossan, "What Victory? What God? A Review Debate with N. T. Wright on *Jesus and the Victory of God*," *SJT* 50 (1997): 346–47.

57. John Riches, *Jesus and the Transformation of Judaism* (New York: Seabury, 1982), 1–19.

58. Colin Brown, "Quest of the Historical Jesus," in *DJG*, 337.

actually read them instead of trusting our chroniclers who typically do little more than make sweeping generalizations about the supposed three quests, generalizations that self-servingly make our own time and place the great τέλος of questing history. Do we really need to raise our own self-esteem by lowering our esteem for the dead?

Although there is indeed a contemporary quest for Jesus, it is not manifest that there is really so much new or distinctive about it. Certainly the current search is not a thing easily fenced off from its predecessors; it has no characteristic method; and it has no body of shared conclusions — differences in opinion being now almost as common and ineradicable as differences in taste.[59] Contemporary work also has no common set of historiographical or theological presuppositions. And trying to locate its beginning is like trying to find the origins of modern science: the ever-present continuity with and debt to the past make convenient divisions into neat periods suspect. Given that there are always trends in research no less than in fashion, I am sure one could draw a line at 1990, find some common features in the books written about Jesus since then, and declare that we have actually entered a fourth quest. This would be an unprofitable exercise, but no more so than much of our current map-making.

Sometimes history does suggest that we divide it in a particular way. Judaism was truly different after 70 CE than it was before, just as the American South was truly different after the Civil War than it was before. At other times, however, the lines we pencil over history for our own practical ends, lines that beguile because they are convenient, are also delusive. More often than not the patterns we espy in history are, like Providence, less than evident. They are then phantasms conjured by our seemingly innate desire to bring order out of chaos, in our case the chaos that is the discipline of New Testament studies. But sometimes everything is a maze; and what if, in these pluralistic times — when researchers are less often the members of schools,[60] when there are no more dominating figures such as Dodd or Bultmann to lead the rest of us, when most are

---

59. Jürgen Roloff, *Jesusforschung am Ausgang des 20. Jahrhunderts* (Bayerische Akademie der Wissenschaften Philosophisch-historische Klasse Sitzungsberichte; Munich: Bayerischen Akademie der Wissenschaften, 1988), 20, even opines that the distance now between much American and Continental scholarship is such that it is no longer possible to speak of "a unified direction for research."

60. I will admit, however, that the Jesus Seminar has functioned as a sort of "school," despite the disagreements among its members.

is antiquated and needs to be questioned. That some of those features appear in books decades old[69] whereas others are absent from significant current works[70] should do more than give us pause. Our lists look tendentious because they are. They are products of misguided ingenuity and a failure to see that the age of the easy generalization and of the authentic consensus is over.[71]

My own conviction is that it has not been very helpful to divide all the post-Schweitzerian activities into chronological segments or different quests. It is much more useful to lay aside the diachronic and take up the synchronic, to abandon periodization for a typology that allows us to classify a book, whether from the 1920s or the 1990s, with those akin to it. Perhaps we might lump together the books that present Jesus as a liberal social reformer, or those that present him as a forerunner of Christian orthodoxy, or those that reconstruct him as an eschatological Jewish prophet, or those that liken him to a Cynic-like sage, or those that regard him as having been a political revolutionary, and so on.[72] Even here, however, our generalizing descriptions would inevitably hide as much as they reveal; so if we ever imagine them to be anything other than cartoon histories for neophytes, then we deceive ourselves, and the truth is not in us.

---

openness and a special interest in the social sciences characterize current studies. In fairness to Telford, he is reporting what others have claimed, and he himself goes on to observe that in view of the lack of uniformity in methodologies and results it would nonetheless "be unwise to claim at this stage" that the trends observed constitute the basis of a "third quest." "Time will tell," he writes (60).

69. Points (b)–(e) marked much of the earlier conservative British tradition, and (f) is equally true of the works of Jeremias and Rudolf Otto. Telford himself wonders whether (d) and (g) adequately typify present work. He further expresses some reservations about even some of the trends he does detect.

70. Point (a), for instance, does not apply to the writings of Marcus Borg or Tom Wright. Perhaps the most justified of the various generalizations is (g), for there is indeed an interdisciplinary openness among many. My own work, for instance, interprets Jesus with the aid of parallels from millenarian movements, and Crossan uses data from studies of peasants and of Mediterranean society to fill out his reconstruction. One must keep in mind, however, that many important scholars, including Meier, Sanders, and Wright, continue to work on Jesus without calling upon much interdisciplinary assistance.

71. On some of the misuses of alleged consensuses, see John C. Poirier, "On the Use of Consensus in Historical Jesus Studies," *TZ* 56 (2000): 97–107.

72. For instances of this sort of typology, see Irvin W. Batdorf, "Interpreting Jesus since Bultmann: Selected Paradigms and their Hermeneutic Matrix," in *Society of Biblical Literature 1984 Seminar Papers* (ed. Kent H. Richards; Chico, CA: Scholars Press, 1984), 187–215; John Wick Bowman, *Which Jesus?* (Philadelphia: Westminster, 1970); and Reumann, "Great Quest."

THE SECULARIZING OF JESUS

Having said all this, I should like, before closing, to remark upon an increasingly common hermeneutical move in the literature on Jesus. Its advent does not undo the promiscuous diversity of the present, for it is far from being ubiquitous, but its appearance in scattered works does perhaps say something about the present moment. I advert to what I call the secularizing of Jesus. By this I do not mean that nonreligious publishers now give us books on Jesus and that presumably they garner readers from outside the church. Nor do I mean that non-Christians now contribute to our discussions, although that is happily true enough. What I mean rather is this: many texts that have, for two thousand years, invariably received explicitly religious interpretations do so no longer. In other words, they are now sometimes given diminished theological content. Let me briefly illustrate with seven random instances:

1. The parable of the Sower recounts the four different fates of seeds that fall in different places.[73] The allegorical interpretation that accompanies the parable in the Synoptics turns the narrative into a lesson about preaching the gospel. In stark contrast to this theological understanding, Charles Hedrick has argued that our parable, which fails to remark upon the farmer's plowing or God's intervention, "tends to subvert a religious view of the natural processes, a view that looks to God as the source of the blessings and the curses of nature, a view that sacramentalizes the cosmos."[74] Indeed, "because of its secularity and its tacit failure to acknowledge God's sovereignty over nature and to insist on the fulfillment of an individual's holy obligations to God in order to ensure the harvest, the story resonates with impiety. Hence the story subverts the faith of Israel by challenging its fictive view of reality."[75] For Hedrick, Jesus' parable actually opposes the Shema (Deut 6:4–6; 11:13–21), which promises divine intervention to make crops prosper if one wholeheartedly loves and serves God.

2. In Matthew and Luke, the parable of the Unexpected Burglar functions as a warning to watch for Jesus' eschatological return.[76] The Jesus Seminar, however, does not attribute an apocalyptic eschatology to Jesus,

---

73. Matt 13:3–9; Mark 4:3–9; Luke 8:5–8; *Gos. Thom.* 9.
74. Charles W. Hedrick, *Parables as Poetic Fictions: The Creative Voice of Jesus* (Peabody, MA: Hendrickson, 1994), 177.
75. Ibid., 185.
76. Matt 24:43–44 and Luke 12:39–40 (Q); cf. *Gos. Thom.* 21 and 1 Thess 5:2–6.

so it concludes: "The root metaphor itself in [Luke 12] v. 39 could have come from Jesus but it would have been understood on his lips in a secular sense."[77] What that sense might have been they do not tell us.

3. The parable of the Wheat and Weeds is, in Matthew, about the last judgment.[78] This is made plain in the allegorical interpretation of Matt 13:36–43: "The one who sows the good seed is the Son of man; the field is the world, and the good seed are the children of the kingdom; the weeds are the children of the evil one, and the enemy is the devil; the harvest is the end of the age. . . . " If one sets aside this allegory, however, other interpretations become possible. Among them is the recent proposal of R. David Kaylor: The parable is "a social critique of the patterns of land tenure developed during the period immediately prior to Jesus' lifetime."[79]

4. The parable of the Tenants of the Vineyard is about a man who plants a vineyard and then leases it to tenants.[80] Later he sends for his portion of the produce. The tenants ignore his requests and mistreat the messengers. Finally, the owner returns, destroys the tenants, and gives the vineyard to others. This story is, in the canonical Gospels, an allegory about faithlessness and judgment, and Christian readers have traditionally understood the householder to stand for God, the tenant farmers to stand for Jewish leaders, the rejection of the servants to stand for the rejection of prophets, and so on. Yet some now suppose that these equations were not implicit in the original parable, and that the theological sense may in fact be an ecclesiastical overlay. According to Bruce J. Malina and Richard Rohrbaugh, for example, "If at the earliest stage of the gospel tradition the parable embedded here was not a riposte to enemies in Jerusalem, it may well have been a warning to landowners expropriating and exporting the produce of the land."[81]

---

77. Robert Funk, Roy W. Hoover, and the Jesus Seminar, *The Five Gospels: The Search for the Authentic Words of Jesus* (New York: Macmillan, 1993), 342. On 287 Jesus is called a "secular sage" who used "secular proverbs," and on 201 we read that in debate his "responses were more secular than legal in character."

78. Matt 13:24–30; cf. *Gos. Thom.* 57.

79. R. David Kaylor, *Jesus the Prophet: His Vision of the Kingdom on Earth* (Louisville: Westminster/John Knox, 1994), 143.

80. Matt 21:33–46; Mark 12:1–12; Luke 20:9–19; *Gos. Thom.* 65–66.

81. B. J. Malina and R. L. Rohrbaugh, *Social-Science Commentary on the Synoptic Gospels* (Minneapolis: Fortress, 1992), 164. An economic interpretation also appears in J. D. Hester, "Socio-Rhetorical Criticism and the Parable of the Tenants," *JSNT* 45 (1992): 27–57.

5. Within its Matthean and Lukan contexts, the parable of the Hidden Talents is filled with transparent religious symbols.[82] The master is Jesus. His slaves represent the church, whose members have received various responsibilities. The master's departure is the departure of the earthly Jesus. The period of the master's absence is the age of the church, his return is the Parousia of the Son of Man, and the rewards for the good servants stand for heavenly rewards the faithful receive at the great assize. The punishment of the evil slave represents those within the church who, through their sins of omission, condemn themselves to eschatological darkness. Scholars have long thought that Jesus, if he authored the parable, must have meant something a bit different. Recently William R. Herzog II has proposed that originally the parable praised the third servant, the one who hides his talent, because he does not participate in the exploitation of the economic system. For Herzog, hearers of this parable might have asked: "How would you react to a whistle-blower? Would a former retainer find a welcome in a peasant village? Or would the former hostilities suffocate even the possibility of a latter-day coalition? Do the people of the land realize the role played by retainers? Do they understand how their bitter animosity toward them plays into the hands of the ruling elite? Can peasants and rural poor folks realize how their interests can be tied to the very class of people whom they despise?"[83]

6. In Matt 10:26 and Luke 12:2, Jesus says that nothing covered up will not be uncovered, and that nothing secret will not become known. Most commentators find in these words a somber allusion to the final judgment, when all will come to light. Burton Mack agrees that this is the right reading for the second level of Q. But for the primary level, he declares that the saying was far less loaded: it was "general cautionary advice."[84]

7. Often in the Gospels Jesus refers to himself as "the Son of Man." Most Christians traditionally have understood this in terms of the incarnation: Jesus was not only the Son of God but also a true human being. Until recently most modern scholarship preferred instead to interpret the expression as being either a title from Jewish eschatological

---

82. Matt 25:14–30; Luke 19:11–27.
83. William R. Herzog II, *Parables as Subversive Speech: Jesus as Pedagogue of the Oppressed* (Louisville: Westminster/John Knox, 1994), 167–68.
84. Burton Mack, *The Lost Gospel: The Book of Q and Christian Origins* (San Francisco: HarperSanFrancisco, 1994), 166.

expectation (cf. the Son of man in *1 Enoch*) or an allusion to Daniel 7 and the eschatological vindication of the saints. On either reading the term is full of religious connotations. At present, however, a large body of contemporary scholars has argued that, at least for Jesus himself, the expression may have been nothing more than a common Aramaic idiom, a roundabout way of speaking of oneself.[85] In other words, in and of itself the expression had no theological meaning.

The preceding seven examples, to which it would be easy to add, illustrate a trend. As one would expect in an increasingly secular age, in which transcendent realities for so many are distant or even altogether illusory, there is an increasing number of what may be fairly called secular readings of some Gospel texts. This is not to imply that the proponents of those interpretations would not consider themselves religious, only that they are sometimes forwarding interpretations that shove our attention away from traditional theological, christological, and eschatological concerns.

Now it is always possible that, just as modernity has in other ways brought us new knowledge about the past, so here too; and I do not wish in this context to contest any of the interpretations just introduced, although I indeed find none of them persuasive. Maybe our secular outlook and the ever-diminishing influence of traditional ecclesiastical readings are helping us to see things our predecessors were blind to, such as ancient economic realities. I in fact think this is sometimes the case. At the same time, one must wonder how often we are once again, like the liberal nineteenth-century questers we look down upon as naive, remaking Jesus in our own image. Are we not victims of our own contemporary vogues? Do we not see less traditional theology than earlier exegetes because today we are less theological? Do not secular readers make for secular readings? People began to see artificial canals on Mars precisely when we began building lots of canals on earth. And there are no artificial canals on Mars.

I do not believe in the new and improved secular Jesus. The earliest extant interpretations of the Jesus tradition are all what one may fairly call religious. This is because the authors of those interpretations were all consumed by thoughts about the invisible God, supernatural interventions, and eschatology or the afterlife. In some ways they indeed were

---

85. See, e.g., Douglas R. A. Hare, *The Son of Man Tradition* (Minneapolis: Fortress, 1990).

what one may fairly call "unworldly," more interested in prayer than in economics, in eschatological rewards than in Roman politics. I do not mean here to extricate religion from the rest of ancient life, for such cannot be done. But there is undeniably a sense in which the Sermon on the Mount, let us say, is more religious than the legal texts among the Elephantine papyri; and surely it is says something that the ratio of θεός to Καῖσαρ in the New Testament is 30:1.

One good explanation for the religiosity of the extant texts, and the explanation I accept, is that Jesus himself was a deeply religious personality, who interpreted everything in terms of an unseen world, and that he and the traditions about him attracted like-minded others. If I may so put it, Jesus would have found the themes of Aldous Huxley's *Perennial Philosophy* more interesting than the themes of Karl Marx's *Das Kapital*. We might accordingly do well to ask ourselves to what extent our competence to find Jesus requires an "ability to appreciate a distinctly religious personality,"[86] and to what extent our growing secularity may sometimes constrict that ability.[87]

BOOKS ON JESUS, 1907–1953

E. D. Burton, *The Life of Christ* (1907); William Sanday, *The Life of Christ in Recent Research* (1907); A. T. Robertson, *Epochs in the Life of Christ* (1907); James Denney, *Jesus and the Gospel* (1908); Johannes Weiss, *Christus* (1909); C. G. Montefiore, *Some Elements of the Religious Teaching of Jesus* (1910); E. F. Scott, *The Kingdom and the Messiah* (1911); Paul Fiebig, *Die Gleichnisreden Jesu im Licht der rabbinischen Gleichnisse* (1912); George Holley Gilbert, *Jesus* (1912); Wilhelm Heitmüller, *Jesus* (1913); H. L. Jackson, *The Eschatology of Jesus* (1913); Paul Wernle, *Jesus* (1916); T. R. Glover, *The Jesus of*

---

86. Rowlinson, "The Continuing Quest of the Historical Jesus," 42.

87. In this connection I find interesting some remarks of Gary Gilbert, in his online (*Review of Biblical Literature* [*RBL*] 6 [2003]) review of John Dominic Crossan and Jonathan L. Reed, *Excavating Jesus: Beneath the Stones, Behind the Texts* (New York: HarperSanFrancisco, 2001): "We do well to remember that . . . materialistic categories often played little if any role in acts of rebellion among Jews. In the 40s, shortly after Jesus' execution, Jewish peasants neglected their farms and were willing to die not because of the exploitation of the land or the economic injustice imposed by the wealthy elites in the large cities but in protest over Gaius Caligula's desire to erect a statue of himself in the Jerusalem temple. Religious ideals, here the sanctity of the temple, more than a response to economic, political, or social injustice, often spurred Jews to engage in acts of resistance, both violent and nonviolent" (online: http://www.bookreviews.org/pdf/3227_3625.pdf; accessed June 26, 2003).

History (1917); W. Manson, *Christ's View of the Kingdom of God* (1918); H. G. Enelow, *A Jewish View of Jesus* (1920); F. C. Grant, *The Life and Times of Jesus* (1921); Adolf Schlatter, *Die Geschichte des Christus* (1921); Gustaf Dalman, *Jesus-Jeschua* (1922); Burton Scott Easton, *Christ and His Teaching* (1922); Joseph Klausner, *Yeshu ha-Notsri* (1922); A. C. Headlam, *The Life and Teaching of Jesus Christ* (1923); A. H. McNeile, *Concerning the Christ* (1924); James Moffatt, *Everyman's Life of Jesus* (1924); E. F. Scott, *The Ethical Teaching of Jesus* (1924); Maurice Goguel, *Vie de Jésus* (1925); B. W. Bacon, *The Study of Jesus* (1926); Shirley Jackson Case, *Jesus: A New Biography* (1927); Joseph Warschauer, *The Historical Life of Christ* (1927); Maurice Goguel, *Critique et Histoire* (1928); M.-J. Lagrange, *L'évangile de Jésus-Christ* (1928); W. Michaelis, *Täufer, Jesus, Urgemeinde* (1928); Walter E. Bundy, *Our Recovery of Jesus* (1929); B. W. Bacon, *Jesus the Son of God* (1930); B. H. Branscomb, *Jesus and the Law of Moses* (1930); Burton Scott Easton, *Christ in the Gospels* (1930); P. Feine, *Jesus* (1930); Joachim Jeremias, *Jesus als Weltvollender* (1930); Robert Eisler, ΙΗΣΟΥΣ ΒΑΣΙΛΕΥΣ ΟΥ ΒΑΣΙΛΕΥΣΑΣ (2 vols.; 1929–30); James Mackinnon, *The Historic Jesus* (1931); T. W. Manson, *The Teaching of Jesus* (1931); H.-D. Wendland, *Die Eschatologie des Reiches Gottes bei Jesus* (1931); F.-M. Braun, *Où en est le problème de Jésus?* (1932); F. C. Burkitt, *Jesus Christ* (1932); C. A. H. Guignebert, *Jésus* (1933); James Stewart, *The Life and Teaching of Jesus Christ* (1933); Rudolf Otto, *Reich Gottes und Menschensohn* (1934); C. H. Dodd, *The Parables of the Kingdom* (1935); Joachim Jeremias, *Die Abendmahlsworte Jesu* (1935); W. O. E. Oesterley, *The Gospel Parables in the Light of their Jewish Background* (1936); H. J. Cadbury, *The Peril of Modernizing Jesus* (1937); P. Couchoud, *Jésus* (1937); C. H. Dodd, *History and the Gospels* (1938); P. Gardner-Smith, *The Christ of the Gospels* (1938); G. Lindeskog, *Jesusfrage im neuzeitlichen Judentum* (1938); H. D. A. Major, T. W. Manson, and C. J. Wright, *The Mission and Message of Jesus* (1938); Vincent Taylor, *Jesus and His Sacrifice* (1938); Percival Gardner-Smith, *The Christ of the Gospels* (1939); Martin Dibelius, *Jesus* (1939); A. T. Cadoux, *The Theology of Jesus* (1940); W. Grundmann, *Jesus der Galiläer und das Judentum* (1940); C. C. McCown, *The Search for the Real Jesus* (1940); Rudolf Meyer, *Der Prophet aus Galiläa* (1940); G. Ogg, *The Chronology of the Public Ministry of Jesus* (1940); C. J. Cadoux, *The Historic Mission of Jesus* (1941); J. Leipoldt, *Jesu*

Verhältnis zu Griechen und Juden (1941); John Knox, *The Man Christ Jesus* (1942); W. Michaelis, *Der Herr verzieht nicht die Verheissung* (1942); Anthony Flew, *Jesus and His Church* (1943); William Manson, *Jesus the Messiah* (1943); John Wick Bowman, *The Intention of Jesus* (1943); A. E. J. Rawlinson, *Christ in the Gospels* (1944); H. B. Sharman, *Son of Man and Kingdom of God* (1944); W. G. Kümmel, *Verheissung und Erfüllung* (1945); E. C. Colwell, *An Approach to the Teaching of Jesus* (1946); F.-M. Braun, *Jesus* (1947); H. J. Cadbury, *Jesus: What Manner of Man?* (1947); Jean G. H. Hoffmann, *Les vies de Jésus et le Jésus de l'histoire* (1947); G. Lundström, *Guds Rike i Jesu Förkunnelse* (1947); John Wick Bowman, *The Religion of Maturity* (1948); C. J. Cadoux, *The Life of Jesus* (1948); George S. Duncan, *Jesus, Son of Man* (1948); C. W. F. Smith, *The Jesus of the Parables* (1948); S. H. Hooke, *The Kingdom of God in the Experience of Jesus* (1949); E. J. Goodspeed, *A Life of Jesus* (1950); A. M. Hunter, *The Work and Words of Jesus* (1950); H. A. Guy, *The Life of Christ* (1951); J. Finegan, *Rediscovering Jesus* (1952); T. W. Manson, *The Servant-Messiah* (1953); Ernst Percy, *Die Botschaft Jesu* (1953).

BOOKS ON JESUS, 1954–1979

R. H. Fuller, *The Mission and Achievement of Jesus* (1954); Vincent Taylor, *The Life and Ministry of Jesus* (1954); W. E. Bundy, *Jesus and the First Three Gospels* (1955); W. Grundmann, *Die Geschichte Jesu Christi* (1956); H. A. Guy, *The Life of Christ* (1957); Ethelbert Stauffer, *Jesus and His Story* (German, 1957); E. Barnikol, *Das Leben Jesu der Heilsgeschichte* (1958); J. Schneider, *Die Frage nach dem historischen Jesus in der neutestamentlichen Forschung der Gegenwart* (1958); Rudolf Schnackenburg, *Gottes Herrschaft und Reich* (1959); H.-W. Bartsch, *Das historische Problem des Lebens Jesu* (1960); H. Ristow and K. Matthiae, eds., *Der historische Jesus und der kerygmatische Christus* (1960); H. Zahrnt, *Es begann mit Jesus von Nazareth* (1960); Morton Scott Enslin, *The Prophet from Nazareth* (1961); F. Hahn, W. Lohff, and G. Bornkamm, *Die Frage nach dem historischen Jesus* (1962); J. Jervell, *Den historiske Jesus* (1962); X. Léon-Dufour, *Les Évangiles et l'histoire de Jésus* (1963); Hugh Anderson, *Jesus and Christian Origins* (1964); A. Finkel, *The Pharisees and the Teacher of Nazareth* (1964); Otto Betz, *Was wissen wir von Jesus?* (1965);

A. Strobel, *Die moderne Jesusforschung* (1966); C. K. Barrett, *Jesus and the Gospel Tradition* (1967); S. G. F. Brandon, *Jesus and the Zealots* (1967); E. W. Saunders, *Jesus in the Gospels* (1967); D. Flusser, *Jesus in Selbstzeugnissen und Bilddokumenten* (1968); Eduard Schweizer, *Jesus* (German, 1968); H. Braun, *Jesus* (1969); W. Trilling, *Fragen zur Geschichtlichkeit Jesu* (1969); Harvey K. McArthur, *In Search of the Historical Jesus* (1969); Hans-Werner Bartsch, *Jesus* (1970); C. H. Dodd, *The Founder of Christianity* (1970); Howard Clark Kee, *Jesus in History* (1970); G. Baumbach, *Jesus von Nazareth im Lichte der jüdischen Gruppenbildung* (1971); Leander E. Keck, *A Future for the Historical Jesus* (1971); Étienne Trocmé, *Jésus de Nazareth vu par les témoins de sa vie* (1971); J. Blank, *Jesus von Nazareth* (1972); J. Bowker, *Jesus and the Pharisees* (1973); Richard H. Hiers, *The Historical Jesus and the Kingdom of God* (1973); F. Schnider, *Jesus der Prophet* (1973); Geza Vermes, *Jesus the Jew* (1973); Karl Kertelge, ed., *Rückfrage nach Jesus* (1974); E. Schillebeeckx, *Jezus: Het verhaal van een levende* (1974); Georg Strecker, ed., *Jesus Christus in Histoire und Theologie* (1975); Joachim Gnilka, *Wer ist doch Dieser?* (1976); W. Grimm, *Weil ich dich liebe* (1976); A. Nolan, *Jesus before Christianity* (1977); H. Leroy, *Jesus* (1978); Ben F. Meyer, *The Aims of Jesus* (1979)

T W O

THE PROBLEM OF AUDIENCE

Precious words drift away from their meaning.
— GEORGE HARRISON

AN OLD INTERPRETATION

Do the difficult imperatives of Jesus, a reader of the Gospels might ask, impinge equally upon all? One venerable approach insists that they do not. Maldonatus, for instance, thought that the Sermon on the Mount, whose stridency has always haunted readers,[1] addresses the disciples alone, a circumstance he believed to be full of hermeneutical significance: Jesus made demands of his immediate followers that he did not make of others.[2] While all must heed the commandments that are requisite for salvation, some imperatives are instead, in accord with the distinction between *praeceptum Domini* and *consilium* in 1 Cor 7:25, "evangelical counsels." Such counsels are for those with a special religious calling. Jesus, according to Maldonatus, "carefully distinguished between precepts and counsels. When he gives a precept, he does not say, 'If you will be perfect' but 'If you will enter into eternal life.' When he gives a counsel he does not say, 'If you will enter into life' but 'If you will be perfect.' He gives eternal life as a reward for keeping the commandments; but to the observance of counsels, not life eternal, but 'treasure in heaven.' "[3]

Maldonatus did not, of course, invent this interpretation. He rather found it in medieval commentaries, where it matched the writers' social reality. The Middle Ages knew two sorts of believers. There were the

---

1. Cf. already Trypho in Justin, *Dial.* 10.2 (ed. Marcovich; PTS 47:87): "I am aware that your precepts in the so-called Gospel are so wonderful and so great, I suspect that no one can keep them; for I have carefully read them."
2. Juan Maldonatus, *Commentarii in Quatuor Evangelistas* (London: Moguntiae, 1853), 1:66.
3. Ibid., 1:266–67.

so-called "religious," such as hierarchs, monks, nuns, and ascetics; and there were those who were not "religious," meaning everybody else. Seeing, as one would expect, their own reflections in the biblical text, exegetes often took Jesus to be addressing the two different groups in two different ways. Comments similar to those of Maldonatus appear in Bonaventure, Thomas Aquinas, and many others writers.[4]

Protestants, with their emphasis upon the priesthood of all believers, have consistently maligned the old, medieval interpretation. Their polemic has indeed often been merciless, as in Luther's commentary on the Sermon on the Mount.[5] But later Roman Catholics, such as Juan de Valdés, also criticized the traditional approach.[6] And in our own time, more and more Catholic theologians have come to view it without enthusiasm, partly no doubt because of modern ideas about democracy and equality.[7] Although the *Catechism of the Catholic Church* still accepts the distinction between counsels and precepts,[8] the approach of Maldonatus and like-minded others seems to belong to the dead past, according to the minds of most Scripture scholars, of whatever religious persuasion. We no longer live in a world with two distinct classes of believers, so our own *Sitz im Leben* does not encourage us to find such in the texts.

---

4. Bonaventure, *Comm. in Luc.* 18.31–34 in *Doctoris Seraphici S. Bonaventure Opera Omnia* (ed. Quaracchi), 7:82–86; Aquinas, *Summa* 2.1, q. 107, art. 2; q. 108, art. 4. Cf. Dorotheus of Gaza, *Disc.* 1.12 (ed. Regenault and de Préville; SC 92:164–66); Bede, *Tabern.* 1.6 (25.25) (ed. Holder; CCSL 119A: 24); idem, *Hom. L* 1.13 (ed. Hurst; CCSL 122:90); Aelred of Rievaulx, *Spec. carit.* 3.34 (80) (ed. Hoste and Talbot; CCCM 1:144–45); Haymo of Faversham, *Hom. sanct.* 8 (PL 118:777A–78B); and Cornelius à Lapide, *The Great Commentary*, vol. 1 (London: John Hodges, 1876), 245. See further Brigitta Stoll, *De Virtute in Virtutem: Zur Auslegungs- und Wirkungsgeschichte der Bergpredigt im Kommentaren, Predigten und hagiographischer Literatur von der Merowingerzeit bis um 1200* (BGBE 30; Tübingen: Mohr-Siebeck, 1988), 114–25; also E. Dublanchy, "Conseils évangéliques," in *Dictionnaire de théologie Catholique*, vol. 3 (ed. A. Vacant, E. Mangenot, and É. Amann; Paris: Letouzey et Ané, 1938), cols. 1176–82.

5. Martin Luther, *The Sermon on the Mount (Sermons) and the Magnificat* (ed. Jaroslav Pelikan; Luther's Works 21; St. Louis: Concordia, 1956), 3–4, 128–29. Cf. Calvin, *Inst.* 2.8.56–59 (ed. Benoit; 2:184–88).

6. Juan de Valdés, *Dial. de doctr. crist.*, fols. 21v–22v, 41v–42v.

7. Karl Rahner's discussion of the evangelical counsels in *Theological Investigations*, vol. 8, *Further Theology of the Spiritual Life 2* (London: Darton, Longman, & Todd, 1971), 133–67, stresses that *all* Christians are called to "perfection" in whatever calling they find themselves.

8. *Catechism of the Catholic Church* (2nd ed.; Vatican: Libreria Editrice Vaticana, 2000), 214 (§915). Cf. sections 42–47 of the *Dogmatic Constitution on the Church* (*Lumen gentium*) in the documents of Vatican II.

Notwithstanding modern opinion, I have long suspected that the now-moribund interpretation merits serious attention and that, if it is not wholly true, it is equally not wholly false. The division into two types of believers developed quite early in church history. It shows up already in Gregory the Great, in the Syriac *Book of Steps* (fourth or fifth century), and before that among the Manichaeans.[9] Augustine also recognized such a division,[10] and a century before him, Eusebius wrote this:

> Two ways of life were given by the law of Christ to his church. The one is above nature, and beyond common human living; it admits not marriage, childbearing, property, the possessing of wealth, but wholly and permanently separate from the common customary life of humanity, it devotes itself to the service of God alone in its wealth of heavenly love.... And the other, more humble, more human, permits people to join in pure nuptials and to produce children, to undertake government, to give orders to soldiers fighting for right; it allows them to have minds for farming, for trade, and the other more secular interests as well as for religion; and it is for them that times of retreat and instruction and days for hearing sacred things are set apart. And a kind of secondary grade of piety is attributed to them.[11]

Already Tertullian and Origen, moreover, could distinguish between "advice" and "requirements."[12] Even earlier is the *Didache*, which says in 6.2: "If you are able to bear the whole yoke of the Lord, you will be perfect; but if you are unable, do what you are able to do." Kurt

---

9. On the *Liber graduum*, see Antoine Guillaumont, "Situation et signification du 'Liber Graduum' dans la spiritualité syriaque," in *Symposium Syriacum 1972 célebré dans les jours 26–31 octobre 1972 à l'Institut Pontifical Oriental de Rome* (Orientalia Christiana Analecta 197; Rome: Pontifical Institute of Oriental Studies, 1974), 311–22. For relevant Manichaean sources, see Jes Asmussen, *Manichaean Literature: Representative Texts Chiefly from Middle Persian and Parthian Writings* (Delmar, NY: Scholars' Facsimiles & Reprints, 1975), 26–36. For Gregory the Great, see *Mor. Job* 26.51 (ed. M. Adriaen; CCSL 143B:1305–1306).

10. See Augustine, *De bono conj.* 23 (30) (PL 40:393), and *De sanct. virg.* 14 (PL 40:402–403). Discussion in John Patrick Burchill, "Are There 'Evangelical Counsels' of Perpetual Continence and Poverty? A Study of the Tradition, a Reinterpretation of Mt. 19:10–12, 16–22ff. (and par.), and Implications for a Biblical Basis of Religious Life" (STD diss., Dominican House of Studies, Washington, DC, 1975), 31–36. Cf. Ambrose, *De viduis* 12 (PL 16:256C); Jerome, *Adv. Jov.* 1.9 (PL 23:222B–C).

11. Eusebius, *Dem. ev.* 1.8 (ed. Heikel; GCS 23:39). Cf. Cyprian, *Hab. virg.* 23 (ed. G. Hartel; 3rd ed.; CSEL 3.1:203–204).

12. Tertullian, *Ad uxorem* 2.1 (ed. Kroymann; CSEL 70:110–11); Origen, *Comm. Matt.* 15.13 (ed. Klostermann; GCS 40:382–85); *Comm. Rom.* on 3:3 (ed. Heither: FC 2.2:68–74).

Niederwimmer takes this line to refer back to the largely dominical commandments of *Did.* 1.3b–2.1: the Didachist has no illusions about the inability of some to heed the hard words of the Jesus tradition.[13]

A sort of double standard also evidently appeared in pre-Christian Judaism. The sectarians responsible for the Dead Sea Scrolls seemingly divided themselves into two groups — those at the Qumran settlement near the Dead Sea and those scattered in the camps. The former apparently lived by certain rules not incumbent upon the latter. Even though the two texts are ideologically close, the *Damascus Document* legislates for a different way of life than does the *Rule of the Community.* Our best guess is that the sectarians at Qumran, who had separated themselves from the world, lived by rules more strict than those who remained in and about the cities, and yet both groups belonged to the same religious movement.[14]

Not only are there premedieval examples of Jews and Christians making different demands of different people,[15] but the Jesus tradition itself distinguishes an inner circle from a wider public, and it has Jesus sometimes ask of one group things he does not ask of the other.[16] This is most obviously the case in the various missionary discourses in the Synoptics: Matt 10:1–42; Mark 6:6–13; Luke 9:1–6; 10:1–20. I deem it well-nigh incredible that the detailed instructions in these closely related texts were ever indiscriminately directed at a broad Galilean audience, peasant or otherwise. These collections rather presuppose, and the evangelists themselves highlight, a distinction between missionaries, whom

---

13. Kurt Niederwimmer, *The Didache: A Commentary* (Hermeneia; Minneapolis: Fortress, 1998), 122–23.

14. For a plausible reconstruction, see Geza Vermes, *The Dead Sea Scrolls: Qumran in Perspective* (Cleveland: Collins & World, 1978), 87–109. Here we are actually dealing with a cross-cultural phenomenon. Buddhism, for instance, knows the distinction between monks and laity and promulgates different rules for each.

15. One suspects that, if we knew more about the Sadducees, we would find that they "were content to defend and observe their special traditions both in their private lives and when they were exercising some public office — but without claiming that their special traditions were obligatory for all Jews and therefore should be imposed on all Jews in their daily lives." So John Meier, *A Marginal Jew: Rethinking the Historical Jesus,* vol. 3, *Companions and Competitors* (New York: Doubleday, 2001), 405. The Pharisees were presumably a bit different, for while they "did not consider the common people or other Jews heinous sinners or beyond the pale simply for not agreeing to follow Pharisaic practice," they nonetheless "struggled to have their views accepted by the common people" (so Meier, ibid., 316).

16. Whether one thinks of this inner circle as the Twelve or as a larger group including the Twelve or doubts the historicity of the Twelve makes no difference for the present investigation.

Jesus is instructing, and their potential audiences, whom he is not instructing. The orders to go without purse and knapsack and sandals and staff and to exorcize are not general imperatives for everyone. Neither Jesus nor his disciples require the missionized to become like the missionaries. They do not tell everyone to travel from village to village or to proclaim the kingdom or to do without necessities. On the contrary, the messengers accept the hospitality of people who can afford to serve them, the hospitality of individuals who are living at home and have not abandoned their customary lives.[17] One is reminded of 1 Cor 9, which applies a direction from the missionary discourse specifically to "those who proclaim the gospel" (v. 14).[18]

The missionary discourses, which surely reflect things that Jesus said,[19] indicate that he sometimes instructed his closest followers in ways that he did not instruct others, a circumstance that harmonizes well with the general impression the tradition otherwise leaves. But how do we interpret this circumstance, and what are the implications for understanding Jesus and understanding the canonical Gospels?

TEACHING FOR COWORKERS

There is no good reason to doubt that Jesus and his disciples traveled from place to place. Even Q, despite having little narrative, testifies that Jesus and those around him were on the move. Matt 8:5 = Luke 7:1 places Jesus in Capernaum, and Matt 11:23–24 = Luke 10:15 presupposes that Capernaum has responded negatively to Jesus and/or his disciples. Matthew 10:5–10, 16 = Luke 10:3–10 has him speak of workers being dispatched, of them being on their way, of them greeting no one on the road, and of them eating whatever is set before them in whatever town they are in. Matthew 11:21 = Luke 10:13 presupposes that Chorazin and Bethsaida have heard Jesus and/or his disciples. And Matt

---

17. See, e.g., Matt 10:7–13 = Luke 10:5–9 (Q); Mark 7:24–30; 14:3, 13–15; Luke 7:36; 10:38–42; 19:1–10; John 11. This fact raises questions about much of the reconstruction of Jesus in John Dominic Crossan and Jonathan L. Reed, *Excavating Jesus: Beneath the Stones, Behind the Texts* (San Francisco: HarperSanFrancisco, 2001); cf. E. P. Sanders's review in *The New York Review of Books* 50, no. 6 (2003): 49–51.

18. On this see my book, *The Jesus Tradition in Q* (Harrisburg, PA: Trinity, 1997), 104–11.

19. See Ferdinand Hahn, *Mission in the New Testament* (SBT 47; London: SCM, 1965), 33–36; and Rudolf Laufen, *Die Doppelüberlieferungen der Logienquelle und des Markusevangeliums* (BBB 54; Königstein: P. Hanstein, 1980), 260–68.

23:37–39 = Luke 13:34–35 has Jesus address Jerusalem directly, from which we may infer his sometime presence there.

Mark's account of the ministry offers more of the same: Jesus is in Capernaum (1:21; 9:33), the land of the Gerasenes (5:1), Nazareth (6:1), Bethsaida (6:45; 8:22), Genesaret (6:53), the region of Tyre (7:24), Sidon (7:31), the region of the Decapolis (7:31), Dalmanutha (8:10), Caesarea Philippi (8:27), the region beyond the Jordan (10:1), Jericho (10:46), Jerusalem (11:1), and Bethany (11:11–12; 14:3).

While the origin of these Markan notices is a matter for speculation,[20] Mark 6:6 is surely correct to remark that Jesus "went about among the villages teaching" (cf. John 7:1). As is implicit in his recurring "Follow me" (Matt 8:21 = Luke 9:59 (Q); Mark 1:17; 2:14), Jesus and his disciples carried on a mission that took them from one locale to another. They sought to promulgate a message beyond one or two villages. Christianity's missionary impulse goes back to the pre-Easter period.

Recent study of the Jesus tradition has revealed that portions of it reflect the different situations of the itinerants and the householder.[21] This circumstance does not just mirror the post-Easter situation; it also reflects the missionary work of Jesus himself.[22] Some people who embraced his cause were, at least for a time, called away from their everyday lives to serve him. Others who accepted his proclamation — surely the vast majority — did not leave home. They rather continued to live their lives where they had lived them all along, and there is no cause to imagine that

---

20. Most of them presumably come from Mark's tradition. If the stories in which they appear go back to local communities in the places named (an opinion to which I am disinclined), then the geographical settings were not originally part of those stories: one names a place only if it is not where one now is.

21. See, e.g., John Dominic Crossan, *The Birth of Christianity: Discovering What Happened in the Years Immediately after the Execution of Jesus* (San Francisco: HarperCollins, 1998), 291–417; Stephen J. Patterson, *The Gospel of Thomas and Jesus* (Sonoma, CA: Polebridge, 1993), 158–214; and Gerd Theissen, *Sociology of Early Palestinian Christianity* (Philadelphia: Fortress, 1978). For criticism of Theissen, see Richard A. Horsley, *Sociology and the Jesus Movement* (2nd ed.; New York: Continuum, 1994); and Thomas Schmeller, *Brechungen: Urchristliche Wandercharismatiker im Prisma soziologisch orientierter Exegese* (SBS 136; Stuttgart: Katholisches Bibelwerk, 1989). Future work will also have to address the criticisms of William E. Arnal, *Jesus and the Village Scribes: Galilean Conflict and the Setting of Q* (Harrisburg, PA: Trinity, 2001). Although I find Arnal too skeptical, many of his criticisms of itinerancy as an explanatory category for much of the Jesus tradition merit serious reflection. In this essay, however, I am not concerned with the precise nature or extent of itinerancy in the early church. All that matters for my purposes herein is that Jesus and his disciples, in carrying on their work, sometimes moved from place to place.

22. Cf. Crossan, *Birth*, 407: "The dialectic of itinerants and householders ... goes back as early into the tradition as I can trace the evidence. It goes back into the life of the historical Jesus; it is, in fact, the program of the kingdom."

Jesus disapproved of them doing this. The tradition does not depict him enjoining everyone to accompany him (cf. Mark 9:38–40), nor does it have him demanding that all abandon their normal lives to become itinerants. There were, it appears, disciples in the strict sense, that is, people who literally followed Jesus, and then there were sympathizers who did not hear the call, "Follow me." Some individuals indeed were, at least according to Mark 2:11; 5:19; and 8:26, told to return home. And the saying in Mark 13:15–16, for which there may be a Q parallel in Matt 24:17–18 = Luke 17:31–32, presupposes that the end will find believers on housetops and in fields. This scene fits the notion "that Jesus expected the majority of believers to go on living a normal life in the interim."[23] Inclusion in the kingdom did not require tagging along after Jesus. The situation is somewhat analogous to that of Paul, who did not impose his way of life upon others. The apostle was an unmarried convert who, along with a handful of coworkers, ministered to settled communities. Nowhere in his extant correspondence does he urge readers to abandon kith and kin.

In my files I have a copy of a letter that C. H. Dodd sent to W. D. Davies, in which the former, with his usual cogency, wrote:

> I was interested in your suggestion that the apparent reduction of the "radical" element may not always be due to later development, but that Jesus may Himself have taught on two levels. I had been feeling about, myself, after some such "dualism" in the teaching, but I was putting it rather differently. On the one hand some sayings seem to make demands for absolute renunciation as the *sine qua non* of discipleship, or of entrance into the Kingdom of God, and yet Jesus often seems to have let people go on quietly at home. Zacchaeus having promised reasonable restitution, was not asked to sell up and join the march. The *basilikos* of Capernaum, though he "believed," was not asked to abandon his family and give up his office. Can it be that after all there *was* a kind of "double standard" — the heroic absolute for the *corps d'elite* on whom fell the terrible responsibility of sharing directly in the Messianic crisis — and a *halakah* for those for whom "receiving the Kingdom of God" meant a concentration of moral effort upon daily duties

---

23. So Benedict T. Viviano, "The Historical Jesus in the Doubly Attested Sayings: An Experiment," *RB* 103 (1996): 407. Cf. also Matt 24:40–41 = Luke 17:34–35 (Q).

falling short of the heroic? The *"Schonanbruch"* [already begin-ning] of the Kingdom and the imminence of judgment applies [*sic*] to both, but not necessarily with the same implications for actual conduct.[24]

These words commend themselves. While one often asks more of one-self than others, as Jesus clearly did, the Synoptics show us that he also asked more of those nearest to him. Even the Reformers, despite their op-position to a two-tiered ethic, recognized this at certain points. Writing, for instance, on Jesus' demand that the rich man give up all his goods, Calvin rejected the Catholic distinction between counsels and precepts. Yet, he acknowledged that "our Lord in that passage is not proclaiming a general statement that is applicable to everyone, but only to the person with whom He is speaking."[25] Calvin could not, given his ideology, find in Jesus' word an "evangelical counsel," but he did agree with his oppo-nents that Jesus' word was not directly addressed to everyone.[26] In line with this, although the Lukan Jesus declares, "None of you can become my disciple if you do not give up all your possessions" (14:33), Luke nonetheless lets Zacchaeus give up only half of his possessions, presum-ably because the rich toll collector is not being called to discipleship in the strict sense (19:8–9).

There must be quite a few statements in the Synoptics that were never intended to apply to everyone. One such statement appears in the slight call story in Matt 8:21–22 = Luke 9:59–60 (Q), which is reminiscent of Elijah calling Elisha in 1 Kgs 19:19–21. A would-be disciple makes what appears to be a wholly reasonable request: "Lord, first let me go and bury my father." Jesus responds with the seemingly outrageous dec-laration: "Follow me, and let the dead bury their own dead." Now one can, if so inclined, take this novel and startling line to imply something about Jesus' attitude toward the dead or burial in general. According

---

24. Letter of C. H. Dodd to W. D. Davies, May 28, 1964.

25. Calvin, *Contra la sect phant. et furieuse des Lib.* 21 (Calvini Opera, 7:216). He goes on: "It is utter folly to extract a universal doctrine from a passage that was meant to test the heart of a particular person" (217). Luther similarly refused to find in Matt 19:12 a rule for a particular group while yet admitting that the verse regards celibacy as a personal choice; see *De votis monasticis Martini Lutheri iudicium 1521*, in Werke 9:580–91 (= Luther's Works 44:261–72).

26. This remains a common judgment of exegetes; cf. Bernhard Lohse, *Askese und Mönchtum in der Antike und in der alten Kirche* (Religion und Kultur der alten Mittelmeerwelt in Parallelforschugen 1; Munich: R. Oldenbourg, 1969), 117–18; and Rudolf Schnackenburg, *The Moral Teaching of the New Testament* (New York: Crossroad, 1965), 50.

to Kathleen Corley, he regarded certain customs surrounding treatment of the dead, such as secondary burial and the veneration of the tombs of prophets, as extravagant.[27] This resembles the interpretation I once ran across in an essay of Jorge Luis Borges: "To condemn the pompous vanity of funerals," Jesus "said that the dead will bury the dead."[28]

Corley's evidence, however, is not irrefragably convincing. She cites Matt 23:27 = Luke 11:44 (Q: "Woe to you, for you are like unmarked graves, and people walk over them without realizing it"); Matt 23:29 = Luke 11:47 (Q: "Woe to you! For you build the tombs of the prophets"); Matt 24:28 = Luke 17:37 (Q: "Wherever the corpse is, there the vultures will gather"); Matt 23:9 (which includes: "Call no one your father on earth"); and *Gos. Thom.* 42 ("Become passersby"). These verses fail to stand up, under cross-examination, as wholly creditable witnesses to a negative attitude toward widespread custom. Matthew 23:27 = Luke 11:44 is a simile, not a statement about practice. Similarly, Matt 23:9 (which may be Matthean redaction) belongs to a section treating honorifics, not burial. The implications of *Gos. Thom.* 42 remain infolded; certainly it does not explicitly teach anything about burial.[29] And Matt 24:28 = Luke 17:37 is notoriously enigmatic. Byron McCane can take this proverb to mean that the divinity is displeased unless human remains receive some form of ritual disposition.[30] Even the purport of Matt 23:29 = Luke 11:47 is not obvious. This line criticizes those who build the tombs of the prophets — not for building those tombs but for being hypocrites. Our sources, moreover, otherwise assume that Jesus' followers continued both to practice mourning rituals and to view burial as an act of religious devotion.[31] And how likely is it that one who believed

---

27. Kathleen E. Corley, *Women and the Historical Jesus: Feminist Myths of Christian Origins* (Santa Rosa, CA: Polebridge, 2002), 73–77. Corley takes the saying in Matt 8:21–22 = Luke 9:59–60 (Q) to refer to secondary burial. For this view see esp. Byron R. McCane, " 'Let the Dead Bury Their Own Dead': Secondary Burial and Matt 8:21–22," HTR 83 (1990): 31–43.

28. Jorge Luis Borges, "The Apocryphal Gospels," in *Selected Non-Fictions* (ed. Eliot Weinberger; New York: Penguin, 1999), 515.

29. According to Corley, *Women*, 75, "become passersby" may "well allude to the phrase 'passersby' common in ancient grave epitaphs. The point would be to keep on walking." This is an intriguing interpretation, but its probability is hard to determine.

30. Byron R. McCane, *Roll Back the Stone: Death and Burial in the World of Jesus* (Harrisburg, PA: Trinity, 2003), 65.

31. See, e.g., Mark 6:29 and Matt 27:57–61 par. On the lamentation of the women at Jesus' tomb, see Corley, *Women*, 107–39.

in the resurrection of the dead would have denigrated concern for the bodies of the dead?[32]

We may, then, doubt the reading of Corley and Borges and return to the traditional commentators, patristic, Catholic, and Protestant, who have typically refused to read Matt 8:21–22 or Luke 9:59–60 as a general or normative remark about burial. They have rather understood Jesus' imperative to reflect only a concrete moment, to be "a one-time only requirement,"[33] a demand made to one individual in a unique situation.[34] In other words, Christian exegetical tradition has rightly understood Jesus' demand to be not universal but particular. It is part of a call story and no more enjoins Galilean peasants to neglect burial or to abandon certain burial customs than summoning the sons of Zebedee away from their father's boat was a swipe at the fishing industry. Jesus, with the consciousness of a prophet, called a certain individual away from a sacred obligation, because for that individual something else was more important, something to be attended to immediately: service to Jesus and his cause. In the words of Ulrich Luz, "This harsh saying of Jesus was not intended to give general instructions about how people should act any more than the demand to give up everything and to follow Jesus was a requirement for everybody. Instead, the followers of Jesus, itinerant prophets, were specially called to proclaim the kingdom of God, and along with this came blunt symbolic actions that portray the deep divide between the kingdom of God and the world."[35]

Jesus' difficult teaching about families also surely reflects the unique demands he placed upon his closest followers. According to Matt 10:37 = Luke 14:26 (Q), Jesus once said: "Hate [your] father and mother." This is antinomian if taken as a general declaration, for it would then

---

32. For Jesus' belief in the resurrection, see Dale C. Allison Jr., *Jesus of Nazareth: Millenarian Prophet* (Minneapolis: Fortress, 1998), 136–41.

33. E. P. Sanders, *The Law from Jesus to the Mishnah: Five Studies* (London: SCM, 1990), 4. Cf. Martin Hengel, *The Charismatic Leader and His Followers* (New York: Crossroad, 1981), 61–6.

34. This is why Augustine, in his treatise on the subject, *De cura pro mortuis gerenda* (ed. J. Zycha; CSEL 41), justifiably refers nowhere to the Matthean or Lukan passage.

35. Ulrich Luz, *Matthew 8–20* (Hermeneia; Minneapolis: Fortress, 2001), 19–20. Cf. Jürgen Becker, *Jesus of Nazareth* (New York: de Gruyter, 1998), 285 ("Matt 8:21–22 par. does not say . . . that the Decalogue with its command to honor one's parents has become generally meaningless. Its view is more likely that there are circumstances in which the Kingdom of God and the Torah have competing claims. When that happens, the Kingdom of God takes precedence and denies the previously valid claims of the Law"); also Jacques Schlosser, *Jésus de Nazareth* (2nd, rev. ed.; Paris: Agnès Viénot Éditions, 2002), 208–9.

blatantly contradict the Decalogue's imperative to "honor your father and mother" (Exod 20:12; Deut 5:16), upon which it is clearly modeled.[36] But if Jesus were an antinomian, the existence and nature of early Jewish Christianity become inexplicable; and Mark at least depicts Jesus explicitly endorsing the fifth commandment: 7:9–13; 9:17.[37] Jesus' striking command to hate is much more likely to have its *Sitz im Leben* in his call to missionary labor (cf. Matt 9:37–38 = Luke 10:2 [Q]). In Mark 1:16–20, the summons to James and John is, in effect, a call to forsake father Zebedee, to leave him alone in his boat and alone in his business. And in Matt 8:21–22 = Luke 9:59–60 (Q), just discussed, the call to discipleship requires following Jesus immediately, even if that means neglecting burial or reburial of one's parent.

Becoming a companion of Jesus required leaving one's home and its obligations. Conflict was inevitable. This partly explains Jesus' characterization of the present as one of division among families: "There will be five in one house, three against two and two against three. For I came to divide a father from his son and a son against his father, a mother against her daughter and a daughter against her mother, a mother-in-law against her daughter-in-law and a daughter-in-law against her mother-in-law" (Matt 10:34–36 = Luke 12:51–53 [Q]).[38] This was no general declaration about human experience, as though Jesus thought it good or necessary for members of his audience as a rule to despise parents. It instead is an interpretation of the concrete experience of those who suffered the social, economic, and psychological consequences of leaving father and mother to join themselves to Jesus.

Matthew 6:25–33 = Luke 12:22–31 (Q) supplies another, albeit less obvious example of words that make more sense if they were originally composed for individuals who had left home to follow Jesus. This poetic unit asserts that although ravens and lilies do not sow or reap or work or spin, they yet are fed and dressed in splendor. What can this impractical wisdom, if we may indeed call it wisdom, mean? One might urge, against Matt 12:42 = Luke 11:31 (Q), that Jesus here appears as Solomon's lesser, not his greater, for the startling assurances seem no more sagacious

---

36. See my *The Intertextual Jesus: Scripture in Q* (Harrisburg, PA: Trinity, 2000), 62–64.
37. See further chapter 5 (below).
38. On this text see my article "Q 12.51–53 and Mk 9:11–13 and the Messianic Woes," in *Authenticating the Words of Jesus* (ed. Bruce Chilton and Craig A. Evans; NTTS 28.1; Leiden: Brill, 1998), 289–310.

than, say, leading people to expect being fed, like Elijah, by ravens. But to give Jesus the benefit of the doubt, the analogy, if it is to carry any conviction at all, surely presupposes that the hearers, like the birds and flowers, are not toiling, not working for a living. As David Catchpole observes, the passage does not sound like advice for normal existence, peasant or otherwise, but rather implies "abandonment of life-sustaining work."[39] Luz asks, "Why does Jesus say that birds do not do the work of men, and that lilies do not do the work of women? This makes sense only if it is applied to men and women who have left their ordinary work for the sake of the kingdom of God."[40] Implicit is nonapplication to everyone else. One could understand Jesus encouraging people who lived according to the way of life outlined in the missionary discourse of Matt 10:7–16 = Luke 10:3–12 (Q; cf. Mark 6:6–13), and one could imagine him attempting to lighten their anxiety about food, drink, and clothing. As general religious instruction, however, the relevance or even meaning of most of the sayings in Luke 12:22–31 (Q) remain curious and difficult to fathom. The history of interpretation confirms this.[41]

Besides the missionary discourses and the three other units just introduced, it stands to reason that there are probably additional texts, probably many additional texts, that Jesus — if he authored them — designed not for the public at large but for the little group around him, or

---

39. David R. Catchpole, "The Question of Q," *STRev* 36 (1992): 40. Catchpole goes on to speak, surely justly, of "this frankly unrealistic teaching."

40. Ulrich Luz, *Matthew in History: Interpretation, Influence, and Effects* (Minneapolis: Fortress, 1994), 29. Cf. Joachim Jeremias, *New Testament Theology: The Proclamation of Jesus* (New York: C. Scribner's Sons, 1971), 236; Heinz Schürmann, "Das Zeugnis der Redenquelle fur die Basileia-Verkündigung Jesu," in *Logia: Les Paroles de Jésus — The Sayings of Jesus* (ed. Joël Delobel; BETL 59; Leuven: University Press, 1982), 158; Gerd Theissen, *Sociology of Early Palestinian Christianity* (Philadelphia: Fortress, 1978), 13; and Dieter Zeller, *Die weisheitlichen Mahnsprüche bei den Synoptikern* (FB 17; Würzburg: Echter, 1977), 92–93. According to John S. Kloppenborg, *The Formation of Q: Trajectories in Ancient Christian Wisdom Collections* (SAC; Philadelphia: Fortress, 1987), 239, Q (cf. Luke) 12:22b–28 is among those texts that "may have had their *Sitz im Leben* in the instructions given to and carried by wandering charismatic preachers." Migaku Sato, *Q und Prophetie: Studien zur Gattungs- und Traditionsgeschichte der Quelle Q* (WUNT 2.29; Tübingen: Mohr-Siebeck, 1988), 218–19, 389–90, believes that although the unit originally addressed disciples in the narrow sense, in Q it came to be instruction for the entire community. Contrast Paul Hoffmann, "Die Sprüche vom Sorgen in der vorsynoptischen Überlieferung," in *Tradition und Situation: Studien zur Jesusüberlieferung in der Logienquelle und den synoptischen Evangelien* (Münster: Aschendorff, 1995), 88–106. He argues just the opposite: in Q, the words were for missionaries, but Jesus himself — Hoffmann accepts the authenticity of Q (cf. Luke) 12:22c–d, 24, 27–28, 29, 30b — was concerned with the overcoming of anxiety in the conditions of daily life.

41. See Ulrich Luz, *Matthew 1–7: A Commentary* (Minneapolis: Augsburg, 1989), 1:409–11. Perhaps I may be permitted to add that the sermons I have heard on this text have confirmed this conviction: I have found none of them persuasive.

for potential members of it. The following are, it seems to me, among the better candidates — although given the nature of the evidence we can do no more than make educated guesses. In view of the limited scope of this chapter, I offer little more than a short list with seven representative entries.

- Matthew 6:9-13 = Luke 11:2-4 (Q), the Lord's Prayer. The prayer for "daily bread," which probably alludes to the well-known story in Exod 16, where God is the source of manna, would be particularly appropriate for itinerants who had to live off the uncertain charity of others. For them, daily bread might become a real issue (cf. Mark 2:23-28), and the memory of God having fed the saints of old would be great reassurance. In line with this, Luke 11:1 interprets Jesus' prayer as analogous to a prayer that the Baptist purportedly gave, not to the public at large, but to his disciples (ἐδίδαξεν τοὺς μαθητὰς αὐτοῦ).[42]

- Matthew 10:27 = Luke 12:3 (Q), things said in the dark will be heard in the light. Matthew's version of this saying is clearly addressed to missionaries: "What I say to you in the dark, tell in the light; and what you hear whispered, proclaim from the housetops." In Luke the saying is a general prophecy of eschatological reversal: "Whatever you have said in the dark will be heard in the light, and what you have whispered behind closed doors will be proclaimed from the housetops." Scot McKnight has argued that Luke's wording and sense are original, that it is Matthew who turned the eschatological into the missionary.[43] Yet the International Q project follows Matthew rather than Luke. In addition, the immediate Q context addresses missionaries,[44] and that Matthew turned a saying that could apply to all believers into one for missionaries alone goes against his redactional tendency in the last half of chapter 10 (see below). So the Q text behind Matt 10:27 and Luke 12:3 was probably, at least in Q, an exhortation to missionaries; and that likewise seems the most plausible setting in the life of Jesus.

---

42. Cf. Origen, *De orat.* 2.4 (ed. Koetschau; GCS 3:302-303): what John taught about prayer he "handed on not to all being baptized but only in secret to those who were not just baptized but also became his disciples."

43. Scot McKnight, "Public Declaration or Final Judgment? Matthew 10:26-27 = Luke 12:2-3 as a Case of Creative Redaction," in *Authenticating the Words of Jesus* (ed. Bruce Chilton and Craig A. Evans; NTTS 38.1; Leiden: Brill, 1999), 363-83.

44. Allison, *Jesus Tradition in Q*, 21-25.

- Matthew 10:38 = Luke 14:27 (Q); Mark 8:34, the call to take up the cross. In Matthew and Mark this saying is about "following" (ἀκολουθέω) Jesus, and Luke's version speaks of being a "disciple" (μαθητής). The version in Mark 8:34, moreover, opens with "if" (εἰ), which makes it not a general imperative but a warning to those persuaded in their own minds that they really want to follow Jesus: they should first reckon with the cost. C. H. Dodd thought that Jesus spoke this word with reference to going up to Jerusalem: "The call to 'carry the cross' is addressed to those who volunteered for service on a particular occasion. Jesus did not expect all those who had come to him in faith to accompany him on this desperate venture nor, if they did not do so, did he mean to disqualify them for a part in the new community."[45]

- Matthew 6:24 = Luke 16:13, the charge not to serve two masters, because one will hate the one and love the other, or be devoted to the one and despise the other. These words would well suit a situation in which Jesus was encouraging someone to join his little band of followers. They would be a good complement to what he says in Matt 8:18–20 = Luke 9:57–58 (Q) and Mark 10:17–22, where he seeks to lure individuals away from home and money so that they can accompany him.

- Mark 1:17, "I will make you fish for people." This belongs to a story in which Jesus calls James and John to follow him and leave their jobs. The context seems entirely appropriate.

- Matthew 13:44–46, the parables of the hidden treasure and costly pearl. Dodd commented on these verses by citing Mark 10:17–30 and "kindred passages," where "Jesus is represented as calling for volunteers to join a cause. It may mean leaving home and friends, property and business; it may mean a vagrant life of hardship, with an ignominious death at the end. Is it folly to join such a losing cause? The parables before us fit such a situation."[46]

---

45. C. H. Dodd, *The Founder of Christianity* (New York: Macmillan, 1970), 104–105. Cf. John Meier, *A Marginal Jew*, vol. 2, *Mentor, Message, and Miracles* (New York: Doubleday, 1994), 64–67. On the dominical origin of the saying about the cross, see Ulrich Luz, "Warum zog Jesus nach Jerusalem?" in *Der historische Jesus: Tendenzen und Perspektiven der gegenwärtigen Forschung* (ed. Jens Schröter and Ralph Brucker; Berlin: de Gruyter, 2002), 417–18.

46. Dodd, *Parables*, 86–87.

- Luke 14:28–32, the parable of reckoning the cost of building a tower before undertaking the task and the parable of the king calculating the outcome of war before waging it. According to Josef Blinzler, "In the double parable, Jesus has in mind only that sort of discipleship which his permanent companions and fellow workers undertook."[47] This matches Luke's interpretation, which follows in 14:33: "So therefore, none of you can become my disciple if you do not give up all your possessions."

As already indicated, the evidence falls short of showing that the seven texts just listed (or others one could cite) must, if Jesus composed them, have been intended for his inner circle of fellow missionaries. It is equally true, however, that one often cannot establish, beyond reasonable doubt, that Jesus must have designed a particular unit for the express purpose of confronting the general public. Providence alone knows the evasive truth. The upshot is regrettable, for the meaning one finds in this or that saying may well depend, as we shall now see, upon the audience that we envisage for it.[48]

HERMENEUTICS

That Jesus said different things to different people, and that he did not ask everyone to do exactly the same thing, may seem so commonsensical as to be banal. Most of my conclusions thus far are, moreover, conventional; perhaps indeed all of my interpretive suggestions could be found elsewhere. Certainly one can easily quote any number of exegetes who have recognized that Jesus did not call everyone to be disciples, or at least to be disciples in the same way.[49] Within the contemporary guild, there

---

47. Josef Blinzler, "Jesus and His Disciples," in *Jesus in His Time* (ed. Hans Jürgen Schultz; Philadelphia: Fortress, 1971), 91. Cf. Dodd, *Parables*, 87, who associates Luke 14:28–33 with the call stories in Matt 8:18–22 and Luke 9:57–62.

48. For some useful comments on problems arising from our ignorance of the original context for the sayings of Jesus, see E. P. Sanders and Margaret Davies, *Studying the Synoptic Gospels* (London: SCM, 1989), 337–44.

49. A sampling: Becker, *Jesus*, 233–34; Blinzler, "Jesus and His Disciples," 91; Günther Bornkamm, *Jesus of Nazareth* (New York: Harper & Row, 1960), 146–48; Martin Dibelius, *Jesus* (Philadelphia: Westminster, 1949), 58–60; Maurice Goguel, *The Life of Jesus* (New York: Macmillan, 1933), 334–37, 584; Hengel, *Charismatic Leader*, 61–63; Heinz-Wolfgang Kuhn, "Nachfolge nach Ostern," in *Kirche: Festschrift für Günther Bornkamm zum 75. Geburtstag* (ed. Dieter Lührmann and Georg Strecker; Tübingen: Mohr-Siebeck, 1980), 120–24; Meier, *Marginal Jew*, 2:80–82; Helmut Merklein, *Die Gottesherrschaft als Handlungsprinzip: Untersuchung zur Ethik Jesu* (2nd ed.; FB 34; Würzburg: Echter, 1981), 60–64; Jürgen Roloff,

is nothing heterodox about my views on this at all. Nonetheless, this plain fact, even when acknowledged, has been given insufficient heed: all too often we have failed to recognize how substantial the hermeneutical implications can be. Let me illustrate with three examples.

Consider Luke 12:8–9 = Matt 10:32–33 (Q): "Anyone who acknowledges me before others, the Son of Man will also acknowledge before the angels; . . . but whoever denies me before others, the Son of man will deny before the angels" (cf. Mark 8:38). For the sake of discussion, let us assume that Jesus said something like this. What might he have meant? The saying has quite different meanings depending upon the audience we assign to it. If we envision Jesus' declaration as a general religious proposition, as it might be if he had originally uttered it before a large Galilean audience, then it would entail that whoever accepts Jesus is saved, and that whoever does not accept him is not saved. Such a sweeping declaration of general import would be, one might fairly claim, a step toward Cyprian's unecumenical conviction that *Salus extra ecclesiam non est.*[50]

We can, however, equally imagine that Jesus spoke Luke 12:8–9 (Q) to his coworkers, perhaps as they set out on their missionary work. The word would then be a warning to stick to their task — one which, to judge from the missionary discourse and the many sayings about hardship and suffering,[51] appears to have been quite difficult (cf. John 6:66). Jesus would have been exhorting them to loyalty. But he would not have been saying anything as loaded as "I am the way, and the truth, and the life. No one comes to the Father except through me" (John 14:6). One reason for understanding the saying in this sense, for seeing it as something other than a universal religious truth, is that the original probably envisaged a situation of persecution for missionaries. The contexts for both Matt 10:32–33 and Luke 12:8–9 concern persecution. This also holds for the parallels in Mark 8:38 and Rev 3:5 (cf. 2 Tim 2:12).

Jesus (Munich: C. H. Beck, 2000), 67–68; E. P. Sanders, "The Life of Jesus," in *Christianity and Rabbinic Judaism: A Parallel History of Their Origins and Development* (ed. Herschel Shanks; Washington, DC: Biblical Archaeology Society, 1992), 69; Sato, *Q und Prophetie*, 375; Schmeller, *Brechungen*, 114; Schnackenburg, *Moral Teaching*, 46–50; Wolfgang Schrage, *The Ethics of the New Testament* (Philadelphia: Fortress, 1988), 49–51; Eduard Schweizer, *Lordship and Discipleship* (SBT 28; London: SCM, 1960), 10; N. T. Wright, *Jesus and the Victory of God* (Minneapolis: Fortress, 1996), 298.

50. Cyprian, *Ep.* 73.21 (ed. Hartel; CSEL 3.1:795). Cf. Becker, *Jesus*, 286.

51. Matt 5:11–12 = Luke 6:22–23 (Q); Matt 5:39–44 = Luke 6:28–30 (Q); Matt 10:19 = Luke 12:11 (Q); Matt 10:28–31 = Luke 12:4–7 (Q); Matt 10:34–36 = Luke 12:51–53 (Q); Matt 23:34–35 = Luke 11:49–51 (Q); Mark 8:31; 9:12–13, 31; 10:30, 35–40; 12:1–10; 13:9–13, 14–20; *Gos. Thom.* 58, 68, 69, 82; etc.

Even in isolation, the combination of "confess" (ὁμολογέω) and "deny" (ἀρνέομαι) might make one think of a court.[52]

Matthew 5:38–42, 43–44 = Luke 6:27–30 (Q), where Jesus commands disciples to turn the other cheek and to go the extra mile, is another text whose meaning is much affected by the audience we posit for it. What was the original context of these famous words? Nothing prohibits us from supposing that Jesus spoke them to the public at large, that, notwithstanding how impractical this may seem, he enjoined everyone in his hearing to forego personal rights, to turn the other cheek, to love their enemies, and so on. There is, however, another possibility, one that is no less plausible. One can interpret Matt 5:38–40, 42 = Luke 6:29–30 as being, like the missionary discourses, instructions for itinerants. On such a reading, Jesus no more asked all to turn the other cheek than he asked all to go about without gold or silver or bread bag. If doing without staff and other necessities turned the disciples into an enacted parable, a concrete display of faith in and utter dependence upon God, this might also have also been the intended upshot of telling them to turn the other cheek, give away cloak, and so on. One admittedly can no more show this to be the case, show that this second reading is the right one, than one can show the first reading to be correct. Does not the imperfect nature of the evidence sadly compel us, on such a matter as this, to be agnostics?

The relevance of audience also appears when we consider Jesus' prohibition of divorce: Matt 5:31–32; 19:9; Mark 10:11–12; Luke 16:18 (Q); 1 Cor 7:7–13. We might interpret this prohibition as something Jesus expected of everybody. This is, in fact, how theologians, following Matt 19 and Mark 10, have read the rule throughout Christian history. They may well be right. Yet we can equally imagine that the injunction against divorce initially emerged from and addressed a very specific problem within a very small group of people.[53] Jesus' traveling company included men and women who must have kept close quarters. Some of them were presumably single, but some of them, such as Peter, were away from their spouses (cf. Mark 1:29–30). The situation was potentially scandalous, as appears from Matt 11:19 = Luke 7:34 (Q); Mark 2:15–16; and Matt

---

52. See Otto Michel, "ὁμολογεῖν," *TDNT* 5 (1968): 207–9; also below, p. 84.
53. In addition to what follows, see my article, "Men with Women: Some Interpretative Possibilities (Matt 5:27–28; Mark 9:43–48; Mark 10:11–12)," in *Feminist Companion to the Jesus Tradition* (ed. Amy-Jill Levine and Vicki Phillips; London: T & T Clark, forthcoming).

21:31.[54] Given this, it is no surprise to find Jesus addressing the problem of sexual lust (e.g., Matt 5:27–28). For the same reason, it is not surprising to find him prohibiting divorce and remarriage.[55] The only way for a disciple to legitimize illicit sexual desire would be to make it licit through marriage. But the word against divorce disallows that option. Forbidding the dissolution of marriages eliminates the one recourse that married followers would have had if they wanted to leave one union for another. And surely we would expect such a ban from Jesus, who commended those who had made themselves "eunuchs for the sake of the kingdom of heaven" (Matt 19:12).[56]

As the foregoing examples show, one's interpretation of a text may depend heavily upon the audience one envisages it addressing. The point stands whether or not one accepts my conjectures about this or that unit. Unfortunately, when it comes to particular texts, our utmost endeavors can produce little more than modest speculations about the original audience(s). The facts are too often scantly indicative of the original *Sitz im Leben*. For although our sources often instruct us about Jesus' audience, form- and redaction-criticism have shown us that they are uncertain guides in the matter. Some have, admittedly, thought that modern scholarship has been too pessimistic here. T. W. Manson believed it still possible to learn that certain words and expressions characterized Jesus' teaching to his disciples, that other words and expressions characterized things he said to the general public, that yet other words and phrases characterized his discourse for religious leaders who opposed him.[57] J. Arthur Baird, armed with computer statistics, later sought to support and further Manson's claims.[58] Their work on this matter, however, has not netted converts.

One difficulty involved in recovering the original audience of a saying of Jesus is that the canonical writers, scarcely unimpeachable authorities,

---

54. See Kathleen E. Corley, in *DJG*, s.v. "Prostitute"; as well as her book *Private Women, Public Meals* (Peabody, MA: Hendrickson, 1993).

55. Cf. Heinz Schürmann, "Neutestamentlichen Marginalien zur Frage nach der Institutionalität, Unauflösbarkeit und Sakramentalität der Ehe," in *Studien zur neutestamentlichen Ethik* (ed. Thomas Söding; SBANT 7; Stuttgart: Katholisches Bibelwerk, 1990), 123.

56. On Matt 19:12, see esp. Josef Blinzler, "Εἰσὶν Ἐυνοῦχοι," *ZNW* 48 (1957): 254–70.

57. T. W. Manson, *The Teaching of Jesus: Studies in Its Form and Content* (Cambridge: Cambridge University Press, 1967), 320–27.

58. J. Arthur Baird, *Audience Criticism and the Historical Jesus* (Philadelphia: Westminster, 1969). Part of the problem with this book is that the recurrent use of over five dozen idiosyncratic abbreviations makes reading a Herculean task. I doubt that anyone other than the author has ever fully understood it.

show a pronounced tendency to make as many of his words relevant to as many as possible. The desire is understandable, indeed unavoidable: as a text moves forward through history, it necessarily loses its first audience and must, if it is to continue its existence, gain new audiences. In this way, through the literary law of self-preservation, the particular becomes the general. Christians throughout the ages have found themselves in the Pauline correspondence, even though Paul wrote not encyclicals for all generations but occasional letters to particular congregations about their very particular problems. Words written to a few have become words appropriated by the many.

This same movement toward the universal already appears in the canonical Gospels themselves, as Matthew's Sermon on the Mount demonstrates. Much of its content was presumably directed originally to insiders, and while the Matthean setting, following Q, seemingly betrays knowledge of this fact (Matt 5:1–2), Matthew's closing, 7:28–8:1, in which he tells us that the crowd marveled, expands the audience. In accord with this, 28:16–20, which tells the disciples to teach all that Jesus has commanded, and which must include the contents of the Sermon, leaves no room for doubt. Everyone should heed Matt 5–7.

Matthew 10 supplies another clear illustration of this phenomenon. Verses 5–25 explicitly address missionaries, and they offer largely specialized instruction: the missionary should do this, the missionary should do that. But to state the obvious, not all Christians were missionaries, and concrete advice on where to go and not to go, on what to take and not to take, would not have been of pressing relevance for most of Matthew's readers. So the potential audience of 10:5–25 seems restricted. Matthew 10:26–42 is, however, different. Although still ostensibly directed to the missionary, the whole section contains imperatives that potentially own a wider audience, and the very last verse reveals that the broadening of the discourse is intentional: "And whoever gives to one of these little ones even a cup of cold water only because he bears the name of Christ, truly I say to you, he will not lose his reward" (v. 42). Since the "little ones" are Christian missionaries (cf. v. 41), verse 42 is not a word for them but for others — those who, although not missionaries, may, if they will, share in and further the Christian mission by supporting the heralds of the gospel. Matthew has made sure that the discourse to missionaries also addresses those not engaged in mission.

Matthew's universalizing hermeneutic appears elsewhere in the Jesus tradition. Joachim Jeremias, for example, made a good case that the Synoptics show a tendency to convert parables that Jesus addressed to opponents into parables for believers.[59] And I have argued elsewhere for an analogous makeover in Q: the Sayings Gospel took up logia originally spoken to itinerants and made them general instruction for Christians.[60]

At this juncture it may not be out of place to pause for a theological point. The universalizing tendency on display in the canon is one answer to the worry that assigning significant parts of the Jesus tradition to a small group of disciples makes "the seriously challenging sayings of Jesus...not relevant to ordinary social relations."[61] The words just quoted are from Richard Horsley, who believes that Gerd Theissen's work on itinerants "is a modern domestication of 'early Palestinian Christianity.'" Theissen, in Horsley's eyes, diverts attention "from the evidence of concrete problems... such as hunger and indebtedness, problems that the Jesus tradition ostensibly addresses, to the religious-ethical response of a handful of itinerant charismatics."[62] Horsley, like Luther protesting against the old monastic interpretation of Jesus' commands, is unhappy with a seemingly less-demanding Jesus, with the possibility that many of the harder or more radical imperatives of Jesus were never intended for common consumption.

Against Horsley's conviction that sayings such as Matt 8:18–22 = Luke 9:57–60 (Q) "were surely addressed to a broader audience than a few dozen wandering charismatics,"[63] the entirety of this essay may stand as an argument. And against his apparent assumption that words originally spoken to a small group cannot be generally relevant, or must be of reduced relevance, the movement of the Jesus tradition itself gives the lie. This is because the Gospels, composed decades after Jesus' departure, cannot address his pre-Easter coworkers but only believers who never knew him, and whose circumstances were doubtless most diverse and certainly not identical with the circumstances of those who followed

---

59. Joachim Jeremias, *The Parables of Jesus* (2nd rev. ed.; New York: C. Scribner's Sons, 1972), 33–42.

60. Allison, *Jesus Tradition in Q*, 30–36. Luke, by contrast, seems less prone to universalize some of Jesus' more radical teachings; see Luise Schottroff and Wolfgang Stegemann, *Jesus and the Hope of the Poor* (Maryknoll, NY: Orbis, 1986), 67–87.

61. Richard A. Horsley, *Sociology and the Jesus Movement* (2nd ed.; New York: Continuum, 1989), 39.

62. Ibid., 40–41.

63. Ibid., 44.

Jesus about Galilee. So a broadening of the audience and a reinterpretation of the sayings of Jesus, including the radical sayings, are inevitable on any reading of the evidence.[64] If, on the contrary, original audience determined relevance, we could appropriate nothing from the ancient world: meaning would die with the death of the first hearers.

Beyond this general hermeneutical point, recognition that many of Jesus' harder sayings were originally for a narrow group scarcely requires us to speak of a two-tiered ethic.[65] It makes much more sense to speak of one ethic with different demands for different callings. Jesus' disciples must have been subject to the ethical demands he made upon all his hearers, and the additional requests he made of a few hardly constituted new or different moral principles. It is true that a Jesus who called only some away from their parents or from married lives or from their businesses appears less radical than a Jesus who asked such things of all. Yet he presumably did ask all his hearers to put God before all others things, to love their neighbor, to beware of mammon, to guard intentions, to be humble, and so on. It can be only in such general imperatives as these — not in commands to go without a staff or not to bury a parent or to travel without money or to cast out demons — that any continuing relevance of Jesus' moral teachings must lie.[66]

AUDIENCE AND JUDGMENT

So far I have concerned myself with the different sorts of things Jesus may have said to his immediate followers as opposed to the larger circle of his adherents, sympathizers, and the general public. At this point I should like to consider how he might have spoken to those who opposed him and his cause. The matter is of some interest for reconstructing Jesus' eschatology.

---

64. Cf. Schmeller, *Brechungen*, 115 (Easter "led to the identification of following [*Nachfolge*] and faith" and so to a new formulation and new interpretation in which "all of Jesus' words, even the radical demands, are now relevant and binding for all believers"); and Schnackenburg, *Moral Teaching*, 47–48.

65. So too Schmeller, *Brechungen*, 114; Schnackenburg, *Moral Teaching*, 505–51; and Heinz Schürmann, *Jesus — Gestalt und Geheimnis: Gesammelte Beiträge* (ed. Klaus Scholtissek; Paderborn: Bonifatius, 1994), 79–80.

66. Cf. Daniel J. Harrington and James F. Keenan, *Jesus and Virtue Ethics: Building Bridges between New Testament Studies and Moral Theology* (Lanham, MD: Sheed & Ward, 2002), 52–53. For further hermeneutical reflections on a pastoral level, see Peter Milloy, *Disciples and Other Believers* (Grand Forks, ND: Century Creations, 2000).

"It is in the archaic collections imbedded in Q," James M. Robinson has argued, "that one can with the most assurance speak of material that goes back to sayings of Jesus himself."[67] Foremost among these collections is Q 12:22–31, the section on care. Closely related are the Lord's Prayer (Q 11:9–13) and the Sermon on the Plain (Q 6:27–49). For Robinson, the agreeable Jesus of these early sayings or clusters is not the same as the less-agreeable Jesus of the final Q or the Q redaction. Following the work of Dieter Lührmann, Robinson believes that the appealing, archaic collections are overlaid with a different theology.[68] The older materials demand forgiveness because God forgives, and they enjoin one to love enemies. But the redactor of Q, ignoring the theological grounding of such imperatives, planted discord by affixing sayings that teach something else. God ceases, in the final form of Q, to love all indiscriminately. Less than infinitely patient, the Divinity is instead bent upon punishing the wicked in due season. Woes now balance blessings; judgment ousts pity. In this way the pristine theology is — although this is not Robinson's own phrasing — polluted and spoiled.

For Robinson, two different brands of material appear in Q, and they must be from different manufacturers: only one group can have the stamp of Jesus. And the sort that prevails on this score, the sort that must be dominical, belongs happily to the so-called archaic collections. They lack the regrettable "judgmentalism" of, for example, Q 3:8; 11:49–51; 13:28–29, 34–35, and they contain no dreadful disparagement of "this generation" (Q 7:31; 11:29–32, 50–51).

There are at least two separate issues here. The first is literary. Although I have my doubts, it may be, on purely literary grounds, that the units speaking of eschatological deprivation or reflecting a harsh Deuteronomistic view of things are later additions to Q.[69] The second

---

67. James M. Robinson, "The Critical Edition of Q and the Study of Jesus," in *The Sayings Source Q and the Historical Jesus* (ed. A. Lindemann; BETL 158; Leuven: Leuven University Press, 2001), 44. In addition to what follows see chapter 3 (below), in which I show that Robinson is heir to an interpretive tradition that goes back at least as far as the poet Shelley. (Q texts are referred to by their Lukan chapter and verse.)

68. Dieter Lührmann, *Die Redaktion der Logienquelle* (WMANT 33; Neukirchen-Vluyn: Neukirchener Verlag, 1969). Robinson is quite clear that he himself is fond of the theology of the archaic collections, and that he holds a prejudice against the alleged overlay and regards it as inferior.

69. See further John S. Kloppenborg Verbin, *Excavating Q: The History and Setting of the Sayings Gospel* (Edinburgh: T & T Clark, 2000), 143–53. Although many now start from Kloppenborg's fundamental conclusion as though it were a foundational fact, others of us

issue, however, is historical and theological. If one were to decide, with Robinson, that all the references to chastisement come from a secondary stage, how would we then make the historical determination that those references have a different origin than the dominical materials that derived from an earlier stage? We cannot, without further ado, equate the first stage of Q with a beneficent Jesus, the secondary stage with a mean-spirited community. To draw a parallel, Luke's being later than Q scarcely proves that Jesus authored none of Luke's non-Q material.

If I understand Robinson aright, he considers the fearsome sayings about judgment to be from the community instead of Jesus not because — or at least not only because — they belong to a secondary stage of Q, but rather because they stand in theological tension with the allegedly archaic clusters, which represent Jesus rather well. One might respond, however, by asking whether we should reconstruct the past by assuming that Jesus must have been, to our way of thinking, theologically consistent. Does not such an assumption savor more of the academic study than real life, in which all of us are, if we are honest, paragons of unconscious inconsistencies? The requirement to love one's enemies exists alongside harrowing threats of divine judgment in Q, in the Gospels of Matthew, Mark, and Luke, and in the Pauline Epistles; and if the two-sided authors of those texts could tolerate and even promote the tension that Robinson espies in Q, we may well wonder about the presumption that Jesus was altogether different. In the next chapter I shall observe that there is a seeming contradiction in the Wisdom of Solomon between its amiable affirmations of God's universal compassion and its dreadful prophecies of divine vengeance. One wonders what Robinson would make of this dramatic contradiction. Does it suffice to disclose more than one hand in Wisdom? Did one contributor betray the theology of another? Or was one and the same person his own theological Judas? The latter circumstance is, I think, the more likely. Logic may be the historian's guide, but often the all-too-human truth is off the

---

remain unpersuaded and so must instead regard it as an influential pseudo-fact. See Paul Hoffmann, "Mutmassungen über Q: Zum Problem der literarischen Genese von Q," in *The Sayings Source Q and the Historical Jesus* (ed. A. Lindemann; BETL 158; Leuven: Leuven University Press, 2001), 255–88. Kloppenborg's analysis of Q's history, incidentally, is a bit like several popular analyses of the Matthean and Johannine traditions: the strongest polemic is located in the later stages; things go from bad to worse. Whether this intriguing convergence of tradition-histories, or at least their popularity among many of us, says anything about the present academic moment may be a question worth asking.

rational map — which circumstance, if I may be allowed the aside, is what keeps historians humble and history interesting.

I now return to the question of audience and its bearing on Robinson's argument. Let us, for the sake of discussion, concede that there are, roughly speaking, two types of materials: one that breathes hot judgment, and one that features divine and human mercy. We can, as does Robinson, assign disparate origins to each. Yet Q itself attributes both sorts of utterance to Jesus, and I should like to trust the Sayings Source far enough at least to ask whether this is so unlikely. Could Jesus himself have spoken in varied ways?

Consider the Sermon on the Plain in Q 6:27–49 and the discourse against the Pharisees in Q 11:39–52. The two exhibit great differences in tone and outlook. One is emboweled with mercy and consolation. The other is full of judgment and contains what some call a Deuteronomic view of history. Such differences could certainly bespeak different origins. I suggest, however, that they might equally reflect different audiences and so different rhetorical situations. The mood and strategy of Galatians are not the mood and strategy of Phil 1–2, yet Paul wrote both. Similarly, Isaiah of Jerusalem composed oracles of woe for Assyria (e.g., 31:8–9), but he also composed oracles of weal for Israel (e.g., 9:1–7; 11:1–16). That is, one and the same prophet produced two different sorts of oracles because he had different things to say to different audiences. The Jesus tradition may offer something similar.

Parts of the Sermon on the Plain were, I have urged, originally addressed to disciples in the proper sense. Many of its sayings, like the remainder of Robinson's so-called "archaic collections," can certainly be understood as challenges to sympathizers. Given this, it is only natural that the theme of judgment is peripheral. Jesus is speaking to those who are already on his side, who have made the decision for him. Rebuking them with threats of damnation would not serve his purpose. In fact, the one warning in the Sermon on the Plain — the parable of the two builders, Matt 7:24–27 = Luke 6:47–49 (Q) — speaks of salvation as well as failure: there is not only a house that collapses but also one that does not collapse. This parable of exhortation is best understood as it has so often been preached, as addressing those who have already thrown in with Jesus. It is designed to keep adherents in the way that they are already headed. The hortatory similes are a means of encouraging them to finish what they have begun. In other words,

Q 6:47–49 is a bit like the warning in Luke 9:61–62: If you have put your hand to the plow, you should not look back.

The words of judgment against the Jewish leaders in Q 11:39–52 have a quite different character, doubtlessly because they directly address, if only fictively, an altogether different audience — not faithful insiders but recalcitrant opponents.[70] The woes, like the threatening rebukes of the Baptist in Matt 3:7–10 = Luke 3:7–9 (Q), address themselves to outsiders, to those who have made up their minds to oppose Jesus. It would make no sense for those woes, then, to encourage such people in the way they are going, or to tell them that God will take care of them. Nor would it make sense to demand of them ethical behavior that presupposes a positive response to Jesus and his message. They rather need to be motivated to change their ways. Q 11:39–52 does this, like the proclamation of Jonah, through an unqualified, dire threat of judgment. So the woes differ from the Sermon on the Plain largely because the audiences are so different.

One can, with this in mind, ask whether the tensions between Robinson's two different sorts of clusters might reflect the different rhetorical strategies of one speaker in different situations. We certainly do not imagine that if, as Luke 11:1 assumes, John the Baptist had disciples, he spoke to them the words of Matt 3:7 = Luke 3:7: "Brood of vipers! Who warned you to flee from the wrath to come?"[71] John must have used a very different tone with his own disciples as well as with others who had already submitted to his baptism.

And so may it have been with Jesus. He could have thought that some people, because of their negative response to him, needed to be warned about judgment, and that others, because of their positive response to him, needed to hear something else, such as encouragement and moral

---

70. One must of course distinguish here between both the literary and original audiences on the one hand and the real audience — hearers or readers of the text — on the other. Q speaks not to Jewish leaders but to followers of Jesus, who in effect overhear words ostensibly directed to others. On how different audiences will hear differently sayings about judgment and how in fact a declaration of judgment for some will be a declaration of salvation for others, see Michael Wolter, " 'Gericht' und 'Heil' bei Jesus von Nazareth und Johannes dem Täufer: Semantische und pragmatische Beobachtungen," in *Der historische Jesus: Tendenzen und Perspektiven der gegenwärtigen Forschung* (ed. Jens Schröter and Ralph Brucker; Berlin: de Gruyter, 2002), 355–92. Wolter helpfully distinguishes between those addressed and those who hear and observes that the sayings of judgment were preserved by the faithful, who clearly found their own meaning in them.

71. Cf. Paul Hollenbach, "Social Aspects of John the Baptist's Preaching Mission in the Context of Palestinian Judaism," *ANRW* 2.19.1 (1979): 861–62.

demand. Context really does, to belabor the obvious, dictate what we say. I have seen lots of tombstones that refer to heaven, but none that speak of hell. This by no means entails that no one responsible for those inscriptions believed in hell, only that mention of the prospect is appropriate in some contexts, inappropriate in others. In like fashion, I doubt that condemnations of "this generation" and rebukes based upon a Deuteronomic view of history have their most natural origin in words for disciples. So one can urge that at least some of the differences that Robinson observes between various clusters in Q owe something to a change in audience, not a change of speaker. Q mirrors the fact that Jesus had more than one rhetorical demeanor.

I do not wish to be misunderstood here. Imagining different audiences for the different materials Robinson distinguishes does not eliminate the theological tension that he feels, which it would be idle to deny. It should, however, make more plausible that such tension could exist within one individual, namely, Jesus himself. It is not easy to envisage someone telling an audience that God loves the wicked in one sentence and then, in the next sentence, renouncing the wicked with the prospect of perdition. I think we can, however, envision someone emphasizing to compatriots God's universal compassion on one occasion and then, on some other occasion, say in debate with opponents, warning those opponents that God's judgment upon them is impending, that without repentance they may become grist for the eschatological mill.[72]

---

72. Cf. the way in which Paul's statements on justification by faith and on judgment by works, which are often thought to stand in tension, occur in different contexts and serve different purposes; on this, see Nigel Watson, "Justified by Faith; Judged by Works — An Antinomy?" *NTS* 29 (1983): 209–21; also below, p. 72. Cf. also David Winston, *The Wisdom of Solomon* (AnBib 43; Garden City, New York: Doubleday, 1979), 13, explaining the different views in Wis 6–19 and 1–5: the latter "was probably designed as a broadside against assimilated Alexandrian Jews who had turned their backs on their spiritual heritage....In this case the emphasis was bound to be on the divine wrath." The former, however, in seeking to comfort other Jews, naturally concentrated on divine mercy.

Perhaps it is not out of place to refer here to my own experience. In discussing the problem of evil in the classroom, I have sometimes argued, quite seriously, that God must be in something analogous to a Zen trance, or akin to the Buddhist monks who have so transcended normal consciousness as to be able to sit perfectly still while enduring self-immolation in fire; otherwise, the divinity would scream with the pain of the world and bring all to a halt. At other times I have sympathetically explored the meaning of Pascal's assertion that Jesus Christ is on the cross until the end of time. It was many years before these two radically different views of God showed up in the same lecture, and only then did I suddenly realize that the one seemingly voids the other. In retrospect, the fact seems incredible as I pride myself, like Dorothy's scarecrow, with having a brain. But there it is.

Although I accept the critical opinion that the sources cannot be relied upon to tell us to whom Jesus spoke this or that saying, it is worth observing that Q itself, as Kloppenborg has observed,[73] seems to feel that the strongest statements about judgment are most apposite for the crowds or opponents, not the disciples. For example, all of the sayings about "this generation" are addressed to the crowds or opponents:

- Q 7:31 ("To what shall I liken this generation, and what is it like?") belongs to a discourse for "the crowds" (τοὺς ὄχλους, 7:24).
- 11:29 ("This generation is...evil") and the next three verses all address themselves to those who have demanded from him a sign (11:16).
- 11:30 ("For as Jonah became a sign to the Ninevites, so also will the Son of Man be to this generation").
- 11:31 ("The queen of the South will be raised at the judgment with this generation and will condemn it").
- 11:32 ("The Ninevites will arise at the judgment with this generation and will condemn it").
- 11:50 ("blood...may be required of this generation"): this verse and the next are at the end of a discourse featuring a series of woes, including "Woe to you Pharisees!" (11:39, 42, 43).
- 11:51 ("blood...may be required of this generation").

In like fashion, although the woes in Q 10:13–14 ("Woe to you, Chorazin! Woe to you, Bethsaida!") and 15 ("And you, Capernaum, will you be exalted to heaven?") are part of the missionary discourse, addressing not the disciples but cities that have opposed Jesus and/or his missionaries — "Woe to you, Chorazin," and so on. Even though at this point the cities are not present in the narrative as actors, they are addressed in the second person. The result, however awkward, is that the rebukes are not for missionaries but for unbelievers in Jesus.[74]

Q does, admittedly, contain words of judgment not directly addressed to opponents. Yet in each case those words envisage the possibility of salvation as well as judgment. They function either as calls to decision,

---

73. Kloppenborg, *Formation*, 167–68, 238–39.
74. Cf. the woes in Luke (Q?) 6:24–26: these address not the disciples but the rich, the full, the laughing, and those well spoken of.

in which case they would be appropriate for the general public, or as exhortations to stay the course, in which case they would be appropriate for sympathizers and/or disciples. Here Q 12:5 is typical: "Fear the one who is able to destroy both the soul and body in Gehenna." This verse belongs to a discourse that proffers encouragement (cf. v. 4 = Matt 10:28: "Do not fear those who kill the body but cannot kill the soul"). Those addressed — surely they are missionaries (see above) — are not being told that they will be destroyed in Gehenna but are rather being moved to fear God in such a way that other fears are expelled. Matters are similar in Q 17:34–35 = Matt 24:40–41: "Two men will be in the field; one is taken and one is left. Two women will be grinding at the mill; one is taken and one is left." Whether being taken or being left is the better fate, it is clear that only some are judged, and others are saved. So the saying envisions the possibility of redemption, which hearers should be motivated to lay hold of.

By reflecting upon the issue of audience, I have not established the authenticity of any of the Q sayings that Robinson assigns to the community. I have rather done something much easier, which is to make a point about rhetoric. Robinson's argument is weaker than it first appears once we take into account the varied nature of Jesus' audiences. A resourceful Jesus, we may think, spoke differently to his disciples than to the crowds, and differently to the crowds than to his opponents. Presumably what he had to say about judgment, if he had anything to say at all, varied accordingly. Whether he did in fact so speak is the subject of the next chapter.[75]

---

75. In an exchange on X-Talk dedicated to chapters 2–4 of this book, Robert Schacht offered that maybe some of the tensions between the sayings about judgment and other portions of the tradition could reflect a change in Jesus' own message. "If Jesus' ministry did extend to three years and not just one, it would be rather remarkable if his message did not change at all in response to the 'feedback' he was getting from his audience(s). Even if Jesus himself did not change his views at all, he might still have changed his presentation in response to whatever patterns of resistance he experienced."

There has long been discussion of whether or not Jesus suffered something like a Galilean crisis. See Franz Mussner, "Gab es eine galiläische Krise?" in *Orientierung an Jesus: Zur Theologie der Synoptiker: Fur Josef Schmid* (ed. Paul Hoffmann with Norbert Brox und Wilhelm Pesch; Freiburg: Herder, 1973), 238–52. In the nineteenth century it was quite common to discuss changes in Jesus' thought and tactics, changes presumably occasioned by the falling away of the Galilean populace, which was read out of John 6. Indeed, according to Luigi Salvatorelli, "From Locke to Reitzenstein: The Historical Investigation of the Origins of Christianity," *HTR* 22 (1929): 303, the notion that Jesus' "preaching ministry passed through a stage of success and one of failure" was standard fare in German lives published 1860–90. Other developmental schemes have also appeared in the literature. Albert Schweitzer saw Jesus as changing strategies in midstream after his disciples returned from their mission and the end became overdue. Even the conservative Albert Descamps, in "Aux origines du ministère: La pensée de Jésus," *RTL* 2 (1971): 3–45, found evidence of Jesus modifying his view of the future. See also Anton Vögtle, "Exegetische Erwägungen über das Wissen und das Selbstbewusstsein Jesu," in *Gott in Welt: Festgabe für Karl Rahner* (ed. Johannes Baptist Metz; Freiburg: Herder, 1964), 1:608–67. In this work the first period of Jesus' ministry is the attempt to convert Israel; in the second period he knows he will die. More recently, some members of the Jesus Seminar, echoing earlier critics, have urged that, whereas the early Jesus embraced the apocalyptic theology of John the Baptist, he came later to a very different view of things. Whatever one makes of such proposals, it seems unlikely that Jesus was always, if I may so put it, in the same frame of mind. And it is not implausible to suppose that he was, for example, disappointed in negative responses to his ministry, and that this is indeed the genesis of some of the sayings about judgment, if any are dominical.

Much recent Q research, which starts with John Kloppenborg's three-layered stratification of Q, and which assigns most of the judgment sayings to Q's second stage, takes those sayings to reflect the disappointment and disillusionment of the Q community with the Jewish response to its mission. In this way, the old scheme, in which the forecasts of judgment betoken the Galilean crisis, is transferred from the historically rejected Jesus to the historically rejected Q people. This is a natural move to make if one does not, for whatever reason, trace judgment sayings to Jesus. My only point here, however, is that it almost inevitable to read some sayings as signs of change in someone's attitude.

Consider, for instance, Matt 11:20–24 = Luke 10:13–15 (Q). It is hard to read this as anything other than a testimony to dashed expectations. If one assumes for the sake of discussion that the text goes back to Jesus, what follows? Surely he conducted his ministry in the hope that he would be heard and heeded. He can hardly have carried on his mission and sent forth messengers fully persuaded that all the effort would be empty, that "this generation" would mostly disbelieve him. So if Jesus, who viewed his mission as of the utmost importance, did not get the response he expected, the disappointment would have been acute, and Q 10:13–15 could then be its verbal embodiment.

Having said all this, however, the gist of the present chapter remains unaffected. All my argument needs is the proposition that Jesus spoke differently to ill-disposed outsiders than to well-disposed insiders. It should make no difference whether this or that saying comes from this or that period of the ministry. Jesus' words to outsiders probably did vary from one phase of his public life to another, and it would be reasonable to locate the harshest utterances in a later period; but they would in any event be addressed to the unsympathetic.

THREE

THE PROBLEM OF GEHENNA

When was hell anything but murky?
— FRANCISCO DE QUEVEDO

We have heard ... of some who have endured breaking on the
Wheel, ripping up of their Bowels, fleaing alive, racking of Joynts,
burning of Flesh, pounding in a Mortar, tearing in pieces with Flesh-
hooks, boyling in Oyl, roasting on hot fiery Gridirons, etc. And yet
all these, tho' you should superad thereto all Diseases, such as the
Plague, Stone, Gout, Strangury, or whatever else you can name
most torturing to the Body, ... they would all come short ... of that
Wrath, that Horror, that unconceivable Anguish which the Damned
must inevitably suffer every Moment, without any Intermission of
their Pains, in Hellish Flames.
— JOHN SHOWER

I believe that in our unthinkable destiny, ruled by such infamies as
bodily pain, every bizarre thing is possible, even the perpetuity of
a Hell, but that it is sacrilegious to believe in it.
— JORGE LUIS BORGES

THE ISSUE

That hell is a languishing belief, and not just of late, is scarcely news.[1]
Universalism made good strides in the seventeenth century. In the optimistic eighteenth century, Jonathan Edwards may still have heartily

---

1. See Philip C. Almond, *Heaven and Hell in Enlightenment England* (Cambridge: Cambridge University Press, 1994); St. George Mavart, "Last Words on the Happiness in Hell: A
Rejoinder," *The Nineteenth Century* 33 (January–June 1893): 637–51; Geoffrey Rowell, *Hell*
and the Victorians: A Study of the Nineteenth-Century Theological Controversies concerning
Eternal Punishment and the Future Life (Oxford: Clarendon, 1974); D. Walker, *The Decline*
of Hell: Seventeenth-Century Discussions of Eternal Torment (Chicago: University of Chicago
Press, 1964).

threatened people with hell, but he also had to defend the horrible prospect from its many detractors.[2] By the nineteenth century, when even "the most strenuous of the Orthodox" were "busily depopulating hell,"[3] the Romantic poets could use "hell" as a metaphor while fervent opponents of the church could cite it as reason for writing off Christianity.[4] Toward the end of the century, Gladstone remarked that the place had been relegated "to the far-off corners of the Christian mind,... there to sleep in deep shadow, as a thing needless in our enlightened and progressive age."[5]

In the twentieth century, most mainline Protestant preachers and theologians effectively dismissed divine punishment by avoiding the topic whenever possible. When hell managed to come up anyway, some theologians, such as the members of the Doctrine Commission of the Church of England (1995), ruled that it "is not eternal torment" and, further, that "annihilation might be a truer picture of damnation."[6] Other apologists urged, seemingly against the New Testament texts in which people are thrown into Gehenna, that judgment must be self-imposed: God allows the damned to exercise their freedom and to go wherever they please, which is hell, not heaven.[7] Still others dispensed with nuanced reinterpretation and simply came to believe that — here I quote Walter

---

2. "The Eternity of Hell Torments," in *The Works of President Edwards* (New York: Leavitt, Trow, 1849), 4:266–79.

3. Washington Gladden, "Under the Laws of His Own Moral Nature, and by His Own Volition, Man Fixes His Own Destiny," in *That Unknown Country, or What Living Men Believe concerning Punishment after Death* (Springfield, MA: C. A. Nichols, 1888), 383.

4. "The Legend of Hell is...a powerful enemy of the Christian religion, as it has for generations been the most general cause of the widespread repudiation of the Churches which marks the modern era." So Percy Dearmer, *The Legend of Hell: An Examination of the Idea of Everlasting Punishment, with a Chapter on Apocalyptic* (London: Cassell, 1929), 72–73.

5. W. E. Gladstone, *Studies Subsidiary to the Works of Bishop Butler* (New York: Macmillan, 1896), 206. For the amelioration of hell among the theologians, see David J. Powys, "The Nineteenth and Twentieth Century Debates about Hell and Universalism," in *Universalism and the Doctrine of Hell: Papers Presented at the Fourth Edinburgh Conference in Christian Dogmatics, 1991* (ed. Nigel M. de S. Cameron; Carlisle, U.K.: Paternoster, 1992), 93–138.

6. The Doctrine Commission of the General Synod of the Church of England, *The Mystery of Salvation* (Church House Publishing, 1995), 198.

7. See, e.g., W. H. Auden, "Anger," in *The Seven Deadly Sins* (ed. Angus Wilson et al.; New York: William Morrow, [1962]), 84–87; and Michael Ramsey, *Canterbury Essays and Addresses* (London: SPCK, 1964), 38–39. One can already find this idea among theologians of the nineteenth century; see, e.g., Charles Hodge, *Systematic Theology* (New York: Scribner, Armstrong, 1875), 3:537. Yet, the parable of the wedding feast, Luke 14:16–24 = Matt 22:1–14 = *Gos. Thom.* 64, does depict self-exclusion, and this seems to be how things work in John's Gospel; cf. 3:18 ("the one who does not believe is condemned already"). Origen, *Princ.* 2.10.4 (ed. Görgemanns and Karpp; TzF [Texte zur Forschung] 24:426–30), clearly knows this idea. Cf. John Scotus Erigena's *De divina praedestinatione*.

Wink — "belief in a place of eternal torments is unworthy of the highest forms of Christian faith."[8] Jürgen Moltmann went further: "The logic of hell is, in my opinion, in the last resort atheistic."[9] It indeed seems that hell "has now been thrown so much into the background, it has been so modified and softened and explained away, that it scarcely retains a shadow of its ancient repulsiveness."[10] The gates of Hades have not prevailed but have rather fallen off their hinges, and the prison of shrieks and groans they once guarded is quiet and empty. Hell has indeed been harrowed. It is, in fine, "finished," and "after 2,000 years of horrifying performances the play will not be repeated."[11]

Given that so many people nowadays dislike hell but still like Jesus, it is not surprising that some modern reconstructions no longer depict him as a believer in eschatological or postmortem punishment. One could here be cynical and wonder to what extent the wish has cultivated the conclusion, a conclusion that certainly goes against the impression that the canonical Gospels leave.[12] After all, "people almost invariably arrive at their beliefs not on the basis of proof but on sentiment.... We believe little except that which pleases us" (Pascal). Maybe a Jesus who says nothing about hell is the artifact of interested historians who themselves have nothing to say about hell, or at least nothing good to say. Yet the matter is not resolved with this all-too-easy sort of ad hominen retort, for there are some interesting critical issues here.[13] Those who doubt that Jesus believed in hell and employed it in his teaching are not without

8. Walter Wink, "A Reply," *Christian Century*, August 14–27, 2002, 44.

9. Jürgen Moltmann, "The End of Everything Is God: Has Belief in Hell Had Its Day?" *ExpTim* 108 (1997): 264.

10. W. E. H. Lecky, *History of the Rise and Influence of the Spirit of Rationalism in Europe* (London: Longmans, Green, 1865), 1:341. This observation was made in the 1860s, and time has only added to its force.

11. Piero Camporesi, *The Fear of Hell: Images of Damnation and Salvation in Early Modern Europe* (University Park, PA: Pennsylvania State University Press, 1991), vi. Popular opinion polls sometimes record a surprisingly prevalent belief in a hell. For example, a 2003 Fox News poll reported that 74 percent of Americans still believe in hell. If this is accurate, one wonders how deep or important or relevant this belief generally is: one can believe things that do not much matter. Another recent poll by the Barna Research Group in 2003 reported that of those who do believe in hell, less than half of one percent seriously thinks he or she may end up there.

12. For this impression see Alan M. Fairhurst, "The Problem Posed by the Severe Sayings Attributed to Jesus in the Synoptic Gospels," *SJT* 23 (1970): 78–79.

13. And the argument can be turned around. I know a NT scholar who thinks hell is a good idea and who indeed prefers it in its everlasting form. It thus is no surprise that he has argued in print that Jesus said a good deal about judgment and believed in hell. I know another colleague who has written books on Jesus and confides that, although hell makes him uneasy, he nonetheless wants Jesus to believe in it. This is because his personal theology requires that

their arguments — even if many recent books on him ignore these and simply pass over the subject in silence.[14]

THE ARGUMENTS

One motive for skepticism has to do with the coherence of Jesus' thought. Can it be that a mind profoundly enamored of the love of God and counseling charity toward enemies concurrently accepted and even promoted the dismal idea of a divinely imposed, unending agony? If, as it seems, Jesus muted the element of vengeance in his eschatological language; if, in accord with the tradition about him, he proclaimed that God seeks the prodigal and graciously rains upon the unjust; and if, in the early sources, he shows no interest in either Joshua or Judges, books featuring violent holy war — then surely we might wonder whether he would have been comfortable with a traditional hell. Jesus was an exorcist and healer. As such, he sought to ameliorate human suffering, which an eternal hell, to the contrary, abets immeasurably. Do we not have here, as many have remarked, a conspicuous and bona fide contradiction?[15] And should this contradiction not provoke misgiving about what goes back to Jesus and what does not?

To my imperfect knowledge, the earliest argument along these lines is about two hundred years old. It comes not from a theologian or biblical scholar but from a Romantic poet, Percy Bysshe Shelley, who lived before anyone knew the ABC's of source or redaction criticism. In his essay "On Christianity," he argued that the evangelists "impute sentiments to Jesus

---

there be no great distance between the Synoptics and the historical Jesus; and as the Synoptics purport that Jesus spoke about hell, my friend needs him to have done so.

14. See the survey of Marius Reiser, *Jesus and Judgment: The Eschatological Proclamation in Its Jewish Context* (Minneapolis: Fortress, 1997), 1–16. On 3 he speaks of a "silent fadeout."

15. See, e.g., William Rounseville Alger, *A Critical History of the Doctrine of a Future Life* (Philadelphia: George W. Childs, 1864), 527 (arguing that Jesus could have taught judgment according to works but not eternal punishment); R. H. Charles, *Eschatology: The Doctrine of a Future Life in Israel, Judaism and Christianity: A Critical History* (New York: Schocken, 1963), 367; John Hick, *Evil and the God of Love* (rev. ed.; New York: Harper & Row, 1978), 346; Ian Ramsey, "Hell," in *Talk of God* (Royal Institute of Philosophy Lectures, vol. 2, 1967–1968; London: Macmillan, 1969), 208–9; Hastings Rashdall, *Conscience and Christ: Six Lectures on Christian Ethics* (London: Duckworth, 1916), 294, 305; James M. Robinson, "The Critical Edition of Q and the Study of Jesus," in *The Sayings Source Q and the Historical Jesus* (ed. A. Lindemann; BETL 158; Leuven: Leuven University Press, 2001), 27–52; Frederick A. M. Spencer, *The Future Life: A New Interpretation of the Christian Doctrine* (New York: Harper & Brothers, 1935), 128, 135; William Strawson, *Jesus and the Future Life* (2nd ed.; London: Epworth, 1970), 100.

Christ which flatly contradict each other." Jesus, according to Shelley, "summoned his whole resources of persuasion to oppose" the idea of injustice inherent in hell; Jesus believed in "a gentle and beneficent and compassionate" God, not in a "being who shall deliberately scheme to inflict on a large portion of the human race tortures indescribably intense and indefinitely protracted."[16] "The absurd and execrable doctrine of vengeance seems to have been contemplated in all its shapes by this great moralist with the profoundest disapprobation."[17]

Perhaps the most comprehensive case for this conclusion appears in an old book that, while still on the shelves of some libraries, has almost ceased to be remembered. In *The Lord of Thought* (1922), Lily Dougall and Cyril W. Emmet argued that the Synoptic passages that depict a punishing God are additions to the true tradition.[18] Rejecting the possibility that Jesus had "a confused mind, in which traditional beliefs existed unchallenged side by side with newer and more vital ideals which . . . contradict them,"[19] the authors surmised that Jesus abandoned traditional conceptions of divine judgment. The discrepant tone of divine retribution is a regrettable "accretion which has crept in during some of those various stages through which Christ's words passed before they reached their present form."[20] We must chose between the God of Jesus and the God of the Gospel writers.

---

16. Percy Bysshe Shelley, "On Christianity," in *The Prose Works of Percy Bysshe Shelley* (ed. E. B. Murray; Oxford: Clarendon, 1993), 1:260, 253. Given Shelley's knowledge of deistic writers, one suspects that this argument may not be original with him; certainly some of the early Deists distinguished the teachings of Jesus from the eschatological teaching of his followers. I have, however, yet to come across Shelley's precise argument in any earlier work I have read. Two Shelley experts, Nora Crook of East Anglia and Michael Neth of Middle Tennessee State University, in personal correspondence, are inclined to think that Shelley's thought here is not precisely paralleled in any of the books he had read. The nearest parallel I have found is in Thomas Morgan, *The Moral Philosopher in a Dialogue* (London: the author, 1737), 439–40; see p. 124, n. 45 herein. I do not know, however, whether Shelley had read Morgan, whose name is neither on the list of "Shelley's Reading" in *The Letters of Percy Bysshe Shelley* (2 vols.; ed. Frederick L. Jones; Oxford: Clarendon, 1964), 1:467–88; nor on "The Shelleys' Reading List" in *The Journals of Mary Shelley, 1814–1844* (2 vols.; ed. Paula Feldman and Diana Scott-Kilvert; Oxford: Clarendon, 1987), 2:630–84.

17. Shelley, "On Christianity," 252–53.

18. Lily Dougall and Cyril W. Emmet, *The Lord of Thought: A Study of the Problems Which Confronted Jesus Christ and the Solution He Offered* (London: SCM, 1922). A few years later Percy Dearmer made the same argument in the second half of his entertaining *The Legend of Hell*.

19. Dougall and Emmet, *Lord of Thought*, 190.

20. Ibid., 235. Cf. Dearmer, *Legend*, 258: "If our Lord had taught such a doctrine — if he had taught that God's love of the world would so fail, and his power would so fail,

Is all this just reading between the lines and then dismissing half the lines because they do not fit with what we have found between them? Or does one part of the tradition demand, because of irreconcilable differences, a divorce from the other part? The verdict of Dougall and Emmet has this at least in its favor, that the feeling animating it is not confined to post-Enlightenment moderns. Origen, Didymus the Blind, Gregory of Nyssa, Diodore of Tarsus, Evagrius, Theodore of Mopsuestia, and Isaac of Nineveh all hoped for a universal reconciliation, partly because of their conviction that God loves everyone, even the wicked — a conviction the canonical Gospels implanted in them.[21] Isaac has the most arresting things to say on the subject and is the most eloquent. He contends that the God of Jesus Christ has no anger, no wrath, no jealousy; that God is above retribution; and that God, being like a father, can never act out of vengeance or hatred.[22] "If it is a case of love, then it is not one of requital; and if it is a case of requital, then it is not one of love."[23] Again, "God is not one who requites evil, but He sets aright evil: the former is the characteristic of evil people, while the latter is characteristic of a father."[24] In short, "it is not (the way of) the compassionate Maker to create rational beings in order to deliver them over mercilessly to unending affliction (in punishment) for things of which He knew even

---

that evil and misery would persist unsubdued in an endless eternity, while the vast majority of mankind writhed and blasphemed in stark agony for ever and ever, victims to the angry will of a frustrated Divinity — if he had taught anything like this, his 'good news' would have been a mass of unresolved contradictions, he would have been a false prophet incoherently mixed with a true one, and the God he proclaimed would have been a false god."

21. Origen, *Princ.* 2.10.8; 3.6.3 (ed. Görgemanns and Karpp; TzF 24:436–38, 648–50); *Cels.* 8.72 (ed. Marcovich; 588–90); *John* 2.13 (ed. Preuchsen; GCS 10:68); Didymus, *1 Petr.* ad 1:12 (PG 39:1759B), ad 3:22 (1770B–C); *Ps.* ad 36:36 (PG 39:1340C); Gregory of Nyssa, *Or. catech.* 26 (ed. Winling; SC 453:261–63); *Anim. et res.* (PG 46:69C–72B, 88A, 100A–101A, 104B–105A); *Mort.* (PG 46:524–25); *Vit. Mos.* 2:82 (ed. Daniélou; SC 1:154); Diodore, *Frag. dog.* (see Abramowski, *ZNW* 42 (1949): 59–61; and cf. Solomon, *Book of the Bee* 60 (ed. Budge; 162–63); Evagrius, *Keph. gnost.* Syr. 2.2.84; 2.5.20; 2.6.27 (ed. Guillaumont; PO 134/28.1:95, 185, 229); *Ep.* 59.3 (ed. Frankenberg, 608–9); Theodore of Mopsuestia, *Contra def. pec. orig.* (PG 66:1005–12; cf. Solomon, *Book of the Bee* 60 [ed. Budge; 161–62]); Isaac of Nineveh, *Second* 39–40 (ed. Brock; CSCO 544:151–68). See also Gregory of Nazianzus, *Orat.* 40 (PG 36:412A–B), and the references to Stephanus, Bishop of Edessa, Georgius of Arbela, Ebed Jesu of Soba, and Timotheus II, patriarch of the Nestorians in Giuseppe Simone Assemani, *Bibliotheca orientalis Clementino-vaticana: in qua manuscriptos codices syriacos, arabicos, persicos, turcicos, hebraicos, samaritanos, armenicos, aethiopicos, graecos, aegyptiacos, ibericos, & malabaricos* (Rome: Typis Sacrae Congregationis de Propaganda Fide, 1719–28), 3:323; 4:344.

22. Isaac of Nineveh, *Second* 39–40 (544:151–68). Cf. Gregory of Nyssa, *V. Macr.* (PG 46:100C).

23. Isaac of Nineveh, *Second* 39.17 (544:160).

24. Ibid., 39.15 (544:160).

before they were fashioned, (aware) how they would turn out when He created them — and whom (nonetheless) He created."[25]

In view of Isaac and his predecessors, we cannot dismiss as peculiarly modern the sense of a tension between the God who makes the sun rise upon all and the God who destroys both body and soul in Gehenna. In line with this are old Apocrypha, such as the *Greek Apocalypse of the Virgin*, in which God allows tormented sinners a respite during Pentecost or Lent or on Sundays.[26] Surely this happy thought was borne of the feeling that the divine goodness must ameliorate hell, at least a bit. It is the same with those popular apocalypses, such as the *Apocalypse of Peter* and the Armenian *Apocalypse of Paul*, in which saints pray sinners out of hell.[27] Here compassion vanquishes pain. Given texts such as these — as well as the rabbinic authorities who limit hell's duration[28] and the feeling of some early Christians, such as Marcion, that the God of compassion cannot be the God of vengeance — it is not unthinkable that a first-century Galilean Jew also had qualms about the matter.[29] Other Jews certainly expressed dismay. According to *2 Bar.* 55:7, when Baruch heard "the announcement of the punishment of those who have

---

25. Ibid., 39.6 (544:155).

26. *Greek Apoc. Vir.* 30 (ed. M. R. James; 126). Cf. *Vis. Paul* 44 (ed. Silverstein and Hilhorst; 160–61); and Prudentius, *Cat.* 5.125–26: There is "often holiday from punishment in hell." Discussion in Theodore Silverstein, *Visio Sancti Pauli* (SD 4; London: Christophers, 1935), 79–81.

27. *Apoc. Pet.* 14 Rainer frag. (ed. James, *JTS* 32 [1931]: 271); Arm. *Apoc. Paul* (form 4) 35 (trans. Leloir; CCSA 3:171–72): Mary and Paul pray everyone out of hell. Cf. *Sib. Or.* 2.330–39: "Whenever they ask the imperishable God to save men from the raging fire and deathless gnashing he will grant it, and he will do this. For he will pick them out again from the undying fire and set them elsewhere and send them on account of his own people to another eternal life with the immortals"; *Ep. Apost.* 40 (ed. Schmidt; TU 43:18–19: Jesus says to the apostles, "I will hear the request of the righteous concerning them [the sinful dead]"); Coptic *Apoc. Elijah* 5:28 (ed. Steindorff; TU 17:102: "Grace will occur. In those days, that which the righteous will ask for many times will be given them"); *Tanna d. El.* 15 (Elyyahu Rab. 3: The righteous will pray to life the wicked who attended synagogue). For Augustine's knowledge of such ideas, see *Civ.* 21.17ff. (ed. Dombart and Kalb; CCSL 48:783ff.).

28. *m. 'Ed.* 2:10: "The judgment of the unrighteous in Gehenna shall endure twelve months"; *t. Sanh.* 13:4; *b. Roš. Haš.* 17a: "Wrongdoers among the Jews as well as among the Gentiles suffer in Gehenna for twelve months"; *y. Sanh.* 10:3; *Midr. Prov.* 17; *Tanna d. El.* 15 (Elyyahu Rab. 3): "Some of the wicked will be sentenced for thirty days, some for sixty days, some for three months and some for six months." Akiba's paradoxical remark in *m. 'Abot* 3:15 — "The world is judged by goodness, but all is according to the excess of [good or bad] works" — calls attention to a perceived conflict between justice and mercy.

29. See further Richard Bauckham, "The Conflict of Justice and Mercy: Attitudes to the Damned in Apocalyptic Literature," in *The Fate of the Dead: Studies on the Jewish and Christian Apocalypses* (NovTSup 93; Leiden: Brill, 1998), 132–48. Marcion's God, however, does not prevent sinners from falling into the fire of this world's creator; see Adolf von Harnack, *Marcion: The Gospel of the Alien God* (Durham, N.C.: Labyrinth, 1990), 90–91.

transgressed," he did not rejoice in self-satisfaction but became "wholly terrified." Second Esdras (= 4 Ezra) shows us the same horrified response to the injustice of conventional eschatological expectations and the seer's resultant feeling that human beings should not have been created (7:62–69; cf. 8:4–19; 10:9–17). Surely, at least in theory, it is not ahistorical to imagine that Jesus, who in Ed Sanders's words was "a kind and generous man,"[30] might have been equally distraught.

Source and redaction criticism supply another reason, one much more concrete, for wondering whether Jesus really taught anything about divine punishment.[31] The following are the Synoptic texts that clearly presuppose a personal or collective judgment either after death or at the end of the present age.[32]

Texts Commonly Assigned to Q[33]

- Luke 10:12 = Matt 10:15: "I say to you: It shall be more bearable on that day for Sodom than for that town."

- Luke 10:14 = Matt 11:24: "Yet it shall be more bearable at the judgment for Tyre and Sidon than for you."

---

30. E. P. Sanders, *The Historical Figure of Jesus* (Allen Lane: Penguin, 1993), 192.

31. Here the second half of Dearmer's *Legend of Hell* makes some telling points and remains instructive for its overall impression, even if it is dated.

32. Throughout this essay I shall make no distinction between personal and collective eschatology, which exist side by side in the Jesus tradition (as in so much ancient Jewish and Christian literature), nor between Gehenna and Hades. On the equation of the latter two places in the canonical Gospels, see W. J. Boyd, "Gehenna — according to Jeremias," in *Studia Biblica 1978*, part 2, *Papers on the Gospels: Sixth International Congress on Biblical Studies* (ed. E. A. Livingstone; JSNTSup 2; Sheffield: JSOT, 1980), 9–12; and Alan E. Bernstein, *The Formation of Hell: Death and Retribution in the Ancient and Early Christian Worlds* (Ithaca, NY: Cornell University Press, 1993). It is the later church fathers who clearly distinguish Hades and Gehenna; see Henri Crouzel, *Les fins dernières selon Origène* (Brookfield, VT: Gower, 1990), 291–331. I reject and will leave to the side the view of T. Francis Glasson, *The Second Advent: The Origin of the New Testament Doctrine* (2nd ed.; London: Epworth, 1947), 127–34, that Jesus taught about a judgment running through history, to which some of the texts listed allegedly refer. I also pass over sayings, such as Luke 19:41–44, that advert or may advert to historical and national judgment; for these, see Marcus J. Borg, *Conflict, Holiness and Politics in the Teaching of Jesus* (Lewiston, NY: E. Mellen, 1984), 265–76. I further omit from my list sayings that, while they seem to me to point to or to presuppose the last judgment, do not do so in the view of others. Examples are Luke 6:37–38 = Matt 7:1–2 (Q; cf. Mark 4:24); Luke 6:47–49 = Matt 7:24–27 (Q; on this, see n. 91); Luke 11:19 = Matt 12:27 (Q); Luke 14:11 = Matt 23:12 (Q?; cf. Luke 18:14; *Gos. Thom.* 59, 70); Luke 17:33 = Matt 10:39 (Q; cf. John 12:25); Luke 19:26 = Matt 25:29 (Q); Mark 8:35; 9:42; 10:31; Luke 6:24–26.

33. I have based most of my translations upon the Greek text of Q according to *The Critical Edition of Q: Synopsis* (ed. James M. Robinson, Paul Hoffmann, and John S. Kloppenborg; Leuven: Peeters, 2000). On occasion, however, I have gone my own way.

- Luke 10:15 = Matt 11:24: "And you, Capernaum, will you be exalted to heaven? Into Hades you will come down."

- Luke 11:31 = Matt 12:42: "The queen of the South will be raised at the judgment with this generation and condemn it, for she came from the ends of the earth to listen to the wisdom of Solomon, and behold, something greater than Solomon is here!"[34]

- Luke 11:32 = Matt 12:41: "The men of Nineveh will arise at the judgment with this generation and condemn it; for they repented at the preaching of Jonah, and behold, something greater than Jonah is here."

- Luke 12:5 = Matt 10:28 (cf. *2 Clem.* 5:4): "But fear . . . the one who is able to destroy both the soul and body in Gehenna."

- Luke 12:8–9 = Matt 10:32–33 (cf. Mark 8:38): "Anyone who acknowledges me before men, the Son of Man will also acknowledge before the angels. . . . But whoever denies me before men, the Son of Man will deny before the angels."

- Luke 12:10 = Matt 12:31 (cf. Mark 3:28–29): "And whoever says a word against the Son of Man, it will be forgiven him; but whoever speaks against the Holy Spirit, it will not be forgiven him."

- Luke 12:46 = Matt 24:50: "The master of that slave will come on a day that he does not expect and at an hour he does not know, and he will cut him to pieces and give him an inheritance with the faithless."

- Luke 12:58–59 = Matt 5:25–26: "And the assistant will throw you into prison. I tell you, you will never get out until you pay the last penny."

- Luke 13:24 = Matt 7:13–14: "Enter through the narrow door, for many will seek to enter, and few are those who enter through it."

- Luke 13:25, 27 = Matt 7:22–23 (cf. Matt 25:10–12; *Gos. Thom.* 75): "When the householder has arisen and locked the door, and you begin to stand outside and knock on the door, saying: Master, open for us, and he will answer you: I do not know you. . . . And he will say to you: I do not know you. Get away from me, you who work lawlessness."

---

34. Both Luke/Q 11:31 and 32 refer to the eschatological judgment, although this is sometimes denied; see Reiser, *Jesus and Judgment*, 211–12.

- Luke 13:28 = Matt 8:12: "There will be weeping and gnashing of teeth when you shall see Abraham and Isaac and Jacob in the kingdom of God but you yourselves thrown out."[35]

- Luke 17:27, 30 = Matt 24:38–39: "For as in those days they were eating and drinking, marrying and giving in marriage, until the day Noah entered the ark and the flood came and took them all, so will it also be on the day the Son of man is revealed."[36]

- Luke 17:34–35 = Matt 24:40–41 (cf. *Gos. Thom.* 61): "I tell you, there will be two men in the field; one is taken and one is left. Two women will be grinding at the mill; one is taken and one is left."

- Luke 19:26 = Matt 25:29 (cf. Mark 4:25; *Gos. Thom.* 41): "To everyone who has, more will be given; but from the one who does not have, even what he has will be taken from him."

Texts from Mark

- 9:43 (cf. Matt 18:8): "If your hand causes you to stumble, cut it off; it is better for you to enter life maimed than to have two hands and to go to hell, to the unquenchable fire."

- 9:45 (cf. Matt 18:8): "And if your foot causes you to stumble, cut it off; it is better for you to enter life lame than to have two feet and to be thrown into hell."

- 9:47–48 (cf. Matt 18:9): "And if your eye causes you to stumble, tear it out; it is better for you to enter the kingdom of God with one eye than to have two eyes and to be thrown into hell, where their worm never dies, and the fire is never quenched."

- 12:40: "They will receive the greater condemnation [κρίμα]."

Texts from Matthew Alone

- 5:22: "If you are angry with a brother, you will be liable to judgment; . . . and if you say, 'You fool,' you will be liable to the hell of fire."

---

35. In Luke 13:28 "the weeping and gnashing of teeth" expresses the regret of those who are excluded from the eschatological banquet. In Matt 8:12 the phrase describes what goes on in the place of torment itself: "thrown in the outer darkness, where there will be weeping and gnashing of teeth."

36. Cf. the agraphon in Justin, *Dial.* 47.5 (ed. Marcovich; PTS 47:148): "In whatever situations I find you, I shall judge you."

- 7:19 (cf. 3:10; Luke 3:9): "Every tree that does not bear good fruit is cut down and thrown into the fire."
- 12:36–37: "On the day of judgment you will have to give an account for every careless word you utter; for by your words you will be justified, and by your words you will be condemned."
- 13:42 (cf. *Gos. Thom. 57*): "They will throw them into the furnace of fire, where there will be weeping and gnashing of teeth."
- 13:49–50: "The angels will ... throw them [the evil] into the furnace of fire, where there will be weeping and gnashing of teeth."
- 15:13: "Every plant that my heavenly Father has not planted will be rooted up."
- 22:13: "Bind him hand and foot, and throw him into the outer darkness, where there will be weeping and gnashing of teeth."
- 23:15: "Woe to you! ... You make the new convert twice as much a child of hell as yourselves."
- 23:33: "You brood of vipers! How can you escape being sentenced to hell?"
- 24:51: "He will cut him in pieces and put him with the hypocrites, where there will be weeping and gnashing of teeth."
- 25:30 (contrast Luke 19:27 [Q]): "As for this worthless slave, throw him into the outer darkness, where there will be weeping and gnashing of teeth."
- 25:41 (cf. *2 Clem.* 4:5): "Depart from me into the eternal fire prepared for the devil and his angels."
- 25:46: "These will go away into eternal punishment."

Texts from Luke Alone

- 6:25: "Woe to you who are full now, for you will be hungry. Woe to you who are laughing now, for you will mourn and weep."
- 12:20: "But God said to him, 'You fool! This very night your life is being demanded of you. And the things you have prepared, whose will they be?' "
- 12:47–48: "That slave who knew what his master wanted, but did not prepare himself or do what was wanted, will receive a severe beating.

But the one who did not know and did what deserved a beating will receive a light beating."

- 16:23–24: "In Hades, where he was being tormented, he looked up and saw Abraham far away, with Lazarus by his side. He called out, 'Father Abraham, have mercy on me, and send Lazarus to dip the tip of his finger in water and cool my tongue, for I am in agony in these flames.'"

- 16:28: "They will not also come into this place of torment."

While sixteen of these texts come from Q, only four are from Mark; and Mark's three lines about Gehenna all belong to the same complex, 9:43–48. Eschatological punishment is most prominent in Matthew. Not only does Matthew, unlike Luke, take over all of the relevant Markan texts, but he also has many additional lines of his own, and almost half the texts that name Gehenna in the Synoptics are his alone. Assuming the priority of Mark and Q, Matthew has added about a dozen new references to eschatological punishment, and surely many are redactional. Furthermore, the Lukan parallels to Matt 24:51 and 25:30 are much less developed in their eschatological imagery. Instead of "He will cut him in pieces and put him with the hypocrites, where there will be weeping and gnashing of teeth," which we find in Matt 24:51, Luke 12:46 has the less elaborate: "The master... will cut him in pieces, and put him with the unfaithful." Similarly, though Matt 25:30 has "As for this worthless slave, throw him into the outer darkness, where there will be weeping and gnashing of teeth," Luke 19:27 lacks both "the outer darkness" and "weeping and gnashing of teeth." Instead it says: "But as for these enemies of mine who did not want me to be king over them — bring them here and slaughter them in my presence." So it seems fairly clear, at least for those of us who suppose that Matthew followed Mark, that the further we get from Jesus, the more hell there is. Consider the chart on the following page, which is rather suggestive regarding Matthew's contribution to the words of Jesus.

What one finds in Matthew when compared with Mark and Luke, one can likewise discover, if so motivated, in Q itself. John Kloppenborg has persuaded many that the Sayings Source contained two major types of materials — prophetic words that announce the impending judgment of this generation on the one hand, and on the other hand wisdom-like utterances addressed to the community that concern self-definition and

Word or Phrase	Matthew	Mark	Luke
ἀπώλεια (of eschatological punishment)	1	0	0
γέεννα	7	3	1
κλαυθμὸς καὶ ὁ βρυγμὸς τῶν ὀδόντων	6	0	1
κόλασις (of eschatological punishment)	1	0	0
πῦρ (of eschatological punishment)	8	2	0
πῦρ αἰώνιον	2	0	0
σκότος ἐξώτερον	3	0	0

general comportment toward the world.[37] The latter were, according to Kloppenborg, the formative component of Q. The prophetic sayings arrived later. This matters because such a reconstruction might encourage one so inclined to assign most or even all of Q's sayings about divine punishment to the community's second stage and then to deny them to Jesus. Kloppenborg himself would not argue so simply. He is quite careful not to identify segments of the first stratification of Q with the historical Jesus and everything else with Jesus' later followers.[38] But others have been less circumspect, and acceptance of Kloppenborg's analysis would certainly be consistent with skepticism about the originality of the sayings that announce eschatological or postmortem judgment.

James Robinson has recently emphasized the contrast in Q between what he calls the "judgmentalism" of a later redactional layer and the spirit of earlier materials.[39] "Those parts of Q that have, over the years, been recognized as the archaic collections, seem to have been ignored by the redactor, where God passing judgment has replaced God taking pity on sinners!"[40] For Robinson, the tension between judgment and mercy in Q does not betray an inconsistency in Jesus' own mind but reflects rather the difference between Jesus himself and some of his interpreters — the same verdict that Shelley rendered. "Jesus' vision of a caring Father who is infinitely forgiving and hence shockingly evenhanded in dealing with the bad as well as the good, may have been lost

---

37. John S. Kloppenborg, *The Formation of Q: Trajectories in Ancient Christian Wisdom Collections* (SAC; Philadelphia: Fortress, 1987). But for criticism, see Paul Hoffmann, "Mutmassungen über Q: Zum Problem der literarischen Genese von Q," in *The Sayings Source Q and the Historical Jesus* (ed. A. Lindemann; BETL 158; Leuven: Leuven University Press, 2001), 255–88.

38. Kloppenborg, *Formation*, 245; idem, "The Sayings Gospel Q and the Question of the Historical Jesus," *HTR* 89 (1996): 337.

39. Robinson, "Critical Edition of Q," 27–52. In addition to what follows, see chapter 2, "The Problem of Audience" (above).

40. Robinson, "Critical Edition of Q," 40.

from sight a generation later, as a result of the grueling experience of the Jewish war, understood as God's quite judgmental punishment of Israel."[41] Again, "Jesus' basic insight into the ever-loving and forgiving nature of God would seem to have been lost from sight as the age-old view of God undergirding retaliatory justice again asserted itself."[42] In this way the Jesus who spoke of Gehenna is, with scarcely concealed applause in the background, executed upon the scaffold of criticism.

ASSESSING THE ARGUMENTS

Such then are some of the arguments one might invoke to deny that Jesus said anything much about hell. What do we make of them? The argument from consistency is of great interest theologically. Speaking for myself, I see little prospect of harmonizing Jesus' God of catholic compassion with the God who tosses the lost into the eschatological incinerator. Isaac of Nineveh's musings, as I shall indicate in due course, make perfect sense to me. I nonetheless doubt that my being nonplussed about this issue is a suitable guide to the reconstruction of history. All of us are bundles of seeming contradictions, from which generalization I see no reason to exempt Jesus. It would be unimaginative and foolhardy to subdue him with the straightjacket of consistency. If, for instance, we were to hold to the authenticity of Matt 5:22, where Jesus prohibits anger and insulting others, would we be bound to infer that Mark 3:5 ("He looked around at them with anger") must be pure fabrication, or that Jesus could never have railed against the scribes and Pharisees and insulted them as he does in Luke 11 and Matt 23, or that he could not have overturned tables in the temple?

It is useful to recollect the contradictions that a few older critics found in some Jewish and Christian apocalypses, contradictions that were the basis for dubious compositional theories, such as G. H. Box's analysis of 4 Ezra and R. H. Charles's analysis of Revelation.[43] We cannot infer, on the basis of our own logic, what someone else's logic must have dictated, especially someone from a very different time and place. Jesus' ways need

41. Ibid., 43.
42. Ibid., 42–43.
43. R. H. Charles, *A Critical and Exegetical Commentary on the Revelation of St. John* (2 vols.; ICC; Edinburgh: T & T Clark, 1920); G. H. Box, "4 Ezra," in *The Apocrypha and Pseudepigrapha of the Old Testament* (ed. R. H. Charles; Edinburgh: T & T Clark, 1913), 2:542–624.

not be our ways.[44] We must distinguish between a tension that he might
have tolerated — and that his followers certainly did tolerate — from a
contradiction that we personally may not abide. This is all the more so
in the present case, for the Jesus tradition contains no explicit rejection
of hell. To go by the New Testament, if Jesus opposed divine judgment,
his protest was stunningly ineffectual.

We would do well to remember that the Christian tradition is full of
people who have waxed eloquently about God's love one minute and
then threatened people with divine vengeance the next. Paul penned
1 Cor 13, but he also spoke about "the wrath that is coming" (1 Thess
1:10; cf. 2:16; 5:9). The redactor of the Sermon on the Mount, with its
God who rains upon the unjust as well as the just, speaks of the weeping
and gnashing of teeth fully six times. And Luke, who preserves Q's Sermon on the Plain, with its imperative to love even enemies, also passes
down the tale of the rich man and Lazarus, with its flames of agony.
From a later time, I think of the curious case of Bernard of Clairvaux.
He wrote exquisitely beautiful words about love and yet sponsored the
Second Crusade with zest and had no qualms about consigning Abelard
ad inferos.[45] Even the kindly Francis of Assisi warned of hell.[46]

Furthermore, Gregory of Nyssa and Isaac of Nineveh and their kin,
despite their qualms, retained a place for hell, albeit a delimited one. In
my opinion, Gregory and Isaac would not have believed in hell if they
had felt the freedom to do without it; postmortem punishment remains
foreign to their innermost and distinctive characters and to their central
images of God. Yet they did not do away with hell, for they evidently felt
obliged to make the best of what their tradition had handed them. They
are perhaps a bit like the author of 4 Ezra. Despite his incisive skepticism and his profound conviction that God's dealings with humanity are
unfair, he could not break with his tradition. Instead of giving up divine
retribution, he put aside his feelings and, in the end, resigned himself to

---

44. See further Jack T. Sanders, "The Criterion of Coherence and the Randomness of
Charisma: Poring through Some Aporias in the Jesus Tradition," *NTS* 44 (1998): 1–25. See
also Gerd Lüdemann, *Jesus after Two Thousand Years: What He Really Said and Did* (Amherst,
NY: Prometheus Books, 2001), 691.

45. Bernard, *Ep.* 188.2 (ed. Leclercq and Rochais; 11).

46. See his "Letter to the Rulers of the Peoples," in *Francis of Assisi: Early Documents*,
vol. 1, *The Saint* (ed. Regis J. Armstrong, J. A. Wayne Hellmann, and William J. Short; New
York: New City, 1999), 58.

taking consolation from a Job-like ignorance and an apocalyptic world-view. We can imagine something similar with Jesus. If, as is likely enough, he had ever heard the end of Isaiah (66:24: "And they shall go out and look at the dead bodies of the people who have rebelled against me; for their worm shall not die, their fire shall not be quenched, and they shall be an abhorrence to all flesh") or the last chapter of Daniel (12:2: "Many of those who sleep in the dust of the earth shall awake, some to everlasting life, and some to shame and everlasting contempt"), or if he was familiar with the sort of eschatological expectations found in 1 Enoch and other apocalypses, he would have known about Gehenna; and he may well have accepted the prospect as carrying the authority of his divinely-inspired tradition. Dispensing with Gehenna may have been, given his cultural setting, something he never seriously contemplated.

We must take full account of Jesus' Jewish and biblical heritage. After declaring that the Lord is "a God merciful and gracious, slow to anger, abounding in steadfast love and faithfulness, keeping steadfast love for the thousandth generation, forgiving iniquity and transgression and sin," Exod 34:6-7 immediately follows with this frightful and incongruent thought: God will "by no means clear the guilty, but visits the iniquity of the parents upon the children, and the children's children, to the third and the fourth generation." Deuteronomy 32:39 says, much more succinctly, "I kill and I make alive; I wound and I heal." In like manner, the book of Wisdom castigates sinners and revels in their judgment while at the same time offering this unsurpassed declaration of God's universal care:[47] "But you have compassion over all, because you can do all, and you overlook the sins of human beings with a view to their repentance. For you love all that exists, and loathe nothing which you have created; for if you had hated anything you would never have fashioned it. How could anything have endured, had it not been your will, or that which was undesignated by you have been preserved? But you spare all because they are yours, O Sovereign Lord, lover of all that lives; for your imperishable spirit is in them all" (11:23–12:1). It is beyond me how the person who wrote these remarkable words could also depict God as scornfully laughing at the unrighteous, as dashing them to the ground, as turning them into dishonored corpses, as wrathfully assailing them with

---

47. Discussion in Moyna McGlynn, *Divine Judgement and Divine Benevolence in the Book of Wisdom* (WUNT 2.139; Tübingen: Mohr Siebeck, 2001).

sword, lightning, and hailstorms (4:18–19; 5:17–23; cf. 16:15–24). But there it is.[48]

There is also a very instructive and analogous problem in the New Testament Epistles. Commentators since Origen have knit their brows over the presence in Paul's letters of justification by faith and judgment by works.[49] Many have espied here a "contradiction," others a "paradox."[50] While some have tried to eliminate or reduce the inconsistency, the truth is that, when the apostle refers to the eschatological judgment, "he looks at it in two different aspects. Which aspect is foremost depends on the needs of the rhetorical situation. Such rhetorical flexibility defeats attempts to discover absolute systematic consistency [in] Paul's conceptions of God's final judgment."[51] In other words, Pauline theology is, in one significant respect, in seeming tension with itself—which is not at all remarkable: even the most systematic thinkers can be deconstructed. Now students of Paul are stuck with the problem because the relevant texts belong to the undisputed letters. But who can doubt that, if those letters were instead known to be the end products of an oral tradition that mixed the teachings of Paul with the thoughts of his admirers, some critics would confidently inform us that the remarks on judgment by works, being in conflict with those on justification by faith, must be secondary, or vice versa? The thesis, although understandable, would be erroneous; and it bears a resemblance to what Robinson and others have posited for the Jesus tradition.

What about the argument from source and redaction history, from the fact that sayings about hell attached themselves to the tradition as time moved on? This should indeed give us pause. Ultimately, however, it does not make up our minds, for the question is not whether tradents added references to divine punishment. They assuredly did. The issue

---

48. The unity of the Wisdom of Solomon "is now the consensus." So David Winston, *The Wisdom of Solomon* (AnBib 43; Garden City, NY: Doubleday, 1979), 13.

49. See Kent L. Yinger, *Paul, Judaism, and Judgment according to Deeds* (SNTSMS 105; Cambridge: Cambridge University Press, 1999), 6–15.

50. See, e.g., Rudolf Bultmann, *Theology of the New Testament* (New York: C. Scribner's Sons, 1951), 1:75: "It is noteworthy and indicative of the extent to which Paul keeps within the framework of general Christian preaching, that he does not hesitate, in at least seeming contradiction to his doctrine of justification by faith alone, to speak of judgment according to one's works." Also see H. A. A. Kennedy, *St. Paul's Conceptions of the Last Things* (London: Hodder & Stoughton, 1904), 201: Paul's invocation of the last judgment is part of a "profound paradox."

51. David W. Kuck, *Judgment and Community Conflict: Paul's Use of Apocalyptic Judgment Language in 1 Corinthians 3:5–4:5* (NovTSup 66; Leiden: Brill, 1992), 239.

is instead whether, in so doing, they were elaborating upon something that was there from the beginning or rather attaching a foreign element that altered the character of the tradition. That Christians contributed sayings about hell to the tradition is, clearly, no unimpeachable proof that Jesus himself did not also do so.[52]

MORE ARGUMENTS

If the arguments against eschatological punishment belonging to Jesus' proclamation do not force assent, what about the case on the other side? There is, to begin with, an argument from continuity. Many have urged that Jesus' position between John the Baptist, for whom the imminent judgment was central, and the early church, which longed for the Parousia, makes most sense on the supposition that Jesus himself was much concerned with eschatology.[53] One can construct related arguments about hell. John the Baptist, if we can trust Q, concerned himself with the salvation of individuals in the face of the coming judgment. Luke 3:7 = Matt 3:7 reports that he warned his hearers to flee from the wrath to come; and in Luke 3:17 = Matt 3:12, we find the Baptist saying: "His winnowing fork is in his hand, and he will clear his threshing floor and gather the wheat into his granary, but the chaff he will burn with fire that can never be put out." Paul too thought that if some were headed for life, others must be not so destined: Rom 2:5 ("You are storing up wrath for yourself on the day of wrath"), 8–9 ("For those who are self-seeking and who obey not the truth but wickedness, there will be wrath and fury. There will be anguish and distress for everyone who does evil"); 14:10 ("We will all stand before the judgment seat of God"); 1 Thess 1:10 (Jesus "rescues us from the wrath that is coming"); 2 Thess 1:9 ("the punishment of eternal destruction"); etc. Now because Jesus submitted to John's baptism and praised him extravagantly (Luke 7:24-35; Matt 11:7-19: Q), and because Paul's Letters are our earliest

---

52. Here I cannot discuss the details of Q's compositional history and the questions one might ask of Robinson (see pp. 47–55 above). I observe, however, that Luke 12:5 = Matt 10:28, which refers to destruction in Gehenna, belongs to the collection in Q (cf. Luke) 12:2–12, which Kloppenborg assigns to Q1, and the verse seems integral to its context.

53. See, e.g., Dale C. Allison Jr., *Jesus of Nazareth: Millenarian Prophet* (Minneapolis: Fortress, 1998), 39–40, 102–113; and E. P. Sanders, *Jesus and Judaism* (Philadelphia: Fortress, 1985), 91–95. On the significant continuity between Jesus and John the Baptist, see my article, "John and Jesus: Continuity and Discontinuity," *Journal for the Study of the Historical Jesus* [*JSHJ*] 1, no. 1 (2002): 6–27.

written witnesses to the Christian movement, is there not some presumption that Jesus, like both his predecessor and his successor, fretted about
people flunking the divine judgment? Jürgen Becker asks, "What kind
of historical view of Primitive Christianity would we be left with if we
juxtapose a message of Jesus that was purified of all traces of judgment
and a dark and brooding Primitive Christianity that so easily and in so
many ways speaks of God's judgment?"[54]

In addition to the argument from continuity, one might appeal to a
criterion of manifold or recurrent attestation. Belief in hell or wrath-
ful judgment appears, as already indicated, in all the Synoptic sources.
Furthermore, John's Gospel, while it nowhere mentions "Hades" or
"Gehenna," presupposes a divine judgment and recompense for the lost.
That believers will "not perish but have eternal life" (3:16; cf. 10:28;
11:26) implies that unbelievers will, to the contrary, perish and not have
eternal life. Both 5:28–29 ("The hour is coming when all who are in
their graves will hear his voice and will come out ... those who have
done evil, to the resurrection of condemnation") and 12:48 ("The one
who rejects me and does not receive my words has a judge; on the last
day the word that I have spoken will serve as judge") confirm this. And
15:6 ("Whoever does not abide in me is thrown away like a branch and
withers; such branches are gathered, thrown into the fire, and burned")
probably, despite the doubts of many modern commentators, adverts to
Gehenna.[55]

Divine judgment does not appear in a mere isolated verse or two in
the canonical Gospels; it instead is a significant element of the Jesus tradition as we have it. The theme recurs in Matthew, Mark, Luke, and
John; it is central to the earliest source, Q; and it may even appear in the
Gospel of Thomas at one point (57: "On the day of harvest the weeds
will appear, they will be pulled and burned"). While Reiser's estimate —
"more than a quarter of the traditional discourse material of Jesus is
concerned with the theme of the final judgment"[56] — seems overgener-
ous to me, one can hardly characterize the theme as marginal. It appears,
moreover, in diverse genres — in parables (e.g., Q 13:25–27; Matt
25:41, 46; Luke 16:23–24, 28), in prophetic forecasts (Q 10:12–15;

---

54. Jürgen Becker, *Jesus of Nazareth* (New York: de Gruyter, 1998), 50.

55. See Raymond E. Brown, *The Gospel according to John (xiii–xxi)* (AB; Garden City, NY: 1970), 679.

56. Reiser, *Jesus and Judgment*, 304.

11:31–32; Matt 13:42, 50), in admonitions to insiders (Q 12:5; 13:24; Mark 9:43–48; Matt 5:22), and in rebukes of outsiders (Q 13:28; Matt 23:15, 23; Luke 6:25). Some might think this evidence enough that divine judgment and Gehenna had a place in Jesus' proclamation. I myself am so inclined, for I am not sure how we find Jesus if we can altogether excise a theme or motif consistently attested over a wide range of materials.[57] In Gerd Theissen's words, "All in all, there is no reason to deny that Jesus preached judgment. The tradition of this is too broad."[58]

Others, however, would protest that this is too easy, and not without reason. The criterion of multiple attestation, although we usually neglect the fact, cuts both ways. The more a motif is attested, the more reason we have to surmise its popularity among Christians; and how can early Christian fondness for something be, without further ado, evidence about Jesus?[59] In the present case, why not regard the many references to judgment, some of which are clearly secondary, as proof of the popularity of the theme in the churches? And why not, with that in mind, then apply the criterion of dissimilarity to discredit attributing to Jesus words about divine judgment? In this way we could dissociate him from a belief that seems to so many to involve "insane concentrated malignity on the part of God."[60]

Although I do not commend this line of reasoning, our guild's tradition requires that we do more than just pile up units in the hope that somehow quantity will establish an origin with Jesus. Although we have a large number of sayings about the "Son of Man," that has settled nothing. One cannot expect it to be different with anything else. In the end, most of us want to be able to cite some texts that plausibly give the sense of a few things Jesus said. So which, if any, of the many texts I have cited above satisfy on that score?

---

57. See further Allison, *Jesus*, 1–94. Cf. Sanders, *Jesus*, 176: "It is my own view that we cannot recover Jesus' view merely by picking and choosing among the sayings. In particular, I think it impossible to reject any of the major categories completely."

58. Gerd Theissen and Annette Merz, *The Historical Jesus: A Comprehensive Guide* (Minneapolis: Fortress, 1998), 269.

59. Cf. Jens Schröter, "The Historical Jesus and the Sayings Tradition: Comments on Current Research," *Neot* 30 (1996): 158: "A multiple attestation proves a strong interest of the tradents in this piece of tradition but not its origin from the historical Jesus."

60. W. M. W. Call, *Reverberations. Revised, with a Chapter from My Autobiography* (London: Trübner, 1875), 12.

The older I become, the less I trust anyone's ability to answer this sort of question, to trace the history and origin of particular sayings. I have lost my youthful "faith in the omnipotence of analytical decomposition."[61] It is not so easy to establish that any particular saying goes back to Jesus, and it is not so easy to establish that any particular saying does not go back to him. Most of our attempts thus to argue are wearisome speculation; and my current considered opinion is that most of the sayings in the Synoptics are what I would call possibly authentic: we cannot show that they come from Jesus, and we equally cannot show that they come from the church. In any case a few sentences in a short space will not do the trick, and the scope of this chapter prohibits thorough examination. So I content myself with citing three sayings that many have felt comfortable assigning to Jesus — one a threat to outsiders in Q, one an admonition to insiders in Mark, and one a parable from L. The Q text is Luke 13:28 = Matt 8:12, which warns some group that it will not recline with Abraham, Isaac, and Jacob in the kingdom but instead will be thrown into the outer darkness, where there will be weeping and gnashing of teeth. The Markan text is 9:43–48, which hyperbolically counsels cutting off hand, foot, and eye because being maimed is better than going to hell, to the unquenchable fire, where the worm never dies. The Lukan text is 16:19–31, the episode of the rich man and Lazarus, which has the former in Hades, a place of torment and agony. It would, admittedly, be silly to comb this morality tale — which takes up traditional elements and indeed comes ultimately from Egypt[62] — for details about the afterlife. At the same time, and granting latitude in interpretation, one has difficulty imagining Jesus using this story if he did not believe in both an afterlife and in postmortem punishment. Indeed, "one of the truths enshrined in the parable" is that "death is not the end of the moral account, but its continuation, with the possibility of firm adjustment and even reversal."[63]

If Q 13:28 or Mark 9:43–48 or Luke 16:19–31 fairly reflects something Jesus said, then he spoke of some sort of hell. I shall not attempt

---

61. Paul A. Weiss, *Inside the Gates of Science and Beyond: Science in Its Cultural Commitments* (New York: Hafner, 1971), 214.

62. The central thesis of Hugo Gressmann, *Vom reichen Mann und armen Lazarus: Eine literargeschichtliche Studie* (Berlin: Königlichen Akademie der Wissenschaft, 1918), is still persuasive.

63. J. Gwyn Griffiths, "Cross-Cultural Eschatology with Dives and Lazarus," *ExpTim* 105 (1993): 10.

herein to establish the authenticity of these three sayings — none of which, by the way, the Jesus Seminar colors red or even pink.[64] I can, however, refer, for what it is worth, to others who would demur from the conclusions of the Seminar[65] and, beyond that, state that, in my own personal judgment, the case for Mark 9:43–48 in particular seems solid. The language is vivid and shocking. My mind's eye sees a bloody stump and an empty eye socket when it encounters these words. If Jesus said them, they would stick in the memory. The language is also hyperbolic, because neither Jesus nor early Christians known to us counseled people to mutilate their physical bodies. And the hyperbolic is characteristic of Jesus. Also characteristic is the moral earnestness of Mark 9:43–48: Jesus was dead serious about things. Lastly, the uncompromising demand for self-sacrifice is also typical. I cannot, then, see any good reason to deny the complex to him — unless it is the conviction that he could not have had Gehenna in his rhetorical arsenal.[66]

After coming to this conclusion and siding with those who think that Jesus spoke about hell, I am certain that my partial and imperfect outline of some of the relevant arguments will not, in the end, change anybody's mind. Little in our contentious field is clear to demonstration; and regarding Jesus and Gehenna, we do not come to the question free of judgments about Jesus in general. Many of us, myself included, believe that the sort of eschatological or even apocalyptic Jesus that Johannes Weiss and Albert Schweitzer promoted, with his descendants in the works of Rudolf Bultmann, Joachim Jeremias, and Ed Sanders, is close to the truth. Many others — most members of the Jesus Seminar, for example — believe that this line of research has not unearthed the

---

64. Robert W. Funk, Roy W. Hoover, and the Jesus Seminar, *The Five Gospels: The Search for the Authentic Words of Jesus* (New York: Macmillan, 1993). Red means Jesus said something. Pink means he may have said it or something like it.

65. On Q 13:28–29, see John Meier, *A Marginal Jew: Rethinking the Historical Jesus*, vol. 2, *Mentor, Message, and Miracles* (ABRL; New York: Doubleday, 1994), 311–17, although his equation of the "many" with Gentiles is problematic. For the authenticity of Mark 9:43–48, see Werner Zager, *Gottesherrschaft und Endgericht in der Verkündigung Jesu: Eine Untersuchung zur markinischen Jesusüberlieferung einschließlich der Q-Parallelen* (BZNW 82; Berlin: de Gruyter, 1996), 210–13; and cf. Jacques Schlosser, *Le règne de Dieu dans les dits de Jésus* (EB; Paris: J. Gabalda, 1980), 2:632–33.

66. Certainly the rejoinder that the cutting off of bodily members is excommunication and so reflects an ecclesiastical context does not carry conviction. Contrast Funk et al., *The Five Gospels*, 86. This interpretation, which goes back to Irenaeus, *Adv. haer.* 4.27.4 (ed. Rousseau; SC 100:750–52), and Origen, *Comm. Matt.* 13.24–25 (ad 18:8–9; ed. Klostermann; GCS 40:244–49), derives from Paul's discussion of "the body of Christ" and has nothing to do with the Markan context.

facts, that the historical Jesus was somebody else. My point is that those who find more to applaud than to boo in Schweitzer will surely have greater sympathy for my arguments than those with another take on things. This is only natural. We do not and cannot evaluate the details apart from the big picture with which we begin. So if one's big picture is closer to, let us say, that of John Dominic Crossan or of Marcus Borg or of Stephen Patterson than to mine, my arguments will scarcely suffice to alter one's view. It is in part because I start with a Jesus who is a millenarian prophet, and because I know that millenarian prophets typically divide the world into two camps, the saved and the unsaved, that I give a hospitable reception to the case for affirming Jesus' belief in a God who will, at death or the final judgment, have bad news for some. In the end, then, the debate about Gehenna grows into a debate about the big picture we start with — a large subject that is, it goes without saying, fraught with complexity and so best left for another occasion.[67]

SOME DETAILS

If we do come to the conclusion, as did Bultmann, that "Jesus shares the idea of a fiery Hell into which the damned are to be cast,"[68] what more can we say? It is one thing to affirm *that* Jesus believed in Gehenna, another to recover precisely *what* he believed about it.

We would do well, before tackling this question, to keep in mind that nowhere does the tradition turn Gehenna into a topic in and of itself. It remains undeveloped, in the shadows of an impressive obscurity. It is never the subject of a discourse, nor does Jesus dwell upon it at any length. It is always rather a serviceable assumption shared by the audience, a dreaded thing invoked to admonish or rebuke. Jesus, unlike the *Apocalypse of Peter* and Dante's *Inferno*, never fills in the details — just as he refrains from offering expanded descriptions of the coming utopia he calls the kingdom of God. Are there degrees of torment (cf. Luke 12:47–48)? Does the punishment fittingly correspond to the crime, as in the later apocalypses and Dante (*contrapasso*)? Do the righteous revel in the spectacle of the wicked being defeated, as already in Isa 66:24

---

67. For my own reflections on this issue, see Allison, *Jesus*, 1–94; also, my contributions to *The Apocalyptic Jesus: A Debate* (ed. Robert J. Miller; Santa Rosa, CA: Polebridge, 2001), 17–29, 83–105.

68. Rudolf Bultmann, *Theology of the New Testament*, 1:7.

(which Mark 9:48 quotes) and infamously in later Christian writers?[69] Is the fire literal, as in Augustine and Wesley, or figurative, as in Origen and Calvin?[70] Can people in hell ever get out?[71] Can the righteous pray them out, as in the famous story of Gregory the Great successfully interceding for the emperor Trajan?[72] Would Jesus have been distraught or bemused or even delighted that later commentators found purgatory in Luke 12:59 = Matt 5:26 ("You will never get out until you have paid the very last penny"; cf. Matt 18:34)? Did he suppose that torment will be eternal, that the wicked will be ever dying, never dead?[73] Or, as the only occurrences of "eternal fire" and "eternal punishment" are confined to Matthew (25:41 and 46 respectively), and as "Their worm never dies" and "The fire is never quenched" in Mark 9:48 are of doubtful import and may in any case be secondary additions,[74] did he, like Arnobius and certain rabbis, think that the fires of hell would consume the wicked and

---

69. For Jewish texts, see *1 En.* 27:3; 62:12; *Jub.* 23:30; *T. Mos.* 10:10; *Apoc. Abr.* 31:4. Christian sources include *2 Clem.* 17:5–7; *Apoc. Pet.* 13:2; Tertullian, *De spec.* 30 (ed. Turcan; SC 332:316–28, a dreadful passage famously quoted by Gibbon and thereafter by all the polemical English literature written against the traditional, popular hell); Augustine, *Civ.* 20.21–22 (ed. Dombart and Kalb; CCSL 48:736–41); Gregory the Great, *Hom. ev.* 40.8 (PL 76:1309A–B); Aquinas, *Sum. Theo.* Suppl. q. 94, art. 1; Peter Lombard, *Sent.* 4.50.7 (PL 192:962); Robert Bellarmine, *De aeterna felicitate sanctorum* 4.2. See further below, 94–95; and Robert Joly, *Christianisme et philosophie: Études sur Justin et les Apologistes grecs du deuxième siècle* (Université libre de Bruxelles, Faculté de philosophie et lettres 52; Bruxelles: L'Université de Bruxelles, 1973), 171–82. Contrast the *Hebrew Apocalypse of Elijah* (trans. Buchanan, 440): God "will move the temple a great distance away from the destruction of the age, so that the righteous will not hear the voice of the crying of the wicked and seek mercy for them. They will be as though they never existed."

70. Augustine, *Civ.* 20.21 (ed. Dombart and Kalb; CCSL 48: 740); John Wesley, *Explanatory Notes upon the New Testament* (London: Epworth, 1950), 171 (ad Mark 9:44); Origen, *Comm. Matt.* 72 (ad 25:35–41; ed. Klostermann; GCS 38:171–72); Calvin, *Inst.* 3.25.12 (ed. Benoit; 495–96). To my knowledge, the rabbis tended to think of Gehenna's fire as literal: *Mek.* on Exod 20:18; *b. Ber.* 57b; *b. Menaḥ.* 100a; *b. Pesaḥ.* 54a; *b. 'Erub.* 19a; *b. Šabb.* 39a; *Hell* 20 (*Beit ha-Midrash* 5:50–51) (trans. Gaster; 599–605); etc. Just how literal the fire of hell could be appears from Gregory the Great, *Dial.* 4.36 (ed. Vogüé and Antin; SC 265:122): Sicily has "more craters burning with the fires of torment than any other region.... These are becoming larger every day, for as the end of the world approaches, it seems that the openings of hell are enlarged so as to receive the great number of lost souls who will be gathered there to be cast into eternal punishment."

71. Cf. *Num. Rab.* 18:20: "In the time to come, the Holy One, blessed be he, will take them [the company of Korah] out [of Gehenna]."

72. Ps.-John of Damascus, *Fide dormierunt* (PG 95:261D–264A); and Anon. Monk of Whitby, *V. Greg.* 29 (ed. Colgrave; 126–28).

73. For "eternal" punishment see 4 Macc 9:9; 10:11; 12:12; Josephus, *J.W.* 2.155; *Apoc. Abr.* 31:3; *b. Roš. Haš.* 17a.

74. The line is close to Isa 66:24 LXX and may be a Markan addition. The textual tradition bears witness to similar additions; thus the Textus Receptus reproduces Mark 9:48's quotation from Isa 66:24 also in vv. 44 and 46, both of which modern editions omit.

then burn out?[75] If so, how long would that take? And in the meantime, would sinners get any respite, something they ask for in *1 Enoch* 63? Will they perhaps, as in some medieval Jewish sources, get time off for the Sabbath?[76]

These questions go unasked and so unanswered. Jesus, as far as we can ascertain, discreetly paid them no heed. His interests were elsewhere.

---

75. See n. 28 and Arnobius, *Adv. gent.* 2.14 (ed. Oehler; 65–66). That Jesus expected the extinction of the wicked was the conclusion of both J. Arthur Baird, *The Justice of God in the Teaching of Jesus* (Philadelphia: Westminster, 1963), and Strawson, *Future Life*. So also Bernard Robinson, "Hell and Damnation: Biblical Concepts of Hell," *ScrB* 32, no. 1 (2002): 31: "The matter is not susceptible of proof, but it seems likely that Jesus himself accepted the prevalent Jewish notion of *Gehenna*, but in a weak version (destruction by fire; annihilation)." This was already seemingly the tentative opinion of J. H. Leckie, *The World to Come and Final Destiny: The Kerr Lectures, Delivered in the United Free Church College, Glasgow during Session 1917–1918* (Edinburgh: T & T Clark, 1918), 113–14. Cf. *1 En.* 98:9–10; *Ps. Sol.* 3:10–12; 13:11; 4 Ezra 12:33; 13:38; *t. Sanh.* 13:4–5 (which has some sinners annihilated after twelve months but the worst of them punished forever); *m. Sanh.* 10:3; *Gen. Rab.* 6:6. Even the import of Matt 25:41, 46 (whose origin with Jesus is hardly a given) and Mark 9:48 remain unclear to me. To turn from the Gospels to Augustine's influential, analytical discussion in the *City of God* is to leave paraenetical rhetoric for philosophical analysis and to enter an altogether different world, which is where so much exegetical discussion has been mired ever since. Having said this, and if one must hazard an opinion, it is intriguing that some texts speak both of destruction and everlasting fire or punishment — which is reason for us not to press the language, or reason to envisage a punishment that is eventually terminated, or reason to imagine that the point is to express an eternal result, not an eternal process; cf. 1QS 4:12–14; *1 En.* 10:11–16; 91:9; Philo, *Praem.* 85–91; Ps.-Philo, *LAB* 16:3; 63:4; Matt 3:12; 7:13; 10:28; Rev 20:10, 14. This is apart from the observation that Gregory of Nyssa, Evagrius, and the other church fathers who tended toward universalism, and who were much more reflective and careful about their language than any of the NT writers, could yet speak of "eternal" or "inextinguishable" fire; and that, as Origen in *Comm. Rom.* 6.5 (ed. Heither; FC 2.3:224–26) already recognized, αἰώνιος and its Semitic equivalents sometimes mean something other than what we mean by "everlasting"; see, e.g., Exod 21:6; Deut 15:17; 1 Sam 1:22; 27:12; Isa 32:14–15; Jonah 2:6; 1 Macc 14:41; Rom 16:25; *Jub.* 5:10; *2 Bar.* 40:3; also Henry D. A. Major, "ΑΙΩΝΙΟΣ. Its Use and Meaning Especially in the New Testament," *JTS* 18 (1916): 7–23. Modern commentators do not take Isa 66:24, which is the basis of Mark 9:48, to imply everlasting affliction. Probably Henry Barclay Swete, *Commentary on Mark* (London: Macmillan, 1913), 213, was right to assert that, in Mark 9:43–48, "the question of the eternity of the punishment does not come into sight." See further Wilhelm Michaelis, *Versöhnung des Alls: Die frohe Botschaft von der Gnade Gottes* (Bern: Siloah, 1950), 41–48, 53–63. But for another view see Scot McKnight, "Eternal Consequences or Eternal Consciousness?" in *Through No Fault of Their Own?* (ed. William V. Crockett and James G. Sigountos; Grand Rapids: Baker, 1991), 147–58. Apart from the exegetical issue, there is the philosophical problem. Talk of "everlasting" hell transfers our mundane understanding of time onto the transcendent world; but measuring hell by days and hours may be no more sensible than measuring heaven in terms of feet and inches.

76. For such respite see *b. Sanh.* 65b; *Gen. Rab.* 11:5; *Pesiq. Rab.* 23:8; *Hell* 20 (*BhM* 5:50–51) (trans. Gaster; 604); and Israel Lévi, "Le repos sabbatique des âmes damnées," *REJ* 25 (1892): 1–13; 26 (1893): 131–35. For Christian parallels see n. 26. It is worth observing that this idea of time off, which later appears in Cardinal Newman, "conceives of penalty not as an inward condition due to the action of moral law, but as a thing imposed from without, and so capable of being relieved by the exercise of external power." So Leckie, *World to Come*, 126–27.

"The truth of the matter seems to be that the thoughts of Jesus about the future of human souls did not generally travel far beyond the moment of the Kingdom's coming."[77] In Bousset's words, "He was no painter of the colossal."[78] Even apart from this, to pretend to elicit doctrinal specifics from mythologically laden imperatives that make incidental use of conventional ideas of divine punishment is a rather peculiar undertaking. It asks from texts, which intend to be "efficacious rather than accurate,"[79] more than they intend to give; it seeks for what cannot be found. When I speak of my "unquenchable thirst" or a speaker going on "forever," there is really no need for philological analysis, and why the "unquenchable fire" or the "everlasting fire" of the Jesus tradition is any different is far from obvious to me. Further, I am much impressed by F. W. Farrar's old survey of what the church fathers had to say about hell.[80] In case after case he exposes their vagaries and inconsistencies, large and small. He shows how hard it is to make unqualified generalizations, even about Augustine.[81] How much more difficult must it be with Jesus, whose teaching survives only in secondhand fragments. It was a long time after him before theologians sorted out the details of hell.[82]

That Jesus, in any event, did not much meditate upon the finer points of Gehenna, that it was not for him a subject of independent reflection, is consistent with the thoroughly conventional nature of his purported language about the place, as the parallels show:

---

77. Rashdall, *Conscience*, 305.

78. W. Bousset, *Jesus* (London: Williams & Norgate, 1906), 121. Cf. 123: "In many points of detail we are left quite in the dark as to his real views."

79. The phrase is from Stephen F. Teiser's " 'Having Once Died and Returned to Life': Representations of Hell in Medieval China," *Harvard Journal of Asiatic Studies* [*HJAS*] 48 (1988): 443, where it is used to describe the function of some Chinese artistic depictions of the underworld. Here there is truth in the insistence of Emil Brunner, *Eternal Hope* (London: Lutterworth, 1954), 183–84, that a word of challenge should not be confused with a word of doctrine.

80. F. W. Farrar, *Mercy and Judgment: A Few Last Words on Christian Eschatology with Reference to Dr. Pusey's "What Is of Faith?"* (New York: E. Dutton, 1881), 222–95.

81. For a survey of some of the problems with Origen and Maximus the Confessor, see Frederick W. Norris, "Universal Salvation in Origen and Maximus," in Cameron, *Universalism*, 34–72. The writings of both fathers contain seemingly contradictory statements about hell and universal salvation.

82. Cf. Farrar, *Mercy and Judgment*, 233: The testimonies to hell "grow in definiteness and horror with each succeeding century, until we come at last to the unmitigated atrocities of the Dialogues of Gregory the Great, the Elucidarium, the writings of Bede, and the vision of Dante."

- "Gehenna" as the place of punishment: *1 En.* 27:2–3; *Sib. Or.* 1:104; 2:292; 4:186; *2 Bar.* 59:10; 85:13; *t. Sanh.* 13:3; *m. Qidd.* 4:14; *m. 'Ed.* 2:10; *b. Soṭah* 4b; *b. 'Erub.* 19a; etc.

- "Fire" as a feature of Gehenna or postmortem punishment: Isa 66:24; *1 En.* 10:13; 54:1–6; 90:24; 1QS 2:8; *Sib. Or.* 1:103; 2:295; Ps.-Philo, *LAB* 38:4; 4 Ezra (2 Esd) 7:36; *2 Bar.* 44:15; *Apoc. Abr.* 15:6; etc.

- Being "thrown" into eschatological fire: *1 En.* 54:1–6; 90:25; 91:9; 98:3; Luke 3:9 = Matt 3:10 (attributed to John the Baptist); *2 En.* 63:4

- "Darkness" as a characteristic of Gehenna or postmortem punishment: *1 En.* 103:7; 1QS 2:8; 4:13; 4QM1 frags. 8–10 1:15; *Sib. Or.* 2:292; *Ps. Sol.* 14:9; 15:10; Wis 17:21; Josephus, *J.W.* 3.375; etc.

- The wicked cry and/or gnash teeth: Ps 112:10; *1 En.* 108:3; *Sib. Or.* 2:297–99, 305–306; *y. Sanh.* 10:3; *Midr. Eccl.* 1:15.1; cf. also Job 16:9; Ps 35:16; 37:12

The Jesus tradition adds nothing new to the Jewish lore about Gehenna.[83] As Leckie wrote nearly a hundred years ago: Jesus' "predictions of Gehenna are not different in any respect from similar prophecies in the Jewish books. Indeed, they are singularly wanting in any feature that might associate them with the personality of the Saviour. We cannot find in them any image or thought which is not traditional."[84]

Having acknowledged that large areas of ignorance will continually resist inquiry, we may still pursue two issues. The first is this: How exactly does Gehenna function in the proclamation of Jesus? The second is: Who exactly runs the risk of going there?

As to the function of Gehenna, it would please me to discover that Jesus used hell less as a threat to outsiders than as a challenge to insiders.[85] And we can read a few texts this way. Mark 9:43–48, with its call

---

83. A mechanical application of the criterion of dissimilarity might, for this reason, discourage attributing these items to Jesus. Popular and theological writings have long done something similar. See, e.g., Leckie, *World to Come*, 109–10. From the fact that Jesus' "predictions of Gehenna are not different in any respect from similar prophecies in the Jewish books" (see above), Leckie surmises that "it is impossible to say that all these references to Gehenna and its torments are couched in the very words of Jesus. They do not, as a rule, bear the imprint of His mind, being expressed in terms which are entirely traditional."

84. Ibid., 109.

85. Cf. the formulation of Joseph Ratzinger, *Eschatology: Death and Eternal Life* (Washington, DC: Catholic University Press of America, 1988), 217.

to guard against sin, is one. Q 12:5, which counsels fearing not one's enemies but the one who can destroy in Gehenna, is another. The content of most of the sayings, however, seems to concern and/or address outsiders. We can perhaps imagine most of these logia as calls to repentance (e.g., Q 11:31–32; 13:24, 25–27; 17:30, 34–35; Luke 16:19–31).[86] "A threat of punishment" can be, and often is in the Jewish prophets, "a paradoxical way of inducing the people to conform to the pattern of God's law in the future, and so gain divine wealth."[87] This is why some of Jesus' sayings about judgment are also sayings about reward (see below).

Yet a couple of logia may have a different character. Q 10:13–15, the woes on Galilean cities, and especially Q 13:28, the rebuke of those who will not enjoy the eschatological banquet with the patriarchs, could express resignation or even exasperation, defeat rather than hope.[88] Instead of opening the door to repentance, these two logia may rather shut it. So those of us who suppose that Q 10:13–15 and 13:28 are faithful to the memory of Jesus[89] will have to face the possibility, if we are honest, that he invoked divine punishment not just to exhort but also to write some people off.

There is, nonetheless, room for doubt about this, even apart from the question of whether or not Q 10:13–15 and 13:28 go back to Jesus. The doubt comes from our ignorance of the original *Sitz im Leben*. Consider, as an illustration of the problem, Q 12:8–9 (cf. Mark 8:38): "Anyone who acknowledges me before men, the Son of Man will also acknowledge before the angels. . . . But whoever denies me before men, the Son of man will deny before the angels." How might this warning of judgment

---

86. I should emphasize the words "imagine" and "perhaps." Within the Sayings Source, Q 11:39–52 does not hold forth the chance of repentance; the woes are for insiders who are united by the condemnation of outsiders. But that need not have been the pre-Easter situation. Once again, the problem of the original rhetorical situation is beyond our recovery, so the interpretation remains doubtful.

87. So Jože Krašovec, *Reward, Punishment, and Forgiveness: The Thinking and Beliefs of Ancient Israel in the Light of Greek and Modern Views* (VTSup 78; Leiden: Brill, 1999), 785. He continues: "Threats of punishment are for this reason usually found combined with promises of reward." Cf. Reiser, *Jesus and Judgment*, 305–6.

88. Theissen and Merz, *Jesus*, 266, judge that "only in the woe on the Galilean cities . . . does Jesus seem to have anticipated God's final verdict." Cf. Reiser, *Jesus and Judgment*, 230, 306.

89. On Q 10:12–15, see esp. Christian Riniker, *Die Gerichtsverkündigung Jesu* (Europäische Hochschulschriften 23.653; Bern: P. Lang, 1999), 301–3. On Q 13:28, see idem, 85–91, as well as Meier in n. 65 (above). With Riniker, I contend that a saying that condemns rather than calls to repentance cannot, for that reason alone, be denied to Jesus.

have served Jesus, if he uttered it?[90] Everything depends upon the audience and context, which are lost to history. If Jesus spoke this word to itinerants, to members of his inner circle, then it would hardly be a general soteriological statement. It would rather be an exhortation to disciples, in the face of opposition or hardship, not to fail in their appointed mission. One can, however, equally imagine Jesus using Q 12:8–9 to call the undecided to repentance: If you do not heed what I am saying, then you run a terrible risk; if you respond rightly, things will go well. Yet one can also envisage a third scenario. Jesus could have hurled our logion in judgment upon opponents, upon those who had not and clearly would not recognize his mission. In such a case, Q 12:8–9 would have been a way of rebuking and dismissing them, of declaring that they would be denied before the angels of God.

Once we recognize the extent to which context contributes to meaning and, further, admit how little we know about the original settings of Jesus' sayings, we will have little confidence in our speculations about how Q 10:13–15 and 13:28 or other sayings about judgment must have functioned. They are like Jonah 3:4. Without the wider story, we would hardly know whether "Yet forty more days and Nineveh will be destroyed" is a blanket denunciation or, as it so happens, a conditional warning that issues in repentance. The problem with Jesus is that his words, unlike Jonah 3:4, have drifted away from their first moorings. So all we can do is hazard the likely generalization that he sometimes used hell to motivate sympathizers, that at other times he used it to induce the undecided to obedience, and that he *may* likewise, on occasion, have been actuated by a motive less congenial to us and used it in order to turn the page and go on.

Apart from the problematic issue of how this or that logion first functioned, I take it for granted that Jesus, like so many through the ages, invoked the threat of eschatological punishment in order to incite people to change or to keep them going in the way that they should go. The purpose of telling a parable in which one house, upon being assailed by floods and wind, stands firm, while another, upon being beset similarly, falls into ruin, is to get people to stick to a certain

---

90. Cf. above, p. 42. The most helpful treatment of this saying remains Rudolf Pesch, "Über die Autorität Jesu: Eine Rückfrage anhand des Bekenner- und Verleugnerspruchs Lk 12,8f par.," in *Die Kirche des Anfangs: Für Heinz Schürmann* (ed. Rudolf Schnackenburg, Josef Ernst, and Joachim Wanke; Freiburg: Herder, 1978), 25–55. Pesch argues for an origin with Jesus.

path.[91] Most of us, living after Shaftesbury and Kant, like to imagine that we should do the good for its own sake: *Virtus sibi ipsi praemium.* We understand Wittgenstein's remark that "ethical reward and ethical punishment... must reside in the action itself."[92] We may even admire the sentiment of the Sufi Rabi'a: "God, if I worship Thee in fear of hell, burn me in hell. And if I worship Thee in hope of Paradise, exclude me from Paradise; but if I worship Thee for Thine own sake, withhold not Thine everlasting Beauty."[93] Jesus, however, did not say anything quite like this.[94] While he may have made love of God the supreme motive for righteousness, he did not make it the sole motive, and eudaemonism is not foreign to his thought. He evidently believed, as Origen put it, that the purpose of the subject of punishments is "to induce those who have heard the truth to strive with all their might against those sins which are the causes of punishment."[95] One understands the sentiment — once expressed in the proverb, "The fear of hell peoples heaven" — even if one is uncomfortable with it. The fear of punishment in the afterlife has presumably often been an effective prod, as the pagan critics of religion observed long ago.[96] According to Pusey, "The dread of hell peoples heaven: perhaps millions have been scared back from sin by the dread of

---

91. Cf. Luke 6:47–49 = Matt 7:24–27. Regarding this saying from Q, Joachim Gnilka, *Jesus of Nazareth: Message and History* (Peabody, MA: Hendrickson, 1997), 152, observes: "The pressing thing in this contrast is that there is hardly any doubt that it depicts the imminent, eschatological judgment, which elsewhere is seen as analogous to the flood (Matt 24:38f. par.)." He adds in a footnote: "Those who take the image to refer to any repetitive threat rob it of its decisive eschatological emphasis."

92. Ludwig Wittgenstein, *Tractatus logico-philosophicus* 6.422 (London: Routledge, 1961), 147.

93. As quoted by Aldous Huxley, *The Perennial Philosophy* (New York: Harper & Row, 1970), 102. Cf. *m. 'Abot* 1:3: "Be not like servants who serve the master on condition of receiving a gift, but be like servants who serve the master not on condition of receiving."

94. Yet for the argument that "the rewards that Jesus offers" are not eschatological but rather "intrinsic to the deeds for which they are the reward," see Robert W. Funk, "Rewards Are Intrinsic," *The Fourth R* 15, no. 2 (2002): 18. Accordingly to Funk, "Jesus does not speak explicitly about the fate of persons after death."

95. Origen, *Cels.* 8.48 (ed. Marcovich; 562–63). Cf. Justin Martyr, *1 Apol.* 12 (ed. Marcovich; PTS 38:48–49). Elsewhere, Origen makes it plain that, on his view, the threat of punishment is an accommodation to the masses — something like the Buddhist concept of "skillful means," a provisional teaching for the unenlightened; it is for those who cannot otherwise turn from their sins: *Cels.* 5.15; 6.25–26 (ed. Marcovich; 331–32, 402–3).

96. See Critias frag. 25 (ed. Diels/Kranz; 2:386–88); Lucretius, *De rer. nat.* 1.102–26; and cf. Augustine, *Conf.* 6.16 (ed. O'Donnell; 67). But one should not exaggerate this element in the history of Christianity; see Clement F. Rogers, *The Fear of Hell as an Instrument of Conversion* (London: SPCK, 1939). And there is the other side, too: instead of promoting conversion, hell has sometimes promoted unbelief: if Christianity requires a hell, and if hell is not to be believed, then Christianity is not to be believed.

it."[97] This verdict is not idiosyncratic, which is why there is a tradition of "hellfire sermons." Josephus wrote: "The good are made better in their lifetime by the hope of a reward after death, and the passions of the wicked are restrained by the fear that, even though they escape detection while alive, they will undergo never-ending punishment after their decease" (*J.W.* 2.157). Although we may wish it were otherwise, perhaps the lament in 1741 of William Dodwell had some truth in it: "It is but too visible, that since men have learnt to wear off the Apprehension of Eternal Punishment, the Progress of Impiety and Immorality among us has been very considerable."[98] Jesus, like Dodwell, apparently believed in hell's utility, if that is the right word, just as he believed in the efficacy of eschatological reward.[99] Jesus took human fear for granted and made it serve his proclamation, confronting his hearers with the possibility of an odious fate — just as he acknowledged the human hope for happiness and promised its fulfillment in the kingdom of God. For him, the issue was not whether there would or would not be recompense. For him the issue was what sort of recompense one would receive.

To keep perspective, we should not lose sight of the fact that eschatological loss is only the underside of eschatological gain, and that the latter dominates Jesus' preaching. Judgment is secondary. Mark 1:15 rightly summarizes Jesus' kerygma as announcing the kingdom, not Gehenna, and the Lord's Prayer asks for the former to come, not the latter.[100] Yet despite the asymmetry, the one presupposes the other. Indeed, in some respects the two can become antithetical correlatives: "Being saved from hell is the kingdom. And being without the kingdom is hell."[101] Consider the following texts:

---

97. E. B. Pusey, *What Is of Faith as to Everlasting Punishment? In Reply to Dr. Farrar's Challenge in His 'Eternal Hope,'* 1879 (3rd ed.; Oxford: James Parker, 1880), 19. Cf. the story of conversion Pusey tells on 3–4.

98. As quoted in Walker, *Decline*, 3. According to Paul Johnson, *The Quest for God: A Personal Pilgrimage* (New York: HarperCollins, 1996), 159, "Certainly when the doctrine of Hell went into its long historical decline, from the seventeenth century onwards, those who studied the facts of crime and evil felt its waning power was significant."

99. Wilhelm Pesch, *Der Lohngedanke in der Lehre Jesu vergleichen mit der religiösen Lohnlehre des Spätjudentums* (Münchener Theologische Studien 1.7; Munich: Karl Zink, 1955).

100. Cf. the formulation of Günter Rusher, "Hat Jesus die Hölle gepredigt? Gericht, Vorherbestimmung und Weltende im frühen Christentum," *Zeitschrift für Neues Testament in Universität, Kirche, Schule, und Gesellschaft* [ZNT] 9 (2002): 28: Jesus does not proclaim hell, but he does speak of it.

101. Isaac of Nineveh, *First* 88 (trans. Wensinck; 59).

Reward	Punishment
Q 12:8–9	
Whoever acknowledges me in public the Son of Man will acknowledge.	Whoever denies me in public will be denied.
Q 13:28–29	
Many will come [and] recline with Abraham in the kingdom.	You will be thrown out, [with] wailing and grinding of teeth, into the darkness.
Q 17:33	
Those who lose their life will find it.	Those who find their life will lose it.
Q 19:26	
To everyone who has will more be given.	From the one who does not have even what he has will be taken from him.
Mark 9:43–48	
to enter life to enter life to enter the kingdom of God	to go to Gehenna to be thrown into Gehenna to be thrown into Gehenna
Luke 16:19–31	
in Abraham's bosom Now he is comforted here.	in Hades You are in agony.

These sayings reflect the logic of eschatological soteriology. If some will become little children and enter the kingdom, others will not;[102] and in a Jewish context, what else can that mean except eschatological destruction or punishment?[103] To lose the kingdom is to gain Gehenna. For if there is life, there is also death. If the humble will be exalted, the exalted will be humbled. The first become last. Promise and reward cannot be separated. So reminding people "of the judgment to come by means of warnings" and "bringing to their mind the kingdom of heaven so that they may desire it" belong to the same proclamation. "Explaining the rewards of the good so that people may yearn for them" and "showing to them the power of judgment, that they may restrain

---

102. See Mark 10:15 (cf. John 3:3, 5; *Gos. Thom.* 22, 46); Mark 10:23–24.
103. See Reiser, *Jesus and Judgment*, 26–163.

themselves"[104] serve the same end. It is altogether natural that Jesus or somebody after him fashioned woes to balance the beatitudes of the Sermon on the Plain (Luke 6:20–26).

But who, we may now ask, ran the risk of going to Gehenna in Jesus' opinion? It was not the Gentiles en masse. There is no trace in the tradition of the belief, found in some Jewish works (*Jub.* 24:29–30; *1 En.* 90:19; 1QM), that they will be excluded from the kingdom; and the existence of an early mission to Gentiles confirms that Jesus shared the spirit of the book of Jonah and did not anticipate their eschatological annihilation. So it must have been some segment of the Jewish people that, in his eyes, courted danger. The sources encourage us to believe that it was precisely certain Jews who opposed him and his cause — his enemies — who were headed for disaster. Jesus, we may think, condemned not unbelief but disbelief; he threatened not those who did not know of him but those who knew of him and rejected him.

That Jesus had enemies is wholly likely, for it is wholly unlikely that the early church invented the slander in the Gospels, that Christians concocted the accusation that Jesus was a friend of toll collectors and sinners, that he was a glutton and a drunkard, that he cast out demons by the prince of demons. These calumnies must be memory. Given this, it goes without saying that Jesus cannot have looked kindly at those who said such things. What follows? If Jesus believed in a hell of some kind, and if he had enemies, surely he consigned the one to the other. What good is a hell if one's enemies are not in it? One recalls 1QH 15(7):12, where the hymnist (the Teacher of Righteousness?) declares, "At the judgment you pronounce as guilty all those who harass me, separating the just from the wicked through me."

Like John the Baptist, Jesus did not believe that Jews were saved solely by virtue of descent from father Abraham.[105] Like other Jewish teachers, he must have believed that one could lose one's place within the covenant; and surely, in his own mind, rejection of him and his cause entailed such loss. This is clearly the purport of Q 10:12, which denounces Jews who reject Jesus' messengers; of Q 10:13–15, which threatens Galilean

---

104. So Ephraem the Syrian, *Ep. ad Publ.* 23 (ed. Brock; 293).

105. The following comments correct my earlier thoughts on this subject; see "Jesus and the Covenant: A Response to E. P. Sanders," *JSNT* 29 (1987): 57–78; reprinted in *The Historical Jesus* (ed. Craig A. Evans and Stanley E. Porter; Sheffield: Sheffield Academic Press, 1996), 61–82.

cities because they have responded feebly to his ministry; and of Q
11:31–32, which censures those not repenting at something greater than
the preaching of Jonah. In these cases, as in the sayings about "this generation,"[106] it is opposition to Jesus' eschatological mission that puts
people in jeopardy. It is likely that this was also the original import of Q
12:10 = Mark 3:28–29, the saying about blasphemy against the Holy
Spirit. If Jesus thought of himself as the eschatological prophet of Isa
61, anointed by the Spirit to proclaim good news in the latter days,[107]
then the saying about blasphemy against the Spirit probably envisages
serious opposition to his own ministry. Other sins might be forgiven; but
how could one refuse to embrace the Spirit-inspired proclamation of the
kingdom and still enter it?

Assigning one's opponents to Gehenna seems to have been standard
fare in the ancient sources, so in this respect Jesus belonged to his world.
In the Dead Sea Scrolls, those headed for destruction are, above all, the
enemies of the sect.[108] *First Enoch* 62 condemns "the kings, the gover-
nors, the high officials, and the landlords" (vv. 1, 3) and previsions that
the "Lord of Spirits . . . will deliver them to the angels for punishments
in order that vengeance shall be executed on them — oppressors of his
children and his elect ones" (vv. 10–12; cf. 94:9; 95:6–7; 96:8). It is the
same in the Mishnah. The exceptions to the rule, that all Israel has a
place in the world to come, are first those who discount the teachings of
the Mishnah's contributors: "He that says that there is no resurrection
of the dead prescribed in the Law, and he that says that the Law is not
from heaven, and an Epicurean" (*m. Sanh.* 10:1).

If Jesus envisioned the punishment of his opponents, he probably also
thought that Gehenna held a place for those with certain moral failings.[109] Jeremias observed that "the numerous words of judgment in the
gospels are, almost without exception, not directed against those who
commit adultery, cheat, etc., but against those who vigorously condemn

---

106. Luke 7:31 = Matt 11:16; Luke 11:29–32 = Matt 12:38–42; Luke 11:49–51 = Matt
23:34–36; Mark 8:12, 38; 9:19. See Evald Lövestam, *Jesus and 'This Generation': A New
Testament Study* (ConBNT 25; Stockholm: Almqvist & Wiksell, 1995).

107. See A. E. Harvey, *Jesus and the Constraints of History* (Philadelphia: Westminster,
1982), 120–53.

108. Cf. 4QPsa 3:12; 4:1–2; 1QH 11 (3):14–18; 12 (4):18–20; 1QpHab 10:9–13; 11:12–
15.

109. Cf. Josephus, *J.W.* 3.375; Greek *3 Bar.* 4:16; *b. Šabb.* 33a.

adultery and exclude cheats from the community."[110] Yet there are, as
Jeremias admitted, exceptions. The sins of Mark 9:43–48 are not sins
against Jesus and his cause but instead sins of eye, hand, and foot. These
must be moral failings of some kind.[111] The situation is presumably similar in Mark 9:42, where Jesus envisions a great millstone around the
neck of one who has set a stumbling block before a little one. Likewise,
in Luke 16:19–31 the rich man is in Hades not because he has rejected
Jesus but because, as verse 25 says: "During your lifetime you received
your good things, and Lazarus in like manner evil things; but now he is
comforted here, and you are in agony."[112] With this one may compare
Mark 10:25: "It is easier for a camel to go through the eye of a needle
than for a rich man to enter the kingdom of God." This implies that
some sins growing from wealth may barricade the way to the kingdom.
Matthew 25:31–46 also belongs here, for the exegetes who identify the
unfortunates in this text with Christians or missionaries are almost certainly wrong. This depiction of the great assize, which may in part go
back to Jesus,[113] teaches that judgment will fall upon those who have
not taken care of the hungry, the ill-clothed, the naked, and so on.[114]
So the redactional Matt 7:19, which declares that "every tree that does
not bear good fruit is cut down and thrown into the fire," likely reflects
one aspect of Jesus' proclamation. Whether we can harmonize this with
justification by faith seems to me doubtful. But we should state the facts
as they are, not as we should like them to be.[115]

---

110. Joachim Jeremias, *New Testament Theology: The Proclamation of Jesus* (New York:
C. Scribner's Sons, 1971), 151.

111. For the argument that the unit condemns sexual sins, see Allison, *Jesus*, 178–82.

112. See Richard Bauckham, "The Rich Man and Lazarus: The Parable and the Parallels,"
NTS 37 (1991): 225–46.

113. See W. D. Davies and Dale C. Allison Jr., *A Critical and Exegetical Commentary on
the Gospel according to Saint Matthew* (ICC; Edinburgh: T & T Clark, 1997), 3:417–22; and
Riniker, *Gerichtsverkündigung*, 438–54.

114. See Arland J. Hultgren, *The Parables of Jesus: A Commentary* (Grand Rapids:
Eerdmans, 2000), 309–30.

115. Although many Christian theologians, including Augustine and Aquinas, have offered
the frightful estimate that most human beings are bound for perdition, we cannot, I am happy
to report, with confidence ascribe such a view to Jesus, even if the idea of *massa damnata* was
not foreign to his world; cf. 4 Ezra 7:47–51; 8:1–3, 55; 9:20–22; 2 *Bar.* 44:15; 48:43; *b. Sanh.*
97b; *b. Menah.* 29b. The proof texts have been Matt 7:13–14 and 22:14. The former derives
from Q 13:24, and nothing requires us to turn the latter into a general statement about all
humanity. "Enter through the narrow door. Many (of all human beings ever born) will seek to
enter and few (of them) will enter it" is no more plausible on the lips of Jesus than is "Enter
through the narrow door. Many (among you listening to me) will seek to enter and few (of
you) will enter it." The function of Q 13:24 is not in any case to measure an eschatological

REFLECTIONS

It is one thing to learn what the historical Jesus likely believed, another to know what we should believe for ourselves. Perhaps, then, some reflections on this vexatious subject of hell, which sensible people seldom now discuss, are not out of place.

Those within my Christian tradition who have profited neither from modern works on comparative religion nor from the theological discussions of the last three hundred years will deny that our imagined, conventional hell, "which the natural heart revolts against and struggles against,"[116] is mythological, deny that it is one of those "forms of expression which are inadequate to the matter it is intended to convey."[117] They will have to fret, in the manner of Augustine, over the different senses of αἰώνιος and the precise connotations of ἀπώλεια.[118] They will further have to explain to themselves why, if they take the fire to be literal, the Bible does not compel them to believe in an immortal underground

quantity but to motivate more people to repent, to go through the narrow door. The text is, as the current edition of the *Catechism of the Catholic Church* (2nd ed.; Vatican: Libreria Editrice Vaticana, 2000), 1036, says, "a call to conversion"; it works, so to speak, to undo itself. As for Matt 22:14, it belongs solely to M and, beyond that, the meaning may well be "All are called, but not all are chosen"; see Edmond Boissard, "Note sur l'interpretation du texte 'Multi sunt vocati, pauci vero electi,'" *Revue Thomiste* 52 (1952): 569–85; and Ben F. Meyer, "Many (= all) are called, but few (= not all) are chosen," *NTS* 36 (1990): 89–97. In addition to these exegetical points, the relevant sayings, unlike Augustine's doctrine, do not plainly presuppose that humanity is "one mass of perdition." Jesus was probably optimistic about the salvation of the Gentile world (see p. 88); he almost certainly expected the return of the lost tribes of Israel (see Allison, *Jesus*, 141–45); and his hyperbolic statements about "this generation" (see n. 106) are not about humanity in general but a particular group in a particular place at a particular time.

116. Charles Hodge, *Systematic Theology* (New York: Scribner, Armstrong, 1874), 3:870.

117. Brunner, *Eternal Hope*, 115.

118. Although I have not seen this done, one could invoke relativity theory to show how the wicked will both suffer forever and be annihilated. At the end of days, Captain Almighty God builds a celestial ark, puts the righteous in it, squishes the wicked and some tormenting demons into the center of the earth, takes off at near light speed, circumnavigates the universe in five minutes, surpasses light speed for a few seconds (Captain Almighty, aptly named, can do anything), then decelerates and returns to earth. According to relativity theory, five minutes and a few seconds of time on the ark are an eternity on earth, so when the ark docks, the wicked have spent forever in hell. What then? Having fulfilled the prophecies about eternal torment and still needing to fulfill those about destruction, Captain Almighty retrieves a mysterious box from the ark's hold, carefully opens the lid, removes the holy hand grenade stored from the foundation of the world, utters a few solemn words, pulls the sacred pin, and tosses the thing out the window. The wicked and the sin-wracked universe disappear, and now Captain Almighty can make all things new. Alternatively, the good Captain might rather want, upon returning to earth, to save the wicked and so fulfill those Pauline texts that speak of all being saved, thus resolving a different contradiction. This is all juvenile nonsense; but it is unclear to me how those who take the biblical statements about hell literally could recognize it as nonsense, or how they could fail to laud this brilliant resolution of a hoary exegetical conundrum.

worm.[119] What, however, of the rest of us, for whom mere scripturalism is not enough? What if we know that hell, precisely because it belongs to the world to come and so lies beyond what eye has seen and ear heard, must belong to mythological thinking? What if we are incredulous that the nature of God's eternal future can be compressed into a few strong figures of speech found in the Bible? What if we believe that we "must have a broader basis than the halting reconciliation of ambiguous and opposing texts... believe that reason, and conscience, and experience, as well as Scripture, are books of God, which must have a direct voice in these great decisions"?[120]

Part of the problem with hell is that it is a paraenetical motif and mythological idea that unfortunately grew into a sober doctrine; and since we now know its mythological character, it can be a doctrine no longer. If, then, we are not to discard it utterly, we must explore its meaning as a metaphor or symbol.[121] Gehenna is, in this respect, like the garden of Eden, which retains an important place in the religious imagination but not in the real world. Just as the primeval paradise is part of the Bible's mythological interpretation of human origins, so also is Gehenna part of the Bible's mythological interpretation of human destiny. The retrospect is not in our past, and the prospect is not in our future. Both are purely theological ideas, matters of meaning, whether the biblical writers understood this or not.

We know well enough why the human — and mostly male — imagination has conjured hell. The place belongs to worldwide mythology — the Christian hell certainly owes much to Egyptian, Iranian, and Greek sources — because there is darkness in the recesses of the mind: nightmares, hellish visions, and sinister psychological experiences are part of the human condition.[122] There is also the undoubted fact that this world too often sees justice undone, and some "deeds that cry out to heaven

119. Cf. *Vis. Paul* 42 (ed. Silverstein and Hilhorst; 156): "I saw there the worm that does not sleep, and in that place was gnashing of teeth." *Apoc. Mos.* A 40 (trans. Gaster, 582) afflicts the tormented with giant black worms. Augustine, *Civ.* 20.22 (ed. Dombart and Kalb; CCSL 48:748), observes that "some people" take both the fire and the worm literally, although he prefers (for no good reason) to take the former literally, the latter figuratively — an opinion which thereafter dominated Western theological opinion.

120. Frederic William Farrar, *Eternal Hope: Five Sermons Preached in Westminster Abbey, November and December, 1877* (London: Macmillan, 1879), 64.

121. Cf. the approach of Ninian Smart to "Heaven," in *Talk of God* (Royal Institute of Philosophy Lectures, vol. 2, *1967–1968*; London: Macmillan, 1969), 226–38.

122. Here Aldous Huxley, *The Doors of Perception and Heaven and Hell* (New York: Harper & Row, 1963), 133–40, is particularly helpful.

also cry out for hell."[123] The dreadful underworld of retribution is sometimes "the poetry of indignation,"[124] a vision of the oppressed who now live in their own hell and dream of a world in which balance is restored. Such a vision can express the divine discontent that rolls through all things.

The difficulty is that hell typically makes us, to say the least, less than magnanimous when it is used, as it typically is, to condemn those with allegiances other than our own.[125] It solidifies our alienation from others who honestly see the world differently and, as in Tertullian and Dante, becomes the fantasy of our enemies getting what we deem to be their just desserts. "Hell is the consummation of revenge."[126] Even worse, hell can justify the mistreatment of others. Queen Mary I of England remarked: "As the souls of heretics are hereafter to be eternally burning in hell, there can be nothing more proper than for me to imitate the Divine vengeance by burning them on earth."[127] Matthew's several redactional references to fire and darkness no doubt mirror his hostile feelings for his religious opponents, whom he took to be beyond all hope and worthy of languishing in God's infernal wrath. The Sermon on the Mount would seem to know better, but then the ideals of the sermon typically extend beyond our reach.

Hell is also problematic because it has inevitably titillated morbid human instincts. The *Apocalypse of Peter* and Bosch's paintings entertain us with the violent and the grotesque in ways analogous to contemporary horror films.[128] We somehow enjoy their hideous, nauseating disgusts,

---

123. Peter Berger, *A Rumor of Angels: Modern Society and the Rediscovery of the Supernatural* (Garden City, NY: Doubleday, 1970), 67.

124. So Farrar, *Eternal Hope*, 64.

125. See Richard K. Fenn and Marianne Delaporte, "Hell as a Residual Category: Possibilities Excluded from the Social System," in *The Blackwell Companion to Sociology of Religion* (ed. Richard K. Fenn; Oxford: Blackwell, 2001), 336–60.

126. Robert G. Ingersoll, *The Ghosts and Other Lectures* (Peoria, IL: C. Farrell, 1878), ii.

127. Quoted by Alger, *Critical History*, 515.

128. "It is impossible to examine the oeuvre of Hieronymous Bosch without thinking: how this great artist loved Hell — and how impoverished his work would have been without it! . . . He loved Hell — it was his work, his life, his creative universe — and though he set about depicting it as a place of horror, which would produce in those who studied it revulsion and the desire to repent while there was still time, he also made it a place of beauty of colour and form, of scintillating detail and ingenuity. . . . His lakes of evil and exploding cities of doom and fire are so exciting, the colours so exquisite, the eye is so irresistibly drawn into the picture, to dwell there on its fascinating details, that I wonder how many errant souls were actually frightened by Bosch into a better life." So Johnson, *Quest for God*, 158. Does not our love of the morbid partly explain why James Joyce's sermon on hell in *A Portrait of the Artist as a Young Man* (Oxford: Oxford University Press, 2000) has attracted so much attention?

enjoy holding in our imaginations, in the words of the Spiritual Exercises of Ignatius, "a vivid portrayal . . . of the length, breadth, and depth of hell."[129] Such sinister and vulgar entertainments were no more edifying in their old religious contexts than they are in their modern secular settings.[130]

Even more odiously, hell — in its popular, ordinary acceptation — has depicted a transcendental violence[131] that has issued in a transcendental paradox, a God who loves all yet insatiably tortures some. This appalling conundrum, as many or even most Western Christians since the last quarter of the nineteenth century have instinctively felt, is not an irreducible tension to be tolerated but a plain inconsistency to be dissolved. Genuine mystery is one thing, stark contradiction another.[132] Jonathan Edwards, who confesses that, in his youth, he thought an eternal hell unjust, hardened his heart and later asserted that "it is now our duty to love all men, though they are wicked; but it will not be a duty to love wicked men hereafter."[133] Does this make any sense? Samuel Hopkins, sadly speaking for many in our tradition, claimed that "the divine vengeance and eternal punishment that shall be inflicted on the wicked . . . in the clear and full view of the redeemed" will be a means of "exciting and greatly increasing their love, joy and praise."[134] How many of us can

---

129. From the fifth exercise of the first week. The text goes on to encourage seeing, hearing, smelling, tasting, and feeling various features of hell, including the fire, the shrieks, the stench of filth, and the melancholy.

130. We might do well to remember, however, that people of former ages, who knew cruel penal practices and experienced much more illness and shorter life spans than most of us in the modern West, would feel less instinctive revulsion about a hell of misery. A better life makes for a less-wrathful God. This is part of a larger fact: because the world is always changing, some ideas are more congenial to some times and places than are others.

131. This phrase is from John Dominic Crossan in Miller, *Apocalyptic Jesus*, 64. See also Crossan's article, "Eschatology, Apocalypticism, and the Historical Jesus," in *Jesus Then and Now: Images of Jesus in History and Christology* (ed. Marvin Meyer and Charles Hughes; Harrisburg, PA: Trinity, 2001), 91–112.

132. Here I distinguish my own perception of a contradiction from the perceptions of others, who have held the two things together; see above, 69–72.

133. So Edwards, "The End of the World Contemplated," in *Works* (New Haven: Yale University Press, 1957ff.), 4:293. For the comment that, in childhood, he found everlasting torment to be "a horrible doctrine," see "Personal Narrative," in *A Jonathan Edwards Reader* (ed. John E. Smith, Harry S. Stout, and Kenneth Minkema; New Haven/London: Yale, 1995), 283.

134. Samuel Hopkins, *The Works of Samuel Hopkins* (New York: Garland, 1987), 2:457. Cf. Ephraem the Syrian, *Ep. ad Publ.* 21 (ed. Brock; 291): "The vision of the eye is also permitted there to come and go, giving pain or joy to either side — the good regard their own lot as all the better when they see the wicked, and they rejoice all the more in it (their own lot)." The idea is depicted in some Renaissance paintings. Is it possible to imagine a more selfish and sadistic thought than this? Cf. the lack of feeling in the Icelandic *Elucidarius* 3:20

return a hearty "Amen" to this? Richard Baxter added that God will join with us in laughing and mocking and rejoicing over the calamitous fate of the wretched.[135] This profoundly disturbing sentiment, this delight in seeing others harpooned by God's justice, is as irrational and unchristian as Rubens's astounding painting of Saint Francis crouched around and protecting the world from a Jesus Christ who wants to attack it with thunderbolts. Baxter, like Edwards and Hopkins, sounds like an adherent of Moloch. If, in accord with the Golden Rule, we do not want people in hell because we do not want to be there ourselves, then we would surely mourn if anyone were to go there,[136] and how can we approve of what we would mourn?[137]

Most of us cannot worship a god who fails to fulfill his own imperative to overcome evil with good, a god who does things to human beings that we would never dream of doing to a dog, a god whose postmortem penal colony, in its artistic representations, reminds us of nothing so much as the death camps of the Holocaust.[138] It is altogether appropriate that traditional depictions of hell put demons, not angels, in charge of the ghastly show. Their deity has morphed into his adversary, the devil. The supposed justice of this cosmic sheriff is a superfluity of injustice. Certainly attempts to make everlasting punishment commensurate with the sins of finite beings, or to show that such punishment is better

---

(ed. Firchow; 82): "Even if a father sees his son or a son his father in torment; a mother her daughter, or a daughter her mother; a man his wife, or a wife her husband, they are no more grieved than when we see fish playing in a pool." See also Almond, *Heaven and Hell*, 97–98, and the references in n. 69.

135. Richard Baxter, *The Saints' Everlasting Rest* (New York: R. Carter & Brothers, 1855), 267–68. This book's barbaric chapter on the torments of hell was once in circulation as an independent tract.

136. Cf. Clement of Alexandria, *Strom.* 7.12.78.3 (ed. A. Le Boulluec; SC 428:240: "showing pity upon those who are chastised after death"); and *Vis. Paul* 20, where there is weeping in heaven over those who miss the promises of God.

137. Aquinas, *Summa* 3 suppl. 94.3, concedes that the saints will not rejoice directly in the punishment of the wicked, but he goes on to contend, unpersuasively, that they will rejoice "by considering therein the order of the divine justice and their own deliverance, which will fill them with joy. And thus the divine justice and their own deliverance will be the direct cause of the joy of the blessed, while the punishment of the damned will cause it indirectly."

138. For an instructive, eye-opening collection of horrific opinions about what hell is like, see Thomas J. Sawyer, *Endless Punishment: In the Very Words of Its Advocates* (Boston: Universalist Publishing House, 1880). For the argument that "in the camps the millenary pornography of fear and vengeance cultivated in the Western mind by Christian doctrines of damnation was realized," see George Steiner, "A Season in Hell," in *In Bluebeard's Castle: Some Notes towards the Definition of Culture* (New Haven: Yale, 1971), 27–56, esp. 55. Whatever one makes of this thesis, it is clear that long, medieval meditation upon the tortures of hell contributed to the tortures of the Inquisition. See further Lecky, *Rationalism in Europe*, 349–68, whose remarks on the psychological effects of a horrific hell merit pondering.

than annihilation, have been far-fetched, nothing more than "the little Subtleties and Quirks of the Metaphysicians."[139] An eternal hell hardly comports with Jesus' assertion that "the measure you give will be the measure you get."

So what do we say? We cannot deny that the Bible has a hell, nor that Jesus preached judgment. Yet, we can (1) observe that the later Christian lore about hell, with its numerous and substantive parallels in the mythological hells of other religions,[140] goes far beyond anything that the biblical texts and Jesus, both innocent of sadism, taught.[141] (2) Decline to purchase the divine justice at the expense of the rest of God's attributes — "the Christian teaching surely is that the highest spiritual attitude is not justice but forgiveness."[142] And (3) urge that Jesus' characteristic teaching about nonviolence and love of enemy deconstructs the retributive postmortem torture chamber of our tradition. "We who believe in Christ know nothing more certainly than the character of God. We know that He is perfect love, perfect equity. We are quite justified in refusing to believe about Him anything which would be inconsistent with the highest goodness we can conceive."[143] This forces us to play text against text. The Bible does not speak with one voice, and the canon within the canon moves us to reject a divine justice that requires a divine violence.[144]

Yet this is not all that we should say. Hell is more than an old, disconcerting myth that, once scrutinized and found wanting, henceforth means nothing. This is because it presupposes a fundamental conviction

---

139. Thomas Burnet, *A Treatise concerning the State of Departed Souls* (London: John Hooke, 1730), 351. See further Marilyn McCord Adams, "Hell and the God of Justice," *RelS* 11 (1975): 433–47; as well as the humane and sensible letter from John Foster to E. White (September 24, 1841), printed in *The Life and Correspondence of John Foster* (ed. J. R. Ryland; New York: J. Wiley, 1849), 2:262–70.

140. For instructive illustrations see Daigan and Alicia Matsunaga, *The Buddhist Concept of Hell* (New York: Philosophical Library, 1972), esp. 80–136 and the prints in the middle of the book.

141. Here again, the work of Farrar, *Mercy and Judgment*, remains profitable.

142. John Baillie, *And the Life Everlasting* (London: Oxford, 1934), 243.

143. Charles Gore, *The Religion of the Church as Presented in the Church of England* (Milwaukee: Young Churchman, 1917), 82. Cf. Silas K. Hocking, "What Is Hell Like?," in *Is There a Hell? by Leaders of Religious Thought* (London: Cassell, 1913), 15: "The hell of the Scriptures has to be interpreted by the revealed character of God, and anything inconsistent with that character must be assumed to be wrong. God must be consistent with Himself, and the hell such as our fathers learned makes God out to be worse than any heathen deity ever conceived."

144. See further my article, "Rejecting Violent Judgment: Luke 9:52–56 and Its Relatives," *JBL* 121 (2002): 459–78.

that requires careful nurture. Hell is, in the Bible, a penalty imposed at the eschatological judgment. It is punishment due a crime, with staggering consequences. One cannot imagine a stronger statement of human responsibility: what we do really matters, and our accountability does not forsake us. Few things are further from the spirit of our age than this. Although the sort of deterministic materialism Laplace expounded — which eliminates all free acts and so seemingly all genuine moral responsibility — no longer holds sway, modern psychology and sociology have successfully shown how much we seem to be products of circumstances beyond our control. Modern medicine, moreover, is often able to trace disorders back to chemical imbalances and so remove them from the realm of personal responsibility. It is unsurprising that the word "sin," which presupposes such responsibility, does not frequent our lips today.[145] Sin is doing as poorly as hell, and partly for the same reason. In our world the courts routinely entertain reduced penalties or even acquittal because, for instance, it is known that a defendant, although guilty, was abused as a child or suffers from a neurochemical disorder.

I raise no objection to such juridical verdicts, which are often the inevitable upshot of new learning. The problem is that we willingly let such learning erode our fragile sense of moral responsibility. We, like Adam and Eve, are happy to place blame elsewhere. But while we must, it goes without saying, not evade undoubted advances in knowledge and the qualifications they entail, we equally cannot acquiesce to the superficial proposition that, in general, we are unaccountable for our deeds. If we were to educate children according to the worldview Clarence Darrow enunciated in his infamous sentencing speech in the Leopold and Loeb case,[146] with its exposition of environmental determinism, the results would be intolerable. "Our moral sanity is at stake in our conviction that the issues which confront us are tremendous, that our choice is real

---

145. Most famously observed by Karl Menninger, *Whatever Became of Sin?* (New York: Hawthorn, 1973). But the observation was hardly new; see already F. R. Tennant, *The Concept of Sin* (Cambridge: Cambridge University Press, 1912), 277–81, on "The Decay of the Sense of Sin"; and much before that, in the wake of the Deists, William Wilberforce, *A Practical View of the Prevailing Religious System of Professed Christians* (London: T. Cadell, Jun. and W. Davies, 1797).

146. *Clarence Darrow's Sentencing Speech in State of Illinois v. Leopold and Loeb* (Minnetonka, MN: Professional Education Group, n.d.).

and that the forfeits of wrong choice are real."[147] Here common sense is
on the side of our religious tradition and its hell. Without responsibility
there can be neither right nor wrong, neither praise nor blame. And hell,
whatever its defects, rightly lays the burden of responsibility upon us.
It blames us for the wrong, just as heaven praises us for the right. The
thought of divine judgment undoes frivolity and confronts us with the
import of our actions. It is the antithesis of the sentimentalism and lack
of seriousness that everywhere today conspire to wither responsibility.
Hell furthermore tells us that God is something other than an amiable
chap who looks the other way no matter what. So hell has always had
its fitting functions — and it is not at all clear what else can effectively
fulfill those functions. This is what Berdyayev meant when he wrote
that the "modern rejection of hell makes life too easy, superficial and
irresponsible."[148]

But hell also has to do with the world to come. It presupposes the
transcendence of death. Those who no longer believe in an afterlife must
necessarily limit their musings on hell to this-worldly matters. What,
however, of those of us who cannot dissociate Christianity from hope
for something beyond the grave? What do we make of hell if we know
it to be mythological?

The Christian tradition, as I understand it, does not offer prosaic
knowledge about the afterlife. Heaven, no less than its polar opposite, is a myth, a projection of the religious imagination. To say that,
in the matter of what lies before us, we see in a glass darkly, is perhaps
to be optimistic. We certainly cannot map the afterlife with the words
of mediums, and the jury is still deliberating about near-death experiences — which include, interestingly enough, hellish as well as heavenly
encounters.[149] But we must not confuse the prosaic with the theological,
as do those who still vainly imagine that Genesis and modern science

---

147. Sir Walter Moberly, *The Ethics of Punishment* (London: Faber & Faber, 1968), 362.
His whole discussion, on 329–67, of "The Conception of Eternal Punishment" is more helpful
than most theological discourses on this subject.

148. Nicolas Berdyayev, *The Destiny of Man* (New York: Harper & Row, 1960), 266. Cf.
the related sentiment in Immanuel Kant, *Religion within the Limits of Reason Alone* (New
York: Harper & Row, 1960), 53: the antithesis between heaven and hell "serves to prevent us
from regarding good and evil, the realm of light and the realm of darkness, as bordering on
each other and as losing themselves in one another by gradual steps."

149. Bruce Greyson and Nancy Evans Bush, "Distressing Near-Death Experiences," *Psychiatry* 55 (February 1992): 95–110. On the role of such experiences in worldwide depictions
of hellish afterlives, see James McClenon, *Wondrous Events: Foundations of Religious Belief*
(Philadelphia: University of Pennsylvania Press, 1994), 168–84.

have something to do with each other. If we were to learn someday that near-death experiences are often veridical or that some ghosts are real — surely our faith allows latitudinarianism about such matters — we would still be left to do theology, to interpret the facts in Christian terms.

Hell sensibly extends moral responsibility into the next world. I say sensibly because this is the only way to prevent eschatology from making a mockery of the present world. I do not know what befell Mother Teresa of Calcutta when she died, nor what has become of Joseph Stalin. But the same thing cannot have come upon both. If there is any moral rhyme or reason in the universe, all human beings cannot be equally well off as soon as they breathe their last and wake again. The next life continues this life; it does not start at square one. So moral reflection within a theological context demands, what Jewish and Greek history witnessed, that Sheol evolve into heaven and hell, and that Hades become divided into different sections for different sorts.[150] Hell, which outrages our moral sensibilities, is paradoxically a product of those same sensibilities. It is a postulate of the conscience. It calls for divine justice to make things right, and it solemnly expresses the profound significance of our moral and religious decisions, a significance that crosses even the cordon of death, and goes so far that it raises the possibility of an ongoing alienation from God. In these particulars, hell makes good sense.

Perhaps — who knows? — the divine benevolence continues to let itself be circumscribed by human freedom in the next life. Perhaps it does so even to the point of allowing the self-absorbed to continue in their sad way.[151] But if so, God nonetheless must continue to be φιλάνθρωπος and so love them. The superstition that the divinity wishes to heal the sick only until their bodies give out or they meet with an accident is strange indeed. "What is there in the act of dying that it should change the mind of God towards us?"[152] So whatever inward loss or deprivation or discipline God permits to fall upon the dead, it cannot be the retributive violence of the traditional hell that profits sufferers nothing. "Shall not

---

150. The same moral reasoning also leads to speculation about purgatory and different levels of heaven and hell.

151. I cannot, however, understand how such a state could be eternal; cf. Marilyn McCord Adams, "Horrors in Theological Context," *SJT* 55 (2002): 475–76; and Eric Reitan, "Eternal Damnation and Blessed Ignorance: Is the Damnation of Some Incompatible with the Salvation of Any?" *RelS* 38 (2002): 429–50.

152. Dearmer, *Legend*, 268. Cf. Alger, *Critical History*, 535: "What is it, the instant mortals pass the line of death, that shall transform this Divinity of yearning piety and beneficence into a devil of relentless hate and cruelty?"

the Judge of the earth do right?" If God is good, by which I mean not good in some abstract sense but good to every individual,[153] then God's dealings with us must always be for some useful end, which eternal and unremedial retribution is not.[154] Such retribution would rather be "the consummation of a frightful dualism of the entire creation, ... an eternal sign of discord, internal disharmony and alienation; an incompleteness of the act of creation itself. ... An eternal hell would likewise be a hell for God, a hell for divine love."[155]

Dives, after death, saw his mistakes, felt remorse, and sought to serve others (Luke 16:27–28). This must be God's hope for even the worst of us.[156] Nothing else rings true if the Transcendent Pity sincerely wills that not one of these little ones should perish.

Excursus 1

PERCY BYSSHE SHELLEY AND THE HISTORICAL JESUS

Having referred, in the preceding chapter, to Shelley's thoughts on Jesus and hell, I here add a few modest comments concerning his work on the historical Jesus in general. I do this because New Testament scholars seem to have altogether overlooked the great poet; at least I cannot recall any survey of the quest paying him heed. The circumstance is unfortunate

---

153. Contrast Augustine, *Civ.* 11.18 (ed. Dombart and Kalb; CCSL 48:337), who can interpret the evil fate of evil creatures as enriching the experience of the redeemed; cf. Gregory the Great, *Hom. ev.* 40.8 (PL 76:1309A), who uses the same analogy as Augustine: the background enhances the picture. This makes the lost akin to slaves: they are not of value in themselves but only insofar as they profit others.

154. Here Origen's understanding of justice as always remedial is helpful; see *Princ.* 2.5 (ed. Görgemanns and Karpp; TzF 24:340–54). In this particular Origen is presumably indebted to Clement of Alexandria; cf. *Strom.* 4.24.154.1–2 (ed. van den Hoek; SC 463:314); 6.6.46.3; 6.6.52.1; 12.99.2 (ed. Descourtieux; SC 446:154, 166, 258).

155. Waclaw Hryniewicz, *Nadzieja zbawienia wszyskich: Od eschatologii lęku do eschatalogii nadziei* (Warsaw: Verbinum, 1990), 103; as quoted by Christopher Garbowski, "Tolkien's Eschatology of Hope: From Ragnarok to Joyous Subcreation," in *Apocalyptic in History and Tradition* (ed. Christopher Rowland and John Barton; JSNTSup 43; Sheffield: Sheffield University Press, 2002), 278.

156. Cf. the exegesis of Hans Denck, *Ordnung Gottes 3*, in *Schriften 2. Teil: Religiöse Schriften* (ed. W. Fellmann; Quellen und Forschungen zur Reformationsgeschichte 24.6.2; Gütersloh: C. Bertelsmann, 1956), 93–94.

not only because it unjustly fails to acknowledge Shelley's interesting contribution, but also because some of his conclusions and the means he employs to reach them have their parallels in more recent work.

Shelley's most extended venture into the Gospel traditions is his essay entitled "On Christianity."[157] Probably written in 1817, it was left incomplete and not published until 1859, years after his death.[158] My purpose here is not to review the major themes of the piece but rather more simply to call attention, from the standpoint of New Testament studies, to some of his critical assumptions and arguments regarding the historical Jesus.

For Shelley, what Jesus taught matters much more than what he did. The consequent abridging of the data, the reduction of interest to teaching alone, is partly due to a reluctance, not unexpected in a post-Humean world, to discuss "the supernatural events which the historians of this wonderful man subsequently asserted to have been connected with every gradation of his career" (*PW*, 1:246).[159] Yet no less important is Shelley's conviction that most of the story of Jesus is "not unparalleled in the annals of mankind," for "every religion and every revolution can furnish with regard to some of its most important particulars a parallel series of events." That is to say, every religion and revolution fabricates some version of the tale of "a man of ardent genius, and impatient virtue [who] perishes in stern and resolute opposition to tyranny, injustice and superstition" (*PW*, 1:247). So although Jesus' story is "full of heart-moving truth" (*PW*, 1:246), it does not, by reason of its typicality, attract much of Shelley's attention. Instead, the poet, like some Deists and Enlightenment philosophes, cares much more about "the comprehensive morality" of Jesus' "doctrines which essentially distinguish him from the crowd of

---

157. In what follows I use the edition on 246–71 of *The Prose Works of Percy Bysshe Shelley* [*PW*] (ed. E. B. Murray; vol. 1; Oxford: Clarendon, 1993).

158. Jane Gibson Shelley, *Shelley Memorials: From Authentic Sources: To Which Is Added, an Essay on Christianity, Now First Printed* (London: Smith, Elder, 1859). Against David Lee Clark, "Shelley's Biblical Extracts," *Modern Language Notes* 66 (1951): 435–41, most scholars do not identify "On Christianity" with the so-called "Biblical Extracts" sent to publisher Thomas Hookham in 1812 but never printed. See Murray's comments in *PW*, 1:460–61, 462.

159. Shelley explicitly brackets not only miracles but also the question of Jesus' divinity. His tone is quite different in the earlier *Notes to Queen Mab* (London, 1812–13) and elsewhere, where he derides belief in miracles and plainly rejects Jesus' divinity; see, e.g., *The Complete Works of Percy Bysshe Shelley*, vol. 1, *Poems* (ed. Roger Ingpen and Walter E. Peck; London: Ernest Benn, 1927), 152–55. The reserve in "On Christianity" is presumably a rhetorical ploy: Shelley is trying not to lose the favor of his envisioned audience.

martyrs and of patriots who have exulted to devote themselves for what they conceived would contribute to the benefit of their fellowmen" (*PW*, 1:246).[160]

What exactly are those distinguishing "doctrines," some of which Shelley says are "unexampled" (*PW*, 1:246)?[161] Being a critical reader, he does not identify the discourses in the canonical Gospels with the speech of the historical Jesus. He nowhere, for example, cites or even clearly alludes to the Gospel of John.[162] Anticipating a multitude of scholars after Strauss, he leaves the Fourth Gospel entirely out of account: it ill-suits his purposes. Focus is rather on the Synoptics — yet not on the Synoptics in their entirety, and not even on the Synoptic teachings in their entirety. Again, in accord with ensuing scholarship, only certain sayings in the Synoptics, in Shelley's judgment, go back to Jesus:

> It cannot be precisely ascertained to what degree Jesus Christ accommodated his doctrines to the opinions of his auditors, or in what degree he really said all that he is related to have said. He has left no written record of himself, and we are compelled to judge from the imperfect and obscure information which his biographers, persons certainly of very undisciplined and undiscriminating minds, have transmitted to posterity. These writers, our only guides, impute sentiments to Jesus Christ which flatly contradict each other.[163]

---

160. "Jesus, the alleged Messiah and self-styled Son of God, seemed to the deist an excellent moralist, but not a supernatural agent." So Roland N. Stromberg, *Religious Liberalism in Eighteenth-Century England* (Oxford: Oxford University Press, 1954), 57.

161. I am unsure how we should reconcile the proposition that Jesus offered "unexampled teaching" with Shelley's later statement that Jesus promulgated "the doctrines of every just and compassionate mind that ever speculated on the social nature of man" (*PW*, 1:260). Cf. "On the Doctrines of Christ," in *PW*, 1:273: "Nothing would be gained by the establishment of the originality of Jesus Christ's doctrines but the casting of a suspicion upon its practicability."

162. "Insomuch therefore as ye love one another, ye may enjoy the community of whatsoever benefits arise from the inventions of civilized life" (*PW*, 1:264) could allude to John 13:34; 15:12, 17; but the comment is made in passing, and the sequence of the words "Ye love one another" also appears in the AV in 1 Pet 1:22, while "love one another" occurs more than once in both the Pauline and Johannine Epistles.

163. *PW*, 1:260. In "A Refutation of Deism," Shelley, presumably drawing upon a Deist he had read, offers another argument against the reliability of the New Testament witnesses: "The Gospels contain internal evidence that they were not written by eyewitnesses of the event which they pretend to record. The Gospel of St. Matthew was plainly not written until some time after the taking of Jerusalem, that is, at least forty years after the execution of Jesus Christ." His evidence is Matt 23:35, which he takes (wrongly in my judgment) to refer to the Zachariah who died in the Jewish War, according to Josephus, *J.W.* 4.334–44 (*PW*, 1:108).

Despite his acknowledgment that we cannot always separate the wheat from the chaff, cannot always recover exactly what Jesus said, Shelley nonetheless regards the following ten logia — eight from Matthew's Sermon on the Mount — as coming from Jesus himself. They all have to do with ethics, and Shelley can co-opt each one for his own vision of social justice:[164]

- "Blessed are the pure in heart, for they shall see God" (Matt 5:8 KJV). Shelley, denying that that the words concern the afterlife, supposes them to say "no more than the most excellent philosophers have felt and expressed — that virtue is its own reward" (*PW*, 1:250–51).

- "Love your enemies, bless those who curse you, . . . that ye may be the sons of your heavenly Father, who makes the sun to shine on the good and on the evil, and the rain to fall on the just and the unjust" (Matt 5:44–45, cited in a form that conflates Matthew with Rom 12:14; cf. also Luke 6:28). Shelley interprets as follows: "You ought not to love the individuals of your domestic circle less, but to love those who exist beyond it, more. Once make the feelings of confidence and affection universal and the distinctions of property and power will vanish" (*PW*, 1:264–65).[165]

- Jesus "instructed his disciples to be perfect as their father in Heaven is perfect" (cf. Matt 5:48). This means that "the perfection of the human and the divine character is . . . to be the same: man by resembling God fulfills most accurately the tendencies of his nature, and God comprehends within itself all that constitutes human perfection. Thus God is a model thro' which the excellence of man is to be measured, whilst the *abstract* perfection of the human character is the type of the *actual* perfection of the divine" (*PW*, 1:259).

- "Think not that I am come to destroy the law and the prophets: I am not come to destroy but to fulfill. Till Heaven and Earth pass away, one jot or one tittle shall in no wise pass from the law till all be fulfilled" (cf. Matt 5:17–18 KJV). Jesus allegedly used this as a

---

164. *PW*, 1:260. Cf. Shelley, Letter to Miss Hitchener, February 27, 1812: "I have often thought that the moral sayings of Jesus Christ might be very useful, if selected from the mystery and immorality which surrounds them."

165. For a dramatic poetic incarnation of this, see Shelley's "Prometheus Unbound," where Prometheus forgives Jupiter, who has bound him in Tartarus.

rhetorical ploy to gain the crowds' sympathy before he went on "to abrogate the system of the Jewish [law]" (*PW*, 1:263).[166]

- "The spirit of the Lord is upon me because he hath chosen me to preach the gospel to the poor, he hath sent me to heal the broken-hearted, to preach deliverance to the captives, and recovery of sight to the blind, and to set at liberty them that are bruised" (cf. Luke 4:18 KJV, quoting Isa 61:1). This is not a christological declaration for Shelley but "an enunciation of all that Plato and Diogenes have speculated upon of the equality of mankind" (*PW*, 1:263).

- Jesus "descants upon" the system of Jewish law "as a code of moral conduct, which it professed to be, and absolutely selects the law of retaliation as an instance of the absurdity and immorality of its institutions" (Matt 5:38–39; *PW*, 1:262–63).

- "Take therefore no thought for the morrow, for the morrow shall take thought for the things of itself. Sufficient unto the day is the evil thereof" (Matt 6:34 KJV). This calls for "a pure and simple life," exposing "the miseries and mischiefs of that system which makes all things subservient to the subsistence of the material frame of man" (*PW*, 1:266–67).

- "Sell [all] that thou hast,... give [it] to the poor,... and follow me" (Matt 19:21 KJV). Shelley, in a Jacobinic spirit, construes this as being about equality (*PW*, 1:269)[167]

- "No man can serve two masters" (Matt 6:24 KJV). This means "that it is impossible at once to be high-minded and just, and wise, and comply with the accustomed forms of human society, seek honour, wealth or empire either from the idolatry of habit, or as the direct instruments of sensual gratification" (*PW*, 1:267–68).

- "Clothing and food and shelter are not... the true end of human life.... In this respect the fowls of the air and the lilies of the field are examples for the imitation of mankind. They are clothed and fed by the Universal God.... Your heavenly father knoweth that you have need of these things" (cf. Matt 6:25–33 KJV). Shelley divines here

---

166. Setting Jesus against Judaism was another commonplace of the Deists; see Stromberg, *Religious Liberalism*, 61, 78–81.

167. Shelley also cites this text in "An Address to the Irish People" (*PW*, 1:26), where he comments: "This is not to be understood literally. Jesus Christ appears to me only to have meant that riches have generally the effect of hardening and vitiating the heart; so has poverty."

"the right of every human being to possess, and that in the same degree," life's necessities (*PW*, 1:266–68).

All of these passages are, in a way that foreshadows *Formgeschichte*, considered apart from their literary contexts. This move, which values parts of the tradition more than the literary wholes, implicitly denies the historical value and spiritual inspiration of the Synoptic evangelists and allows Shelley great latitude in his own noncanonical elucidations: Meaning need not depend upon evangelical context. Scripture need not be interpreted by Scripture.

In addition to crediting Jesus plainly as the author of several sayings, Shelley indicates that Jesus had an eschatological outlook, although the details remain vague. To all appearances human beings die, go down to the grave, and molder in a heap of senseless dust. But "Jesus Christ asserts that these appearances are fallacious, that a gloomy and cold imagination alone suggests the conception that thought can cease to be. Another and a more extensive state of being, rather than the complete extinction of being, will follow from that mysterious change which we call death" (*PW*, 1:255). Shelley, although he does not endorse this dream, does not dismiss it either: "How magnificent and illustrious is the conception which this bold theory suggests to the contemplation, even if it be no more than the imagination of some sublimest and most holy poet, who impressed with the loveliness and majesty of his own nature, is impatient, discontented, with the narrow limits which this imperfect life, and the dark grave they have assigned forever as his melancholy portion" (*PW*, 1:256). In setting forth Jesus' eschatological expectations, Shelley fails to cite any particular texts. At this point, apparently, he is summarizing the general impression the tradition has left upon him — a wholly reasonable thing to do, in this writer's judgment.

Given his recognition of the secondary elements in the Gospels, how does Shelley sort the variegated items, that is, assess which Synoptic texts go back to Jesus and which do not? At one point he observes that the evangelists "insert in the midst of a strain of impassioned eloquence, or sagest exhortation, a sentiment only remarkable for its naked and driveling folly. But it is not difficult to distinguish the inventions by which these historians have filled up the interstices of tradition, or corrupted the simplicity of truth, from the real character of the object of their rude amazement."[168] This verdict assumes — as obvious and without argument, but perhaps with implicit appeal to the poet's own sense of artistic instinct — that Jesus was an eloquent sage, and that any "naked and driveling folly" that we find in the Gospels must be from someone else. This conviction is an early ancestor of what we know as the criterion of dissimilarity. Shelley has no doubt that Jesus' teachings were unconventional, were distinctively different from "the gross imaginations of the vulgar" (*PW*, 1:250).[169] We can distinguish them from traditional Jewish thought (see p. 166) as well as from the lamentably incompetent Christian commentary now parasitic upon them.

A second principle that Shelley clearly follows is that of coherence. The poet adamantly insists that some parts of the tradition cannot go back to Jesus because they fail to cohere with what we otherwise know him to have taught. Again and again Shelley reverts to Matt 5:38–48, which prohibits vengeance and depicts God as being good to the unjust. And again and again he avers that "the mild and gentle Author" (*PW*, 1:253) of those verses could never have believed in or commended any sort of retributive hell. A God glutted with vengeance contradicts "the whole tenor" of Jesus' "doctrines and his life overflowing with benevolence and forbearance and compassion!" (*PW*, 1:253). "Jesus Christ would hardly have cited as an example of all that is gentle and beneficent and compassionate a being who shall deliberately scheme to inflict on a large portion of the human race tortures indescribably intense and indefinitely protracted, ... who shall inflict them too without any mistake as to the true nature of pain, without any view to future good, ... merely because it is just!" (*PW*, 1:253). Although Shelley does not cite chapter and verse, this firm conviction entails that the numerous Gospel texts envisaging future divine judgment are not from Jesus. They originated rather with early Christians, who in this matter learned less from Jesus than has Shelley.

---

168. *PW*, 1:260. Cf. Shelley, "A Defense of Poetry," in *Shelley's Poetry and Prose: Authoritative Texts, Criticism* (ed. Donald H. Reiman and Neil Fraistat; 2nd ed.; New York: Norton, 2002), 224: "The scattered fragments presented to us by the biographies of this extraordinary person are all instinct with the most vivid poetry. But his doctrines seem to have been quickly distorted."

169. These and other relevant comments of Shelley should be part of the history told by Gerd Theissen and Dagmar Winter, *The Quest for the Plausible Jesus: The Question of Criteria* (Louisville: Westminster John Knox, 2002).

We have no cause to imagine, Shelley readily concedes, that Jesus was the exception to the rule that human beings are bundles of inconsistencies. "It is not here asserted that no contradictions are to be admitted to have place in the system of Jesus Christ between doctrines promulgated in different states of feeling or information, or even such as are implied in the enunciation of a scheme of thought various and obscure thro' its immensity and depth. It is not asserted that no degree of human indignation ever hurried him beyond the limits which his calmer mood had placed to disapprobation against vice and folly."[170] What Shelley does affirm, however, is that Jesus had an "essential character," and anything too alien from that character cannot come from him (*PW*, 1:261). Given this take, the initial critical task must be "to form a general image of his character and of his doctrines and refer to this whole the distinct portions of action and speech by which they are diversified" (*PW*, 1:260). If I understand these words aright, they foreshadow the recent argument that the safest way to reconstruct the historical Jesus is first to establish an interpretive framework or sketch a general portrait and only then to evaluate individual sayings and purported events within that framework or as a part of that sketch.[171]

However that may be, Shelley's appeal to consistency is clearly an antecedent of the criterion of coherence as later critics developed it. Norman Perrin wrote: "Material from the earliest strata of the tradition may be accepted as authentic if it can be shown to cohere with material established as authentic by means of the criterion of dissimilarity."[172] The corollary of this principle is that items failing to cohere with material established as original on other grounds should be ascribed to the community. If saying X does not cohere with saying Y, and if saying Y goes back to Jesus, then saying X cannot go back to Jesus. This is the logic Shelley adopts when dogmatically insisting that Jesus had no place for eschatological or retributive judgment. Lily Dougall, Cyril W. Emmet,

---

170. *PW*, 1:260–61. Cf. the caution of John Meier, *A Marginal Jew: Rethinking the Historical Jesus*, vol. 1, *The Roots of the Problem and the Person* (New York: Doubleday, 1991), 176–77, regarding negative use of the criterion of coherence to eliminate items from the original tradition: we should not demand of Jesus an artificial consistency.

171. See Dale C. Allison Jr., *Jesus of Nazareth: Millenarian Prophet* (Minneapolis: Fortress, 1998), 39–58.

172. Norman Perrin, *Rediscovering the Teaching of Jesus* (New York: Harper & Row, 1967), 43.

Percy Dreamer, and James Robinson have more recently, as we have seen, argued in much the same way.

The outcome of Shelley's methodology can surprise no one brought up on Schweitzer's *Von Reimarus zu Wrede* (ET, *The Quest of the Historical Jesus*). Reconstructing the Galilean can mean executing a self-portrait, entitling it "Jesus," and admiring the result.[173] Of this Shelley is no doubt guilty. "The Jesus that Shelley reconstructs is to a large extent a projection of his own self-image as an apostle of enlightenment defying inquisitorial college dons, authoritarian judges, and the quislings of the Anglican hierarchy."[174] "On Christianity" offers us a social reformer who was, congenially for Shelley, "an ardent genius," a "poet," and a "spirit seeking after truth" (*PW*, 1:247, 251, and 249 respectively). His chief interests were virtue, knowledge, and happiness; he promoted nonviolence and social equality; and he was conveniently apathetic about christological dogma and miracles.[175] Furthermore, if Shelley finds the moral teachings of the Old Testament to be dated and unworthy of esteem, then in this Jesus also was Shelley's precursor, having allegedly done his broad-minded best to counter those teachings (*PW*, 1:263–64). Shelley can also regard his own Jesus with affection because of a shared and hearty disgust of the gross miscarriage of divine justice known as hell. Jesus "summoned his whole resources of persuasion" (*PW*, 1:252–52) to repel the odious myth that a schizophrenic Providence will punish some and reward others. Likewise, Shelley — who was, it has been said, obsessed with hell[176] — vigorously argued against divine vengeance in a postmortem torture chamber.

---

173. Shelley's admiration for Jesus should be evident from this excursus. On his negative remarks about Jesus, all of which appear to have come from a time before he wrote "On Christianity," see David Lee Clark, ed., *Shelley's Prose* (New York: New Amsterdam, 1988), 11–16.

174. Byron Shelley, *Shelley and Scripture* (Oxford: Clarendon, 1994), 57.

175. Cf. the summary in Thomas Paine, *The Age of Reason*, in *The Writings of Thomas Paine* (ed. Moncure Daniel Conway; New York: G. Putnam's Sons, 1896), 4:40: Jesus "called men to the practice of moral virtues, and the belief in one God. The great trait in his character is philanthropy."

176. See Leslie D. Weatherhead, *The After-World of the Poets: The Contribution of Victorian Poets to the Development of the Idea of Immortality* (London: Epworth Press, 1929), 48–78. On 58, Weatherhead writes: "We have made an attempt to count in his complete works, both prose and poetry, all the subjects directly related to religion. Of all mention of these subjects, over fifty per cent. are definite references to hell..." Whatever the personal reasons for Shelley's fixation with and opposition to hell (his Christian mother, one may observe, appears to have been a universalist), he was philosophically opposed to tracing good and evil to the same source.

As for theology in the proper sense, Jesus' sophisticated conception of God, in Shelley's mind, differed greatly from the general conceptions abroad in his day: "The word God according to the acceptance of Jesus Christ...is the interfused and overruling Spirit of all the energy and wisdom included within the circle of existing things....He every where represents this power as something mysteriously and illimitably pervading the frame of things" (*PW*, 1:250). This analysis, which at best reads between the Synoptic lines and imposes a foreign idiom upon them, well describes the God whom Shelley, under Spinoza's influence, elsewhere confessed himself to believe in.[177]

One final word about Shelley. Some of the Deists he had read were wholly destructive. They criticized the Bible in order to do away with it. Baron d'Holbach, for example, had no interest in recovering a serviceable Jesus. It was otherwise with Shelley, for whom parts of the Bible retained a genuine fascination. Like those Enlightenment thinkers who reinterpreted Jesus as a great moral teacher, he frowned upon the church and yet admired its Savior. He thought that the evangelists had, sadly, gotten much wrong and that, ever since, "demagogues" have led Christians astray. After the communal experiment in Acts 2:44, which attempted to carry forward Jesus' vision of equality, "the transitory glow of enthusiasm...faded from the minds of men," and "precedent and habit resumed their empire [and] broke like a universal deluge on the shrinking and solitary island" (*PW*, 1:269). "The demagogues of the infant republic of the Christian sect attaining thro' eloquence or artifice to influence among its members, first violated, under the pretence of watching over its integrity, the institutions established for the common and equal benefit of all" (*PW*, 1:270). Jesus' original, inspired program withered all too soon after its promising germination.

Given the failure of the churches — and, incidentally, his preference for Jesus over Paul — Shelley's goal was not to do away with everything in the Gospels but rather to seek the real Jesus behind the ecclesiastical dogma, the historical genius beneath the mythological overlay, the remarkable moral hero who "opposed with earnest eloquence the panic fears and hateful superstitions which have enslaved mankind for ages"

---

177. See Shelley, *Shelley and Scripture*, 17. Shelley's famous atheism was a rejection only of the traditional Christian God, not a rejection of all conceptions of divinity.

(*PW*, 1:256). Shelley — in words that very much remind us of some recent reconstructions of the historical Jesus — believed that he had found him: "We discover that he is the enemy of oppression and falsehood, that he is the advocate of equal justice, that he is neither disposed to sanction bloodshed or deceit under whatsoever pretences their practice may be vindicated. We discover that he was a man of meek and majestic demeanor, calm in danger, of natural and simple thoughts and habits, beloved to adoration by his adherents, unmoved and solemn and serene" (*PW*, 1:260).

FOUR

APOCALYPTIC, POLEMIC, APOLOGETICS

Theological dogma is so intimately concerned with the most precious interests of life that the tendency to intolerance of free enquiry persists more obstinately in this than in other spheres. It is natural that it should be so, but the effort required to escape prejudice is an effort which must be made, not least in the interests of those dogmas which it is hoped to defend.
— Percival Gardner-Smith

But one thing is quite certain: if that belief in the speedy second coming of the Messiah which was shared by all parties in the primitive Church, whether Nazarene or Pauline, which Jesus is made to prophesy, over and over again, in the Synoptic gospels; and which dominated the life of Christians during the first century after the crucifixion; — if he believed and taught that, then assuredly he was under an illusion, and he is responsible for that which the mere effluxion of time has demonstrated to be a prodigious error.
— Thomas H. Huxley

If the history of philosophy is any guide, arguments for conclusions that people are very reluctant to accept have an extremely poor track record with respect to actually convincing anybody.
— Michael Rea

Tomorrow is a long, long time if you're a memory.
— Neil Young

INTRODUCTION

Academic discussion of the historical Jesus has, for the past one hundred years, preoccupied itself with two questions. The first concerns

111

the historical character of the relevant sources. How much do they
allow us to know about Jesus? The second question, which Johannes
Weiss and Albert Schweitzer bequeathed to us, has to do with apocalyptic[1] or eschatology.[2] Did Jesus believe the final judgment and its
attendant events, such as the resurrection of the dead, were imminent,
and if so, to what extent did his proclamation and ministry mirror such
a conviction?

---

1. In previous writings I have used "apocalyptic" to designate a cluster of themes and
expectations — cataclysmic signs and suffering, resurrection of the dead, universal judgment,
heavenly redeemer figures, a divine utopia — which developed in postexilic Judaism, typically in
association with belief in a near end. An "apocalyptic Jesus" would then be one who promoted
and largely lived out of such themes and expectations. In this chapter, however, I use the
term more loosely to characterize any picture of Jesus that bears a strong resemblance to the
reconstructions of Johannes Weiss and Albert Schweitzer.

2. Johannes Weiss, *Jesus' Proclamation of the Kingdom of God* (Philadelphia: Fortress,
1971 [ET of *Die Predigt Jesu vom Reiche Gottes*, 1892]); Albert Schweitzer, *The Quest of the
Historical Jesus* (Minneapolis: Fortress, 2001 [ET of *Geschichte der Leben-Jesu-Forschung*,
1906, 1913, 1950]). One should bear in mind, however, that Schweitzer's narrative — which
tells the story so that his own work becomes the great telos of his history, with Weiss as
Schweitzer's very own John the Baptist — discreetly underestimates the extent to which others
besides himself and Weiss already recognized a strong eschatological element in the teaching
of Jesus. See the complaints of Paul Wernle, in his review of Schweitzer in *TLZ* 38 (1906):
501–6. It was after all recognition of the eschatological Jesus in the Synoptics and fear of it
that explains the lifework of Timothée Colani (1828–88). In his publications he argued that
the "Son of Man" was not messianic, that none of the sayings about a second advent go
back to Jesus, that Jesus had a spiritual understanding of the kingdom, and that Mark 13
is a Jewish-Christian tract, not testimony to Jesus. And Oskar Holtzmann, *The Life of Jesus*
(London: Adam & Charles Black, 1904; ET of *Leben Jesu*, 1901), could assert independently of
Schweitzer that "the starting point of Jesus' preaching is . . . to be found in its eschatology: 'The
end of the existing world is immediately at hand, therefore repent ye.' In that case we must
regard the eschatological discourses in the preaching of Jesus as being (to use a metaphor)
not merely accidental offshoots, but the roots which support the trunk of the tree. It was, we
cannot doubt, with eschatological discourses that Jesus came forward in the first instance"
(160n). Again, "The passing away of Jesus' contemporaries not only proved that he had been
mistaken in certain of his sayings; it proved more than this, because the motive force of his
preaching had been the thought of the speedy coming of the judgment, of the nearness of
the kingdom of God. The expectation had been the determining factor in his own preaching
of repentance, as well as in that of his apostles" (506). Cf. James Martineau, *The Seat of
Authority in Religion* (4th rev. ed.; London: Longmans, Green, 1898): The problem of Jesus
and apocalyptic is "well known, not perhaps without sorrowful regrets, by every reader of
the synoptic gospels" (327), and the coming kingdom "is more than the subject of a parable
here, and a denunciation of a blessing there; it is, throughout, the very spring of conviction that
disposes of his will, and shines through all his public compassions and lonely devotions" (328).
Passages of similar purport appear before Schweitzer in Renan, H. J. Holtzmann, W. Bousset,
and others. Schweitzer was not new in pushing eschatology to the center. His contribution was
to make it dramatically and unashamedly the sun around which every single word and deed
of Jesus orbited. Incidentally, it would be useful if someone were to collect the early German
reviews of Schweitzer's work — such as those of Jülicher, Wernle, Windisch — and translate
them into English. While we all know the deficiencies of Schweitzer's own reconstruction,
far fewer of us know the deficiencies in his history of research, some of which those reviews
highlight.

Although in my mind these two controverted questions are inextricably related, in this context I attempt, as far as is possible, to isolate and concentrate on the second. My purpose in doing so is not to take an excursion among the arguments and ask what the truth might be — a subject about which I have elsewhere said much and will herein say no more.[3] I intend rather to review some of the theological convictions that have encouraged or discouraged fondness for a fervently eschatological Jesus.

One rarely reads a book on Jesus without feeling that there is, for the author, immense interest in the outcome. E. F. Scott's optimistic assertion that "we have learned to approach the question [of Jesus and apocalyptic] dispassionately"[4] is as ridiculously false now as when Scott penned it eighty years ago. Weiss and Schweitzer did not produce equanimity but provoked an uproar, and it has never quieted. Almost everyone who has written about Jesus since 1900 has become embroiled in the fracas, and those traveling the straight and narrow road of bona fide impartiality on this issue are few. It is no secret that intense theological interests have always environed our quest for Jesus. So what precisely has been at stake theologically with regard to the great eschatological question?

PRO

I begin with those who have sketched for us a Jesus who lived and spoke in the grip of the impending consummation. Perhaps we do well to remember that such a Jesus appeared originally among people outside the church, people wishing to attack those inside the church. If one wants to discredit a religion, discredit its founder. Show, for example, that the founder was wrong about something, preferably something important.

Of all the things that the New Testament is clearly mistaken about, the most obvious is its conviction, plainly expressed in a good number

---

3. Dale C. Allison Jr., *The End of the Ages Has Come: An Early Interpretation of the Passion and Resurrection of Jesus* (Philadelphia: Fortress, 1985), 100–14; "A Plea for Thoroughgoing Eschatology," *JBL* 113 (1994): 675–92; "Jesus and Eschatology," *BRev* 12, no. 5 (1996): 34–41, 54; "The Eschatology of Jesus," in *Encyclopedia of Apocalypticism*, vol. 1, *Origins of Apocalypse in Judaism and Early Christianity* (ed. John J. Collins and Bernard McGinn; New York: Continuum, 1998), 267–302; *Jesus of Nazareth: Millenarian Prophet* (Philadelphia: Fortress, 1998); and my contributions to *The Apocalyptic Jesus: A Debate* (ed. Robert J. Miller; Santa Rosa, CA: Polebridge Press, 2001).

4. E. F. Scott, "The Place of Apocalyptical Conceptions in the Mind of Jesus," *JBL* 41 (1922): 137.

of places, that the consummation is near to hand. In the seventeenth
century, the expositor Matthew Poole wrote: "The apostles ordinarily in
their epistles speak of the world as nigh to an end in their age, though
it hath since continued more than sixteen hundred years; which would
incline one to think, that they thought it would have been at an end
before this time."[5] The risen Jesus himself says a full three times in Rev
22: "I come quickly" (vv. 7, 12, 20; cf. 3:11). The speaker has failed to
keep this promise; and the fact has not escaped notice, which is why 2 Pet
3 knows of "scoffers" who ask, "Where is the promise of his coming?
For ever since our ancestors died, all things continue as they were from
the beginning of creation" (v. 4).[6] While we can only wonder about
the identity of these so-called "scoffers,"[7] we certainly do understand
their critique. The Babylonian Talmud, in the name of Rabbi Samuel
ben Nahmani, rebukes those who say, "Since the predetermined time
has arrived, and yet he [Messiah] has not come, he will never come" (*b.
Sanh.* 97b); and William Miller lost most of his embarrassed followers to
disillusionment when Jesus failed to return to earth on October 2, 1844.
Being wrong about the date of the end is a discrediting experience. We
do not need Deuteronomy to surmise that "if a prophet speaks in the
name of the Lord but the thing does not take place or prove true, it is a
word that the Lord has not spoken" (Deut 18:22).

Whether the "scoffers" in 2 Pet 3 had in mind words credited to
Jesus himself is unknown, although some commentators have suspected
this. It is, however, perfectly clear that there was, in the early church,
awareness that some prophecies attributed to him were problematic.
John 21:22–23 reflects consternation that the Beloved Disciple has died
even though Jesus has not yet returned: "So the rumor spread in the
community that this disciple would not die. Yet Jesus did not say to
him that he would not die, but, 'If it is my will that he remain until
I come, what is that to you?'" Obviously, in the background is some
saying such as Mark 9:1: "There are some standing here who will not

---

5. Matthew Poole, *A Commentary on the Holy Bible* (London: Henry G. Bohn, 1846),
3:572 (on 1 Cor 10:11). Poole exempts Jesus himself from this error; see 45 (on Matt 10:23)
and 166 (on Mark 9:1).

6. When the author, in response, goes on to affirm that "with the Lord one day is like
a thousand years" (1 Pet 3:8), he effectively euthanizes imminent expectation. Remaining a
doctrine, it ceases to be felt.

7. For various possibilities, see Richard J. Bauckham, *Jude, 2 Peter* (WBC 50; Waco, TX:
Word, 1983), 154–57.

taste death until they see that the kingdom of God has come with power." Somebody reasonably enough understood this or something like it to mean that not all of Jesus' disciples would die before the consummation.

We do not know whether John 21 was designed to dispel doubt within the church or to confute criticism from without or both, but that some non-Christians at a later date imputed eschatological error to Jesus is not in doubt. In his attack on Christianity, the Neoplatonist Porphyry (233–301) not only ridiculed Paul for misreading the eschatological clock; he also made Jesus guilty of the same misperception. Porphyry's argument about Matt 24:14, an argument preserved in the work of Macarius Magnes, comes down to this: Jesus says that the gospel will be preached throughout all the creation, and then the end will come. But the gospel has indeed been preached throughout all the creation, and the end has nonetheless failed to arrive. QED: Jesus was wrong. One would like to know what Eusebius, in his lost response to Porphyry, had to say about this.[8]

The attempt to gut Christianity by finding false forecasts in the Gospels also appears centuries later with the Deists of the seventeenth and eighteenth centuries. Hermann Samuel Reimarus is the most famous of them, but because of Schweitzer's history, he has received far too much credit: much of Reimarus's reconstruction of Jesus just expands the work of his English predecessors.[9] So let me first refer here to one of them, Matthew Tindal (1653–1733). Tindal came to destroy not just the law and the prophets but also the New Testament. One of his weapons was the argument that Jesus and his apostles were mistaken insofar as they expected the second coming not centuries down the line but in the near

---

8. For the Greek text, see Macarius Magnes, *Apoc.* 4.3 (ed. Blondel; 161). R. Joseph Hoffmann, *Porphyry's Against the Christians: The Literary Remains* (Amherst, NY: Prometheus Books, 1994), 71, offers this translation: "It is as servile a piece of work as ever came from a drudge in a factory: 'The Gospel of the kingdom shall be preached in all the world, and then the end will come.' Consider that every corner of the world has heard of the gospel; that everyone — everywhere — has the finished product — but that the end has not come and will never come. This saying should be whispered, not said aloud." For Eusebius, see Jerome, *Comm. Matt.* 24.16–18 (ed. Bonnard; SC 259:192–94); Socrates, *Hist. eccl.* 3.23 (PG 67.445B); Philostorgius, *Hist. eccl* . 8.14 (ed. Bidez; GCS 21:115).

9. See below, n. 12. See also Colin Brown, *Jesus in European Protestant Thought, 1778–1860* (SHT 1; Durham, NC: Labyrinth, 1985), 29–55. Perhaps it was under the spell of his champion Strauss that Schweitzer began his review with Reimarus, for this is where the story also begins in Strauss's *Das Leben Jesu für das deutsche Volk*.

future.[10] Tindal was a proponent of the religion of reason, which he insisted had to be both universal and unchanging. In promoting this up-to-date yet allegedly primordial faith, he was obliged to censure the religion of revelation, which meant criticizing the Bible. It was his desire to do away with traditional, dogmatic Christianity that led him to latch onto unfulfilled prophecies in the New Testament, including the Gospels (he cited Matt 24:3, 33–36; 26:64). Tindal asked, regarding the tardy Parousia, "If most of the Apostles, upon what Motives soever, were mistaken in a Matter of this Consequence; how can we be absolutely certain, that any one of them may not be mistaken in any other Matter? If they were not inspir'd in what they said in the Writings concerning the then coming of Christ; how could they be inspir'd in those Arguments they build on a Foundation far from being so? And if they taught their Times were the last, no Direction they gave, cou'd be intended to reach further than their own Times."[11]

Reimarus (1694–1768) also had as his aim the discrediting of traditional, orthodox Christianity.[12] Like Tindal, whom he had read, he criticized the behavior of biblical worthies such as Moses — deriding the latter, for instance, as a murderer (cf. Exod 2:11–12). He mocked the miracles of the Bible, sarcastically observing, among other things, that the author of the Pentateuch "kills all Pharaoh's cattle three times running. Each time not a single beast is left alive, but in his fertile

---

10. Matthew Tindal, *Christianity as Old as the Creation: Or, the Gospel a Republication of the Religion of Nature* (2nd ed.; London: n.p., 1732), 233–36.

11. Ibid., 236. Cf. Anonymous (Paul Henri Thiry, Baron d'Holbach), *Ecce Homo! or, A Critical Enquiry into the History of Jesus Christ* (2nd ed.; London: D. I. Eaton, 1813), 190: "Critics maintain also that it was false to say near eighteen hundred years ago that the end of the world was near, and more false still to affirm that the great Judge would arrive before the apostles could have time to make the tour of the cities of Israel." On 188 the author has Jesus say to his apostles, "Speak of the end of the world; this will intimidate women and poltroons."

12. For what follows, see the complete edition of Reimarus's apology as edited by Gerhard Alexander: *Apologie oder Schutzschrift für die vernünftigen Verehrer Gottes* (2 vols.; Frankfurt am Main: Insel, 1972). For a convenient English translation of the sections dealing principally with the historical Jesus, see Charles H. Talbert, ed., *Reimarus, Fragments* (trans. Ralph S. Fraser; Philadelphia: Fortress, 1970). Schweitzer's exaggerated claims for Reimarus's originality have left the general impression that the latter inaugurated modern critical thinking about the historical Jesus. Most of Reimarus's claims about Jesus, however, appear in the writings of English Deists he had read; see August Chr. Lundsteen, *Hermann Samuel Reimarus und die Anfänge der Leben-Jesu Forschung* (Copenhagen: O. C. Olsen, 1939), 95–148. Already Paul Wernle, in his review of Schweitzer in *TLZ* 38 (1906): 502, complained that Schweitzer had neglected Reimarus's predecessors. On the whole question of English Deism and German theology, see Christopher Voigt, *Der englische Deismus in Deutschland* (BHT 121; Tübingen: Mohr Siebeck, 2003).

imagination there are always fresh ones ready to be demolished again."[13] Reimarus was especially on the lookout for contradictions in the canonical accounts of Jesus' resurrection. Matthew's tale, in chapter 28, of women arriving at the tomb to a great earthquake, a terrified guard, and a descending angel does not, Reimarus emphasized, sound much like Mark 16; Luke 24; or John 20.

Central to Reimarus' skeptical critique was the eschatological nature of Jesus' message. Reimarus argued that the ambition of Jesus, like that of John the Baptist, was "awakening the people to the speedy arrival of the long-hoped-for deliverer" and "making them eager for his coming."[14] In the event, however, Jesus and his disciples "found themselves mistaken and deceived."[15] The fullness of time was emptied. The end that came upon the would-be Messiah was not the restoration of Israel but the torture of crucifixion. Jesus had been gazing at a mirage. Yet, in the aftermath the disciples, not taking No for an answer, faked the resurrection and invented the notion of a spiritual redeemer and spiritual kingdom. Their deception did not fool Reimarus: "If Christ neither has nor does come again to reward the faithful in his kingdom, then our belief is as useless as it is false."[16]

If one can — as did Porphyry, Tindal, and Reimarus — sponsor a strongly eschatological Jesus for polemical reasons,[17] it is equally possible to defend such a Jesus for apologetical ends. Consider the case of Joachim Jeremias, one of the more important questers in the era after Schweitzer. We may fairly offer three generalizations about him. First, Jeremias was conservative with regard to the general reliability of the Synoptics. He may have distrusted many of the miracle stories,[18] but he believed that "our sources are sufficient to enable us to bring out the basic ideas of the preaching of Jesus with some degree of probability."[19] Indeed, he even argued that certain linguistic and stylistic features

---

13. Reimarus, *Fragments*, 231.

14. Ibid., 141.

15. Ibid.

16. Ibid., 228.

17. One should observe that non-Christians have continued to cite the failed expectations of the Gospels as invalidating Christian faith; see, e.g., Bertrand Russell, *Why I Am Not a Christian and Other Essays on Religion and Related Subjects* (New York: Simon & Schuster, 1957), 15–17.

18. Joachim Jeremias, *New Testament Theology: The Proclamation of Jesus* (New York: C. Scribner's Sons, 1971), 86–92.

19. Ibid., 1.

of the early Jesus tradition "show so much faithfulness and such respect towards the tradition of the sayings of Jesus that we are justified in drawing up the following principle of method: In the Synoptic tradition it is the inauthenticity, and not the authenticity, of the sayings of Jesus that must be demonstrated."[20]

The second relevant fact about Jeremias is that his own species of Christian theology required a conservative historiography. Here are his words on the place of the historical Jesus in theology: "We must continually return to the historical Jesus and his message. The sources demand it; the kerygma, which refers us back away from itself, also demands it. To put it in theological terms, the incarnation implies that the story of Jesus is not only a possible subject for historical research, study, and criticism, but [also] demands all of these. We need to know who the Jesus of history was, as well as the content of his message."[21] Clearly, Jeremias's theology needs some trustworthy sources.

My third point about Jeremias is that his Jesus is a direct descendant of Albert Schweitzer's Jesus. The parables, for example, are eschatological texts on Jeremias's reading; many of them are about obtaining salvation or losing it in the face of the looming eschatological catastrophe and last judgment.[22] And this is what Jeremias sees throughout the Synoptic record as a whole. Indeed, Jesus adopted, according to Jeremias, some of the "details" of "apocalyptic": he announced the messianic woes, the resurrection of the dead, the last judgment, the punishment of the devil and his angels, and the renewal of the world.[23]

Now, what does this third point have to do with the first two? How is Jeremias's apocalyptic Jesus related to a faith that the Synoptic tradition needs to be, as his theology demands and as his historical studies seek to show, relatively reliable? If one wants to regard the canonical Gospels as generally accurate icons of Jesus, if in fact one's theology depends upon them being so, then a Jesus much engaged with eschatology is a foregone conclusion.[24] One may put it this way. If Mark's Jesus utters the so-called

---

20. Ibid., 37.

21. Joachim Jeremias, "The Search for the Historical Jesus," in *Jesus and the Message of the New Testament* (ed. K. C. Hanson; Minneapolis, MN: Fortress, 2002), 8.

22. Joachim Jeremias, *The Parables of Jesus* (2nd rev. ed.; London: SCM, 1972).

23. Jeremias, *New Testament Theology*, 241–49.

24. One recalls that Schweitzer argued for his own Jesus by combating the skepticism of William Wrede, even to the point of defending the historicity of Matt 10 down to the smallest detail.

little apocalypse in chapter 13, with its detailed eschatological scenario; and if Luke's Jesus strings together sayings about the days of Noah and the days of Lot and how they typify the coming catastrophe (17:20–37); and if Matthew's Jesus promises that the disciples will not finish going through the towns of Israel before the Son of man comes (10:23) and otherwise preoccupies himself with such things as eschatological rewards and punishments then surely, if the Synoptics are the good guides that Jeremias desires them to be, Jesus must have had much to say about eschatological judgment and recompense, thought of as imminent. To deny this would be, on a conservative evaluation of the Synoptics, to enlarge intolerably the distance between Jesus and his witnesses. In short, because the Synoptics have more than a few sayings with what one may fairly call an apocalyptic orientation, those with a personal theology entailing great faith in the Synoptics will find such an orientation in Jesus himself.[25]

(One need not interpret the eschatological materials as Jeremias did. Tom Wright's conservative view of the historicity of the Synoptics also leads him to accept as authentic just about everything in them, in his case even Mark 13.[26] The difference from Jeremias is that Wright, in a manner reminiscent of C. H. Dodd and some of the church fathers,[27] finds a lot more metaphor in the language of Jesus' eschatological expectations. Still, Wright is akin to Jeremias in that a particular view of Synoptic historicity means an apocalyptic Jesus.)

There are additional theological concerns that have sometimes encouraged making peace with an apocalyptic Jesus. One is this: Such a Jesus can be a good weapon with which to bludgeon opponents for their defective theology. As illustration, let me go back a hundred years to F. C. Burkitt (1864–1935), Professor at Trinity College, whose failure to be cited much anymore is no reflection of his onetime importance,

---

25. Kirsopp Lake, "Albert Schweitzer's Influence in Holland and England," in *The Albert Schweitzer Jubilee Book* (ed. A. A. Roback; Cambridge, MA: Sci-Art, 1945), 438, observed that, after Schweitzer, those "who were conservative in criticism and believed that in the main the Gospel of Mark is history" necessarily ended up with an eschatological Jesus.

26. N. T. Wright, *Jesus and the Victory of God* (Philadelphia: Fortress, 1996).

27. There are also close parallels between Wright's work and that of several nonacademics. See, e.g., J. Stuart Russell, *The Parousia: A Study of the New Testament Doctrine of Our Lord's Second Coming* (2nd ed.; London: T. Fisher Unwin, 1887); and Max R. King, *The Spirit of Prophecy* (Warren, OH: Warren Printing, 1971).

which was considerable.[28] Burkitt, whose preface to W. Montgomery's translation of *Von Reimarus zu Wrede* warmly welcomed Schweitzer to England, dismissed the so-called liberalism of his day. He reckoned it "a religion not of science but of sentiment. It wanted to find itself in a free world governed by a kind personal God, who would distribute a happy personal immortality to everyone."[29] Such religion was a useless "compromise between traditional Christianity and present-day philosophy, formed by taking some things out of Christianity and some things out of our modern world."[30] Burkitt, who labeled himself "Catholick," was not a traditional conservative; he wholeheartedly embraced historical criticism. His problem with liberalism was not its modern methods but rather his belief that, whatever Christianity should be, it should be something other than one more manifestation of the zeitgeist. What good is the church if its central teachings are available in the contemporary culture at large? Burkitt could not abide the deistically inspired, common liberal portrait of a Jesus who, as an example of unsurpassed goodness and pure morality, as a purveyor of the perfect scheme of ethical truth,[31] simply confirmed what good people might otherwise believe without benefit of the gospel.

What did Burkitt offer in place of the liberal synthesis and its to-his-mind tepid Jesus? He enthusiastically championed the enthusiastic prophet of Weiss and Schweitzer. Despite that figure's mistakes about eschatological particulars, Burkitt argued that we can never do without hope in the divine utopia. It is the foundation of the gospel, the most important thing in the world, and "as long as we believe in our hearts that our property, our arts, our institutions, our buildings, our trust-deeds, are the most permanent things in this world, so long we are not in sympathy with the Gospel message."[32] Given this view of things, one understands Burkitt's sympathy for Schweitzer's sort of otherworldly

28. For an overview of Burkitt's views on eschatology, see Mark D. Chapman, *The Coming Crisis: The Impact of Eschatology on Theology in Edwardian England* (JSNTSup 208; Sheffield: Sheffield Academic Press, 2001), 81–101. Schweitzer's own evaluation of Burkitt — "Professor Burkitt brought to bear on my views a purely scientific interest" (*Out of My Life and Thought: An Autobiography* [New York: H. Holt, 1933], 63) — is clearly mistaken.

29. F. C. Burkitt, *"The Failure of Liberal Christianity" and "Some Thoughts on the Athanasian Creed"* (Cambridge: Bowes & Bowes, 1910), 12.

30. Ibid., 20.

31. Burkitt wondered whether "the portrait of our Lord which...Liberal Christians have sketched will pass muster at the bar of scientific criticism as wholly human" (ibid., 26).

32. F. C. Burkitt, "The Eschatological Idea in the Gospel," in *Essays on Some Biblical Questions of the Day by Members of the University of Cambridge* (London: Macmillan, 1909),

Jesus, who has no hope in or theory of human progress. An apocalyptic Jesus is irreducibly religious; he dwells in and speaks from and to an imaginative world that can never be annulled by economics, politics, or culture.[33]

One also understands why some with more orthodox opinions also early on lauded Schweitzer, whose Jesus had such an exalted self-conception, so much so that he imagined himself able to turn the wheel of history. For Herbert Relton, "the Eschatological movement under the leadership of Johannes Weiss and Schweitzer threatens to make it impossible hereafter for Liberal criticism to come to rest in a purely humanitarian view of the Person of Christ. The Eschatologists are seeking to do full justice to the self-witness of Christ and the transcendental character of His claims."[34] In other words, Schweitzer's eschatological Jesus not only leaves the liberals bereft of their liberal Jesus but also simultaneously shows us that Jesus imagined himself to be somebody.[35]

210–11. Dodd's use of "Good Time Coming" in his early work, *The Gospel in the New Testament* (London: National Sunday School Union, n.d.), 18–20, shows the influence of Burkitt upon him.

33. Cf. William E. Arnal, "Making and Re-making the Jesus-Sign: Contemporary Markings on the Body of Christ," in *Whose Historical Jesus?* (ed. William E. Arnal and Michel Desjardins; Studies in Christianity and Judaism [SCJ] 7; Wilfrid Laurier University Press, 1997), 315. Of J. N. Figgis, the Anglican theologian and historian, it has been remarked that "an eschatological interpretation of the historical Jesus was part of a broader emphasis on mystery and the supernatural as the indispensable essence of Christianity" (so Chapman, *Coming Crisis*, 141). One could say the same of George Tyrrell. According to J. Warschauer, "The Present Position of Liberal Theology in Great Britain: A Study of Tendencies," *AJT* 16 (1912): 351, "The eschatological theory was a veritable godsend to the opponents of liberal theology — the first stroke of good fortune they had known for years, the first setback to criticism of the modern school.... The eschatological hypothesis was welcomed in England because it seemed to signify 'the failure of liberal Christianity.'" Cf. the editorial in *ExpTim* 52 (1941): 322: Weiss and Schweitzer "proved that the mysterious, otherworldly elements in our Lord's teaching cannot be eliminated by any method that is genuinely scientific. And this clearly showed that, whatever Jesus was, He was not a mild moralistic figure who fits easily into modern idealism. The story of His life and death quivers with catastrophe, judgment, and the powers of another world."

34. Herbert M. Relton, *A Study in Christology: The Problem of the Relation of the Two Natures in the Person of Christ* (London: SPCK, 1917), 236–37.

35. Relton cites C. W. Emmet, *The Eschatological Question in the Gospels: And Other Studies in Recent New Testament Criticism* (Edinburgh: T & T Clark, 1911), 73: "Eschatology certainly emphasizes the fact, which is coming to be recognized more and more from other points of view, that even the Synoptists do not set before us a merely Human Teacher or Prophet, and that Christology is not a late and mistaken development. It ascribes to Jesus Himself the claims to be more than man." Schweitzer himself, one may observe, was unconcerned with this sort of apologetic. In fact, in *Out of My Life*, 73, Schweitzer presents himself as a liberal Protestant, convinced that even if liberal Protestantism "has to give up identifying its belief with the teachings of Jesus in the way it used to think possible, it still has the spirit of Jesus not against it but on its side."

Geerhardus Vos went so far as to declare that Weiss and Schweitzer "have strikingly vindicated the right of supernaturalists, Augustinians, Calvinists to claim Jesus as their own."[36] I suppose this sort of thinking is partly why most so-called conservative Christians seemingly prefer Ed Sanders's Jesus, who takes himself to be the king of Israel, over the Jesus of the Jesus Seminar, who does not take himself to be such.

Let me add a footnote to Burkitt. It will serve as a reminder that one motive may lie beside others. To say that Burkitt found Schweitzer's work a means by which to criticize liberal theology is not to say that no other impulse animated him. We do well to remember that Schweitzer's Jesus showed up at a time when there was a growing knowledge of and interest in Jewish apocalyptic literature;[37] and Burkitt, who wrote a book entitled *Jewish and Christian Apocalypses*,[38] shared such interest. With this in mind, consider the following words of C. W. Emmet, penned in 1911:

> It may turn out that the charge of modernizing, and of false modernizing, will lie at the door of those who ascribe to Him [Jesus] their own absorbing interest in the recently studied apocalyptic literature, rather than of those who hold that He came to reveal the Fatherhood of God, and the joy of communion with Him. The study of the Jewish Apocalypses is the *dernier cri*, and the New Testament student is just now steeped in eschatology. There is a danger in our taking our own enthusiasm and transferring it bodily to Jesus. We assume that He was nourished on apocalyptic literature as His Bible, and breathed daily an atmosphere impregnated by the ideas of the Book of Enoch. Is it not possible that a future generation will reproach the eschatologist himself with creating a Christ after his own likeness?[39]

---

36. Review of Schweitzer in *Princeton Theological Review* 9 (1911): 141. On 140 is this: "The apocalyptic and the eschatological further stand for a very pronounced and definite conception of salvation. A Christ who derived the ideals and impulses of His life from these, must have laid claim not to the rank of a mere prophet or teacher or ethical reformer, but to that of a veritable Savior."

37. See James H. Charlesworth, *The Old Testament Pseudepigrapha and the New Testament* (Harrisburg, PA: Trinity, 1998), 6–10.

38. F. C. Burkitt, *Jewish and Christian Apocalypses* (London: H. Milford, 1914). On 14–15 we find this: "What is wanted . . . in studying the Apocalypses is, above all, sympathy with the ideas that underlie them, and especially with the belief in the New Age. And those who believe that in Christianity a near Era really did dawn for us ought, I think, to have that sympathy."

39. Emmet, *Eschatological Question*, 34.

We should not forget that Weiss and Schweitzer were the beneficiaries of new, accessible German translations of the Jewish apocalypses; and surely someone today could write a paragraph like Emmet's about our current enthusiasm for the *Gospel of Thomas*.

I add one more reason why an apocalyptic Jesus has had theological appeal for some. Once one gets around the scandal of a missed date, and indeed lives with it for a while, one can get used to it. Meanwhile, it may occur, or rather has occurred, that it is the end of a story that determines the meaning of what has gone before. If that is so, then associating Jesus with eschatology may be a natural way of stressing his finality and meaning.[40] Twentieth-century theologians often reinterpreted biblical statements about the last things in terms of the cosmic or the eternal (Karl Barth) or of existential decision or personal encounter (Rudolf Bultmann). Perhaps the most explicit transformation of the eschatological or apocalyptic into a claim for ultimacy occurs in the theology of Wolfhart Pannenberg. He once wrote: "Only at the end of all events can God be revealed in his divinity, that is, as the one who works all things, who has power over everything. Only because in Jesus' resurrection the end of all things, which for us has not yet happened, has already occurred can it be said of Jesus that the ultimate already is present in him, and so also that God himself, his glory, has made its appearance in Jesus in a way that cannot be surpassed."[41] As Pannenberg amply proves, this sort of theology welcomes an apocalyptic Jesus with open arms.[42]

CON

Let me now turn to the other side of things. If some have had theological reasons for hoping that Weiss and Schweitzer were going down the right road, others have had theological reasons for hoping that they

---

40. With what follows, cf. John S. Kloppenborg Verbin, "A Dog among the Pigeons: The 'Cynic Hypothesis' as a Theological Problem," in *From Quest to Q: Festschrift James M. Robinson* (ed. Jon Ma. Asgeirsson, Kristin de Troyer, and Marvin W. Meyer; BETL 146; Leuven: Leuven University Press/Peeters, 2000), 112–14.

41. Wolfhart Pannenberg, *Jesus — God and Man* (2nd ed.; Philadelphia: Westminster, 1977), 69.

42. Cf. Seán Freyne, "Galilean Questions to Crossan's Mediterranean Jesus," in Arnal, *Whose Historical Jesus?* 90: "In the absence of an eschatological dimension to Jesus' utterances, it would be impossible to see how any christological claims could be grounded in his earthly life, which is precisely the issue that gave rise to the quest for the historical Jesus in the first place as both an ecclesiastical and an academic exercise."

went badly astray.[43] Who wants "the eschatological nightmare"[44] of an errant Jesus, a Jesus akin to William Miller? As we have seen, John 21 already fights against the notion that Jesus might have been mistaken about something. Its strategy is to say that he was misunderstood: "Yet Jesus did not say to him that he would not die, but, 'If it is my will that he remain until I come, what is that to you?' " This shifting of eschatological error from Jesus to others is a common move in exegetical history.[45]

Strong, inveterate prejudices, it goes without saying, can be aroused here.[46] A miscalculating Jesus is mephitic, a cause for Christian stumbling. He is, so many believe, at best regrettable, at worst damnable. Voltaire, like Celsus, used him in his case against Christianity.[47] Henry Sidgwick gave up Christian orthodoxy because he determined, forty

43. In addition to what follows, see Richard H. Hiers, "Eschatology and Methodology," *JBL* 85 (1966): 170–84; and Klaus Koch, *The Rediscovery of Apocalyptic* (SBT 2.22; London: SCM, 1972), 57–97; also the helpful survey of early responses to Schweitzer: Werner Georg Kümmel, "Die 'Konsequente Eschatologie' Albert Schweitzers im Urteil der Zeitgenossen," in *Heilsgeschehen und Geschichte: Gesammelte Aufsätze*, vol. 1, *1933–1964* (ed. Erich Grässer, Otto Merk, and Adolf Fritz; Marburg: N. G. Elwert, 1965), 328–39.

44. The phrase is that of Warschauer, "Present Position," 354.

45. See Allison, *Jesus*, 166–67, with fn. 269. In addition to the writers cited there, see Konstantin Wieland, *Hat Jesus geirrt? Ein Lösungsversuch zur Parusiefrage* (Dillingen an der Saar: J. Keller'sche Buchhandlung, 1911), 63–64; and Hans Urs von Balthasar, "Jesus, the Absolutely Singular," in *The Von Balthasar Reader* (ed. Medard Kehl and Werner Löser; Edinburgh: T & T Clark, 1982), 139. The earliest modern example of this in connection with eschatology that I have yet discovered is in Thomas Morgan, *The Moral Philosopher in a Dialogue* (London: the author, 1737), 439–40. For Morgan, Jesus preached "a complete system of moral Truth and Righteousness, Justice and Charity — as the Rule of Equity and Rectitude, by which Men were to be rewarded or punished in the final Judgment by God himself, as the most powerful, wise, and righteous Creator, Governor, and Judge of the world." But Jesus' "Disciples and Followers soon fell into very odd Notions about him, and reported several Things of him, that were neither consistent with his character and general Design, nor with the Religion which he had preached and propagated." In addition to making Jesus divine and attributing to him miracles he did not do, the early Christians "made Christ himself a false prophet. They made him prophesy of the End of the World, and of his second Coming to Judgment, as a Thing very shortly to happen during that present Generation. In a Word, they understood and reported every Thing that he said according to their own Prejudices and false Opinions concerning the Messias." These assertions, unfortunately left undeveloped, are remarkably congruent with those of many contemporary historians of Jesus. On 400–401, Morgan argues that Jesus never taught the everlasting suffering of the wicked but rather their extermination.

46. Instructive here is the history of interpretation of sayings that appear to announce a near end; see Martin Künzi, *Das Naherwartungslogion Markus 9,1 Par.: Geschichte seiner Auslegung: Mit einem Nachwort zur Auslegungsgeschichte von Markus 13,30 Par.* (BGBE 21; Tübingen: Mohr-Siebeck, 1977).

47. See, e.g., *Examen important de milord Bolingbroke ou le tombeau du fanatisme*, chap. 16 (= Voltaire, *Mélanges* [Paris: Gallimard, 1961], 1061–62); further references in Alfred J. Bingham, "Voltaire and the New Testament," *Studies on Voltaire and the Eighteenth Century* 24 (1963): 199. Whether Voltaire borrowed this argument from Lord Bolingbroke or some other Deist, I have been unable to learn.

years before Schweitzer, that Jesus had been mistaken in his eschatological convictions: this was the coup de grâce to his faith.[48] Wilhelm Weiffenbach, responding to the eschatological Jesus of Strauss, felt that such a figure impaired "the religious-ethical greatness of Jesus."[49] In 1914 Hastings Rashdall wrote, "I do not see how the Christ of Schweitzer or of Tyrrell can be 'the Way, the Truth and the Life' to anybody."[50] C. W. Emmet similarly thought it improbable that "a Jesus dominated by an error and living for an illusion can ever retain the reverence of the world." The "Jesus of eschatology it is difficult either to admire or to love; worship Him we certainly cannot."[51] W. R. Inge summed up Schweitzer's book in one word: "blasphemous."[52] Here is C. J. Cadoux, in the 1940s: "If it is hard to see the Christ of tradition in the Jesus of liberalism, how much harder is it to see him in the deluded visionary whom Schweitzer put in his place?"[53] The evangelical George Eldon Ladd, three decades later, shook the dust of Schweitzer from his feet with these words: "To imagine that one sees on the horizon the rosy blush of the breaking dawn and in its faint light sets out upon a journey only to wander in the darkness of midnight is utter deception.... If Schweitzer was correct in his analysis of Jesus' message, he was right in the conclusion that the historical Jesus was the victim of a gross error and can have little relevance for the twentieth century."[54]

---

48. So Charles Gore, *Belief in Christ* (New York: C. Scribner's Sons, 1922), 137n1, attributing this knowledge to a personal conversation with Sidgwick. According to James Martineau, *The Seat of Authority in Religion* (London: Longmans, Green, 1898), 327, writing in 1898, the knowledge that Jesus expected a "speedy return" is "well known, not perhaps without sorrowful regrets, by every reader of the synoptic gospels."

49. Wilhelm Weiffenbach, *Der Wiederkunftsgedanke Jesu: Nach den Synoptikern kritisch untersucht und dargestellt von Wilhelm Weiffenbach* (Leipzig: Breitkopf & Härtel, 1873), iv.

50. Hastings Rashdall, "The Creeds," *Modern Churchman* 4 (1914): 211.

51. Emmet, *Eschatological Question*, 72, 77. Cf. the foreword to Wieland, *Hat Jesus geirrt?*

52. W. R. Inge, review of W. Sanday's *Christologies Ancient and Modern*, *JTS* 11 (1910): 586. He went on to comment: "It has now appeared in English, not, as might have been expected, under the auspices of the Rationalist Press Association, but with commendations from Divinity Professors of both our great Universities."

53. C. J. Cadoux, *The Historic Mission of Jesus: A Constructive Re-Examination of the Eschatological Teaching in the Synoptic Gospels* (New York: Macmillan, 1941), 6. In "Is It Possible to Write a Life of Christ? A Second Answer," *ExpTim* 53 (1942): 177, his phrase is, "a deluded eschatological fanatic."

54. George Eldon Ladd, *The Presence of the Future: The Eschatology of Biblical Realism* (Grand Rapids: Eerdmans, 1974), 125–26. This egregious misstatement of fact, that Jesus, for Schweitzer, "can have little relevance for the twentieth century," betrays the depth of prejudice that haunts our subject, and the inability of people with one view to understand people with another view.

I remember my own teacher, the late W. D. Davies, expressing a similar concern. He was anxious that I not end up with a Jesus who had an overabundance of eschatological expectations and who kept a calendar. He did not much like the figure who strides through my book *Jesus of Nazareth: Millenarian Prophet*, a book that makes me Schweitzer's ally. It was Davies's least favorite of my publications. Although never so blunt, he must have felt the same way as Markus Bockmuehl, who in a review of my work wrote that Allison's "Jesus remains in the end a poor idealistic blighter whose misguided religious zeal got the better of him."[55]

It is not just people one might label conservatives who continue to find a Schweitzerian Jesus, apparent victim of a "monstrous deception,"[56] intensely problematic. John Dominic Crossan, although he has been more than cordial about our disagreements, is also unhappy with my sort of Jesus. His reasons are candidly theological as well as historical. He has, for example, asserted that I could never claim that God vindicated Jesus: "Having said that Jesus and all other millenarian prophets were wrong (so far), you could hardly claim that God raised Jesus from the dead to prove he alone was transcendentally wrong."[57] Crossan is asserting that if Jesus really was off target about the date of the consummation, it will be impossible to do much with him theologically.[58] (This conviction, interestingly enough, and for whatever reason, much less commonly extends itself to Paul or to other canonical writers.[59])

If miscalculation of the end has often been an obstacle to accepting a strongly eschatological Jesus, another impediment has been his regular association with the word "apocalyptic." That word has dreadful associations for many.[60] Many have pounced upon it with something

---

55. Markus Bockmuehl, review of *Jesus of Nazareth*, *JTS* 51 (2000): 640.

56. The phrase is from Martin Dibelius, *Jesus* (2nd ed.; Berlin: de Gruyter, 1949), 61, "ungeheure Täuschung." Cf. 130, "ungeheurer Irrtum."

57. John Dominic Crossan, in Miller, *Apocalyptic Jesus*, 55.

58. Cf. Robert J. Miller, "Is the Apocalyptic Jesus History?" in *The Once and Future Faith* (ed. Karen Armstrong; Santa Rosa, CA: Polebridge, 2001), 101–16.

59. Although traditional dogma has in fact also wanted to keep Paul free from all eschatological error; see, e.g., Henry Denzinger, *Enchiridion symbolorum: Definitionum et declarationum de rebus fidei et morum* (31st ed.; Barcelona: Herder, 1960), 619–20.

60. I myself fear it, for I worry what others will read into it when I use it. This is why, when I wrote the first draft of *Jesus of Nazareth: Millenarian Prophet*, "apocalyptic" did not put in a single appearance. I did not want others mistakenly to infer, from my use of the word, that I was associating Jesus directly with books belonging to the apocalyptic genre, or that I thought he had a detailed blueprint for the future and knew exactly how and when it would unfold. But

close to rage. Kierkegaard wrote, "It is the believer who is nearer to the eternal, while the apocalyptic visionary is farthest from the eternal."[61] It matters not for us what precisely Kierkegaard meant by "apocalyptic visionary" (*Apokalyptiker*); the point is simply his pejorative use of the word, which harmonizes with "the prevailing ecclesiastical and theological tradition," which regards "apocalyptic" as deplorable, "strange and bizarre,"[62] "morbid,"[63] a "suspicious symptom of tendencies toward heresy."[64] That prejudiced ecclesiastical and theological tradition has also infected New Testament studies. Here is disparagement from Werner Kümmel: "The apocalypticist stands in danger of portraying God's aim in the world in too unambiguous and unified a manner."[65]

One could go on and on, citing theologians and historians who believe that "apocalyptic," however they define it, is a thing most miserable,

---

a scholar I hold in high esteem moved me to change my mind and, wisely or not, I inserted the word. The problem is that when one links Jesus with the word "apocalyptic," readers see in it all of their own, stereotypical ideas about "apocalyptic," whether you have associated them with your Jesus or not. Then the simplistic antitheses crowd the stage, and communication is diminished. Someone will assert, for instance, "Well, the apocalypses have A and B, Jesus does not have A and B, so he could not have been apocalyptic." Erich Haupt, *Die eschatologischen Aussagen Jesu in den synoptischen Evangelien* (Berlin: Reuther & Reichard, 1895), 157, argued that Jesus, unlike Jewish apocalyptic, wrote no history of the future, was otherworldly, made no calculations, and spoke from intuition. E. F. Scott flatly asserted that "the apocalyptic view" is "that no forces for good are working in the present," and since Jesus taught that God does not let "a sparrow fall to the ground without His knowledge," the "fundamental beliefs of apocalyptic were...foreign to the mind of Jesus" ("Apocalyptical Conceptions," 139–40). According to James Moffatt, *The Theology of the Gospels* (New York: C. Scribner's Sons, 1913), 67, Jesus "believed in a God who was by no means the distant deity of conventional apocalyptic, but a living, loving Father." H. A. Guy, *The New Testament Doctrine of the "Last Things": A Study in Eschatology* (London: Oxford University Press, 1948), 85, spoke of "the wild ideas of the apocalyptists" and then comforted readers by distinguishing between "apocalyptic" and "eschatology" and observing that Jesus did not learn his eschatology from visions. W. D. Davies, *Christian Origins and Judaism* (Philadelphia: Westminster, 1962), 20, argued that Jesus could not be "an Apocalyptic visionary" and author of the "bizarre Apocalyptic elements" in the Synoptics because he was not a "simple, untutored carpenter" but a scholar — implying that apocalyptic visionaries could not be scholars! These sorts of simplistic generalizations, which show imperfect knowledge of and certainly no sympathy for the Jewish apocalypses, are all over the literature.

61. *Søren Kierkegaards Samlede Værker* (ed. A. B. Drachman, J. L. Heiberg, and H. O. Lange; Copenhagen: Gyldendalske Boghandel Nordisk Forlag, 1901–6), 10:78. Kierkegaard is contrasting believers who can be contemporary with themselves, living in the present, with individuals who in their wishes and longings and delusions live toward the future.

62. Frederick C. Grant, *The Gospel of the Kingdom* (New York: Macmillan, 1940), 116.

63. James Mackey, *Jesus, the Man and the Myth: A Contemporary Christology* (New York: Paulist Press, 1979), 126.

64. Gerhard Ebeling, "The Ground of Christian Theology," in *Apocalypticism* (ed. Robert W. Funk; JTC 6; New York: Herder & Herder, 1969), 51.

65. Werner Georg Kümmel, *Introduction to the New Testament* (rev. ed.; Nashville: Abingdon, 1975), 474.

and surely associated with the "fanatical" and "fantasy."[66] Some sixty years ago, John Wick Bowman observed that the term "apocalyptic" is "suggestive to the modern mind of the visionary and the bizarre." He went on: "There is some ground for the modern shrinking from this type of literature."[67]

If Schweitzer's sort of Jesus has lost allegiance because of his regular association with a word that carries dubious connotations for many, there is also the fact that his Jesus is further linked to any number of ideas that many find theologically uncongenial, even "grotesque."[68] One might be perturbed that, in some respects, such a Jesus shares company with modern fundamentalists, such as the readers of the Left Behind series, whose uninformed fancies are captive to a never-to-be-realized eschatological scenario. "Anyone who finds a futuristic eschatology impossible today does not want to find one in the New Testament."[69] Or one might fret that such a Jesus focused on judgment and really believed in hell, ideas that are not much in vogue in our pluralistic, relativistic world.[70] Or one might be anxious that a Jesus with too much eschatology had an exalted self-conception, that he indeed imagined himself to be an apocalyptic figure, maybe even, as the Synoptics have it, the central figure in the apocalyptic drama. John Knox thought that such a possibility involved "serious psychological difficulties. Could so sane a person [as Jesus] have entertained such thoughts about himself?"[71] David Friedrich

66. Cf. Hans Conzelmann, "On the Analysis of the Confessional Formula in 1 Corinthians 15:3–5," *Int* 20 (1966): 23: The origins of Christian theology are "neither apocalyptic fantasies nor spiritual experiences however intensive."

67. John Wick Bowman, *The Intention of Jesus* (Philadelphia: Westminster, 1943), 51.

68. Emmet, *Eschatological Question*, 29: "The impression which Schweitzer's theory makes on different readers varies greatly. Some find it merely grotesque from first to last." I am reminded of how "grotesque" so many modern readers have found the many miracles stories in Gregory the Great's *Dialogues*, and how in response some critics have wrongly argued the Pope could not have written them.

69. Koch, *Rediscovery*, 83–84.

70. See further chapter 3 (above).

71. John Knox, *The Death of Christ: The Cross in New Testament History and Faith* (New York: Abingdon, 1958), 58. Cf. 67 and 70–71: "I, for one, simply cannot imagine a sane human being, of any historical period or culture, entertaining the thoughts about himself which the Gospels, as they stand, often attribute to him or even the thoughts which the modern critical scholars who have been cited [T. W. Manson, George S. Duncan, Oscar Cullmann] can suppose him to have had." It is easy to find similar statements, such as that of Benjamin Wisner Bacon, *Jesus the Son of God* (New York: H. Holt, 1930), 24: The "word and work" of Schweitzer's Jesus "can barely be distinguished from fanaticism"; cf. Frederick C. Grant, *The Gospel of the Kingdom* (New York: Macmillan, 1940), 67: Grant wants to "relieve the historical Jesus of intolerable contradictions and an unsupportable burden of unreality. He was certainly no mad fanatic, no deluded pretender to a celestial and really mythical title, no claimant to a

Strauss posed the riddle of self-exaltation: If Jesus sincerely foretold his own second coming on the clouds of heaven, then "he is for us nothing but a fanatic; if, without any conviction on his part he said it of himself, he was a braggart and an imposter."[72] Hermann Werner said much the same thing: Jesus "makes himself the future judge of the whole human race and presents as impending his triumphant return on the clouds of heaven," all of which is evidence of a sort of fanaticism (*Schwärmerei*) found in "institutions of the insane."[73]

Yet another theological gripe against an apocalyptic Jesus is the perception of his inherent violence. Certainly there is a lot of carnage in the old Christian and Jewish apocalypses, in which the good typically comes only after all hell breaks loose. In Revelation the blood comes up to the bridles of the horses (14:20). Crossan has been passionate in his concern that an apocalyptic Jesus may implicitly condone violence. How do you make the world right without violently attacking wrongs? How do you exalt the debased without violently debasing the exalted?[74]

Let me sum up many of the misgivings people have had about an apocalyptic Jesus with comments Walter Bundy made in 1929:

> The modern mind, as it turns to Jesus' picture of the future, feels that the form of his faith in the kingdom of God is too fanciful and fantastic. It takes offense at the spectacular scenery in which Jesus has cast his faith. His eschatology strikes the modern mind as too highly imaginary, as so saturated with a sheer supernaturalism that

---

throne which did not exist, no prophet of a coming judgment to be carried out by a heavenly figure seated on the clouds with whom he identified himself — which judgment never took place, never could take place." Again, on 156 Grant writes: "The Jesus of 'thoroughgoing eschatology' is and remains a deluded fanatic, disguise it how we will, and simply ceases to command respect as a moral and religious leader." Burton Mack, *A Myth of Innocence: Mark and Christian Origins* (Philadelphia: Fortress, 1988), 70, remarks that "many have thought such an announcement [an imminent end] and such an announcer crazy."

72. David Friedrich Strauss, *A New Life of Jesus* (London: Williams & Norgate, 1865), 322; cf. 331. The word "fanatic" comes up again and again in critics of Schweitzer. See, e.g., Benjamin W. Bacon, *The Story of Jesus and the Beginnings of the Church: A Valuation of the Synoptic Record for History and for Religion* (New York: Century, 1927), 254: "I am afraid the great popularity of this conception of Jesus as a deluded fanatic is still all too successful." For Schweitzer's own discussion of this issue, see his *The Psychiatric Study of Jesus: Exposition and Criticism* (Boston: Beacon, 1948); on 27 he remarks that many have thought his Jesus to be a victim of a "system of fantasies [*Wahnsystem*]." Perhaps the richest collection of relevant material on this theme appears in Walter E. Bundy, *The Psychic Health of Jesus* (New York: Macmillan, 1922).

73. Hermann Werner, *Die psychische Gesundheit Jesu* (Berlin: Edwin Runge, 1909), 44.

74. Crossan in Miller, *Apocalyptic Jesus*, 56–69.

it is quite out of harmony with the modern world-view. When Jesus begins to speak of the kingdom of God as a supernatural order that is to be introduced by a superhuman agent, the Son of man, who is to come on the clouds attended by angels and surrounded by great glory, the modern mind feels that he is speaking in a language that is wholly foreign and strange to its understanding.[75]

I am unsure what to make of the so-called "modern mind" because the expression presumes an agreement that has never existed. Yet Bundy's statement certainly stands as an apt disclosure of how many felt in his day and still feel in ours. It is no mystery why so many have been so anxious to exorcise the apocalyptic Jesus from the earliest tradition. Is it not better to have a desirable Jesus without error and a Synoptic tradition with flaws than a Synoptic tradition without flaws and an undesirable Jesus with error? How many times have I imagined hearing a sigh of relief from pages in which an author explains why Mark 13 — which, it is often thought, "in its present form offers a most promising field for attacks upon Christianity"[76] — cannot go back to Jesus?

Here there is often an ironic agreement here between more liberal and more conservative readers. The former may avoid an apocalyptic Jesus by attributing the discourse to the church; the latter may achieve the same end by allegorizing. Both sides eliminate a Jesus who meant what Mark 13 plainly says. There are also the conservatives who become liberal when writing about this chapter. Vincent Taylor, for one, tended to find history everywhere in Mark except chapter 13, an exception that allowed him happily to lift from Jesus' shoulders "the glittering apocalyptic robe with which primitive Christianity clothed Him, and with which He is still draped in popular Christian expectation."[77]

I mention one more factor that has helped to ostracize the apocalyptic Jesus and has made him an unwelcome guest in many books and articles. Schweitzer made a bad thing worse and offended a host of Christians when he claimed that Jesus had an "interim ethic," that his moral teaching was inextricably bound up with his belief in a near end.[78] It might

---

75. Walter E. Bundy, *Our Recovery of Jesus* (Indianapolis, IN: Bobbs-Merrill, 1929), 178.
76. E. C. Dewick, *Primitive Christian Eschatology: The Hulsean Prize Essay for 1908* (Cambridge: Cambridge University Press, 1912), 181.
77. Vincent Taylor, "The Apocalyptic Discourse of Mark xiii," *ExpTim* 60 (1949): 98.
78. Oddly enough, Heathcote William Garrod, *The Religion of All Good Men* (New York: McClure, Phillips, 1906), in a nearly forgotten book that nonetheless anticipates much later

be natural to disregard families and money if they are soon to dissipate in the eschaton. But if Jesus promulgated an ethic for the interim, if he did not leave behind a set of general precepts or principles designed for every time and place, what good is his counsel? Not much, in the minds of many.[79] "Can any moralist, firmly persuaded of the imminent dissolution of the world and all things, frame an ethical code adequate for all time?"[80] Presumption of a negative response explains the vehement resistance to Schweitzer's claims — often misunderstood — about an interim ethic. According to one early critic, Francis Greenwood Peabody, if Schweitzer were right, "the ethics of the Gospels would give us a teaching, not designed for this world, but preparatory for another; an 'Interim-ethics,' appropriate for those who looked for some great catastrophe, but not to be taken seriously by those who have waked from the apocalyptic dream. The best way of conduct on the approach of an earthquake is not the best rule of conducting a stable world."[81] Julius Wellhausen was adamant: Jesus, unlike his followers, was not consumed by eschatology, and his "ethics certainly were not, as ignorant individuals have recklessly asserted, provisional asceticism, and beyond that point superfluous. His ethics were the eternal will of God, in heaven as on earth."[82]

---

discussion, claimed to be the first to observe that "only the intense and fierce conviction of the immediate coming of the 'Kingdom of Heaven,' and the end of all things, could have given birth to the ethical system formulated, or adumbrated, by Christ." This thought, Garrod avowed, "has never hitherto, so far as I know, been put into words because the ethical criticism of Christianity has scarcely yet begun" (177). I have not been able to learn whether Garrod was being dishonest, was deceiving himself, or did in truth come to his conclusions independently of Schweitzer. Or perhaps he had read and then forgotten Otto Pfleiderer's Gifford lectures, in which Jesus' apocalyptic eschatology is used to explain his ascetic-like tendencies and other-worldly ethic: *Philosophy and Development of Religion* (Edinburgh: W. Blackwood, 1894), 2:101–2.

79. See the survey of resistance in Richard H. Hiers, *Jesus and the Future: Unresolved Questions for Understanding and Faith* (Atlanta: John Knox, 1981), 50–61.

80. Garrod, *Religion of All Good Men*, 179.

81. Francis Greenwood Peabody, "New Testament Eschatology and New Testament Ethics," in *Transactions of the Third International Congress for the History of Religions* (Oxford: Clarendon, 1908), 308. Cf. A. W. F. Blunt, *The Gospels and the Critic* (London: Oxford University Press, 1936), 46: "It is an unconvincing simplification to present the moral teaching in the Gospels as only incidental and temporary in its reference. Can we really agree that Jesus laid down no moral principles for universal application, and that the very idea of a system of Christian morals is a mistake?"

82. Julius Wellhausen, *Einleitung in die drei ersten Evangelien* (Berlin: George Reimer, 1905), 107.

AGAINST UNDULY SIMPLIFYING

Having outlined some of the theological reasons why some have wanted to embrace an apocalyptic Jesus while others, instead, have longed to push him away, I now issue several caveats. All four of them warn us against making simplistic estimates of people's motives.

My first caveat is that human beings are complex, and sometimes they are conflicted within themselves. Recall Jeremias. Despite the theological grounding of his eschatological Jesus, that Jesus troubled him, as he candidly admitted in an article published in 1975.[83] Jeremias believed Jesus to be the incarnate Son of God. This christological dogma entailed a dilemma. How could God incarnate be mistaken in his eschatological expectations? In struggling with this quandary, Jeremias made three apologetical moves. He argued (1) that Jesus' belief in the nearness of the end was only the outer clothing of a spiritual judgment regarding God's active grace in the present;[84] (2) that Jesus believed in a God whose will is not fixed and unalterable but a gracious God who, in response to human need, can hasten the end or delay it;[85] and (3) that Jesus' error was part of the incarnation; it derived from his true humanity.[86] Now, one's estimate of the plausibility of these propositions is wholly irrelevant for our purposes. Nor do I have space to speculate on the depth of Jeremias's

---

83. Joachim Jeremias, "Die Naherwartung des Endes in den Worten Jesu," in *Kerygma und Mythos*, vol. 6.6, *Aspekte der Unfehlbarkeit: Kritische Untersuchungen und Interpretationen* (ed. Franz Theunis; TF 56; Hamburg: Herbert Reich, 1975), 144.

84. In modern discussions of Jesus, this distinction between the outer clothing and the inner reality appears again and again, often as talk about the kernel and the husk. It seems to go back to Johann Salomon Semler (1725–91), who perhaps took over the general concept from the Deists. Thus Thomas Morgan, *The Moral Philosopher in a Dialogue* (London: the author, 1737), 394–95, thought it good "if Men would only take in the Substance and Essentials of it [Christianity], and either leave out, or not much insist on the Circumstantials." Some such conceptualization appears inevitable given our cultural distance from the biblical past. The most famous use of it may be in Adolf Harnack, *What Is Christianity?* (New York: Harper & Brothers, 1957). Alfred Loisy, *The Gospels and the Church* (New York: C. Scribner's Sons, 1904), criticized Harnack on just this particular. While Loisy was justified from the point of view of the historian, there remains a legitimate and even necessary theological question if we are seeking to translate texts from one time and place into the idiom of another time and place. Although Schweitzer sometimes spoke against separating the permanent essence of Jesus from its transitory trappings, he still could speak in terms of reclothing the religious truth of Jesus; see *Out of My Life and Thought*, 53.

85. Cf. Dewick, *Eschatology*, 142: The Son of man did not come on the clouds of heaven (Matt 10:23) because the moral conditions essential to its coming, namely, repentance, were unfulfilled (cf. 180–81).

86. Jeremias, "Naherwartung," 142–45. Related remarks appear in *New Testament Theology*, 139–41. There was nothing new about this approach to the problem. For an earlier example see Baron Friedrich von Hügel, *Essays and Addresses on the Philosophy of Religion*, First Series (London: J. M. Dent & Sons, 1921), 125–26.

conviction about them.[87] Pertinent only is the observation that Jeremias would surely, all else being equal, have been happier with a Jesus who committed no error and did not clothe his sentiments in language that seems so culture-bound.[88] So Jeremias had to choose between the lesser of two evils, between a mistaken Jesus and a mistaken Synoptic tradition, between assigning unrealized hopes to his Lord or plucking out lots of verses and throwing them away. Why he preferred the former course of action to the latter, in contrast to others who have preferred the latter to the former, I cannot say. We can imagine someone with conservative theological leanings going either way on this issue, just as we can envisage someone else with a more liberal bent heading down either path. My point, however, is that Jeremias was not wholly comfortable with his own reconstruction. If his eschatological Jesus harmonized nicely with some aspects of his theology, it also created cognitive dissonance. We cannot, then, simply claim that he produced a Jesus in his own theological image, after his likeness. Speaking for myself, although I have written a book with the title *Jesus of Nazareth: Millenarian Prophet*, I am no millenarian prophet; and a Jesus without eschatological error would certainly make my life easier. I might, for instance, be able to tell some of my relatives, without them shuddering aghast, what I really do for a living.

My second caveat is that, if motives are sometimes disharmonious, other times they are just not apparent. I agree with Schweitzer about much, but I wonder about his assertion that "there is no historical task which so reveals a man's true self as the writing of a Life of Jesus."[89] Although he has written two important books on Jesus, I am uncertain, for example, what makes Ed Sanders tick.[90] He has been discreetly

---

87. In *New Testament Theology*, 310–11, Jeremias characterizes the disciples' experience of Jesus' resurrection in these terms: It was "the dawn of the eschaton. They saw Jesus in shining light. They were witnesses of his entry into glory. In other words, *they experienced the parousia.*" This would seem to supply yet another way of explaining Jesus' eschatological predictions — they were in some way fulfilled at Easter. Yet in his later article, "Naherwartung," this thought plays no role.

88. Cf. H. Latimer Jackson, *The Eschatology of Jesus* (London: Macmillan, 1913), 348: "If pain be occasioned to devout souls when some of His recorded utterances are referred by criticism to the piety of the early Christians, how much more so when sayings which criticism accounts genuine on His lips are thrown into the crucible of historical research — only that it may be said of them that they reveal beliefs and conceptions more or less current in His day."

89. Schweitzer, *Quest*, 4.

90. E. P. Sanders, *Jesus and Judaism* (Philadelphia: Fortress, 1985); idem, *The Historical Figure of Jesus* (London: Penguin, 1993). On page 2 of the former he writes: "I am interested in the debate about the significance of the historical Jesus for theology in the way one is interested

silent about his personal theology, if he has any at all. So I do not know whether, apart from professional honor, he has much at stake in what he has written about the historical Jesus. Sometimes we keep our theological cards close to the vest, even when writing books on Jesus. And sometimes there may not be any theological cards at all.

I even find it hard to pin down the motives of the great Schweitzer himself, despite all the biographical information we have about him.[91] Here I can quote Schweitzer again, this time against his own assertion that writing about Jesus reveals one's character as nothing else does: "Of that which constitutes our inner life we can impart even to those most intimate with us only fragments; the whole of it we cannot give, nor would they be able to comprehend it. We wander through life together in a semi-darkness in which none of us can distinguish exactly the features of his neighbor."[92] Who would disagree? People are containers of mystery.

Having said this, we can still speculate about what drove Schweitzer. He once wrote: "I live my life in God, in the mysterious divine personality which I do not know as such in the world, but only experience as mysterious Will within myself."[93] Someone who does not find God at large in the world might well be attracted to an otherworldly Jesus. In line with this, Schweitzer also said that Jesus' words are relevant for all times and places precisely because they "contain the expression of a mind for which the contemporary world with its historical and social circumstances no longer had any existence."[94] This was, for Schweitzer, the great virtue of an imminent expectation that others have so often thought to be a vice.[95]

---

in something that he once found fascinating. The present work is written without that question in mind, however."

91. But for some interesting observations, see David L. Dungan, "Albert Schweitzer's Disillusionment with the Historical Reconstruction of the Life of Jesus," *PSTJ* 29 (1976): 27–48.

92. Albert Schweitzer, *Memoirs of Childhood and Youth* (New York: Macmillan, 1963), 109–10.

93. Albert Schweitzer, *The Philosophy of Civilization*, vol. 2, *Civilization and Ethics* (London: Adam & Charles Black, 1923), xviii. These words of self-description are close to what he says of Jesus himself in *Christianity and the Religions of the World* (New York: George H. Doran, 1923), 32: For Jesus, God "is a dynamic Power for good, a mysterious Will, distinct from the world and superior to the world."

94. Schweitzer, *Quest*, 400.

95. Only a few have picked up on this point, which has always seemed to me to be theologically profound. But see B. H. Streeter, "The Historic Christ," in *Foundations: A Statement of Christian Belief in Terms of Modern Thought: By Seven Oxford Men* (B. H. Streeter et al.;

I nonetheless remain unclear as to what extent a personal theological agenda advanced Schweitzer to his Jesus. One suspects that his otherworldly ideology was partly a product of his otherworldly Jesus. Schweitzer claimed that Jesus' "significance for us is that He fights against the spirit of the modern world, forcing it to abandon the low level on which it moves even in its best thoughts and to rise to the height when we judge things according to the superior will of God, which is active in us, and think no more in terms of human utilitarianism but solely in terms of having to do God's will — becoming forces of God's ethical personality."[96] My bet is that this evaluation of things was not firmly in place before Schweitzer's historical Jesus showed up but instead came later; it was the interpretation of an apparent discovery, not the motivating impulse behind that discovery. But whether this is so or not, motives can remain obscure.

I come now to my third caveat, which I should like to underline: motives need not be ideological. Some people, for instance, can take this or that position on an issue not because they care about the issue but because they enjoy playing devil's advocate. Furthermore, people often do things — maybe most things they do — simply out of habit. This matters so much for our purposes because we may justly suspect that many or even most New Testament scholars hold the view of Jesus that they do because it was instilled in them at a young age by their education. And once they came to see things a certain way, they found it difficult to change their minds. Intellectual inertia can be obstinate. Ask yourself: Can you name any important historians of Jesus whose views in their fifties or sixties were radically different from their views in their twenties or thirties?

London: Macmillan, 1913), 119–20: "The summits of certain mountains are seen only at rare moments when, their cloud-cap rolled away, they stand out stark and clear. So in ordinary life ultimate values and eternal issues are normally obscured by minor duties, petty cares, and small ambitions; at the bedside of a dying man the cloud is often lifted. In virtue of the eschatological hope our Lord and His first disciples found themselves standing, as it were, at the bedside of a dying world. Thus for a whole generation the cloud of less interests was rolled away, and ultimate values and eternal issues stood out before them stark and clear.... The majority of men in all ages best serve their kind by a life of quiet duty, in the family, in their daily work, and in the support of certain definite and limited public and philanthropic causes. Such is the normal way of progress. But it has been well for humanity that during one great epoch the belief that the end of all was near turned the thoughts of the highest minds away from practical and local interests, even of the first importance, like the condition of slaves in Capernaum or the sanitation of Tarsus."

96. Schweitzer, *Christianity and the Religions of the World*, 35.

Imagine with me a young graduate student in a department of religion. She becomes convinced that Schweitzer was close to the truth — or, as the case may be, not close to the truth — because a revered professor, whose arguments she has not the means to rebut, persuades her of this. Once her paradigm about Jesus is in place, a cognitive bias will also be in place. We all see what we expect to see and want to see — like highly prejudicial football fans who always spot more infractions committed by the team they are jeering against than by the team they are cheering for.[97] A professor of paleontology once praised a student with these words: "She has no preconceptions, so her observational skills are excellent." If we hold a belief, we will notice confirming evidence, especially if we are aware that not everyone agrees with us. Disconfirming evidence, to the contrary, makes us uncomfortable, and so we are more likely to miss, neglect, or critically evaluate it.[98] We do not see things as they are but as we construe them to be. After a period of time, then, one might anticipate that our graduate student will have collected her own evidence for her professor's belief and become all the more persuaded of its correctness. As soon, moreover, as she communicates her views in public fashion, such as by tutoring undergraduates or publishing a paper, she may be set for life — especially as one's self-perception as an expert, the psychologists tell us, typically enlarges self-confidence.[99] The prospect of embarrassment from publicly admitting error can make it

97. See Albert H. Hastorf and Hadley Cantril, "They Saw a Game: A Case Study," *Journal of Abnormal and Social Psychology* 49 (1967): 129–34. They conclude: "It is inaccurate and misleading to say that different people have different 'attitudes' concerning the same 'thing.' For the 'thing' simply is *not* the same for different people.... We do not simply 'react to' a happening.... We behave according to what we bring to the occasion, and what each of us brings to the occasion is more or less unique. And except for these significances which we bring to the occasion, the happenings around us would be meaningless occurrences, would be 'inconsequential.' "

98. See Charles G. Lord, Lee Ross, and Mark Lepper, "Biased Assimilation and Attitude Polarization: The Effects of Prior Theories on Subsequently Considered Evidence," *Journal of Personality and Social Psychology* 37 (1979): 2098–2109. They begin by claiming that people who hold strong opinions on complex issues "are likely to examine relevant empirical evidence in a biased manner. They are apt to accept 'confirming' evidence at face value while subjecting 'discomforting' evidence to critical evaluation, and as a result to draw undue support for their initial positions from mixed or random empirical findings" (2098). On page 2108 they affirm that "once formed, impressions about the self, beliefs about other people, or theories about functional relationships between variables can survive the total discrediting of the evidence that first gave rise to such beliefs.... Beliefs can survive the complete subtraction of the critical formative evidence on which they were initially based." These should be sobering thoughts for all of us.

99. James V. Bradley, "Overconfidence in Ignorant Experts," *Bulletin of the Psychonomic Society* 17 (1982): 82–84.

hard to admit error to oneself, to undertake the difficult cognitive task of rearranging data into a new pattern after one has long been looking at an old pattern. If, in the near future, someone truly demonstrates that my sort of Jesus cannot be the historical Jesus, others would no doubt be quicker than me to home in on the truth. I would have to reconfigure my entire reconstruction of early Christianity, a task requiring courage and prolonged intellectual effort. Maybe I would not be up to it. I find this troubling. It raises embarrassing questions to which I have no answer. I am stuck with nothing better than what Chesterton says somewhere: "The nearest we can come to being impartial is to admit that we are partial."

I have a fourth and final caveat, and it is the most important. People can be, like cats, genuinely, greedily curious, and surely the desire to learn things of interest really does partly animate some of us. I think that, if we could call up Albert Schweitzer's ghost as Saul called up Samuel, and if we were to quiz his shade about his reconstruction of Jesus, he would assuredly depone that he thought he had, in all honesty, found the truth: his Jesus was above all a solution to many important historical riddles.[100]

Since Ed Sanders and John Dominic Crossan are not dead, we could also call them up — on the phone; and if we were to ask them the same question, I am confident that they too would express their conviction that they have come close to the historical truth. Now as Sanders and Crossan have fundamental disagreements, at least one of them must be fundamentally wrong. But being wrong does not mean one has not been looking for the truth, which after all may be difficult to find. The corridors of history are dark.

If one wants to call the appetite for truth just another ideology, so be it. But no one should pretend that people cannot be interested in what really happened, or that they cannot learn new things, or that they cannot change their minds about deeply held theological convictions. Jesus of Nazareth was or was not influenced by Cynic philosophy. He did or did not think that the consummation was at hand. He did or did not think of himself as Israel's eschatological king. It is the business of the conscientious historian addressing these questions to answer them, when that is possible, honestly, whatever the theological payoff or lack

---

100. Cf. Schweitzer, *Out of My Life and Thought*, 65. Here he mentions his "painful consciousness" of the implications.

thereof may be. Doing real history means diligently staring into the face of the uncongenial as well as the congenial, the unedifying as well as the edifying, the useless as well as the useful.

In this connection I think of Johannes Weiss. It has been said of him that he "was able to keep the historical and theological questions radically distinct in his own mind."[101] It is hard to disagree. In the preface to the second edition of his book on the proclamation of Jesus (1900), where he claims that his work was accompanied by "distressing personal conflict," he declares that Albrecht Ritschl's understanding of the kingdom of God cannot be identified with Jesus' understanding of the kingdom. Yet Weiss goes on to endorse Ritschl: his interpretation is "the most suitable to awaken and sustain for our generation the sound and nourishing religious life that we need."[102] Here Weiss indicates that his own view is not Jesus' view. I admire this confession of distance from Jesus. The unflinching honesty remains refreshing to this day, when many still assume (as I know from personal experience) that if you contend that Jesus believed something, then you must believe it too. Everything we know about Weiss indicates that he reluctantly entered the grim portals of imminent eschatology while he was conscientiously working as an historian. Some may think that he misconstrued the evidence (I do not); but I cannot see that what he took to be a discovery appeared from anything other than a desire to recover history.

I now bring this excursus of caveats to a halt by dissociating myself from any investigation of theology or ideology that deteriorates into ad hominem attack. We can become amateur seat-of-the-pants psychologists and conjecture interminably about what motivated this scholar or that writer. We can ponder the zeitgeist in which Schweitzer lived

---

101. Richard H. Hiers and David Larrimore Holland, "Introduction" to Johannes Weiss, *Jesus' Proclamation of the Kingdom of God* (Philadelphia: Fortress, 1971), 5. According to William Baird, *History of New Testament Research*, vol. 2, *From Jonathan Edwards to Rudolf Bultmann* (Minneapolis: Fortress, 2003), 229, "Weiss followed historical criticism with both rigor and reluctance: he did not like what he found!"

102. Johannes Weiss, *Die Predigt Jesu vom Reiche Gottes* (2nd rev. ed.; Göttingen: Vandenhoeck & Ruprecht, 1900), v. Cf. idem, *Jesus' Proclamation*, 135: "That which is universally valid in Jesus' preaching, which should form the kernel of our systematic theology is not his idea of the Kingdom of God, but that of the religious and ethical fellowship of the children of God. This is not to say that one ought no longer to use the concept 'Kingdom of God' in the current manner. On the contrary, it seems to me, as a matter of fact, that it should be the proper watchword of modern theology. Only the admission must be demanded that we use it in a different sense from Jesus.' "

and moved and had his being, or wonder about the connection between Crossan's peasant Jesus in the midst of an oppressive Roman colonialism and Crossan's own Irish past. In the end, however, Crossan and Schweitzer and the rest have, in their works on Jesus, ostensibly written not about themselves but about him, and they move toward their conclusions by means of arguments, which stand or fall independently of the theology or ideology that may have helped nurture them. We show our fellow historians disrespect if we do not respond in kind, that is, if we imagine our chief task to be the perilous investigation of authors rather than the critical evaluation of their arguments.[103]

γνῶθι σαυτόν

It is one thing to ponder the motives of others; it is something else again to imitate Saint Augustine, look inside oneself, and negotiate the whats and whys of one's own life. Which of the two tasks is easier, that of evaluating oneself or others, or which task one is more likely to succeed at, I honestly do not know. I should momentarily like, nonetheless, to discard the historian's gown, divest myself of all pretense to impartiality, and reflect briefly upon my own pilgrimage. I hope the reader allows this very postmodern indulgence on the ground that it illustrates all of the caveats that I have just introduced.

I first encountered Albert Schweitzer's *Quest for the Historical Jesus* when I was sixteen or seventeen. By chance I happened upon the book in a Methodist church library and, out of sheer curiosity, took it to school to read during twelfth-grade study hall. My chief memory is of the section on Paulus, which made me smile with condescension. What I thought of Schweitzer's own reconstruction, the passing of the years has dimmed. The one person I spoke to about it at the time cannot reboot my memory, for sadly he is prematurely dead. I do recall, however, that as I closed Schweitzer's book, I felt that I had read something both entertaining and important.

When I went off to the local college, Wichita State University, I was soon enough fascinated by the critical commentaries on the Gospels and

---

103. Here I should like to direct readers to J. H. Hexter, *Doing History* (Bloomington: Indiana University Press, 1971), 77–106; this effectively cuts through a lot of nonsense and skepticism regarding our ability to recover the past.

the literature on Jesus and, when not in the classroom, passed most of my days happily reading from dawn past dusk. Of the writers I encountered, I found Rudolf Bultmann,[104] C. H. Dodd,[105] and Joachim Jeremias[106] to be the most engaging on the subject of eschatology. The order in which I first read their books lamentably escapes the reach of my memory, but the general impressions these scholars left remain clear.[107]

I came away from Bultmann thinking that, despite his apodictic method, his short sketch of Jesus as an eschatological prophet,[108] although surely correct in what it affirmed, could be enlarged. This conviction reflected my own theological wants. Although I had no illusions about biblical inerrancy — I was the child of liberal Presbyterians, and my fleeting time in evangelical circles never remade me — I still wanted the canonical Gospels to be better sources for Jesus than Bultmann allowed. I did not want to come out where I later learned that Strauss had come out, convinced that "after removing the mass of mythical parasites of different kinds that have clustered round the tree, we see that what we before considered branches, foliage, colour, and form of the tree itself belonged for the most part to those parasitical creepers, and instead of its true condition and appearance, we find, on the contrary, that they have swept away its proper foliage, sucked out the

---

104. I remember especially going over sections of Bultmann's *History of the Synoptic Tradition* (rev. ed.; Oxford: Blackwell, 1963) again and again. Being even then much more interested in Jesus than in Paul, I found less interesting his *Theology of the New Testament* (2 vols.; New York: C. Scribner's Sons, 1951–55), which has so much more on the latter than the former. My own personal copy of *Jesus Christ and Mythology* (New York: C. Scribner's Sons, 1958) has not only my own marks and comments from my college days but also those of a close friend; clearly I thought the book important enough to lend to someone else so we could then talk about it.

105. C. H. Dodd, *The Apostolic Preaching and Its Developments: Three Lectures* (Chicago: Willett, Clark, 1937); and idem, *Historical Tradition in the Fourth Gospel* (Cambridge: Cambridge University Press, 1963) particularly delighted me. Regarding his reconstruction of Jesus, I paid more attention to *The Parables of the Kingdom* (New York: C. Scribner's Sons, 1961) than to *The Founder of Christianity* (London: Collins, 1971). *The Founder* gives Dodd's conclusions; *The Parables* offers more arguments to engage.

106. Joachim Jeremias's *New Testament Theology* captivated me from beginning to end, and I learned it well. His *The Eucharistic Words of Jesus* (rev. ed.; New York: C. Scribner's Sons, 1966) left me chastened, aware of how complex critical issues can be; I felt for the first time that "to try and substantiate almost any story as historical fact, even if it is true, and to produce complete certainly about it, is one of the most difficult tasks and in some cases is impossible" (Origen, *Cels.* 1.42 [ed. Marcovich; 42]).

107. Schweitzer is not on the list because, after reading him in high school, I did not return to his *Quest* until graduate school.

108. Bultmann, *Theology*, 1:3–32.

sap, crippled the shoots and branches, and consequently that its original figure has entirely disappeared."[109]

As for Dodd's reconstruction of Jesus' eschatology, I construed it as a sort of Platonic reading of Schweitzer.[110] I found it beguiling and wished it were true — I have always found Plato congenial — but I suspected that it was not. It seemed to me that Dodd had, if I may so put it, the outer history right but the inner history wrong. I could not disagree that "the impression which we gather from the Gospels as a whole is that Jesus led His followers up to the city [Jerusalem] with the express understanding that a crisis awaited them there which would involve acute suffering both for them and for Him."[111] Nor did I doubt that Jesus anticipated divine vindication. But when Dodd went on to spiritualize all this, I took him, against his intention, to be speaking for himself, not Jesus. Dodd claimed that some of the old Jewish visionaries seem to be describing "that which lies beyond history altogether." He then asked, "Must we assume that they always intended their visions of the end, unlike their visions of coming events within history, to be taken with the strictest literalness, or does a consciously symbolic element still persist...? It does however seem probable that the more deeply spiritual their outlook was, the more clearly they must have been aware that the ultimate reality lies beyond anything that the mind of man can conceive, and that any form in which he can imagine it must remain strictly symbolic."[112] I rejected this

---

109. Strauss, *New Life*, 431–32. When one runs across such colorful passages as this in Strauss, one cannot but wonder to what extent Schweitzer's own penchant for extended metaphors and (in the words of a reviewer of the first German edition) *glänzend Sprache* derive from imitation of his predecessor, whom he admired so much.

110. In the 1960 Preface to *Parables*, Dodd makes clear that his "work began by being orientated to the problem as Schweitzer had stated it" (vii).

111. Ibid., 41.

112. Ibid., 81. Cf. his *Founder*, 121–26. Perhaps it is not out of place to observe that we often fail to recognize the extent of Dodd's indebtedness to his predecessors for his "realized eschatology." Much of its contents can be found in British writers in the first decade of response to Schweitzer; see, e.g., Ernst von Dobschütz, *The Eschatology of the Gospels* (London: Hodder & Stoughton, 1910), who instead of "realized eschatology" speaks of "transmuted eschatology." Two important themes in Dodd, Jesus' spiritualization of apocalyptic language and the disciples' failure to understand, appear again and again in the literature. See e.g. Edwin Abbott, *The Son of Man, or Contributions to the Study of the Thoughts of Jesus* (Cambridge: Cambridge University Press, 1910), 728: "Our modern notions of Christ's eschatology are often based on an underrating of the extent to which He used material imagery and of the extent to which He was absorbed — whereas His disciples were by no means similarly absorbed — in Spiritual thought." "The error [in understanding apocalyptic language] was natural for disciples unable to apprehend the intensity with which Jesus gazed into spiritual things — realizing their reality and certainty of fulfillment, apart from any definite details and time."

interpretation not because I knew then what I know now, that millenarian movements are typically quite literal in their expectations, at least initially. It was rather my native skepticism plus Schweitzer's lengthy lesson about reading ourselves into Jesus that made me so suspicious of Dodd: it just sounded too apologetically convenient to be convincing.[113] I did not want to be guilty of following "a preconceived determination to find in the gospel nothing but the essentials of one's own religion."[114] I did not want to be a primitive villager who, when confronted with the truth from a larger world beyond, cannot acknowledge it. I wanted the courage, if it came to it, to agree with what Strauss said when he wrote that given "our Christian habits of thought," some discovery "might be bitter to our taste; but if it comes out as an historical result our habits would have to give way."[115]

I recall with special affection my initial encounter with Jeremias's portrait of Jesus, as outlined in *New Testament Theology*; for me it was the most persuasive and fecund reconstruction I had theretofore encountered, even though I was aware that some of it sounded like apologetics. The habit of making Jesus unique by contrasting him with his native religion often depended upon a caricature of Judaism, as my Jewish Studies professor, Robert Goldenberg, helpfully showed me. Still, Jeremias augmented my growing feeling that my own work, like his, would travel in the ruts left by Schweitzer's eschatological wagon. Indeed, it is apparent, looking back, that it was while reading and rereading Jeremias's *New Testament Theology* that I was seduced into identifying the historical Jesus as an apocalyptic figure. The explanation is straightforward. Time after time, Jeremias's interpretation of this saying or that theme within the framework of a near end made compelling sense, certainly more sense than the ecclesiastical readings I had grown up with.

While doing my reading in New Testament, studying philosophy, and being introduced to the general history of religions, I was, off and on, attending a Protestant church, and I was quite aware that a fallible Jesus was not what my friends in that church believed in. Nor was he what

---

113. See further Allison, *Jesus*, 167–69. It has occurred to me that perhaps metaphorical interpretations of Jesus' eschatology have come solely from within the church; readings from Jewish or secular scholars have tended to be more literal.

114. Loisy, *Gospels*, 65–66.

115. Strauss, *New Life*, 323.

I had heretofore believed in. Midway through college, however, I happened upon the writings of Wolfhart Pannenberg, which I immediately consumed. His theology is a sophisticated, philosophical interpretation of apocalyptic that stays within the Christian orbit. Because I enjoyed his rigorous and spacious mind and could conceive of the possibility that he was right about many things, my anxiety about a mistaken Jesus was much reduced. Where I would have ended up without Pannenberg I cannot say. Would I have been able to continue serving two masters, the historical-critical method and the Christ of faith? It may well have been, in retrospect, Pannenberg's theology that gave me leave to explore with a less timorous mind the then-painful issues and, in the end, to become a convert, if not without some reluctance, to an apocalyptic Jesus. I may thus illustrate the comment that Burkitt made regarding Jesus' eschatology: "It is one of those questions about which men find it hard to judge by the evidence alone, until they are assured that the conclusion to which the evidence seems to point will not land them in disaster."[116]

Recently, James Robinson, writing in defense of a Jesus who can be for us "a serious person worthy of a hearing," has characterized "Albert Schweitzer's deluded and mistaken apocalypticist" as "queer, though those with the still-prevalent eschatological orientation for Jesus do not face up to this fact."[117] As one with such an orientation, and who knows full well its implications, the comment leaves me nonplussed. Jesus became apocalyptic for me not because I willed it but because I found him. He, queer or not, was the fact that I thought I had to face up to, and I take some pride in having done so. What one wants to believe in the present should not be any guide to what one finds in the past, and Robinson really cannot think otherwise. I prefer to think his comment careless.

I should add that, while doing my undergraduate work, I was quite familiar with scholars who, like Robinson, had not found the eschatological Jesus of Schweitzer or of Jeremias convincing. My New Testament Professor was David Suter, who had studied under Norman Perrin and learned much from him: so I learned much from him, too. Although Perrin himself was a pupil of Jeremias, Perrin's writings promoted a very

---

116. Burkitt, "Eschatological Idea," 210.
117. James M. Robinson, "Afterword," to Birger A. Pearson, *The Gospel according to the Jesus Seminar* (Institute for Antiquity and Christianity, Occasional Papers 35; Claremont, CA: Institute for Antiquity and Christianity, 1996), 46.

different understanding of Jesus' eschatology.[118] I did not buy it. In my last year of college, in fact, I wrote a long critical essay on the eschatology of Jesus, offering criticism of Perrin.[119] His application of the criterion of dissimilarity seemed illegitimate to me; his explanation of the Son of Man sayings, which denied to Jesus any of the future logia, appeared to me to be particularly weak;[120] and his reconstructed Jesus had a modern flavor that made me suspicious. I was not persuaded that Jesus offered no picture of the eschatological future, nor that his message really had nothing to do with the time of the kingdom's coming. Perrin never made my imagination feel that it had gone back to the first century.

In the same essay in which I criticized Perrin, I also engaged an early article of Crossan, "The Servant Parables of Jesus."[121] Crossan — who in my mind has always been a name to conjure with, always been the most dexterous and formidable of what I sometimes think of as, on the matter of Jesus' eschatology, the opposition establishment — argued that Jesus spoke "out of the ancient prophetic eschatology precisely in order to oppose and deny the current apocalyptic eschatology. . . . He was not announcing that God was about to end the world (i.e., for us, the planet), but he was proclaiming God as the One who shatters world repeatedly and always. If, for instance, he forbade calculations of the signs of the end, it was not calculations nor signs he was opposed to, but end."[122] This struck me, if I may simplify, as reading too much into the texts, and only after all the texts that could not abide such a reading had already been eliminated. I suppose that this is also more or less my evaluation

---

118. See esp. Norman Perrin, *Jesus and the Language of the Kingdom: Symbol and Metaphor in New Testament Interpretation* (Philadelphia: Fortress, 1976); and idem, *Rediscovering the Teaching of Jesus* (New York: Harper & Row, 1976).

119. Pages 106–112 of my first book, *End of the Ages*, go back to a section of this paper, which was written for a class with Suter on the comparative study of apocalyptic. I was fascinated by Suter's materials and found the approach brightly illuminating. I am always disappointed by scholars who list some of the real difficulties involved in comparing religious materials from different times and places and then refuse even to try. See further Robert A. Segal, "In Defense of the Comparative Method," *Numen* 48 (2001): 339–73.

120. Norman Perrin's article, "Mark 14:62: The End Product of a Christian Pesher Tradition?" in *A Modern Pilgrimage in New Testament Christology* (Philadelphia: Fortress, 1974), 10–22, still seems to me to illustrate a constant failing among members of the guild, myself no doubt included. All too often we seem to assume that if we can imagine history to have unfolded in a certain way, then history did in fact unfold that way.

121. John Dominic Crossan, "The Servant Parables of Jesus," in *Society of Biblical Literature 1973 Seminar Papers* (ed. George MacRae; Cambridge, MA: Society of Biblical Literature, 1973), 2:94–118.

122. Crossan, "Servant Parables," 109.

of much of Crossan's later work,[123] although I nevertheless have found it exceedingly profitable to engage him. Certainly, his criticisms of me have clarified in my own mind some things that would otherwise have remained foggy.[124]

I have asked myself whether I would have turned out differently had I focused on Perrin and Crossan before Jeremias. I do not know the answer. Jeremias had already formed my general outlook before I worked my way through the arguments of Crossan and Perrin. Maybe I had too soon become somewhat overconfident in my own judgments, and maybe like the hypothetical graduate student introduced above, my already-formed opinions Jesus constituted a cognitive bias that prevented me from doing full justice to competing paradigms. My bias, I am certain, made it harder to be fair to those with another view.

My predilection for the Schweitzerian tradition was, in any case, firmly established before I went to graduate school at Duke. This is one reason, I suppose, why I was immune to the doubts of the man I went there to work with, W. D. Davies, who himself had studied under Dodd. I was an unusually unpliable student, and Davies never managed to pass on to me his unease with Schweitzer who, although named only a dozen times in my doctoral thesis, is everywhere present. I have not changed a lot since then. I believe now what I did then, that, in Jesus' mind, the things of this world were coming to an end, and the world without end was beginning. This is not to say — here is my distance from Schweitzer — that Jesus was an eschatological machine who produced only eschatological products. He was rather an eschatological prophet who typically but not invariably spoke and acted in the light of his eschatological expectations.

(I now regret my earlier endorsement of Schweitzer's phrase "thoroughgoing eschatology." Jesus was not a monomaniac. Much in his teaching was eschatological, but not everything was. Most of his ethical imperatives, for instance, cannot be reduced to eschatology, even though their eschatological context gave them an added urgency. The same is true of several of the major themes and motifs of his ministry, including his depiction of God as a caring father; his demand that people love, serve, and

---

123. See Allison, *Jesus*, 10–33.
124. See Crossan's response to my work in Miller, *Apocalyptic Jesus*, 48–69, 119–23, 137–42, 157–60.

forgive others; and his special regard for the unfortunate. Good sense forbids stretching the evidence to an undue extent, or reducing the complex to the simple, the many to the one.[125])

Despite the role that cognitive partiality has undoubtedly played in keeping me close to where I began so long ago, I can say with full conviction that I did not come to my reconstruction because of my theology. Rather, my theology changed and continues to change to accommodate my historical studies.[126] Although from youth I have had a certain fondness for eccentrics, I nonetheless have always found apocalyptic prophets and millenarian leaders foreign and disturbing; and I have never, at least as an adult, expected Jesus to come on the clouds of heaven. So in my study I did not verify the Jesus of my own piety. Although I wanted Jesus to be right about everything, I concluded that he had not been. Like Jeremias, my faith was challenged by this result. Yet, hoping to be more committed to the truth than to my own orthodoxy, I was able to overcome my predisposition in this particular. I do not fully fathom why this was so. Pannenberg's thought surely helped, and so too my not having been brought up in a fundamentalist or evangelical environment. But I would also guess that I carried on my work within a native cynicism that Schweitzer had reinforced: I suspected that any Jesus of whom I was too fond could not be the real Jesus. I was worried about the human proclivity to rationalization, which can be a weakness of the strongest minds. So I embraced the uncongenial. My Christology did not, then, produce my Jesus, nor did my Jesus confirm my Christology. On the contrary, my religious beliefs evolved in order to accommodate themselves to my conclusions as a critical historian.

Elsewhere I have written, "A Jesus who proclaimed the nearness of the end in the first century must have been a real human being. This is no small point. Docetism may have been condemned long ago as a heresy, but it has never gone away. Much of the popular Christianity I have known seems to think that Jesus was at least three-fourths divinity,

---

125. See further my comments in Miller, *Apocalyptic Jesus*, 101–103.

126. The claim that theology or faith can somehow be independent of historical research has never seemed plausible to me, in part because the proposition itself is a response to the challenges that modern historical criticism has bred. My own view is consistent with that of James F. Keating, "Epistemology and the Theological Application of Jesus Research," in *Christology: Memory, Inquiry, Practice* (ed. Anne M. Clifford and Anthony J. Godzieba; Maryknoll: Orbis, 2003), 18–43: Although historical conclusions about Jesus are not foundational for theology, they remain potentially important.

no more than one-quarter human being. If we go back to the ancient church, it wasn't much better. The theologians who confessed Jesus' true humanity balked at the implications.... Here is one point at which the Fathers failed us."[127] I teach at a seminary, and most of the student orthodoxy that I encounter is in fact ill-concealed docetism, which I hold in contempt: it is a lie. Now at some point it occurred to me that an errant Jesus was a rather effective antidote to a piety that denies Jesus' humanity. Yet I assuredly did not reconstruct my Jesus with the goal of dismantling the docetism of misinformed students. I did not say to myself, "Allison, how can you fight all this silly and noxious docetism? Well, why not discover that Jesus made a mistake? That ought to do it." The theological application rather trailed my historical conclusions. It was the cart, not the horse. Use came after discovery.

That I have employed an apocalyptic Jesus for this or that theological end does not, I should like to emphasize, mean that I see eye to eye with him on everything. Clearly I do not. Like Weiss, I do not identify Jesus' beliefs with my own beliefs. I remember what Schweitzer wrote: "In defiance of what the words of the text said we managed to interpret the teaching of Jesus as if it were in agreement with our own worldview. Now, however, it must be clear to us that we can only harmonize these two things by an act, for which we claim the right of necessity."[128] Schweitzer was surely right. Jesus comes from another time and place; I accordingly do not expect his beliefs simply to match mine.

For me, Jesus' eschatological convictions belong to, for lack of a better word, mythology, even though such a thought is foreign to the way in which his own mind must have looked at the last things. He surely construed his eschatological expectations much as most premoderns construed Gen 1–3, that is, more or less literally.[129] But just as the mythological character of Genesis does not bar us from interpreting and appropriating the text, so too is it with the old eschatological expectations: what they took literally, I must take figuratively. I understand biblical eschatology to be akin to Platonism. Both are mythological ways of directing us beyond this world, to a larger reality about which we cannot speak literally because it transcends our mundane minds, which after all have evolved in order to interact with the material world around

---

127. See Miller, *Apocalyptic Jesus*, 147–48.
128. Schweitzer, *Out of My Life and Thought*, 67.
129. See Allison, *Jesus*, 152–69.

us.[130] I would also assert that "the idea embodied in the Eschatology of Jesus — the embodiment belonging to its own day — is that of the ulti-mate triumph of God."[131] It does not matter, however, whether others think these fair readings or not. The point is that, for better or worse, my historical studies have modified cherished beliefs instilled in me as a child. I am accordingly not now who I once was. My research has shaped my ideology as much as my ideology has shaped my research.

---

130. In all this I find myself in essential agreement with George Tyrrell, *Christianity at the Cross-Roads* (London: Longmans, Green, 1913). This in turn means that, in the end, I am close to Dodd, the big difference being that I regard my interpretation as my interpretation, not that of Jesus.

131. Jackson, *Eschatology*, 350.

FIVE

TORAH, *URZEIT, ENDZEIT*

*I have yet to see any problem, however complicated, which
when you look at it in the right way, did not become still more
complicated.*
— PAUL ANDERSON

*For every problem, there is a neat, simple solution, and it is
always wrong.*
— H. L. MENCKEN

THE PROBLEM

Shortly after the crucifixion, the Jewish law became, for the Christian
communities, a matter of debate. Some, compelling Gentiles to live like
Jews, required circumcision (cf. Acts 15:1; Gal 6:12). Others, such as
Paul, promoted a gospel for the uncircumcised (cf. Gal 2:7). There were,
further, moderates between the extremes. The so-called apostolic decree
of Acts 15 did not impose circumcision, but it did, echoing Levitical rules
for resident aliens, outlaw certain foods and ban intercourse with near
kin.[1] Luke presents this decree as a consensus. Many modern scholars,
more critical, have reckoned it a compromise or worse.

How are the various positions in the early Jesus movement related
to the teaching of Jesus? If, as Matt 5:18 has it, Jesus taught that not
one letter or stroke will pass from the law until heaven and earth pass
away, then the radicalism of the Hellenists and Paul must have been
a secondary development, without pre-Easter precedent. But if, on the
contrary, Jesus was a radical who, as Mark 7:19 claims, pronounced all

---

1. Cf. Lev 18, and for a brief survey of opinion on the origin and meaning of this decree,
see C. K. Barrett, *A Critical and Exegetical Commentary on the Acts of the Apostles* (ICC;
Edinburgh: T & T Clark, 1998), 2:709–12.

foods clean, then in the matter of Torah there was profound discontinuity between his thought and the conservativism of James and like-minded Jewish Christians.[2] Put a bit differently, if Jesus abolished the law, as Mark seems to say, then how do we explain Paul's opponents in Galatia and the imposition of the apostolic decree? And if, as Matthew has it, Jesus wholeheartedly endorsed the law down to its minutiae, then how do we account for the law-free apostle to the Gentiles?

One should freely confess that there need be no necessary continuity between what Jesus taught about the law and what some of his followers taught about it. We cannot ascribe everything in early Christianity to its founder. We can no more praise him for all that went right than we can blame him for all that went wrong. His followers sometimes reaped where he did not sow. In the present case, however, this observation does not halt the discussion.[3] For the early traditions about Jesus contain a striking antinomy. There are sayings that strongly sanction the Mosaic Torah. There are likewise sayings that seem to undermine it. So different sides in the post-Easter debate are mirrored in traditions that at least purport to derive from Jesus himself.

One sensible explanation for this circumstance is that participants in the ecclesiastical disputes renovated the tradition to suit their own theological tastes. Do we not see Matthew making Jesus as observant as possible?[4] And do we not see Mark making Jesus as liberal as possible?[5] Yet the story of Jesus and Torah is much more complex than this.[6] It does not suffice to say that radicals made the tradition more radical or that conservatives made it more conservative, or even that both things

---

2. One should keep in mind, however, that at least according to Josephus, *Ant.* 20.200, James himself was executed with others accused of being παρανομησάντων, "lawbreakers."

3. Cf. D. Marguerat, "Jésus et la loi dans le mémoire des premiers Chrétiens," in *La mémoire et le temps: Mélanges offerts à Pierre Bonnard* (ed. Daniel Marguerat and Jean Zumstein; MdB 23; Geneva: Labor et Fides, 1991), 55–74, whose goal in reconstructing Jesus' attitude toward the law is to find a position that explains the diversity within the early church.

4. Those who think that Q 16:17 and 11:42c are editorial additions can see the same revising impulse in Q; see Christopher Tuckett, *Q and the History of Early Christianity: Studies on Q* (Edinburgh: T & T Clark, 1996), 404–24.

5. For an overview of Mark's view of the law, see Heikki Sariola, *Markus und das Gesetz: Eine redaktionskritische Untersuchung* (AASF dissertationes humanarum litterarum 56; Helsinki: Suomalainen Tiedeakataemia, 1990).

6. Matters are muddied even further by the ambiguities that surround what one means by "law" or "torah." See Philip S. Alexander, "Jewish Law in the Time of Jesus: Towards a Clarification of the Problem," in *Law and Religion: Essays on the Place of the Law in Israel and Early Christianity by Members of the Ehrhardt Seminar of Manchester University* (ed. Barnabas Lindars; Cambridge: James Clark, 1988), 44–58.

happened — although we can be quite sure that they did. The original tradition was not a blank slate waiting for Christian scrawl. Although Torah was not the central theme of Jesus' proclamation,[7] he did teach some memorable things that bear both directly and indirectly on the law, and being memorable they were not forgotten. Indeed, Jesus himself contributed to the later confusion, for if he sometimes sounded like a faithful disciple of Moses, other times he did not sound so faithful. Early Christians had trouble sorting out the law because Jesus left them a lot of sorting to do. Showing that this was the case and explaining how — or rather beginning to explain how — it could be so are the goals of this chapter.[8]

Leaving aside until later the difficult issue of what Jesus himself really said or did, I shall begin with Mark's view of things, and in particular with the attitude of his Jesus toward the Decalogue. This is altogether appropriate, for Jewish tradition had long regarded the Ten Words written by God's finger as standing for the law in its entirety. The Decalogue was the foundation of Israel's legislation, a list of the broad principles or "categorical law" behind the detailed "case law."[9] Already the Pentateuch puts the Ten Commandments at the front of its corpus of ordinances, as an introduction, and they are repeated a second time, in Deut 5:6–21.[10] Philo subsequently called the Ten Words "heads summarizing the particular laws" (*Decal.* 19–20), and he claimed that the Ten Commandments "are summaries of the laws which are recorded in the sacred books and run through the whole of the legislation" (*Decal.* 154; cf. *Spec.* 1.1). From a later time, *Tg. Ps.-J.* on Exod 24:12 has God declare: "I will give to you [Moses] the tablets of stone upon which are hinted the rest of the law and the six hundred and thirteen commandments."[11] Given

---

7. See Daniel Kosch, *Die eschatologische Tora des Menschensohnes: Untersuchungen zur Rezeption der Stellung Jesu zur Tora in Q* (NTOA 12; Göttingen: Vandenhoeck & Ruprecht, 1989), 474–75.

8. For a recent survey of the entire, convoluted subject, see William R. G. Loader, *Jesus' Attitude toward the Law* (WUNT 2.97; Tübingen: Mohr Siebeck, 1997). For a briefer introduction to some of the problems, see John Meier, "The Historical Jesus and the Historical Law: Some Problems within the Problem," *CBQ* 65 (2003): 52–79.

9. Cf. Patrick D. Miller, "The Place of the Decalogue in the Old Testament and Its Law," *Int* 43 (1989): 229–43. Only the Ten Commandments are delivered directly to Israel by God's own voice.

10. On the centrality of the Decalogue for Deuteronomy, see Eduard Nielsen, *The Ten Commandments in New Perspective* (SBT 2.7; London: SCM, 1968), 44–51.

11. Cf. *Cant. Rab.* 14:2: the Decalogue implies the 613 commandments.

the representative status of the Ten Commandments, it may be prove profitable to learn what Mark's Jesus says or implies about them.[12]

THE CONSERVATIVE JESUS

Jesus, in Mark 7, castigates some Pharisees and scribes with this observation: "You have a fine way of rejecting the commandment of God in order to keep your tradition! For Moses said, 'Honor your father and mother'; and, 'Whoever speaks evil of father or mother must surely die.' But you say that if anyone tells father or mother, 'Whatever support you might have had from me is Corban' (that is, an offering to God) — then you no longer permit doing anything for a father or mother, thus making void the word of God through your tradition that you have handed on" (vv. 9–13). Here Jesus' opponents earn rebuke precisely because their human tradition has led them to neglect one of the Ten Commandments.

Just a few verses later, Mark's Jesus takes his disciples aside and says to them: "It is from within, from the human heart, that evil intentions come: fornication, theft, murder, adultery, avarice, wickedness, deceit, licentiousness, envy, slander, pride, folly. All these evil things come from within, and they defile a person" (vv. 21–23). The second, third, and fourth items in this list — theft, murder, adultery — also occur together in the Decalogue: "You shall not murder. You shall not commit adultery. You shall not steal" (Exod 20:13–15). So within the space of just a few verses, in Mark 7:9–13 and 21–23, Jesus teaches the validity of four of the Ten Commandments.[13]

Something similar happens in chapter 10. When a rich man asks Jesus, "What must I do to inherit eternal life?" Jesus responds, "You know the commandments: 'You shall not murder; You shall not commit adultery; You shall not steal; You shall not bear false witness; You shall not defraud; Honor your father and mother'" (vv. 17–19). Of these six imperatives, five belong to the Ten Commandments. When we set them beside the list of sins in chapter 7, Jesus accentuates fully half of the Decalogue. He enjoins the honoring of parents and repudiates murder, adultery, theft, and false witness.

---

12. On the Decalogue in Mark, see Sariola, *Gesetz*, 151–82.

13. Although Jesus also condemns covetousness, which the Decalogue likewise prohibits, Mark's word is the noun πλεονεξία (v. 22) whereas the LXX of Exod 20:17 and Deut 5:21 have the verb ἐπιθυμέω.

The next Markan passage to consider is 12:28–31, where a scribe asks Jesus, "Which commandment is the first of all?" Jesus responds by citing and endorsing Scripture: "The first is, 'Hear, O Israel: The Lord our God, the Lord is one; and you shall love the Lord your God with all your heart, and with all your soul, and with all your mind, and with all your strength.' The second is this, 'You shall love your neighbor as yourself.' There is no other commandment greater than these." What would ancient hearers have made of this combination of two famous texts, Deut 6:4–5 ("love the Lord") and Lev 19:18 ("love your neighbor")?[14]

These are well-known sentences from the Torah. To cite them together may constitute nothing less than an endorsement of the Torah in its entirety. Jesus is in fact, if one may so put it, being deliberately unprovocative here, for he is calling attention to two scriptural texts that were popular summaries of religious duty.[15] But this is not all that may be said, for Jesus' double commandment should probably be related to the Ten Commandments in particular.

In their biblical contexts, both Lev 19 and Deut 6 associate themselves with the Decalogue. In Deut 6:6–9, "these words" — "Keep these words . . . recite them . . . bind them as a sign on your hand . . . and write them on the doorposts" — have sometimes been taken to include the Ten Commandments, which Moses delivers in the previous chapter — a circumstance that helps explain why some ancient phylacteries and mezuzot contained the Decalogue.[16] As for Lev 19, it seems to build upon the Decalogue.[17] Certainly there are correlations between the latter and the former. As *Lev. Rab.* 24:5 puts its, "The Ten Commandments are included in" Lev 19.[18]

---

14. Some late Jewish sources bring these two verses together; see Ephraim E. Urbach, "The Role of the Ten Commandments in Jewish Worship," in *The Ten Commandments in History and Transmission* (ed. Ben-Zion Segal and Gershon Levi; Jerusalem: Magnes, 1985), 175. But these are too late to bring into the discussion here. Perhaps they indeed reflect Christian influence.

15. Cf. Jürgen Roloff, *Jesus* (Munich: C. H. Beck, 2000), 98–99.

16. Cf. Moshe Weinfeld, *Deuteronomy 1–11* (AB 5; New York: Doubleday, 1991), 340.

17. For a survey of modern opinion, see Jacob Milgrom, *Leviticus 17–22* (AB; New York: Doubleday, 2000), 1600–1602.

18. *Lev. Rab.* 24:5 goes on to correlate Exod 20:2 with Lev 19:3; Exod 20:3 with Lev 19:4; Exod 20:7 with Lev 19:12; Exod 20:8 with Lev 19:3; Exod 20:12 with Lev 19:3; Exod 20:13 with Lev 19:11, 16 and 20:10; Exod 20:13 with Lev 19:11; Exod 20:13 with Lev 19:16; and Exod 20:14 with Lev 19:18. Also, *Ps.-Phoc.* 3–8 first summarizes the Decalogue, then 9–41 rewrites much of Lev 19. According to P. W. van der Horst, *The Sayings of Pseudo-Phocylides* (SVTP 4; Leiden: Brill, 1978), 66, "For Ps.-Phoc. Lev XIX was a kind of summary of the Torah or a counterpart of the Decalogue."

But what do first-century Jewish sources have to say here? Philo, as already observed, believed the Decalogue to be a précis of the entire Mosaic legislation. He also thought that the Decalogue itself can be summarized, that the Ten Words can in fact be reduced to two. As have so many since, the Alexandrian exegete split the commandments into "two sets of five, which he [God] engraved on two tables" (*Decal.* 50; cf. 106). The first set of five, each one of which names Yahweh,[19] contains the prohibition of other gods, the ban on graven images, the interdiction against taking the Lord's name in vain, the injunction to keep the Sabbath, and the commandment to honor one's father and mother. The second set of five, none of which mentions God's name, forbids adultery, murder, theft, false witness, and covetousness (*Decal.* 51).

Philo's twofold division is more than formal. The partitioning is also thematic. The first set of injunctions is "more concerned with the divine" (*Decal.* 121). The "second" set has to do with "the duties of individual to individual" (106). Or as he says in *Her.* 168, "The Ten Words...are divided equally into two sets of five, the former comprising duties to God, and the other duties to humans." This twofold explanation, with its typical Hellenistic focus on duty to God and to humanity, brings us near Mark 12:28–31.

And there is more. Philo characterizes the two chief duties in terms of love (*Decal.* 108–110). Those who heed the first five words are "lovers of God" (φιλόθεοι). Those who heed the last five words are "lovers of people" (φιλάνθρωποι). This interpretation, which Philo offers as though obvious or well-known, makes plain that the summary of Torah may itself be summarized, that the Decalogue embodies two demands — to love God and to love neighbor. The parallel to Mark 12:28–31 is all the closer in that, for Philo, the commandments concerning love of God are a "first (προτέρᾳ) set," and those concerning love of humanity are a "second (δευτέρᾳ) set" whereas, in Mark, Deut 6:4 ("and you shall love the Lord your God") is the "first" (πρώτη) commandment, and Lev 19:18 ("You shall love your neighbor as yourself") is the "second" (δευτέρα) commandment. Philo, then, would have construed the commandments to love God and neighbor as together a synopsis of the Decalogue, a resume of the two tables given to Moses.

---

19. *Pesiq. Rab.* 21.2–3 observes that God's name appears only in the first five commandments.

There are good reasons to suppose that others besides Philo would similarly have understood Mark 12:28–34 in the same way.

1. The Ten Commandments, which Jewish and Christian piety and theology have long regarded as the quintessence of proper religious and moral behavior, have conventionally been divided into two parts. The Hebrew Bible itself informs us that Moses carried the Ten Words down from the mountain on two tablets of stone (Exod 32:15; 34:1; cf. Ps.-Philo, *LAB* 12.10); and Josephus, like Philo, believed that there were five commandments on each (*Ant.* 3.101). This belief was evidently as popular in antiquity as in our own day.[20] The Pentateuch does not, to be sure, indicate that each tablet had, as it were, its own theme; but this idea has been a commonplace. Much like Philo, Gerhard von Rad urged that the Decalogue falls into two sections, the first having to do with "man's duties to God," the second with "man's duties towards man."[21] The same notion appears in Calvin,[22] earlier in Aquinas,[23] and much earlier in Irenaeus.[24] It is in fact everywhere in the Christian theological tradition.[25] Here then the modern historian, von Rad, is simply reiterating — how far he himself was aware of this, I do not know — the old ecclesiastical tradition that naturally[26] bifurcates the Ten Commandments. The first five have to do primarily with God, whom they mention again and again.[27] The other five concern primarily human relationships.

2. Early Christian paraenesis sometimes makes use of only the final four or five commandments and in this way implies awareness of a distinction between the two parts of the Ten Words. Examples include Matt

---

20. Cf. *Cant. Rab.* 5:14. *Pesiq. Rab.* 21:18 correlates the first five commandments with the second five commandments. Augustine, however, and after him much Roman Catholic tradition, assign the first three to the first table, and the final seven to the second; see Nielsen, *Ten Commandments*, 33–34. Although Ptolemy, in his *Epistle to Flora*, does not divide the Decalogue into two sets of five, he nonetheless thinks of two sorts of imperatives — one of things to avoid, another of things to do: Epiphanius, *Pan.* 33.5.3 (ed. K. Holl; GCS 25:454).

21. G. von Rad, *Old Testament Theology* (New York: Harper & Row, 1962), 1:191.

22. Calvin, *Inst.* 2.8.51–53 (ed. Benoit; 2:181–83): The holiness enjoined by the Decalogue is comprehended "under two heads," love of God and love of neighbor as expressed in Deut 6:5 and Lev 19:18.

23. Aquinas, *De decem parae.* 4.11. Cf. *Summa* quaest. 101, art. 11.

24. Irenaeus, *Haer.* 4.16.3 (ed. A. Rousseau; SC 100:564); see further below.

25. Cf. Juan de Valdés, *Dial. de doctr. crist.* fol. 38r.; etc.

26. It is even more natural because our hands constantly present us with two sets of fives. Cf. Shakespeare, *Henry VI*, part 2, scene 3, where the Duchess says, "Was't I! yea, I it was, proud Frenchwoman: Could I come near your beauty with my nails, I'd set my ten commandments in your face."

27. "The Lord your God" appears in each of the first five commandments and in none of the second five. Cf. n. 19.

19:18–19 par.; Rom 13:9; Eph 6:1–3; *Did.* 1:2–3:6; Pliny, *Ep.* 10.96; and Theophilus of Antioch, *Autol.* 1.2 (ed. M. Marcovich; PTS 44:17).

3. According to Paul in Rom 13:9, "The commandments, 'You shall not commit adultery; You shall not murder; You shall not steal; You shall not covet'; and any other commandment, are summed up in this word, 'Love your neighbor as yourself.'" Here, to quote Charles Cranfield, "the particular commandments of the 'second table' of the Decalogue are all summed up in the commandment to love one's neighbour as oneself (Lev 19.18)."[28] This is exactly what Philo would have found in Mark 12:31. The point would be all the more forceful if, as some have suspected, Rom 13:9 depends upon the tradition passed on in Mark 12:28–31.[29] For then the apostle's use of Lev 19:18 as a rubric for the second half of the Decalogue would be a reading of the Jesus tradition.

4. Paul was not the only early Christian to associate Lev 19:18 with the final four or five words. Matt 19:18–19 cites the same commandments as does Paul, adds the imperative to love father and mother, and then cites Lev 19:18 as the general rule that contains the preceding particulars. Similarly, Jas 2:8–13 (also plausibly dependent upon the Jesus tradition at this point[30]) refers to Lev 19:18 as "the royal law" and then cites the prohibitions of adultery and murder as instances of that law.[31] And then there is the *Didache*. It opens by citing Deut 6:5 (love God, *Did.* 1:2a) and Lev 19.18 (love neighbor, *Did.* 1:2b) and then instances, in illustration of the latter, commandments from the second half of the Ten Words (2:1–2).[32] The same exegetical tradition, that is, use of Lev 19:18 to characterize the final four or five commandments, appears also in Aristides, Tertullian, Gregory of Nyssa, and Benedict of Nursia, to name four later sources.[33] Obviously, the commandment to love "your neighbor" (πλησίον σου), as quoted in Mark 12:31, was

---

28. C. E. B. Cranfield, *A Critical and Exegetical Commentary on the Epistle to the Romans* (ICC; Edinburgh: T & T Clark, 1979), 2:677.

29. So James D. G. Dunn, *Romans 9–16* (WBC 38B; Dallas: Word, 1988), 779.

30. Peter H. Davids, "James and Jesus," in *Gospel Perspectives*, vol. 5, *The Jesus Tradition outside the Gospels* (ed. David Wenham; Sheffield: JSOT, 1984), 72–73.

31. Luke T. Johnson, "The Use of Leviticus 19 in the Letter of James," *JBL* 101 (1982): 48.

32. *Did.* 1:3–6 is an interpolation; the link between Lev 19:18 and the Decalogue was even closer in an earlier form of the tradition; see Kurt Niederwimmer, *The Didache* (Hermeneia; Minneapolis: Fortress, 1998), 30–52.

33. Aristides, *Ep.* 15 (ed. J. Armitage Robinson; TS 1:13); Tertullian, *Adv. Jud.* 2.3–4 (ed. Tränkle; 5–6); Gregory of Nyssa, *Vit. Mos.* 1.48 (ed. J. Daniélou; SC 1:84); Benedict, *Regula* 4.2–7.

widely regarded among early Christians as a summary of the second half of the Decalogue. Just as obvious is the exegetical explanation. If Lev 19:18 commands one to love "your neighbor" (רֵעֶךָ, πλησίον σου), "your neighbor" (רֵעֶךָ, πλησίον σου) appears thrice in the decalogue in Exod 20:16–17, four times in the parallel in Deut 5:20–21.[34]

5. Unlike Matt 22:37 and Luke 10:27, the text of Mark 12:29 introduces the double commandment to love with words from Deut 5:6: "Hear, O Israel: The Lord our God, the Lord is one." This reminds us that the commandment to love God is from the Shema, a liturgical text for ancient as for modern Jews. Indeed, the sources tell us that the Shema — consisting of Deut 6:4–9 + 11:13–21 + Num 15:37–41 — was recited every day at sunrise and sunset.[35] This matters for our purposes because of the solid evidence that the Shema was, in some circles, firmly linked with the Decalogue. Already in the Tanak, the Shema closely follows the version of the Ten Words in Deut 5, and commentators often take the great imperative in the Shema (Deut 6:4–5) to be a positive restatement of the Decalogue's first commandment.[36]

That at least some Jews around the turn of the era perceived a close kinship between the Decalogue and the Shema is evidenced by the Nash papyrus (first or second century BCE, from Egypt, in Hebrew). This combines, on a single sheet (perhaps used for lectionary purposes), the Ten Commandments and the Shema.[37] With this, one may compare 4QPhyl[b], which contains in part Deut 5:1–6:9, both the Decalogue and the Shema.[38] No less important, rabbinic sources inform us — and in this particular there is no reason to my knowledge to disbelieve them — that in the Second Temple period recitation of the Shema followed

---

34. Cf. how Ps.-Ephraem, *Comm. Exod.* 7 ad 20:17 (ed. E. G. Mathews; CSCO 26:82), passes from Exod 20:17 to Jesus' quotation of Lev 19:18.

35. Cf. *m. Ber.* 1–4; *b. Ber.* 21b, 47b; also perhaps Philo, *Spec.* 4.141; Josephus, *Ant.* 4.212. But for caution and for the argument that the Shema had not, by the first century, "attained the prominence that was to be ascribed to it from the third century onward as part of the twice-daily creedal affirmation of a fundamental tenet of the Jewish faith," see Paul Foster, "Why Did Matthew Get the Shema Wrong? A Study of Matthew 23:37," *JBL* 122 (2003): 309–33.

36. The theme of loving God unites the Shema with the second commandment, in Exod 20:6 = Deut 5:10: "showing steadfast love to the thousandth generation of those who love me and keep my commandments."

37. W. F. Albright, "A Biblical Fragment from the Maccabean Age: The Nash Papyrus," *JBL* 56 (1937): 145–76.

38. See Karl Georg Kuhn, *Phylakterien aus Höhle 4 von Qumran* (AHAW, Philosophische-Historische Klasse 1; Heidelberg: Carl Winter, 1957), 11–15.

recitation of the Decalogue.[39] So the liturgical creed of Jews in the NT period summarized the faith by quoting the Ten Commandments and the Shema.

6. A large and impressive cloud of witnesses within the Christian tradition has regularly taken Deut 6:4 and Lev 19:18 to sum up the purport of the Decalogue.[40] These include the current *Catechism of the Catholic Church*,[41] the 1928 *Book of Common Prayer* (in its catechism), the systematic theologies of Thomas Watson (1692) and John Gill (1769–70),[42] the works of Matthew Henry (1662–1714) and Jonathan Edwards (1703–58),[43] the commentaries of Matthew Poole (1624–79) and Cornelius à Lapide (1562–1637),[44] the *Heidelberg Catechism* (1562) and the *Westminster Confession* (1646–47),[45] and still earlier, the writings of John Calvin (1509–64), Thomas Aquinas (1225–74), and Rabanus Maurus (776–856).[46] Here we have to do with a very old tradition, as established by its appearance in the *Apostolic Constitutions*, a fourth-century compilation of earlier sources. In 2.36 of this ancient collection, the faithful are enjoined to keep the Ten Commandments. A partial list of them, mixed with other exhortations, follows. The catalog is prefaced by "Love the one and only God with all your strength," words from Deut

39. See, e.g., *m. Tamid* 5.1; *b. Ber.* 12a. Cf. the prohibition of reciting the Decalogue with the Shema in *Sipre Deut.* 34 (on Deut 6:5–6); and see Yigal Yadin, *Tefillin from Qumran (X Q Phyl 1–4)* (Jerusalem: Israel Exploration Society, 1969), 32–35. Many have thought this a response to Christian teaching; cf. *y. Ber.* 1.3; *b. Ber.* 12a; and Geza Vermes, *Post-Biblical Jewish Studies* (SJLA 8; Leiden: Brill, 1975), 169–77. The traditional association of the Shema and Decalogue is reflected in Christian literature; see, e.g., Methodius of Olympus, *Symp.* 8.13 (ed. H. Musurillo; SC 95:236).

40. Cf. Ian Green, *The Christian's ABC: Catechisms and Catechizing in England c. 1530–1740* (Oxford: Clarendon, 1996), 427; and Arthur Penrhyn Stanley, *Christian Institutions: Essays on Ecclesiastical Subjects* (London: John Murray, 1881), 347–48.

41. *Catechism of the Catholic Church* (2nd ed.; Vatican: Libreria Editrice Vaticana, 2000), §§ 2055, 2067.

42. Thomas Watson, *A Body of Practical Divinity* (5th ed.; Glasgow: D. Niven for J. Johnston, 1797), 209 (question 42); John Gill, *A Body of Doctrinal and Practical Divinity, or, A System of Practical Truths Deduced from Scripture* (London: Whittingham & Rowland for Button & Son & Whittingham & Arliss, 1815), 262 (4.6.3).

43. Matthew Henry, *Matthew Henry's Commentary on the Whole Bible*, vol. 5, *Matthew to John* (New York: Fleming H. Revell, n.d.), ad Matt 22:34–40; Jonathan Edwards, *Charity and Its Fruits* (ed. Paul Ramsey; New Haven: Yale University Press, 1989), 138 (1.2.2).

44. Matthew Poole, *A Commentary on the Holy Bible* (McLean, VA: MacDonald Publishing, 1962), 3:82; Cornelius à Lapide, *The Great Commentary of Cornelius à Lapide* (2nd ed.; London: John Hodges, 1876–86), 3:26.

45. *Westminster Confession* § 21; *Heidelberg Catechism* 3.14–6 (questions 93–112).

46. Rabanus Maurus, *Comm. Matt.* 6.4 (PL 107:1062B–C); Thomas Aquinas, *De decem parae.* 4 (the first three commandments concern love of God, the last seven love of neighbor); Calvin, *Inst.* 2.8.11 (ed. Benoit; 2:143–44).

6:5. Moreover, the commandment to love one's neighbor (Lev 19:18) is inserted immediately after "Honor your father and mother." Here, then, our exegetical tradition seems already in place.[47]

An even earlier and happily even clearer witness is Irenaeus, at the end of the second century. He says that "the meaning of the Decalogue" was "written in the hearts and souls" of the patriarchs, which means that "they loved the God who made them and did no injury to their neighbor."[48] He also affirms that, when the Israelites received the Ten Commandments, the purpose was to enjoin "love of God" and to teach "just dealings with our neighbor."[49] For Irenaeus, as for Philo, the substance of the Decalogue can be reduced to two items, duty to (= love of) God and duty to neighbor. Moreover, "to love the God who made them" is a variant of Deut 6:5, known also from the *Didache*,[50] and "did no injury to their neighbor" is a free rendering of Lev 19:18, influenced by a negative form of the so-called Golden Rule.[51] Irenaeus, then, although he may not have read Philo, knows the same interpretative tradition that Philo knows.[52]

---

47. *Apost. Const.* 2:36 (ed. Funk; 121, 123). Cf. Benedict, *Reg.* 4.1–7: In enumerating the so-called "instruments" of good works, he first cites the commandment to love God; then, second, the commandment to love one's neighbor; and then, third, the second half of the Decalogue.

48. Irenaeus, *Haer.* 4.16.3 (ed. A. Rousseau; SC 100:564): "Justi autem patres, virtutem decalogi conscriptam habentes in cordibus et animabus suis, diligentes scilicet Deum qui fecit eos et abstinentes erga proximum ab injustitia."

49. Irenaeus, *Haer.* 4.16.3 (ed. A. Rousseau; SC 100:566, 568).

50. *Did.* 1:2; cf. Justin, *1 Apol.* 16.6 (ed. M. Marcovich; PTS 38:56).

51. Cf. Rom 13:9–10; Irenaeus, *Haer.* 4.16.3 (ed. A. Rousseau; SC 100:564–66); *Ps.-Clem. Hom.* 12:32 (ed. B. Rehm; GCS 41:190–91); Cyprian, *Dom. or.* 28 (ed. G. Hartel; CSEL 3.1: 288); Augustine, *Serm. Dom.* 2.22.75 (ed. A. Mutzenbecher; CCSL 35:173). Matthew could tag both the Golden Rule and Lev 19:18 as the sum of the Law and the Prophets (7:12; 22:39).

52. On Irenaeus and Philo see David T. Runia, *Philo in Early Christian Literature: A Survey* (CRINT; Assen: Van Gorcum, 1993), 116–18. Justin, *Dial.* 44 (ed. M. Marcovich; PTS 47:142), may be an even earlier Christian witness than Irenaeus: "A certain injunction (ἐντολή) was ordained for the reverence of God (θεοσέβειαν) and the practice of righteousness" (δικαιοπραξίαν)." But Justin does specify the identity of this injunction.

Many Jewish and Christian texts bring together duty to God and duty to neighbor, sometimes expressed as love of God and neighbor, other times as holiness and justice, or piety and righteousness: *Jub.* 7:20; 20:2; 36:7–8 — on these texts from *Jubilees*, see Michel Testuz, *Les idées religieuses du livre des Jubilés* (Geneva: E. Droz, 1960), 102–5; *Let. Aris.* 229; *T. Iss.* 5:2 — "Love the Lord and your neighbor" follows references in 5:1 to "God's law [νόμον]" and "God's commands [ἐντολάς]"; 7:6; *T. Dan* 5:3; *T. Naph.* 8:4–7, 9–10 (?); *T. Benj.* 3:1–3 — see M. de Jonge, "The Two Great Commandments in the Testaments of the Twelve Patriarchs," *NovT* 44 (2002): 371–92; Philo, *Virt.* 51, 95; *Abr.* 208; Josephus, *J.W.* 2.139; 7.260; 9.236; *Ant.* 15.375; etc. To judge from his comments, E. P. Sanders in *Judaism: Practice and Belief, 63 BCE — 66 CE* (London: SCM, 1992), 192–93, 517, would probably take most of these as summaries of the Decalogue. I am not so sure; but cf. Theophilus of Antioch, *Autol.* 3.9

All of the foregoing leads to the inference that, when Mark's Jesus, in 12:28–34, sums up everything in terms of loving God and loving neighbor, he is summarizing and so endorsing the Decalogue. The result is consistent with the other Markan passages we have looked at.

Yet, if this is the case, what do we make of the Markan stories in which Jesus seems to work on the Sabbath? How do his Sabbath activities accord with his approval of the Decalogue? Are his opponents right to accuse him of transgression? In Mark 1:21–28 Jesus performs an exorcism on a Sabbath. In 1:29–31 he heals Peter's mother-in-law on a Sabbath. In 2:23–28 his disciples pluck grain on a Sabbath. And in 3:1–6, also on a Sabbath, he heals a man with a withered hand. While the first two episodes generate no opposition, the latter two do. Why? And how does Jesus defend himself?

The issues here quickly become opaque, and I cannot herein weary the reader by minutely examining the relevant episodes. A few quick comments nevertheless may be hazarded. The episode in Mark 2, where Jesus' disciples pluck grain on the Sabbath, naturally occasions protest: "The Pharisees said to him, 'Look, why are they doing what is not lawful on the sabbath?'" (v. 24). Many if not most learned Jews would have understood plucking to be reaping, which the Tanak was thought to prohibit on the Sabbath.[53] What then is Jesus' response? He does not say, as did many later Christians, that the Sabbath has been abolished.[54] Nor does he say, as did some so-called heretics, that the true God did not institute the Sabbath. Jesus does not attack the Sabbath but instead appeals to David and the hunger of his men in 1 Sam 21.[55] Jesus seems to be saying that one imperative can trump another imperative, that

---

(ed. M. Marcovich; PTS 44:109), where the first part of the Decalogue illustrates "piety," the second half "doing good" and "righteousness."

53. Cf. Exod 34:21: "Six days you shall work, but on the seventh day you shall rest; even in plowing time and in harvest you shall rest"; CD A 10.22–23: "No one shall eat on the Sabbath day except that which is already prepared. He shall eat nothing lying in the fields"; Philo, *Mos.* 2.22: "It is not permitted to cut any shoot or branch, or even a leaf, or to pluck any fruit whatsoever"; *m. Šabb.* 7:2: "The main classes of work are forty save one: sowing, ploughing, reaping, binding sheaves, threshing, winnowing, cleansing crops...." In Exod 16:23–26, no manna is to be gathered on the Sabbath.

54. Cf. Col 2:16–17 (?); Ignatius, *Magn.* 9; Justin, *Dial.* 23.3 (ed. M. Marcovich; PTS 47:108); Epiphanius, *Pan.* 30.32 (ed. K. Holl; GCS 25:377–79); canon 29 of the Council of Laodicea; etc.

55. Cf. already the anti-Marcionite exposition of Irenaeus, *Haer.* 4.8.3 (ed. A. Rousseau; SC 100:470–76).

human need can, in some cases, overrule a commandment — in this case
Sabbath-keeping — which, it is assumed, remains intact.[56] As Tertullian
put it, Jesus "finds excuse" for his disciples on account of "human necessity" and "associates David and his followers with his own disciples
in fault and in indulgence."[57] Perhaps we can say that Jesus chooses the
lesser of two evils or, what amounts here to the same thing, the greater
of two goods: It is more important to feed hungry messengers of the
kingdom than to keep a conventional Sabbath.

We are not told how effective Jesus' audience took his riposte to
be. We may wonder if many, few, or none accepted the force of the
analogy between Jesus' disciples plucking corn out of hunger on the
Sabbath and David's hungry company breaking the Torah by eating the bread of the presence, which only the priests, by law, can
eat. But one thing is clear: Jesus does not perceive himself here as
an antinomian. Not only does he affirm that the Sabbath is divinely
ordained (2:27: "The sabbath was made for humankind"), but also Jewish law in its wisdom certainly knew that Sabbath observance might
be the lesser of two goods and so, in the rabbinic terminology, one
might "override" or "supersede" the Sabbath law (cf. *m. Pesaḥ.* 6:1–2:
דוחין את השבת).[58] This principle allowed the Maccabeans to fight on the
Sabbath.[59] It allowed the Mishnah to rule that a physician can attend
a patient if that patient's life is in danger,[60] and further that, if the

---

56. Cf. Paul Heger, *The Pluralistic Halakah: Legal Innovations in the Late Second Com-
monwealth and Rabbinic Periods* (SJ 22; Berlin: de Gruyter, 2003), 98n: "Contrary to the
rabbinic system, whose purpose was to avoid a direct confrontation with the law, Jesus deduced from his comprehension of the divine law an authorization to act unreservedly against
the law in order to alleviate suffering.... He pleaded for the relativity of the law and was not
concerned with its formal disregard, when such disregard was perceived as necessary and justified." On rabbinic discussions of David's action, see M. Casey, "Culture and Historicity: The
Plucking of the Grain (Mark 2.23–28)," *NTS* 34 (1988): 1–23.

57. Tertullian, *Marc.* 4.12.8 (ed. E. Evans; OECT, 314. Cf. 4.12.1 311: "There could
have been no discussion as to why he was breaking the Sabbath, if it had been his duty to
break it.... The reason for their surprise then was that it was not his business ... to assail the
Sabbath."

58. דוחין את השבת and related expressions occur often in rabbinic literature: *Mek.* on Exod
31:12, 15; *m. Tem.* 2:1; *b. Sukkah* 43a; *b. Šabb.* 131a; etc.

59. See 1 Macc 2:39–41; Josephus, *J.W.* 2.517; *Ant.* 12.276–77. Contrast *Jub.* 50:12–13;
1 Macc 2:29–38; 2 Macc 6:11; *m. Šabb.* 6.2, 4. See further Robert Goldenberg, "The Jewish
Sabbath in the Roman World," *ANRW* 11.19.1 (1979): 430–34.

60. See *Mek.* on Exod 31:12; *m. Yoma* 8:6; *b. 'Abod. Zar.* 27b; *b. Sanh.* 74a: One may
transgress various commandments to save one's life, except for idolatry, incest, and murder.
Keeping the Sabbath is not on the lists. Cf. *b. Yoma* 85a.

eighth day after birth is a Sabbath, circumcision should be performed anyway.[61]

Incidentally, some critics reckon it unlikely that Jesus and his disciples were, on the occasion of Mark 2:23–28, if it really happened, truly famished.[62] Laying aside for now discussion of whether Mark 2:23–28 is or is not built out of historical reminiscence, I do not share this skepticism. Not only does the analogy with David presuppose genuine need but also, in the Synoptic instructions for missionaries, Jesus sends out itinerants without food or money. In the Sayings Source, Jesus exhorts followers not to worry about what they are to eat or what they are to drink (Matt 6:25–34 = Luke 12:22–32), and why should he so exhort unless they are anxious about eating or drinking? Similarly, would the brevity of the Lord's Prayer permit a petition for daily bread (Matt 6:11 = Luke 11:3 [Q]) if daily bread were never a real problem? It is entirely plausible that, just as Paul the missionary sometimes found himself hungry and thirsty (2 Cor 11:27), so similarly Jesus and his disciples, who relied upon the hospitality of others, were occasionally less than full.[63]

To return, however, to the problem of the Sabbath, what of Mark 3:1–6? Here Jesus heals a man simply by saying: "Stretch out your hand." That some would have regarded this as work is implicit in what follows, and the Mishnah certainly equates practicing medicine with work.[64] Jesus, furthermore, does not deny the equation. Yet this scarcely means that he is, in principle, on the side of Sabbath-breaking. He rather appeals to compassion as raising an exception to the rule of Sabbath law: "Is it lawful to do good or to do harm on the sabbath, to save life or to kill?" This does not satisfy the Pharisees and Herodians in Mark 3. For even if they accept the principle that "whenever there is doubt whether life is in danger, this overrides the Sabbath" (*m. Yoma*

---

61. See *m. Šabb.* 19:1–3.

62. D. M. Cohn-Sherbok, "An Analysis of Jesus' Arguments concerning the Plucking of Grain on the Sabbath," *JSNT* 2 (1978): 35.

63. Cf. T. W. Manson, *The Sayings of Jesus* (London: SCM, 1949), 190: "Surely what is described [in Mark 2:23–28]...is not just a quiet sabbath afternoon stroll. Should we not rather think of Jesus and His disciples really journeying from one place to another on the missionary work of the Kingdom? Should we not think of the plucking of the corn, not as an idle pastime, but as something done to satisfy real hunger?" To the question, "Why did the disciples not go somewhere else to eat?" one possible answer is that they knew of no friendly welcome nearby.

64. So *m. Šabb.* 14:3–4; cf. *t. Šabb.* 12:8–14; and see further above, n. 59.

8:6), the man with the lame hand is not near death. Surely Jesus could, one supposes, wait another day (cf. Luke 13:14). Still, as already indicated, the idea that humanitarian concern can interfere with Sabbath observance was comfortably at home in Judaism. Pentateuchal Sabbath legislation already reflects compassion for unfortunates (Exod 23:12; Deut 5:14–15). Some rabbis thought it permissible to carry the sick on the Sabbath. 4Q265 frag. 2 1.7–8 allows one to throw a garment to a man who has fallen into water (cf. *b. Šabb.* 128b). In *Eccl. Rab.* 9:7, Abba Tahnah exalts mercy over Sabbath observance by carrying a man afflicted with boils into the city; while his conscience bothers him, a *bat qōl* endorses his action and invalidates his guilt. Probably few if any would have disputed the principle that human need can stretch the Sabbath rules, only perhaps its applicability to the case in Mark 3. Jesus does not, furthermore, glory in his shame and say, "Well, you're right after all; I guess I do want to obliterate the Sabbath." Instead, he implies that what he does is permitted, lawful (Mark 3:4, ἔξεστιν). He does not assail Sabbath observance but cites a circumstance that, in his view, qualifies such observance. Again, Tertullian got it right: Jesus explains the circumstances that condition observing the divinely ordained Sabbath.[65]

One final text in Mark invites notice, although it has nothing to do with the Decalogue. In Mark 1:40–45, Jesus heals a leper and then instructs him: "See that you say nothing to anyone; but go, show yourself to the priest, and offer for your cleansing what Moses commanded, as a testimony to them" (v. 44). We need concern ourselves neither with the command to be quiet, which belongs to Mark's messianic secret, nor with the meaning of the closing phrase, "as a testimony to them," the ambiguity of which is notorious. All that counts is Jesus' order to adhere to Lev 14, which instructs priests on the examinations of leprosy and legislates the appropriate offerings for healing. Here Mark's Jesus freely insists, "even in a purely ritual context, on strict adherence to the Torah."[66] As Eusebius put it: "Our Lord could not have said to the leper, 'Go and show yourself to the priest and offer the gift which Moses

---

65. Tertullian, *Marc.* 4.12.14 (ed. E. Evans; OECT, 316). Cf. Goldenberg, "Sabbath," 426n54: "No one in the story seems to raise the question 'whether' such exceptions were allowed. The issue turns entirely on determining the proper circumstances."

66. Geza Vermes, *The Religion of Jesus the Jew* (Minneapolis: Fortress, 1993), 18.

commanded'... if he did not consider it right for the legal observances to be carried out there as in a holy place worthy of God."[67]

Having introduced some of the relevant Markan passages that present us with a conservative Jesus, I next call attention, if only briefly, to three texts in Q that do the same thing. The first is Matt 5:17–18 = Luke 16:17, which *The Critical Edition of Q* reconstructs as follows: "[[But it is easier for]] heaven and earth [[to]] pass away [[than for one iota or]] one serif of the law to fall."[68] Q's Jesus here explicitly affirms the Torah's abiding validity. Comment is scarcely needed. Q 16:17 anticipates the sort of blameless, law-observant speaker we find in most of Matthew's Gospel. This is all the more true when one considers the Q context. Q 16:17 follows Q 16:16, which states that the Law and the Prophets were until John (cf. Matt 11:12–13). Just as Matt 5:17–20 is a way of alerting readers that Matt 5:21–48 is not the undoing of the Decalogue or any other part of Moses, so also Q 16:17 is clearly a way of saying that Q 16:16 does not entail any abrogation of Torah.

The second Q text worth remarking upon is Matt 23:23 = Luke 11:42, for which *The Critical Edition* prints: "Woe to you, Pharisees, for you tithe mint and dill and cumin, and [[give up]] justice and mercy and faithfulness. But these one had to do, without giving up those."[69] Even if the precise tithing practices referred to may be unclear, these words, like Q 16:17, sound quite conservative. The extracanonical halakah on tithing is neither dismissed nor belittled. It instead is affirmed. Tithing is not undone by the weightier matters of the law but subordinated to them. Indeed, Q in this place seems "to assert that the ceremonial aspect of the Law is on a par with the rest."[70]

The third Q text belongs to the Lord's Prayer. Although the secondary literature seems to have missed this, one line in the Our Father — "Hallowed be your name" (Matt 6:9 = Luke 11:2) — should perhaps be linked with the third commandment: "You shall not make wrongful use of the name of the Lord your God" (Exod 20:7 = Deut 5:11). Christian commentators through the ages have regularly read "Hallowed be

---

67. Eusebius, *Dem. ev.* 8.2 (401c) (ed. Heikel; GCS 23:388).

68. James M. Robinson, Paul Hoffmann, and John S. Kloppenborg, eds., *The Critical Edition of Q: Synopsis* (Minneapolis: Fortress, 2000), 468. Helpful for the reconstruction of this text is Petri Luomanen, *Entering the Kingdom of Heaven: A Study on the Structure of Matthew's View of Salvation* (WUNT 2.101; Tübingen: Mohr Siebeck, 1998), 70–80.

69. *Critical Edition*, 266.

70. Tuckett, *Studies*, 410.

your name" as a general or unspecified call to honor God — as though it meant simply, "May we honor you." Perhaps they have been right. Perhaps already by Jesus' time such a phrase would have served as the sort of conventional religious language that fails to provoke concrete thought.

There is, however, another possibility. In a first-century Jewish context, "your name" might well not have been so vague. It may instead have called to mind the tetragrammaton, יהוה (Yahweh). This sacred name, "the glorious and honored and great and splendid and amazing and mighty name which created heaven and earth and everything together" (*Jub.* 36:7), was a topic unto itself, the subject of much reflection. A good deal of superstition surrounded the name, which some avoided while others used it in magical invocations.[71] Rabbinic tradition recalled that it was pronounced only once a year, by the high priest in the holy of holies on the Day of Atonement. All others were forbidden to say it.[72] Now, the Lord's Prayer does not spell out what hallowing God's name might precisely mean. Yet "Hallowed be your name" does appear to put Jesus in the company of Jews who conscientiously observed the third commandment's stipulations about the divine name.

To conclude this section: the Jesus of Mark and Q embraces the Decalogue in its entirety (Mark 12:28–31), reiterates many of its individual demands (Mark 7:9–13, 21–23; 10:17–19; Q 11:2), observes a Levitical rule (Mark 1:44), declares the ever-binding force of even the least item in the Torah (Q 16:17; cf. 11:42), and refutes criticism that his behavior is lawless (Mark 2:23–28; 3:1–6).

THE RADICAL JESUS

The Jesus tradition, however, does not just feature a conservative Jesus. Cohabiting that tradition with him is a liberal Jesus. If Jesus in Mark 7 accuses others of not honoring parents, the same criticism seems to rebound against him in Mark 3. Here he goes home, and his family (οἱ παρ' αὐτοῦ) comes to restrain him, for the rumor is about that he is

---

71. Many examples may be found in Joseph Naveh and Shaul Shaked, *Amulets and Magic Bowls: Aramaic Incantations of Late Antiquity* (Jerusalem: Magnes, 1985); idem, *Magic Spells and Formulae: Aramaic Incantations of Late Antiquity* (Jerusalem: Magnes, 1993).

72. See *t. Yoma* 2:2; *m. Sanh.* 10:1; *m. Yoma* 6:2; *m. Soṭah* 7:6; *m. Tamid* 3:8; 7:2; *b. Yoma* 39b. Cf. Josephus, *Ant.* 2.276: "God revealed to him [Moses] his name...of which I am forbidden to speak."

"out of his mind" (3:21). When Jesus learns that his mother and siblings have come for him, he asks scornfully, "Who are my mother and my brothers?" (v. 33). He then answers himself: "Here are my mother and my brothers! Whoever does the will of God is my brother and sister and mother" (vv. 34–35). This is hardly honoring one's mother. We are light-years from *b. Qidd.* 31b, according to which R. Joseph, when he heard the footsteps of his mother, exclaimed, "I rise up before the Shekinah which is approaching."

While the tension between Jesus and Torah remains only implicit in Mark 3:34–35, it is otherwise in 10:2–12. Here Jesus prohibits divorce, which Moses permits (Deut 24:1–4).[73] "What God has joined together, let no one separate. . . . Whoever divorces his wife and marries another commits adultery against her; and if she divorces her husband and marries another, she commits adultery" (Mark 10:9, 11–12). While these words condemn the sin of adultery, so that in this respect Jesus aligns himself with Moses, Jesus is quite clear also that, in another particular, the law implicitly allows adultery and so needs upgrading. "If remarriage after a divorce means adultery, then this means that the Mosaic permission of divorce is a permission for adultery."[74] Moses allowed one to write a certificate of dismissal and to obtain a divorce only because of their "hardness of heart" (Mark 10:5), "but from the beginning it was not so" (10:6). While Jesus goes on to justify his ruling by appealing to Genesis, this mending of a temporal rift in the Torah is not halakhic business as usual. Jesus can criticize Moses.

Probably the most radical line in Mark's Gospel is 7:15: "There is nothing outside a person that by going in can defile, but the things that come out are what defile." As an isolated utterance, this sentence will bear several interpretations.[75] But in its Markan context, there is this editorial comment: "Thus he declared all foods clean" (7:19). This interpretation leaves no doubt that, at least in Mark's eyes, the declaration in

---

73. Contrast Matt 5:31–32 and 19:3–9, which allow divorce for exceptional circumstances.

74. Martin Hengel and Roland Deines, "E. P. Sanders' 'Common Judaism,' Jesus, and the Pharisees," *JTS* 26 (1995): 13n34.

75. For attempts to keep it within Jewish law, see Menahem Kister, "Law, Morality, and Rhetoric in Some Sayings of Jesus," in *Studies in Ancient Midrash* (ed. James L. Kugel; Cambridge, MA: Harvard University Press, 2001), 150–54; and W. D. Davies and Dale C. Allison Jr., *A Critical and Exegetical Commentary on the Gospel according to Saint Matthew* (ICC; Edinburgh: T & T Clark, 1991), 2:527–31. For a possible setting within the context of a debate about Pharisaic purity, see John C. Poirier, "Why Did the Pharisees Wash Their Hands?" *JJS* 47 (1996): 217–33.

7:15 "is flatly denying the ceremonial law of defilement"[76] and so entails "revocation of the OT kosher laws."[77]

Given the provocative nature of Mark 3:34–35; 7:15; and 10:2–12, one should perhaps return to the Sabbath conflicts in Mark and ask whether they are really as tame as urged earlier. Consider again Mark 2:23–28, where the disciples pluck grain on the Sabbath. Jesus' defense of his followers does, assuredly, eliminate the possibility that he disrespects Moses. He certainly issues no general rule abolishing the Sabbath — which is why, incidentally, some of his female followers attend to his tomb only after the Sabbath: they are seemingly still Sabbath-observant (Mark 16:1).

This is not, however, the whole story. When his disciples pluck grain on the Sabbath, Jesus does not deny that they are transgressing a divinely sanctioned custom.[78] Nor does he defend himself by pleading that lives are in danger, that the disciples are indeed near death. Nor does he dispute that "it is not permitted to cut any shoot or branch, or even a leaf, or to pluck any fruit whatsoever" (Philo, *Mos.* 2.22). Nor does he say: "This is not work." Instead, conceding that his opponents have raised an objection needing an answer, he argues, appealing to David's precedent, that his disciples in the circumstances are justified in temporarily disregarding authoritative custom. Hunger, in this instance, justifies transgression of the Sabbath. Not only does Jesus admit the infraction, but he also does not hasten to add an apologetical epilogue. He does not say: "If it were not for this extreme emergency, I'd be observant," or "Don't worry; this is the first time I've ever done this, and it will be the last," or "While this is a regrettable exception to Sabbath observance, there aren't many other justifiable exceptions." Without some such diplomatic assurance, which would be easy enough to add, and which one might expect from a law-observant Jew, readers are left wondering what Jesus really thinks. Why does he bend the rules?

Here I must distance myself from some recent scholars who have asserted that nothing Jesus does in the Synoptics on the Sabbath would

---

76. Barnabas Lindars, "All Foods Clean: Thoughts on Jesus and the Law," in *Law and Religion: Essays on the Place of the Law in Israel and Early Christianity* (Cambridge: James Clarke, 1988), 65.

77. Joel Marcus, *Mark 1–8* (AB 27; New York: Doubleday, 2000), 458.

78. Cf. Tom Holmén, *Jesus and Jewish Covenant Thinking* (Biblical Interpretation Series [BIS] 55; Leiden: Brill, 2001), 101–2.

have offended anybody, at least deeply.[79] The claim that Jesus commits
no serious transgression because he himself does not work fails to account either for the accusations of the opponents — Can this be wholly
tendentious? — or for Jesus' response, which is not "We haven't done
anything to offend anybody." Given the Synoptic accounts, and given
that Sabbath observance was not uniform, it seems preferable to acknowledge that some in Jesus' time and place found some of the things
he did on the Sabbath objectionable.[80] We should also, if we are thinking
of the *Sitz im Leben Jesu*, keep in mind the words of Jürgen Becker:

> No one in that day commissioned a scholarly opinion or charged a
> neutral commission with the task of examining whether his words
> and deeds fit within the variety of Early Jewish interpretations of
> the Law as an independent, historical development, or whether
> Jesus de facto put himself outside the pale of Judaism and thus
> was an apostate of sorts. That sort of question was not considered,
> since the issue was not historical impartiality. Jesus was simply one
> of the competing voices. Every group based its judgment about him
> on its own position, i.e., in partisan terms. The question was: Given
> our goals, do we want to coexist with him, or do we want to op-
> pose him? Those who were not satisfied with the entire program
> were then quick to judge. There is, therefore, no historical basis for
> the recent claim that, since Jesus' view of the Law fits within what
> we know of Early Judaism, the stories of conflict over the Law in
> all four gospels must have been later creations.[81]

We should not expect Jesus' opponents to be any more objective than is
the Matthean Jesus with his complaints about the scribes and Pharisees
in Matt 23.

Despite its conservative elements, Q, like Mark, contains items that
seem dissonant with the conservative Jesus introduced above. In addition to the unqualified prohibition of divorce, which it shares with Mark

---

79. See, e.g., David Flusser, in collaboration with R. Steven Notley, *Jesus* (3rd ed.; Jerusalem: Magnes, 2001), 61–64; E. P. Sanders, *Jewish Law from Jesus to the Mishnah: Five Studies*
(London: SCM, 1990), 6–23; idem, *Jesus and Judaism* (Philadelphia: Fortress, 1985), 264–66.
80. See further Lutz Doering, *Schabbat: Sabbathalacha und -praxis im antiken Judentum
und Urchristentum* (TSAJ 78; Tübingen: Mohr Siebeck, 1999), 446–50; and Berndt Schaller,
"Jesus und der Sabbat," in *Fundamenta Judaica: Studien zum antiken Judentum und zum
Neuen Testament* (SUNT 25; Göttingen: Vandenhoeck & Ruprecht, 2001), 129–33.
81. Jürgen Becker, *Jesus of Nazareth* (New York: de Gruyter, 1998), 278.

(Q 16:18; see above), there is, for instance, the little call story in Matt 8:21–22 = Luke 9:59–60. A would-be disciple makes what appears to be a wholly reasonable request: "Lord, let me first go and bury my father." Jesus harshly responds: "Follow me, and let the dead bury their own dead." These disquieting words have long scandalized commentators, who have freely exercised their imaginations to revise their sense.[82] Maybe the Aramaic has been mistranslated.[83] Or perhaps the Greek has suffered corruption.[84] Maybe the man's father is sick and not yet dead, so that the inquirer will not be free to follow Jesus for days or even weeks. Or perhaps the father is hale and hearty, and his son is saying that he has to stay home to take care of his parents in their old age.[85] Or maybe the father has just now died and Jesus is disallowing the obligatory six days of bereavement.[86] Again, perhaps Jesus knows that the man has brothers who will take care of the dead man.[87] Or maybe the potential disciple is involved in exhumation and a secondary burial.[88]

It would be imprudent to dismiss such suggestions as impossible. It would be even more imprudent to accept any of them as likely. They must all stand under the suspicion of being rationalizations designed to extract the offense. Martin Hengel is probably closer to the truth when he surmises that "Let the dead bury their own dead" could have been taken, by any so inclined, as "an attack on the respect for parents which is demanded in the fourth commandment."[89] E. P. Sanders has issued a

---

82. See the survey of Hans G. Klemm, "Das Wort von der Selbstbestattung der Toten: Beobachtungen zur Auslegungsgeschichte von Mt. VIII.22 Par.," *NTS* 16 (1969): 60–75.

83. For various options see ibid.; Herbert W. Basser, "Let the Dead Bury Their Dead: Rhetorical Features of Rabbinic and New Testament Literature," in *Approaches to Ancient Judaism*, NS, vol. 5, *Historical, Literary, and Religious Studies* (ed. Herbert W. Basser and Simcha Fishbane; Atlanta: Scholars Press, 1993), 79–95; and David M. Goldenberg, "Retroversion to Jesus' Ipsissima Verba and the Vocabulary of Jewish Palestinian Aramaic: The Case of *Mata'* and *Qarta'*," *Bib* 77 (1996): 64–83.

84. Cf. L. Hermann, "Correction du k en a dans une phrase de Jésus," *REA* 82 (1981): 283: the νεκρούς (dead) has replaced an original νεαρούς (young men).

85. John Wesley, *Explanatory Notes upon the New Testament* (London: Epworth, 1950), 47: "It is not certain that his father was already dead. Perhaps his son desired to stay with him, being very old, till his death." Cf. George Wesley Buchanan, *The Gospel of Matthew* (Lewiston: Mellon Biblical Press, 1996), 1:398.

86. So Joachim Jeremias, *New Testament Theology: The Proclamation of Jesus* (New York: C. Scribner's Sons, 1971), 132.

87. Herman N. Ridderbos, *Matthew* (Grand Rapids: Zondervan, 1987), 173.

88. For this possibility see Byron R. McCane, " 'Let the Dead Bury Their Own Dead': Secondary Burial and Matt 8:21–22," *HTR* 83 (1990): 31–43. See also the discussion on 34–36 (above).

89. Martin Hengel, *The Charismatic Leader and His Followers* (New York: Crossroad, 1981), 8.

similar verdict: "At least once Jesus was willing to say that following him superseded the requirements of piety and of the Torah. This may show that Jesus was prepared, if necessary, to challenge the adequacy of the Mosaic dispensation."[90]

Markus Bockmuehl has recently criticized Hengel and Sanders for their influential conclusions regarding "Let the dead bury their own dead."[91] Bockmuehl emphasizes that the Torah itself contains two exceptions to the command to bury one's parents: Lev 21:11–12 exempts high priests; Num 6:6 exempts Nazirites. He further argues that Hengel failed to show that, at the time of Jesus, there was any relaxation of those two prohibitions. The implications of all this are, however, unclear. It would surely be far-fetched to draw any connection between the historical Jesus and legislation for high priests, and Bockmuehl wisely tries not to do this. Furthermore, while the Jesus tradition may, to the contrary, contain some things reminiscent of Nazirite vows — the abstinence in Mark 14:25 and the refusal in Matt 27:34 to take a drink — we can hardly classify Jesus as a Nazirite.[92] Beyond that, in Q 9:59–60 it is not Jesus himself but a potential disciple who is being challenged not to bury his father. When all is said and done, it remains true, as Bockmuehl writes, that "burial of the dead was in the first century viewed as a universal duty and an important act of kindness, and that not to be buried was widely considered the ultimate disgrace."[93] Given this, the demand to abdicate responsibility for a father's burial would surely have provoked pious Jews to wonder about Jesus and the Decalogue.[94] It is true that "the notion of a special religious duty transcending even basic family obligations is one that would have been culturally familiar to Jesus' audience, regardless of whether they agreed with him or not."[95] Yet the fact remains that in Q 9:59–60 the special religious duty is following

---

90. Sanders, *Jesus and Judaism*, 255. See further Menahem Kister, " 'Leave the Dead to Bury Their Own Dead,' " in Kugel, *Studies in Ancient Midrash*, 43–56. Although Kister finds parallels to Q 9:59–60 in traditions about Abraham leaving his father, the tension with the Decalogue remains, especially in view of Jesus' challenging formulation.

91. Markus Bockmuehl, *Jewish Law in Gentile Churches: Halakah and the Beginning of Christian Public Ethics* (Edinburgh: T & T Clark, 2000), 23–48.

92. Although given that the usual duration of a Nazirite vow was one month, one could hold that Jesus, although not a lifelong Nazirite, took a vow at the Last Supper.

93. Bockmuehl, *Jewish Law*, 27–28.

94. This is all the more so if, as it appears, Q 9:59–60 is designed to recall 1 Kgs 19:19–21 and make Jesus demand more than Elijah; see Dale C. Allison Jr., *The Intertextual Jesus: Scripture in Q* (Harrisburg, PA: Trinity, 2000), 142–45.

95. Bockmuehl, *Jewish Law*, 47.

Jesus; it is loyalty to him or his cause that transcends one of the Ten Words. This may not be antinomianism, at least from his own point of view, but it is hardly halakhic conservativism.[96]

There is also, to understate the matter, nothing conservative about Luke 14:26: "Hate [your] father and mother."[97] Commentators old and new have consistently wrestled with the tension between this verse and the famous commandment to "honor your father and your mother" (Exod 20:12; Deut 5:16). Chrysostom asked, "What then? Are not these things contrary to the Old Testament?" He answered: "It is a sacred duty to render them [parents] all other honors; but when they demand more than is due, one ought not to obey.... [Jesus is] not commanding simply to hate them, since this was quite contrary to the law, but rather 'When one desires to be loved more than I am, hate him in this respect.'"[98] Ulrich Luz, in summarizing the history of the interpretation of our verse in its Matthean guise, remarks that, in ecclesiastical tradition, there is an order of those to be loved: God, father, mother, children, and "only in cases of necessity should one transgress the commandment to love parents. As a matter of principle the first table of the ten commandments comes before the second, at the beginning of which stands the commandment to love parents. Only then, when parents hinder us from doing the will of God, may the fourth commandment be rescinded."[99]

Given that our line has, over the centuries, incessantly put commentators in mind of the Decalogue, one cannot avoid wondering whether it was intended to do so, whether it was provocatively formulated in deliberate contrast to the commandment to honor father and mother. This would seem to be the case, for not only does the content make the scripturally literate ponder the relationship to Exod 20:12 = Deut 5:16, but the sentence's very structure moves us to do this.

Luke 14:26: μισεῖ τὸν πατέρα ἑαυτοῦ καὶ τὴν μητέρα
Exod 20:12 LXX: τίμα τὸν πατέρα σου καὶ τὴν μητέρα
Deut 5:16 LXX: τίμα τὸν πατέρα σου καὶ τὴν μητέρα σου

---

96. For further comment on Bockmuehl's position, see Crispin H. T. Fletcher-Louis, "'Leave the Dead to Bury their own Dead': Q 9.60 and the Redefinition of the People of God," *JSNT* 26 (2003): 39–68.

97. It is interesting that Bockmuehl, *Jewish Law,* 46, quotes the secondary form in Matt 10:37: "Whoever loves father or mother more than me is not worthy of me."

98. Chrysostom, *Hom. Matt.* 35:3 (PG 57:406).

99. Ulrich Luz, *Matthew 8–20* (Hermeneia; Minneapolis: Fortress, 2001), 112–13.

Both lines consist of a verb + τὸν πατέρα + personal pronoun ending in -ου + καί + τὴν μητέρα. This construction occurs in the Greek Bible (LXX) in the Decalogue (Exod 20:12 = Deut 5:16), in quotations of that line (e.g., Mark 7:10; 10:19; Luke 18:20), in Luke 14:26 (Q), and judging by my vain *Thesaurus linguae graecae* search, nowhere else. So Luke 14:26 rewrites Exod 20:12 par. by substituting "hate" for "honor."

What does one make of this curious fact? And is it possible to harmonize the Markan Jesus, who twice commends honoring parents, with the Jesus of Q 14:26, who solemnly demands hatred of parents? While I concur with Sanders that "Leave the dead to bury their own dead" should be reckoned "a onetime only requirement,"[100] Q 14:26 is seemingly different. It does not come with a context that allows us to blunt it in the same way. Matthew and Luke at least understand the unqualified effrontery as some sort of generalization, not an isolated imperative for an isolated and peculiar circumstance.

Another line from Q that raises questions about Jesus' faithfulness to the law is Q 16:16, which *The Critical Edition* reconstructs as follows: "The law and the prophets <<were>> until John. From then on the kingdom of God is violated and the violent plunder it."[101] Within Matthew's Gospel, with its unambiguous endorsement of the Torah (5:17–20), this saying (see 11:13) is difficult to interpret. Perhaps it is only a way of saying that the kingdom of God has entered the present: promise has become fulfillment. But the rhetoric remains provocative — deliberately so, one suspects — and interpreters from early times have, naturally enough, seen in Matt 11:13 or its Lukan parallel an implicit criticism of the law.[102] David Catchpole probably goes too far when he judges that "no one with traditional Jewish theological reflexes would have generated the saying in question."[103] Nevertheless, and even if "the law and the prophets were

---

100. Sanders, *Law*, 4. See above, 168–71.
101. *Critical Edition*, 466.
102. See Tertullian, *Jejun.* 2 (ed. A. Reifferscheid and G. Wissowa; CSEL 20:275): Tertullian's opponents cite Matt 11:13 = Luke 16:16a in arguing for the abolition of certain OT observances; and idem, *Pud.* 8 (ed. A. Reifferscheid and G. Wissowa; CSEL 20:228): the "burdens" of the law were until John.
103. David R. Catchpole, "The Law and the Prophets in Q," in *Tradition and Interpretation in the New Testament: Essays in honor of E. Earle Ellis for his 60th Birthday* (ed. Gerald F. Hawthorne and Otto Betz; Grand Rapids: Eerdmans, 1987), 87.

until John" is foil for the main point, so that Jesus is not issuing a clear and direct verdict about Torah,[104] Q 16:16 does assume a displacement. The Law and the Prophets are no longer the center of religious attention; something else — the kingdom — now is that center.

The radical Jesus appears not only in Mark and Q. There is also relevant special material in M and L. Luke, for instance, recounts a unique Sabbath conflict in 13:10–17. In this, the leader of a synagogue objects that healing on the Sabbath is doing work on the Sabbath. Jesus does not deny the equation. He instead appeals to his audience's experience: "Does not each of you on the sabbath untie his ox or his donkey [cf. Deut 5:14] from the manger, and lead it away to give it water? And ought not this woman, a daughter of Abraham whom Satan bound for eighteen long years, be set free from this bondage on the sabbath day?" (13:15–16). In this episode, as in Mark 2:23–28, Jesus observes one imperative and so fails to observe another. While he does not reject the trumped commandment, he does acknowledge exceptions to it — just as his Pharisaic opponents do in Mark 7:11–13 when they put Corban before honoring parents. In other words, Jesus recognizes that two commandments may sometimes conflict with each other, in which case one must choose between them. This in and of itself implicitly concedes that the law is not perfect, or at least not perfectly applicable: circumstances may compel disobedience. Moreover, a reader of Luke, with its several Sabbath conflicts, will come away thinking that Jesus likes to go out of his way to make this point about conflicting imperatives. After all, he presumably could, one fancies, wait a day to heal.[105] What agenda, then, lies behind the deliberate provocation?

One feels the law's inadequacy even in Matthew's Gospel, despite the declaration in 5:17–20. In 5:21–26 and 27–30, Jesus passes from murder to anger and from adultery to lust. Here Torah is certainly not broken. Indeed, the one who observes Jesus will necessarily observe Moses all the more. As Augustine observed, "The one who does not commit adultery

---

104. Cf. David Kosch, *Die Gottesherrschaft im Zeichen des Widerspruchs: Traditions- und redaktionsgeschichtliche Untersuchung von Lk 16,16//Mt 11,12f bei Jesus, Q und Lukas* (Bern: P. Lang, 1985), 48.

105. On the other hand, if we are thinking about the historical Jesus, perhaps we should not too quickly dismiss the possibility that sometimes he was in one place for one day only, and if that happened to be a Sabbath, then that was his only time to heal the sick in that place.

in the heart much more easily guards against committing adultery in actual fact. So he who gave the later precept confirmed the earlier; for he came not to destroy the law, but to fulfil it."[106] The same holds for the relation between anger and murder. And yet, when Jesus formulates his imperatives as contrasts with Moses, he is clearly signaling that Moses does not suffice. God demands more than the Torah demands, which is why Jesus demands more than Moses does.

Even this, however, is not as far-reaching as what we find in Matt 5:33–37. This prohibits swearing (cf. Jas 5:12), and it does so by paraphrasing Moses, who does not forbid it (cf. Exod 20:7; Lev 19:12; Num 30:3–15; Ps 50:14). Although one who does not swear breaks no commandment, to deny the utility of oaths seems a plain rejection of Scripture.[107] Both the commandment not to make wrongful use of the name of the Lord and the commandment not to bear false witness assume the validity of taking oaths. Further, God and the saints swear in the Bible. In Gen 14:22, Abraham declares, "I have sworn to the Lord, God Most High, maker of heaven and earth, that I would not take a thread or a sandal-thong of anything that is yours." In Gen 22:16, the angel of the Lord appears to Abraham and says, "By myself I have sworn, says the Lord: Because you have done this, and have not withheld your son, your only son, I will indeed bless you" (cf. Exod 6:8; Isa 45:23). One understands why Theophylact decided that, at the time of Moses, "it was not evil to swear. But after Christ, it is evil."[108]

---

106. Augustine, *Serm. Dom.* 1.12.33 (ed. A. Mutzenbecher; CCSL 35:36).

107. Yet care must be taken here because some Jewish sources also are uneasy with the oath. Already Eccl 5:5 says that "it is better that you should not vow than that you should vow and not fulfill it." Even more reservation appears in Sir 23:9: "Do not accustom your mouth to oaths"; Philo, *Decal.* 84: "To swear not at all is the best course and most profitable to life, well suited to a rational nature which has been taught to speak the truth so well on each occasion that its words are regarded as oaths; to swear truly is only, as people say, a 'second-best voyage,' for the mere fact of his swearing casts suspicion on the trustworthiness of the man"; and *m. Demai* 2:3: Those who wish to fulfill the law should not be "profuse in vows." Regarding the Essenes, Josephus tells us that "any word of theirs has more force than an oath; swearing they avoid, regarding it as worse than perjury, for they say that one who is not believed without an appeal to God stands condemned already" (*J.W.* 2.135). Philo, like Coleridge later ("The more oath-taking, the more lying"), observed that frequent swearing is really a sign of untrustworthiness (*Spec.* 2:8).

108. Theophylact, *Comm. Matt.* ad 5:33–37 (PG 123:200B). For a similar view from later times, see William Penn's learned "A Treatise of Oaths," in *The Select Works of William Penn* (London: William Philipps, 1825), 2:29–127.

THE HISTORICAL JESUS AND RHETORIC

We have seen that, on the one hand, the canonical Gospels portray a law-observant Jesus who teaches the Decalogue and even upholds the Torah in its entirety. On the other hand, this same Jesus plays fast and loose with the commandment to honor one's parents, finds multiple occasions on which to depart from Sabbath law, uses a formula that starkly contrasts his own words with those of Moses, and disallows oath-taking and divorce, which the Tanak allows. What then should we think?

Complex problems do not have simple answers, and this is a complex problem. We cannot even eliminate the possibility that Jesus himself was not perfectly clear or always consistent about the issues, that he approached Torah not in a principled fashion but on a case-by-case basis, in view of circumstances.[109] I nonetheless offer some preliminary reflections. They cannot be the whole truth, but I hope that they have some truth in them.

It would probably be unwise to equate the real Jesus either with the radical Jesus alone or with the conservative Jesus alone.[110] The latter equation requires denying to Jesus the imperative to let the dead bury their own dead (Q 9:60), the saying about hating father and mother (Q 14:26), the comment that the Law and the Prophets were until John (Q 16:16), and the prohibition of divorce (Q 16:18; cf. Mark 10:11–12) — or offering implausibly lame interpretations of these traditions. *The Five Gospels*, the product of the Jesus Seminar's voting, which many do not believe was overly generous, colors the first two of these sayings pink, indicating "Jesus probably said something very like" them.[111] The Seminar's gray print — not included in the primary data base, but some of the content may be useful for determining who Jesus was — for the prohibition of divorce, with its parallel in 1 Cor 7:10–11, is idiosyncratic.

---

109. Cf. Daniel Marguerat, "Jésus et la Loi dans la mémoire des premiers chrétiens," in *La mémoire et le temps: Mélanges offerts à Pierre Bonnard* (ed. Daniel Marguerat and Jean Zumstein; Geneva: Labor et Fides, 1991), 62–63.

110. Cf. the statement of Jacques Schlosser, *Jésus de Nazareth* (2nd, rev. ed.; Paris: Agnès Viénot Éditions, 2002), 190–91. Contrast Flusser, *Jesus*, whose conservative Jesus fails to explain Paul; as well as Herbert Braun, *Jesus of Nazareth: The Man and His Time* (Philadelphia: Fortress, 1979), 53–72, whose Jesus, with his indifference to religious law and even an "extreme unjewishness" (54) in some matters of ritual, cannot account for law-abiding Jewish Christians.

111. Robert W. Funk, Roy W. Hoover, and the Jesus Seminar, *The Five Gospels: The Search for the Authentic Words of Jesus* (New York: Macmillan, 1993), 353 on Luke 14:26, and 316 on Luke 9:61.

Surely Jesus prohibited divorce and remarriage.[112] We can, moreover, be fairly confident that Q 16:16 goes back to something he said.[113] In short, the radical Jesus seems to be the real Jesus.

What, then, do we make of the conservative Jesus? Is he too the real Jesus? Or is he rather the post-Easter projection of conservative churches? This last possibility is not so easily laid to rest. Surely Jesus did not compose Matt 5:17, with its ringing endorsement of the Law and the Prophets;[114] and some scholars would doubtlessly be fairly comfortable in denying also that Jesus told a leper to show himself to a priest as Moses commanded (Mark 1:40–45), accused opponents of not honoring father and mother (Mark 7:9–13), told a rich man that the way to life was keeping the commandments (Mark 10:17–19), summed up God's demand by citing two representative passages from Torah (Mark 12:28–31), affirmed the abiding validity of Torah (Q 16:17), and endorsed tithing as long as one also embodied justice, mercy, and faithfulness (Q 11:42). One should, however, have qualms about smothering the conservative Jesus with such wide-ranging skepticism. Q 16:17 and the end of Q 11:42 ("But these one had to do, without giving up those") are admittedly not likely to be from Jesus,[115] and the origin of Mark 7:9–13 is hardly clear.[116] One can nevertheless make a decent case that Mark 10:17–22, where Jesus quotes from the Decalogue, preserves memories about him. Bultmann for one found here a "genuine apothegm."[117] It is also not clear to me that Mark 1:40–45, where Jesus follows the Levitical legislation on leprosy, is nothing but a legend.[118]

There is, moreover, cause to suspect that Jesus, as Mark 12:28–31 has it, may have summed up the divine demand by appeal to Deut 6:5 and Lev 19:18. Some have thought that the combination of these two

---

112. See David R. Catchpole, "The Synoptic Divorce Material as a Traditio-Historical Problem," *BJRL* 57 (1974): 92–127.

113. See Kosch, *Die Gottesherrschaft*, 20–21, 46–47. Cf. John Meier, *A Marginal Jew*, vol. 2, *Mentor, Message, and Miracles* (New York: Doubleday, 1994), 157–63.

114. See already David F. Strauss, *A New Life of Jesus* (London: Williams & Norgate, 1865), 287–90.

115. On Q 11:42, see Holmén, *Covenant*, 114–15; and Kosch, *Tora*, 130–31, 144–45. But for the possibility that Q 16:17 comes from Jesus, see Arthur J. Dewey, "Quibbling over Serifs: Observations on Matt 5:18//Luke 16:17," *Forum* 5, no. 2 (1989): 109–20.

116. See esp. Roger Booth, *Jesus and the Laws of Purity: Tradition History and Legal History in Mark 7* (JSNT 13; Sheffield: Sheffield Academic Press, 1986).

117. Rudolf Bultmann, *History of the Synoptic Tradition* (rev. ed.; New York: Harper & Row, 1963), 21–22.

118. See Davies and Allison, *Matthew*, 2:9, 11–12; and cf. Luke 17:11–14.

biblical texts betrays a Jewish Hellenistic *Sitz im Leben.*[119] The chief argument for this conclusion is that non-Palestinian sources, reflecting the conventional Greek pair, εὐσέβεια καὶ δικαιοσύνη, often sum up moral obligation in terms of duty to God and duty to one's fellow human beings.[120] Yet just this sort of dual summation had already, before Jesus, entered Palestinian Judaism, as *Jubilees* demonstrates:

- 7:20: Noah teaches his children to "bless the one who created them and honor father and mother, and for each to love his neighbor."

- 36:7–8: Isaac makes his sons swear to "fear" and "worship" God, and promise "that each one love his brother with compassion and righteousness."[121]

Beyond these parallels from *Jubilees,* "the twofold commandment fits well into the rest of Jesus' preaching. The radical theocratic message of the dawn of the kingdom of God does not allow obligations to other masters, and Jesus extended the concern for the neighbour which is called for to the limits of the possible."[122] While this hardly establishes that Mark 12:28–31 does in fact go back to Jesus, there is equally no justification for safely conducting business on the assumption that it does not go back to him.

There is further warrant for denying that Jesus was, without further ado, a nomistic liberal.[123] One is that, as explained at the beginning of this chapter, it is perhaps harder to account for the heated debates over law in the early church if Jesus was nothing but a radical who loosed

---

119. So C. Burchard, "Das doppelte Liebesgebot in der frühen christlichen Überlieferung," in *Der Ruf Jesu und die Antwort der Gemeinde* (ed. E. Lohse et al.; Göttingen: Vandenhoeck & Ruprecht, 1970), 39–62; and Helmut Merklein, *Die Gottesherrschaft als Handlungsprinzip: Untersuchung zur Ethik Jesu* (2nd ed.; FB 34; Würzburg: Echter, 1981), 100–104.

120. See the texts cited in n. 52.

121. Cf. the discussion of the relationship between the social commitments and faith in God in *t. Šeb.* 3:6, which takes up Lev 6:1–3, and the suggestive commentary of Herbert W. Basser, *Studies in Exegesis: Christian Critiques of Jewish Law and Rabbinic Responses, 70–300 C.E.* (Brill Reference Library of Ancient Judaism; Leiden: Brill, 2000), 86–90. It is possible that the relevant passages in the *Testaments of the Twelve Patriarchs* (see n. 52) ultimately go back to Palestinian Jewish sources (cf. the discovery of *Aramaic Levi* at Qumran), but they may also be the work of second-century Christians, so I leave them aside here. For an introduction to the problem, see Harm W. Hollander, *Joseph as an Ethical Model in the Testaments of the Twelve Patriarchs* (SVTP 6; Leiden: Brill, 1981), 7–9.

122. So Gerd Theissen and Annette Merz, *The Historical Jesus: A Comprehensive Guide* (Minneapolis: Fortress, 1998), 388.

123. In addition to what follows, see Peter Fiedler, "Die Tora bei Jesus und in der Jesusüberlieferung," in *Das Gesetz im Neuen Testament* (ed. Karl Kertelge; QD 108; Freiburg: Herder, 1986), 71–87.

himself from the ties of Torah. How then would we explain that even according to Paul, who "was not able apparently to appeal to any specific word or act of Jesus during His ministry which would clarify His championing of Gentile Christians,"[124] Jesus' existence was "under the law" (Gal 4:4)?[125] Another reason is that, from any point of view, the original tradition is full of quite difficult, austere, uncompromising imperatives. Whatever else Jesus did, he did not teach a relaxed ethic or rid anyone of moral responsibility. The man who forbade remarriage and oath-taking may have been qualifying Moses, but the strictness of his principles are not in doubt. So although Matt 5:20 is Matthean redaction, it probably does not distort the truth. In many ways, Jesus demanded more, not less.

Additionally relevant are the several stories of Sabbath conflict that come from Mark, L, and John: Mark 2:23–28; 3:1–6; Luke 13:10–17; 14:1–6; John 5:1–18; 9:1–17. Christopher Tuckett has written concerning these texts: "If all the sabbath debates are reflections of early Christian controversies, and if none goes back to Jesus, we have to face the problem of explaining why then sabbath controversies dominate (at least part of) the gospel tradition but are notable by their (almost total) absence from nongospel Christian literature in the first century (e.g., the epistles, the *Didache*, etc.). It seems much more plausible to argue that sabbath controversies do go back to Jesus in some shape or form."[126]

This is a sensible statement, and it is supported by the work of Sven-Olav Back. His survey of early Christian positions on the Sabbath shows that, outside of the canonical Gospels, there are three opinions regarding

---

124. W. D. Davies, *Christian Origins and Judaism* (Philadelphia: Westminster, 1962), 53. See further Gerhard Dautzenberg, "Gesetzkritik und Gesetzesgehorsam in der Jesustradition," in Kertelge, *Gesetz*, 46–70, though not all of his arguments are equally persuasive. On the other side, Paul's ability to gain approval from Peter and James (Gal 2) tells against Jesus being too conservative; cf. Schlosser, *Jésus*, 212.

125. Cf. Hermut Löhr, "Jesus und der Nomos aus der Sicht des entstehenden Christentums: Zum Jesus-Bild im ersten Jahrhundert n. Chr. und zu unserem Jesus-Bild," in *Der historische Jesus: Tendenzen und Perspektiven der gegenwärtigen Forschung* (ed. Jens Schröter and Ralph Brucker; Berlin: de Gruyter, 2002), 340. According to James D. G. Dunn, *The Epistle to the Galatians* (BNTC; Peabody, MA: Hendrickson, 1993), 216, in Gal 4:4 "the Jewishness of Jesus, and indeed his practice as a devout Jew, is emphasized: it was by his sharing in Israel's subjection to the law during his life, as by his sharing in the status of the outcast from the law in his death ([Gal] iii.13), that his death and resurrection were able to effect redemption."

126. Christopher M. Tuckett, "Q and the Historical Jesus," in Schröter and Brucker, *Der historische Jesus*, 233. See further Holmén, *Covenant*, 97–100, and Schaller, "Sabbat," 140–44. Jesus also heals on a Sabbath in Mark 1:21–28, 29–31; and 6:1–6, although these stories make no mention of controversy.

Sabbath practice: (1) Christians should keep the Sabbath (Paul's opponents in Galatia). (2) Jewish Christians should keep the Sabbath (the "weak" in Rome; probably Matthew). (3) Gentile Christians should not keep the Sabbath; Jewish Christians need not do so (Paul and the author of Colossians).[127] The point is that "no one argues for a 'liberal' sabbath practice," which is what the Synoptics seem to promote. The issue in the churches, to the extent of our knowledge, "is not how the sabbath should be observed, but whether it should be observed at all."[128] In other words, the Synoptic stories fail to promote any position on Sabbath observance that is otherwise attested — which is some evidence for supposing they say something about Jesus and not just the church.[129]

The relevance of this conclusion is that the memory of Jesus creating controversy on the Sabbath comes with the attendant memory that he did not respond to critics by contemptuously dismissing the Sabbath out of hand. Nowhere does he say: "We can break the Sabbath with impunity because the Sabbath does not matter." He rather defends himself, arguing in ways that he expects his hearers to understand, if not necessarily agree with: "Have you never read what David did?" (Mark 2:25). "Is it lawful to do good or to do harm on the sabbath?" (3:4). "Does not each of you on the sabbath untie his ox or his donkey from the manger, and lead it away to give it water?" (Luke 13:15). "If one of you has a child or an ox that has fallen into a well, will you not immediately pull it out on a sabbath day?" (Luke 14:5; cf. Matt 12:11 — from Q?).[130] Jesus defends himself even in John, where he appeals to halakhic precedent — custom allows circumcising on the Sabbath (7:19–24). If then we accept the testimony that Jesus offended some people on the Sabbath, we should also accept the testimony that he denied being a libertine.[131] He justified his Sabbath behavior as exceptional, not typical, and he did not announce the termination of the Sabbath.

If all this is correct, the easy way to solve our problem, which would be to sort into the post-Easter pile all of the traditions that represent

---

127. Sven-Olav Back, *Jesus of Nazareth and the Sabbath Commandment* (Åbo: Åbo Akademi University Press, 1995), 57–67.

128. Ibid., 61.

129. See further ibid., 85–90, 117–19, 128–30, 141–42.

130. See further Schaller, "Sabbat," 142–43, who observes that the Synoptic tendency to argue about the Sabbath by using arguments from the greater to the lesser has parallels in rabbinic arguments about the Sabbath. For detailed exegesis of Luke 14:5 = Matt 12:11–12, see Back, *Sabbath*, 131–42.

131. Cf. Doering, *Schabbat*, 445–46.

Jesus as respectful of Torah, is not prudent. One might, as yet another alternative, imagine that he was once friendly to the Torah and later changed his mind,[132] or alternatively, that he became less hostile as time passed. But there is no good evidence for either option. We seem stuck with a Jesus who both observed and in some cases even intensified Torah and yet also in other cases relaxed Torah.[133] He himself, then, is the contriver of our dilemma.

One possible way of accounting for the conflicting signals in the tradition involves thinking less about theology and more about rhetoric. Some of us are wont to think of ancient Jews, at least the pious ones, as though they were modern fundamentalists, so that they would never have sounded as revolutionary as Jesus sometimes does. But this is misperception. Some Jews not only felt free to rewrite Scripture — illustrative are *Jubilees* and the *Life of Adam and Eve*, both of which freely transform Genesis — but some also were further able, in the words of Michael Fishbane, to use "authoritative Torah-teaching as a didactic foil."[134] Indeed, "the Jewish device of twisting Scripture, of subjecting the earlier canon to radical reinterpretation by means of subtle reformulations, is now recognized as central to the Bible as a whole."[135] When Job gripes, "What are human beings, that you make so much of them, that you set your mind on them?" (7:17), is not he recalling the famous Ps 8, "What are human beings that you are mindful of them, mortals that you care for them?" (v. 4) and thereby inverting and mocking the liturgy?[136] Psalm 144, in rewriting Psalm 18, turns it from a thanksgiving into a complaint.[137] Joel 3:9–10 ("Prepare war.... Beat your plowshares into swords, and your pruning hooks into spears") prophesies war in the language of a famous prophecy of peace (Isa 2:4 = Mic 4:3: "They shall beat their swords into plowshares, and their spears into pruning hooks ... neither shall they learn war any more"). Joel makes similar rhetorical moves elsewhere, as when he transfers prophetic threats against Babylon (Isa

---

132. Cf. M. Hubaut, "Jésus et la loi de Moïse," *RTL* 7 (1976): 401–25.

133. Cf. Theissen and Merz, *Historical Jesus*, 359–72.

134. Michael Fishbane, "Torah and Tradition," in *Tradition and Theology in the Old Testament* (ed. Douglas A. Knight; Philadelphia: Fortress, 1977), 277.

135. David G. Roskies, *Against the Apocalypse: Responses to Catastrophe in Modern Jewish Culture* (Cambridge, MA: Harvard University Press, 1984), 19.

136. Paul E. Dion, "Formulaic Language in the Book of Job: International Background and Ironical Distortions," *SR* 16 (1987): 190–91.

137. Eberhard Baumann, "Struktur-Untersuchungen im Psalter II," *ZAW* 62 (1950): 148–51.

13:6) and Egypt (Ezek 30:2) into warnings against Jerusalem (Joel 1:15), and when the prophecy that the wilderness will be turned into Eden (Isa 51:3; Ezek 36:35) becomes a prophecy that Eden will be turned into a wilderness (Joel 2:3).[138] Jonah seems to revise the narrow understanding of divine grace within Joel 2:1–17 — unless it is Joel 2:1–17 that is narrowing the more universal understanding of Jonah.[139] Isa 40:28 declares that God needs no rest, 45:7 that God creates darkness — about-faces from the primeval history.[140] "The oracular formula in Isa. 56.4 signals the announcement of a new word of YHWH, a word that annuls the legal stipulations of Deut. 23.2–9."[141] Daniel 12:4 foretells that at the end (קץ), "many will be running back and forth [ישטטו], and knowledge will increase." This takes up Amos 8:12 — at the end קץ, v. 2) "they will run back and forth [ישוטטו], seeking the word of the LORD, but they shall not find it" — and so turns prophetic pessimism into words of hope.[142]

Examples of the seeming subversion of Scripture also appear outside of the Bible. 1QpHab 7:2 goes against the plain sense of Hab 2:2 ("Write the vision; make it plain on tablets") when it says, "The fulfillment of the end-time he did not make known to him" (the prophet Habakkuk).[143] 4Q393 modifies Neh 9:16–25 so that whereas the latter "asserts that God did not abandon his people despite their disobedience, but enabled them to dispossess kingdoms and peoples and take possession of their houses and fields, 4Q393 frg. 3 complains that God has forsaken his people. Consequently, the very things which Nehemiah 9:22–25 announces that God gave to the Israelites are the things for which 4Q393 petitions."[144] *Ascen. Isa.* 3:8–9 makes this observation: "Moses said, 'There is no

---

138. Hans Walter Wolff, *Joel and Amos: A Commentary on the Books of the Prophets Joel and Amos* (Hermeneia; Philadelphia: Fortress, 1977), 11.

139. Thomas B. Dozeman, "Inner-Biblical Interpretation of Yahweh's Gracious and Compassionate Character," *JBL* 108 (1989): 207–23.

140. Moshe Weinfeld, "God the Creator in Gen. 1 and in the Prophecy of Second Isaiah," *Tarbiz* 37 (1968): 105–32 (in Hebrew).

141. Brooks Schramm, *The Opponents of Third Isaiah: Reconstructing the Cultic History of the Restoration* (JSOTSup 193; Sheffield: Sheffield Academic Press, 1995), 124.

142. For possible examples of Jeremiah using Psalms ironically, see William L. Holladay, *The Psalms through Three Thousand Years: Prayerbook of a Cloud of Witnesses* (Minneapolis: Fortress, 1993), 41–45. But also see the criticism of Jerome F. D. Creach, "Like a Tree Planted by the Temple Stream: The Portrait of the Righteous in Psalm 1:3," *CBQ* 61 (1999): 34–46.

143. W. H. Brownlee, *The Midrash Pesher of Habakkuk* (SBLMS 24; Missoula: Scholars Press, 1979), 109.

144. Daniel K. Falk, "Biblical Adaptation in 4Q392 *Works of God* and 4Q393 *Communal Confession*," in *The Provo International Conference on the Dead Sea Scrolls: Technological Innovations, New Texts, and Reformulated Issues* (ed. Donald W. Parry and Eugene Ulrich; STDJ 30; Leiden: Brill, 1999), 144.

man who can see the Lord and live' [Exod 33:20]. But Isaiah has said, 'I have seen the Lord, and behold I am alive [Isa 6:1, 5].' " The *Testament of Abraham*, in order to teach its lessons about mortality, turns the reflexively obedient Abraham of Genesis into an example of self-centered disobedience, and to make a better story, it adds hundreds of years to the patriarch's life span and has him dying before, not after, Sarah.[145]

According to R. Jeremiah, in *b. B. Meṣi'a* 59b, it is written in the Torah, "After the majority one must incline." But the text here cited, Exod 23:2, in fact says, "After the majority you will not incline." *b. Giṭ.* 56b has Rabbi Ishmael teach: "You [God] heard the blaspheming and insults of that wicked man and kept silent. 'Who is like you, O Lord, among the mighty [באלים, Exod 15:11]'? [Read rather,] 'Who is like you among the mute [באלמים].' " Even the Targumim sometimes engage in what has been called "converse translation," making the Bible say the opposite of what it actually means.[146] In *Tg. Onq.* on Gen 4:14, for instance, Cain's remark that he will "be hidden from your [God's] face" (so MT) becomes, "It is impossible to hide from before you." And in the Targum on Mal 2:16, the MT's statement that God hates divorce is turned into "But if you hate her, divorce her."

Early Christian literature also contains examples of the reversal of scriptural subtexts, and many of these are often ironic. Matthew 2:6 inserts οὐδαμῶς, "not at all," into its quotation of Mic 5:2, so that Micah remarks upon Bethlehem's insignificance whereas Matthew — who elsewhere affirms the continuing authority of the Law and the Prophets (5:17–20) — outright denies it. In Rom 10:6–8, Paul transmutes the exhortation to do the law in Deut 30:11–14 ("It is not in heaven. . . . Neither is it beyond the sea. . . . No, the word is very near to you; it is in your mouth and in your heart for you to observe it") into a statement about his law-free gospel. A less obvious but still striking example occurs in Revelation, if one considers the book in its entirety. The Apocalypse throughout "draws extensively on the temple chapters of Ezekiel 40–48, while denying the existence of the very thing these chapters are about," a new temple (see Rev 21:22).[147]

---

145. See my commentary, *The Testament of Abraham* (Commentaries on Early Jewish Literature; Berlin: de Gruyter, 2003), 50–51, 66, 394.

146. Michael L. Klein, "Converse Translation: A Targumic Technique," *Bib* 57 (1976): 515–37.

147. Steve Moyise, *The Old Testament in the Book of Revelation* (JSNTSup 115; Sheffield: Sheffield Academic Press, 1995), 114.

Returning now to Jesus, I suggest that some of his radical utterances belong to a rhetorical tradition within Judaism. Religious Jews were quite capable of saying some surprising things, of turning Scripture upside down and inside out, of unraveling sacred texts and then reweaving the threads. They did this in order to startle, to drive home a point, and to find permanent lodging in memories. And is Jesus not doing this when he transforms the pious "Honor your father and your mother" into the provocative "Hate [your] father and mother" (Luke 14:26)? Or when he puts his teaching into the form "You have heard that it was said to those of ancient times....But I say to you" (Matt 5:21–22)? Whatever else they may be, these words of Jesus are loud and daring rhetoric. While "I say such and such" may be interesting, "I say such and such even though Moses said something else" is eloquently arresting. If you are sleeping, it is going to wake you up.

CONFLICTING IMPERATIVES

There is more to Jesus, however, than a rhetorical manner of discourse. Something more is going on in the Sabbath controversies and in the demand that a man not bury his father but leave the dead to bury their own dead. Jesus was, I submit, keenly interested, in his own way, in the problem of competing moral imperatives.[148] We moderns often speak of choosing between the lesser of two evils. Do I bear false witness when it will save a life? Or do I abet a murder by telling the would-be assassin that his intended victim is hiding in my closet? Unless I am Augustine or Kant, I choose the smaller sin and bear false witness. Lying is wrong; but I lie if it saves an innocent life: I prefer the lesser transgression.

And so it is with Jesus.[149] Jesus nowhere extols breaking the Sabbath, but he breaks it if doing so restores a human body to wholeness or feeds the hungry. Again, parents should be honored, as the Decalogue enjoins (see Mark 10:17–19); but if showing such honor hinders hearkening to

---

148. To my knowledge, the modern scholar who has seen this most clearly is Vermes, *Religion,* 21: "The controversial statements turn...on conflicting laws"; idem, 28–29, regarding Matt 8:21–22 = Luke 9:59–60: "We are faced with a clash of requirements....In the case of such conflicting duties, the responsibility for the unavoidable 'disobedience' to one of the precepts can be laid only at God's doorstep."

149. As contrary to instinct as this seems, Jesus belongs with those in the (non-Augustinian) Christian tradition who have recognized that some important moral imperatives are not absolute; on this see Boniface Ramsey, "Two Traditions on Lying and Deception in the Ancient Church," *Thomist* 49 (1985): 504–33.

the call to discipleship, then it must slide. Salvation prevails over the Sabbath; discipleship outweighs filial obligation. As Chrysostom said, in commenting on Matt 8:21–22: "Jesus forbade him, not as commanding him to think lightly of the honor due to our parents, but as signifying that nothing ought to be to us more urgent than the things of heaven" — which in this case means literally following Jesus.[150] One command must decrease because another must increase.

Judaism knew all too well that commandments can conflict with each other, and that therefore to break the Torah was not to abolish it. The Hasidim did not abolish the Sabbath when they went to war on Saturday (1 Macc 2:29–48). Nor were their actions intended in any way to nullify the authority of the Torah or to lessen the sanctity of the Sabbath. They rather faced a moral dilemma: Do we sin by breaking the Sabbath, or do we sin by letting the nation perish? They chose the lesser of two evils, breaking the Sabbath, in order to obtain the greater of two goods, the life of the nation. This was not lawlessness but the subordination of one imperative to another imperative. Later, in a less-anxious setting, the rabbis debated at leisure the tensions between the various commandments and which have priority over which. What do you do, for example, when your father implores you to do something that desecrates the Sabbath? Do you dishonor your father, or do you dishonor the Sabbath (*b. Yebam.* 5b)? And do you circumcise a male infant on the eighth day if that day is the Sabbath? Which commandment should you break (*m. Šabb.* 18:3; 19:1–3)? Sometime imperatives just cannot be harmonized, and the rabbis knew it.

The discussions in the Mishnah and the Talmud concern clashes that come up in the normal course of Jewish life and ritual. It is otherwise in the Gospels. The rabbis discussed which one of two competing commandments comes first when circumstances force a reluctant choice. But when Jesus compels people to choose between imperatives, it is seemingly because he himself has deliberately created a conflict that requires decision. In the words of David Flusser, Jesus "knew how to create situations that would highlight aspects of his teaching."[151] As I see it, he

---

150. Chrysostom, *Hom. Matt.* 27.3 (PG 57:347–48). The subject of when one should disobey one's parents, who are owed obedience, was common in the Hellenistic world; cf. Aristotle, *Eth. nic.* 9:2; Seneca the Elder, *Controv.* 2.1.20; Aulus Gellius, *Noct. att.* 2.7.1; *Ps.-Clem. Hom.* 4:8.

151. Flusser, *Jesus*, 62. This probably explains why the tradition remembers a number of occasions on which Jesus heals on a Sabbath: Mark 1:21–28, 29–31; 3:1–6; Luke 13:10–17;

heals on the Sabbath precisely in order to make a statement. Similarly, he crafts the conditions of discipleship so that they necessarily interfere with honoring parents. And when he prohibits divorce, he compels hearers to choose between himself and Deuteronomy.

But why? Why make problems for yourself and others? Why create situations in which one cannot honor father and mother or observe the normal Sabbath? Why read the Bible so that the primeval will of God revealed in Gen 2–3 is not in accord with the later legislation in Deut 24? In *Antigone*, Sophocles depicts competing duties in order to reveal the tragic nature of human existence; what was Jesus' motive for doing something similar?

THE END AND THE BEGINNING

If Judaism knew about competing imperatives, it also knew about discrepant accounts of God's will. In contrast with Gen 1:29 ("I have given you every plant yielding seed that is upon the face of all the earth, and every tree with seed in its fruit; you shall have them for food"), Gen 9:3 grants permission for the post-Edenic world to eat meat: "Every moving thing that lives shall be food for you; and just as I gave you the green plants, I give you everything. Only, you shall not eat flesh with its life, that is, its blood." As it says in *Gen. Rab.* 34:13: "Adam, to whom flesh to satisfy his appetite was not permitted, was not admonished against eating a limb torn from the living animal. But the children of Noah, to whom flesh to satisfy their appetite was permitted, were admonished against eating a limb torn from a living animal." So there are two different directives on food, one directive for Eden, one for after Eden. Similarly, Deuteronomy promulgates divine precepts for the king, yet other portions of Scripture regard kingship as God's reluctant concession to Israel's frailty (cf. Judg 8:22–23; 1 Sam 8:4–22). So the Torah can be, and has been, viewed as containing divine concessions to human sin or compromises for it, as promoting less than the ideal human behavior.[152]

To my knowledge, however, old Jewish texts nowhere declare that such concessions have come and gone, whereas this is just what Jesus

---

14:1–6; John 5:1–47; 9:1–41. Contrast Holmén, *Covenant*, 104–5, who labels the Sabbath incidents as "casual" and evidence of Jesus' "indifference" to the Sabbath; they were not, for Holmén, the upshot of a deliberate strategy.

152. David Daube, "Concessions to Sinfulness in Jewish Law," *JJS* 10 (1959): 1–13.

says. He does it in part because of his eschatological worldview. The law, designed for the ordinary purposes of life, cannot be unaffected by the coming of God's reign, which brings the extraordinary. If the kingdom is at hand, then the renewal of the world is nigh; and if the renewal of the world is nigh, then paradise is about to be restored; and if paradise is about to be restored, then concessions to sin should no longer be needed.[153] This is certainly the implicit logic of Mark 10:1–12. As *Barn.* 6:13 has it, "The last things [will be] like the first," and because, for Jesus, the last things have come, then so have the first. Hence Jesus requires a prelapsarian ethic: "From the beginning it was not so" (Matt 19:8). Insofar as the law contains concessions to the fall, it requires repair.[154] So Jesus forbids divorce.

This conviction also illuminates Matt 5:33–37, where Jesus prohibits oaths. The presupposition of the oath is the lie, for if everyone always told the truth, it would never occur to anybody to take an oath. Oath-taking assumes that there are two types of statements, one of which demands commitment — the oath — and one of which need not — the statement without an oath. But in a sin-free world, a world like Eden or paradise regained, human beings would be invariably committed to every statement; and if they were so committed, then the superstition of the oath would be redundant. There will be no swearing in heaven. As it says in Zeph 3:13, "They shall do no wrong and utter no lies, nor shall a deceitful tongue be found in their mouths." The point is recognized in the earliest extracanonical reference to our saying. Justin Martyr takes Jesus' prohibition of swearing to mean that we should "always [be] speaking the truth."[155] In short, Jesus' prohibition of swearing is akin to his prohibition of divorce. Both set forth a prelapsarian standard that revokes a temporary concession in the Torah. Just as Hillel purportedly abrogated the Mosaic law about releasing debts every Sabbatical Year

---

153. Becker, *Jesus*, 279–80, objects that Jesus did not promote a primal or Edenic Torah because then we would expect him to be a vegetarian and to oppose circumcision. But why suppose that if Jesus, on some matters, thought in terms of something like a primal Torah, he must have been consistent and thought of everything in those terms? Jesus was a human being, not a thinking machine.

154. Cf. the interpretation of Sanders, *Jesus and Judaism*, 256–60.

155. Justin, *1 Apol.* 16.5 (ed. M. Marcovich; PTS 38:56). Cf. Becker, *Jesus*, 295: "The purpose is not primarily to get people to avoid swearing; it is to get them to tell the absolute truth before God and before their neighbors, since only this kind of truth-telling is appropriate to the Kingdom of God."

for the sake of life in this world, so Jesus formulated imperatives that leave behind the Mosaic law for the sake of life in the world to come.

One wonders whether the (presumably once independent) saying in Mark 2:27 — "The sabbath was made for humankind, and not humankind for the sabbath" — likewise reflects a recovery of "God's intention in creation."[156] "The sabbath was made for humankind" (τὸ σάββατον διὰ τὸν ἄνθρωπον ἐγένετο) sends one back to the creation story in Gen 1–2.[157] The implicit logic seems to be this: When God's purpose in establishing the Sabbath is rightly fathomed, it can override the prohibition of work. Is there not an analogy here with Mark 10:6, where Jesus also trumps an imperative by harking back to the beginning?[158]

One recalls that, in Judaism, rest is a major eschatological motif.[159] Indeed, the Sabbath is, as in some of the church fathers, often spoken of as a foretaste and symbol of the coming era of redemption,[160] just as that era is conceived of as a great Sabbath. *m. Tamid* 7:4 declares that the world to come will be a "day that shall be wholly all Sabbath and rest in the life everlasting."[161] The conception of God's future world as a great Sabbath, which is part of the *Urzeit* = *Endzeit* mythology, is part and parcel of the notion that the last age of the world will be its

---

156. So Marcus, *Mark 1–8*, 245. Cf. 246: "It may be that Mark thinks that Jesus restores the compassionate aspect of the original Sabbath, which in the interim has been effaced by a human hard-heartedness that has transformed the good Sabbath into a source of destruction." On the difficult questions regarding the historicity and tradition-history of Mark 2:23–28, see Doering, *Schabbat*, 409–16. Doering thinks that the passage has grown up around the authentic saying in v. 27. For the case that Mark 2:23–26 instead represents a stylized report of an incident from Jesus' life, to which v. 27 and later v. 28 were added, see Davies and Allison, *Matthew*, 2:304–5.

157. Cf. the repeated use of ἐγένετο in Gen 1:3–2:7 LXX; also Isa 48:7 LXX; John 1:3 (πάντα δι᾽ αὐτοῦ ἐγένετο); and Doering, *Schabbat*, 418. Whether or not the text presupposes the sequence in Genesis — God creates humankind then institutes the Sabbath — Mark 2:27 in MSS W b (cf. sy^s) notably uses ἐκτίσθη instead of ἐγένετο.

158. Christian Dietzfelbinger, "Von Sinn der Sabbatheilungen Jesu," *EvT* 38 (1978): 296.

159. Cf. Heb 4:1–11; 4 Ezra 7:36, 38; 8:52; 2 *Bar.* 73:1; 2 *Clem.* 5:5; 6:7; and see esp. Otfried Hofius, *Katapausis: Die Vorstellung vom endzeitlichen Ruheort im Hebräerbrief* (WUNT 11; Tübingen: Mohr Siebeck, 1970), 59–74.

160. Cf. *LAE* 51:2; '*Abot R. Nat.* A 1; *b. Ber.* 57b; *Gen. Rab.* 17:5. See the discussion in Samuele Bacchiocchi, "Sabbatical Typologies of Messianic Redemption," *JSJ* 17 (1986): 153–76; and Theodore Friedman, "The Sabbath: Anticipation of Redemption," *Judaism* 16 (1967): 443–52. For OT anticipations see Jon Laansma, "*I Will Give You Rest*": *The Rest Motif in the New Testament with Special Reference to Mt 11 and Heb 3–4* (WUNT 2.98; Tübingen: Mohr Siebeck, 1997), 65–67. Cf. Irenaeus, *Haer.* 4.16.1 (ed. A. Rousseau; SC 100:562); Origen, *Hom. Num.* 23.4 (ed. L. Doutreleau; SC 461: 124, 126).

161. Cf. *Barn.* 15:4–5; Irenaeus, *Haer.* 5.30.4 (ed. A. Rousseau; SC 153:386).

seventh age.[162] It might be natural, then, for Jesus, who saw his miracles as manifestations of the kingdom of God,[163] to consider Sabbath healings as particularly appropriate symbols or realizations of that kingdom.[164] Whether that is the case or not, salvation (cf. the ψυχὴν σῶσαι of Mark 3:4) and deliverance from Satan (cf. Luke 13:16) are certainly, for Jesus, eschatological realities (cf. Matt 11:4–6 = Luke 7:22–23 [Q]; Matt 12:28 = Luke 11:20 [Q], and so they manifest the restoration of the creation. Surely we must assume that Jesus interpreted his Sabbath healings "in the same way as he interpreted other healings of his. There is no reason to avoid this assumption. That is, the Sabbath healing acts were in the view of Jesus closely connected to the kingdom of God. Indeed, they were manifestations of the Kingdom."[165]

There are Jewish analogies to this sort of thinking. *m. Šabb.* 6:4 contains this ruling: On the Sabbath "a man may not go out with a sword or a bow or a shield or a club or a spear; and if he went out [with one of these] he is liable to a Sin-offering. R. Eliezer says: They are his adornments. But the Sages say: They are naught save a reproach, for it is written, 'And they shall beat their swords into plowshares, and their spears into pruning hooks; nation shall not lift up sword against nation, neither shall they learn war anymore' " (Isa 2:4). Here one's behavior on the Sabbath should anticipate the conditions of the messianic age and/or world to come, in which Isaiah's oracle will be realized. As *Gen. Rab.* 35:7 and 44:17 put it, the Sabbath is "partial realization of the world to come."

---

162. See *T. Abr.* (rec. short) 7:16; *T. Levi* 17–18 (?); *Barn.* 15:4–5; Irenaeus, *Haer.* 5.28.3 (ed. A. Rousseau; SC 153:356); Hippolytus, *Comm. Dan.* ad 4:23–24 (ed. Lefèvre; SC 14:187–89); Augustine, *Civ.* 22.30 (ed. Dombart and Kalb; CCSL 48:864–65); *b. Sanh.* 97a; *Pirqe R. El.* 19. See the discussion in D. S. Russell, *Method and Message of Jewish Apocalyptic* (OTL; London: SCM, 1964), 224–29; and Jean Daniélou, *The Theology of Jewish Christianity* (London: Darton, Longman & Todd, 1964), 396–404.

163. See Matt 11:2–6 = Luke 7:18–23 (Q) and the discussions of these texts in Allison, *Intertextual Jesus*, 53–57, 109–14.

164. For others who suggest a link between Jesus' Sabbath controversies and his eschatological proclamation, see Dietzfelbinger, "Sinn," 294–98; Doering, *Schabbat*, 454–56; Harald Riesenfeld, *The Gospel Tradition* (Philadelphia: Fortress, 1970), 115–22; Schaller, "Sabbat," 146–47; Schlosser, *Jésus*, 203.

165. Back, *Sabbath*, 177. Cf. the formulation of Jürgen Roloff, *Jesusforschung am Ausgang des 20. Jahrhunderts* (Bayerische Akademie der Wissenschaften, Philosophisch-historische Klasse Sitzungsberichte; Munich: Bayerischen Akademie der Wissenschaften, 1988), 33–34: "With his own interpretation, Jesus wants to bring into focus the true sense of the Sabbath. It is a gift of the Creator, a sign of salvation for human beings, and a reference to the future fulfillment."

Another display of this sort of thinking appears in the Shammaite ruling that one should not kill anything on the Sabbath. According to *t. Šabb.* 16:21, "R. Simeon b. Eleazar says, 'Beth Shammai says, "They do not kill a moth on the Sabbath." ' " Similarly, in *b. Šabb.* 12a, the Shammaite R. Eliezer b. Hyrcanus says: "If one kills vermin on the Sabbath, it is as if he killed a camel." According to Theodore Friedman, this prohibition of killing on the Sabbath, even the killing of an insect, "reflects the notion that the perfect peace and harmony that will prevail between man and all living creatures in the world-to-come must prevail on the Sabbath, the foretaste of that world."[166] Although Jesus sponsors an action rather than prohibits one, his rationale, I suggest, is much the same as what Friedman assigns to the Shammaites.

That for Jesus the coming of the kingdom indeed impinges upon the law appears from a line in the Sayings Source already introduced. Matt 11:12–13 reads: "From the days of John the Baptist until now the kingdom of heaven has suffered violence, and the violent take it by force. For all the prophets and the law prophesied until John came." Luke 16:16 has this: "The law and the prophets were in effect until John came; since then the good news of the kingdom of God is proclaimed, and everyone tries to enter it by force." These two closely related lines clearly go back to an original that distinguished between the time of the Law and the Prophets on the one hand and the time of the kingdom on the other. This seems to imply that, in some sense, the time of the Law has been superseded. Things are not now as they always have been, Torah included.

In line with this, in Matt 11:11 and Luke 7:28 (Q) Jesus can declare that no one born of women has arisen who is greater than John the Baptist. This is, to understate the matter, a remarkable utterance, even outrageous. Can John really be greater than Abraham, who is perfect or blameless or pure from sin in *Jub.* 23:10; Wis 10:5; Pr Man 8; and *T. Abr.* (rec. long) 10:13–14? Can he be greater than the lawgiver, who is reckoned divine (θεός) in some sense by Philo (*Mos.* 1.158; *Mut.* 129; etc.), and who is nearly omniscient in rabbinic literature? In *Ezek. the Tragedian* 68–80 (in Eusebius, *Praep. ev.* 9.29), Moses sits on God's

---

166. Friedman, "Sabbath," 448. Cf. Bacchiocchi, "Typologies," 156. It is intriguing, given what was said above about Jesus' prohibition of oaths, that Friedman finds in *y. Demai* 4:1 a prohibition of lying on the Sabbath and then explains this as yet another correlation between the Sabbath and the world to come.

throne, holds the divine scepter, and numbers the stars. Judaism defined itself in terms of the past, in terms of its great heroes such as Moses and David, and in terms of stupendous miracles such as the parting of the Red Sea and the giving of the law on Sinai. In the Gospels, however, the new outshines the glorious past. To use Jesus' parable, the new wine cannot be put into new wineskins without bursting them (Mark 2:22). The center of gravity has moved from the past, where Moses was, to the present, where Jesus is. How can the law remain unaffected?

One final text in which Jesus' eschatological vision seems to impinge upon the law, at least implicitly, is Mark 12:18–27, where he announces that in the future the saints will neither marry nor be given in marriage, but instead will be like the angels in heaven.[167] Sexual intercourse was, in first-century Judaism, largely thought of as serving the purpose of procreation, not pleasure,[168] and angels (usually conceived of as male[169]) were thought of as deathless. It followed that intercourse for the angels was unnecessary and would only have been self-indulgence. So too, according to the Markan text, shall it be for the saints in the world to come. After becoming deathless like the holy ones in heaven,[170] they will no longer need to reproduce. Intercourse will be no more. The saints, like the good angels who "restrained themselves" (*2 Bar.* 56:14) when the bad angels fell (Gen 6:2), will forever be chaste (cf. *b. Ber.* 17a). Now, all of this matters for us because the Torah contains law concerning marriage, married life, and children; and if, in the world to come there will be no more marriage, there will be no more married life and no more children; and if all this is so, then those portions of Torah that legislate concerning those matters will no longer have any sphere of application. Mark does not make the point explicit, but it takes only a moment's

---

167. For the argument that this text goes back to something Jesus said, see J.-G. Mudiso Mbâ Mundla, *Jesus und die Führer Israels: Studien zu den sog. Jerusalemer Streitgesprächen* (NTAbh 17; Münster: Aschendorff, 1984), 71–109; and O. Schwankl, *Die Sadduzäerfrage (Mk 12,18–27 parr): Eine exegetisch-theologische Studie zur Auferstehungserwartung* (BBB 66; Frankfurt am Main: Athenäum, 1987), 466–587.

168. Full documentation is in Dale C. Allison Jr., "Divorce, Celibacy, and Joseph," *Studies in Matthew: Interpretation Past and Present* (Grand Rapids: Baker Academic, 2005).

169. Recall the male names for the angels — Michael, Gabriel, Raphael, Uriel, et al. — and 1 Cor 11:2–16, where unveiled females (but not males) evidently tempt the angels. Also, *Jub.* 15:27 informs us that the angels were born circumcised. According to an old interpretation of the myth in Gen 6:2, the wicked angels engaged in sexual intercourse with human females (*1 En.* 6–7; etc.).

170. The thought that eschatological destiny will be angelic is well-attested: Wis 5:5 (assuming that "sons of God" = angels); Acts 6:15; 4QSb 4:25; 4Q511 frg. 35; *1 En.* 104:1–6; *2 Bar.* 51:5, 10; *2 En.* 22:10; *T. Isaac* 4:43–8, etc.

reflection to see that in this particular the *Endzeit*, as Jesus conceives it, will make a portion of the law irrelevant in practice.

INTENTION AND PRIORITIES

Jesus probably understood his teaching in the light of the Jewish expectation of eschatological wisdom and knowledge.[171] This is the best explanation of Q 10:23–24: "Blessed are the eyes that see what you see! For I tell you: Many prophets and kings wanted to see what you see, but never saw it, and to hear what you hear, but never heard it." More particularly, Jesus' view may be linked with the traditional expectation that an eschatological figure will bring eschatological instruction. Isaiah 42:1–4 says that the servant will bring חורה (*tōrah*) — a passage that Matthew at least thought fitting for Jesus (12:18–21). 4Q175 implies that the Qumran community expected an eschatological prophet like Moses, of whom God said: "I will put my words into his mouth, and he shall tell them all that I command them" (Deut 18:15, 18). 11QMelch. 2:15–21 prophesies the coming of "an anointed one, a prince" (cf. Dan 9:25) who will instruct those who mourn in Zion (cf. Isa 61:2–3). In *1 En.* 51:3 we see the Elect One, the Son of Man, sitting on God's throne, and we are told that "from the conscience of his mouth shall come out all the secrets of wisdom" (cf. 46:3; 49:3–4). *Ps. Sol.* 17:43 foretells that the Messiah's "words will be purer than the finest gold, the best. He will judge the peoples in the assemblies, the tribes of the sanctified. His words will be as the words of the holy ones, among sanctified peoples." According to *Tg. Onq.* on Gen 49:11, those who "carry out the Torah" will be with the Messiah "in study." And *Tg. Isa.* on 53:5 says that peace will come through the Messiah's teaching, and that those who "gather around his words... will be forgiven."[172] One should also not overlook John 4:25, where a Samaritan woman, in conversation with Jesus, expresses her

---

171. See Hos 6:2–3 LXX; Hab 2:14; 1QpHab 7:1–5; 11:1–2; Matt 11:25 par.; 13:35. There is much relevant material in Raymond E. Brown, *The Semitic Background of the Term "Mystery" in the New Testament* (FBBS; Philadelphia: Fortress, 1968).

172. Cf. *Gen. Rab.* 98:9: "When he, about whom it is written, 'Lowly and riding upon an ass' [Zech 9:9] will come... he will elucidate for them the words of the Torah... and elucidate for them their errors. R. Hanina said: 'Israel will not need the teachings of King Messiah in the world to come, for it is said, "Unto him the nations shall seek" [Isa 11:10] — not Israel.' If so, why will King Messiah come, and what will he come to do? To gather the exiles of Israel and to give them thirty commandments." Additional rabbinic texts in Str-B 4.1:1–3.

faith that, when the Christ comes, "he will proclaim all things to us" (cf. *Memar Marqah* 4:12).

None of these passages openly declares that the eschatological future will add to or change the Torah. But Isa 56:1–8, which in Jesus' day would have been understood as eschatological,[173] plainly depicts the undoing of Deuteronomy's exclusion of eunuchs from the temple: "Deut 23:1–3 is replaced by a new prophetic *torah* by which both foreigners and eunuchs . . . are welcomed into the worshipping community."[174] Further, a few rabbinic texts say that certain sacrifices and festivals will cease,[175] that the laws covering things clean and unclean will be revised,[176] or even that there will be a new Torah.[177] Some later Jewish teachers certainly did entertain thoughts about eschatological alterations of the Torah. If they did so, then maybe Jesus — like perhaps Paul[178] — anticipated them.

---

173. Mark 11:17 has Jesus himself quoting Isa 56:7. The Targum on Isa 56:8 adds a reference to the ingathering of the exiles.

174. Grace I. Emmerson, *Isaiah 56–66* (OTG; Sheffield: Sheffield Academic Press, 1992), 15.

175. *Yal.* on Prov 9:2: "All the festivals will cease except Purim"; *Lev. Rab.* 9:7: "In the time to come, all sacrifices will be annulled, but that of thanksgiving will not be annulled, and all prayers will be annulled, but that of thanksgiving will not be annulled."

176. *Midr. Ps.* on Ps 146:4: "In the world to come God will again permit the eating of that flesh which he has forbidden"; *Lev. Rab.* 13:3: "In the time to come, the Holy One, blessed be he, will make a banquet for his righteous servants, and whoever has not eaten *nebēlah* [meat from an invalidly slaughtered animal] in this world will have the privilege of enjoying it in the world to come."

177. Targum on Isa 12:3: "And you will accept a new teaching with joy from the chosen ones of righteousness"; Targum on Cant 5:10: "new traditions which he will make known to his people on the great day"; *Midr. Qoh.* 2:1: "All the Torah which you learn in this world is vanity in comparison with Torah learned in the world to come"; *Yal.* on Isa 26:2: "God will sit and expound a new Torah which he will give, on days, by the hand of the Messiah." See further W. D. Davies, *Torah in the Messianic Age and/or the Age to Come* (SBLMS 7; Philadelphia: Society of Biblical Literature, 1952); and A. Diez-Macho, "En torno a las ideas de W. D. Davies sobre el Sermón de la Montaña," in W. D. Davies, *El Sermon de la Montaña* (Madrid: Cristiandad, 1975), 201–8. But for caution and a warning on how marginal such texts are in the rabbinic corpus, see Peter Schäfer, "Die Torah der messianischen Zeit," *ZNW* 65 (1974): 27–42.

178. Cf. Gal 6:2: "Bear one another's burdens, and in this way you will fulfill the law of Christ [τὸν νόμον τοῦ Χριστοῦ]." The Hebrew equivalent, תורתו של משיח, appears in *Midr. Qoh.* 11:8: "The Torah which a man learns in this world is vanity compared with the Torah of the Messiah." Is the identity of phrase coincidence? Gal 6:3 could be the proof that pre-Christian Judaism already spoke of the Messiah's Torah, especially as the expression is so surprising within the larger context of Galatians. Of this, however, we must remain unsure: independent invention of the same phrase cannot be deemed impossible. Yet Paul, whatever he meant by it, could indeed refer to Jesus Christ as having his own *nomos*; cf. 1 Cor 9:21; *Barn.* 2:6; Justin, *Dial.* 11.2; 12.3. See further Heinz Schürmann, "'Das Gesetz des Christus' (Gal 6,2)," in *Neues Testament und Kirche: Für Rudolf Schnackenburg* (ed. Joachim Gnilka; Freiburg: Herder, 1974), 282–300.

We may justifiably believe that he did. For not only is he an eschato-logical prophet who modifies Torah, as when he disallows oath-taking and divorce, but Jesus also is particularly interested in the interiority of the Torah. In Joseph Klausner's words, Jesus *overemphasizes* this idea.[179] Jesus seeks to shift attention from murder to anger, from adultery to lust. He wants people to reflect upon the light within, or the lack thereof (Matt 6:22–23 = Luke 11:34–35 [Q]), for he believes that what is inside defiles (Mark 7:15). How does this "constant and emphatic dwelling on the inward disposition"[180] relate to eschatology?

Jeremiah 31:31–34 famously prophesies the interiorization of the law: "The days are surely coming, says the LORD, when I will make a new covenant with the house of Israel and the house of Judah. It will not be like the covenant that I made with their ancestors when I took them by the hand to bring them out of the land of Egypt — a covenant that they broke, though I was their husband, says the LORD. But this is the covenant that I will make with the house of Israel after those days, says the LORD: I will put my law within them, and I will write it on their hearts; and I will be their God, and they shall be my people." According to Jeremiah, a new covenant will someday be established, and the Torah will then be engraved internally (cf. the related idea in Ezek 36:26–27). According to Jesus, the kingdom of God has come, and the law must be effective even within one's heart. It does not surprise us that the author of Hebrews and Justin Martyr claimed the fulfillment of Jer 31:31–34 in what Jesus wrought (Heb 8:8–12; 10:16–17; Justin, *Dial.* 11.3 [ed. M. Marcovich; PTS 47:88]), nor that the tradition of the Lord's Supper common to Luke and Paul alludes to Jeremiah's "new covenant" (Luke 22:20; 1 Cor 11:25).

So far I have urged that Jesus' attitude toward the law should be correlated with his eschatological outlook. The coming of the kingdom explains the return to Edenic standards, the prohibitions of divorce and oath-taking, and some other seemingly impractical demands. Eschatol-ogy also clarifies Jesus' focus, in explicit contrast with Moses, upon intention, for the internalization of the Torah is an eschatological ex-pectation of Jeremiah. But there is yet another way in which eschatology and Torah are linked. The kingdom of God, as the pearl and the hidden

---

179. Joseph Klausner, *Jesus of Nazareth: His Life, Times, and Teaching* (London: Macmillan, 1925), 393.

180. C. H. Dodd, *The Founder of Christianity* (London: Fontana, 1971), 84.

treasure illustrate, matters far more than anything else (Matt 13:44–46; *Gos. Thom.* 109). To find it means to find everything, and to lose it means to lose everything. Now, because the kingdom matters more than anything else, the call to obtain it and for the disciples to assist others in obtaining it must outweigh all other demands. This is why Jesus can hyperbolically demand hatred of parents, and why he can call a man to neglect his father's burial: it is the eleventh hour, the prophet is here today, and he will not be here tomorrow. So this is the only chance to heed his call to discipleship. When obligation to parents might interfere with the cause of Jesus, then such obligation must lapse. Zebedee and business as usual must be left in the boat. Like every other obligation, filial responsibility abdicates in the face of eschatological need. One can no more serve the kingdom and parents than one can serve God and mammon.

The Talmud contains the following, in *b. Yebam.* 90b: "Come and hear: Him you will listen to [Deut 18:15], even if he tells you, 'Transgress any of all the commandments of the Torah' as in the case for instance of Elijah on Mount Carmel [in 1 Kgs 18 Elijah sacrifices outside the temple], obey him in every respect in accordance with the needs of the hour." In this startling passage, the Talmud teaches that, in a time of crisis, the prophet like Moses may have to go against Moses, may have to do what the Torah does not want to be done.[181] Now there can be no greater crisis than the coming of the kingdom and the end of the old world. So the explicit logic of the Talmud is analogous to the implicit logic of Jesus. Whatever interferes with preparing for the new era must, even if it stands in the Decalogue, defer to the greater that has come.

The idea here is, I believe, implicit in Matt 10:34-36 = Luke 12:51-53 (Q): "There are five in one house, three against two and two against three. For I came to divide a father from his son and a son against his father, a mother against her daughter and a daughter against her mother, a mother-in-law against her daughter-in-law and a daughter-in-law against her mother-in-law."[182] This transparent adaptation of Mic

---

181. There is a related logic in *b. Yebam.* 79a: "It is proper that a letter be rooted out of the Torah so that thereby the heavenly name will be publicly hallowed."

182. For this reconstruction of Q and what follows, see further my article, "Q 12.51–53 and Mk 9:11–13 and the Messianic Woes," in *Authenticating the Words of Jesus* (ed. Bruce Chilton and Craig A. Evans; NTTS 28.1; Leiden: Brill), 289–310.

7:6 situates the eschatological motif of family strife[183] in the ministry of Jesus. Now, if Jesus said something like this with reference to his own situation, it could only be because, as we otherwise infer, he and some of his followers had become alienated from their families (cf. Mark 3:31–35). Such alienation was the upshot of conflict between familial loyalty and adherence to Jesus' proclamation of the kingdom, which in the case of some involved abandoning life as they had theretofore known it. The sons of Zebedee heeded Jesus, not their father, whose business they deserted (Mark 1:19–20) — a circumstance that the saying about division puts in eschatological perspective. If one has to obey Jesus and so honor him rather than one's parents, that is because, in accord with eschatological expectation, the dawning age of peace does not come until after the present period of strife, which includes strife within families.

FINAL COMMENTS

1. *Historical.* This chapter has covered a lot of ground and unfortunately had to run rapidly over most of it when it would have been safer to stroll leisurely and inspect everything along the way. But we have seen enough to learn that Jesus was neither a conservative nor a liberal because he was both. The one label without the other is a misnomer, for while his eschatological convictions turned him into an occasional radical, because the demands of the kingdom sometimes created tension with Torah and tradition, Jesus was also a conservative, a fact that needs no comment other than that he was a pious Jew, and how could a pious Jew not respect Moses? A Jew calling Jews to repentance, a Jew "for whom the ethical ideal was everything,"[184] had to acknowledge the authority of the Torah.

Here at this chapter's end let me return to the beginning and again ask, What about the debates in the early church? Those who felt duty bound to the law would not have found themselves rebuked by Jesus. For he exhorted his hearers to keep the commandments. And on the several occasions when he broke Torah, he did so without abolishing it. It was a question of deciding between two legitimate imperatives, not between a good commandment and a bad commandment. Further, in

---

183. *Sib. Or.* 8.84; Mark 13:12; 4 Ezra 5:9 Arm.; *m. Soṭah* 9:15; *b. Sanh.* 97a; Targum on Mic 7:6.

184. Klausner, *Jesus,* 389.

the few instances where eschatology requires revision of Torah, the one who obeys Jesus will not disobey Moses. What law does one break if one does not divorce one's wife or refuses to take an oath? So Jesus, in the words of Matt 5:17–20, does not come to abolish the Law and the Prophets.

At the same time, the Christians who promoted a law-free mission could have taken heart from memories of Jesus. For they could have recalled that he was an imaginative interpreter of Torah, that he occasionally relaxed this or that commandment, that he replaced a couple of Mosaic imperatives with Edenic imperatives, and that his demands exceeded the Torah, thereby implying that Moses is not enough. All this is, admittedly, a long way from the law-free Gentile gospel, about which Jesus had nothing to say. Yet we may believe that the traditions underlining the limitations of Torah and the memory of Jesus' liberalism played some role in the church's own liberalism; and that Jesus' subordination of the law to eschatology was one factor in the eventual recognition — even, according to Paul, recognition by the three Jerusalem pillars, James, Peter, and John, who had some knowledge of the historical Jesus (Gal 2:9) — that the Gentile followers of God need not live like Torah-observant Jews.

2. *Theological*. Marcion upheld the radical Jesus. Tertullian defended the conservative Jesus. Neither knew the historical Jesus, who was much more complex. He was, as we have seen, neither a radical who spoke against the God of Moses nor a traditionalist confined to conventional readings of Torah. He rather lived with an eschatological vision in which the God of the future had begun to act differently than in the past. There was continuity because Jesus' God was Israel's God. To this extent, Tertullian's instinct was right. But there was also discontinuity because this old God, in changing the world, was doing some brand-new things. In this regard, Marcion was not wholly wrong.

Readers of the Gospels have long sensed discrepancies between certain features in the Jesus tradition and certain aspects of the Old Testament revelation. The God who sends rain upon the just and unjust seems unlike the God who sponsors the violence of Joshua and Judges.[185] Though the Elijah of Kings calls down fire from heaven (2 Kgs 1:10, 12), the

---

185. It is perhaps not coincidence that the early Jesus tradition shows no interaction with these two OT books.

Jesus of Luke rebukes such an action (Luke 9:51–56).[186] Many so-called heretics found these sorts of contrasting behaviors cause for positing two different Gods. More recently, Jack Miles has woven such contrasts into a literary narrative in which the New Testament shows us a God who has, under duress, altered his character: "Though Jesus speaks as if God is now as he always has been, he is in fact revealing (or enacting) an enormous change in God."[187]

Miles's fascinating literary approach, in which the God incarnate in Jesus suddenly rejects the difference between neighbor and enemy, amity and hostility, is rather novel. Others who have acknowledged the real contradictions between the two Testaments have instead more typically appealed to "progressive revelation" and located the apparent changes in human perception of Providence rather than in the Divine Being itself. But however one construes the opposition between the Testaments, it is Jesus himself who hands us the problem. We see in him neither the same God doing the same things nor a different God doing different things. We instead see the old God doing new things. For Miles, this is a literary phenomenon. For proponents of progressive revelation, it is a theological phenomenon. For the historical Jesus, it is an eschatological phenomenon: the Law and the Prophets were until John, and since then a new reality is displacing the old.

Jesus' belief that revelation can in effect become dated, as well as his recognition — and indeed promotion of the idea — that ethical imperatives cannot always be harmonized, led to his implicitly critical stance vis-à-vis some aspects of the Torah. That stance is theological precedent for those of us who cannot wish away the tensions between the Testaments but rather feel compelled critically to scrutinize them in the full light of day. It is of course far beyond the proper scope of this chapter to undertake such scrutiny. All I can do is observe that Jesus himself, while seeking to remain faithful to the God of Israel, freely participated in his people's critical discussion of its own tradition.

---

186. See my article "Rejecting Violent Judgment: Luke 9:52–56 and Its Relatives," *JBL* 121 (2002): 459–78.

187. Jack Miles, *Christ: A Crisis in the Life of God* (New York: Knopf, 2001), 96–97.

SIX

RESURRECTING JESUS

The attitude of my own mind is inconsistent and, so far as these stories are concerned, I cannot help having a slight inclination for things of this kind, and indeed, as regards their reasonableness, I cannot help cherishing an opinion that there is some validity in these experiences in spite of all the absurdities involved in the stories about them.
— IMMANUEL KANT

I have tried to present both sides of these questions; or rather, all possible sides, for ... there seems to be no black-and-white, no yea-and-nay, and every apparently straight path branches off into a dozen different directions.
— PAUL TABORI

Instead of disputing the facts, we must try to explain them. But whatever explanation we offer, we soon find ourselves in very deep waters indeed.
— H. H. PRICE

THE QUESTION

What might it mean to say that Jesus rose from the dead?[1] This is no recondite question. When I speak to audiences about the historical Jesus, I am sometimes asked to confirm individuals in their belief that the resurrection must be understood as some sort of metaphor. Surely, they

---

1. My first book, *The End of the Ages Has Come: An Early Interpretation of the Passion and Resurrection of Jesus* (Philadelphia: Fortress, 1985), contains an excursus on "Belief in the Resurrection of Jesus" (163–68). The present chapter serves as a belated defense of positions first briefly staked out there. At the same time, and although this is quite a long chapter, the following pages offer no more than the sketch of an outline. The subject is so vast and so complex that herein I must at every turn bypass a hundred questions and ignore most of the secondary literature, of the making of which there is no end.

198

query, we no longer need believe the unbelievable, believe in a literal empty tomb and the energizing of a corpse. Are these not incredible artifacts from the age of legends? Others, to the contrary, are anxious for me to reassure them that the resurrection is not incredible but a solid historical fact. The tomb was empty, the body was gone, and surely God was responsible: no other explanation makes sense. Does not Paul in 1 Cor 15 teach that "if Christ has not been raised" — not metaphorically raised but really raised — then we are still in our sins, and that "if for this life only we have hoped in Christ, we are of all people most to be pitied" (vv. 17, 19)?

What should I say?[2]

OPTIONS

My initial response to inquiry about Jesus' resurrection is usually, if time permits, to outline briefly what others have said, and that is how I shall begin herein. The main plot can be quickly told.[3] Until the Enlightenment, Orthodox, Roman Catholic, and Protestant Christians accepted the New Testament accounts of Jesus' resurrection as historically accurate down to their details and interpreted those details literally. Things began to change about three hundred years ago. Disillusioned with the feuding branches of European Christendom, oriented to doubt by Cartesian philosophy, and enamored with the successes of materialistic science, rationalism began to replace Christianity as the central ideology

---

2. Some, on theological grounds, would dismiss the following discussion as illegitimate because it involves evaluating evidence surrounding the theological claim that Jesus rose from the dead. In my defense, I am, as an historian, the victim of my own curiosity. Historical criticism may not establish theological assertions, but that does not dissolve my desire to learn what I can about the past. Against Karl Barth, *Church Dogmatics* (Edinburgh: T & T Clark, 1958), 4/2:150, I also do not know how to refrain from reading the biblical texts "without imposing questions which they themselves do not ask." Impudent cross-examination is for me inevitable. Cf. A. J. M. Wedderburn, *Resurrection* (London: SCM, 1999), 3–23.

3. Partial surveys of earlier work include William Lane Craig, *The Historical Argument for the Resurrection of Jesus during the Deistic Controversy* (Lewiston, NY: E. Mellen, 1985); and Paul Hoffmann, "Die historisch-kritische Osterdiskussion von H. S. Reimarus bis zu Beginn des 20. Jahrhunderts," in *Zur neutestamentlichen Überlieferung von der Auferstehung Jesu* (ed. Paul Hoffmann; Weg der Forschung 522; Darmstadt: Wissenschaftliche Buchgesellschaft, 1988), 15–67. Much of the twentieth-century discussion is reviewed in John E. Alsup, *The Post-Resurrection Appearance Stories of the Gospel-Tradition: A History-of-Tradition Analysis with Text-Synopsis* (Calwer theologische Monographien, Reihe A, Bibelwissenschaft 5; Stuttgart: Calwer, 1975), 19–54.

in the West, at least among the intellectual elite. This rationalism, emboldened by Protestant critiques of Catholic wonders, had no place for miracles, understood as the violation of natural law. So there was certainly no place for the greatest Christian miracle of all, the resurrection of Jesus. That event must be, many came to think, a myth in the guise of history; it must belong not to the real world but solely to the religious imagination.

It is one thing to doubt, another to explain; one thing to reject the Easter proclamation as beyond belief, another to tell a story that, without calling upon the supernatural, accounts for the origin of that proclamation. And since doubt, just like faith, needs to justify and console itself, there has since the Enlightenment been no dearth of attempts to euthanize early Christian belief in Jesus' literal resurrection, to prove it to be just another pious belief inadequate to the facts. In response, there have also been myriad attempts to justify the traditional conviction.

Almost everybody agrees that we need a good story. If we are to account for the birth of the church, we must, one way or the other, get Jesus raised from the dead, at least in the minds of the disciples. But recovering exactly what or even approximately took place two thousand years ago is tough work, for history appears to have taken a very strange turn here. Although Pilate and the Roman authorities surely anticipated that crucifixion would halt Jesus and his cause, it did not. So what surprising series of events frustrated their expectation? Surely C. D. Broad was right: "*Something* very queer must have happened soon after the crucifixion, which led certain of the disciples and St. Paul to believe that Jesus had survived in some supernatural way."[4] But what? The question holds its proud place as the prize puzzle of New Testament research.

"No trail of historical research," according to E. C. Hoskyns and F. N. Davey, "has been more zealously trodden over than this, or with more disparate results."[5] Leaving to one side the first part of this claim, I dispute the second part: it is overstatement. Although the laborers have not been few, the harvest has not been so plentiful. The thousands of books and articles dedicated to Jesus' resurrection have not, despite their

---

4. C. D. Broad, *Religion, Philosophy and Psychical Research: Selected Essays* (London: Routledge & Kegan Paul, 1953), 230.

5. Edwyn Clement Hoskyns and Francis Noel Davey, *Crucifixion-Resurrection: The Pattern of the Theology and Ethics of the New Testament* (ed. Gordon S. Wakefield; London: SPCK, 1981), 280.

manifold differences, produced a plethora of truly disparate hypotheses. Indeed, almost all of the elucidations of belief in Jesus' resurrection can, for convenience, be placed within one of seven categories:[6]

1. *Orthodox belief*. First of all, there is the conventional Christian account, hallowed by centuries of creedal recitation. Many within the churches have continued to hold the traditional, apostolic line because they have seen no compelling reason to let go of it; for them, orthodox opinion continues to commend itself. Tom Wright is the most prominent recent example of this.[7] He, like Wolfhart Pannenberg before him,[8] has defended both the reality of the empty tomb and the objectivity of the appearances. Many in the pews, surely most in the American pews, would no doubt go along with him. Without an empty tomb, they are sure, Christian faith is empty.

2. *Misinterpretation*. Others have thought that the Christian proclamation rests ultimately upon some mundane circumstance attending Jesus' burial or connected with his tomb that prescientific Christians, more pious than thoughtful, more credulous than disinterested,[9] misinterpreted. Is it not more reasonable to think that there was some faulty observation or misinterpretation, some illusion or unconscious distortion of the facts, than that a dead man became undead? Jesus' tomb, for instance, could have been emptied by other than supernatural means.

---

6. Here I leave aside the mythological proposals, according to which Jesus did not exist and the traditions about him are modeled on myths of dying and rising gods. On these myths see now Tryggve N. D. Mettinger, *The Riddle of Resurrection: "Dying and Rising Gods" in the Ancient Near East* (ConBOT 50; Stockholm: Almqvist & Wiksell, 2001). On 220–21 Mettinger confirms the common verdict that the resurrection of Jesus is not "a mythological construct."

7. N. T. Wright, *The Resurrection of the Son of God* (Minneapolis: Fortress, 2003).

8. Wolfhart Pannenberg, *Jesus — God and Man* (2nd ed.; Philadelphia: Westminster, 1977), 88–114.

9. The early, deistic protests again and again come back to the uneducated nature of the first Christians; cf. Anonymous (Paul Henri Thiry, Baron d'Holbach), *Ecce Homo! or, A Critical Enquiry into the History of Jesus Christ* (2nd ed.; London: D. I. Eaton, 1813), 259: "An indefatigable credulity was the most prominent trait in their character." On 273 he speaks of "imbecile people, incapable of reasoning, fond of the marvelous, and of too limited understandings to escape the snares laid for their simplicity." While this sort of polemic, which is presumably ancient (cf. Acts 4:13), is today happily out of bounds, we do need to keep in mind the words of John Hick, *The Metaphor of God Incarnate: Christology in a Pluralistic Age* (Louisville: Westminster/John Knox, 1993), 16: "This was a time of excited and sometimes (from the typical twentieth-century standpoint) fantastic beliefs and practices to whose atmosphere we have a clue in the uninhibited enthusiasms of contemporary Pentecostalism and the unshakeable certainties of marginal sects expecting the imminent end of the world. In that early apocalyptic phase of the Christian movement the canons of plausibility were very different from those operating within today's mainline churches."

Perhaps Jewish authorities removed the body and quietly disposed of it because they did not want it venerated.[10] Or maybe it was a gardener who took the corpse, for reasons forever unknown.[11] When the tomb was subsequently found vacated, belief in the resurrection was born. Such belief in turn fostered subjective visions among people who perhaps were not perfectly in their wits: Peter and his distraught friends hallucinated Jesus. A similar proposal has it that the women went to the wrong tomb, with the same result,[12] or, with the same result again, that Joseph of Arimathea kept Jesus' body in his family tomb for a day and then moved it to its final resting place, which circumstance evidently never came to anyone's attention.[13]

One can also envisage a sorcerer, keen on body parts for magical rituals, stealing Jesus' corpse.[14] Not only might the remains of a holy man

10. So D. Gerald Bostock, "Do We Need an Empty Tomb?" *ExpTim* 105 (1994): 201–4. He argues that the leaders then spread the rumor that the disciples had stolen the body.

11. Tertullian, *Spect.* 30 (ed. Reifferscheid and Wissowa; CSEL 20: 29), knows opponents who claim that Jesus was removed by a gardener so that his lettuce plants would not be trampled by the pious crowds visiting the site! Is John 20:13–15 already an answer to something like this it? Despite Hans von Campenhausen, *Tradition and Life in the Church: Essays and Lectures in Church History* (Philadelphia: Fortress, 1968), 66–68, the answer is probably No. See Robert M. Price, "Jesus' Burial in a Garden: The Strange Growth of a Tradition," *Religious Traditions* 12 (1989): 17–30.

12. So famously Kirsopp Lake, *The Historical Evidence for the Resurrection of Jesus Christ* (London: Williams & Norgate, 1907), 241–52. The young man who said to the women, "He is not here; behold the place where they laid him," was trying to tell them what had happened; but misunderstanding and fear, later compounded by imagination, turned the young man into an angel and his message into an announcement of resurrection. I am unaware of any contemporary scholar who takes seriously this suggestion, which is pure speculation. Lake himself wrote: "These remarks are not to be taken as anything more than a suggestion of what might possibly have happened" (252). For an adequate refutation, see J. C. O'Neill, "On the Resurrection as an Historical Question," in *Christ, Faith and History: Cambridge Studies in Christology* (ed. S. W. Sykes and J. Clayton; Cambridge: Cambridge University Press, 1972), 210. I observe, however, that today's popular Christian literature does often contain stories in which, or so it seems to me, people turn mundane events into miracles and, in retrospect, perceive other human beings as angels from heaven. For a likely example, in which a busboy is taken to be an angel, see Mickey Rooney, *Life Is Too Short* (New York: Villard, 1991), 279–80; and further, Rense Lange and James Houran, "Role of Contextual Mediation in Direct Versus Reconstructed Angelic Encounters," *Perceptual and Motor Skills* 83 (1996): 1259–70. Although Lake's hypothesis has never been popular, it did not go without support; see, e.g., Percival Gardner-Smith, *The Narratives of the Resurrection: A Critical Study* (London: Methuen, 1926), 133–39, 179–82.

13. So Oskar Holtzmann, *The Life of Jesus* (London: Adam & Charles Black, 1904), 499; Joseph Klausner, *Jesus of Nazareth: His Life, Times, and Teaching* (New York: Macmillan, 1925), 357; Guillaume Baldensperger, *Le tombeau vide: La légende et l'histoire* (Paris: F. Alcan, 1935). I have been unable to obtain a copy of the original presentation of this thesis: Anonymous, "Versuch über die Auferstehung Jesu," *Bibliothek für Kritik und Exegese des Neuen Testaments und älteste Kirchengeschichte* 2 (1799): 537–51.

14. Cf. Apuleius, *Metam.* 2.20; *PGM* 4:2140–44; and see Richard Carrier, "The Guarded Tomb of Jesus and Daniel in the Lion's Den: An Argument for the Plausibility of Theft," *Journal*

have been particularly tempting — recall the power of Elisha's bones in 2 Kgs 13:20–21, of Thomas's bones in *Acts Thom.* 170, and later superstition about the healing powers of relics — but the remains of the executed were also thought particularly powerful (cf. *PGM* 4.1885–1886). Jesus was desirable on both counts. Furthermore, necromancers, "who were, almost by necessity, body snatchers,"[15] had a special interest in those who died violent deaths.[16] Tomb robbery was a problem in antiquity, even when wealth was not involved (cf. Chariton, *Chaer.* 2.5.10); and the so-called Nazareth inscription, whatever its immediate occasion, confirms the circumstance for first-century Palestine.[17]

Another conjecture is that the crucified Jesus never really died.[18] In Mark 15:44–45, Pilate wonders that Jesus is so soon dead. Maybe, then, a few have guessed, he was not dead. What Poe called "premature burial" was, in earlier times, frightfully more common than we would like to suppose (cf. *Sem.* 8:1). So perhaps Jesus revived in the cool air of the tomb to make his exit, and then later his vacated sepulcher was discovered. Or perchance he ran into some people who naively mistook him to be returned from the dead — although how a flagellated, half-dead victim of the hideous torture of crucifixion could impress others

---

of Higher Criticism 8 (2001): 304–18. David Whittaker, "What Happened to the Body of Jesus?" *ExpTim* 81 (1970), 307–10, guesses that criminals snatched the body but is vague on their motives.

15. So George Luck, *Arcana Mundi, Magic and the Occult in the Greek and Roman Worlds* (Baltimore: Johns Hopkins University Press, 1985), 167.

16. See Hans Dieter Betz, "Zum Problem der Auferstehung Jesu im Lichte der griechischen magischen Papyri," in his *Hellenismus und Urchristentums* (Gesammelte Aufsätze 1; Tübingen: Mohr Siebeck, 1990), 241–45.

17. See Bruce M. Metzger, *New Testament Studies: Philological, Versional, and Patristic* (NTTS 10; Leiden: Brill, 1980), 75–92.

18. See esp. Karl Heinrich Georg Venturini, *Natürliche Geschichte des grossen Propheten von Nazareth* (2nd ed.; Bethlehem [Copenhagen]: Schubothe, 1806), 4:169–312; Samuel Butler, *The Evidence for the Resurrection of Jesus Christ* (ed. Robert Johnsonte; Garrarads Cross: Colin Smythe, 1980); John L. Cheek, "The Historicity of the Markan Resurrection Narrative," *JBR* 27 (1959): 191–200; and, more recently, M. and T. A. Lloyd Davies, "Resurrection or Resuscitation?" *Journal of the Royal College of Physicians of London* 25, no. 2 (1991): 167–70; J. Duncan M. Derrett, *The Anastasis: The Resurrection of Jesus as an Historical Event* (Shipston-on-Stour, Warwickshire, UK: Drinkwater, 1982); Michael A. Persinger, "Science and the Resurrection," *The Skeptic* 9, no. 4 (2002): 76–79, arguing that Jesus had temporal lobe epilepsy; and Barbara Thiering, *Jesus and the Dead Sea Scrolls* (San Francisco: HarperSanFrancisco, 1992). The basic idea goes back to earlier times; see *The Second Treatise [Logos] of the Great Seth*; Origen, *Cels.* (ed. Marcovich; 128–29); Qur'an 4.157. For a full and entertaining discussion of books featuring the thesis that Jesus never died, see Gerald O'Collins and Daniel Kendall, "On Reissuing Venturini," *Greg* 75 (1994): 241–65. A variant of this theme appears in Hugh J. Schonfield's best-selling *The Passover Plot: New Light on the History of Jesus* ([New York]: B. Geis Associates, 1965); he posits that Jesus schemed to survive crucifixion and did so, although this exit strategy left him in no shape to live much longer.

as triumphant over death is hard to envisage.[19] Despite the obvious difficulty, the hypothesis of a docetic death is an old one. Whether or not Mark 15:44–45 (Pilate "learned from the centurion that he was dead") already served to answer detractors who surmised that Jesus had never really expired,[20] Origen later had to address the problem, in *Cels.* 2.56 (ed. Marcovich; 128–31).

One other reductive scenario involving an empty tomb is that, as Matt 27:51 has it, there was an earthquake when Jesus died. Maybe, then, after he was buried, an aftershock opened a crack in his sepulchre, which crack ingested his body and then slammed right back over it. Visitors, later misled by an unoccupied tomb, came to believe as true a thing utterly false. Seismic activity would additionally explain why, as the Gospels have it, the stone before his tomb rolled back seemingly of its own accord.[21]

3. *Hallucinations.* Much more popular, at least in recent times, has been a third approach. This holds that it was not the empty tomb that begot hallucinations but hallucinations that begot the empty tomb. We know that sometimes people see things that are not there, so why not the disciples? If Freud said that we cannot imagine our own deaths, maybe the disciples could not imagine the death of their beloved teacher. One recalls that, according to Origen, the Dositheans, about whom we know all too little, denied the death of their messianic leader, Dositheus.[22] Maybe then we should give a psychological reading to Acts 2:24, which declares

---

19. Josephus, *Vita* 420–21, tells us that when he intervened with Titus to have three crucifixion victims taken down, the most careful treatment still left two dead. Cf. Herodotus, *Hist.* 7.194; and see further David Friedrich Strauss, *The Life of Jesus Critically Examined* (Philadelphia: Fortress, 1972), 733–39.

20. Cf. John 19:33–35. Mark 15:44–45, which has no Matthean or Lukan parallel, may be a post-Markan addition; see Craig A. Evans, *Mark 8:27–16:20* (WBC 34B; Nashville: T. Nelson, 2001), 515–16. If so, perhaps it was inserted precisely to counter the polemic that Jesus had not died. That Jesus rose "on" or "after the third day" might also be understood to prove that he was really dead; see below, 232. One need not think here only of anti-Christian polemic: doctrinal Docetists also denied Jesus' death; see Irenaeus, *Haer.* 1.24.4 (ed. Rousseau and Doutreleau; SC 264:328).

21. Both Gerhard Lohfink, "Die Auferstehung Jesu und die historische Kritik," *BibLeb* 9 (1968): 46; and Paul Wilhelm Schmiedel, "Resurrection- and Ascension-Narratives," in *Encyclopaedia Biblica* (ed. T. K. Cheyne and J. Sutherland Black; New York: Macmillan, 1903), 4:4067, mention this theory in passing. Although neither attributes the conjecture — which Schmiedel labels "a mere refuge of despair" — to any named scholar, I observe that Reinhold Seeberg, *Christliche Dogmatik* (Erlangen: Deichert, 1925), 2:205, seems to entertain it as a real possibility.

22. Origen, *Comm. Jo.* 13.27 (ed. Blanc; SC 222:122). See further Stanley Jerome Isser, *The Dositheans: A Samaritan Sect in Late Antiquity* (SJLA 17; Leiden: Brill, 1976), 31–32, 46.

that it was impossible for death to hold Jesus in its power: the disciples just could not imagine him being gone for good. Perhaps Jesus' followers externalized their deep conviction that "he cannot be dead, therefore he is alive."[23]

Whereas a guilty subconscious punished Macbeth by conjuring the face of Banquo, maybe, at the beginning, a grieving, guilty Peter — who had denied his lord — conjured the face of Jesus; but instead of administering self-reproof, Peter projected exactly what he needed for healing: a forgiving Jesus, which the uncritical, superstitious disciple sincerely thought real.[24] Under a psychological necessity to restore his emotional equilibrium, Peter turned his subjective impression into a mythic objectification. Without knowing it, he became his own oracle and forgave himself.

A sort of mass hysteria, the product of emotional contagion, followed, with others as victims of their overluxuriant imaginations also claiming to see Jesus, although he was nothing but a figment of their optical delusion.[25] Visionary claims can be mass produced,[26] and if we like we can imagine that those who saw Jesus may have thereby coped with their disillusionment and stress, gained attention, and enhanced their status.[27] So Peter's individual reality soon became, without any notable interference from Providence, the communal reality, the sacred canopy of Galilean peasants who had as children been brought up on the far-fetched miracles of the

---

23. Charles Guignebert, *Jesus* (New York: Knopf, 1935), 527. This is certainly more plausible than the absurd suggestion that Jesus hypnotized the disciples to have, after his death, posthypnotic visions. Ian Wilson, *Jesus: The Evidence* (London: Weidenfeld & Nicolson, 1996), 150, imagines this fantasy only to withdraw it immediately.

24. Cf. Ernest Renan, *The Apostles* (New York: Bretano's, 1898), 42–58, who claimed: "A man of penetration might have announced on that Saturday that Jesus would arise" (44). He, however, thought Mary Magdalene instead of Peter to be the real instigator.

25. That there was a high concentration of resurrection appearances in a relatively short period of time and then fewer or none at all does in fact match the pattern of many episodes of collective delusion: initial report, then rapid multiplication of experiences, then rapid cessation. See Norman Jacobs, "The Phantom Slasher of Taipei: Mass Hysteria in a Non-Western Society," *Social Problems* 12 (1965): 318–28; and Nahum Z. Medalia, "Diffusion and Belief in a Collective Delusion: The Seattle Windshield Pitting Epidemic," *American Sociological Review* 23 (1958): 180–86.

26. Cf. Otto Pfleiderer, *Philosophy and Development of Religion* (Edinburgh: W. Blackwood, 1894), 2:116, with reference to the resurrection of Jesus: "It is a well-known fact of experience that states of the extraordinarily excited life of the soul, and in particular religious enthusiasm and ecstasy, have a sort of infectious character, and master whole assemblies with elemental power."

27. Cf. Frieda L. Gehlen, "Toward a Revised Theory of Hysterical Contagion," *Journal of Health and Social Behavior* 18 (1977): 27–35.

Hebrew Bible and then as adults followed a reputed wonder-worker. "Did not their prepossessed imaginations make them see what did not exist?"[28] The matter might not be much different than a Bigfoot scare: once there is one report, another may follow, and then another and another, although we may well doubt the veracity of what is related.[29] Certainly, unknown giant, hairy hominids, even if they exist, can scarcely exist in sufficient numbers to account for the numerous sightings of Bigfoot that people all over the world testify to every year.[30] An even better parallel would be some of the episodes involving sightings of the Virgin Mary. Even the Roman Catholic Church has condemned many of the less-sober reports of the Blessed Mother as arising from prodigal hysteria.[31] Maybe it was the same with Jesus' followers: fantasy was confused with reality; collective delusion took over. Celsus, the second-century critic of Christianity, already envisioned this possibility,[32] and such was the skeptical view of David Friedrich Strauss in the nineteenth century, and such is the verdict of Gerd Lüdemann in our own day.[33] The denial of death, which

---

28. So Anonymous, *Ecce Homo!* 259. See further Charles T. Gorham, *The First Easter Dawn: An Inquiry into the Evidence for the Resurrection of Jesus* (London: Watts, 1908). Gorham's essay is, incidentally, one of the best skeptical treatments of the resurrection; unfortunately, it has never received much attention.

29. See James R. Stewart, "Sasquatch Sightings in South Dakota: An Analysis of an Episode of Collective Delusion," in *Exploring the Paranormal: Perspectives on Belief and Experience* (ed. George K. Zollschan, John F. Schumaker, and Greg F. Walsh; Dorset: Prism, 1989), 287–304. The comparison of Jesus' resurrection with sightings of Bigfoot appears in Michael Goulder, "The Baseless Fabric of a Vision," in *Resurrection Reconsidered* (ed. Gavin d'Costa; Oxford: Oneworld, 1996), 48–61; idem, "Did Jesus of Nazareth Rise from the Dead?" in *Resurrection: Essays in Honour of Leslie Houlden* (ed. Stephen Barton and Graham Stanton; London: SPCK, 1994), 58–68.

30. See the regularly updated log of North American, Canadian, and international sightings online: http://www.bfro.net/GDB/.

31. René Laurentin, *The Apparitions of the Blessed Virgin Mary Today* (2nd ed.; Dublin: Veritas, 1991), 141–46.

32. Origen, *Cels.* 2.55, 60 (ed. Marcovich; 128–29, 132).

33. Strauss, *Life of Jesus*, 739–44; Gerd Lüdemann, *The Resurrection of Jesus: History, Experience, Theology* (Minneapolis: Fortress, 1994); idem, "Psychologische Exegese oder: Die Bekehrung des Paulus und die Wende des Petrus in tiefenpsychologischer Perspektive," in *Bilanz und Perspektiven gegenwärtiger Auslegung des Neuen Testaments: Symposion zum 65. Geburtstag von Georg Strecker* (ed. Friedrich Wilhelm Horn; Berlin: de Gruyter, 1995), 91–111. Cf. also Carl Holsten, *Zum Evangelium des Paulus und Petrus* (Rostock: Stiller, 1868), 3–237; Maurice Goguel, *The Birth of Christianity* (London: George Allen & Unwin, 1953), 29–86; Reginald W. Macan, *The Resurrection of Jesus Christ: An Essay in Three Chapters* (London: Williams & Norgate, 1877); Selby Vernon McCasland, "Peter's Vision of the Risen Christ," *JBL* 47 (1928): 41–59; H. C. Snape, "After the Crucifixion or 'the Great Forty Days,'" *Numen* 17 (1970): 188–99; and many others. Petr Pokorný, *The Genesis of Christology: Foundations for a Theology of the New Testament* (Edinburgh: T & T Clark, 1987), 125n149, is right to observe that recent proponents of the subjective vision theory "bring nothing essentially new in comparison with Goguel."

came by way of subjective visions, gave rise to Christianity.[34] The story of the empty tomb, not found in Paul, can then be a late legend, a pure postulate of the faith fabricated by credulous visionaries.

One should add that many contemporary Christians have been able to domesticate this point of view: what was once polemic aimed at their faith no longer troubles them. Karl Martin Fischer, for instance, declares that the nature of the visions of Peter and his companions are of interest only to historians and perhaps psychologists, not theologians. The issue has nothing to do with his Christian faith, which is not grounded in what happened in the psyches of the first disciples.[35]

4. *Deliberate deception.* A fourth hypothesis, promoted today by next to nobody,[36] involves not self-delusion but the deliberate deception of others. Thomas Woolston (1669–1733) and H. S. Reimarus (1694–1768), both deistic antagonists of Christian orthodoxy who enjoyed swashbuckling their way through centuries of dogma, concluded that some of Jesus' followers secretly stole his body by night.[37] While Jesus was with them, they had learned that power, honor, and free meals come

---

34. In his first book on the resurrection, Lüdemann seemingly does not exclude the possibility that some so-called paranormal experiences, including presumably early Christian encounters with Jesus, might be more than subjective (this "remains to be seen"); see *Resurrection*, 183. I find no trace of this possibility in his second, more-popular book: *What Really Happened to Jesus? A Historical Approach to the Resurrection* (Louisville: John Knox Westminster, 1995).

35. Karl Martin Fischer, *Das Ostergeschehen* (2nd ed.; Göttingen: Vandenhoeck & Ruprecht, 1980), 88–91. Cf. the indifference of Rudolf Bultmann, "New Testament and Mythology," in *Kerygma and Myth* (ed. Hans Werner Bartsch; London: SPCK, 1953), 42; Ingo Broer, " 'Der Herr ist dem Simon erschienen' (Lk 24,34): Zur Entstehung des Osterglaubens," *SNTU (Studien zum Neuen Testament und seiner Umwelt)* 13 (1988): 81–100; and Paul Hoffmann, "Einführung," in Hoffmann, *Überlieferung*, 13; and the use of "hallucination" by Gordon D. Kaufman, *Systematic Theology: A Historicist Perspective* (New York: Scribner's, 1968), 411–34. Contrast Friedrich Schleiermacher, *The Christian Faith* (New York: Harper & Row, 1963), 2:420: Those who reject the literal resurrection and "prefer to suppose that the disciples were deceived and took an inward experience for an outward" ascribe "to them such weakness of intellect that not only is their whole testimony to Christ thereby rendered unreliable, but also Christ, in choosing for Himself such witnesses, cannot have known what is in men."

36. But Richard Carrier, "Guarded Tomb," thinks this a possibility. See p. 208.

37. Thomas Woolston, *A Sixth Discourse on the Miracles of Our Saviour* (2nd ed.; London: the Author, 1729); Hermann Samuel Reimarus, *Reimarus: Fragments* (ed. Charles H. Talbert; Philadelphia: Fortress, 1970), 199, 248–58. For Woolston, Jesus himself had prophesied his own resurrection, and his disciples did him the favor of fulfilling his forecast. Something like this scenario seems already implicit in the comments of Celsus in Origen, *Cels.* 2.55 (ed. Marcovich; 127–28). Cf. also Anonymous, *Ecce Homo! 256–57.* Given the views of Woolston and other English Deists, such as Peter Annet, it is not true that Reimarus was "the first modern scholar to deny outright the Resurrection of Jesus conceived as the rising of a body from the tomb" (Rowan Williams, "Resurrection," in *The Oxford Companion to Christian Thought* [ed. Adrian Hastings; Oxford: Oxford University Press, 2000], 617).

to religious leaders, and they did not want the crucifixion to put them out of a business they enjoyed. So they conspired to steal his corpse, which allowed them to proclaim the resurrection and to declare, despite the crucifixion, the impending second coming. Credulous dupes believed them. Already Matt 28:11–15 has Jewish opponents of Christianity claim that the disciples came and pirated the body away.

(This is not, to be sure, a very plausible hypothesis. Already effectively dispatched by William Paley in the eighteenth century, it has never deserved credence.[38] Not only does it seem unlikely that the frightened followers of Jesus would have braved an illegal act,[39] but one can hardly doubt the sincerity of Paul, and he clearly did not doubt the sincerity of Peter, at least in this matter. The only version of this far-fetched hypothesis that could be taken seriously would have it that a single disciple or admirer, wanting to restore Jesus' good name, removed the body without knowledge of the deed coming to Peter and most of the others. Such is the view of Richard Carrier, who thinks that "from among what may have been over seventy people in Jesus' entourage, it is not improbable that at least one of them would be willing to engage in such a pious deceit."[40])

5. *Genuine visions.* Some have offered, as a fifth account of things, that, while the story of the empty tomb is legendary, the visions were veridical, real. The disciples did encounter a triumphant, postmortem Jesus, who sought to communicate with them. This was the view of C. J. Cadoux, who wrote that "the least difficult explanation of these appearance seems to me to regard them as real manifestations given to his followers by Jesus himself, not by means of the presence of his physical body resuscitated from the empty tomb, but by way of those strange processes sufficiently attested to us by psychical research, but as yet very imperfectly understood."[41] Hans Grass famously came to a similar conclusion, although he preferred the language of theology to the language of psychical research. According to Grass, the tomb was not emptied, but God did grant the disciples visions of

---

38. William Paley, *Paley's Evidences of Christianity* (ed. Charles Murray Nairne; New York: Robert Carter & Bros., 1855), 377.

39. See Bruce M. Metzger, "Nazareth Inscription," in *New Testament Studies.*

40. Carrier, "Guarded Tomb," 306–7.

41. C. J. Cadoux, *The Life of Jesus* (West Drayton, Middlesex: Penguin, 1948), 165. See further the works of Badham, Hyslop, Lake, Lodge, Perry, Weatherhead, and Zorab in n. 293.

the victorious Jesus who, upon bodily death, had entered into the life of God.[42]

6. *Belief in God's vindication.* The rival accounts introduced so far all focus, naturally enough, on events following the crucifixion. But a sixth approach begins rather in the pre-Easter period.[43] Rudolf Pesch, following Klaus Berger,[44] found traces of a tradition of a dying and rising prophet in Mark 6:14–16 (Herod and others think that Jesus is John the Baptist risen from the dead); Rev 11:7–12 (two prophets are slain and then rise after three and a half days); and some other, later sources;[45] and Pesch argued that this tradition was known by the disciples, who regarded Jesus as God's eschatological prophet. So when, in the event, he suffered and died, his disciples naturally postulated God's vindication of him. The disciples' faith, established before Good Friday, eventually produced the legends of Easter. The tomb was not empty, and all the appearance stories in the Gospels are late. Pesch also contended that the unelaborated ὤφθη of 1 Cor 15:3–8 need not refer to visionary experiences: it is rather part of a formula of

---

42. Hans Grass, *Ostergeschehen und Osterberichte* (2nd ed.; Göttingen: Vandenhoeck & Ruprecht, 1962), 233–49. For earlier presentations of this standpoint, see Hermann Christian Weisse, *Die evangelische Geschichte: Kritisch und philosophisch bearbeitet* (Leipzig: Breitkopf & Härtel, 1838), 1:426–38; Theodore Keim, *The History of Jesus of Nazara, Considered in Its Connection with the National Life of Israel* (London: Williams & Norgate, 1876–1883), 6:323–65 (Keim famously used the phrase "telegrams from heaven"); and G. H. C. MacGregor, "The Growth of Resurrection Faith. II," *ExpTim* 50 (1939): 282–83. This is also the view, if I understand him aright, of John Shelby Spong, *Resurrection: Myth or Reality? A Bishop's Search for the Origins of Christianity* (San Francisco: HarperSanFrancisco, 1994), 255–56. I am not sure how to classify John J. Pilch, "Appearances of the Risen Jesus in Cultural Context: Experiences of Alternate Reality," *BTB* 28 (1998): 52–60. His thesis is that "the Resurrection appearances of the Risen Jesus are experiences of him in alternate reality by his contemporaries. Phrased differently, they are human experiences in alternate states of consciousness." Pilch is so keen on interpreting the texts in terms of the ancient Mediterranean world instead of modern Western science that he avoids any clear statement as to how we, who do not live in the ancient Mediterranean world, should understand for ourselves the first Easter experiences.

43. A related idea occurs in the polemical *Toledoth Jesu*, which implies that the disciples originally proclaimed Jesus' ascension to heaven simply because he had prophesied it. Their faith was then unwittingly bolstered by a gardener who moved Jesus' body. See Günter Schlichting, *Ein jüdisches Leben Jesu: Die verschollene Toledot-Jeschu-Fassung Tam ū-mūʾād: Einleitung, Text, Überlieferung, Kommentar, Motivsynopse, Bibliographie* (WUNT 24; Tübingen: Mohr Siebeck, 1982), 152, 154.

44. Klaus Berger, *Die Auferstehung des Propheten und die Erhöhung des Menschensohnes: Traditionsgeschichtliche Untersuchungen zur Deutung des Geschickes Jesu in frühchristlichen Texten* (SUNT 13; Göttingen: Vandenhoeck & Ruprecht, 1976).

45. Discussion in Johannes M. Nützel, "Zum Schicksal der eschatologischen Propheten," *BZ* 29 (1976): 59–94.

legitimation.[46] Resurrection faith came neither from visions — there need not have been any — nor from discovery of an empty tomb — that is legend[47] — but from the continuing conviction that if God's eschatological prophet has died to salutary effect, he must also be exalted to God.[48]

Several other recent scholars agree that belief in the resurrection was more a continuation of pre-Easter faith in the historical Jesus than the product of peculiar events after the crucifixion.[49] Stephen Patterson represents this point of view: "The *presupposition* for any claim about resurrection is not appearance stories, empty tombs, and the like. Resurrection, as vindication, presupposes only that a righteous person has been killed in faithfulness to a divine cause. In a dissident Jewish context,

---

46. Objections in Joseph Plevnik, "Paul's Appeal to His Damascus Experience and 1 Cor. 15:5–7: Are They Legitimations?," *TJT* 4 (1988): 101–11. My own judgment is that while the appearances may have been used as legitimation, their content cannot be reduced to such. The ecclesiological function does not annul the christological statement. Cf. Anton Vögtle, "Wie kam es zum Osterglauben?" in Anton Vögtle and Rudolf Pesch, *Wie kam es zum Osterglauben?* (Düsseldorf: Patmos, 1975), 44–68; and see below, 237–39. For another attempt — based upon an analysis of the speeches in Acts — to argue for the secondary nature of the appearance tradition, see William O. Walker, "Postcrucifixion Appearances and Christian Origins," *JBL* 88 (1969): 157–65.

47. Cf. Rudolf Pesch, *Das Markusevangelium* (HTKNT 2.2; Freiburg: Herder, 1977), 2:521–28, 536–40; idem, "Das 'leere Grab' und der Glaube an Jesu Auferstehung," *IKZ* 11 (1982): 6–20.

48. Rudolf Pesch, "Zur Entstehung des Glaubens an die Auferstehung Jesu," *TQ* 153 (1973): 201–28. For Pesch's initial response to his critics, see his "Stellungnahme zu den Diskussionsbeiträgen," *TZ* 153 (1973): 270–83. For his theological reflections on the resurrection, see his chapter on "Tod und Auferstehung," in Rudolf Pesch and Herbert A. Zwergel, *Kontinuität in Jesus: Zugänge zu Leben, Tod und Auferstehung* (Freiburg: Herder, 1974), 35–94 (a volume bearing the Catholic imprimatur).

49. See esp. Peter Fiedler, "Vorösterliche Vorgaben für den Osterglauben," and Ingo Broer, " 'Seid stets bereit, jedem Rede und Antwort zu stehen, der nach der Hoffnung fragt, die euch erfüllt' (1 Pet 3,15): Das leere Grab und die Erscheinungen Jesu im Lichte der historischen Kritik," in *"Der Herr ist wahrhaft auferstanden" (Lk 24.34): Biblische und systematische Beiträge zur Entstehung des Osterglaubens* (ed. Ingo Broer and Jürgen Werbick; SBS 134; Stuttgart: Katholisches Bibelwerk, 1988), 9–28 and 29–62, respectively; also Stephen J. Patterson, "Why Did Christians Say: 'God Raised Jesus from the Dead'?" *Forum* 10 (1994): 135–60; Henk Jan de Jonge, "Visionary Experience and the Historical Origins of Christianity," in *Resurrection in the New Testament: Festschrift J. Lambrecht* (ed. R. Bieringer, V. Koperski, and B. Lataire; BETL 155; Leuven: Leuven University Press/Peeters, 2002), 35–53. De Jonge accepts the argument of Joost Holleman, *Resurrection and Parousia: A Traditio-Historical Study of Paul's Eschatology in 1 Corinthians 15* (NovTSup 84; Leiden: Brill, 1996), that there was a pre-Christian tradition (different from the one Berger reconstructed) concerning the non-eschatological resurrection of just individuals. For older reconstructions that can be construed as ancestors in Pesch's family tree, see Wilhelm Bousset, *Kyrios Christos* (Nashville: Abingdon, 1975), 50–51; and Nathaniel Schmidt, *The Prophet of Nazareth* (New York: Macmillan, 1905), 392–98. Schmidt regards both the story of the opened tomb and the appearance traditions as secondary and asserts that "the ultimate cause" of belief in the resurrection was "the ineradicable impression of the personality of Jesus."

this is all one needs. The followers of Jesus could have said 'God raised Jesus from the dead' on the day he died, and probably did."[50]

Although English-speaking scholarship seems to have mostly missed the debate,[51] Pesch's work has been much discussed in Germany.[52] Pesch himself found his critics persuasive, because he later forwarded an alternative explanation, although once again it grounds resurrection faith first in the historical ministry of Jesus, not in post-Easter experiences.[53] Jesus and his followers, according to Pesch, expected the eschatological consummation to arrive in the near future, when tribulation and death for many would be followed by, in accordance with their interpretation of Dan 7, Jesus' coming as the Son of Man on the clouds of heaven.[54] After the crucifixion, Peter and other disciples realized the Parousia in

---

50. Patterson, "God Raised Jesus," 142. Although my reasons for saying this will not appear until later, I wonder if Patterson's words are not an illustration of exaggerated hindsight. "In hindsight, people consistently exaggerate what could have been anticipated in foresight. They...tend to view what happened as being inevitable." So Baruch Fischhoff, "For Those Condemned to Study the Past: Reflections on Historical Judgment," in *Fallible Judgment in Behavioral Research* (ed. Richard A. Schweder; San Francisco: Jossey-Bass, 1980), 83.

51. Including Wright, *Resurrection*, who mentions Pesch only at 4n3; the item in the bibliography under Pesch's name appears to be to a book written rather by Anton Vögtle. The only significant discussions in English known to me are John Galvin, "Resurrection as Theologia Crucis Jesu: The Foundational Christology of Rudolf Pesch," *TS* 38 (1977): 513–25; idem, "The Origin of Faith in the Resurrection of Jesus: Two Recent Perspectives," *TS* 49 (1988): 25–44; Francis J. Moloney, "Resurrection and Accepted Exegetical Opinion," *Australian Catholic Record* 58 (1981): 191–202; and E. Ruckstuhl, "The Resurrection of Jesus," in *Ecumenical Institute for Advanced Theological Studies, Yearbook 1973/1974* (Jerusalem: Tantur Ecumenical Institute, 1974), 143–57.

52. See the list of relevant works in Rudolf Pesch, "Zur Entstehung des Glaubens an die Auferstehung Jesu: Ein neuer Versuch," *FZPhTh* 30 (1983): 80n8; and Hans-Willi Winden, *Wie kam und wie kommt es zum Osterglauben? Darstellung, Beurteilung und Weiterführung der durch Rudolf Pesch ausgelösten Diskussion* (Disputationes theologicae 12; Frankfurt am Main: P. Lang, 1982).

53. Pesch, "Neuer Versuch," 73–98. Although here Pesch abandons his earlier thesis, his explanation is laconic: "My proposal for discussion has, in the extensive and intense debate of the past few years, shown itself to be untenable" (84).

54. See further Rudolf Pesch, *Simon-Petrus: Geschichte und geschichtliche Bedeutung des ersten Jüngers Jesu Christi* (Päpste und Papsttum 15; Stuttgart: Anton Hiersemann, 1980), 52–55. Although Pesch does not refer to others who have thought this, he is not alone. Very similar ideas appear in Philipp Seidensticker, *Die Auferstehung Jesu in der Botschaft der Evangelisten: Ein traditionsgeschichtlicher Versuch zum Problem der Sicherung der Osterbotschaft in der apostolischen Zeit* (Stuttgart: Katholisches Bibelwerk, 1967); Hans-Werner Bartsch, *Das Auferstehungszeugnis: Sein historisches und sein theologisches Problem* (TF 41; Hamburg: Herbert Reich, 1965); idem, "Historische Erwägungen zur Leidensgeschichte," *EvT* 22 (1962): 449–59; idem, "Inhalt und Funktion des Urchristlichen Osterglaubens," *NTS* 26 (1980): 180–96; idem, "Inhalt und Funktion des Urchristlichen Osterglaubens," *ANRW* 2.25.1 (1982): 794–890. The notion that the resurrection appearances were not of the man Jesus or the crucified Jesus but of Jesus as the glorified Son of Man already appears in Adolf von Harnack, "Die Verklärungsgeschichte Jesu, der Bericht des Paulus (I. Kor. 15,3ff.) und die beiden Christusvisionen des Petrus," *SPAW.PH* (Berlin, 1922): 70 (= Hoffmann, *Überlieferung*, 103).

their own experience. They had visions of Jesus enthroned in heaven, in fulfillment of his words about the Son of Man.[55] In this way they came to believe in his resurrection and, at some point, posited, without historical discovery, his empty tomb. Pesch, one should note, is a Roman Catholic who contends that God can communicate in various and sundry ways, including via hallucinations.[56]

7. *Rapid disintegration of the body plus visions.* The final option I introduce not because it is representative but because it is, on the contrary, novel and so may stand for the several truly idiosyncratic hypotheses that have failed to garner respect or support. According to the Roman Catholic John Michael Perry, Jesus' soul did in fact triumph over death, and he was able to communicate this to the disciples through veridical visions.[57] His body, being unnecessary for life in the world to come, rotted in the tomb. In Jesus' time and place, however, most Jewish people mistakenly believed that survival required a body; so for the disciples to embrace the truth of Jesus' victory over death, God had to arrange things so that the tomb would be void. God did this by hurrying up the natural processes of decay. The body remained where Joseph of Arimathea laid it, but its disintegration was so rapid that, when the tomb was entered shortly after Jesus' interment, it appeared that its occupant had vanished. According to Perry, this hocus-pocus did not constitute a violation of natural law.

Surely Perry's singular thesis represents the triumph of ingenuity over good sense. It seems to me, for what little it is worth, that it would have been much easier for a powerful Deity to trick the women into going to the wrong tomb, or to have had an earthquake conveniently swallow

---

55. In my judgment, the evidence for this is sparse indeed. With the exception of Matt 28:16–20, the encounters with the risen Jesus in the canonical Gospels are, unlike Rev 1, devoid of Son of Man and enthronement motifs — although Bartsch's claim (see previous note) that ὤφθη + dative in 1 Cor 15:3–8 recalls pre-Solomonic theophanies (see n. 149) and so belongs to an *Endzeit-Urzeit* scheme is worth considering.

56. Cf. Gerhard Lohfink, "Der Ablauf der Ostereignisse und die Anfänge der Urgemeinde," *TQ* 160 (1980): 165–68. According to Lohfink, the alternative, natural versus supernatural vision, is false: God "does not abandon the structures, laws, constructions, and final causes of the world but instead acts precisely through them and with their help and in cooperation with them. Thus an authentic vision is both a work of the human being and the work of God." One understands the point: those who thank God for food before meals typically do not envisage supernatural events taking place between farm and table.

57. John Michael Perry, *Exploring the Identity and Mission of Jesus* (Kansas City, KS: Sheed & Ward, 1996), 176–213.

the corpse.[58] One might further ask why God failed to raise up Jewish prophets to promote the immortality of the soul à la Socrates rather than the resurrection of the body à la Daniel. But what is the point of further discussing an unattractive position without adherents?[59]

So much then for the various options.[60] Can we deem one more probable than another?

CONFESSION

Because this is a case where one's religious prejudices inevitably get in the way of dispassionate analysis, a case of unusual enormity where it is

---

58. Another option: the spiritualist Charles Lakeman Tweedale, in *Man's Survival of Death, or, The Other Side of Life* (5th ed.; London: Spiritualist Press, 1947), 482–87, has the angel who rolled the stone away dispose of Jesus' useless body.

59. Yet Perry's theory has a forerunner in the curious work of the Jehovah's Witness, Charles Taze Russell, *Studies in the Scriptures* (Allegheny, PA: Watchtower Bible & Tract Society, 1908), 2:129: "Our Lord's human body was . . . supernaturally removed from the tomb; because had it remained there it would have been an insurmountable obstacle to the faith of the disciples, who were not yet instructed in spiritual things — for 'the spirit was not yet given' (John 7:39). We know nothing about what became of it, except that it did not decay or corrupt (Acts 2:27, 31). Whether it was dissolved into gases or whether it is still preserved somewhere as the grand memorial of God's love, of Christ's obedience, and of our redemption, no one knows." See also Leslie D. Weatherhead, *The Resurrection of Christ in the Light of Modern Science and Psychical Research* (London: Hodder & Stoughton, 1959), 43–51: Jesus' body dissipated into gas. In a way, the views of Perry and Russell and Weatherhead are in continuity not only with Luther's view that the glorified body of the risen Christ is ubiquitous, not confined to any particular space and time (God's "right hand" is everywhere), but also with those who have argued that, since human beings cannot see spiritual bodies, the resurrected Jesus, before the ascension, used his old material body when communicating with his followers but later discarded it; see, e.g., Edward Meyrick Goulburn, *The Doctrine of the Resurrection of the Body* (Oxford: J. Vincent, 1850), 163–74. If I understand him, Hugh Montefiore, *The Womb and the Tomb* (San Francisco: Fount, 1992), 165, also thinks some such scenario possible; so too perhaps Pierre Masset, "Immortalité et l'âme, resurrection des corps: Approches philosophiques," *NRTh* 105 (1983): 334, who characterizes the resurrected form of Jesus as "occasionnelle," its only use being to shore up the disciples' faith. This reminds one of the old view that the risen Jesus consumed food but did not need to: he ate for "economy" (οἰκονομία); so John of Damascus, *De fide orth.* 4.1 (ed. Kotter; PTS 12:172).

60. Margaret Barker's *The Risen Lord: The Jesus of History as the Christ of Faith* (Valley Forge, PA: Trinity, 1997), is another example of an idiosyncratic hypothesis. She uncovers a mystic experience of resurrection at the baptism and argues that Jesus rose before he died. We have also been promised a future book from Robert Greg Cavin and Carlos A. Colombetti, arguing that "Jesus had an unknown twin who faked the resurrection" (Robert Greg Cavin, "A Logical Analysis and Critique of the Historical Argument for the Revivification of Jesus," unpublished paper delivered to the 1995 Pacific Region meeting of the American Philosophical Association). A. N. Wilson, *Jesus* (New York: W. W. Norton, 1992), 244, has already suggested something similar. For some additional idiosyncratic hypotheses that are more entertaining than enlightening, see Gary R. Habermas, "The Late Twentieth-Century Resurgence of Naturalistic Responses to Jesus' Resurrection," *TJ* 22 (2001): 179–96. No doubt more is to come: each generation enjoys rewriting the records of the defenseless dead, especially when those records belong to a religious collection many enjoy debunking.

hard not to take sides, it is sensible to ask discussants to set aside their usual discretion and disclose what side they are rooting for. So before turning to the historical issues, I wish to be candid about my personal inclinations in this matter. I am not inhumanly impartial, and there are reasons why I should very much like to believe in the literal resurrection of Jesus and reckon it more than a symbol, more than just a way of saying that his cause continues or that he lives on in the memory of the church.

My first reason is the conviction that the teaching of Jesus, which as a Christian I am committed to, may well hang in the air without a dramatic, postmortem endorsement. The eschatological pattern of humiliation and suffering followed by vindication runs throughout his proclamation.[61] The hungry become filled. Mourners are comforted. The humble are exalted. More particularly, Jesus looks forward to his own vindication at the resurrection of the dead, thought of as near.[62] Given all this, his torture without his vindication, his execution without his resurrection, would surely, in the minds of most of his public, have invalidated his eschatological optimism — especially since he ended his life on a cross and so perhaps was, according to Deut 21:13, under the curse of God (Gal 3:13; cf. 11QTemple 64:12). The situation would have been even graver if he was remembered as having cried out, near death, "My God, my God, why have you forsaken me?" (Mark 15:34). My own guess is that some of Jesus' closest followers would have continued to hope for his vindication at the general resurrection of the just, but surely a wider public would not have gone along.[63] One remembers that the apostasy of Sabbatai Sevi, his death, and then the death of his prophet, Nathan of Gaza, turned Sabbateanism from a mass movement into a small, insignificant, esoteric religion. To this extent, Luke 24:21, which records disillusionment following the crucifixion, rings true: "We had hoped that he was the one to redeem Israel." Without proclamation of the resurrection, probably only a few would have summoned the inner resources to reckon Jesus anything other than a false prophet, and so his cause might eventually have been lost to oblivion.

---

61. Dale C. Allison Jr., *Jesus of Nazareth: Millenarian Prophet* (Minneapolis: Fortress, 1998), 131–36.

62. See Allison, *End of the Ages*, 137–40; idem, *Jesus*, 136–41, 147–51.

63. See further Allison, *End of the Ages*, 164–66; and below, 321–24.

Unlike the wisdom sayings of Proverbs, Jesus' sometimes other-worldly, sometimes ascetical, often eschatological, often counterintuitive teachings — "Love your enemies," do not be "angry," do not divorce and remarry — are not self-validating.[64] On the contrary, they are at every turn debatable.[65] They further self-destruct if the humble, including Jesus himself, are never exalted. So the crucifixion and Jesus' cry of dereliction require a sequel. If they do not receive one, most of Jesus' speech loses much of its plausibility, and he becomes just another futile dreamer, a messianic pretender whose words may be dismissed as fantasy. But if the resurrection is the sequel, then God has "transformed the fate of the lost Jesus by openly and finally acting out in the person of Jesus the image of God that Jesus had espoused."[66]

The early Christian claim that Jesus rose from the dead confirms my point. Let me put it this way. Either God raised Jesus from the dead, or the disciples somehow got the job done in their imaginations. If it was God, then the Deity thought that crucifixion was not the appropriate finale to the story of Jesus, that something in his history cried out for a different ending. If, however, it was disciples who, through deceit or self-deception, raised Jesus into Christian mythology, then clearly they felt the same way: something was wrong with death having the last word with their master, so they persuaded themselves and others that it had not. In either case, whether it was God or the disciples, crucifixion was deemed to be the wrong denouement. Resurrection was needed.

A second personal reason for wanting Jesus to have been literally raised is that I like the sort of God who would do such a thing. I am reluctantly a cryptic Deist. My tendency is to live my life as though God made the world and then went away. It is hard for me to see the hand of Providence either in human history or in individual lives, including my own. My hope, however, is that I am in this particular blind and that the Creator is not as indifferent and distant as appears to me. So I would

---

64. Matt 5:44, 22; Mark 10:11–12; cf. David Catchpole, *Resurrection People: Studies in the Resurrection Narratives in the Gospels* (London: Darton, Longman & Todd, 2000), 215: "The historical Jesus *might* have been essentially a teacher in the wisdom tradition, but if so his mission would have needed no divine endorsement, for wisdom teaching is part of the common stock of human reflection."

65. See the commonsense objections of Baron d'Holbach, *Ecce Homo!* 151–70 (which anticipate Nietzsche). Cf. already the ironic criticism of the Jewish opponent in Justin Martyr, *Dial.* 10.2 (ed. Marcovich; PTS 47:87): The commands in the Gospels are so great that no one can keep them.

66. Jürgen Becker, *Jesus of Nazareth* (New York: de Gruyter, 1998), 363.

welcome an intervening God who, at least for a bit, cares more about making a point than keeping the so-called laws of nature, welcome a "ceaselessly imaginative God"[67] who comes out of hiding for a moment to break the monotony of death and to do something truly wonderful. I like happy endings, and this would be a very happy ending indeed.[68]

I also fancy the particular point that this happy ending seems to make. A resurrection from the dead could theoretically be an inexplicable quirk, a statistical aberration, the realization of an infinitesimal possibility, as in Stanislov Lem's novel *The Investigation*.[69] That is presumably how we would have to regard the resurrection of any random individual, about which most people would not care a penny, much less start a religion worth dying for. But God does not raise just anyone. The Deity, according to the New Testament, instead raises precisely Jesus of Nazareth, which implies an endorsement of that man's character, of the values incarnate in him, values that resonate with my deepest religious sentiments. As John Austin Baker has written:

> The nature of existence is such that the only credible God is one whose values are those exemplified in Jesus. If Herod the Great had risen from the dead, this would not have been tolerable to reason as a testimony to God. For a God who ratified monstrosity might explain the evil in the world; he could never satisfy us as a source of goodness. But the God who ratifies the values incarnate in Jesus . . . can be seen as having a good purpose which gives meaning to the evil in the world.[70]

Yet another reason that I should like to believe in the nonmetaphorical resurrection of Jesus is that this makes a compelling statement for the goodness of creation and so against *contemptus mundi*. To transfigure a

---

67. The phrase is that of Arthur A. Cohen, "Resurrection of the Dead," in *Contemporary Jewish Religious Thought: Original Essays on Critical Concepts, Movements, and Beliefs* (ed. Arthur A. Cohen and Paul Mendes-Flohr; New York: C. Scribner's Sons, 1987), 811.

68. Finding it all but impossible to demarcate the normal from the abnormal, I personally do not exclude a priori the possibility of a fantastic event or "miracle." Many, by contrast, are deeply troubled by phenomena not recognized by mainstream science as well as by an intermittently interventionist Deity; cf. Lüdemann, *Resurrection*, 12, who up front makes clear his agreement with Hume: the philosopher "demonstrated" that no testimony can establish a miracle (cf. 59). Hume's arguments, however, are, despite their long-running popularity, fatally flawed; see the critical treatment of John Earman, *Hume's Abject Failure: The Argument against Miracles* (Oxford: Oxford University Press, 2000).

69. Stanislov Lem, *The Investigation* (New York: Avon, 1976).

70. John Austin Baker, *The Foolishness of God* (Atlanta: John Knox, 1975), 278.

crucified corpse is another way of saying, with Gen 1, that the material world, despite all the evil we see in it, is nonetheless good. God does not abandon matter but redeems it. My Christian tradition has too often denigrated the physical through an unbalanced Platonism. In the second century such denigration took the form of Docetism, which drained Jesus of his humanity. In later times it took the form of excessive modesty and unwarranted shame concerning human bodies. The resurrection, which involves God caring for flesh and blood, neatly deconstructs these and related errors. It says that, despite the ills and sins flesh is heir to, despite the burden our arthritic bones become as we progress into old age, Gen 1 has it right, so much so that the creator of matter must be the redeemer of matter. Belief in the resurrection should allow one to recite the words of *b. Ber.* 60b without discomfiture: "Blessed is he who formed human beings in wisdom and created in them many orifices and many cavities."

A final cause for my finding the literal resurrection of Jesus congenial is that it entails his surviving death; and hope for a life after this one is, despite all of modernity's objections to it, very near the center of my own faith. I cannot believe in a good God and simultaneously disbelieve in a life beyond this one. Otherwise, I find this world irredeemably bleak. I know that many now find this conviction old-fashioned and superfluous. Some of my friends, with undisguised condescension, feel sorry for me. They regret that, in my weakness, I find meaning and hope in what is to them a fringe belief. It is enough, they say, that others will remember us, or that we will live in the memory of God. To want more is the sin of self-ishness.[71] And in any case, the philosophers and the neurophysiologists have made conventional immortality implausible.[72] To think otherwise is not to think but rather to wish the truth away. Given all we now know, to die must be to fall

> Into the Blank where life is hurled
> Where all is not, nor is again![73]

---

71. So Krister Stendahl, "Immortality Is Too Much and Too Little," in *The End of Life: A Discussion at the Nobel Conference Organized by Gustavus Adolphus College, St. Peter, Minnesota, 1972* (ed. John D. Roslansky; Amsterdam: North Holland, 1972), 73–83.

72. See Paul Edwards, "The Dependence of Consciousness on the Brain," in *Immortality* (ed. Paul Edwards; Amherst, NY: Prometheus, 1997), 292–307.

73. William Hope Hodgson, *The House on the Borderland* (Amsterdam: Coppens & Frenks, 2001), 20.

But I am with the tradition on this one. I cannot agree with John Dominic Crossan, who thinks about life after death what he thinks about UFO's: he does not know and he does not care.[74] For me, on the contrary, this is an issue of tormenting sharpness. Most days I sympathize with Dante in the *Convito*: "I say that of all idiocies, that which holds that after this life there is no other is most stupid, most vile, and most damnable."[75] The emergence in early Judaism of a robust faith in an afterlife of rewards and punishments was a way of maintaining belief in God's goodness and justice despite the agonies and unfairness of this world, a way of maintaining "that even a mortal life of disprivilege can have meaning and value."[76] The move is theologically compelling. In Michael Wyschogrod's words, "Either death wins or God saves."[77] John Hick is fully justified to argue that the denial of a life after this one is "the worst possible news for humanity as a whole," for it implies that "the human situation is irredeemably bleak and painful for vast numbers of people."[78] God cannot be thought good in any authentic sense of that word if the world as it is, this desert in which so many briefly live, suffer, die, and are forgotten, is the alpha and the omega, the beginning and the end. And I want God to be, as Jesus believed, profoundly good. The heartbreaks and horrors and injustices of this age cannot be squared with the doctrine of a consoling Providence unless all is not as it seems to be, unless there is something more than death and extinction. "Does God treat some people like garbage, casting them aside into nothingness without anything good ever happening to them?"[79]

Perhaps the relatively comfortable or well-to-do, such as the old Sadducees or many modern academics, can feel generally content with what they have and say to themselves, when they are through with life, "It

---

74. John Dominic Crossan, in *The Apocalyptic Jesus: A Debate* (ed. Robert J. Miller; Santa Rosa, CA: Polebridge, 2001), 158.

75. Cf. the depth of feeling in Joseph Butler, *The Analogy of Religion, Natural and Revealed* (London: James, John & Paul Knapton, 1736), 301: "Whether we are to live in a future State...is the most important Question which can possibly be asked."

76. Byron R. McCane, *Roll Back the Stone: Death and Burial in the World of Jesus* (Harrisburg, PA: Trinity, 2003), 137. See further Claudia Setzer, "Resurrection of the Dead as Symbol and Strategy," *JAAR* 69 (2001): 65–102.

77. Michael Wyschogrod, "Resurrection," *ProEccl* 1 (1992): 109.

78. John Hick, *The Fifth Dimension: An Exploration of the Spiritual Realm* (Oxford: Oneworld, 1999), 24–25. See further the remarks of Broad, *Religion*, 114–15, which are all the more poignant given Broad's religious agnosticism and personal desire not to survive bodily death.

79. William C. Placher, *Jesus the Savior: The Meaning of Jesus Christ for Christian Faith* (Louisville: Westminster John Knox, 2001), 159.

is enough." The malnourished, the enslaved, those whose dreams have died, and those who never approach three score and ten must often feel quite differently about things, as must death-bound, cancer-ridden children and their grief-stricken parents, who will never recover. For myriads, "death is the ultimate absurdity, the total annihilation of everything that a human life distinctively represents";[80] and miserable human beings, seemingly orphaned by a Kafkaesque universe, are justifiably malcontents. Many of them, sensibly enough, deny God's existence or God's goodness. Others hope for what they cannot see, a life beyond and after this earthly necropolis where God will no longer appear to mock broken hearts, where God instead will undo the sufferings of the present time. I sympathize with the former and side with the latter, as does a Jesus who is truly resurrected from the dead. The resurrection is the denial of death, and I want to deny death, or at least its finality.

DOUBTS

If I have motives for wanting to believe in the literal resurrection of Jesus, it is also true that certain considerations make me less than enthusiastic.[81] In other words, here I am a bit schizophrenic. One problem is a prejudice generated by all the nonsense, all "the literalistic pseudo-biological fantasies"[82] traditionally associated with belief in the resurrection, a belief

---

80. Neil Gillman, *The Death of Death: Resurrection and Immortality in Jewish Thought* (Woodstock, VT: Jewish Lights, 1997), 248.

81. The following comments place me within a large class of Christians from the last two centuries who have doubted or expressed reservations about belief in "the resurrection of the flesh." On this change of opinion, see Kirsopp Lake, *Immortality and the Modern Mind* (Cambridge, MA: Harvard University Press, 1922), 38–44; also Paul Badham, *Christian Beliefs about Life after Death* (London: Macmillan, 1976), 85–94. For the parallel development in Jewish theology, see Gillman, *Death*, 189–214. At the same time, there has also been a revival, at first in response to nineteenth-century philosophy and theology, and then in concession to the perceived demands of contemporary science and philosophy, of support for a materialistic anthropology and a physicalist resurrection among many Christian thinkers, an anthropology many have hailed (wrongly) as what the Bible teaches after all. See, e.g., most of the contributions to Warren S. Brown, Nancey Murphy, and H. Newton Malony, *Whatever Happened to the Soul? Scientific and Theological Portraits of Human Nature* (Minneapolis: Fortress, 1998), esp. the introduction by Murphy on 1–30; also the interesting observations of Gisbert Greshake, "Das Verhältnis 'Unsterblichkeit der Seele' und 'Auferstehung des Leibes' in problemgeschichtlicher Sicht," in Gisbert Greshake and Gerhard Lohfink, *Naherwartung, Auferstehung, Unsterblichkeit: Untersuchungen zur christlichen Eschatologie* (QD 71; Freiburg: Herder, 1975), 98–112. Again, for parallel Jewish developments, see Gillman, *Death*, 215–41.

82. The phrase is from Will Herberg, *Judaism and Modern Man: An Interpretation of Jewish Religion* (New York: Farrar, Straus & Young, 1951), 230.

that originated in connection with hope for a millennium or this-worldly kingdom of God,[83] a hope that, in its ancient form, I cannot share. Some rabbinic texts, recognizing the fact that human bodies inevitably, over time, become scattered and disintegrate, teach that all that needs to endure is the tip of the coccyx bone, about which the following tale is told:

> Hadrian — may his bones rot — asked R. Joshua b. Hananiah, "From what part in the body will the Holy One, blessed be he, make a person sprout up in the age to come?" He said to him, "He will make him sprout out of the nut of the spinal column." He said to him, "How do you know this?" He said to him, "Bring one to me, and I will explain it to you." He put it [the nut brought to him] into the fire, yet it did not burn up. He put it into water, yet it did not dissolve. He pulverized it between millstones, yet it was not crushed. He put it on a block and smashed it with a hammer. The block split, the hammer was cleft, yet it remained undamaged.[84]

Some rabbis also postulated that, since the resurrection will take place on the Mount of Olives (cf. Zech 14:4–5), and since many or rather most Jews are buried outside the Holy Land, God will surely make tunnels under the earth through which the bones of those in the Diaspora will roll into the land. "When the dead rise, the Mount of Olives will be cleft, and all Israel's dead will come up out of it, also the righteous who have died in exile; they will come by way of a subterranean passage and will emerge from beneath the Mount of Olives."[85] This is quaint, or rather bizarre, as are the rabbinic discussions of whether the resurrected will appear nude or clothed[86] and whether God at the resurrection will start

---

83. On the link between resurrection and the millennium in early Christianity, see J. G. Davies, "Factors Leading to the Emergence of Belief in the Resurrection of the Flesh," *JTS* 23 (1972): 448–55; and (with more caution) Horacio E. Lona, *Über die Auferstehung des Fleisches: Studien zur frühchristlichen Eschatologie* (BZNW 66; Berlin: de Gruyter, 1993), 261–62. It is no coincidence that Origen countered chiliasts in developing his own doctrine of a spiritual resurrection, or that, much later, Maimonides, in his *Treatise on the Resurrection*, argued that resurrected bodies would be needed in the messianic kingdom but not in the world to come.

84. *Gen. Rab.* 28:3. Cf. *Lev. Rab.* 18:1; *Eccl. Rab.* 12:5.

85. *Tg. Cant.* 8:5; cf. *y. Kil.* 9:3; *y. Ketub.* 12:4.

86. See *b. Ketub.* 111b; *b. Sanh.* 90b; *Pirqe R. El.* 33. Cf. *Sem.* 9.23: "In the same clothes in which one descends to Sheol will he appear in the age to come." It is probably against this background that we should interpret R. Gamaliel II's attempt to curb spending too much on burial clothes: cf. *b. Ketub.* 8b; *b. Mo'ed Qaṭ.* 27b; Saadia Gaon, *Book of Beliefs and Opinions* 7.6 (trans. Rosenblatt; 276–77).

with the bones or with the flesh (*Gen. Rab.* 14:5). One finds it all but impossible to restrain a condescending smile.

My own Christian tradition is just as full of similar nonsense.[87] Athenagoras, in defending the resurrection, faced the problem of cannibalism. What if a cannibal eats a saint and then converts? To which Christian body does the ingested matter belong in the world to come? Is the swallowed meal magically returned to its original owner, or does it stay assimilated to its new proprietor? The church father solved this dilemma by contending that human flesh cannot be digested, so God will happily never have to face the problem.[88] Is this not one theological opinion that science has indisputably falsified? One wonders what, were he alive today, old Athenagoras would make of organ donation.

English folklore holds that some people, in accord with their belief in eschatological reversal, have had themselves buried head down so that they will be right side up on the last day.[89] Others have had themselves buried facing Jerusalem, so that they will be facing the right direction when Jesus returns. All this matches the literalism on display in some Christian art which, evoking John 5:28–29 and anticipating some modern horror films about zombies, depicts bodies and parts of bodies emerging from the cemetery sod.[90] But my favorite illustration of misguided resurrection belief comes from a colleague. He avows that, in one Boston graveyard, there is a cemetery with a very wealthy family buried in a circle. All of the members are interred standing upright, faces looking inward, toward each other. This arrangement is to spare

87. See the sympathetic treatment by Caroline Walker Bynum, *The Resurrection of the Body in Western Christianity, 200–1336* (New York: Columbia University Press, 1995).

88. Athenagoras, *Res.* 5–8 (ed. Marcovich; 29–33). Later theologians continued to discuss whether food actually becomes part of the substance of one's body; see Kieran Nolan, *The Immortality of the Soul and the Resurrection of the Body according to Giles of Rome* (SEAug 1; Rome: Studium Theologicum Augustinianum, 1967), 105–23. Augustine, *Civ.* 22.12 (ed. Dombort and Kalb; CCSL 48:832), called the problem of cannibalism "the most difficult question" posed by unbelievers; cf. 22.20 (840). See also the discussion in Saadia Gaon, *Book of Beliefs and Opinions* 7.7 (trans. Rosenblatt; 277–83): There is more than enough matter to go around, so human bodies do not have to share any; further, God sees to it that a person's constituent parts are not mixed up with other materials. Incidentally, the structure of the argument Saadia is answering is remarkably like the Sadducean objection in Mark 12:18–27, with matter instead of wife: a man lives and dies; some of his matter is passed on to another man, who then dies; some of that man's matter then enters into a third man, who then dies; and so on. In the resurrection, to whom will the matter belong?

89. Jacqueline Simpson, "The World Upside Down Shall Be: A Note on the Folklore of Doomsday," *Journal of American Folklore* 91 (1978): 559–67.

90. That this is a very old artistic tradition appears from the north wall of the Dura-Europos synagogue and its literal reading of Ezek 37.

the blue-blooded snobs from having to cast glances at all the riffraff round about them who at the last trump will annoyingly be raised alongside them.

One cannot fairly criticize an idea by ridiculing its distortions, so let me turn to what is a real theological problem: the necessary discontinuity between Jesus' bodily resurrection and the proposed resurrection of the rest of us — despite the tradition's emphasis upon continuity (cf. 1 Cor 15:23, 48–49; Ign. *Trall.* 9.2).[91] If Jesus' rescue from death involved the transformation of freshly dead flesh, the same cannot be true for the rest of us. Suppose resurrection morning is next Monday. At that time the sainted Polycarp of Smyrna, burned as a martyr two millennia ago, will according to the creed be resurrected to life in the world to come. But what can that mean? Polycarp's physical body no longer exists. Maybe the atoms persist (although given the "foamy" nature of space at the subatomic level and the indeterminate or statistical nature of bosons and fermions, this is not at all clear). But the body those atoms constituted has ceased to be, exactly in the same sense that the World Trade Center no longer exists: it is gone. So what will be raised?[92] If a sugar cube, dissolved in tea, is then drunk, surely it has, in every nontrivial sense of the words, ceased to be; and another sugar cube reconstituted from its old atoms would be just that, another sugar cube. Why is the resurrection of the elements of a body disintegrated and dispersed abroad and once again part of the nitrogen cycle any different? As 2 Sam 14:14 says, "We must all die; we are like water spilled on the ground, which cannot be gathered up."

"It is no exaggeration to say that a historical survey of philosophical discussions of the resurrection would, in large part, be a survey of discussion about how a body that has been destroyed could possibly

---

91. The following doubts are ancient; theologians have constantly discussed them. For an early, influential, and unpersuasive attempt to answer them, see Augustine, *Civ.* 22.12 (ed. Dombort and Kalb; CCSL 48:832). For a later example see James Boggs, *The Resurrection of the Redeemed and Hades* (Philadelphia: J. B. Lippincott, 1872); his solution to the old objections anticipates Rupert Sheldrake's theory of morphogenic fields! Bertrand Russell, "An Outline of Intellectual Rubbish," in *Unpopular Essays* (New York: Simon & Schuster, 1950), 77–78, uses the old problems to discredit Christian faith.

92. According to 2 *Bar.* 50:2, "The earth will surely give back the dead at that time; it receives them now in order to keep them, not changing anything in their form. But as it has received them so it will give them back." One can only wonder about an author unacquainted with or able blithely to ignore the everyday processes of decay that turn corpses into skeletons and skeletons into dust.

be numerically identical with a body that exists long after the destruction."[93] It is not clear to me that this discussion has supplied us with any good answers. Many have nevertheless continued to believe that God will, at the world's end, gather the scattered particles of the saints from the four winds and reconstitute the bones and sinews and cover them with skin and then breathe into them the breath of life. Augustine and many others have believed, in the words of the Scots Confession of 1560, "The Eternal our God sall stretche out his hand on the dust, and the dead sall arise uncorruptible, and...in the substance of the selfe same flesh that every man now beiris, [all shall] receive according to their warkis, glory or punishment."[94] George Herbert spoke his faith this way:

> What though my body run to dust?
> Faith cleaves unto it, counting ev'ry grain
> With an exact and most particular trust
> Reserving all for flesh again.[95]

Yet this seems, if taken literally, a very peculiar faith in an altogether superfluous activity — especially if, as modern scientists claim, every atom of every element is wholly interchangeable with every other atom of that element. The atoms and molecules in Polycarp's body at his death were all different from those he possessed at, say, age twenty. So if God wanted to do so, could not God make three Polycarps, one from the martyr's atoms when he was thirty, another from when he was fifty, another from when he was seventy? Which one would be the real Polycarp? Beyond that muddle, Polycarp's body while yet animated consisted, at any given time, of an ever-moving, Heraclitean stream of molecules;[96] so his identity never inhered in his purely physical stability over time. Why then should God bother to make sure that his redeemed body — which would

---

93. So Michael J. Murray, "The Resurrection of the Body and the Life Everlasting," in *Reason for the Hope Within* (ed. Michael J. Murray; Grand Rapids: Eerdmans, 1999), 270–71.

94. *The Scots Confession, 1560* (ed. G. D. Henderson; Edinburgh: Saint Andrews Press, 1960), 52.

95. George Herbert, *The Country Parson; The Temple* (New York: Paulist, 1981), 165. Cf. Augustine, *Enchir.* 89 (CCSL 46:96–97): The elements of "the earthly matter which on the soul's departure becomes a corpse...will return to the same body from which they were separated."

96. This is not just modern knowledge. In discussing the resurrection, Origen, as preserved in Epiphanius, *Pan.* 64.14.2–6 (ed. K. Holl; GCS 31:423–24), speaks of the body as a river that is scarcely the same from day to day.

need to include atoms and molecules that have been in other bodies before and after Polycarp — be some edition of his past mundane body?[97]
Furthermore, if there is anything like a soul, then surely Polycarp's identity must lie in it, not elsewhere. But if there is nothing like a soul, if
Polycarp is his body, then once that body is burned and destroyed and
scattered, Polycarp no longer exists, so any resurrected Polycarp will be
only his duplicate.[98]

Peter van Inwagen, in defending the resurrection of the body, recognizes that the difficulties here are genuinely baffling. Since he rejects the
traditional notion of a soul, this philosopher's escape is to suggest that
"perhaps at the moment of each man's death, God removes his corpse
and replaces it with a simulacrum which is what is burned or rots. Or
perhaps God is not quite so wholesale as this: perhaps He removes for
'safekeeping' only the 'core person' — the brain and central nervous system — or even some special part of it."[99] This theft and cold storage
for later use at the last trump has a bad smell. It sounds a bit like the
rabbis on the coccyx bone, and if this is where literal bodily resurrection
leads us, then surely something is wrong. Isaiah may have said that God
is hidden, but this deceptive, body-snatching Deity strikes one as over
the top.[100]

---

97. The issue here is the thorny one of material identity; on the profound philosophical
puzzles involved, see Michael C. Rea, ed., *Material Constitution: A Reader* (Lanham, MD:
Rowman & Littlefield, 1997).

98. See further Peter van Inwagen, "The Possibility of Resurrection," *International Journal
for the Philosophy of Religion* 9, no. 2 (1978): 114–21; reprinted in idem, *The Possibility of
Resurrection and Other Essays in Christian Apologetics* (Boulder, CO: Westview, 1998), 45–
51. Reverting to the old cannibal conundrum, van Inwagen observes that "a wicked man who
read his Aquinas might hope to escape punishment in the age to come by becoming a lifelong
cannibal," for this would guarantee that all his atoms would, in the world to come, go into the
bodies of others. I find it telling that Murray, "Resurrection of the Body," 261–86, in upholding
a "reassembly" view of resurrection, can offer no satisfactory account of it. The objections are,
he concedes, indeed powerful. He then urges: "That we cannot see how resurrection is supposed
to go, that we cannot explain what God does to bring an annihilated body back into existence,
does not imply that God's doing this is impossible; it implies only that we are ignorant" (276).
I do not find this an encouraging argument.

99. Van Inwagen, "Resurrection," 121.

100. More substantially, van Inwagen's theory is, from his own point of view, an attempt
to defend a biblical doctrine, yet surely it does not match the statements and ideas of the
biblical writers. This is also true of the more plausible fission model of resurrection proposed by
Dean W. Zimmerman, "The Compatibility of Materialism and Survival: The 'Falling Elevator'
Model," *Faith and Philosophy* 16 (1999): 194–212; his model has the additional problem of
drawing to itself Calvin's warning about those who exhibit "a licentious indulgence in free
and subtle speculation" regarding the resurrection (*Inst.* 3.25.8). Zimmerman may or may not
supply an adequate notion of survival from a materialistic point of view, but a theory that
leaves human corpses in the ground forever to rot can hardly be identified with the traditional

My own considered opinion is that staking our postmortem identity to a literal resurrection because the Bible tells us so is akin to insisting on finding science in Genesis or seeing blueprints for the future in Revelation. I further believe, although this does not suit the reigning intellectual dogmas, that human identity is not constituted by the present physical body, which body will not be required in order to survive death.[101] I believe, rightly or wrongly, in a future existence free from the constraints of material corporeality as we have hitherto known them. A new *sōma pneumatikon* (1 Cor 15:44), as Origen interpreted this, does not strike me as outrageous;[102] but its material continuity with our present physical body makes no sense. What is the point of spatiotemporal continuity and how can it be possible if our future is not in the present space and time?[103] Apart from a scriptural fundamentalism, I see no reason why we should, on the other side of the grave, need to come back for our rotting or disassembled corpses. And moving then from the general to the particular, if I believe that the survival of human beings does not depend upon strict physical continuity, then does not Jesus' literal resurrection make him the exception, an anomaly, an aberration? I understand why Kirsopp Lake wrote: "If we hope for this [a resurrection] in our case in such a way as to resuscitate the human flesh which will be laid in the

---

confession of belief in *carnis resurrectionem*. What good is a materialist thesis if it cannot make a corpse stand up again?

101. I am wholly cognizant of the enormity of this claim within the present intellectual milieu. Herein all I can do to explain myself is refer to a few works that defend positions compatible with my own: Stephen E. Braude, *Immortal Remains: The Evidence for Life after Death* (London: Rowman & Littlefield, 2003); R. W. K. Paterson, *Philosophy and the Belief in a Life after Death* (London: Macmillan, 1995); John R. Smythies, *The Wall of Plato's Cave* (Aldershot: Avebury, 1994); John R. Smythies and John Beloff, *The Case for Dualism* (Charlottesville: University of Virginia Press, 1989); Charles Taliaferro, *Consciousness and the Mind of God* (Cambridge: Cambridge University Press, 1994); Mark B. Woodhouse, *Paradigm Wars: Worldviews for a New Age* (Berkeley, CA: Frog, 1966).

102. On Origen's views, which were later caricatured and condemned, see Henri Crouzel, "La doctrine origénienne du corps ressuscité," *Bulletin de littérature ecclésiastique* 81 (1980): 241–66; see also Wright, *Resurrection*, 518–27.

103. Contrast the *Westminster Confession*, which declares that Jesus "rose from the dead, with the same body in which he suffered; with which also he ascended into heaven" (8.4). The language is naturally taken to imply a movement from here to there within the same space and same time with the same body. This was certainly the traditional understanding — "The ancients assigned to the gods the heaven and the upper region as being the only immortal place" (Heraclitus apud Aristotle, *Cael.* 284a11). This is why Augustine had to defend the notion of physical bodies living on high without ground under them: *Civ.* 13.18; 22.11 (ed. Dombort and Kalb; CCSL 48:400–401, 829–31). The rejection of heaven as a place above us, although a modern commonplace, was rare before the Enlightenment; Gregory of Nyssa may have been an exception. Contrast Wright, *Resurrection*, 655, who doubts that ancient Jews thought of heaven as above their heads.

ground, we must postulate the same for the 'first-born from the dead.' If we do not believe, and would not desire this for ourselves, it is illogical that we should believe that it was so for him."[104] Broad was even more blunt: "The body of Jesus did not decay in the tomb, but was transformed; whilst the body of every ordinary man rots and disintegrates soon after his death. Therefore, if men do survive the death of their bodies, the process must be utterly unlike that which took place when Jesus survived His death on the cross. Thus the analogy breaks down in every relevant respect, and so an argument from the resurrection of Jesus to the survival of bodily death by ordinary men is utterly worthless"; it is "one of the world's worst arguments."[105]

One is all the more puzzled about a literal resurrection of Jesus because, at least according to the canonical testimony, his resurrected body possesses properties that we do not associate with physicality. He can, to be sure, be touched (Luke 24:39; John 20:20, 27), and he eats (Luke 24:41–43; cf. John 21:13). Yet he also appears suddenly out of nowhere, and he disappears into thin air just as abruptly (Luke 24:31, 36, 51; John 20:19, 26; Acts 1:9).[106] In Matt 28:1–10, he seems to be gone before the angel rolls away the stone, which implies, unless there was a back door, that he passed through the solid rock.[107] John 20:6–7 may, in like manner, imply that Jesus' "body had in some way disappeared from, or passed through, the cloths and left them lying as they were."[108] All this makes us think of something other than a physical body — although I

---

104. Lake, *Resurrection*, 253; cf. 245–46, 253; and G. W. H. Lampe, "Easter: A Statement," in *The Resurrection: A Dialogue by G. W. H. Lampe and D. M. MacKinnon* (ed. William Purcell; Philadelphia: Westminster, 1966), 58–59.

105. Broad, *Religion*, 236–37. Others, however, would turn everything around: since Jesus' resurrection was physical, ours must also be physical.

106. Calvin's argument, in his *Commentary on John* ad loc. (*Calvin's Commentaries* [ed. Torrance and Torrance], 5:202), that Jesus does not pass through the locked door in John 20:19, is tendentious and motivated by antagonism toward the Roman Catholic doctrine of the ubiquitous presence of Christ.

107. Luther emphasized this point in *Confession concerning Christ's Supper* (ed. Jaroslav Pelikan; Luther's Works; St. Louis: Concordia, 1961), 37:216–17.

108. C. K. Barrett, *The Gospel according to St. John* (2nd ed.; Philadelphia: Westminster, 1978), 563. Contrast John 11:44: Lazarus is still bound in his grave clothes. Chrysostom, *Hom. Jo.* 85.4 (PG 59:465), argues that thieves would not have first stripped the body or neatly rolled up the removed items. Cf. Cyril of Alexandria, *Comm. John* ad loc. (ed. Pusey; 3:109). For a modern attempt to turn the grave clothes into an apologetical proof, see Henry Latham, *The Risen Master* (Cambridge: Deighton, Bell, 1901), 29–96.

Because John 20:5–7 leaves Jesus' old clothes in the tomb, and because he presumably does not stand naked before Mary Magdalene, one has to ask questions about postmortem clothing (which was actually a subject of debate in medieval times); cf. Trevor Williams, "The Trouble

concede that modern science has made matter itself deeply mysterious — as do the facts that the appearances are intermittent, not continuous, and that, in Acts 9:7, Paul sees something the others do not.[109] This does not obviously accord with the belief that "Christ did truly rise again from death, and took again His body, with flesh, bones, and all things appertaining to the perfection of man's nature."[110] On the contrary, and at the very least, the Gospel stories imply that Jesus' "relationship to his body and to the world is infinitely more protean and pluriform than can be expressed in terms applicable to other embodied persons."[111] Origen, trying to make sense of the texts, surmised that the risen Jesus "existed in a sort of intermediate body, between the grossness of that which he had before his sufferings and the appearance of a soul uncovered by such a body" (*Cels.* 2.62 [ed. Marcovich; 133]).

No less puzzling if one stresses the bodily continuity between the pre- and the post-Easter Jesus is that the latter is not always recognized as the former. This is truly peculiar. When Jesus appears to the Twelve in Matt 28:16–20, some doubt.[112] When Jesus walks down the Emmaus road with Cleopas and another, unnamed disciple, the two disciples fail to recognize him (Luke 24:13–27). They catch on only when he sits with them at table and then vanishes (24:30–31). Mary Magdalene also initially does not perceive who Jesus is in John 20:14. How does one explain these traditions, which contrast strikingly with the story of the transfiguration, where Peter somehow instantly recognizes Moses and Elijah? Although the commentators give us a smorgasbord here, none of the entrées is very appealing.[113] Augustine suggested a divinely imposed

with Resurrection," in *Understanding, Studying and Reading: New Testament Essays in Honour of John Ashton* (ed. Christopher Rowland and Crispin H. T. Fletcher-Louis; JSNTSup 153; Sheffield: Sheffield Academic Press, 1998), 219–35.

109. Although in Acts 22:9 we read: "Now those who were with me saw the light but did not hear the voice of the one who was speaking to me."

110. This is the Fourth Article of Religion in *The Book of Common Prayer* (1928). Cf. Theodore Beza, *Confession de foi du chrétien* 3.25: "Glorification brought immortality to the body of Jesus Christ . . . but this did not change the nature of his true body, a body confined to one certain space and having bounds."

111. Luke Timothy Johnson, *Living Jesus: Learning the Heart of the Gospel* (San Francisco: HarperSanFrancisco, 1999), 20.

112. The Greek is οἱ δὲ ἐδίστασαν. On whether this refers to all or some of the disciples or to still others with them, see the commentaries.

113. For an overview of the history of interpretation, see Kathy Anderson, "Recognizing the Risen Christ: A Study of the Non-Recognition/Recognition Motif in the Post-Resurrection Appearance Narratives (Luke 24:13–35; John 20:11–18; and John 21:1–14)" (master's thesis, Pittsburgh Theological Seminary, 2004). See also Wedderburn, *Resurrection*, 29–37.

blindness and cited 2 Kgs 6:15–19, where the Arameans cannot see the angelic army all about them.[114] John Trapp thought Mary could not see well because she had tears in her eyes.[115] John Gill suggested that the two people on the Emmaus road did not know what was going on because their eyes were downcast in sadness.[116] Thomas Sherlock offered the pedestrian elucidation that Cleopas and his companion and Jesus were walking "side by side, in which Situation no one of the Company has a full View of another."[117] Frederic Godet thought Jesus had a new wardrobe, which made him unfamiliar: clothes make the man, I guess.[118] To be fair, more common than these detective-novel solutions — or at least more common in the past, when Ps.-Mark 16:12 ("he appeared in another form," ἐν ἑτέρᾳ μορφῇ) was still thought to be an original part of the Gospel — has been the supposition that Jesus' body was transformed and so altered in appearance.[119] This, however, is to say that it became what it was not before; and if it was not what it was before, then why should we be so anxious to stress the physical continuity in the first place?

FORMULAS, CONFESSIONS, APPEARANCE STORIES

So much by way of preface. What do the texts themselves tell us, and what should we ourselves think about them? The relevant data, which

---

114. Augustine, *Quaest. Hept.* 1.43 (ed. Zycha; CSEL 28.3:24).

115. John Trapp, *A Commentary on the Old and New Testaments* (London: Richard D. Dickinson, 1868), 5:417.

116. John Gill, *Gill's Commentary* (Grand Rapids: Baker, 1980), 5:584. Murray J. Harris, *Easter in Durham: Bishop Jenkins and the Resurrection of Jesus* (Exeter: Paternoster, 1985), 20, says difficulty in recognition arose from distance, dimness of light, and preoccupation with grief, among other factors.

117. Thomas Sherlock, *The Tryal of the Witnesses of the Resurrection of Jesus* (11th ed.; London: J. & H. Pemberton, 1743), 68.

118. Frederick Louis Godet, *Commentary on the Gospel of John* (3rd ed.; New York: Funk & Wagnalls, 1886), 2:416–17. Even more ridiculous is the suggestion — beyond bizarre yet offered in all seriousness — of Geraldine Dorothy Cummins, *The Resurrection of Christ: An Explanation of This Mystery through Modern Psychic Evidence* (London: L.S.A. Publications, 1947), that the strenuous effort it took to rise from the dead aged Jesus considerably. The only response to this can be dumbstruck admiration for human ingenuity, even when it is in the cause of nonsense.

119. E.g., Raymond E. Brown, *The Gospel according to John* (AB 29A; Garden City, NY: Doubleday, 1966), 2:1009; and Brooke Foss Westcott, *The Gospel of the Resurrection: Thoughts on Its Relation to Reason and History* (7th ed.; London: Macmillan, 1891), 162–63 (implying, incidentally, that the use of "flesh and bones" instead of "flesh and blood" in Luke 24:39 hints at a bloodless body). Cf. Goulburn, *Resurrection*, 174–82.

can only be concisely introduced here, fall into three categories — the primitive formulas and confessions about the resurrection, the stories of Jesus appearing to others, and the traditions about the empty tomb. Setting aside the issue of the empty tomb for later, here are the data from the first two categories.

Formulas and Confessions

1. Several early Christian texts supply variants of a simple sentence:

θεός (ὁ) (God [who]) as the subject +

ἐγείρειν (to raise) as the verb (in both finite and participial forms) +

(τὸν) Ἰησοῦν (Jesus) or Χριστόν (Christ) or αὐτόν (him) as the object +

ἐκ (τῶν) νεκρῶν (from the dead) as a prepositional qualifier

This formula is attested in Rom 4:24; 6:4; 8:11 (*bis*); 10:9; Gal 1:1; Eph 1:20; Col 2:12; 1 Thess 1:10; 1 Pet 1:21; and Pol. *Phil.* 2.1. A shorter version of this standard sentence, without the qualifier, "from the dead," also appears: Acts 3:26; 10:40; 13:33; 1 Cor 6:14; 15:15; and 2 Cor 4:14.

The antiquity of θεὸς [ὁ] ἤγειρεν τὸν Ἰησοῦν ἐκ [τῶν] νεκρῶν — which is already interpretation rather than a straightforward statement of experience — is established by its appearance in Paul's earliest extant Epistle, 1 Thessalonians, as well as by its occurrence outside his writings (Acts, 1 Peter, Polycarp). The formula presumably goes back to the earliest Aramaic community, as Klaus Wengst has argued. It resembles clauses from standard Jewish confessional statements, such as the last line of the Shema ("I am the Lord your God, who brought you out of Egypt"; cf. Num 15:41) and Isa 45:6–7, which is taken up into the first blessing before the morning Shema ("the one fashioning light and darkness ... I am the Lord, the one who is doing these things").[120] In each case the form is:

---

120. Klaus Wengst, *Christologische Formeln und Lieder des Urchristentums* (Gütersloh: Gerd Mohn, 1972), 27–48. Cf. also Exod 16:6 ("the Lord who brought you out of the land of Egypt"); Deut 8:14 ("God, who brought you out of the land of Egypt"); Jer 16:14 and 23:7 ("the Lord ... who brought the people of Israel up out of the land of Egypt"; the phrase is reworked in 16:15 and 23:8); Pss 115:15; 121:2 ("the Lord, who made heaven and earth").

God as subject (+ who) + salvific act. There is also a resemblance between the Christian affirmation and the famous line in the second benediction of the Shemoneh Esreh, "Blessed are you, O Lord, who raises the dead [ברוך אתה יי מחיה המתים]."

"God raised Jesus from the dead" is an assertion without warrant. The formulation speaks about God and Jesus — about half the time there is no christological title — without stating how anyone learned about what transpired between them. Nothing is said, for instance, of appearances.[121] So the phrase "God raised Jesus from the dead" has no epistemological prop and in itself does not serve an apologetical end. This fact, as well as the regular connection with the confessional verb πιστεύω (believe)[122] and the existence of liturgical Jewish parallels, are consistent with a setting in Christian worship.[123]

2. Also traditional, although more flexible, was a statement of contrast between Jesus' death and his resurrection. First Thessalonians 4:14 and Rom 8:34 says that Jesus died and rose, Rom 4:25 that he was put to death for believers' trespasses and raised for their justification, 1 Cor 15:3–4 that he "died for our sins...and that he was raised on the third day." The simple scheme also appears in Acts 3:15: "You killed the Author of life, whom God raised from the dead" (cf. 2:22–24; 4:10; 5:30–31; 10:39–40; 13:28–30); in Ign. *Rom.* 6.1: "I seek him who died for our sake; I desire him who rose for us"; and in Pol. *Phil.* 9.2: "who died on our behalf and was raised by God for our sakes." It is also embedded in the formal, antithetical passion predictions in the Gospels (Mark 8:31 par.; 9:31 par.; 10:33–34 par.) as well as in Mark's conclusion, 16:6: "who was crucified. He has been raised." Because of the multiple attestation and its appearance in Paul's earliest letter, all presumption is in favor of supposing that we have here, as with "God raised Jesus from the dead," a very primitive way of speaking.[124]

---

121. Stephen Patterson, *The God of Jesus: The Historical Jesus and the Search for Meaning* (Harrisburg, PA: Trinity, 1998), 218–19, argues that "the simple, primitive resurrection tradition has priority over the appearance tradition," at least "conceptually." Even if this is correct, I do not see how it follows from this that "it is very unlikely that the resurrection proclamation arose in response to stories of Jesus' appearance."

122. Rom 4:24; 10:9; Eph 1:19–20; 1 Pet 1:21; Pol. *Phil.* 2.1.

123. See further Paul Hoffmann, "Auferstehung Jesu Christi," *TRE* 4 (1979): 478–89; A. B. du Toit, "Primitive Christian Belief in the Resurrection of Jesus in the Light of Pauline Resurrection and Appearance Terminology," *Neot* 23 (1989): 309–30.

124. Although Wengst, *Formeln*, 92–104, argues for an origin in the "Hellenistic-Jewish community."

It is intriguing that, in three of the passages just listed, Nazareth is mentioned and reference is made to crucifixion:[125]

Mark 16:6: "You are looking for Jesus of Nazareth, who was crucified. He has been raised."

Acts 2:22–24: "Jesus of Nazareth... you crucified.... But God raised him up."

Acts 4:10: "Jesus of Nazareth, whom you crucified, whom God raised from the dead."

This may not be coincidence. Given that the speeches in Acts are not devoid of old materials, it could be that 2:22–24 and 4:10 as well as Mark 16:6 preserve a kerygmatic sentence from a time and place where Jesus was still popularly known as "Jesus of Nazareth."

3. The two formulas just introduced are of negligible use for our purposes. They establish the antiquity of a couple of ways of speaking but convey no concrete information as to what historical or psychological circumstances might have encouraged their genesis. We may find more help in a third formula. Quite a few texts assert that Jesus' resurrection took place "on the third day" (τῇ ἡμέρᾳ τῇ τρίτῃ; Matt 16:21; 17:23; 20:19; Luke 9:22; 13:32; 18:33; 24:7, 46; Acts 10:40; 1 Cor 15:4) or "after three days" (μετὰ τρεῖς ἡμέρας; Matt 27:63; Mark 8:31; 9:31; 10:34). What gave rise to this way of speaking?[126]

One's first thought is that perhaps the true course of events gave rise to the formulations about "three days" or "the third day." Maybe they reflect the conviction that Jesus' tomb was found empty on the third day after his death,[127] or — although we never read that he "appeared to

---

125. Cf. Jean Delorme, "Résurrection et tombeau de Jésus: Marc 16,1–8 dans la tradition évangélique," in P. de Surgy, P. Grelot, M. Carrez, A. George, J. Delorme, and X. Leon-Dufour, *Le résurrection du Christ et l'exégèse moderne* (LD 50; Paris: Cerf, 1969), 120–21.

126. For a survey of critical opinion, see E. L. Bode, *The First Easter Morning: The Gospel Accounts of the Women's Visit to the Tomb of Jesus* (AnBib 45; Rome: Biblical Institute, 1970), 105–26.

127. So, e.g., William Lane Craig, "The Historicity of the Empty Tomb of Jesus," *NTS* 31 (1985): 42–49; Birger Gerhardsson, "Evidence for Christ's Resurrection according to Paul: 1 Cor 15:1–11," in *Neotestamentica et Philonica: Studies in Honor of Peder Borgen* (ed. David E. Aune, Torrey Seland, and Jarl Henning Ulrichsen; Leiden: Brill, 2003), 83; Martin Hengel, "Das Begräbnis Jesu bei Paulus und die leibliche Auferstehung aus dem Grabe," *Auferstehung — Resurrection* (ed. Friedrich Avemarie and Hermann Lichtenberger; WUNT 135; Tübingen: Mohr Siebeck, 2001), 132–33; Lohfink, "Auferstehung," 45; W. Nauck, "Die

so-and-so on the third day" — that the first sighting of the risen Lord then took place. All four canonical Gospels, however, have Jesus die on a Friday and rise from the dead by or before Sunday morning, a sequence that, while it may just perhaps be harmonized with "on the third day,"[128] does not account for the variant, "*after* three days." Given the difficult chronological fit, some have proposed that the specification was originally intended imprecisely and meant only "a little while,"[129] others that it alluded to Hos 6:2 (cf. Tertullian, *Adv. Jud.* 13.23 [ed. Tränkle; 36]) or to a tradition of divine deliverance coming on or after three days,[130] others that it was proof that Jesus was really dead,[131] and still others that it goes back to something that Jesus said, something which was close enough to what seemingly happened as to be later appropriated.[132] As these are all good possibilities, the most we can infer with any confidence is that Christians found three-day language appropriate because they believed that very little time elapsed between Jesus' crucifixion and God's vindication of him. This is some reason to suppose the Gospels correct when they represent Easter faith as emerging very soon, indeed within a week, after the crucifixion.

    4. First Corinthians 9:1 is strikingly similar to two verses in John:

Bedeutung des leeren Grabes für den Glauben an den Auferstandenen," *ZNW* 47 (1956): 264; Wedderburn, *Resurrection*, 50–53.

128. For the principle that part of a day may be counted as the whole of a day, see Gerhard Delling, ἡμέρα, *TDNT* 2 (1964): 949–50.

129. For "three days" meaning a short time, see J. B. Bauer, "Drei Tage," *Bib* 39 (1958): 354–58; and R. Gradwohl, "Drei Tage und der dritte Tag," *VT* 47 (1997): 373–78. Cf. Acts 25:1; 28:7, 12, 17; Josephus, *Ant.* 8.408; *LAB* 56:7; *T. Job* 31:2; *4 Bar.* 9:14; *T. Sol.* 20:7.

130. Karl Lehmann, *Auferweckt am Dritten Tag nach der Schrift: Früheste Christologie, Bekenntnisbildung und Schriftauslegung im Lichte von 1 Kor. 15,3–5* (QD 39; Freiburg: Herder, 1968), 176–81, 262–90; Harvey K. McArthur, "On the Third Day," *NTS* 18 (1971): 81–86.

131. *Sem.* 8:1 v. 1. records the habit of visiting graves "until the third day" in order to prevent premature burial (examples of which *Semaḥoth* gives). This custom is undoubtedly related to the folk belief, presupposed by John 11:17, 39; *T. Job* 53:7; and *4 Bar.* 9:12–14, that the soul of an individual remains near its body for three days after death. *Gen. Rab.* 100:7 reads: "Up to the third day the soul keeps returning to the body, thinking that it will go back in"; cf. *y. Mo'ed. Qat.* 3:5; *Tanḥ.* Gen 10:4; *Lev. Rab.* 18:1.

132. Cf. the predictions of the temple's restoration on or three days after its destruction (John 2:19; Mark 14:58 par.) and see esp. Joachim Jeremias, "Die Drei-Tage Worte der Evangelisten," in *Tradition und Glaube: Das frühe Christentum in seiner Umwelt: Festgabe für Karl Georg Kuhn zum 65. Geburtstag* (ed. Gert Jeremias, Heinz-Wolfgang Kuhn, and Hartmut Stegemann; Göttingen: Vandenhoeck & Ruprecht, 1971), 221–29. There is not enough evidence to show that the third day has anything to do with pre-Christian stories of gods dying and rising, although Bousset, *Kyrios Christos*, 56–60, still thought this possible; see Mettinger, *Riddle*, 214–15.

John 20:18: "I have seen the Lord [ἑώρακα τὸν κύριον]."

John 20:25: "We have seen the Lord [ἑωράκαμεν τὸν κύριον]."

1 Cor 9:1: "Have I not seen Jesus our Lord? [οὐχὶ Ἰησοῦν τὸν κύριον ἡμῶν ἑόρακα;]."

One can ask whether the coincidence between Paul and John preserves a primitive way of announcing the resurrection in the first person and so perhaps one's apostolic status as well. One might even wonder whether the original, firsthand reports of the resurrection took the form of "I/we have seen the Lord," in which case "the Lord" would presumably have meant something closer to "the teacher" (cf. John 13:13–14) than to the exalted judge of the world. Unfortunately, however, speculation on this matter is unprofitable. The sparse attestation of the formula, if indeed we should speak of a formula, permits only questions, not answers.

5. There is, fifth, the tradition in 1 Cor 15:3–8:

[3]For I handed on to you as of first importance what I in turn had received:
that Christ died for our sins in accordance with the Scriptures,
[4]and that he was buried,
and that he was raised on the third day in accordance with the Scriptures,
[5]and that he appeared to Cephas,
then to the twelve.
[6]Then he appeared to more than five hundred brothers at one time, most of whom are still alive, though some have died.
[7]Then he appeared to James,
then to all the apostles.
[8]Last of all, as to one untimely born, he appeared also to me.

This overview of foundational events has its close, sequential parallel in Acts 13:28–31[133] and incorporates, as almost universally recognized,

---

133. Acts 13:28, killed   1 Cor 15:3, died
Acts 13:29, laid in a tomb   1 Cor 15:4, buried
Acts 13:30, raised him from the dead   1 Cor 15:4, raised
Acts 13:31, he appeared   1 Cor 15:5, he appeared

a pre-Pauline formula.[134] Not only does Paul plainly say this (1 Cor 15:3), but he also uses words and expressions here that he does not use elsewhere: "sins" in the plural (ἁμαρτιῶν), "according to the scriptures" (κατὰ τὰς γραφάς), ἐγείρω ("was raised") in the perfect (ἐγήγερται) instead of the aorist, "he was seen/appeared" (ὤφθη), and "the twelve" (τοῖς δώδεκα). There has been much debate over the extent of the tradition before Paul. Verses 6b and 8 must be the apostle's own additions. But what else is secondary, or what if anything Paul has subtracted, or what stages the complex passed through before it reached Paul, we do not know.[135] We also do not know whether any part of the unit goes back to a Semitic original, as Joachim Jeremias urged, or whether Hans Conzelmann was right to deny this.[136] The one thing we can be assured of is that "since Paul has visited Peter and the Christian community in Jerusalem about five to six years after the crucifixion of Jesus, the tradition which he reports…can, at least, not contradict what he heard then."[137] Indeed, Paul knew Peter and James and presumably others who claimed to have seen the risen Jesus. First Corinthians 15:3–8 is not folklore.

Whatever the tradition-history of the passage and despite its brevity, 1 Cor 15:3–8 tells us that Paul and others were interested not just in the "thatness" of the appearances but also in their relative order (τῇ ἡμέρᾳ τῇ τρίτῃ…εἶτα…ἔπειτα…ἔπειτα…εἶτα…ἔσχατον)[138] as well as in the identities of important percipients: Cephas, the Twelve, James.

Perhaps Acts 13:28–31 shows us how the old formula behind 1 Cor 15:3–8 was taken up into public proclamation.

134. For another view see Robert M. Price, "Apocryphal Apparitions: 1 Corinthians 15:3–11 as a Post-Pauline Interpolation," *Journal of Higher Criticism* 2 (1995): 66–99. Among other things, Price unpersuasively argues that the tension between 1 Cor 15:3–11 (Paul's gospel is tradition) and Gal 1:1, 11–12 (Paul did not receive his gospel from human beings) demands that the whole section be excised as secondary.

135. For the issues see John Kloppenborg, "An Analysis of the Pre-Pauline Formula in 1 Cor 15:3b–5 in Light of Some Recent Literature," *CBQ* 40 (1978): 351–57; and Jerome Murphy-O'Connor, "Tradition and Redaction in 1 Cor 15:3–7," *CBQ* 43 (1981): 582–89. Many believe, with some justification, that an early form ended with "to Peter and the Twelve"; see esp. Wilhelm Pratscher, *Der Herrenbruder Jakobus und die Jakobustradition* (FRLANT 139; Göttingen: Vandenhoeck & Ruprecht, 1987), 29–46.

136. Joachim Jeremias, *The Eucharistic Words of Jesus* (New York: C. Scribner's Sons, 1966), 102–3; Hans Conzelmann, "On the Analysis of the Confessional Formula in 1 Corinthians 15:3–5," *Int* 20 (1966): 15–25. See further Lehmann, *Auferweckt*, 97–115.

137. Eduard Schweizer, "Resurrection: Fact or Illusion?," *HBT* 1 (1979): 145.

138. Barnabas Lindars, "The Resurrection and the Empty Tomb," in *The Resurrection of Jesus Christ* (ed. Paul Avis; London: Darton, Longman & Green, 1993), 127, suggests that 1 Cor 15:5–7 outlines "the steps whereby the primitive Church came into being": Jesus appeared to Peter; Peter gathered the Twelve; the Twelve gathered a larger group (the five hundred); following an appearance to James, "all the apostles" were commissioned to do

One doubts, furthermore, that these were the only details people knew or cared about. It is, against Ulrich Wilckens, altogether unlikely that "Christ's appearances to Peter, James and Paul were reported in the whole of primitive Christianity only in this short form, in which only the bare fact is mentioned," and that before Paul there were not any "complete stories."[139] Wilckens's inference from 1 Cor 15:3–8, or rather argument from silence, is unconvincing. How likely is it that any Christian group was ever long content with sparse theological assertions unattached to stories and so unillustrated? 1 Cor 15:3–8 must be a summary of traditional narratives that were told in fuller forms elsewhere.

Surely no one would ever have been satisfied with the shorn assertions, "Jesus appeared to Cephas" and "Jesus appeared to five hundred people at once."[140] This is no more plausible than urging that Christians

---

missionary work, and the community moved to Jerusalem. Whether all that is so or not, Paul is surely offering a chronological list; cf. BDAG, s.v., εἶτα §1.

139. Ulrich Wilckens, *Resurrection: Biblical Testimony to the Resurrection: An Historical Examination and Explanation* (Atlanta: John Knox, 1978), 63. This explains, for Wilckens, Mark's failure to narrate an appearance story. Cf. E. P. Sanders, "But Did It Happen?" *The Spectator*, April 6, 1996, 17: "1 Corinthians seems to indicate that Christianity did not require any specific stories at all.... Paul may not have told stories at all. In converting Gentiles, he may have been content to express his conviction that Jesus had appeared to him and others."

140. The appearance to the five hundred might be a reference to Pentecost; so Ernst von Dobschütz, *Ostern und Pfingsten: Eine Studie zu 1 Korinther 15* (Leipzig: J. C. Hinrichs, 1903), 31–43; Lake, *Resurrection*, 203–5; and Lüdemann, *Resurrection*, 100–108. For the history of this hypothesis, see S. MacLean Gilmour, "The Christophany to More than Five Hundred Brethren," *JBL* 80 (1961): 248–52. For criticism, see James D. G. Dunn, *Jesus and the Spirit: A Study of the Religious and Charismatic Experience of Jesus and the First Christians as Reflected in the New Testament* (Philadelphia: Westminster, 1975), 142–46; and C. Freeman Sleeper, "Pentecost and Resurrection," *JBL* 84 (1965): 389–99. For the argument that the appearance to the five hundred should instead be identified with the story in Matt 28:16–20, see Seidensticker, *Auferstehung*, 28; cf. Wright, *Resurrection*, 325: "The appearance to the 500 was an occasion like that reported in Matthew 28.16–20." For the argument that it must in any case have occurred in Galilee, see von Campenhausen, *Tradition*, 48–49.

If the appearance to the five hundred is Pentecost (I am uncertain), and if Acts 2 is not wholly tendentious, then one must wonder about the appropriateness of ὤφθη in 1 Cor 15:6, for Acts 2 recounts no appearance of Jesus. Did a few at Pentecost claim to see Jesus, after which others did likewise? People can, with the passing of time, mistake an image called up by another's speech as an actual experience of their own, especially when the auditor was present at the time of the experience. See D. S. Lindsay, L. Hagen, J. D. Read, K. A. Wade, and M. Garry, "True Photographs and False Memories," *Psychological Science* 15 (2004): 149–54; also Leonard Zusne and Warren H. Jones, *Anomalistic Psychology: A Study of Magical Thinking* (2nd ed.; Hillsdale, NJ: Lawrence Erlbaum Associates, 1989), 117–19. On the general subject of confabulation and false memories, see Daniel L. Schacter, ed., *Memory Distortion: How Minds, Brains, and Societies Reconstruct the Past* (Cambridge, MA: Harvard University Press, 1997). We create false memories all the time even without social pressure. Inexplicably, I have a memory of reading Jonathan Z. Smith's *Drudgery Divine*, published in 1990, in a house I frequented only in the 1960s and early 1970s.

at first said things such as "Jesus went about doing good and healing all who were oppressed by the devil" (Acts 10:38) and only much later enjoyed telling miracle stories about him;[141] or that while Paul and others preached Christ crucified, no supposed particulars about Jesus' martyrdom emerged until decades after the fact, when interest unaccountably set in;[142] or that "he appeared to Cephas" was ever proclaimed without explaining who Cephas was if the audience knew nothing about him. (Later Christian creeds omit the appearances altogether, probably in part because the witnesses were no longer alive.)

Surely Martin Hengel is right regarding 1 Cor 15:3–8: "A Jew or Gentile God-fearer, hearing this formal, extremely abbreviated report for the first time, would have difficulty understanding it; at the least a number of questions would certainly occur to him, which Paul could only answer through the narration and explanation of events. Without clarifying delineation, the whole thing would surely sound enigmatic to ancient ears, even absurd."[143] In harmony with this common sense, which rightly assumes simple human curiosity and a desire on the part of Christians to communicate rather than obfuscate, is the high probability that, although Paul says next to nothing about his own encounter with the risen Jesus in 1 Cor 15, he surely was not, in the right circumstance, averse to offering some details. The apostle does this three times in Acts, and we shall see below that there is every reason to suppose that Luke got this particular right.

The confession in 1 Cor 15:3–8 contains several assertions that, whatever Paul's intention, have often been reckoned evidential.[144] One such

---

141. This illustration I owe to Richard Bauckham, "The Women and the Resurrection: The Credibility of Their Stories," in *Gospel Women: Studies of the Named Women in the Gospels* (Grand Rapids: Eerdmans, 2002), 261.

142. See further below, 236, 373–75.

143. Hengel, "Begräbnis," 127. Cf. Marco Frenschkowski, *Offenbarung und Epiphanie*, vol. 2, *Die verborgene Epiphanie in Spätantike und frühem Christentum* (WUNT 2.80; Tübingen: Mohr Siebeck, 1997), 229; and Gerhardsson, "Evidence," 88–90. Contrast Anton Vögtle, *Biblischer Osterglaube: Hintergründe — Deutungen — Herausforderungen* (ed. Rudolf Hoppe; Neukirchen-Vluyn: Neukirchener Verlag, 1999), 40, who implausibly asserts that imminent eschatological expectation and interest in concrete descriptions of the resurrection christophanies just did not go together. Pheme Perkins, "The Resurrection of Jesus of Nazareth," in *Studying the Historical Jesus* (ed. Bruce Chilton and Craig A. Evans; NTTS 19; Leiden: Brill, 1994), 440, similarly imagines, citing Q 9:59–60, that the tradents of Q were so preoccupied with "the urgent task of preaching the message of God's Reign before the coming of the Son of man in judgment" that this left "no place for their pieties of burial — or interest in Jesus' tomb."

144. Cf. Bultmann's claim that 1 Cor 15:3–8 was Paul's attempt "to prove the miracle of the resurrection by adducing a list of eye-witnesses"; see Bultmann, "Mythology," 39.

assertion is that there were multiple appearances, a minimum of six. Another is that two or three of the appearances were collective — "he appeared...to the twelve. Then he appeared to more than five hundred brothers and sisters at one time.... Then he appeared...to all the apostles"[145] — a point Paul in one case emphasizes (ἐφάπαξ, "at one time"). It is also intriguing that the text has Jesus appearing to James and Paul, and that the latter certainly and the former possibly did not have previous histories of commitment to Jesus.[146] All three of these circumstances have, rightly or wrongly, been reckoned as evidence against supposing that Easter faith was born of wish fulfillment or subjective visions, so we shall have occasion to return to them later.

The previous paragraph assumes that 1 Cor 15:3–8 tells of visual christophanies. As observed already, however, some scholars have emptied the ὤφθη ("let himself be seen," "appeared") of 1 Cor 15 of its normal, visual associations, claiming that as a formula of legitimation it need not advert to real or imagined visions.[147] This is wholly unlikely.[148] Regarding the issue of legitimation, not only can ὤφθη scarcely function to validate the authority of the nameless five hundred (cf. also 1 Tim 3:16: Jesus "seen by angels"), but 1 Cor 15:3–8 may cite prominent or authoritative individuals simply because they were well-known. If Jesus had appeared to the obscure Peleg and to the little-known Serug as well as to the famed Peter and to the important James, we would expect a creed to advert to the latter, not to the former pair. What would

---

145. Often in older works the appearance to "all the apostles" was identified with the ascension; cf. Latham, *Risen Master*, 273–94. More recent critics have sometimes suggested that "all the apostles" = "the Twelve." But it is not even clear that a single appearance is in view. The one good guess we can make is that "the apostles" were "leading missionaries"; so C. F. Evans, *Resurrection and the New Testament* (SBT 2.12; London; SCM, 1970), 51.

146. Although it is commonly supposed that James was no follower of the pre-Easter Jesus, caution is in order; see below, 261–63.

147. See Michaelis for an earlier presentation of the view that when ὤφθη is used "to denote the resurrection appearances there is no primary emphasis on seeing as sensual or mental perception. The dominant thought is that the appearances are revelations, encounters with the risen Lord who herein reveals Himself, or is revealed"; thus W. Michaelis, ὤφθη, *TDNT* 5 (1968): 355–61. Cf. Pesch, "Entstehung," 212–18.

148. See Hans-Werner Bartsch, "Der Ursprung des Osterglaubens," *TZ* 31 (1975): 16–31 (a criticism of Pesch that anticipates Pesch's later position); Karl Heinrich Rengstorf, *Die Auferstehung Jesu: Form, Art und Sinn der urchristlichen Osterbotschaft* (4th ed.; Witten: Luther-Verlag, 1960), 117–27; Franz Mussner, *Die Auferstehung Jesu* (Biblische Handbibliothek 7; Munich: Kösel, 1969), 63–74; and Vögtle, "Wie kam es zum Osterglauben?" in 44–68. Against the idiosyncratic view of Gérard Claudel, *La confession de Pierre: Trajectorie d'une pericope évangélique* (EB 10; Paris: J. Gabalda, 1988), that ὤφθη Κηφᾷ originally referred to the epiphanious pre-Easter ministry, see Jan Lambrecht, "The Line of Thought in 1 Cor 15,1–11," *Greg* 72 (1991): 655–70.

be the point of naming individuals not known to everyone? Regarding the visual connotations of ὤφθη, the verb in Jewish and Christian texts often refers to seeing heavenly beings,[149] and Paul, in 1 Cor 9:1, says that he has "seen [ἑόρακα] Jesus our Lord" (cf. Isa 6:1, 5). Surely this last fact must be decisive in interpreting 1 Cor 15:3–8, where Paul puts his own experience beside those of others. In line with this, Matthew, Mark, Luke-Acts, and John all know traditions about disciples ostensibly *seeing* the risen Jesus.[150] Even were one to judge all of the Synoptic and Johannine stories to be relatively late, surely it is easier to imagine that they represent not some unprecedented interpretation of the confessional ὤφθη but rather stand in some continuity with earlier tradition. Beyond this, it would be unhistorical to downplay the important role of visions within early Christian circles. The earliest Christian writer, Paul, was a visionary.[151] The earliest history of the Christian movement, Acts, attributes multiple visions to the first believers and sees in them the realization of the eschatological prophecy of Joel 2:28: "Your young men shall see visions" (Acts 2:17).[152] The earliest Synoptic Gospel, Mark, may present Jesus himself as a visionary (in Mark 1:10, the baptismal story).[153] Luke 10:18 ("I watched Satan fall from heaven like a flash of

---

149. E.g., LXX Gen 17:1; 18:1; Exod 3:2; Judg 6:12; 13:3 (in the preceding instances ὤφθη renders the niphal of ראה); Tob 12:22; Mark 9:4 par.; Luke 1:11; Acts 7:2, 30, 35; 26:16; Heb 9:28; T. Iss. 2:1. For discussion of LXX usage, see Claus Bussmann, *Themen der paulinischen Missionspredigt auf dem Hintergrund der spätjüdisch-hellenistischen Missionsliteratur* (2nd ed.; Bern: Herbert Lang, 1975), 97–101. It may well be, as several have argued, that the early Christian use of ὤφθη was modeled upon the language of LXX theophanies:

Gen 12:7	ὤφθη κύριος τῷ 'Αβράμ
Gen 26:2	ὤφθη αὐτῷ κύριος
1 Kings 3:5	ὤφθη κύριος τῷ Σαλωμών
1 Kings 9:2	ὤφθη κύριος τῷ Σαλωμών
2 Chron 3:1	ὤφθη κύριος τῷ Δαυίδ
Luke 24:34	ὁ κύριος...ὤφθη Σίμωνι
1 Cor 15:5	ὤφθη Κηφᾷ
1 Cor 15:6	ὤφθη...πεντακοσίοις ἀδελφοῖς
1 Cor 15:7	ὤφθη 'Ιακώβῳ
1 Cor 15:8	ὤφθη κἀμοί

150. See ὁράω in Matt 28:7, 10, 17; Mark 16:7; Luke 24:23, 34, 39; John 20:18, 20, 25, 27, 29; θεωρέω in Luke 24:37, 39; John 20:14; φανερόω in Ps.-Mark 16:12, 14; John 21:1, 14; φαίνω in Ps.-Mark 16:9; Luke 24:11 (cf. Acts 10:40); θεάομαι in Ps.-Mark 16:11, 14; Acts 1:11; δείκνυμι in Luke 24:40; John 20:20; ὀφθαλμοί in Luke 24:16, 31; Acts 1:9; and βλέπω in Acts 1:9.

151. Bernhard Heininger, *Paulus als Visionär: Eine religionsgeschichtliche Studie* (Herders biblischen Studien; Freiburg: Herder, 1996).

152. E.g., Acts 2:17–18; 7:55–56; 9:11–12; 10:3, 9–16, 30; 16:9–10; 18:9; 22:17–18; 23:11; 27:23.

153. Joel Marcus, "Jesus' Baptismal Vision," *NTS* 41 (1995): 512–21.

lightning") almost certainly does.[154] And the three Synoptics, when they tell of Jesus being transfigured, make the disciples visionaries (Mark 9:2–8 par.).[155] Perhaps Q's temptation narrative belongs here, too; at least Origen took Matt 4:1–11 = Luke 4:1–12 to record a vision.[156] However that may be, given the religious enthusiasm of the early Jesus movement and the number of visionary experiences in the New Testament, why balk at the meaning that commentators have customarily and naturally given to ὤφθη over the course of two thousand years?

One final observation about 1 Cor 15. Although its distance from the canonical accounts is often emphasized — there are no women in Paul's account, for example, and the Gospels intimate nothing of an appearance to James — these should not be allowed to obscure the sequential similarities, which can be exhibited this way:

	Matthew	Mark	Luke	John	1 Cor
death	27:45–54	15:33–39	23:44–48	19:28–30	15:3
burial	27:56–61	15:42–47	23:50–55	19:38–42	15:4a
resurrection on third day	28:1–8	16:1–8	24:1–8	20:1–10	15:4b
appearance to individuals	28:9–10	16:7 (?)	24:13–35	20:11–18	15:5a, 7a, 8
appearance to 11 or 12 disciples/apostles	28:16–20	16:7	24:36–51	20:19–22	15:5b, 7b

Amid all the diversity, we seem to have variations upon a common pattern. Paul is perhaps not so far removed from the Gospel traditions as sometimes implied.

Appearance Stories[157]

1. First Corinthians 15:5 speaks without elaboration of an appearance to Cephas (= Peter): ὤφθη Κηφᾷ. The importance of this encounter is

---

154. Ulrich B. Müller, "Vision und Botschaft: Erwägungen zur prophetischen Struktur der Verkündigung Jesu," *ZTK* 74 (1977): 416–48.

155. John J. Pilch, "The Transfiguration of Jesus: An Experience of Alternate Reality," in *Modelling Early Christianity: Social-scientific Studies of the New Testament in Its Context* (ed. Philip F. Esler; London: Routledge, 1995), 47–64.

156. Origen, *Princ.* 4.3.1 (ed. Görgemanns and Karpp; TzF 24:732, 734). His argument is that one cannot see all the world from any one place.

157. Here I pass over the Christic visions of Stephen in Acts 7 and of John in Rev 1 as not being foundational and so not informing us about the origin of belief in Jesus' resurrection. I

indicated by its initial placement,[158] which corresponds to Peter's pride of place on the canonical lists of the Twelve (Matt 10:2–4; Mark 3:16–19; Luke 6:14–16; Acts 1:13). Luke 24:34 refers to this same event: "They [the Eleven] were saying, 'The Lord has risen indeed, and he has appeared to Simon!' " (ὁ κύριος ... ὤφθη Σίμωνι).[159] It is further possible that Mark 16:7, which makes special mention of Peter ("Tell his disciples and Peter that he is going ahead of you to Galilee"), reflects knowledge of a separate appearance to the apostle, although in the Gospel as we have it no such appearance is reported. However that may be, Luke agrees with Paul in putting the appearance to Peter before the appearance to the Eleven as a group.

There is no narrative account of this appearance, although many have found remnants of it behind Matt 16:13–19 (Peter's confession of Jesus and the establishment of the church)[160] or Luke 5:1–11 (the miraculous catch of fish and calling of the first apostles)[161] or 24:13–27 (the appear-

---

also shall not review all those texts sometimes thought to be displaced resurrection stories. For this view of Jesus' transfiguration (Mark 9:2–8 par.), see, e.g., Rudolf Bultmann, *History of the Synoptic Tradition* (rev. ed.; New York: Harper & Row, 1963), 259; and James M. Robinson, "Jesus: From Easter to Valentinus (or the Apostles' Creed)," *JBL* 101 (1982): 8–9. Patterson, *God of Jesus*, 228–29, suggests that the transfiguration actually conflates three appearance traditions — one to Peter, one to James, and one to John. Because I find these views problematic, I shall not review the transfiguration herein; see C. H. Dodd, "The Appearances of the Risen Christ: An Essay in Form-Criticism of the Gospels," in *More New Testament Studies* (Grand Rapids: Eerdmans, 1968), 121–22; and R. H. Stein, "Is the Transfiguration (Mark 9:2–8) a Misplaced Resurrection Account?," *JBL* 95 (1976): 79–96. Also uncertain have been attempts to posit an Easter setting for Matt 16:16–18 (Jesus' blessing of Peter; see n. 160) and Mark 6:45–52 par. (Jesus walking on the water), so I likewise leave them out of account. The most complete case for Mark 6:45–52 originally having a postresurrection setting is by Patrick J. Madden, *Jesus' Walking on the Sea: An Investigation of the Origin of the Narrative Accounts* (BZNW 82; Berlin: de Gruyter, 1997). For a strikingly close modern parallel to what Madden proposes, a parallel in which three witnesses report seeing a recently deceased man walk across a lake, see Sir Ernest Bennett, *Apparitions and Haunted Houses* (London: Faber & Faber, 1939), 37–39.

158. For a survey of modern scholarship on the appearance to Peter, see William Thomas Kessler, *Peter as the First Witness of the Risen Lord: An Historical and Theological Investigation* (Tesi Gregoriana, Serie Teologia 37; Rome: Gregorian University, 1998). On the equation of Peter and Cephas, which a few have occasionally doubted, see my article, "Peter and Cephas: One and the Same," *JBL* 111 (1992): 489–95.

159. Luke 22:31–32, where Jesus exhorts Peter to strengthen his brothers after he has "turned again," is probably an allusion to the event 24:34 mentions.

160. Cf. Reginald H. Fuller, "The 'Thou art Peter' Pericope and the Easter Appearances," *McCQ* 20 (1967): 309–15; Christoph Kähler, "Zur Form- und Traditionsgeschichte von Matth. xvi,17–19," *NTS* 23 (1976): 36–58; and Ernst Stauffer, "Zur Vor- und Frühgeschichte des Primatus Petri," *ZKG* 62 (1943/44): 3–34. For another view see W. D. Davies and Dale C. Allison Jr., *A Critical and Exegetical Commentary on the Gospel according to Saint Matthew* (ICC; Edinburgh: T & T Clark, 1991), 2:604–15.

161. So Grass, *Ostergeschehen*, 79–81; and Gunter Klein, "Die Berufung des Petrus," *ZNW* 58 (1967): 25–30. See further below, 255–58.

ance to Cleopas and an unnamed disciple whom later tradition names "Simon")[162] or John 21:1–17 (the miraculous catch of fish and meal beside the sea).[163] I argue (below) that Luke 5:1–11 and John 21:1–17 are probably informed by an old version of the initial appearance to Peter. If, however, I am wrong about this, and if none of the texts cited is a remnant of Peter's Easter experience, we remain in the dark as to why no early account of that experience — just like no early account of the experience of James[164] — has survived.[165] Perhaps Mark's Gospel originally went beyond 16:8 and did relate the encounter, which later became lost through accidental mutilation.[166] Another suggestion is that there was something about the story, whether or not part of the original Mark, that later Christians disliked, so they deliberately forgot it.[167] Perhaps it exalted Peter's foundational authority too much (cf. Matt 16:16–18) and so was less than congenial to many. Would supporters of James or disciples of Paul treasure a tradition instituting Peter's preeminence? Again, if the story were set on the Sea of Galilee (cf. Luke 5:1–11; John 21:1–17), we would expect at least Luke, who confines his accounts of appearances to Jerusalem, not to narrate it.[168] Hans-Werner Bartsch offers yet another proposal: the original christophany to Peter recounted

---

162. For "Simon" as the name of Cleopas's companion (so already Origen), see Bruce M. Metzger, "Names for the Nameless in the New Testament: A Study in the Growth of Christian Tradition," in *Kyriakon: Festschrift Johannes Quasten* (ed. Patrick Granfield and Josef A. Jungmann; Münster: Aschendorff, 1970), 2:96–97. Some have accordingly thought that Peter was one of the two disciples on the Emmaus road; see Rupert Annand, " 'He was seen of Cephas': A Suggestion about the First Resurrection Appearance to Peter," *SJT* 11 (1958): 180–87; and J. H. Crehan, "St. Peter's Journey to Emmaus," *CBQ* 15 (1953): 418–26.

163. See below, 254–59. The proposal of Renan, *Apostles*, 49, that Peter's visit to the tomb, as recounted in John 20, should be identified with Jesus' appearance to him, remains to my knowledge without endorsement.

164. The account in the *Gospel of the Hebrews* (7) is late and wholly legendary; see below, 261–63.

165. For an overview of opinions, see Kessler, *Peter*, 64–71.

166. Cf. Oscar Cullmann, *Peter: Disciple, Apostle, Martyr. A Historical and Theological Study* (2nd rev. ed.; Philadelphia: Westminster, 1962), 61; Gardner-Smith, *Resurrection*, 16; B. H. Streeter, *The Four Gospels: A Study of Origins* (London: Macmillan, 1924), 355–56. I have long been uneasy with the growing trend to hold that Mark ended at 16:8, and my doubts are now confirmed by the persuasive study of N. Clayton Croy, *The Mutilation of Mark's Gospel* (Nashville: Abingdon, 2003). But what the original ending contained is another question. Cf. the situation with the *Gospel of Peter*: its end is lost, the content unknown.

167. Carl von Weizsäcker, *The Apostolic Age of the Christian Church* (London: Williams & Norgate/G. Putnam's Sons, 1894), 1:11–19.

168. So Emanuel Hirsch, *Osterglaube: Die Auferstehungsgeschichte und der christliche Glaube* (ed. Hans Martin Müller; Tübingen: Katzmann, 1988), 41; and Stauffer, "Primatus Petri," 19.

the fulfillment of hope for the Parousia. Later theology, which moved the Parousia back to the future, had no use for such a story.[169]

Despite the dearth of available details, Lüdemann has recently argued that Peter (who sees a vision in Acts 10) was psychologically primed to project an apparition of Jesus.[170] Those in mourning often think that they have come into contact with a dead friend or relative.[171] The phenomenon is common enough that we may, so Lüdemann says, assume that it happened to Peter. When, moreover, death comes unexpectedly and there is guilt regarding one's relationship to the deceased, and when further a mourner has been heavily dependent upon the deceased, the grieving process can be inhibited. Lüdemann urges that this happened to Peter. Because of his complex situation, the disciple could not let go of his guilt or manage his grief in a normal way. So his unconscious mind conjured the resurrected Jesus to forgive him his sins.

This is an interesting hypothesis, although I do not see that it can be, depending upon one's inclination, either established or falsified.[172] People do often see the recently departed dead, a point to which we shall return; and as Averroës already observed, melancholy and apparitions are sometimes linked; so too stress and hallucinations.[173] Even so, Lüdemann's conjectures regarding Peter's state of mind are just that: conjectures. They do not constitute knowledge. In recent decades contemporary historians have been more leery than their predecessors of the viability of reconstructing and then analyzing the psycho-histories of men and women long dead. Concerning Peter in particular, we have no direct or even indirect access to how he felt or what he thought at any time. Nor do we know how he would have fared on a battery of tests to determine, say, his fantasy-proneness or transliminality.[174] His general psychologi-

---

169. Bartsch, *Auferstehungszeugnis*, 9–15.

170. Lüdemann, *Resurrection*, 97–100.

171. See below, 269–99. Lüdemann himself cites Yorick Spiegel, *Der Prozess des Trauerns: Analyse und Beratung* (Gesellschaft und Theologie, Praxis der Kirche 14; Munich: Kaiser, 1973).

172. The criticisms of M. Rese, "Exegetische Anmerkungen zu G. Lüdemanns Deutung der Auferstehung Jesu," in Bieringer, Koperski, and Lataire, *Resurrection*, 65–67, are far from conclusive.

173. Richard Bentall, "Hallucinatory Experiences," in *Varieties of Anomalous Experience: Examining the Evidence* (ed. Etzel Cardeña, Stevan Jay Lynn, and Stanley Krippner; Washington, DC: American Psychological Association, 2002), 99.

174. Apparitional experients are strongly inclined to fantasize: R. Lange et al., "The Revised Transliminality Scale: Reliability and Validity Data from a Rasch Top-Down Purification Procedure," *Consciousness and Cognition* 9 (2000): 591–617.

cal health and the extent and nature of his psychological trauma after the crucifixion are unavailable to our curiosity.

Lüdemann depicts for us a lonely Peter who, after Jesus' execution, was wrestling with great guilt. While this scenario seems plausible to me, someone else might imagine a postcrucifixion Peter who was thoroughly disillusioned with Jesus and thus angry at being led astray, and beyond that even grateful for not being arrested and punished with his teacher.[175] Perhaps, one might speculate, the disciple's major concern for a time was his own safety. In theory, it could have been his ostensible encounter with Jesus that created guilt or intensified it rather than the other way around. How good would Peter have felt about himself as soon as he believed that God had vindicated the man he himself had denied and abandoned?

Even if, however, we accept Lüdemann's suppositions, we are still left with the question why a hallucination led a first-century Jew to confess that Jesus had been "raised from the dead."[176] Half of the Jewish texts from 200 BCE–100 CE that speak of an afterlife do so without mentioning the resurrection,[177] and there was no single idea about life after death in our period but instead a variety.[178] Immortality of the soul or something akin to it is found as often as not.[179] It would have been easy enough for Peter and those who welcomed his testimony to declare

---

175. Here William Lane Craig, "Closing Response," in *Jesus' Resurrection: Fact or Figment? A Debate between William Lane Craig and Gerd Lüdemann* (ed. Paul Copan and Ronald K. Tacelli; Downers Grove, IL: InterVarsity, 2000), 194, has a point when he suggests this possible scenario: "Any mockery and contempt he [Peter] would face would be not for his failure to go to his death with Jesus — after all, everyone else had deserted him too — but rather for his having followed the false prophet from Nazareth in the first place. Some Messiah he turned out to be! Some kingdom he inaugurated! The first sensible thing Peter had done since leaving his wife and family to follow Jesus was to disown this pretender!"

176. Cf. Catchpole, *Resurrection*, 208–9 — although he seems wrongly to assume that a vision projected by Peter's own mind would not be "earthy" or "realistic" enough to satisfy the concept of "resurrection." The literature on apparitions shows otherwise: phantasms often present themselves as utterly solid and real. See further below, 290–92.

177. See esp. Hans Clemens Caesarius Cavallin, *Life after Death: Paul's Argument for the Resurrection of the Dead in 1 Cor 15*, part 1, *An Enquiry into the Jewish Background* (ConBNT 7.1; Lund: C. W. K. Gleerup, 1974). Stanley E. Porter, "Resurrection, the Greeks and the New Testament," in *Resurrection* (ed. Stanley E. Porter, Michael A. Hayes, and David Tombs; JSNTSup 186; Sheffield: Sheffield Academic Press, 1999), 52–81, is also worth consulting in this connection, although his minimalist readings are often not convincing.

178. See Cavallin, *Life after Death*; and Joseph S. Park, *Conceptions of Afterlife in Jewish Inscriptions* (WUNT 2.121; Tübingen: Mohr Siebeck, 2000). But Richard Bauckham, "Life, Death, and the Afterlife in Second Temple Judaism," in *Life in the Face of Death: The Resurrection Message of the New Testament* (ed. Richard N. Longenecker; Grand Rapids: Eerdmans, 1998), 80–95, sees less variety than many other contemporary scholars.

179. Relevant texts include *1 En.* 9:3, 10; 20:6; 22; 60:8; 62:14–16; 2 Macc 7:9, 36; 4 Macc 7:18–19; 13:17; 16:25; 17:18–19; 18:23; Philo, *Sacr.* 5; *Spec.* 1.345; *Contempl.* 13;

that God had vindicated and exalted Jesus without using the concept of the eschatological resurrection.[180] If, as Lüdemann contends, the first community knew nothing about an opened tomb, Peter and his fellow believers could have said, in a manner reminiscent of *Jub.* 23:31, that while Jesus' bones rested for now in the earth, his spirit was exalted in heaven.[181] Or they could have spoken about Jesus the way the *Testament of Job*, without using the language of resurrection, speaks about its hero: Job's soul was taken to heaven immediately after his death while his body was prepared for burial.[182] This is not, however, what our sources report.[183] Why? This is a question Lüdemann glides over too quickly, and it is not trivial. We shall need to address it ourselves later.

2. First Corinthians 15:5 refers to an appearance to the Twelve without elaboration; so too Mark 14:28 ("After I am raised up, I will go before you to Galilee") and 16:7 ("But go, tell his disciples and Peter that he is going ahead of you to Galilee"). Matthew 28:16–20 tells the story of an appearance to the Eleven in Galilee, and Ps.-Mark 16:14–18

Gig. 14; Wis 3:1–4; *T. Job* 39:12–13; 40:3; 52:8–12; *LAE* 43–47; Luke 16:19–31; 23:42–43; 2 Cor 5:1–10; Phil 1:19–26; Josephus, *Ant.* 18.14; *J.W.* 1.648; 7.344; *T. Abr.* (rec. long) 11–14; 20:9–14; 4 Ezra 7; *b. Ber.* 28b; *'Abot R. Nat.* A 25; *Tg. Ps.-J.* on 1 Sam 25:29.

180. That Jesus' vindication was originally understood as the realization of his Parousia (so, e.g., Hans-Werner Bartsch; see n. 54) or in terms of the noneschatological resurrection of a suffering righteous one or martyr (so Joost Holleman; see n. 49) are suggestions I reject. See Allison, *End of the Ages*, passim. From the beginning Jesus' perceived fate drew to itself the language of the eschatological resurrection. Even if some of Jesus' followers did not have a resurrection-centered theology — for this possibility with regard to the Q tradents, see John Kloppenborg Verbin, *Excavating Q: The History and Setting of the Sayings Gospel* (Edinburgh: T & T Clark, 2000), 363–79 — proclamation of his eschatological resurrection must go back to people who knew Jesus himself and were part of the earliest Jerusalem community, and this is all that matters for the present discussion.

181. Cf. *T. Abr.* (rec. long) 20:10–11; *LAB* 32:9; *Greek LAE* 37–38. This was also said about Muhammad immediately after his death.

182. *T. Job* 52:10–12. Cf. 2 Macc 7:36, where eternal life is gained immediately after death, despite the resurrection being future: 12:43–44. Against Ulrich Kellermann, *Auferstehung in den Himmel: 2 Makkabäer 7 und die Auferstehung der Martyrer* (SB 95; Stuttgart: Katholisches Bibelwerk, 1978), I find no clear evidence that any Jews believed that the resurrection of martyrs would follow immediately upon their death. The disappearance of the bodies of Job's dead children and their glorification in heaven in *T. Job* 39–40 is not the exception. The text fails to use the language of resurrection and is clearly modeled upon popular Hellenistic assumption narratives.

183. Occasional attempts to argue that exaltation language was original and that resurrection language came later do not persuade. The two conceptions existed side by side from the beginning and in several respects were "interchangeable," to use the word of Willi Marxsen, *The Resurrection of Jesus of Nazareth* (Philadelphia: Fortress, 1970), 47. Contrast Fischer, *Ostergeschehen*, 77–88, 97–105.

offers something similar, although no geographical setting is supplied.[184] There are also appearances to the Eleven in Luke 24:36–49 and John 20:19–23, the location in these cases being Jerusalem. All this contributes to what Markus Bockmuehl has called the "narrative mayhem" of the resurrection stories.[185]

It is an interesting question to what extent these several narratives are variants of the same tradition. They do, strikingly enough, all share a similar structure:

	Matthew	Ps.-Mark	Luke	John
Setting	28:16	16:14	24:33–36	20:19
Appearance	28:17	16:14	24:36	20:19–20
Response	28:17	16:14	24:37–41	20:20
Commissioning	28:18–20a	16:15–16	24:44–48	20:21–23
Promise of succor	28:20b	16:17–20	24:49	20:22

If the four accounts are indeed all developments of the same proto-commissioning, a judgment that commends itself,[186] this is probably the event referred to in 1 Cor 15:5 (ὤφθη...τοῖς δώδεκα) and thus "the best attested of all the appearances."[187] According to Gerd Theissen, "There is no doubt that it really happened."[188] It is just possible, however, that there was more than one appearance to the Twelve. If so, 1 Cor 15:5 would presumably advert to the first one, whereas Matt 28:16–20; Ps.-Mark 16:14–18; Luke 24:36–49; and John 20:19–23 could perhaps mingle memories of or traditions about two or more

184. Ps.-Mark 16:9–20 appears to depend upon the Synoptics; see James A. Kelhoffer, *Miracle and Mission: The Authentication of Missionaries and Their Message in the Longer Ending of Mark* (WUNT 2.112; Tübingen: Mohr Siebeck, 2000), 48–156. This does not, however, eliminate the possibility that Mark 16:9–20 also reflects independent oral tradition.

185. Markus Bockmuehl, "Resurrection," in *The Cambridge Companion to Jesus* (ed. Markus Bockmuehl; Cambridge: Cambridge University Press, 2001), 111.

186. So also Raymond E. Brown, *John*, 2:972–75; Albert Descamps, "La structure des récits évangeliques de la résurrection," *Bib* 40 (1959): 726–41; Augustine George, "Les recits d'apparitions aux onze à partier de Luc 24,36–53," in de Surgy et al., *La résurrection*, 75–104; Lake, *Resurrection*, 214–15; Vögtle, *Osterglaube*, 34–38; and many others. Contrast William Lane Craig, *Assessing the New Testament Evidence for the Historicity of the Resurrection of Jesus* (SBEC [Studies in the Bible and Early Christianity] 16; Lewiston, NY: E. Mellen, 1989), 272–76. Helpful is the detailed comparison in Alsup, *Post-Resurrection Stories*, 147–90.

187. Catchpole, *Resurrection*, 210. Pace Patterson, *God of Jesus*, 234, there is no good reason to wonder whether "appeared to the twelve" means that each of the Twelve individually had an experience of Jesus.

188. Gerd Theissen and Annette Merz, *The Historical Jesus* (Minneapolis: Fortress, 1998), 496.

encounters. Positing more than a single encounter, although far from necessary, would be one way of explaining why the variants of the proto-commissioning are set in both Galilee and Jerusalem: maybe the Eleven saw Jesus in both places, and maybe there were stories associated with each locale.[189]

Can we retrieve any historical tidbits from the various versions of appearances to the Eleven? On the assumption that the disciples were not hopelessly and insensibly alienated from the solid world, an apparent vision of or meeting with Jesus may well have generated some confusion or doubt (cf. Matt 28:17; Ps.-Mark 16:14; Luke 24:36–41; John 20:24–29). Such a meeting may also have brought, indeed probably did bring, consolation and joy (cf. Matt 28:20; Luke 24:52; John 20:19–20). One also guesses that an experience begetting belief in Jesus' vindication would almost inevitably have issued in a rebirth of the missionary impulse of the pre-Easter period (cf. Matt 28:19; Ps.-Mark 16:15; Luke 24:47–48; John 20:21).[190] And yet one must acknowledge that doubt, consolation, and mission are all standard fare in Hebrew Bible call narratives. And because those narratives have influenced the stories of Jesus' appearances,[191] the derivation of the motifs referred to could be in large part literary. Convincingly coaxing much history out of the appearances to the Eleven may be beyond us.

3. John's second story of an appearance to the Eleven, the story of doubting Thomas (20:24–29), does not follow the pattern of the other appearances to the Eleven, and it is unparalleled elsewhere. It does not look like an independent account but rather appears "largely spun out of the preceding paragraph."[192] Even were one to come to a different judgment, its apological nature — converting a doubter in a story is a way of addressing doubters in one's audience[193] — renders problematic

---

189. Cf. C. F. D. Moule, "The Post-Resurrection Appearances in the Light of Festival Pilgrimages," *NTS* 4 (1957): 58–61. Moule proposes that the disciples returned from Galilee to the capital for Pentecost. One may alternately surmise that they returned to Jerusalem and stayed there in the hope of the Parousia soon taking place there.

190. Cf. the link between mission and the resurrection appearance to Paul in Acts.

191. See esp. Benjamin J. Hubbard, *The Matthean Redaction of a Primitive Apostolic Commissioning: An Exegesis of Matthew 28:16–20* (SBLDS 19; Missoula, MT: Scholars Press, 1974).

192. Barnabas Lindars, *The Gospel of John* (NCB; London: Oliphants, 1977), 613. Cf. Lüdemann, *Resurrection*, 163–65.

193. Cf. *Ep. Apos.* 11 and the story of Apollonius's postmortem appearance to the doubting youth in Philostratus, *Vit. Apoll.* 8.31.

any attempt to recover an historical event behind it. Further, given the possibility of an antidocetic bent in the rest of the Johannine corpus, it is natural to suspect such here too.[194]

4. Matthew 28:1, 8–10; Ps.-Mark 16:9–11; and John 20:11–18 recount an appearance to Mary Magdalene. While Matthew's version includes another Mary (cf. *Ep. Apos.* 9–10), Ps.-Mark and John refer to Mary alone. The three sources imply that this was the very first appearance, even before Peter's.

It is hard to decide whether we have one or two independent witnesses here. The problem is not Ps.-Mark, which the canonical Gospels have clearly influenced,[195] but John, which some but not others believe here depends upon Matthew.[196] If John does here use Matthew, then Matt 28:8–10 would be our only source for the christophany to Mary, and some have assigned it to Matthean creativity.[197] So it is possible that Matthew made up the tale and that John and Ps.-Mark rewrote it.

Yet it is not at all obvious that John 20:11–18 is a rewrite of Matt 28:8–10, with which it shares so few words;[198] and one hesitates to

---

194. Cf. 1 John 1:1; also Luke 24:37–43; Acts 1:3–4; Ign. *Smyrn.* 3.2; *Ep. Apos.* 11; Jerome, *Vir. ill.* 16 (ed. Richardson; TU 14.1:17); J. K. Elliott, "The First Easter," *HT* 29, no. 4 (April 1979): 216. Lake, *Resurrection*, 222, commented: "The Docetics interpreted the ante-Resurrection life of the Lord in a Docetic manner . . . and the anti-Docetics interpreted the appearance of the risen Lord in anti-Docetic fashion." A docetic background is not, however, demanded by the evidence. The invitation to touch Jesus could serve simply to counter the suspicion that the disciples hallucinated; and the references to Jesus eating and drinking might be on a par with other attempts to correlate Jesus' prophecies with what actually happened; in this case, one could find the realization of the tradition behind Mark 14:25 ("I will never again drink of the fruit of the vine until that day when I drink it anew in the kingdom of God") and Luke 22:16 ("I will not eat it until it is fulfilled in the kingdom of God"). Ecclesiastical commentaries have often related this verse to Luke 24:41–43 and John 21:9–14; cf., e.g., Chrysostom, *Hom. Matt.* 82.2 (PG 58:739).

195. Kelhoffer, *Miracle and Mission*, 48–156.

196. For dependence: Catchpole, *Resurrection*, 157–58; John Dominic Crossan, *The Birth of Christianity: Discovering What Happened in the Years Immediately after the Execution of Jesus* (San Francisco: HarperSanFrancisco, 1998), 552, 560–61; Frans Neirynck, "John and the Synoptics: The Empty Tomb Stories," in his *Evangelica II: 1982–1991: Collected Essays* (BETL 99; Leuven: Leuven University Press/Peeters, 1991), 571–600; idem, "Note on Mt 28,9–10," in his *Evangelica III, 1992–2000: Collected Essays* (BETL 150; Leuven: Leuven University Press/Peeters, 2001), 578–84.

197. Catchpole, *Resurrection*, 41–42; Frans Neirynck, "Les femmes au tombeau: Étude de la redaction matthéenne (Matt. xxviii.1–10)," in *Evangelica: Gospel Studies — Études d'Évangile* (BETL 60; Leuven: Leuven University Press/Peeters, 1982), 273–96.

198. Lake, I believe, hit the truth about John and the Synoptics a hundred years ago: "Possibly he [John] was acquainted with the Synoptic Gospels or with their sources, but, except in one or two cases, made no direct use of them" (*Resurrection*, 9). Nevertheless, this does not help us with individual passages.

categorize Matt 28:8–10 as a purely editorial creation:[199] τρέχω (v. 8) and ὑπαντάω (v. 9) are nowhere else redactional, and one cannot see that the verses forward any clear Matthean theme or interest. "The Evangelist can hardly have felt that the angel's message needed the reinforcement of Jesus Himself, and it is difficult to think of any other reason why it should have been invented."[200] Jesus' words in verse 10 ("Go and tell my brothers to go to Galilee; there they will see me") do nothing but repeat what the angel says in verse 7 and so are redundant.

Even granted that for Mary's christophany we have two independent sources, Matthew and John, one might resist drawing any historical inferences. Mary Magdalene was associated in the tradition with the discovery of the empty tomb and an angelophany (cf. Mark 16:1–8), and it takes slight effort to imagine tradents eventually granting her a christophany even though she never had one.[201]

Jeremias thought otherwise. He found the report of Jesus appearing to Mary "quite credible" and defended his judgment with these words: "Were it a fabrication, the first appearance would not have been said to be to a woman, as women were not qualified to give testimony. There is also a ring of truth about the note that the two experiences of Mary of Magdala, the appearances of the angels and of Christ, at first had no effect: no one believed her (Luke 24.10f., 23; Ps.-Mark 16.10f.). This sounds credible because it does not put the disciples in a good light."[202] C. H. Dodd, appealing not to argument but to his own intuition, issued

---

199. Cf. James D. G. Dunn, *Jesus Remembered* (Grand Rapids: Eerdmans, 2003), 841–43; Joachim Gnilka, *Das Matthäusevangelium* (HTKNT I/1.2; Freiburg: Herder, 1988), 2:492–93; and Roman Kühschelm, "Angelophanie — Christophanie in den synoptischen Grabesgeschichten Mk 16.1–8 par. (unter Berücksichtigung von Joh 20,11–18)," in *The Synoptic Gospels: Source Criticism and the New Literary Criticism* (ed. Camille Focant; BETL 110; Leuven: Leuven University Press/Peeters, 1993), 556–65. For the possibility that Matt 28:8–10 contains part of the lost ending of Mark, see G. W. Trompf, "The First Resurrection Appearance and the Ending of Mark's Gospel," *NTS* 18 (1972): 308–30; also Wright, *Resurrection*, 624. Martin Hengel, "Maria Magdalena und die Frauen als Zeugen," in *Abraham unser Vater: Juden und Christen im Gespräch über die Bibel: Festschrift für Otto Michel zum 60. Geburtstag* (ed. Otto Betz, Martin Hengel, and Peter Schmidt; AGSU 5; Leiden: Brill, 1963), 252, also thinks that Mark's lost ending may have narrated an appearance to Mary.

200. A. E. Morris, "The Narratives of the Resurrection of Jesus Christ," *HibJ* 39 (1941): 318.

201. Cf. Lindars, *John*, 604; and Samuel Vollenweider, "Ostern — der denkwürdige Ausgang einer Krisenerfahrung," *TZ* 49 (1993): 38.

202. Joachim Jeremias, *New Testament Theology: The Proclamation of Jesus* (New York: C. Scribner's Sons, 1971), 306. He cites in support Pierre Benoit, "Marie-Madeleine et les disciples du tombeau selon John 20,1–18," in *Judentum, Urchristentum, Kirche: Festschrift für Joachim Jeremias* (ed. W. Eltester; BZNW 26; Berlin: de Gruyter, 1964), 141–52.

a similar judgment: "I confess that I cannot for long rid myself of the feeling (it can be no more than a feeling) that this *pericopé* has something indefinably first-hand about it."[203]

Although I neither share Dodd's "feeling" nor possess Jeremias' professed ability to hear "a ring of truth," I believe that there are good arguments for thinking that there was an old tradition about a christophany to Mary.[204]

a. Peter's name is first in all of the lists that name the Twelve.[205] This is usually explained by his importance, which was grounded in his being the first to see the risen Jesus. Similarly, Mary Magdalene is always — with the exception of John 19:25, where the principle of order is familiar relationship to Jesus[206] — listed first in the earliest sources:

Matt 28:1	Mary Magdalene and the other Mary
Mark 16:1	Mary Magdalene, Mary the mother of James, Salome
Luke 24:10	Mary Magdalene, Joanna, Mary the mother of James, unnamed others
John 20:1	Mary Magdalene
Gos. Pet. 12:50–51	Mary Magdalene, unnamed female friends

One explanation for Mary's initial placement, especially given the dearth of other stories about her, would be the memory that she first saw Jesus.[207] A competing explanation does not suggest itself.

b. Mark 16:7 (the angelophany) and John 20:17 (the christophany) probably contain variants of the same saying. Both utterances are addressed to Mary Magdalene; both are spoken near the tomb on Easter morning; both direct Mary to speak to the disciples; both describe what Jesus is about to do; and the two are structurally similar:

---

203. Dodd, "Appearances," 115.
204. So also Robert W. Funk, *The Acts of Jesus: The Search for the Authentic Deeds of Jesus* (San Francisco: HarperSanFrancisco, 1998), 478–79; Hengel, "Maria Magdalena," 243–56; and Ulrich Luz, *Das Evangelium nach Matthäus (Mt 26–28)* (EKKNT 1.4; Düsseldorf: Benziger, 2002), 417. Contrast Frenschkowski, *Offenbarung*, 252–53. For a survey of the issue and secondary literature, see Kühschelm, "Angelophanie — Christophanie." Kühschelm thinks that the christophany to the women and the angelophany to them are alternative ways of expressing the same otherworldly experience.
205. Matt 10:1–4; Mark 3:16–19; Luke 6:14–16; Acts 1:13. Cf. also Matt 17:1; 26:37; Mark 5:37; 9:2; 14:33; Luke 8:51; 22:8; John 21:3.
206. Cf. Hengel, "Maria Magdalena," 250.
207. Ibid., 243–56. Observe also the front position of James in Mark 6:3 par.

Mark 16:7   ὑπάγετε
             εἴπατε τοῖς μαθηταῖς αὐτοῦ
             προάγει

John 20:17   πορεύου
             πρὸς τοὺς ἀδελφούς μου καὶ εἰπὲ αὐτοῖς
             ἀναβαίνω

This is some reason to suspect that the angelophany is a version of the christophany or the christophany a version of the angelophany. I observe that, in Matthew, the words of the angel to Mary and of Jesus to Mary are even a bit closer, no doubt due to Matthew's love of parallelism: he consistently assimilates like to like:

28:7   πορευθεῖσαι
         εἴπατε τοῖς μαθηταῖς αὐτοῦ
         προάγει ὑμᾶς εἰς τὴν Γαλιλαίαν
         ἐκεῖ αὐτὸν ὄψεσθε

28:10   ὑπάγετε
         ἀπαγγείλατε τοῖς ἀδελφοῖς μου
         ἀπέλθωσιν εἰς τὴν Γαλιλαίαν
         κἀκεῖ με ὄψονται

c. Tradition has Mary, or Mary and other women, see an angel or the risen Jesus or both:

	Matt	Mark	Ps.-Mark	Luke	John	Gos. Pet.
angelophany	28:1–8	16:1–8		24:1–11	20:1–13	13:55–56
christophany	28:9–10[208]		16:9–11		20:14–18	

Whether Mark — which in its present form fails to narrate any appearances — originally contained a christophany to Mary is an open question for those of us who believe that the book did not originally end at 16:8.[209]

Mary's christophany could have been ignored in parts of the tradition because of a patriarchal prejudice. Carolyn Osiek has conjectured that 1 Cor 15:3–8 fails to mention the empty tomb because "faith is

---

208. Lüdemann, *Resurrection*, 131, seems alone in his claim that Matt 28:9–10 was, in Matthew's tradition, not about Mary Magdalene but rather about the Eleven or another group of disciples.

209. See further Robert H. Gundry, *Mark: A Commentary on His Apology for the Cross* (Grand Rapids: Eerdmans, 1993), 1009–12, who gives some reason for thinking that Matt 28:8–10 may depend upon lost Mark; cf. Trompf, "Resurrection."

based on appearances, not the empty tomb," and "the empty tomb necessitates reliance on the credibility of women, whereas the abundant male experiences of appearances do not.... Once the empty tomb is eliminated, it is not difficult to eliminate also the appearances to the women, which are tied to the tomb narratives and setting."[210] One recalls the comparable silence of Justin's *Dialogue*: the apologist, in discussing the resurrection, nowhere mentions Mary Magdalene or the other women and their experiences, despite his knowledge of Synoptic and Synoptic-like traditions.

One may further speculate that in addition to a patriarchal discrimination, Mary was widely known as one "from whom seven demons had gone out" (Luke 8:2; Ps.-Mark 16:9), and that this discouraged the telling of her christophany. From ancient to modern times, critics of the Christianity have remarked upon the dubious nature of testimony from a former demoniac.[211] Even Matthew, who does report the appearance to Mary, rushes over it in order to get to what for him really matters: the appearance to the male disciples in 28:16–20.

d. Disregarding Mary's christophany, or turning her christophany into an angelophany, could have served to preserve Peter's status as the first to see Jesus. No doubt the memory that Jesus appeared first to Peter helped cement his authority. A desire to safeguard the apostle's status might, then, have been enough to demote Mary's role in the rise of Easter faith. If so inclined, one could appeal in this connection to the researches of Ann Graham Brock.[212] She has argued that the rivalry between Peter and Mary Magdalene — in *Gos. Thom.* 114;[213] *Gos. Mary*;[214] *Pistis Sophia*

---

210. Carolyn Osiek, "The Women at the Tomb: What Are They Doing There?" *ExAud* 9 (1993): 105. Cf. François Bovon, "Le privilege Pascal de Marie-Madeleine," *NTS* 30 (1984): 50–62; and see further Bauckham, "Women," 307–10. Osiek wonders whether the empty tomb stories are tradition from the private world of women, with 1 Cor 15:5–7 from the public world of men.

211. On Celsus see below, 327. For a modern illustration, see Klausner, *Jesus*, 358: "a woman who had suffered from hysterics to the verge of madness."

212. Ann Graham Brock, *Mary Magdalene, the First Apostle: The Struggle for Authority* (HTS 51; Cambridge, MA: Harvard University Press, 2003). Cf. Elisabeth Schüssler Fiorenza, *In Memory of Her: A Feminist Reconstruction of Christian Origins* (New York: Crossroads, 1988), 50–51, 332; and Trompf, "Resurrection," although Trompf thinks that the other Mary of Mark 16:1 was Mary the mother of Jesus and that certain sectors of the early church were not eager to give her family any more authority and so suppressed the christophany to women.

213. *Gos. Thom.* 114: "Simon Peter said: 'Let Mary go out from among us, because women are not worthy of the Life.'" See Brock, *Mary*, 74–80.

214. Berlin Gnostic Codex 7–19: Mary encourages the distraught disciples ("His grace will be with you and will protect you," *Gos. Mary* 9:16–18) and recounts her vision of the risen Lord (10:7–17:7). Then Peter testily responds: "Did he [Jesus] really speak secretly with a

1–3,[215] and other sources from the second century and later — goes back to the New Testament period. She then urges that Luke and the *Gospel of Peter*, both of which report an appearance of Jesus to Peter but not to Mary, exalt Peter's authority and do nothing to raise Mary Magdalene's status. Brock further holds that, although both books mention Mary's angelophany (as opposed to her christophany), neither entrusts her with a mission to inform Peter or the male disciples.[216] Now, I myself am quite unsure that the opposition between Peter and Mary in Gnostic sources tells us anything about first-century debates regarding the authority of women.[217] Even so, it is no stretch of the imagination to suppose that, just as later Easter narratives replaced Mary Magdalene with Mary the mother of Jesus,[218] so earlier narratives, in deference to Peter's authority, reduced Mary's role, either by omitting her christophany or by turning it into an angelophany.

e. Perhaps some consideration should be given to G. W. Trompf's claim that while "fiction surrounds appearances to Peter, James and Mary in apocryphal literature... there are no examples of entirely de-rived appearances to people *for whom no such appearances have already been attested.*"[219] If this conservative convention goes back to the first century, the implication is that Matthew and John would not have recorded an appearance of Jesus to Mary Magdalene unless they knew a tradition to that effect.

To sum up: It is, in Gerd Theissen's words, "more probable that an original tradition of a protophany to Mary Magdalene has been sup-pressed than that it first came into being at a later date."[220] To this I add

---

woman rather than openly with us, and not openly? Are we to [turn] about and all heed her? Has he preferred her to us?" (17:18–22). See Brock, *Mary*, 81–86.

215. See, e.g., *Pistis Sophia* 1:36 (Peter: "We are not able to suffer this woman who takes the opportunity from us, and does not allow anyone of us to speak, but she speaks many times"); and 2:72 (Mary: "I am afraid of Peter, for he threatens me and hates our race"). See Brock, *Mary*, 86–89.

216. See further now J. Verheyden, "Silent Witnesses: Mary Magdalene and the Women at the Tomb in the Gospel of Peter," in Bieringer, Koperski, and Lataire, *Resurrection*, 457–82.

217. See the review of Brock's work by Edith Humphrey, in *RBL*, available online at http://www.bookreviews.org/pdf/3161_3518.pdf (accessed 6/15/04).

218. See Brock, *Mary*, 129–40, discussing the *Acts of Thaddaeus*, Ephraem, Theodoret, Revillout Fragment 14, and the *Book of the Resurrection of Jesus Christ by Bartholomew the Apostle*.

219. Trompf, "Resurrection," 317n5.

220. Theissen and Merz, *Jesus*, 498. According to 497n36, Mark 16:7 implies an appear-ance to Mary Magdalene, for it should be understood this way: "But (you women) go and say to his disciples and to Peter: 'He goes before you into Galilee.' There you (women and

that the story of the women seeing an angel or angels at the tomb may well be a metamorphosis of the story of them seeing Jesus.[221] In spite of Mark 16:8 ("They said nothing to anyone, for they were afraid"),[222] other texts may rightly remember that the women related their experience to the male disciples: Matt 28:10 ("Tell my brothers"); Mark 16:7 ("Tell his disciples and Peter"); Luke 24:9 ("They told all this to the eleven"); and John 20:17 ("Go to my brothers and say to them").[223]

5. Luke 24:13–35, which seems to be summarized in Ps.-Mark 16:12–13, recounts the memorable story of two disciples on the way to Emmaus. This long and captivating narrative is "a little masterpiece of dramatic narrative"[224] and is reminiscent of modern urban legends about phantom hitchhikers who suddenly disappear, only after which their identities are learned.[225] It is so full of Lukan features and dramatic embellishment and so close to Acts 8:26–40 that one might be moved to regard it as a redactional creation.[226] The careful work of David Catchpole, however, has established the existence of a pre-Lukan story behind Luke 24:13–35.[227] Given this, one might hazard the next step and offer that the specificity of the rather obscure "Emmaus" — probably the place mentioned in Josephus, *J.W.* 7.217, although this is far from certain[228] — and the equally obscure "Cleopas"[229] preserve

---

the disciples) will see him, as he said to you." While this reading is consistent with my own conclusions, I nonetheless do not invoke it as evidence. It seems to me more likely that in this verse ὑμᾶς, ὄψεσθε, and ὑμῖν all refer to the same second-person plural, Jesus' disciples.

221. So also Martin Albertz, "Zur Formengeschichte der Auferstehungsberichte," *ZNW* 21 (1922): 259–69. See above, 250–50.

222. On this enigmatic line see below, 303–4.

223. See further below, 335–37.

224. Goguel, *Birth*, 48.

225. Michael Goss, *The Evidence for Phantom Hitch-Hikers* (Willingborough, Northamptonshire: Aquarian, 1984). The motif of an otherworldly being not being recognized is of course common to worldwide folklore and mythology; see 3 Macc 6:18; *T. Job* 52:9; Philostratus, *Vit. Apoll.* 8.31; *Acts Pil.* 15:6; Daniela Flückiger-Guggenheim, *Göttliche Gäste: Die Einkehr von Göttern und Heroen in der griechischen Mythologie* (Bern: P. Lang, 1984).

226. U. Borse, "Der Evangelist als Verfasser der Emmauserzählung," *SNTU* 12 (1987): 35–67. For a list of Lukan linguistic features, see Béda Rigaux, *Dieu l'a ressuscité: Exégèse et théologie biblique* (Studii Biblici Franciscani Analecta 4; Gembloux: Duculot, 1973), 225–27.

227. Catchpole, *Resurrection*, 88–102. Lüdemann, *Resurrection*, 140–45, finds only minimal pre-Lukan tradition. Frenschkowski, *Offenbarung*, 225–28, to the contrary, finds so much evidence of an Aramaic substratum that he wonders whether the evangelist did not hear the story from Cleopas.

228. For various alternatives see Roger David Aus, *The Stilling of the Storm: Studies in Early Palestinian Judaic Traditions* (Binghamton, NY: Global Publications, 2000), 217–30.

229. One might guess that he is the Clopas of John 19:25, whose son Simeon, according to Hegesippus apud Eusebius, *Hist. eccl.* 3.11; 3.32.6; 4.22.4 (ed. Bardy; SC 31:118, 143, 200), succeeded James as bishop of Jerusalem; see Richard Bauckham, "Mary of Clopas (John

historical memory.[230] Yet legend can invent concrete details,[231] and the fact that Luke 24:13–35 belongs to a book that opens with detailed, rich narratives that are mostly fictional (Luke 1–2) is very much to the point. Beyond this, even if one were to find reminiscence in "Cleopas" and "Emmaus," as does Lüdemann,[232] it is hard to see how much more one could say. The edifying story, so illustrative of Lukan themes and interests[233] and so congenial to Christian reflection, is not an obvious entrée into the days following the crucifixion. Although Bultmann took Luke 24:13–35 to contain "the oldest of the Synoptic resurrection stories,"[234] and although Lake urged that the "story of the two disciples who went to Emmaus really represents an experience of two members of the Jerusalem community,"[235] one is at a loss how to confirm their judgments. Keim to the contrary characterized Luke 24:13–35 as "self-condemned by its picturesque legendary style,"[236] and sometimes, one must concede, the more elaborate the story, the less believable the details. I have been unable to come to any decision about the age and origin of the text.

6. John 21:1–17 belongs to a chapter that is either an afterthought or a secondary addition of the evangelist or, more likely, a postscript from someone else.[237] The chapter opens with the story of an appearance of

---

19:25)," in *Women in the Biblical Tradition* (ed. George J. Brooke; Lewiston, NY: E. Mellen, 1992), 231–55. Interestingly enough, according to early tradition, the name of Cleopas's companion was Simon (see n. 162). A few, however, have identified this Simon with Peter and argued that the Emmaus story is actually a version of the first appearance to him; see n. 162. Frenschkowski, *Offenbarung*, 235–38, tentatively accepting the identification of Cleopas as a relative of Jesus, suggests that the story of the Emmaus road functioned to legitimate the authority of the family of Jesus in Jerusalem; this would then explain why Cleopas and his companion are greeted with the news of the postresurrection appearance to Peter (24:34): Luke thus supports Peter's priority as leader of the early church.

230. Cf. Wedderburn, *Resurrection*, 55–56; also the full discussion of E. H. Scheffler, "Emmaus—A Historical Perspective," *Neot* 23 (1989): 251–67.

231. The apocryphal gospels are proof enough; cf. Metzger, "Names for the Nameless."

232. Lüdemann, *Resurrection*, 146–47.

233. B. P. Robinson, "The Place of the Emmaus Story in Luke-Acts," *NTS* 30 (1984): 481–97.

234. Bultmann, *History*, 289.

235. Lake, *Resurrection*, 218. Gardner-Smith, *Resurrection*, 68–69, felt the same way: he thought that the conversation is "true to life," that "a romancer would hardly have been bold enough to invent the petulant tone of Cleopas' question," that the description of Jesus as "a prophet mighty in deed and word before God and all the people" has a "very primitive sound," and further that "We were hoping that it was he who should redeem Israel" likewise sounds ancient.

236. Keim, *Jesus*, 6:295.

237. Jean Zumstein, "La rédaction finale de l'évangile de Jean (à l'exemple du chapitre 21)," in *La communauté johannique et son histoire: La trajectorie de l'évangile de Jean aux deux premiers siècles* (ed. Jean-Daniel Kaestli, Jean-Michel Poffet, and Jean Zumstein; MdB;

Jesus to "Simon Peter, Thomas called the Twin, Nathanael of Cana in Galilee, the sons of Zebedee, and two others of his disciples" (v. 2). In its current context, the episode is peculiar. Jesus has appeared to the disciples, given them their commissioning, and erased all doubt (John 20:22–29). One would expect them to be doing something other than trawling the Sea of Galilee. This is one reason Eugen Ruckstuhl has called John 21:1–17 "perhaps the most mysterious narrative of the New Testament."[238]

Can one reconstruct a pre-Johannine tradition? Those who think of John's Gospel as incorporating tradition from the eyewitness known as the Beloved Disciple, who is prominent in chapter 21, could conjecture that this story ultimately goes back to him.[239] Others, more suspicious of John's link to an eyewitness and less trustful of the Gospel's fidelity to history, will observe the overriding theological interests in the chapter — the proof of Jesus' physicality, the rivalry between Peter and the Beloved Disciple (cf. 13:23–24), the dispelling of cognitive dissonance stemming from the death of the last of the Twelve — and will feel scant confidence in our ability to recover ancient tradition behind John's strange termination.

But before coming to any conclusions about John 21:1–17, one must take into account the parallels with the call story in Luke 5:1–11, which is Luke's fusing of Mark 1:16–20 and a separate tradition.[240] Luke 5:1–11 and John 21:1–17 share much in common:

- Peter, the sons of Zebedee, and other disciples are in a boat near land.
- They have caught nothing after fishing all night.

Geneva: Labor et Fides, 1991), 207–30. As I write, the academic rumor mill has it that an old Coptic ms. ending at John 20:31 has come to light, and that Gesa Schenke will announce this in an article in *Coptica, Gnostica, Manichaica: A Festschrift in Honor of Wolf-Peter Funk on the Occasion of his Sixtieth Birthday* (Bibliothèque Copte de Nag Hammadi Section Études; Paris/Québec: Les Presses de l'Université Laval/Peeters, forthcoming).

238. Ruckstuhl, "Resurrection," 150.

239. See Craig Blomberg, *The Historical Reliability of John's Gospel: Issues and Commentary* (Downers Grove, IL: InterVarsity, 2001), 272–77. While I myself believe that the so-called beloved disciple was an historical figure who played an important role in the history of Johannine Christianity, and while I do not despise the case for identifying him with John the son of Zebedee, I do not share Blomberg's confidence in the general historicity of John's Gospel.

240. For an attempt to isolate Luke's sources from Luke's redaction, see Rudolf Pesch, *Der reiche Fischfang: Lk 5,1–11/Jo 21,1–14: Wundergeschichte, Berufungserzählung, Erscheinungsbericht* (Düsseldorf: Patmos, 1969), 53–86. For work on Luke 5:1–11 and John 21 in the two decades following Pesch, see Frans Neirynck, "John 21," *NTS* 36 (1990): 321–36. Against Neirynck and several other recent writers, I remain unpersuaded that John 21 is largely a rewriting of Luke 5.

- Jesus is on the shore.

- Jesus tells the fishermen to cast out their nets.

- The disciples obey and take in a miraculously large catch.

- In Luke, the nets begin to break or are about to break (διερρήσσετο, 5:6), but in John the nets are not torn.

- Jesus converses with Peter alone.

- In Luke, "Simon Peter" says he is a sinner; John alludes to Peter's denial of Jesus.

- Jesus commissions Peter to catch people (so Luke) or feed Jesus' sheep (so John).

- Peter follows (ἠκολούθησαν, Luke 5:11) Jesus or is told, "Follow me" (ἀκολούθει, John 21:19).

Here we clearly have variants of the same miracle story.[241] While Luke mingled it with Mark 1:16–20, John evidently augmented it with a tradition that featured a meal with the risen Jesus.[242]

The story about the miraculous catch was, according to Pesch, originally set in the pre-Easter period, as it still is in Luke. It was John or John's tradition that postdated it, perhaps because of its resemblance to the source it is now combined with, that being a resurrection narrative that named Peter and featured a meal by a lake.[243] Yet where are the other examples of stories from the ministry being turned into resurrection appearances?[244] It is more plausible that the story about the miraculous catch originally narrated an encounter with the risen Jesus and that Luke moved it to the pre-Easter period. A redactional motive for the relocation is palpable: as Luke confined the Easter stories to Jerusalem, he had no place for a resurrection narrative inescapably set

---

241. Matt 14:28–33 might also reflect knowledge of the same tradition; see Raymond E. Brown, "John 21 and the First Appearance of the Risen Jesus to Peter," in *Resurrexit: Actes du Symposium International sur la Résurrection de Jésus* (Rome 1970) (Vatican: Liberia Editrice Vaticana, 1974), 252–53.

242. Ibid., 248n5, arguing that the second story contained the naming of the disciples (v. 2), the meal of bread and fish (v. 9b), and the recognition of Jesus at a meal (vv. 12–13). For other resurrection traditions that feature a meal, see Luke 24:30–31, 35, 41–43; and the fragment *Gos. Heb.* 7, in Jerome, *Vir. ill.* 2 (ed. Richardson; TU 14.1:7–8); cf. Acts 1:4; 10:41.

243. Pesch, *Fischfang*, 111–13, 131–33.

244. Cf. Günter Klein, *Rekonstruktion und Interpretation: Gesammelte Aufsätze zum Neuen Testament* (BEvT 50; Munich: Chr. Kaiser, 1969), 42–43.

in Galilee. He could retain the story of Jesus and Peter only by placing it in the Galilean ministry.

It is a good bet that the tradition taken up into Luke 5 and John 21 purported to recount the famous first postresurrection appearance to Peter.[245] Here are some reasons:

a. The story features Peter. Although others are present, they remain in the background.[246]

b. The tale is set in Galilee, and that is most likely where the appearance to Peter took place.[247] Even if, as I argue below, the disciples, including Peter, were in Jerusalem the Sunday morning after the crucifixion, all the evidence goes to show that, despite Luke and John, Peter's initial experience with the risen Jesus took place elsewhere. The angelic imperative in Mark 16:7 = Matt 28:7, 10 is surely *ex eventu* and so informed by memory. It entails that the disciples will not meet Jesus until they are in Galilee. One naturally connects this with the similarly retrospective Mark 14:27–28 = Matt 26:31–32: The sheep will be scattered, but Jesus will go ahead of them to Galilee. This assumes that the

---

245. See esp. Brown, "John 21," 246–65; also Brendan Byrne, "Peter as Resurrection Witness in the Lucan Narrative," in *The Convergence of Theology: A Festschrift Honoring Gerald O'Collins* (ed. Daniel Kendall and Stephen T. Davis; New York: Paulist Press, 2002), 19–33; Christian Dietzfelbinger, *Das Evangelium nach Johannes* (ZBKNT 4.1; Zürich: Theologischer Verlag, 2001), 2:355–56; Gardner-Smith, *Resurrection*, 16–18, 145–50, 183–84; Guignebert, *Jesus*, 504–6, 522; Adolf von Harnack, *Luke the Physician, the Author of the Third Gospel and the Acts of the Apostles* (London: Williams & Norgate, 1907), 227–28; Hirsch, *Osterglaube*, 50. Cullmann, *Peter*, 61–62, is uncertain yet not opposed.

246. Ruckstuhl, "Resurrection," 151, suggests that this story recounts "the first appearance of Jesus to Peter and some other disciples, whom the formula tradition (Luke 24,34; 1 Corinthians 15,5) dropped, emphasizing the importance of Peter and his function." See further Brown, "John 21," 251–52, who observes that 1 Cor 15:8 names Paul alone although Acts supplies Paul with companions on the Damascus road. Caroline Bammel, "The First Resurrection Appearance to Peter," in *John and the Synoptics* (ed. Adelbert Denaux; BETL 101; Leuven: Leuven University Press/Peeters, 1992), 620–31, harmonizes the Galilean location in John 21 with Luke 24:34, where the first appearance to Peter must take place in Jerusalem, with the novel suggestion that "Peter, while at Jerusalem, experienced a vision in which he was encountered by the risen Jesus at the Sea of Galilee" (625).

247. See further Fischer, *Ostergeschehen*, 45–55; Lohfink, "Osterereignisse," 162–63; and von Campenhausen, *Tradition*, 47–52. For another point of view, see Bernd Steinseifer, "Der Ort der Erscheinungen des Auferstandenen: Zur Frage alter galiläischer Ostertraditionen," *ZNW* 62 (1971): 232–65. Steinseifer is adequately answered by Thorwald Lorenzen, "Ist der Auferstandene in Galiläa erschienen? Bemerkungen zu einem Aufsatz von B. Steinseifer," *ZNW* 64 (1973): 209–21. The old thesis that "Galilee" might refer to an area near Jerusalem (cf. Josh 18:17), although revived by Pinchas Lapide, *The Resurrection of Jesus: A Jewish Perspective* (Minneapolis: Augsburg, 1983), 112–14, remains without real support. Cf. Fischer, *Ostergeschehen*, 55. So too F. C. Burkitt's theory that Peter encountered Jesus on the way to Galilee and then turned back to Jerusalem: *Christian Beginnings: Three Lectures* (London: University of London Press, 1924), 75–97.

disciples, as in *Gos. Pet.* 14:58–60, quickly returned to Galilee. In harmony with this is John 16:32: "The hour is coming, indeed it has come, when you will be scattered, each one to his own home [εἰς τὰ ἴδια], and you will leave me alone." Here εἰς τὰ ἴδια implies that the disciples, upon abandoning Jesus, will return to their own homes, which means to Galilee, just as John 21 (but not John 20) has it (cf. *Gos. Pet.* 14:59: εἰς τὸν οἶκον αὐτοῦ).

c. The story of the miraculous catch of fish depicts Peter and others going about the work of fishing. This is more than odd if they have already come to belief in Jesus' resurrection. Such belief would surely have brought ordinary life to an abrupt halt and effected resumption of their full-time religious mission. So the logic of the story seems to require that it be the first appearance story. In Brown's words, "The whole atmosphere of 21, where Peter and the others have returned to their native region and have resumed their previous occupation, suggests that the risen Jesus has not yet appeared to them and that they are still in the state of confusion caused by his death."[248]

d. *Gospel of Peter* 12–14 relates that, after the angelophany to the women at the empty tomb, people returned home after the end of the feast. This included Jesus' followers: "But we, the twelve disciples of the Lord, wept and mourned, and each one, grieving for what had happened, returned to his own home. But I, Simon Peter, and my brother Andrew took our nets and went to the sea. And there was with us Levi, the son of Alphaeus, whom the Lord . . . " The text unfortunately breaks off here. But clearly it is moving toward an appearance of Jesus to Peter in Galilee. Even if we think, as I do, that the *Gospel of Peter*, like Ps.-Mark 16:9–20, draws upon the canonical Gospels,[249] it is early enough that it could here nonetheless represent independent oral tradition.

Although the case does not pass beyond a reasonable doubt, I find myself persuaded that Luke 5 and John 21 are descendants of a story purporting to recount Jesus' first postresurrection appearance to Peter. It

248. Brown, "John 21," 246. Cf. Rudolf Bultmann, *The Gospel of John: A Commentary* (Philadelphia: Westminster, 1976), 705: The story was "manifestly originally told of the first . . . appearance of the Risen Jesus to the disciples; it does not presuppose that Jesus had already shown himself once to the disciples, and that they had been charged with their calling and equipped for it. The remarkable uncertainty in the relation of the disciples to Jesus attests the contrary."

249. See Frans Neirynck, "The Apocryphal Gospels and the Gospel of Mark," in *Evangelica II*, 715–72. For the case that this dependence was through oral tradition, see Martha K. Stillman, "The Gospel of Peter: A Case for Oral-Only Dependency?" *ETL* 73 (1997): 114–20.

sadly is not possible to say much more. For one fails to see how we can move from the common tradition behind our two texts to what really happened. If the fact that Jesus was crucified does not guarantee the historicity of details in the passion narrative, so similarly the fact that Peter had a vision of Jesus in Galilee does not establish the veracity of any of the details in Luke 5 or John 21.

7. The three earliest accounts of the ascension are Ps.-Mark 16:19; Luke 24:50–53; and Acts 1:6–11 (cf. *Barn.* 15:9; Mark 16:3 k). The short variant in Ps.-Mark, probably dependent upon Luke-Acts,[250] is not an autonomous story but the conclusion of the appearance to the Eleven in 16:14–18 (cf. the relationship of Luke 24:50–53 to 24:36–49). It in any event is sufficiently bereft of detail to be of no value for this investigation. As for Luke 24:50–53, although some have tried to find pre-Lukan tradition here,[251] the task is futile. Jeremias concluded that verses 50–53 show no "traces of tradition" and that this report of the ascension must be a Lukan composition.[252] It is hard to disagree.

What of Acts 1:6–11? The dialogue in verses 6–8, which as part of the preface states the theme of the book ("You will be my witnesses in Jerusalem and in all Judea and Samaria, and to the ends of the earth"), is clearly Lukan from beginning to end. We must deem it a redactional product that creatively combines elements from Luke 19:11; Isa 49:6; Mark 13:4, 32; and Luke 24:46–49.[253] This leaves only vv. 9–11 to be accounted for. They too have been regarded as editorial,[254] although C. K. Barrett is rather of the opinion that this is "the one place" in the prologue to Acts "where pre-Lucan tradition may reasonably be traced."[255] He does not further specify its scope. Neither does Lüdemann, whom Barrett quotes: Underlying 1:9–11 "is a tradition the form of which can no

---

250. But see Mikael C. Parsons, *The Departure of Jesus in Luke-Acts: The Ascension Narratives in Context* (JSNTSup 21; Sheffield: Sheffield Academic Press, 1987), 145–46.

251. See esp. Rudolf Pesch, "Der Anfang der Apostelgeschichte: Apg 1,1–11: Kommentar-studie," in *Evangelisch-Katholischer Kommentar zum Neuen Testament Vorarbeiten* (Zurich: Benziger, 1971), 3:7–35. He reconstructs a pre-Lukan source behind Acts 1:4a + Luke 24:49b–51 + Acts 1:9b.

252. Joachim Jeremias, *Die Sprache des Lukasevangeliums* (KEK; Göttingen: Vandenhoeck & Ruprecht, 1980), 323.

253. Rudolf Pesch, *Die Apostelgeschichte* (EKKNT 5.1; Zurich: Benziger, 1986), 1:65.

254. Gerhard Lohfink, *Die Himmelfahrt Jesu: Untersuchungen zu den Himmelfahrts- und Erhöhungstexten bei Lukas* (SANT 26; Munich: Kösel, 1971), 133–34, 160–62, 176–210.

255. C. K. Barrett, *A Critical and Exegetical Commentary on the Acts of the Apostles* (ICC; Edinburgh: T & T Clark, 1994, 1998), 1:62.

longer be recognized."[256] Less tentative is Mikeal Parsons: "There was in Luke's tradition a brief narrative describing Jesus' ascension on a cloud from his disciples." Parsons inclines to think that the cloud may be from the tradition, the mountain and angels from Luke, who also assimilated the narrative to Elijah's assumption in 2 Kgs 2:11 and "couched it in eschatological expectations of the nature of Jesus' parousia."[257]

It is hardly possible to decide whether Parsons is right or wrong; here more than elsewhere "we find ourselves in the sphere of hypotheses and conjectures."[258] Only two comments need be added. First, whatever tradition may lie behind Acts 1:9–11, it is not likely to be very old. Only Luke, Acts, and Ps.-Mark have ascension narratives, and there is no earlier trace of their content.

Second, in 1 Cor 15:8, Paul wrote of Jesus appearing to him "last of all" (ἔσχατον), which made him ἔκτρωμα. Whether the latter word means "untimely born" or something else, Paul's formulation implies a belief that the resurrection appearances ceased early on, and that his later experience was an exception to the rule. Evidently he knew of no appearances of Jesus since his own.[259] There is a certain parallel with Acts, where Jesus shows himself on and off for forty days and then ascends to heaven (cf. Ps.-Mark 16:19). "Paul shares with Luke the conviction that there was a closed period of time following the crucifixion when the risen Christ encountered his followers."[260] Yet the implications of this agreement are unclear. Not only do we have evidence that Christians continued to report christophanies (Acts 7:56; Rev 1:9–20), but Acts also itself portrays Paul encountering Jesus several more times (18:9; 22:18; 23:11) , and this may well reflect Paul's personal convictions.

---

256. Gerd Lüdemann, *Early Christianity according to the Traditions in Acts: A Commentary* (Minneapolis: Fortress, 1989), 29. Cf. Gerhard Schneider, *Die Apostelgeschichte* (HTKNT 5.1; Freiburg: Herder, 1980), 1:208–11.

257. Parsons, *Departure*, 144.

258. A. W. Zwiep, *The Ascension of the Messiah in Lukan Christology* (NovTSup 87; Leiden: Brill, 1997), 192.

259. C. F. Evans, *Resurrection*, 46, however, raises the possibility that Paul's statement might be less a remark on what the apostle had learned to be the case than "an expression of Pauline 'egoism,' and of a dogmatic viewpoint about his own person, that with the appearance to himself and with his call to apostleship the period of revelation was over, and what remained was the mission of the gospel to the world until the parousia."

260. Sleeper, "Pentecost," 396. He continues: "Paul differs from Luke in two respects: for him the period is long enough so that he himself is included among the list of resurrection appearances; and he does not identify the event which closes the period as the ascension." See further Daniel Kendall and Gerald O'Collins, "The Uniqueness of the Easter Experiences," *CBQ* 54 (1992): 295–97.

At least 2 Cor 12:8–9 seemingly indicates the apostle's belief that Jesus continued to speak to him. One can only wonder in what ways, if any, Luke and Paul imagined the original christophanies to differ from later experiences.

8. In 1 Cor 15:7, Paul speaks of an appearance to James, who must be the brother of Jesus: the lack of any qualifying phrase demonstrates him to be well-known. Beyond the simple ἔπειτα ὤφθη 'Ιακώβῳ, Paul does not elaborate, and nowhere else does the New Testament refer to this event. One wonders whether unease with the leadership of James in the Jerusalem church has anything to do with the failure of Jesus' appearance to him to leave any trace in the canonical Gospels. Whatever the truth of that, Jerome, *Vir. ill.* 2 (ed. Richardson; TU 14.1:7–8), preserves the following:

> The Gospel entitled "According to the Hebrews," which I recently translated into Greek and Latin, and which Origen often quotes, contains this after the resurrection: "Now the Lord, when he had given the cloth [cf. Mark 15:46 par.] to the servant of the priest [cf. Mark 14:47 par.], went to James and appeared to him. For James had taken an oath that he would not eat bread from that hour in which he had drunk the cup of the Lord until he saw him risen from among those who sleep. Again soon thereafter the Lord said, 'Bring a table and bread,'" and immediately it adds: "He took bread and blessed it and broke it and gave it to James the Just and said to him, 'My brother, eat your bread, for the Son of man is risen from among those who sleep.'"[261]

The legendary character of this story is patent.[262] Not only does Jesus appear to a neutral or hostile outsider ("the servant of the priest"), but the tale also implies, against 1 Cor 15:3–8, that James was the recipient of the first christophany.[263] It further and unbelievably makes the isolated resurrection of Jesus a firm expectation of the pre-Easter period, and it places James at the Last Supper, for which there is otherwise no evidence. The passage can be no guide to what really happened.

---

261. Cf. Gregory of Tours, *Hist. Franc.* 1.21; Ps.-Abdias of Babylon, *Hist. Cert. Apost.* 6.1.

262. See further Pratscher, *Herrenbruder*, 47.

263. But recall the thesis of Harnack, "Verklärungsgeschichte," 62–80 (= Hoffmann, *Überlieferung*, 89–117), that 1 Cor 15:7, which legitimates James, represents a rival statement to 15:5, which gives Peter pride of place.

This leaves us with nothing save the bare-boned 1 Cor 15:7: ἔπειτα ὤφθη ᾽Ιακώβῳ. Much, nonetheless, has often been made of it. Given the plain statement of John 7:5 ("For not even his brothers believed in him") as well as the tension between Jesus and his family reflected in Mark 3:21, 31–34 and implicit in other texts (e.g., Matt 10:34–36 = Luke 12:51–53), many have inferred that the appearance to James was, like the appearance to Paul, a sort of conversion. Reginald Fuller wrote: "It might be said that if there were no record of an appearance to James the Lord's brother in the New Testament we should have to invent one in order to account for his post-resurrection conversion and rapid advance."[264] Apologists for the resurrection have often emphasized that it must have been a christophany that changed James from an outsider to an insider.[265]

This is far from certain. We cannot assume that the tension between Jesus and his family was at all times the same, or that things were not better toward the end than they were at the beginning.[266] Further, Acts 1:14 has Mary, immediately after the crucifixion, with the disciples in Jerusalem, and I am unaware of anyone who has argued that her post-Easter devotion to Jesus, if we accept it as historical, could be explained only by a resurrection appearance. The same holds for James's ἀδελφοί, brothers, referred to in 1 Cor 9:5: the plural implies the prominence of more than just James. Did they also see Jesus?[267] Another possibility is that James joined the Christian community and only subsequently had a vision of Jesus.[268] The frustrating truth is that we just do not know the circumstances of the postmortem appearance to James, only

---

264. Reginald H. Fuller, *The Formation of the Resurrection Narratives* (New York: Macmillan, 1971), 37. Cf. Raymond E. Brown, *The Virginal Conception and Bodily Resurrection of Jesus* (New York: Paulist Press, 1973), 95; Catchpole, *Resurrection*, 210–11; Lohfink, "Auferstehung," 48–49.

265. E.g., Gary R. Habermas, "Explaining Away Jesus' Resurrection: The Recent Revival of Hallucination Theories," *Christian Research Journal* 23, no. 4 (2001), 47; James Orr, *The Resurrection of Jesus* (Cincinnati: Jenings & Graham, 1909), 170; and George Zorab, *Het Opstandingsverhaal in het licht der Parapsychologie* (The Hague: H. Leopold, 1949), 180–90. Contrast Margaret E. Thrall, "Resurrection Traditions and Christian Apologetic," *Thomist* 43 (1979): 205, who uses James's presumed status as a onetime unbeliever in Jesus as a reason for aligning his experience with Paul's: the conflict between conscious and unconscious attitudes provided promising conditions for a vision.

266. See esp. Richard Bauckham, *Jude and the Relatives of Jesus in the Early Church* (Edinburgh: T & T Clark, 1990), 46–57; and John Painter, *Just James: The Brother of Jesus in History and Tradition* (Columbia: University of South Carolina, 1997), 11–41.

267. Zorab, *Opstandingsverhaal*, 180–90, suggests this.

268. Cf. Grass, *Ostergeschehen*, 101–102.

that, if Paul has his facts straight, it took place between the appearances to Peter and Paul; and we can guess that it was a factor in his rise to ecclesiastical power.

9. There is also Paul's experience. Unfortunately and surprisingly, he himself refers to it only in passing, in 1 Cor 9:1; 15:8–10; Gal 1:12, 15–16; and perhaps 2 Cor 4:6.[269] There are also three accounts of his calling or conversion in Acts: 9:1–19 (told in the third person); 22:6–16 (a first-person account); and 26:12–18 (a first-person account, somewhat condensed). These are probably Lukan variations upon a single pre-Lukan tradition.[270] Each version has items that the others omit, and they are not altogether consistent in their details. Most famously, in 9:7 bystanders hear a voice but see nothing, while in 22:9 they see a light but are deaf to the voice.[271] All three accounts, however, concur on the following items:

- Paul persecuted Christians.

- He was on the Damascus road when he saw a light and fell to the ground.

- He heard a voice saying, "Saul, Saul, why do you persecute me?"

- Paul responded, "Who are you, Lord?"

- The voice answered, "I am Jesus, whom you are persecuting."

- Paul rose from the ground.

- The encounter turned Paul's life around and led to his mission to the Gentiles.

We can be fairly certain that the author of Acts had access to a traditional call story that included most or all of the elements just enumerated, a story that, even if expanded with legendary elements and revised by Luke, goes back ultimately to Paul's own narrative.[272] This follows from

---

269. But Wright, *Resurrection*, 284–86, argues that 2 Cor 4:6 is not about Paul's unique call but rather about something common to all Christians. I am not sure the antithesis is warranted.

270. For the many Lukan features, see Charles W. Hedrick, "Paul's Conversion/Call: A Comparative Analysis of the Three Reports in Acts," *JBL* 100 (1981): 415–32.

271. For attempts at harmonization, see the commentaries. For source- and redaction-critical questions, see Heininger, *Paulus*, 211–34.

272. So also Lüdemann, *Resurrection*, 68. Cf. C. K. Barrett, *Acts*, 1:445, who speaks of a "fairly direct tradition from Paul himself." Christoph Burchard, *Der dreizehnte Zeuge: Traditions- und kompositionsgeschichtliche Untersuchungen zu Lukas' Darstellung der*

the correlations between Acts and Paul's own Epistles. Paul himself informs us that he was a persecutor of Christians until his calling (1 Cor 15:9; Gal 1:13). He states that he has seen the risen Jesus, the Son of God (1 Cor 9:1; 15:8; Gal 1:16; cf. Acts 9:17, 20). He attributes his missionary work among the Gentiles to his christophany (Gal 1:16). And he relates that, shortly after his calling, he "returned to Damascus," which implies that his new life began in that city's vicinity (1:17). If, moreover, 2 Cor 4:6 ("God...has shone in our hearts to give the light of the knowledge of the glory of God in the face of Jesus Christ") adverts to Paul's vision of Jesus, this would line up with the accounts in Acts, where Paul sees a supernatural light.

There is yet one more correlation between Paul's Epistles and the accounts of his vision in Acts. In Gal 1:15–16, the apostle says that, "When God, who had set me apart from my mother's womb (ἐκ κοιλίας μητρός μου) and called (καλέσας) me through his grace, was pleased to reveal his Son to me, so that I might proclaim him among the Gentiles, immediately I did not confer with any human being." These words are, as has long been observed, conceptually quite close to Jer 1:4–5: "Before I formed you in the womb I knew you, and before you were born I consecrated you; I appointed you a prophet to the nations." There are, in addition, parallels to the calling of God's servant in Isa 49:1–6: "The Lord called me before I was born, while I was in my mother's womb he named me" (ἐκ κοιλίας μητρός μου ἐκάλεσεν τὸ ὄνομά μου, v. 1); "formed me from the womb [ἐκ κοιλίας] to be his servant" (v. 5); "I will give you as a light to the nations [ἐθνῶν], that my salvation may reach to the end of the earth" (v. 6); and elsewhere Paul also associates his call with phrases from Isa 42. It seems plain enough that Paul thought of his calling as analogous with those of Jeremiah and the servant of Deutero-Isaiah.[273]

Frühzeit des Paulus (FRLANT 103; Göttingen: Vandenhoeck & Ruprecht, 1970), 128–29, concludes that Acts 26:12–18 either goes back to Paul himself or reflects knowledge of his letters. Fergus Kerr, "Paul's Experience: Sighting or Theophany?" *NBf* 58 (1977): 311, is far too skeptical when he doubts that "Luke had much, or any, information from Paul himself" and proposes instead that Luke "turned to the Old Testament for examples of how to tell the story of an encounter with the Lord." More helpful is the argument of Carey C. Newman, *Paul's Glory-Christology: Tradition and Rhetoric* (NovTSup 69; Leiden: Brill, 1992), 165–66: "The way Paul refers to the Christophany implies the recipients of Paul's letters already knew the story of his conversion, and the Christophany may well have formed part of the apostle's preaching (1 Cor. 15:3–8)."

273. See esp. Johannes Munck, *Paul and the Salvation of Mankind* (London: SCM, 1959), 24–33. For Isa 42 as part of Paul's self-conception, see Seyoon Kim, *Paul and the New*

Paul's prophetic self-conception, which he links with his calling on the Damascus road, is also on display in Acts 26, which draws precisely upon Jer 1 and language about Isaiah's servant:

Acts 26:17	ἐξαιρούμενός σε ἐκ τοῦ λαοῦ καὶ ἐκ τῶν ἐθνῶν εἰς οὓς ἐγὼ ἀποστέλλω σε....
Jer 1:7–8, 10 LXX	πρὸς πάντας, οὓς ἐὰν ἐξαποστείλω σε... μετὰ σοῦ ἐγώ εἰμι τοῦ ἐξαιρεῖσθαί σε.... κατέστακά σε σήμερον ἐπὶ ἔθνη.
Acts 26:18	ἀνοίξαι ὀφθαλμοὺς αὐτῶν, τοῦ ἐπιστρέψαι ἀπὸ σκότους εἰς φῶς.
Isa 42:6–7 LXX	εἰς φῶς ἐθνῶν ἀνοῖξαι ὀφθαλμοὺς τυφλῶν... καθημένους ἐν σκότει.

So Paul's interpretation of his own calling is preserved in Acts.[274] Again, it seems clear that Luke's source(s) for Paul's calling must stem ultimately from the apostle himself.

At one point Acts has been thought to contradict Paul's statements about his own calling. "The one thing — and the only thing — Paul says about the experience is that he saw the Lord. Not only do the Acts not mention this fact, they all but exclude it."[275] Whereas in 1 Cor 9:1 Paul says that he has "seen Jesus our Lord," in Acts we read only about a bright light and Jesus' voice. One wonders, however, whether this contradiction is more apparent than real. Paul hoped, in the words of Phil 3:21, that Jesus would change his "body of humiliation that it may be conformed to the body of his glory." Clearly the apostle thought of the risen Jesus as having a body of δόξα, one made of light (cf. 2 Cor 4:6). So although we have no access to exactly what Paul saw or thought he saw, we can imagine either that he saw an indistinct or overwhelming light, or alternatively, that his experience was akin to that of the prophet Ezekiel, who beheld creatures of "human form" in the midst of "a great cloud with brightness around it," with "fire flashing forth continually"

Perspective: Second Thoughts on the Origin of Paul's Gospel (Grand Rapids: Eerdmans: 2002), 101–27.

274. It goes without saying that he must have narrated and interpreted his call retrospectively; his subsequent life would have rewritten his memories of what happened to him on the Damascus road. Helpful here is Terrence L. Donaldson, *Paul and the Gentiles: Remapping the Apostle's Convictional World* (Minneapolis: Fortress, 1997).

275. John Knox, *Chapters in a Life of Paul* (rev. ed.; Macon, GA: Mercer University Press, 1987), 97.

(Ezek 1:4–5). In either case Paul identified this light with the risen Jesus because of the message that came with the vision.[276] As Paul had not known the historical Jesus, one in any event imagines that only a verbal communication would have sufficed to equate a vision or figure of light with Jesus.[277] One recalls that, in the modern literature on near-death experiences, many people see a figure of light to which they give no name, while others call it God or Jesus. Although the experience, whatever its explanation, seems to be relatively stable, the interpretation differs depending upon the individual.

Attempts to explain Paul's conversion have been legion.[278] Many have confidently thought that "of all the miracles of the New Testament," this "is the one which admits of the easiest explanation from natural causes."[279] Some have suggested that the apostle was an epileptic[280] while others have observed that, to judge from 2 Cor 12:2–7 and the picture in Acts, he may be reckoned a visionary.[281] Lüdemann, stressing this

---

276. On the luminous Jesus in early Christianity, see Robinson, "Easter," 5–37. Despite his argument, I am not persuaded that one can trace a straightforward development from luminous appearances to nonluminous, materialistic appearances. For critical comments see William L. Craig, "From Easter to Valentinus and the Apostles' Creed Once More: A Critical Examination of James Robinson's Proposed Resurrection Appearance Trajectories," *JSNT* 52 (1993): 19–39; and Gerald O'Collins, "Luminous Appearances of the Risen Christ," *CBQ* 46 (1984): 247–54.
Incidentally, occasional attempts to link the Easter appearances to so-called near-death experiences are not very illuminating; cf. Gerald O'Collins, "The Risen Jesus: Analogies and Presence," in Porter, Hayes, and Tombs, *Resurrection*, 199–207 (although one of O'Collins's reasons for faulting the analogy — namely, that there are no stories of collectively perceived near-death experiences — betrays ignorance of the relevant literature: while rare, they are not unknown).

277. Jerome Murphy-O'Connor, *Paul: A Critical Life* (Oxford: Clarendon, 1996), 78, is sure that the pre-Christian "Paul had a mental image of Jesus." But mental images are not always clear; they can be quite indistinct.

278. See Eduard Pfaff, *Die Bekehrung des h. Paulus in der Exegese des 20. Jahrhunderts* (Rome: Officium Libri Catholici, 1942).

279. John Stuart Mill, *Three Essays on Religion* (New York: Henry Holt, 1874), 239n.

280. Although this thesis has fallen on hard times, it was once fairly popular, and one is surprised that it has not been reconsidered in the light of what we now know about the so-called Geschwind syndrome in some epilepsy patients; see D. F. Benson, "The Geschwind Syndrome," *Advances in Neurology* 55 (1991): 411–21; and S. G. Waxman and N. Geschwind, "The Interictal Behavior Syndrome of Temporal Lobe Epilepsy," *Archives of General Psychiatry* 32 (1975): 1580–86.

281. In addition to the vision on the Damascus road, Acts gives Paul visions in 16:9–10; 18:9; 22:17–18; 23:11. There perhaps is some doubt as to whether Paul is speaking of himself in 2 Cor 12:2–4; see Michael D. Goulder, "Visions and Revelations of the Lord (2 Corinthians 12:1–10)," in *Paul and the Corinthians: Studies on a Community in Conflict: Essays in Honour of Margaret Thrall* (ed. Trevor J. Burke and J. Keith Elliott; Leiden: Brill, 2003), 303–12. One should in any case observe that Paul himself distinguished his Damascus road experience from later religious experiences; see Dunn, *Jesus and the Spirit*, 97–114.

last point, has argued that Paul's persecution of Christians shows that their message had a profound effect upon him, and the apostle's aggressive response signals unresolved conflict within himself: he was attracted to what went against his religious beliefs. Lüdemann even speaks of Paul's pre-Christian "Christ complex," which finally resolved itself in a hallucination.[282]

Speaking for myself, none of this is implausible; indeed, it makes a great deal of sense.[283] I am put in mind of the conversion to Christianity of the twentieth-century Hindu, Sadhu Sundar Singh. He, like Paul, vigorously opposed the Christian message. He stoned preachers and burned Bibles until the day that he had a dramatic vision of Jesus.[284]

Nonetheless, while Lüdemann's story fits the facts, the facts do not demand it. As others have cautioned again and again, we have no real entry into Paul's pre-Christian state of mind. The autobiographical nature of Rom 7 is notoriously disputed, even if the chapter must to some extent reflect the apostle's personal experience.[285] The only clear statement about his pre-Christian life is in the relatively brief and self-serving Phil

---

282. Lüdemann, *Resurrection*, 79–84. Cf. Goguel, *Birth*, 81–86; and William Walters Sargant, *Battle for the Mind: A Physiology of Conversion and Brainwashing* (Garden City, NY: Doubleday, 1957), 120–22 (Paul's conversion is explicable "in terms consonant with modern psychological observations"). According to Carl Gustav Jung, *Contributions to Analytical Psychology* (London: K. Paul, Trench, Trübner, 1928), 257, "St. Paul had already been a Christian for a long time, only unconsciously; hence his fanatical resistance to the Christians, because fanaticism is only found in individuals who are compensating secret doubts.... That the auditory phenomenon should represent Christ is explained by the already existing Christian complex in the unconscious. The complex, being unconscious, was projected by St. Paul upon the external world as if it did not belong to him." For attempts to understand the appearance stories in terms of Jung's psychology, see Christopher Knight, "Hysteria and Myth: The Psychology of the Resurrection Appearances," *Modern Churchman* 31 (1989): 38–42; and Thrall, "Resurrection Traditions," 197–216.

283. Gary R. Habermas, *The Risen Jesus and Future Hope* (Lanham: Rowan & Littlefield, 2003), 11, objects that Paul's "religious devotion and zeal, his exemplary education, and his choice as the best candidate to lead the persecution of Christians... militate against him being a candidate to produce subjective images of the risen Jesus." This is a very strange assertion. Hallucinating has nothing to do with educational level; religious devotion and zeal are often associated with visions; and conversions of reversal are far from unheard of (see next note).

284. B. H. Streeter and A. J. Appasamy, *The Message of Sadhu Sundar Singh: A Study in Mysticism on Practical Religion* (New York: Macmillan, 1921), 6–8. On conversions that amount to reversals of values and beliefs, a well-known type, and their relevance for Paul's conversion and theology, see John G. Gager, "Some Notes on Paul's Conversion," *NTS* 27 (1981): 697–704. Several have drawn parallels between Sundar Singh and Paul; e.g., see Goguel, *Birth*, 77–80.

285. "Most interpreters now... agree that it would be a mistake to treat the passage autobiographically and to look for matching stages in Paul's own experience." So James D. G. Dunn, *Romans 1–8* (WBC 38A; Dallas: Word, 1988), 382.

3:4–11, which neither says nor implies anything about an internally conflicted Paul. One can, to be sure, observe that this text reflects only Paul's conscious mind, not his unconscious mind. Still, long-distance diagnosis of his psychological state during a time for which we have just residues of evidence is a most uncertain business; and even if we had more and better evidence, nobody's subjective experience is directly available to scientific or historical methods. Lüdemann may think that we "must" seek to uncover "the feelings" and "the emotions" of the first Christians;[286] but this a tall order. I do not see how we can go beyond a few sweeping generalizations.[287]

No less importantly, visions come for all sorts of reasons, and sometimes for no apparent reason at all. Interviews with modern people who have seen apparitions reveal that, more often than not, there was nothing distinctive about their emotional state at the time.[288] A most interesting illustration of this comes from our contemporary, Hugh Montefiore, New Testament scholar and Anglican Bishop. In writing about his own conversion to Christianity from Judaism, a conversion brought about by a vision of Jesus, he has this to say:

> I had no knowledge of Christianity whatsoever.... It [the vision] was certainly not caused by stress: I was in good health, a happy schoolboy with good friends, leading an enthusiastic life and keen on sport as well as work. I do not recall any need to suppress erotic fantasies! I am equally sure that it had nothing to do with my memories, for I had no memories about Jesus. Again, I am sure it was not wish fulfilment, for I was (and still am) proud to be Jewish. I am at a loss to know how it could be psychogenic, although I accept that my brain was the channel through which the experience came about. My sensory input at the time was not at a low ebb. I think it unlikely that the collective unconscious, if it manifested itself in a hallucination, would have taken what for me would have been an alien form. I cannot believe that I was in contact with a ghost, for the figure I saw was alive and life giving.

---

286. Lüdemann, *Resurrection*, 6.

287. For some suggestions of my own, see Excursus 3, below.

288. Eda (= Edie) Devers, "Experiencing the Deceased: Reconciling the Extraordinary" (PhD diss., University of Florida, 1994), 55–56; Celia Green and Charles McCreery, *Apparitions* (London: Edith Hamilton, 1975), 49.

I cannot account for my vision of Jesus by any of the psychological or neurophysiological explanations on offer.[289]

As I have no reason to think these other than honest words, they are a good reminder that sometimes human events remain mysterious. Simple explanations — such as: "Well, it must stem from a pathological condition" — are not always in order.

•

To summarize the previous pages: despite all the details in the fuller accounts in the Gospels and Acts, they do not, upon initial analysis, take us much beyond 1 Cor 15:3–8. For we simply cannot, using our historical-critical tools, determine to what extent the particulars in the accounts preserve old or authentic memory: our instruments are too blunt for such fine work. Even if there are certain recurring themes and motifs,[290] we cannot without further ado equate those with historical events.

Nonetheless, not all the effort is wasted. At least two items, whose historicity Paul substantiates, give us much to ponder. The first is that several people reported christophanies. The second item is that Jesus ostensibly appeared on more than one occasion to more than one person. These appear to be the facts, and they raise the question of how we should explain them. The apologists for the faith say that the sightings of Jesus must, given the reports, have been objective. One person can hallucinate, but twelve at the same time? And dozens over an extended period of time?[291]

SEEING THINGS

These are legitimate questions, and waving the magical wand of "mass hysteria" will not make them vanish. Yet, if the apologists' questions are good, problematic is the assumption, often made, that the resurrection appearances are, because of their multiple witnesses and shared

---

289. Hugh Montefiore, *The Paranormal: A Bishop Investigates* (Leicestershire: Upfront Publishing, 2002), 234–35.

290. See Alsup, *Post-Resurrection Stories*, who plausibly argues that the New Testament resurrection stories belong to a *Gattung* that also appears in certain anthropomorphic theophany narratives of the Hebrew Bible.

291. Cf. Habermas, *Risen Jesus*, 10–11; Paley, *Evidences*, 377; Westcott, *Resurrection*, 114–15; and many others.

nature, without real analogy. There are, on the contrary, many firsthand accounts of several people seeing at once the apparition of a person recently deceased. There are likewise innumerable accounts of various people seeing an apparition over an extended period of time. Indeed, psychical researchers, just like Christian apologists, have long used precisely the same two reported facts — collective appearances and multiple recipients — to argue that certain reported apparitions are somehow veridical.[292] Whether or not they are persuasive, the truth of the matter, welcome or not, is that the literature on visions of the dead is full of parallels to the stories we find in the Gospels. This must mean something. But what?[293]

---

292. E.g., C. D. Broad, "Phantasms of the Living and of the Dead," *Proceedings of the Society for Psychical Research* 50, no. 183 (1953): 60–61; Hilary Evans, *Seeing Ghosts: Experiences of the Paranormal* (London: John Murray, 2002), 95; Erlendur Haraldsson, "Erscheinungen von und Berichte über Begegnungen mit Verstorbenen: Eine Analyse von 357 aktuellen Berichten," in *Aspekte der Paranormologie: Die Welt des Außergewöhnlichen* (ed. Andreas Resch; Innsbruck: Resch, 1992), 464–84; Ian Stevenson, "The Contribution of Apparitions to the Evidence for Survival," *Journal of the American Society for Psychical Research* 72 (1982): 349–50. Reports of collective apparitions are, incidentally, prominent in the literature of parapsychology but not in normal psychology.
    Catholic apologists sometimes appeal to the same criteria — collective perception and manifold witnesses — to validate reported visions of Mary, e.g., those at Pontmain (1870), Fatima (1917), Banneaux and Beauraing (1932–33), and Medjugorje (1981ff.). For some of the difficult problems in this connection, see Herbert Thurston, "Limpias and the Problem of Collective Hallucinations," *Month* 136 (1920): 387–98, 533–41.
    293. This fact has been recognized before, although with various degrees of persuasiveness. Lake, *Resurrection*, 272–76; James H. Hyslop, *Psychical Research and the Resurrection* (Boston: Small, Maynard, 1908), 382–83; Sir Oliver Lodge, *Science and Immortality* (New York: Moffat, Yard, 1908), 265–69; and C. W. Emmet, *The Eschatological Question in the Gospels: And Other Studies in Recent New Testament Criticism* (Edinburgh: T & T Clark, 1911), 124–27 are tentative and undeveloped, as are Cadoux, *Jesus*, 164–66; Broad, *Religion*, 230–31; Alister Hardy, *The Biology of God: A Scientist's Study of Man the Religious Animal* (London: Jonathan Cape, 1975), 216–21; Allison, *End of the Ages*, 167–68; Lüdemann, "Psychologische Exegese," 108–11; Werner Zager, "Jesu Auferstehung — Heilstat Gottes oder Vision?" *Deutsches Pfarrerblatt* 96, no. 3 (March 1996): 120–23; and Crossan, *Birth of Christianity*, xiv–xx. Badham, *Christian Beliefs*, 39–42, although suggestive, is likewise brief. Weatherhead, *Resurrection*, 60–88, is uncritical regarding the historicity of the Gospels and spends unfruitful pages wondering about the dematerialization of Jesus' body. Similar problems beset Tweedale, *Survival*. Jack A. Kent, *The Psychological Origins of the Resurrection Myth* (London: Open Gate, 1999), is marred by a desire to discredit Christianity — cf. the polemic in Origen, *Cels.* 2.55 (ed. Marcovich; 127); and Woolston, *Sixth Discourse*, 29–30 — as well as by a superficial knowledge of the secondary literature on the New Testament, the secondary literature on bereavement, and the secondary literature on apparitions. Michael C. Perry, *The Easter Enigma: An Essay on the Resurrection with Special Reference to the Data of Psychical Research* (London: Faber & Faber, 1959) — a book John A. T. Robinson, *The Human Face of God* (Philadelphia: Westminster, 1973), 130n110, called "important but neglected" — is more helpful and interesting. Like Weatherhead, however, Perry is much too generous with regard to the historicity of the Easter narratives, and his focus is upon the telepathic theory of veridical apparitions forwarded by F. W. H. Myers and other early members of the Society for Psychical Research. More useful because more critical (he denies the historicity of the empty

Putative encounters with the newly departed are, if not exactly everyday events, rather far-flung. The circumstance is often overlooked because, given our current cultural prejudices, many are discouraged from sharing their seemingly paranormal or mystical experiences,[294] including seeming encounters with the dead[295] — a circumstance that allows popular and uninformed stereotypes about so-called "ghosts" to persist.[296] People do not want to be stigmatized, to have others think them shackled to superstition. But the censuring of testimony does not allow us to remain loyal to the realities of human experience; and although the facts are too little known, surveys from various parts of the world indicate that perceived contact with the dead is, however we interpret it, a regular part of cross-cultural experience.[297]

tomb [see 15–24] and interacts with Lake, E. Meyer, Goguel, and other modern scholars) is Zorab, *Opstandingsverhaal*. Also profitable is Peter F. Carnley, "Response," in Stephen T. Davis, Daniel Kendall, and Gerald O'Collins, *Resurrection* (New York: Oxford University Press, 1977), 29–40. For rejection of the correlations, see O'Collins, "Risen Jesus," 207–9, whose comments are flawed by an apparent lack of knowledge of the vast relevant literature (he refers to only two studies). Wright, *Resurrection*, 689–92, although he sees "danger" in connecting too closely meetings with the risen Jesus and other experiences, is primarily interested in showing that such meetings would not have been understood to imply resurrection unless the tomb were known to be empty.

294. For a helpful analysis of the problem, see David Hay, *Religious Experience Today: Studying the Facts* (London: Mowbray, 1990), 52–65.

295. See the comments of A. Grimby, "Bereavement among Elderly People: Grief Reactions, Post-Bereavement Hallucinations and Quality of Life," *Acta psychiatrica Scandinavica* 87 (1993): 76, regarding modern subjects in Sweden: "Despite great care being taken to create confidence in the interview situation, only one subject, a female spiritist, spontaneously reported hallucinations, referring to the frequent 'contacts she had with her dead husband.' Only after being informed about the commonness and normality of post-bereavement hallucinations and illusions did most of the other widows and widowers speak freely, expressing relief from thoughts that they 'might become or be considered insane.'" For full discussion see Devers, "Experiencing the Deceased," 102–14; cf. Edie Devers, *Goodbye Again: Experiences with Departed Loved Ones* (Kansas City, MO: Andrews & McMeel, 1977), 109–26.

296. These stereotypes have interfered with academic discussion of the resurrection appearances insofar as New Testament scholars have often shared them. William Milligan, *The Resurrection of Our Lord* (London: Macmillan, 1901), 76–119, is particularly egregious: almost every (undocumented) generalization he makes about apparitions is false — for example, that they are all momentary, that they must be expected, that they are typically the product of enthusiasm. Similarly, when Habermas, *Risen Jesus*, 11, asserts that "belief, expectation, and even excitement" are typical preconditions for hallucination, this has nothing at all to do with the apparitions of bereavement. I have noticed that apologists typically content themselves with making broad generalizations about visions; they rarely catalog and examine individual reports in any detail; contrast the interesting collection in Arnold Meyer, *Die Auferstehung Christi: Die Berichte über Auferstehung, Himmelfahrt und Pfingsten* (Tübingen: J. C. M. Mohr/Paul Siebeck, 1905), 217–315.

297. Given that in what follows I shall be comparing stories from very different times and places, it is important to note that apparitions of the recently departed are a cross-cultural phenomenon, as appears from worldwide fiction and folklore as well as modern study; see James McClenon, *Wondrous Events: Foundations of Religious Belief* (Philadelphia: University

The last thirty years have witnessed a revolution in the study of this subject. To tell the story, however, we must go back over a century. The English Society for Psychical Research undertook, in 1882, a survey of so-called paranormal experiences among the British population. Their questionnaire, which was the grandparent of all modern public polling, was sent to approximately seventeen thousand people. It asked, "Have you ever, when believing yourself to be completely awake, had a vivid impression of seeing or being touched . . . or hearing a voice; which impression, so far as you could discover, was not due to any external cause?" Of the 15,316 replies, about 10 percent replied in the affirmative. (Given what we now know, this number is surprisingly small.) Of this tenth, 163 reported the apparition of an individual within 24 hours of death. In the follow-up to those 163, fully 9 percent claimed that their vision was shared: one or more persons witnessed the apparition with them.[298]

After this early survey and Eleanor Sidgwick's subsequent major study,[299] several writers, such as the French astronomer Camille Flammarion, dabbled in collecting stories of apparitions and conducted interviews with percipients.[300] The gathering and analysis of relevant testimony was pretty much confined to the parapsychologists until the middle of the twentieth century, when psychologists, medical doctors, and sociologists slowly began to show interest in the subject. In 1944,

---

of Pennsylvania Press, 1994), 39–45; and Karl Osis, "Apparitions Old and New," in *Case Studies in Parapsychology: Papers Presented in Honor of Dr. Louisa E. Rhine at a Conference held on November 12, 1983 at Bryan University Center, Duke University, Durham, North Carolina* (ed. K. Ramakrishna Rao; Jefferson, NC: McFarland, 1986), 74–86. Note the knowledge of bereavement apparitions in Robert Burton, *The Anatomy of Melancholy* (Philadelphia: Claxton, Remsen & Haffelfinger, 1873), 218 (the book was first published in 1621), and the old collection of David Simpson, *A Discourse on Dreams and Night Visions with Numerous Examples both Ancient and Modern* (Macclesfield, UK: Edward Bayley, 1791).

298. Edmund Gurney, Frederic W. H. Myers, and Frank Podmore, *Phantasms of the Living* (London: Trübner's, 1886); Professor Sidgwick's Committee, "Report on the Census of Hallucinations," *Proceedings of the Society for Psychical Research* 10 (1894): 25–422. These two works were later reduced to one book by Eleanor Mildred (Mrs. Henry) Sidgwick, *Phantasms of the Living* (New York: E. Dutton, 1918); I have used the reprint edition of 1962 (see the next note).

299. Eleanor Mildred Sidgwick, "Phantasms of the Living," *Proceedings of the Society for Psychical Research* 86 (1922): 23–473; reprinted as *Phantasms of the Living: Cases of Telepathy Printed in the Journal of the Society for Psychical Research during Thirty-five Years* (New Hyde Park, NY: University Books, 1962).

300. Camille Flammarion, *Death and Its Mystery at the Moment of Death* (New York: Century, 1922). For a later follow-up to and confirmation of the work of Gurney et al., see D. J. West, "A Mass-Observation Questionnaire on Hallucinations," *Journal of the Society for Psychical Research* 34 (1948): 187–96.

E. Lindemann, in an article for the *American Journal of Psychiatry*, reported that several of his patients in bereavement saw their dead loved ones.[301] In 1958, Peter Marris, in *Widows and Their Families*, reported that 36 of the 72 London widows he interviewed reported a strong sense of the presence (SOP) of a dead family member.[302] In 1970, Colin Murray Parkes, in the journal *Psychiatry*, reported that 15 of the 22 widows he spoke with were likewise familiar with SOP, and that often it was all too real.[303] Also in 1970, another study, this one from Japan, reported that fully 18 out of 20 women who had been suddenly widowed had experienced SOP; half had seen their dead husbands.[304]

These several small studies were all eclipsed when Dewi Rees, a British medical doctor, wrote his dissertation at the University of London in 1971 and reported his findings in the *British Medical Journal*. Rees discovered that, of the 293 widows and widowers he interviewed, fully 47 percent of them believed that they had come into contact with their dead spouse. Most of these encounters took place not long after death, but there were also occurrences many years later. A fair percentage of these encounters were full-fledged apparitions.[305]

Rees's work caught the eyes of other researchers, and the time since has witnessed a multiplication of similar studies and related popular works.[306] The upshot is that, in case after case, and from different regions of the globe, we have learned that up to half of all widows and widowers believe that they have run into their dead spouses, that is, have seen them and/or heard them and/or felt their presence. This is clearly a normal part of the mourning process: the bereaved frequently report

---

301. E. Lindemann, "Symptomatology and Management of Acute Grief," *American Journal of Psychiatry* 101 (1944): 141–48.

302. Peter Marris, *Widows and Their Families* (London: Routledge & Kegan Paul, 1958), 14, 22, 24.

303. Colin Murray Parkes, "The First Year of Bereavement," *Psychiatry* 33 (1970): 444–67.

304. Joe Yamamoto, Keigo Okonogi, Tetsuya Iwasaki, and Saburo Yoshimura, "Mourning in Japan," *American Journal of Psychiatry* 125, no. 12 (1969): 1660–65.

305. W. Dewi Rees, "The Hallucinations of Widowhood," *British Medical Journal* 4 (1971): 37–41; idem, "The Bereaved and Their Hallucinations," in *Bereavement: Its Psychosocial Aspects* (ed. Bernard Schoenberg et al.; New York: Columbia University Press, 1975), 66–71. I have read these two articles but have not been able to obtain Rees's dissertation, "The Hallucinatory Reactions of Bereavement" (MD diss., University of London, 1971). Rees discounted experiences in dreams and reports from those who dismissed their experiences as subjective.

306. A sampling: Michael Barbato, Cathy Blunden, Kerry Reid, Harvey Irwin, and Paul Rodriguez, "Parapsychological Phenomena near the Time of Death," *Journal of Palliative Care*

contact with the dead.[307] We have also now learned that such contact is not confined to surviving partners or those in mourning. Indeed, when asked, all parts of the general public report a high incidence — surveys from Western Europe and North America vary anywhere from about 10–40 percent[308] — of apparent contact with the dead through dreams, voices, felt presences, as well as visions while wide awake. These experiences are, moreover, often experienced as quite vivid and real.[309] Widows and widowers, furthermore, actually supply a minority of the relevant

15, no. 2 (1999): 30–37; Gillian Bennett and Kate Mary Bennett, "The Presence of the Dead: An Empirical Study," *Mortality* 5 (2000): 139–57; Julian Burton, "Contact with the Dead: A Common Experience?" *Fate* 35, no. 4 (1982): 65–73; Andrew M. Greeley, *Death and Beyond* (Chicago: Thomas More, 1976), 65–72; idem, *Religion as Poetry* (New Brunswick, NJ: Transaction, 1995), 217–27; Agneta Grimby, "Hallucinations Following the Loss of a Spouse: Common and Normal Events among the Elderly," *Journal of Clinical Geropsychology* 4 (1998): 65–74; idem, "Bereavement," 72–80; Bill Guggenheim and Judy Guggenheim, *Hello from Heaven!* (New York: Bantam, 1995); Haraldsson, "Erscheinungen," 469–84; idem, "Survey of Claimed Encounters with the Dead," *Omega* 19 (1988–89): 103–13; Aniela Jaffé, *Apparitions: An Archetypal Approach to Death Dreams and Ghosts* (Irving, TX: Spring Publications, 1979); Richard A. Kalish, "Contacting the Dead: Does Group Identification Matter?" in *Between Life and Death* (ed. Robert Kastenbaum; New York: Springer, 1979), 61–72; Richard A. Kalish and David K. Reynolds, "Widows View Death: A Brief Research Note," *Omega* 5 (1974): 187–92; D. Klass, "Solace and Immortality: Bereavement and Parents' Continuing Bonds with their Children," *Death Studies* 17 (1993): 343–68; Louis E. LaGrand, *After Death Communication: Final Farewells* (St. Paul, MN: Llewellyn, 1997); William Foster Matchett, "Repeated Hallucinatory Experiences as a Part of the Mourning Process among Hopi Indian Women," *Psychiatry* 35 (1972): 185–94; Richard Olson, Joe A. Suddeth, Patricia J. Peterson, and Claudia Egelhoff, "Hallucinations of Widowhood," *Journal of the American Geriatric Society* 33 (1985): 543–47; John Palmer, "A Community Mail Survey of Psychic Experiences," *Journal of the American Society of Psychical Research* 73 (1979): 221–51; D. Scott Rogo, "Spontaneous Contact with the Dead: Perspectives from Grief Counseling, Sociology, and Parapsychology," in *What Survives? Contemporary Explorations of Life after Death* (ed. Gary Doore; Los Angeles: Jeremy Tarcher, 1990), 76–91; Phyllis R. Silverman and Steven L. Nickman, "Children's Construction of their Dead Parents," in *Continuing Bonds: New Understandings of Grief* (ed. Dennis Klass, Phyllis R. Silverman, and Steven L. Nickman; Washington, DC: Taylor & Francis, 1996), 78–79; Janice Smith, "Ghosts: Their Appearance during Bereavement," *Canadian Family Physician* 23 (1977): 121–22; Merton Strommen and A. Irene Strommen, *Five Cries of Grief* (San Francisco: HarperSanFrancisco, 1993), 47–48. One should also keep in mind surveys revealing that vast numbers of normal people report a variety of hallucinatory experiences or visionary encounters, most not having to do with the dead; see M. M. Ohayon, "Prevalence of Hallucinations and Their Pathological Associations in the General Population," *Psychiatry Research* 97 (2000): 153–64.

307. There is no reason to think the ancient world any different in this connection; cf. Pliny the Elder, *Nat.* 7.179; and see the overview of apparitions in the Jewish and Greco-Roman worlds in Shirley Jackson Case, *Experience with the Supernatural in Early Christian Times* (New York: Century, 1929), 34–66. Also helpful is the collection of stories in H. J. T. Bennetts, *Visions of the Unseen: A Chapter in the Communion of Saints* (London: A. R. Mowbray, 1914), esp. 70–84.

308. Richard A. Kalish and David K. Reynolds, "Phenomenological Reality and Post-Death Contact," *Journal for the Scientific Study of Religion* 12 (1973): 209–21.

309. Interested readers can sample typical stories from the Internet, which offers numerous sites cataloging firsthand encounters; see, e.g., www.beyondreligion.com.

reports, which come from all age groups — children relate these experiences, as do teenagers — and, oddly enough, often have nothing to do with the grieving process. Most striking of all, surveys regularly uncover some people who claim that their experience was shared with others, that more than one person saw an apparition or heard a disembodied voice or felt a presence.[310] Another result of some interest is that religious faith or belief in an afterlife is not a necessary prerequisite of these experiences.[311] Sometimes, on the contrary, people are moved to change their attitude toward death and their opinions about the hereafter.[312]

Perhaps it is not out of line here to relate my own experience. One of my best friends was, in 1987, tragically run over by a drunk driver. After several weeks in a coma, she died, along with her unborn baby. About a week after this, I awakened in the middle of the night. There, standing at the end of my bed, was my friend Barbara. She said nothing; she simply was there. Her appearance did not match the traditional lore about ghosts. She was not faint or transparent or frightening. She was to the contrary beautiful and brightly luminous and intensely real. Her transfigured, triumphant presence, which lasted only a few seconds, gave me great comfort. Although she said nothing, this thought entered my mind: this sight is ineffably beautiful, and any person in that state would be ineffably beautiful. Whatever the explanation, this is just exactly what happened.

This was not my only ostensible encounter with the deceased Barbara. One early afternoon several weeks later, in the full light of day, I was typing in my study, wholly focused on my work. All of a sudden I felt a strong physical presence, which I sensed as being up, behind, and to my left. I immediately knew, I do not know how, that this was Barbara. Unlike the first time, when I saw something and heard nothing, this time I heard something and saw nothing. As clear as could be, my mind somehow picked up the words: "You must go and see Warren [Barbara's

---

310. Kalish and Reynolds, "Phenomenological Reality," 219: Of 434 individuals interviewed, "a total of ten claimed that one or more others shared the experience [of postmortem contact] with them.... Using the entire study population as a base, slightly over 2 percent reported a post-death encounter that was part of the reality of another person present at the time."

311. Barbato et al., "Parapsychological Phenomena," 34; Susan L. Datson and Samuel J. Marwit, "Personality Constructs and Perceived Presence of Deceased Loved Ones," *Death Studies* 21 (1997): 139; and Sherry Simon-Buller, Victor A. Christopherson, and Randall A. Jones, "Correlates of Sensing the Presence of a Dead Spouse," *Omega* 19 (1988–89): 28.

312. Cf. Greeley, *Religion*, 220; Kalish, "Contacting the Dead," 69; also below, n. 330.

distraught husband] right now." Overwhelmed by this communication out of the blue, I instinctively obeyed. I called Warren and made a late luncheon date. In the event he seemed to me to be doing as well as could be expected; there was no emergency that I could see. The voice, however, had been urgent, and I unhesitatingly heeded its request.

I relate all this not so that others may believe that Barbara survived death and spoke to me, nor that readers might regard me as fantasy prone or a victim of mental dysfunction. The point is only that these things really happen, and in my case I know this from firsthand experience. I also know how overwhelmingly real such events can seem — so real that I took them at the time to originate in something other than my own subjectivity and have difficulty thinking otherwise even now, years later.[313]

Perhaps readers will indulge me further if I report on the series of events related to me after brain cancer killed my father, Cliff Allison, in the spring of 1994. My wife, Kris, was with him when he died; I was home with the children. When she returned from the hospital, one of the first things she told me was that, shortly after he was declared dead by the doctors and she was left alone with the body, his spirit somehow returned, hovered near the ceiling, and told her quite clearly that he was overjoyed at finally being free from all his ills.

Three or four days later, my six-year-old son Andrew came to me one evening and told me that he had just seen Grandpa. My father, he said, had just been sitting beside him on a bed, wearing his green bathrobe, the last piece of clothing Andrew had seen him in. My son, who responded to the experience rather matter-of-factly, then told me that Grandpa had shared with him a secret and that he could not tell anyone what it was.

A few weeks after this, my brother John informed me that he had been walking down the street and had plainly heard our father's voice in his head. That voice instructed him about several matters, both personal and of a business nature. My brother had no doubt that the voice, which responded to questions, was real. When, for instance, my brother asked, "What did you think of the funeral, Dad?" the voice said, "I don't know; I got lost." Months later John told me that the voice had returned once

---

313. One may compare the vividness and even "hyperreality" of other sorts of visionary experience; see Simon J. Sherwood, "A Comparison of the Features of Psychomanteum and Hypnagogic/Hypnopompic Experiences," *International Journal of Parapsychology* 11 (2000): 97–121.

more and asked him to call a certain individual and wish her a happy birthday. Upon making the call, John says, he learned it was indeed the woman's birthday.

I shall not continue this narrative any further, except to observe that, months after my father's passing, my mother, Virginia, claimed that he had made his presence known to her, that my daughter, Emily, in 1995, had a vision of her grandfather while she was playing one afternoon in our backyard, and that I also heard from two people outside the family, Bill and Jane, of their alleged encounters with Clifford.

I have inevitably thought of this series of reports when subsequently reading 1 Cor 15. Most of the stories were shared with me independently of each other, and if I were looking for reasons to believe in my father's survival of bodily death, I suppose I could compose a little list like Paul's and regard it as evidential: "Clifford passed away in the hospital, after which he communicated to Kris; then he appeared to Andrew and spoke with him; then he gave guidance to John, after which his presence made itself felt to Bill and Virginia and Jane; and last of all he appeared to Emily; five of them are still alive, although two have died."

Whether one regards my family's stories or those like them as a farrago of nonsense, the hallucinatory projections of self-deceived mourners, or seriously reckons with the possibility that some of them are genuine encounters with the other side, the first point for historians of the New Testament is that the sorts of experiences just recounted are common, and they typically seem quite real to percipients. Moreover, different accounts from various times and sundry places show so many similarities that we are indubitably dealing with a phenomenon about which generalizations can be made, regardless of the etiology one advances.[314]

Although many will be sure to resist compiling parallels between what we find in the Gospels and what we find among the bereaved generally, it is simply not true that the events in the Gospels are "utterly without analogy."[315] Not only is Jesus' resurrection "odd, so that there is some

---

314. See esp. Osis, "Apparitions Old and New."

315. Against Baker, *Foolishness of God*, 251. Contrast also Craig, *New Testament Evidence*, 402–3; Hans Kessler, *Such den Lebenden nicht bei den Toten: Die Auferstehung Jesu Christi in biblischer, fundamentaltheologischer und systematischer Sicht* (new ed.; Würzel: Echter, 1995), 219–36; and *The Encyclopedia of the Lutheran Church* (Minneapolis: Augsburg, 1965), 3:2445, s.v. "Visions": "The appearances of the Risen Christ are never described in the NT as visions; they are in a class by themselves."

reason for comparing it with other odd events,"[316] but the Gospels themselves indeed know the analogy just indicated, because they attempt to
refute it. According to Luke 24:39–43, Jesus cannot be merely a spirit
(πνεῦμα) because he can eat and be handled. John 20:24–29 is similar.
Jesus says to doubting Thomas: "Put your finger here and see my hands.
Reach out your hand and put it in my side. Do not doubt but believe."
Matthew 28:9 ("And coming to him, they took hold of his feet"; cf.
John 20:16, 17 v.l.) might be cut of the same apologetical cloth, for
throughout worldwide folklore, ghosts often have no feet.[317] If the text
presupposes this idea, then the grasping of feet indicates that Jesus is not
a ghost in the popular sense. One may compare the Coptic of *Ep. Apost.*
11, where the risen Jesus says, "You, Andrew, look at my feet and see if
they do not touch the ground. For it is written in the prophet, 'The foot
of a ghost or a demon does not join to the ground' " (cf. Theophylact,
Comm. Matt. ad 28:9–10 [PG 123:481]).

But to protest the parallel is to recognize it, and when one reads the
literature on apparitions, not all of it uncritical, one understands why.
In ways reminiscent of New Testament traditions, there are numerous
reports of apparitions in which the departed[318]

• are both seen and heard,[319]

---

316. Don Cupitt, *Christ and the Hiddenness of God* (Philadelphia: Westminster, 1971),
144.

317. For examples from the literature on modern apparitions, see Timothy Beardsworth,
*A Sense of Presence: The Phenomenology of Certain Kinds of Visionary and Ecstatic Experi-
ence, Based on a Thousand Contemporary First-Hand Accounts* (Oxford: Religious Experience
Research Unit, 1977), 6; Hilary Evans and Patrick Huyghe, *The Field Guide to Ghosts and
Other Apparitions* (New York: Quill, 2000), 52, 62, 82, 86; N. Lukianowicz, "Hallucinations
à Troix," *Archives of General Psychiatry* 1 (1959): 325; Ian Stevenson, "Six Modern Appari-
tional Experiences," *Journal of Scientific Exploration* 9 (1995): 353. Even visions of the Virgin
Mary can come without feet; see Randall Sullivan, *The Miracle Detective: An Investigation of
Holy Visions* (New York: Atlantic Monthly Press, 2004), 76, 84, 114.

318. In what follows I cite illustrations from across the varied literature on apparitions. If
one objects that much of this is from popular writings, the retort is that the New Testament is
itself hardly a collection of critical investigations: I am comparing like with like.

319. Cf. Matt 28:9–10, 16–20; Ps.-Mark 16:14–18; Luke 24:13–49; John 20:11–29;
21:4–23; Acts 1:6–11; William F. Barrett, *On the Threshold of the Unseen* (New York:
E. Dutton, 1917), 145–47; Devers, "Experiencing the Deceased," 64; Green and McCreery,
Apparitions, 80–84, 95–101, 191; Guggenheim and Guggenheim, *Heaven!*, 92, 99, 101, 133,
346; Haraldsson, "Erscheinungen," 476, 481; Hornell Hart and Ella B. Hart, "Visions and
Apparitions Collectively and Reciprocally Perceived," *Proceedings of the Society for Psychical
Research* 41 (1933): 246–47; Jaffé, *Apparitions*, 129; Raymond A. Moody and Paul Perry, *Re-
unions: Visionary Encounters with Departed Loved Ones* (New York: Random House, 1994),
24–29, 89, 99–100, 132–34, 140–41; W. G. Roll, "Encounters with a Talking Apparition,"

- are seen now by one person and later by another,[320]

- are seen by more than one percipient at the same time,[321]

Fate 38, no. 11 (1985): 66–72; William Winter, *The Life of David Belasco* (New York: Benjamin, 1972), 466–68. Habermas, "Explaining Away Jesus' Resurrection," 47, underestimates the prevalence of apparitions that speak: they are not uncommon, at least within bereavement experiences.

The verbal communications of apparitions are often said to be telepathic or heard with the mind, not the ears. They also tend to say little, often only a few words, rarely more than a few lines; this too fits the New Testament stories; cf. H. J. Irwin, *An Introduction to Parapsychology* (Jefferson, NC: McFarland, 1989), 230: "Any spoken communication usually is limited to a few words." This accords with most apparitional experiences lasting less than a minute; cf. Green and McCreery, *Apparitions*, 143. For the opinion that the apparitions of Jesus were originally nonverbal — Ps.-Mark 16:9, 12; and 1 Cor 15:5–8 refer to Jesus appearing but not to him speaking — see Schmiedel, "Resurrection," 4063–64; and the discussion of Vögtle, *Osterglaube*, 72–91. The latter considers this an open question, even though Jesus speaks in every single appearance story in early Christian sources.

320. Cf. Matt 28:9–10, 16–20; Ps.-Mark 16:9–20; Luke 24:13–49; John 20:11–29; 21:1–3; 1 Cor 15:5–8; J. Burton, "Contact with the Dead," 71; Caesarius of Heisterbach, *Dialogue on Miracles* 12.15; Teresa Cameron and William G. Roll, "An Investigation of an Apparitional Experience," *Theta* 2, no. 4 (1983): 74–78; Flammarion, *Death*, 364–65; Guggenheim and Guggenheim, *Heaven!*, 263; Gurney et al., *Phantasms*, 472–73; Lukianowicz, "Hallucinations à Troix," 325; R. C. Morton, "Record of a Haunted House," *Proceedings of the Society for Psychical Research* 8 (1892): 311–32; F. W. H. Myers, "On Recognised Apparitions Occurring More Than a Year after Death," *Proceedings of the Society for Psychical Research* July 8 (1889): 60–62; Paramhansa Yogananda, *Autobiography of a Yogi* (New York: Philosophical Library, 1946), 348–50, 413. For an example of this within the context of a religious enthusiasm akin to that which incubated the early church, see Edwin A. Abbott, *St. Thomas of Canterbury: His Death and Miracles* (London: Adam & Charles Black, 1898), 1:246–47: In a letter sent to the pope shortly after the death of Thomas Beckett, the unknown author, referring to "the frequent testimony of many," writes: "It is said and constantly asserted that after his [Beckett's] Passion he appeared in a vision to many to whom he declared that he was not dead but alive, showing no wounds but only the scars of wounds." Multiple sightings of John of the Cross were also reported in the days after his death; see E. Cobham Brewer, *A Dictionary of Miracles: Imitative, Realistic, and Dogmatic* (Philadelphia: J. Lippincott, 1885), 33–34.

321. Cf. Matt 28:9–10, 16–20; Ps.-Mark 16:12, 14; Luke 24:13–49; John 20:19–29; 21:1–3; Acts 1:6–11; 1 Cor 15:5–7; Devers, "Experiencing the Deceased," 88–89; H. Evans, *Ghosts*, 15–16, 50–51, 64–67, 116, 193, 260–61; Mitch Finley, *Whispers of Love: Inspiring Encounters with Deceased Relatives and Friends* (New York: Crossroad, 1995), 105; Flammarion, *Death*, 339, 349–52, 363; Green and McCreery, *Apparitions*, 40–48; Guggenheim and Guggenheim, *Heaven!*, 330, 334, 338–40; Gurney et al., *Phantasms*, 466–517; Haraldsson, "Erscheinungen"; Hart and Hart, "Visions and Apparitions," 205–49; Lukianowicz, "Hallucinations à Troix," 325; Morton, "Record"; F. W. H. Myers, *Human Personality and Its Survival of Bodily Death* (London: Longmans, Green, 1919), 2:27–31; Louisa E. Rhine, "Hallucinatory Psi Experiences II: The Initiative of the Percipient in Hallucinations of the Living, the Dying, and the Dead," *Journal of Parapsychology* 21 (1957): 35–36; William Oliver Stevens, *Unbidden Guests* (London: Allen & Unwin, 1949), 294; G. N. M. Tyrrell, *Apparitions* (rev. ed.; New York: Collier, 1953), 76–80. In Palmer's survey, fully 12 percent of apparitional experiences were collective; see "Mail Survey," 228. For a modern, collective vision of Jesus, see Phillip H. Wiebe, *Visions of Jesus: Direct Encounters from the New Testament to Today* (New York: Oxford University Press, 1997), 77–82.

Wilckens, *Resurrection*, 113, claims that "in Jewish tradition, visions are always experienced by individuals and not by groups." One is unsure what to make of this statement because one is unsure how to define "vision." Does 3 Macc 6:18, where two angels publicly descend from

- are sometimes seen by some but not all present,[322]
- appear to individuals who did not know them in life,[323]
- create doubt in some percipients,[324]
- offer reassurance and give comfort,[325]

heaven ("visible to all except the Jews"), record a vision? Or are the angels here seemingly concrete, as in Gen 18–19? Is an encounter with a concrete angel a "vision" or not?

322. Cf. Matt 28:17 (?); Acts 9:7; Bede, *Hist. Eccl.* 4.9; *Vita ex Metaphraste* 4, in *Acta sanctorum* January 11 (Bruxelles: Culture et civilization, 1965), 688; Uranius the Presbyter, *Ep.* 3 (PL 53:861); Bonaventure, *Major Legend of St. Francis* 14; Gurney et al., *Phantasms*, 473; Guggenheim and Guggenheim, *Heaven!* 332; Erlendur Haraldsson, "The Iyengar-Kirti Case: An Apparitional Case of the Bystander Type," *Journal of the Society for Psychical Research* 54, no. 806 (1987): 67; Jaffé, *Apparitions*, 87; Lukianowicz, "Hallucinations à Troix," 325; Frank Podmore, *Apparitions and Thought-Transference: An Examination of the Evidence for Telepathy* (London: Walter Scott, 1902), 285; Walter Franklin Prince, *Noted Witnesses for Psychic Occurrences* (New Hyde Park, NY: University Books, 1963), 204–5, 221–22; Rhine, "Hallucinatory," 39; Stevenson, "Experiences," 356.

323. Cf. Acts 9:1–9; 22:6–16; 26:12–18; H. Evans, *Ghosts*, 22–24; Green and McCreery, *Apparitions*, 50–51 (on 178 Green and McCreery generalize that the majority of apparitions are unrecognized); Haraldsson, "Erscheinungen," 481; Hart and Hart, "Visions and Apparitions," 248; Jaffé, *Apparitions*, 105–7, 129; LaGrand, *Communication*, 130, 136; Andrew Mackenzie, *Hauntings and Apparitions* (London: Granada, 1982), 47–74, 75–88, 129–39, 210–33; Myers, "Apparitions," 22–23, 28, 57–58, 61; Prince, *Witnesses*, 283–84; Rhine, "Hallucinatory Psi Experiences," 36. A standard motif in ghost stories is the unknown identity of the ghost.

324. Cf. Matt 28:17; Luke 24:37–38, 41; John 20:20; Acts 9:5; 22:8; 26:15 ("Who are you, Lord?"); Barbato et al., "Parapsychological Phenomena," 34–35; Edie Devers and Katherine Morton Robinson, "The Making of a Grounded Theory: After Death Communication," *Death Studies* 26 (2002): 249; M. Damaris J. Drewry, "Purported After-Death Communication and Its Role in the Recovery of Bereaved Individuals: A Phenomenological Study," *Academy of Religion and Psychical Research 2003 Annual Conference Proceedings* (Bloomfield, CT: Academy of Religion and Psychical Research, 2003), 80, 83; Guggenheim and Guggenheim, *Heaven!*, 7, 90, 132 ("I really didn't know what to make of it at the time"), 331; Haraldsson, "The Iyengar-Kirti Case"; Lukianowicz, "Hallucinations à Troix," 326; Sullivan, *Miracle Detective*, 90; F. G. Tribbe, "The Breadth of Psychical Research Establishes Survival," in *1995 Annual Conference Proceedings: Personal Survival of Bodily Death* (Bloomfield, CN: Academy of Religion and Psychical Research, 1995), 102–103. According to Dewi Rees, *Death and Bereavement: The Psychological, Religious and Cultural Interfaces* (London: Whurr, 1997), 187, some of his patients "rationalized these incidents by saying they had been dreaming, or had pictured the deceased in their mind's eye."

325. Cf. Matt 28:10, 20; Luke 24:38–40; John 20:19–21, 26–27; G. Bennett and K. M. Bennett, "Presence," 151; Eunice Hale Cobb, *Memoir of James Arthur Cobb* (Boston: Sylvanus Cobb, 1852), 124–25; Devers, "Experiencing the Deceased," 69–72; idem, *Goodbye*, 25–26; Finley, *Whispers*, 67; Green and McCreery, *Apparitions*, 99, 200–3; Guggenheim and Guggenheim, *Heaven!*, 78 ("I'll be with you always"), 88, 93, 95–96, 104, 107, 131, 135, 260, 331 ("I am always with you"), 354 ("I feel he is saying, 'I'm here. I will always be here for you'"); Hay, *Religious Experience*, 47; LaGrand, *Communication*, 60, 77; Moody and Perry, *Reunions*, 138; Melvin Morse and Paul Perry, *Parting Visions: Uses and Meanings of Pre-Death, Psychic, and Spiritual Experiences* (New York: Villard, 1994), 119–20; J. B. Phillips, *Ring of Truth: A Translator's Testimony* (New York: Macmillan, 1967), 118–19; on 119 Phillips comments: "It is possible that *some* of the appearances of the risen Jesus were…veridical visions" akin to Phillips' own vision of C. S. Lewis. Accounts often refer to feeling the ongoing presence of the percipient. See further Datson and Marwit, "Personality Constructs," 133, 142; and Rees, "The Bereaved and Their Hallucinations," 69.

- give guidance and make requests or issue imperatives,[326]

- are overwhelmingly real and indeed seemingly solid,[327]

- appear and disappear in unusual and abrupt ways and display what has been called "four-dimensional mobility,"[328]

326. Cf. Matt 28:10, 19–20; Ps.-Mark 16:15–18; Luke 24:25–27, 47–49; John 20:17, 21–23; 21:15–17; Acts 1:8; 9:6; 22:10; 26:16–18; Barbato et al., "Parapsychological Phenomena," 32; W. F. Barrett, *Threshold of the Unseen*, 146; Caesarius of Heisterbach, *Dialogue on Miracles* 12.33; Devers, *Goodbye*, 26–27; Guggenheim and Guggenheim, *Heaven!*, 78, 86, 136, 197, 329; Haraldsson, "The Iyengar-Kirti Case"; Jaffé, *Apparitions*, 59, 140; Elisabeth Kübler-Ross, "Death Does Not Exist," in *The New Holistic Health Handbook: Living Well in a New Age* (ed. Shepherd Bliss et al.; Lexington, MA: Stephen Greene, 1985), 320–21; LaGrand, *Communication*, 79; Archie Matson, *Afterlife* (New York: Harper & Row, 1977), 46–48; Prince, *Witnesses*, 293; Rhine, "Hallucinatory Psi Experiences," 39–49. The postmortem appearances of Teresa of Avila were particularly concerned with offering advice to her followers; see Carlos M. N. Eire, *From Madrid to Purgatory: The Art and Craft of Dying in Sixteenth-Century Spain* (Cambridge: Cambridge University Press, 1995), 479–87.

327. Cf. Matt 28:9; Luke 24:36–43; John 20:17, 20, 24–29; 21:4–14; Jan Connell, *Queen of the Cosmos: Interviews with the Visionaries* (Orleans, MA: Paraclete, 1990), 40 ("My mother came over to me. She put her arms around me and kissed me"); Devers, *Goodbye*, 30 ("There she was, as solid as you or me"), 42, 148 ("He was solid like you or me.... His hand was warm and full of life, not icy the way you might think"); Finley, *Whispers*, 75; Guggenheim and Guggenheim, *Heaven!*, 8 ("I know I touched her, and she had feeling to her"), 92 ("I touched his right arm with my left hand, and I felt a lot of heat coming from his body"), 98 ("She was solid — there was nothing ethereal about her at all"), 100 ("There was nothing ephemeral about him"), 101 ("She appeared solid and real"), 106 ("It was real — there is no question in my mind"), 109 ("Her hand was solid and very warm"), 100 ("solid and firm and real"), 329 ("He seemed very, very solid"), 350 ("very, very real, very solid and distinct and three-dimensional"); Hart and Hart, "Visions and Apparitions," 246–47; Lukianowicz, "Hallucinations à Troix," 327 (the percipient "sometimes would even get out of bed and try to push the hallucinated image of her mother out of her room"); Yogananda, *Autobiography*, 350 (the apparition says, "Here, touch my flesh"), 413–14. Irwin, *Introduction*, 230, generalizes: "Apparitions appear real and solid." People who see apparitions of friends or relatives almost never use the word "ghost" because their experience does not match the traditional lore. It is mentally disturbed individuals who often comment on the *unreality* of their visions. The truth is that "human brains do not need external stimuli in order to create physical or material visionary bodies," so the circumstance that Jesus' "followers could identify him and that they experienced him in bodily form as eating, speaking and walking is no argument in favour of any physical, material body." So Pieter F. Craffert, " 'Seeing a Body into Being': Reflections on Scholarly Interpretations of the Nature and Reality of Jesus' Resurrected Body," *Religion and Theology* 9 (2002): 101; see further below, 289–93. In view of John 20:17, perhaps I should report that in some modern stories an apparition will ask not to be touched, or a percipient will feel that he or she should not touch the vision: Guggenheim and Guggenheim, *Heaven!*, 92, 331 ("No, you cannot touch me now"); Sylvia Hart Wright, *When Spirits Come Calling: The Open-Minded Skeptic's Guide to After-Death Contacts* (Nevada City, CA: Blue Dolphin, 2002), 20 ("No, don't touch me"); Moody and Perry, *Reunions*, 28 ("She would not let me touch her. Two or three times I reached to give her a hug, and each time she put her hands up and motioned me back. She was so insistent about not being touched that I didn't pursue it"); Sylvia Hart Wright, "Paranormal Contact with the Dying: 14 Contemporary Death Coincidences," *Journal of the Society for Psychical Research* 63 (1999): 261 ("No, don't touch me").

328. The phrase is that of H. H. Price, *Essays in the Philosophy of Religion* (Oxford: Clarendon, 1972), 122. Cf. Matt 28:9; Luke 24:31, 36; John 20:19, 26. For illustrations

- are not perceived as apparitional at the beginning of the experience,[329]

- manifest themselves so convincingly that the percipient undergoes changes in belief,[330] and

- are seen less and less as more and more time follows their death, with most appearances (although certainly not all) taking place within a year of the death of the person represented by the apparition.[331]

---

see *De S. Gertrude Virgine* in *Acta sanctorum* March 7 (Bruxelles: Culture et civilisation, 1968), 596–97; *Vita ex Metaphraste* 4 in *Acta sanctorum* January 11 (Bruxelles: Culture et civilization, 1965), 688; J. Burton, "Contact with the Dead," 69; Devers, *Goodbye*, 29–30, 31; Green and McCreery, Apparitions, 135–42; Guggenheim and Guggenheim, *Heaven!*, 16, 89, 91, 92, 99, 108–9, 328, 345–46; Haraldsson, "Erscheinungen," 481; Hart and Hart, "Visions and Apparitions," 245–46; Jaffé, *Apparitions*, 63, 79, 104, 104–106, 139–40; Kent, *Psychological Origins*, 43, 45; LaGrand, *Communication*, 58; Lukianowicz, "Hallucinations à Troix," 326; Harold Owen, *Journey from Obscurity: Memoirs of the Owen Family* (London: Oxford University Press, 1965), 3:198.

329. Cf. Luke 24:30–31; John 20:15; 21:4; *De SS. Andronico et Athanasia Confessoribus in Aegypto* in *Acta sanctorum* October 9 (Bruxelles: Culture et civilization, 1970), 999; Daniel Defoe, "A True Relation of the Apparition of One Mrs. Veal, the Next Day after Her Death, to One Mrs. Bargrave, at Canterbury, the 8th of September 1705," in Charles Drelincourt, *The Christian's Defense against the Fears of Death, with Seasonable Directions How to Prepare Ourselves to Die Well* (21st ed.; London: J. Buckland, 1776), 1–12; H. Evans and P. Huyghe, *Guide*, 92; Green and McCreery, *Apparitions*, 50; Jaffé, *Apparitions*, 79, 86, 138, 140, 163–67; Kübler-Ross, "Death Does Not Exist," 320–21; LaGrand, *Communication*, 130; Moody and Perry, *Reunions*, 24–25.

330. Cf. Luke 24:36–43; John 20:24–29; Acts 9:1–19; 22:6–16; 26:12–18; J. Burton, "Contact with the Dead," 72 ("About 60 percent [of those reporting contact with the dead] of those between the ages of 16 and 60 said their beliefs about the nature of life had changed. This change of attitude was even more pronounced among persons aged 61 to 79 where 81.25 percent reported it"); Douglas J. Davies, *Ritual and Belief: The Rhetoric of Funerary Rites* (2nd ed.; London: Continuum, 2002), 172 ("Since his wife's death he now believes in ghosts, which he did not before"); Devers, "Experiencing the Deceased," 94–96; idem, *Goodbye*, 8; Drewry, "Communication," 77 ("My sister's experience instantly shifted her worldview or paradigm"); Guggenheim and Guggenheim, *Heaven!*, 107 ("I was a card-carrying skeptic before this experience"), 140 ("Immediately, I had a completely different outlook on life, and I knew that I was a changed person"), 337 ("I was a hard-nosed nonbeliever until I had this experience. I didn't think anything like this could ever happen"), 372–73 ("I didn't believe in anything except this life....All of a sudden, I believed!"); Hart and Hart, "Visions and Apparitions," 221 (appearance to one who did not believe in apparitions); Jaffé, *Apparitions*, 163–64; LaGrand, *Communication*, 58 ("I never believed in this sort of thing"), 77 ("She [a grandmother's apparition] changed the way I look at life"); Louis E. LaGrand, *Message and Miracles* (St. Paul, MN: Llewellyn, 1999), 184–85; Moody and Perry, *Reunions*, 28–29.

331. Cf. Acts 1:3; 1 Cor 15:8. See W. F. Barrett, *Threshold of the Unseen*, 144 ("The number of recognized apparitions decreases rapidly in the few days after death, then more slowly, and after a year or more they become far less frequent and more sporadic"); Devers, "Experiencing the Deceased," 50–51; Grimby, "Bereavement," 75; Jaffé, *Apparitions*, 171; Pamela M. Kircher, *Love Is the Link: A Hospice Doctor Shares Her Experience of Near-Death and Dying* (Burdett, NY: Larson, 1995), 73 ("Visitations are...quite common in the days or first few weeks after the death of a close relative"); Dennis Klass and Tony Walter, "Processes of Grieving: How Bonds Are Continued," in *Handbook of Bereavement Research: Consequences, Coping, and Care* (ed. Margaret S. Stroebe, Robert O. Hansson, Wolfgang Stroebe, and Henk Schut; Washington, DC: American Psychological Association, 2001), 436; Meg Maxwell and

What follows from parallels such as this? Some would hope, and others would argue, very little. One can also parade parallels between the resurrection stories and tales from Jewish tradition and Greco-Roman mythology. Do not the various lists of likenesses somehow moderate each other, maybe even cancel each other out? More importantly, do not the analogies suggested above leave the important historical particularities unexplained? Typical encounters with the recently deceased do not issue in claims about an empty tomb, nor do they lead to the founding of a new religion. And they certainly cannot explain the specific content of the words attributed to the risen Jesus. Apparitions do not, furthermore, typically eat or drink,[332] and they are not seen by crowds of up to five hundred people.[333] So, one might contend, early Christianity does not supply us with just one more variant of something otherwise belonging to common experience.

Verena Tschudin, *Seeing the Invisible: Modern Religious and Other Transcendent Experiences* (London: Arkana, 1990), 35. Cf. Green and McCreery, *Apparitions*, 188: "The cases reported to us tend to occur most frequently within a week of the death, and the number falls away as the length of time since the death increases."

332. I speak of the modern literature here (in which there are to be sure occasional exceptions; see, e.g., H. Evans, *Ghosts*, 85); but Gregory J. Riley, *Resurrection Reconsidered: Thomas and John in Controversy* (Minneapolis: Fortress, 1995), 46–47, reminds us that ancient ghosts did in fact have the ability to eat and drink; cf. Homer, *Od.* 11.96; Phlegon, *Mirab.* 2. In much Jewish tradition, incorporeal angels also have this ability; see 292–93 below.

333. Cf. Green and McCreery, *Apparitions*, 41: "There are reports of groups numbering from two up to about eight people seeing the same apparition at the same time, but there are no well authenticated cases of groups much larger than this doing so." The Jesus who appeared in the Muslim village of Kawangware, Nairobi, on June 11 of 1988, for which we have photographic images, must have been an actor. See the picture at http://www.shareintl.org/. The same may hold for the so-called Cummings apparition, witnessed by dozens and dozens of people in Sullivan, Maine, in the year 1800 and thereafter; for knowledge of this we are dependent upon the testimony and interviews of Abraham Cummings, *Immortality Proved by the Testimony of Sense: In Which Is Contemplated the Doctrine of Spectres, and the Existence of a Particular Spectre Addressed to the Candor of This Enlightened Age* (Bath, ME: J. G. Torrey, 1826). Although no less than C. J. Ducasse, *A Critical Examination of the Belief in a Life after Death* (Springfield, IL: Charles C. Thomas, 1961), 154–56, took this episode seriously, reservations are in order, even if one is open-minded about such matters; see Rodger I. Anderson, "The Cummings Apparition," *Journal of Religion and Psychical Research* 6 (1983): 206–19. I must confess, however, that I am at a loss to explain the 1968–69 sightings of the Virgin Mary at St. Mary's Coptic Church in Zeitoun, Egypt; she was reportedly seen by tens of thousands, both Muslims and Christians. See Jerome Palmer, *Our Lady Returns to Egypt* (San Bernadino: Culligan, 1969); also, the photographs at http://www.zeitun-eg.org/stmaridx.htm; and Victor DeVincenzo, "The Apparitions at Zeitoun, Egypt: An Historical Overview," *Journal of Religion and Psychical Research* 11 (1988): 3–13. These Marian sightings were impersonal: the figure did not address individuals. I observe that Michael Carroll, *The Cult of the Virgin Mary: Psychological Origins* (Princeton: Princeton University Press, 1986), 211–16, can do no better than posit a Marian interpretation of "the undeniable reality of a luminous something atop the Church of the Virgin in Zeitoun."

I am not unsympathetic to this rebuttal. I do not believe that the early Christian traditions are wholly accounted for by stories gathered from later times and other places, stories that are themselves of a controversial nature and so, instead of enabling us to explain what we do not understand by way of what we do understand, might be thought to leave us with *ignotum per ignotius*.[334] I also disbelieve that, if only we knew enough about apparitions of the dead in general, we would necessarily know enough about the appearances of Jesus in particular. I make no pretense to having some grand, reductionistic theory that presumes to cover all the facts.

And yet, just as later Christic visions should not be ignored by New Testament scholars,[335] and just as the parallels between the resurrection stories and certain Greco-Roman legends assuredly have their place to play in discussions of Christian origins, so too do we need to learn what we can from the study of apparitions of the dead. The differences or points of contrast between such apparitions and the New Testament data can, in any case, be taken to prove too much. The postmortem manifestation of an unremarkable husband to his isolated widow is not going to generate the same significance as the reappearance of a messianic figure whose followers are living within an eschatological scenario that features the resurrection of the dead.[336] Context begets meaning. When Roger Booth protests that the effect of feeling the presence of a loved one in modern bereavement experiences is not "so cataclysmic as to inspire a continuing course of conduct so contrary to past character, as did the appearances of Jesus to the disciples,"[337] he is right, but his implied

---

334. For some of the difficult questions surrounding the nature and etiology of so-called hallucinations, see C. Andrade, S. Srinath, and A. C. Andrade, "True Hallucinations in Non-Psychotic State," *Canadian Journal of Psychiatry* 34 (1989): 704–6; and G. Asaad and B. Shapiro, "Hallucinations: Theoretical and Clinical Overview," *American Journal of Psychiatry* 143 (1986): 188–97.

335. See esp. the thought-provoking work of Wiebe, *Visions* (which Wright strangely neglects). On 148 Wiebe contends: A "NT criticism that confines its attention to the documentary evidence of the first century alone (biblical and extrabiblical), as though ongoing phenomena could have no relevance to understanding and testing claims coming to us from antiquity, deprives itself of a vital tool." Less helpful than Wiebe's work but still of obvious relevance is the uncritical collection of Christic encounters in Gregory Scott Sparrow, *I Am with You Always: True Stories of Encounters with Jesus* (New York: Bantam, 1995).

336. Cf. James H. Hyslop, *Life after Death: Problems of the Future Life and Its Nature* (New York: E. Dutton, 1918), 71: "An apparition of ordinary people would not impress the multitude, but one of such a personality as Christ is represented to be would excite unusual interest and to the same extent emphasize the meaning of the fact."

337. Roger Booth, *Contrasts — Gospel Evidence and Christian Beliefs* (Settle, North Yorkshire: Paget, 1990), 37–38. Cf. Lapide, *Resurrection*, 124–26.

conclusion is wrong. Similar experiences, if they occur within different interpretive frameworks, may have radically disparate effects. Parallels, one should not need to observe, come with differences.

My own view regarding the resemblances I have catalogued is that, while they may not be our Rosetta Stone, they are nonetheless heuristically profitable. They have their place once we embrace a methodological pluralism, which in this connection means attempting to sort and then explain the data to the best of our abilities from different points of view and within different interpretive frameworks. No one method or set of comparative materials will give us all the answers we seek. We strive rather to learn what we can from each method or set, in the knowledge that each may help us with some part of the picture we are trying to piece together. So in the present case I eschew explaining the appearances of Jesus in terms of typical appearances of the dead — an unfeasible task anyway given our limited knowledge and understanding of apparitions in general — but simply ask what light a wider human phenomenon might shed on some of the issues surrounding the resurrection traditions.

1. Dom Crossan has written: "What are often taken, in the last chapters of the New Testament gospels, as entranced revelations, simply because of the analogy with Paul, are not such at all. They bear no marks of such phenomena (no blinding light, nobody knocked to the ground, no heavenly voices) but are rather quite deliberate political dramatizations of the priority of one specific leader over another, of this leadership group over that general community."[338] Leaving aside the generalization about leadership, which strikes me as overdone,[339] the comment that the New Testament resurrection narratives do not look like visionary accounts will not stand. Reports of apparitions of the dead only occasionally feature a blinding light[340] or a voice from the sky, and I do not recall any such apparition knocking someone to the ground. Such reports do, however, as my catalog of parallels shows, bear many resemblances to what we find in the Gospels. Crossan's generalization should be discarded.

---

338. John Dominic Crossan, *Jesus: A Revolutionary Biography* (San Francisco: HarperSanFrancisco, 1994), 169.

339. See above, 237.

340. Luminous apparitions typically do not obscure sight or shut the eyes; see Jaffé, *Apparitions*, 56–78.

2. Pannenberg speaks for many when he affirms that "the appearances reported in the Gospels, which are not mentioned by Paul, have such a strongly legendary character that one can scarcely find a historical kernel of their own in them."[341] Although this skepticism is not contradicted by my own historical-critical analysis on 239–69, apparitions of the dead, if they are relevant to this subject, introduce some second thoughts. The unexpected appearance and disappearance of Jesus, for instance, and the brevity of the speeches are par for the apparitional course.[342] It is also credible that encounters with the risen Jesus, like some apparitions, produced doubt as well as belief, and likewise plausible that the earthly setting for the canonical stories is not a fiction, for apparitions are typically terrestrial.

To expand on this last point: often the Gospel accounts are dismissed as thoroughly late through something close to this line of reasoning: (a) Paul aligns his experience of the risen Jesus with the experiences of Peter and the Twelve (1 Cor 15:3–8). (b) Paul's vision was of a heavenly Jesus (cf. also Acts 7:54–60; Rev 1:9–20), and he must have seen something that led him to speak of a "spiritual body" (1 Cor 15:44), an oxymoron as mystifying as a square circle.[343] (c) It follows that Peter and the Twelve also saw a heavenly Jesus with a "spiritual body," which explains the texts about Jesus being "glorified": he was thought of as having a heavenly body of light.[344] (d) It also follows that the appearance stories in which Jesus does not appear from heaven and proves himself to be physical are late and apocryphal. (e) They can perhaps be explained as a response to Docetism.[345] One also often reads that,

---

341. Pannenberg, *Jesus*, 89.

342. The postresurrection discourses become longer and longer as we move into the apocryphal and Gnostic gospels of the second centuries and later. I submit that this is because they are further and further away from the original experiences.

343. Augustine, *Ep.* 148.5.16 (ed. Goldbacher; CSEL 44:345–46), confesses that he has not read anything on this perplexing subject that deserves to be either learned or taught. Masset, "Immortalité," 333, labels Paul's "spiritual body" an "alliance incohérente de concepts contradictoires."

344. Cf. Marie-Emile Boismard, *Our Victory over Death: Resurrection?* (Collegeville, MN: Liturgical Press, 1999), 127–28, citing John 12:16, 23; 13:31–32; 17:1, 5; Acts 3:13.

345. This argument was firmly in place already the nineteenth century; see, e.g., Daniel Schenkel, *A Sketch of the Character of Jesus: A Biblical Essay* (London: Longmans, Green, 1869), 318; Christian Hermann Weisse, *Die Evangelienfrage im ihrem gegenwärtigen Stadium* (Leipzig: Breitkopf & Härtel, 1856), 272–92; and Weizsäcker, *Apostolic Age*, 1:1–19. Whatever the origin of the motif of touching the risen Jesus, one wonders whether the motif of eating was in origin not a response to Docetism but instead a way of claiming the fulfillment of an eschatological expectation of Jesus; see n. 194.

for early Christians, the resurrection of Jesus was his ascension (cf. Acts 2:33–36; 5:30–31; Phil 2:9; *Barn.* 15.9), so the Easter witnesses must have seen him in heaven. "As the earliest proclamation does not make any distinction between the resurrection of Jesus and his exaltation to the right hand of God, it is best to assume that the series [in 1 Cor 15:3–8] consists of appearances of the exalted Lord."[346]

Against all this,[347] we cannot assume that earlier Jewish Christians shared Paul's rather sophisticated notion of a "spiritual body"; and in any case the apostle nowhere discusses the nature of the appearances to himself or others. First Corinthians 15:3–8 says only that there were christophanies, not what their apparent origin in space was nor what Jesus looked like. Furthermore, whether or not Leslie Houlden is right to doubt that Paul's encounter "was generally admitted to be of the same sort as its predecessors,"[348] nothing establishes that the apostle or others would have perceived an important distinction between a heavenly appearance and an earthly appearance.[349] This may be the sort of differentiation that occurs to modern scholars but did not occur to early Christians. Even if such a distinction were operative, Jewish and Christian texts often feature heavenly beings descending to earth, and why the resurrected, angelic-like Jesus should have to stay in heaven, away from the faithful, escapes me. In harmony with this, although the extant *Gospel of Peter* breaks off at the end, one guesses that the original ended with an appearance to Peter, Andrew, and Levi on or by the Sea of Galilee (14:60), an appearance related to Luke 5:1–11 and John 21 —

---

346. Barnabas Lindars, "Jesus Risen: Bodily Resurrection but No Empty Tomb," *Theology* 89 (1986): 91–92. While early Christians did sometimes use ascension and resurrection language in functionally similar ways, the different proposal that the most ancient idea was of the ascension of Jesus' soul from the cross — so recently Roger Aus, *Samuel, Saul, and Jesus: Three Early Palestinian Jewish Christian Gospel Haggadoth* (SFSHJ 105; Atlanta: Scholars Press, 1994), 173–87 — should be rejected.

347. Wright, *Resurrection*, also rejects this old line of argument, although not all of his reasons are mine.

348. Leslie Houlden, *Connections: The Integration of Theology and Faith* (London: SCM, 1986), 140. Cf. Catchpole, *Resurrection*, 204: "Paul presents his own experience as equivalent to, but not necessarily identical with, that of the persons listed in [1 Cor 15] verses 5–7." Contrast the gratuitous comment of Emil Brunner, *The Mediator: A Study of the Central Doctrine of the Christian Faith* (Philadelphia: Westminster, 1947), 576: "Can we so easily pass over the plain fact that Paul reckons his encounter with the Risen One ... to be identical with those of the original apostles, and that it is accepted by them as such?"

349. We also have no idea what Peter and James and others who believed they saw Jesus would have made of Paul attaching his name to the list of foundational appearances in 1 Cor 15:3–8.

despite the fact that Jesus has already ascended to heaven straight from the tomb (*Gos. Pet.* 10:40).

Also to be considered, if we wish, is the phenomenology of visionary experience. To judge by modern reports, occasionally an apparition is perceived as being neither distinctly terrestrial nor clearly heavenly in origin. In my own experience, for instance, my dead friend Barbara seemed to have walked into my room from another dimension, a space next door, although I have no idea what that means. Words often fail to capture anomalous or visionary experience. I have run across one narrative in which a woman reports that her deceased husband, in the room with her, was at the same time "in heaven."[350] Some exegetes have been similarly confused about Matt 28:16–20: is Jesus in heaven (cf. Acts 7:55) or on earth?[351]

Despite their myriad disagreements with each other and their late and legendary features, the appearance stories in the canonical Gospels, if reckoned akin to other apparitional accounts, may on account of that kinship be considered not wholly imaginary but instead reminiscent in certain particulars of the original experiences — although delineating those particulars is an uncertain business. Such a conclusion would be consistent with my claim, made earlier, that old appearance narratives probably lie behind 1 Cor 15:3–8. For if the traditions in the Gospels are not the descendants of those narratives, where did they all go? Did the original stories simply disappear, to be replaced by a new batch of tales of a wholly different character? Is it not intrinsically more likely that the narratives known to us, with their parallels in firsthand reports of apparitions, were outgrowths of more primitive narratives? I myself am emboldened by the relevant parallels to reckon with more historical memory in the canonical Easter stories, or rather, more memory in some of their repeated motifs, than I otherwise would. Wedderburn, from another point of view, claims: "The stories cannot just . . . be written off or discounted as pure fiction: there are too many puzzling features about them which are unlikely to be sheer invention, and aspects of them seem to mesh with the historical in such a way that they are indeed woven into the fabric of the history of the early church."[352] I agree.

---

350. Stevenson, "Experiences," 353.
351. See Dunn, *Jesus and the Spirit*, 124.
352. Wedderburn, *Resurrection*, 37. Cf. 39: "There are features of these accounts which defy explanation as mere story and which compel us to take them more seriously as accounts of what happened, features which seem in some measure to establish their claim to historicity."

3. Luke 24:39 has the risen Jesus declare that he is not a πνεῦμα, a spirit. His proof is that he has σάρκα καὶ ὀστέα, flesh and bones. John 20:24–29 is of similar import, and in John 21:9–14, Jesus, returned from the dead, both cooks and serves food. In part because of these texts, Christians through the ages have thought of the resurrection appearances as involving a body as concrete as any run-of-the-mill, normal human body. They have accordingly supposed that the disciples saw Jesus with their normal faculties of visual perception.[353] Much modern scholarship, however, has come to regard the texts just cited as relatively late and apologetical, perhaps even directed at an emerging Docetism; and as already observed, this has in turn cleared the way to understand the first meetings with the risen Jesus as being akin to Luke's version of the encounter of Paul on the Damascus road, where the apostle has what we would call a vision. A trajectory from less literal to more literal can, then, be suggested, with Paul's notion of a spiritual body being closer to the primitive tradition, and the seemingly solid resurrected figures in Luke and John being a later development.[354]

Before offering dissent by considering how apparitions of the dead might bear on this issue, it is useful to recall the old Jewish and Christian texts in which angels are not recognized as such because they seem, to all outward appearances, to be perfectly human,[355] or in which an angel is actually handled and its identity is still not revealed,[356] or in which angels are seen to eat and/or drink.[357] Such stories mean that, apart from the express denial in Luke 24:39, the risen Jesus, in the traditions that have come down to us, does nothing to distinguish himself clearly from

---

353. For a recent defense of this view, see Stephen T. Davis, " 'Seeing' the Risen Lord," in Davis, Kendall, and O'Collins, *Resurrection*, 126–47. Davis is at least correct in claiming that he has the weight of Christian tradition on his side.

354. This idea is fundamental to Grass's influential work, *Ostergeschehen*. Cf. Peter F. Carnley, *The Structure of Resurrection Belief* (Oxford: Clarendon, 1987), 234–49, and the related argument introduced above on 286. Contrast Dunn, *Jesus and the Spirit*, 114–22, who argues that things were more complex, and that one can see both movement away from a more physical interpretation and a turn toward the same.

355. E.g., Gen 18–19; Judg 6:11–24; 13:16; Tob 5:4–5; Heb 13:2; Mark 16:5; *T. Abr.* (rec. long) 2–6.

356. E.g., Gen 18:4 LXX; *T. Abr.* (rec. long) 3:7–9; *Tg. Neof.* 1. on Gen 18:4; Jerome, *Ep.* 66.11 (ed. Hilberg; CSEL 54:661–62).

357. E.g., Gen 18:8; 19:3; Tob 12:19; *T. Abr.* (rec. long) 4:9–10; *Num. Rab.* 10:5; *Pesiq. Rab.* 25:3; Ephraem, *Comm. Gen.* 15.2. Even those who denied that angels eat and drink admitted that, in Gen 18, they at least seemed to do so: Philo, *Abr.* 110, 117–118; *QG* 4.9; Josephus, *Ant.* 1.197; Justin Martyr, *Dial.* 57 (ed. Marcovich; PTS 47:167–68); Ps.-Athanasius, *Confut.* (PG 28:1377A–1380B); *Catena Sinaitica* 1070 and 1074 ad Gen 18:8; *Tg. Neof.* 1 and *Tg. Ps.-J.* on Gen 18:8; *b. B. Meṣiʿa* 86b; etc.

the angels, who were reckoned to be רוחות, πνεύματα, spirits, creatures lacking flesh and blood, and indeed to be ἀσώματος, incorporeal.[358] I note that, in Romanos the Melodist, *Cant.* 42.19 (ed. Grosdidier de Matons; SC 128:478), an angel is described as ἀσώματος yet said to be no φάσμα, no apparition or phantom.

How then would ancient readers have understood the eating, the drinking, and the seeming solidity of the risen Jesus? Maybe the answer lies in the fact that angelic spirits were imagined to be quite different from ghostly human spirits (cf. Matt 14:26; Luke 24:37), and presumably Luke 24:39 has only the latter in mind. That is, the Lukan Jesus denies that he belongs with the specters of popular superstition: he is no fleeting, half-dead, insubstantial, transparent, helpless, restless shade who haunts the earth because he has failed to go to a better place.[359] He instead is robust and fully alive, wholly real.

Just as the seemingly solid nature of the risen Jesus clearly fails to distinguish him from the incorporeal angels, so too, interestingly enough, it does not set him apart from many apparitions. "The majority of visual apparitions" are "opaque rather than transparent," so much so that the figure of the apparition seems "to blot out the part of the real environment behind it, as a real person would."[360] Most apparitions of the dead seen during bereavement are not, in the usual sense of the word, "ghosts" (which is why the bereaved rarely use that word of their experiences). Apparitions instead commonly appear to be just like real human beings. It is accordingly often only their odd arrival, or their sudden disappearance, or their identification with a deceased individual that gives them away. Time and time again people not only hear and see apparitions: they even touch them (cf. the testimonies in n. 327, above). Saint Catharine Labourè reported on the Virgin Mary being seen "en chair et

---

358. *1 En.* 15:4, 6–7; 1QS 3:25; CD 12:2–3; Philo, *Conf.* 174; *Abr.* 118; *QG.* 4.8; Heb 1:14; *T. Abr.* (rec. long) 3:6; Ign. *Smyrn.* 3.2; *T. Sol.* 2:5 v. l. Yet the ancients understood ἀσώματος in only a relative sense. Even the early church fathers, so influenced by Hellenistic dualism, generally allow that angels have bodies of a sort; see F. Andres, *Die Engellehre der griechischen Apologeten des zweiten Jahrhunderts und ihr Verhältnis zur griechisch-römischen Dämonologie* (Paderborn: F. Schöningh, 1914). Pseudo-Dionysius did not believe angels to have matter and form, but it would be wrong to read his sophistication into earlier writers, who tended to think of the soul as quasi-material.

359. Cf. Matt 14:26; and see R. C. Finucane, *Appearances of the Dead: A Cultural History of Ghosts* (London: Junction Books, 1982), 4–28.

360. Green and McCreery, *Apparitions*, 150.

en os,"[361] while the novelist Reynolds Price has said that his encounter with Jesus exhibited "a concrete visual and tactile reality unlike any sleeping or waking dream I've known or heard of."[362] Whatever the experiences behind such claims, the following contemporary story told by a young girl, sleeping with her sister, is not that unusual:

> My grandfather was lying between us, on his back but with his head turned, looking at Janet. I asked him what was the matter, thinking it most strange that he should be in our bed at all. He turned his face towards me, when I spoke, and I put my hand out and started stroking his beard. (He always allowed me to brush it for him as a special treat.) He answered quietly, saying not to jump around too much in case I woke Janet, and that he was only making sure we were alright. It was only then that I remembered that he had died the previous June, and the fear and horror I felt then can be imagined and I started screaming for my mother. The grown-ups passed it off as a bad dream, but I was able to tell them a lot of their conversation of the evening, that had drifted up to me, as I lay awake. I'd like to stress that in no way was I conscious that he was a "ghost." He felt solid, warm and looked and spoke quite naturally.[363]

Even more striking, because of the explicit comparison with the Jesus tradition, are these words from a widow regarding encounters with her dead husband:

> He looked and felt just like when he was living. He didn't look like something you could see through, neither time. He just looked real, alive, real. I put my arms around him, it felt just like you or I, just real. You know like, the Lord reappeared, you know when he died, and he was alive and he asked the man to feel the nail hole in his side. My husband was just as real as if he was here with me now.[364]

Testimony such as this adds some real ambiguity to the stories of people touching the risen Jesus and seeing him eat and drink, even if

---

361. Cited by Karl Rahner, "Visions and Prophecies," in his *Studies in Modern Theology* (Freiburg: Herder, 1965), 133n47.

362. Reynolds Price, *A Whole New Life* (New York: Scribner, 1995), 44.

363. Green and McCreery, *Apparitions*, 53; see further 107–9.

364. Devers, "Experiencing the Deceased," 55.

one takes those stories to enshrine straightforward history.[365] What Karl Rahner wrote on the subject of religious visions in general holds here too: "It is not to be taken as a proof of the corporeality (and divine origin) of the vision if the person seen in it 'speaks,' 'moves' — and even lets himself 'be touched' (for even this happens in purely natural, purely imaginary processes)."[366] Now I personally remain incurably dubious of finding history in the demonstrations of Luke 24 and John 20–21: I rather detect Christian apologetics here, an answer to the criticism that Jesus was just a specter. At the same time, and even though there was quite likely a tendency in the tradition to make the appearances more solid, the comparative study of apparitions might be taken to reinforce the possibility that Luke 24 and John 20–21 preserve the primitive conviction that the risen Jesus seemed to those who encountered him not ethereal but utterly real, even solid.

4. The phenomenology of visions might also be brought to bear on what Tom Wright has called the "transphysicality" of Jesus' resurrected body.[367] Paul envisages for the resurrected saints what he calls a "spiritual body" (1 Cor 15:44), and Wright believes that this idea coheres with the stories in which the risen Jesus is seemingly physical and yet behaves in quite peculiar ways: he can appear out of nowhere and disappear into the same. Wright further argues that the notion of resurrected body seemingly shared by the Gospels and Paul cannot be explained against the background of Jewish thought.[368] It must rather have grown out of reflection on the encounters with the risen Jesus, encounters in which Jesus seemed wholly real, bodily present, while at the same time showing himself capable of transcending normal physical barriers.[369]

Although Wright's main point could well be correct, the phenomenon of "transphysicality" is surely less unexpected than he implies. Whatever else we take them to have been, the appearances were seemingly short-lived and sporadic. Jesus was seen, then he was gone; he would appear, then he would disappear. This matters because, within a Jewish

---

365. Cf. Craffert, "Seeing a Body into Being," 101.

366. Rahner, "Visions," 118.

367. For this and what follows, see Wright, *Resurrection*, 608–15.

368. As an aside, because the subject cannot be entered into here, Wright's argument at this point would be much weakened if, against his analysis, one would see (as I do) in some Jewish resurrection texts a connection with astral immortality.

369. There is a related argument in Baker, *Foolishness of God*, 253–56.

context, such a supernormal facility would remind people of nothing so much as stories about angels, who come and go in mysterious ways (cf., e.g., 2 Macc 3:34). Given, then, that Christians in other ways thought of Jesus as being like an angel,[370] his "transphysicality," his solid reality with unreal abilities, is not so peculiar: if he were like an angel, he would have "transphysicality." This is all the more the case because Jewish sources sometimes modeled human destiny upon the imagined life of angels,[371] and because angels were heavenly dwelling spirits who yet were thought of as physically real — recall that in *Jub.* 15:27 they are circumcised and that a popular exegesis of Gen 6:2 imagined them capable of sexual intercourse with human women. To all this one may further add Cavallin's conclusion: "The popular idea about the grossly materialistic and naïve thoughts concerning the resurrection and postmortem life in Early Judaism has very little foundation. Throughout the sources we find suggestions about the heavenly, transcendent, glorified and spiritual state of the righteous in the new life after death."[372]

Apart from the parallel with angels, we may also keep in mind that modern experiences of apparitions often involve, on the phenomenological level, what might be termed "transphysicality." As indicated on the previous pages, apparitions can be perceived as solid and can even sometimes be touched. And yet they also appear and disappear just like the Jesus of the Gospels and, if I may so put it, live outside this world. So those who regard the encounters with the risen Jesus as related to visionary experiences will be astounded neither at the "transphysicality" of the resurrected Jesus nor by Paul's use of "spiritual body."

5. The study of apparitions does not help us determine whether some or all of the appearances of Jesus were purely subjective or partially derived from a reality independent of the percipients. This is only to be expected as the serious literature on apparitions is itself divided over their nature. The one side is well known. There is no disputing that, on their own, "our brains are capable of generating very vivid, realistic, and compelling imaginary experiences."[373] Various explanations are to hand:

---

370. Charles Gieschen, *Angelmorphic Christology: Antecedents and Early Evidence* (AGJU 42; Leiden: Brill, 1998).

371. See Wisd 5:5 (assuming that "sons of God" = angels); 4QSᵇ 4:25; 4Q511 frg. 35; *1 En.* 104:1–6; *2 Bar.* 51:5, 10; Mark 12:25; Acts 6:15; *T. Isaac* 4:43–48; etc.

372. Cavallin, *Life after Death*, 200. Cf. esp. *2 Bar.* 51:2–3.

373. Sherwood, "Psychomanteum," 115.

Visions can and have been plausibly construed in terms of Freudian theory, as the projection of unconscious wishes; or in terms of biological theory, as resulting from dysfunction of the neurotransmitter dopamine or from a lack of calcium or from the ingestion of ergot or from transient microseizures in the temporal lobe; or in terms of psychological theory, such as the failure of metacognitive ability, the capacity to distinguish between self-generated states and external sources of information.[374] Even without the enlightenment of modern science and psychology, it has long been obvious, as Lewes Lauaterus wrote centuries ago, "that many men doo falsly persuade themselues that they see or heare ghostes: for that which they imagin they see or heare, proceedeth eyther of melancholie, madnesse, weaknesse of the senses, feare, or of some other perturbation."[375] Beyond this, human testimony, including firsthand testimony, is fragile,[376] and anyone who doubts how credulous people can be about what they report themselves or others to have seen should visit the Web site of Share International, with its naive catalogue of contemporary visions of Mary and Jesus.[377] Some people will indeed believe anything.

But there is the other side, too. According to Pannenberg, "The thesis that we must regard all visionary experiences as psychological projections with no basis in reality cannot be regarded ... as an adequately grounded philosophical postulate."[378] This is not an irresponsible assertion. For if one sets aside ill-informed preconceptions and takes the time and exercises the patience to examine carefully the critical literature on apparitions, one discovers numerous well-attested reports, reasonably investigated, where several people at once saw an apparition and later concurred on the details, or where an apparition's words contained information that was not otherwise available to the percipients, or where witnesses independently testified to having seen the same apparition at

---

374. See further Wiebe, *Visions*, 172–211.

375. Lewes Lauaterus, *Of Ghostes and Spirites Walking by Nyiht* (London: Henry Benneyman for Richard V. Vatkyns, 1572), 11.

376. In connection with the literature on apparitions, see Rodger I. Anderson, "How Good Is the Case for Apparitions?" *Journal of Religion and Psychical Research* 6 (1983): 130–36.

377. Online: http://www.shareintl.org/background/miracles/MI_appearances.htm.

378. Wolfhart Pannenberg, *Systematic Theology* (Grand Rapids: Eerdmans, 1994), 2:354. Cf. idem, *Jesus — God and Man*, 95. For others in agreement, see Hilary Evans, *Visions, Apparitions, Alien Visitors: A Comparative Study of the Entity Enigma* (Wellingborough, Northamptonshire: Aquarian, 1984); Hart and Hart, "Visions and Apparitions," 205–49; Paterson, *Philosophy*, 146–60; and esp. Tyrrell, *Apparitions*.

the same place but at different times, or where people saw the apparition of an individual who had just died although they did not know this.[379] It is not obviously true that all so-called visions are purely endogenous, the projection of creative human minds, that they "are grounded on no other Bottom, than the Fears and Fancies, and weak Brains of Men."[380]

Yet even when one allows the force of all this — many will not — we still have the problem of individual cases. For although we might admit that some visionary experiences are veridical, we also know for a fact that many are not. Most of us might well hesitate before crediting the sightings of the postmortem Sabbatai Sevi.[381] How, then, do we make a decision about the early Christian experiences? Did Peter and the others project the risen Jesus? Or did a postcrucifixion Jesus communicate with his own? Or — an alternative the literature does not often contemplate — did perhaps both things happen?

The questions are even more complex than my simple alternatives might imply once we acknowledge the inevitable, that all perception is active construction as opposed to passive reception, and that no human experience can be independent of thoroughly psychological and neurochemical mechanisms.[382] In the present case, it is relevant that perhaps most parapsychologists who accept some apparitions as veridical regard them not as objective but as projections of the percipients in response

---

379. See further William Braud, "Brains, Science, and Nonordinary and Transcendent Experiences: Can Conventional Concepts and Theories Adequately Address Mystical and Paranormal Experiences?" in *NeuroTheology: Brain, Science, Spirituality, Religious Experience* (ed. Rhawn Joseph; San Jose, CA: University of California Press, 2002), 143–58; H. Evans and P. Huyghe, *Field Guide*, 137–52; Green and McCreery, *Apparitions*, 75–79; Alan Gauld, "Discarnate Survival," in *Handbook of Parapsychology* (ed. Benjamin B. Wolman; New York: Van Nostrand Reinhold, 1977), 577–630; David Ray Griffin, *Parapsychology, Philosophy, and Spirituality* (Albany: SUNY, 1997), 209–28; and above all the classics of the field: Gurney, Myers, and Podmore, *Phantasms*; Professor Sidgwick's Committee, "Report on the Census of Hallucinations"; and E. M. Sidgwick, *Phantasms*. One understands why John McTaggart Ellis McTaggart, *Some Dogmas of Religion* (London: Edward Arnold, 1906), 106, could write: "There is much to be said in support of the view that, after all deductions have been made for fraud, error, and coincidence, there is still a sufficient residuum to justify the belief that ... apparitions are in some cases due to the action of the dead man whose body they represent."

380. Henry Bourne, *Antiquitates vulgares: or, The Antiquities of the Common People* (Newcastle upon Tyne: J. White, 1725), 77.

381. I have been unable to learn much about these; but see Gershom Scholem, "Shabbetai Zevi," in *Encyclopedia Judaica* (New York: Macmillan, 1971), 14:1245.

382. See Christopher Knight, "The Resurrection Appearances as Religious Experience," *Modern Believing* 39 (1998): 16–23; and esp. the fascinating discussion of Rahner, "Visions," 113–57.

to a paranormal stimulus.[383] Rahner's understanding of divinely inspired visions seems similar: a vision can be part of the human response to or a secondary effect of the divine activity, "a kind of overflow and echo of a much more intimate and spiritual process."[384]

The pertinent data from the New Testament are, in any case, if we are candid, really quite thin. One can only regret that the sort of detailed ethnographic and psychological facts available to William Christian Jr. in his splendid study of Spanish visions of Mary and saints in 1931 are not at hand.[385] We know enough to dismiss conscious deceit or illness as the cause of Easter faith.[386] But how can we absolutely dismiss, on historical grounds, the possibility of subjective hallucinations and mass wish fulfillment?

It is most often said in response that the first believers could not have hallucinated because too many people were involved and especially because "one may ask whether simultaneous identical hallucinations are psychologically feasible."[387] But this is no adequate rebuttal. The

---

383. For an early presentation, see James H. Hyslop, *Borderland of Psychical Research* (Boston: Herbert B. Turner, 1906), 153–97; cf. the overview of various theories in Mackenzie, *Hauntings*, 17–46.

384. Rahner, "Visions," 138.

385. William A. Christian Jr., *Visionaries: The Spanish Republic and the Reign of Christ* (Berkeley: University of California, 1966). Even Christian, although able to interview some of the old visionaries, laments the loss of much material through selective memory; see 401–2.

386. The American Medical Association, in its standard diagnostic manual, now classifies most bereavement apparitions as "normal": *The Diagnostic and Statistical Manual of Mental Disorders* (4th ed.; Washington, DC: American Psychiatric Association, 1994), 684–85. Cf. Camille B. Wortman and Roxane Cohen Silver, "The Mythos of Coping with Loss Revisited," in Stroebe et al., *Handbook*, 405–29. Studies have shown significant differences between visions of schizophrenics and visions among the general population; see Eiríkur Líndal, Jón G. Stefánsson, and Sigurjón B. Stefánsson, "The Qualitative Difference of Visions and Visual Hallucinations: A Comparison of a General-Population and Clinical Sample," *Comprehensive Psychiatry* 35, no. 5 (1994): 405–8. In the past, Christian apologists have sometimes argued that the disciples did not hallucinate because they were not mentally disturbed; so already Origen, *Cels.* 2.60 (ed. Marcovich; 132); cf. Habermas, *Risen Jesus*, 12 (wrongly asserting that "hallucinations usually result from mental illness or from physiological causes like bodily deprivation"); Pannenberg, *Jesus*, 94–98. The argument is ineffective given that otherwise healthy people experience hallucinations for no discernible cause. See further Vernon M. Neppe, "Psychiatric Interpretations of Subjective Paranormal Perception," *Parapsychological Journal of South Africa* 3 (1982): 6–16; and A. Y. Tien, "Distribution of Hallucinations in the Population," *Social Psychiatry and Psychiatric Epidemiology* 26 (1991): 287–92.

387. Harris, *Easter in Durham*, 24. Cf. C. E. B. Cranfield, "The Resurrection of Jesus Christ," *ExpTim* 101 (1990): 171; George Park Fisher, *The Grounds of Theistic and Christian Belief* (New York: C. Scribner's Sons, 1895), 171–72. Contrast G. W. H. Lampe, *God as Spirit: The Bampton Lectures, 1976* (Oxford: Clarendon, 1977), 153 ("hallucination, even in the case of a large group, is a real possibility"); and see further Michael Martin, *The Case against Christianity* (Philadelphia: Temple University Press, 1991), 95–97; also Zusne and Jones, *Anomalistic Psychology*, 117–19.

plurality of witnesses does not settle anything. Hypnotists can persuade a group of good subjects that they all see the same phantasmal object, and religious enthusiasm can work the same trick.[388] Further, more than one person has sincerely reported having a vision of the departed Elvis Presley.[389] And if counting heads were all the mattered, there would be no question that short, large-headed, bug-eyed aliens have kidnapped thousands of sleeping Americans: the stories are legion. But surely, despite all the testimony, there is room for debate here. As for the New Testament's stories in which Jesus appears to more than one witness, how do we know, without interviewing them, that the Twelve, let us say, saw exactly the same thing on the occasion of Jesus' collective appearance to them? There are examples of collective hallucinations in which people claimed to see the same thing but, when closely interviewed, disagreed on the details, proving that they were after all not seeing exactly the same thing.[390] How do we know that the Twelve, subjected to a critical cross-examination and interviewed in isolation, would all have told the same story?[391] Or would their testimony rather have been riddled with inconsistencies? No one will ever know.

Again, Eduard Schweizer, playing the role of apologist, asserts that while "mass-ecstasies do happen...they are in some way prepared, and this seems not to have been the case after the death of Jesus."[392] Such a remark can only be true of the first encounter, that of Mary Magdalene or Peter, as the case may have been. Once one of them had told of seeing Jesus, then the idea would have been planted in the mind of others, so how can we exclude the thought of psychological contagion? Even the pre-Christian Paul had presumably heard claims of people seeing the risen Jesus.

---

388. Cf. Gurney, Myers, and Podmore, *Phantasms*, 477–78.

389. Raymond A. Moody Jr., *Elvis after Life: Unusual Psychic Experiences surrounding the Death of a Superstar* (Atlanta: Peachtree, 1987). While one may have difficulty taking a book like this seriously, it is largely a collection of interviews, simply a write-up of what people told the author. It is thus a useful statement about human perception and/or testimony, whatever one's doubts about Elvis' postmortem proclivities.

390. See, e.g., Anderson, "Cummings Apparition," 215; E. Bennett, *Apparitions*, 37–39; Green and McCreery, *Apparitions*, 45–47; M. M. Tumin and A. S. Feldman, "The Miracle at Sabana Grande," *Public Opinion Quarterly* 19 (1955): 124–39. There are also numerous examples of collective illusions, of people turning an indistinct thing into something specific.

391. The apologetical literature often assumes that they would tell the same story; e.g., see John J. Johnson, "Were the Resurrection Appearances Hallucinatory? Some Psychiatric and Psychological Considerations," *Churchman* 115 (2001): 227–38. This begs the question.

392. Schweizer, "Resurrection," 147.

Skepticism, however, runs both ways. If the data are too meager for the apologist's needs, they equally do not suffice for the rationalistic antagonists of the church. One can establish without doubt the illusory character of the early Christian experiences only if one's mind is so saturated by a materialistic naturalism that it cannot allow either divine intervention or paranormal phenomena.[393] If one comes to the texts without such a materialistic predisposition, there is nothing in the accounts that determines the nature of the experiences of Peter and the Twelve and the others shortly after Good Friday. Historical knowledge just does not reach that far. We have restricted access to the past, some things are intractable, and this may well be one of them. "We are very unlikely ever to be able either to prove or to disprove the thesis that the appearances were psychologically induced 'subjective visions,' rather than some kind of 'objective vision.' "[394] Some barriers just cannot be crossed. The situation is such, I believe, that nothing would prohibit a conscientious historian from steering clear of both theological and antitheological assumptions, or of both paranormal and antiparanormal assumptions, and simply adopting a phenomenological approach to the data, which do not in and of themselves demand from historians any particular interpretation.[395] Would it be an historical sin to content oneself with observing that the disciples' experiences, whether hallucinatory or not, were genuine experiences that they at least took to originate outside their subjectivity? One can profitably discuss Socrates without denying that he heard a voice and without speculating on the nature of his familiar spirit.

6. One final point about apparitions and the resurrection of Jesus. Surely those who regard all modern postmortem experiences as purely subjective may be strongly inclined to dismiss the resurrection appearances of Jesus in the same way. Long ago Myers wrote:

---

393. Cf. Johannes Weiss, *Earliest Christianity: A History of the Period AD 30–150* (New York: Harper & Brothers, 1959), 1:28: "For those . . . who take account of the modern scientific doctrine of the unbroken sequence of causation, there is scarcely any alternative to the view that these experiences of the disciples were simply 'visions.' The scientific meaning of this term is that an apparent act of vision takes place for which there is no corresponding external object." On 29 he goes on to speak of "delusions, fancies, hallucinations" — although this does not prevent Weiss from finding theological meaning in them.

394. Carnley, "Response," 37.

395. Cf. Pieter F. Craffert, "The Origins of Resurrection Faith: The Challenge of a Social Scientific Approach," *Neot* 23 (1989): 331–48; C. A. Ross and S. Joshi, "Paranormal Experiences in the General Population," *Journal of Nervous and Mental Disease* 180 (1992): 357–61.

Suppose, for instance, that we collect many such histories [of post-mortem encounters], recorded on first-hand evidence in our critical age; and suppose that all these narratives break down on analysis; that they can all be traced to hallucination, misdescription, and other persistent sources of error; — can we then expect reasonable men to believe that this marvelous phenomenon, always vanishing into nothingness when closely scrutinised in a modern English scene, must yet compel adoring credence when alleged to have occurred in an Oriental country, and in a remote and superstitious age?[396]

The obvious answer to Myers's question is that we cannot expect such. One similarly suspects that those of us who believe that some apparitional encounters are not wholly subjective will be more inclined to entertain a nonhallucinatory genesis for the appearances of Jesus, if only because we do not view the world as a closed system or fully explicable in current scientific terms.

AN OPENED TOMB AND A MISSING BODY?

We must next consider the issue of Jesus' tomb, which I have heretofore ignored. It is a great riddle, a problem presented by Providence to the ingenuity of the historians. Yet in reading the secondary literature on the subject, I have often been struck by the assurance with which two opposing camps come to their contrasting conclusions: they resolve the riddle so easily. Many are wholeheartedly convinced that the story of women finding a vacant tomb can be shown to any unbiased observer to be unassailable history. There are just as many who, with raised eyebrows, are incredulous over conservative claims; they are equally sure that the story is apocryphal, without any historical foundation at all. This brimming of confidence on both sides, which is incommensurate with the imperfect data, reflects the deep personal convictions that often attend this particular issue. While some Christians think that the empty tomb is at the heart of their faith, others believe, to the contrary, that it is dead mythology, a mind-boggling irrelevance that distracts us from much more important matters and so needs to be either neglected or disposed of. What counts in the immediately following pages, however,

---

396. Myers, *Survival*, 2:288.

is not the theological or philosophical convictions of the disputants but the arguments that they have been able to muster. It is these that I now review in turn. First, then, some of the reasons for holding that the story of the empty tomb is not early but late, not history but legend.

(I refrain here from taking the pulse of contemporary scholarship. There are passages in the literature asserting that belief in the empty tomb is the consensus of scholarship, others that it is the minority opinion. For myself, I do not know how to count such things, nor in the end do I care. Polling is a poor stand-in for argument, and the belief that the majority must be right is a little like believing in trial by combat.)

1. Informed opinion is divided over how many sources we have for the report of the empty tomb. While there are relevant stories in all four canonical Gospels, those in Matthew and Luke are commonly thought to depend, in whole or in part, upon Mark. So to what extent, if any, the first and third evangelists had to hand non-Markan tradition about an empty tomb is controversial. As for John 20, it could be largely independent of the Synoptics, but that too is wide open for debate.[397] Some infer that John as well as Matthew and Luke probably knew and used Mark and that our only primary source for the unfilled tomb may accordingly be the latter alone.[398] A few, moreover, regard Mark 16:1–8 as redactional.[399] Their judgment, if accepted, clears the way to see behind the four canonical accounts little else but Mark's literary imagination.

On such a view, maybe Mark was, like Paul and some who today take up polemical arms against Jehovah's Witnesses, opposed to the notion of

---

397. For dependence upon John, see Catchpole, Crossan, and Neirynck, as in n. 196.There are an intriguing number of links between John 20 and Luke 24. These include two angels (Luke 24:4; John 20:12), disciples at the grave (Luke 24:24; John 20:3–10), appearance of Jesus to disciples in Jerusalem on the first Easter (Luke 24:36; John 20:19), "stood in the middle" (Luke 24:36; John 20:19), "and saying this he showed them his hands" (Luke 24:40; John 20:20), the theme of joy (Luke 24:41; John 20:20), bestowal of the Spirit (Luke 24:49; John 20:22), the forgiveness of sins (Luke 24:47; John 20:23).

398. So, e.g., John Dominic Crossan, "Empty Tomb and Absent Lord," in *The Passion in Mark: Studies on Mark 14–16* (ed. Werner H. Kelber; Philadelphia: Fortress, 1976), 134–52. In this essay Crossan does not take into account the *Gospel of Peter*, which features prominently in his later work on the passion and resurrection; see, e.g., his *Four Other Gospels: Shadows on the Contours of the Canon* (Minneapolis: Seabury, 1985), 125–81. Given my own judgment that, though the *Gospel of Peter* probably preserves some independent oral tradition, it primarily reworks the four canonical Gospels and does not draw upon an extended, pre-Synoptic passion narrative, I shall consider it only occasionally in what follows.

399. So, for instance, Adela Yarboro Collins, "Apotheosis and Resurrection," in *The New Testament and Hellenistic Judaism* (ed. Peder Borgen and Søren Giversen; Peabody, MA: Hendrickson, 1997), 88–100; and Crossan, "Empty Tomb."

a purely spiritual survival of bodily death. In that case, the evangelist may have created his story in order to implicate Jesus' body unambiguously in his resurrection.[400] Or perhaps his motive was altogether different. Adela Yarboro Collins, calling attention to several ancient texts in which heroes are translated to heaven, has suggested that "the focus on the tomb in Mark may have been inspired by the importance of the graves of the heroes in the Greco-Roman world. Even if the location of the tomb of Jesus was unknown to the author of Mark, and even if there were no cultic observance at the site of the tomb, it would still be important as a literary motif in characterizing Jesus as hero-like."[401]

The reduction of the empty tomb to Markan creativity, whatever the redactional motive postulated, is not a compelling point of view. Not only does the independence or partial independence of John 20 remain a feasible option that commends itself to this writer at least,[402] but the case for the redactional origin of Mark 16:1–8 is unpersuasive, which is why so many Markan scholars, despite their differences on the details, see tradition here.[403] Surely it would be exceptional for Mark to compose

---

400. Goulder, "Baseless Fabric," envisages something like this.

401. Collins, "Apotheosis," 93. Cf. already Neill Q. Hamilton, "Resurrection Tradition and the Composition of Mark," *JBL* 84 (1965): 414–21; and esp. Elias Bickermann, "Das leere Grab," *ZNW* 23 (1924): 281–92 (reprinted in Hoffmann, *Auferstehung*, 271–84). Criticism in Peter G. Bolt, "Mark 16:1–8: The Empty Tomb of a Hero?" *TynBul* 47 (1996): 27–38.

Given the good reasons for thinking that the Corinthians both accepted the resurrection of Jesus and at the same time preferred the immortality of the soul over resurrection of the body, one wonders if they were not simply good Hellenists who thought of Jesus' vindication as the bodily assumption of a hero (cf. Collins's view of Mark 16) and yet, since the fate of a hero was not the rule but the exception, expected for themselves only an immaterial immortality.

402. Despite the work of Frans Neirynck and like-minded others, one can hardly regard John's dependence upon the Synoptics as firmly established. See D. Moody Smith, *John among the Gospels: The Relationship in Twentieth-Century Research* (Minneapolis: Fortress, 1992). Even if John knew one or more Synoptics, he did not copy from them at every turn; my own judgment is that John 20 cannot derive wholly from the Synoptics and Johannine redaction. For a few pertinent considerations, see Alsup, *Post-Appearance Stories*, 95–102; William L. Craig, "The Disciples' Inspection of the Empty Tomb (Lk 24,12.24; Jn 20,2–10)," in Denaux, *John and the Synoptics*, 614–19; and C. H. Dodd, *Historical Tradition in the Fourth Gospel* (Cambridge: Cambridge University Press, 1963), 140–42.

403. See, e.g., Catchpole, *Resurrection*, 4–9; and Pheme Perkins, *Resurrection: New Testament Witness and Contemporary Reflection* (Garden City, NY: Doubleday, 1984), 115–24. My own guess is that Mark 16:1–8 probably derives from a pre-Markan passion narrative; see Édouard Dhanis, "L'ensevelissement de Jésus et la visite au tombeau dans l'évangile de saint Marc," *Greg* 39 (1958): 367–410; and Rudolf Pesch, "Der Schluß der vormarkinischen Passionsgeschichte und des Markusevangeliums," in *L'évangile selon Marc: Tradition et rédaction* (ed. M. Sabbe; BETL 34; Gembloux: Leuven University Press, 1974), 365–409. Contrast Ludgar Schenke, *Auferstehungsverkündigung und leeres Grab* (SBS 33; Stuttgart: Katholisches Bibelwerk, 1969), 11–30. As for what is Markan and what pre-Markan, redaction-criticism has produced quite mixed results. The multitudinous proposals contradict

a key narrative ex nihilo, without some pre-Markan basis. The several hapax legomena are consistent with this supposition,[404] as is the tension between the story's setting — "when the sabbath was over" (16:1), "very early on the first day of the week, when the sun had risen" (v. 2) — and Mark's refrain that the resurrection should take place "*after* (μετά) three days" (8:31; 9:31; 10:34).

2. Mark's story of Jesus' burial and resurrection is, in the judgment of Randel Helms, a late fiction inspired by Dan 6.[405] The correlations may be set forth this way:

Common Element	Mark	Daniel
The law demands the death of God's chosen.	15:1–5	6:6–10
The ruler is reluctant to enforce the law but does so.	15:6–15	6:14–16
Late in the day a sympathetic leader puts the chosen one in a pit or cave and covers it with a stone.	15:42–46	6:17–18
Early in the morning those who care for God's chosen one approach the pit or cave.	16:2	6:19
There is angelic intervention.	16:5–7	6:22
The hero is not dead but lives.	16:1–8	6:19–23

To the extent that one finds these parallels persuasive, so that Mark 15–16 is regarded as a rewriting of Dan 6, to that extent one will be inclined to pigeonhole Mark 16:1–8 as haggadic fiction.

I confess myself unimpressed. There are some handy if rough criteria for determining when one text is using another,[406] and they are not well met in this particular instance. For example, commentators have regularly missed the parallels,[407] the shared vocabulary is minimal, and Dan 6 otherwise plays no role in Mark's Gospel. We should probably shelve Helms's thesis and judge the correlations between Dan 6 and Mark 16

---

each other and may reveal mostly our inability to solve the problem; cf. C. W. Schnell, "Tendencies in the Synoptic Resurrection Tradition: Rudolf Bultmann's Legacy and an Important Christian Tradition," *Neot* 23 (1989): 177–94.

404. In Mark 16:1–8: διαγίνομαι (v. 1), ἄρωμα (v. 1), ἀποκυλίω (vv. 3–4), σφόδρα (v. 4), τρόμος (v. 8).

405. Randel Helms, *Gospel Fictions* (Amherst, NY: Prometheus, 1988), 135–36.

406. Dale C. Allison Jr., *The Intertextual Jesus: Scripture in Q* (Harrisburg, PA: Trinity, 2000), 9–14.

407. There are only occasional exceptions; see, e.g., Ephraem, *Comm. Diss.* 21.21 (ed. Leloir; SC 121:385). Even Albert the Great, who is so intertextually aware, misses this in his *Enarrationes in Marcus*.

to be partly or wholly the upshot of happenstance: it is not so hard to spot parallels between two unrelated texts.[408] It is telling that Michael Goulder can urge, with no more credibility than Helms, that Mark invented the story of Jesus' empty tomb not by rewriting Dan 6 but by mixing together ingredients from Josh 10 and other Scriptures.[409]

3. Mark ends the story of the empty tomb and indeed his entire Gospel with this enigmatic remark: "So they went out and fled from the tomb, for terror and amazement had seized them; and they said nothing to anyone, for they were afraid" (16:8). The words, "they said nothing to anyone," have been construed as a sign that the entire episode was invented at a late date. Mark was in effect saying: "You know what women are like, brethren: they were seized with panic and hysteria, and kept the whole thing quiet. That is why people have not heard all this before."[410]

This third attempted proof is, like the first two, feeble. If 16:8 were an explanation for why people had not previously heard about the empty tomb, presumably Mark would "have made the young man command the women to say that Jesus had been raised, that he was not in the tomb (cf. v. 6). Instead, the young man commanded them to say that Jesus was going ahead to Galilee, where the disciples would see him just as he had said."[411] In other words, "they said nothing to anyone" immediately trails not a command to proclaim the empty tomb but the angel's imperative to tell the disciples about Jesus going before them to Galilee; so the women's failure is more closely connected to the latter than to the former.

Beyond this oft-missed fact, the implications of "they said nothing to anyone" (οὐδενὶ οὐδὲν εἶπαν) — which can be understood as part of Mark's messianic secret[412] — are less than obvious.[413] Because of the

---

408. A more plausible case can be made that Dan 6 has influenced Matthew's story; see Carrier, "Guarded Tomb," 314–17; Wright, *Resurrection*, 640.

409. Michael Goulder, "The Empty Tomb," *Theology* 79 (1976): 206–14 (crediting unpublished work of Austin Farrer). Goulder makes only a passing reference to Dan 6:17.

410. Goulder, "Baseless Fabric," 58. On the history of this hypothesis, see Frans Neirynck, "Marc 16,1–8: Tradition et redaction: Tombeau vide et angélophanie," in *Evangelica*, 247–51. It has remained popular for over a hundred years.

411. Gundry, *Mark*, 1013. For a survey of interpretations of 16:7, see Bode, *Easter Morning*, 39–44.

412. See Broer, "Seid stets bereit," 38–39.

413. Hengel, "Begräbnis," 181, observes the apparent consequence of a literal interpretation, that the author of Mark must have been one of the women at the tomb; otherwise, how could he know something they never communicated? While Hengel is being sarcastic,

prophecy in 14:28, readers surely assume that Jesus did in fact meet the disciples in Galilee. Near to hand, then, is the inference that the angel must after all have gotten his message through to the disciples via the women. One may compare Mark 1:44, where Jesus tells a leper whom he has healed, "Say nothing to anyone" (μηδενὶ μηδὲν εἴπῃς), and yet adds: "Go, show yourself to the priest, and offer for your cleansing what Moses commanded." Clearly, despite the order, "say nothing to anyone," the man, now returned to normal, will have to explain himself to the temple establishment. Bauckham, who cites this as a parallel to 16:7–8, wonders whether "the women take the words of the young man to be an apocalyptic secret that they are to communicate to Jesus' disciples but that is strictly not to be revealed to anyone else."[414] This is quite plausible. Just as 1:44 means "Say nothing to anyone (except the priest)," so 16:8 may well mean the women "said nothing to anyone (except his disciples)." In accord with this, Matthew clearly read Mark so that the message entrusted to the women gets to the men without noticeable delay (cf. 28:16 with 7 and 10).

Whatever interpretation one gives to the enigmatic 16:7, no other logion or story in the canonical Jesus tradition justifies its recent appearance by pretending that people kept quiet about it. Surely R. H. Fuller was right: "The silence of the women can hardly be explained as the Evangelist's device to account for the recent origin of the story [of the empty tomb]; that is altogether too modern and rationalistic an explanation, and assumes that the early Jesus movement was concerned, like the modern historical critics, with conflicting historical evidence. The early church expounded its traditions anew in new situations: it did not investigate them historically in order to discover their origins and Sitz im Leben."[415]

4. Although those who deny the historicity of the empty tomb do not always say this, surely one regular contributor to their doubt is the problem of the miraculous. The story, in its various canonical forms, is

---

Gerd Lüdemann, *Jesus after Two Thousand Years: What He Really Said and Did* (Amherst, NY: Prometheus, 2001), 114, identifies the youth of Mark 16:5 with the naked young man of 14:51–52 and suggests that Mark implies its author's identity with the one who spoke to the women. This explains his knowledge of the secret.

414. Bauckham, "Women," 289. Cf. Catchpole, *Resurrection*, 21–28.

415. Fuller, *Formation*, 53. See further Heinz Giesen, "Der Auferstandene und seine Gemeinde: Zum Inhalt und zur Funktion des ursprünglichen Markusschlusses (16,1–8)," *SNTU* 12 (1987): 119–30; and von Campenhausen, *Tradition*, 61–62.

fantastic. It features not only an angel or angels but a dead man coming back to life. Even in a time and place marked, in retrospect, by superstition, gullibility, and a deep longing for miracles, the proclamation of Jesus' resurrection created doubts (cf. Matt 28:17; Ps.-Mark 16:14; Luke 24:25; John 20:25). Long before Hume, Gregory of Nyssa observed that the natural habit of most people is "to judge the credibility of things said according to the measure of their own experience" (*Vita Macrinae* [ed. Maraval; SC 178:264]). Then as now, experience has taught that corpses do not exit tombs. Skepticism is even more at home in our own time and place, where modern science rules and critical historians have, ever since the Reformation, continually and persuasively converted miracle story after miracle story into unfounded legend. Under the scrutiny of serious historians, the number of purportedly miraculous events has shrunk dramatically or melted away altogether. This matters so much because "the more isolated a phenomenon" the resurrection of Jesus "is understood to be, the more difficult the process of establishing its truth becomes."[416]

All this, however, begs the question we are about, even for those who altogether disallow the possibility of miracles, for there are several non-miraculous explanations for the empty tomb. One does not, as even the New Testament reluctantly implies, have to call upon divine intervention in order to lose Jesus' body or get the stone rolled away (Matt 28:13; John 20:15). As for Mark's young man or angel and his kerygmatic announcement, they can easily enough, if one is so inclined, be judged legendary embellishment for theological edification.[417] As the rest of the Jesus tradition reveals, historical memories can be pressed down and shaken together with mythological motifs. So one may, as have many, regard Mark 16:1–8 as something other than history and still think of its as a Christian write-up and interpretation of the authentic memory that some women found Jesus' tomb opened and empty.[418]

5. While 1 Corinthians 15:4 speaks of Jesus' burial, it says nothing about Joseph of Arimathea, nor does Paul anywhere else refer to an empty tomb. Evidently, the argument runs, Paul did not know about Jesus' grave; and if he did not know about it, then surely no one else

---

416. Maurice Wiles, "A Naked Pillar of Rock," in Barton and Stanton, *Resurrection*, 121.

417. This is not necessarily a literary-critical judgment, for Mark 16:1–8 without the angel is problematic (see n. 542). Rather, facts can be embroidered from the beginning.

418. See esp. L. Schenke, *Auferstehungsverkündigung*, 93–103. The rolling away of the stone must belong to the first telling of the story, for without the tomb being opened, its emptiness could not be discerned.

before him did either. The story of the empty tomb must, it follows, have originated after Paul.[419]

This inference from 1 Cor 15:3–8 and Paul's disregard of the empty tomb is less than overwhelming.[420] It remains an argument from silence regarding a very compressed statement, one mostly bereft of details. Pilate, Jerusalem, and the crucifixion also go unmentioned. One could equally construct the following quite different argument from silence: Had those Corinthians whom Paul sought to correct known or imagined Jesus' corpse to be yet in his grave, then surely, given their rejection of a physical resurrection, they would have brought this forward as a point in their favor, and Paul would have been compelled to answer them. This he did not do.[421]

The apostle often surprises us by what he fails to refer to in the Jesus tradition, even when it would serve his purpose;[422] and certainly we do not, as a general rule, accept as historical only those parts of the Jesus tradition attested by Paul. The apostle's letters say almost nothing about his own encounter with the risen Jesus, even though it was his foundational religious experience, and the author of Acts, who clearly knew and valued the story of the empty tomb, fails in Acts to repeat that story (at best, Acts 2:29–31 and 13:34–37 imply an empty tomb). Our literature, often not abundant with details, does exhibit unexpected holes, and it can be hazardous to infer much from them. Who would deny that James had a post-Easter christophany even though the Gospels do not intimate such? The point is all the more pertinent in the present case as Paul and the old tradition behind 1 Cor 15:3–8 must have known well enough that there was more than one explanation for an empty tomb,

---

419. Cf. Gardner-Smith, *Resurrection*, 12–13; Goulder, "Baseless Fabric," 56; Grass, *Ostergeschehen*, 146–73; Lampe, "Easter," 41–47; Lindars, "Resurrection," in Avis, *Resurrection*, 118, 128; Matti Myllykoski, "What Happened to the Body of Jesus?" in *Fair Play: Diversity and Conflicts in Early Christianity: Essays in Honour of Heikki Räisänen* (ed. Ismo Dunderberg, Christopher Tuckett, and Kari Syreeni; NovTSup 103; Leiden: Brill, 2002), 68; Norman Perrin, *The Resurrection according to Matthew, Mark, and Luke* (Philadelphia: Fortress, 1977), 80; Pokorný, *Christology*, 152–53; Schmiedel, "Resurrection," 4066; Uta Ranke-Heinemann, *Putting Away Childish Things: The Virgin Birth, the Empty Tomb, and Other Fairy Tales You Don't Need to Believe to Have a Living Faith* (San Francisco: HarperSanFrancisco, 1994), 131; and many others. Kenneth Grayston, "The Empty Tomb," *ExpTim* 92 (1981): 254, even argues from Rom 6:4–6 that, for Paul, Jesus' "sinful flesh" was destroyed in the grave.

420. See further below, 314–16.

421. Richard Swinburne, *The Resurrection of God Incarnate* (Oxford: Clarendon, 2003), 161.

422. Dale C. Allison Jr., *The Jesus Tradition in Q* (Harrisburg, PA: Trinity, 1997), 111–19.

which would thus not be a handsome piece of evidence — especially if it was remembered as deriving from the testimony of women.[423]

6. If some Christians had, through visionary encounters with a post-mortem Jesus, come to believe in his resurrection and exaltation, and if they had a physicalist view of resurrection, expecting that "the remains of the departed will...come to light out of the earth" (Ps.-Phoc. 103–104), they may well have inferred at some point that his body was in heaven and so his tomb empty.[424] H. J. Rose reconstructed their ratiocination as follows: "He was not dead, therefore he was not in the grave in which his body had been put; therefore the grave was empty, therefore someone must have found it empty, and also there had been a miracle, therefore a supernatural agency at work; and to people who had, ex hypothesi, no subordinate gods to postulate, the only possible mechanism was the presence of angels."[425]

Christians might, one may suppose, have been able to reason like this without fear of contradiction if the location of Jesus' burial or disposal were unknown, or if too much time had passed since his death. *y. Mo'ed Qaṭ.* 3:5 has the soul leaving the body after three days because by then the appearance of the corpse is already beginning to change. Furthermore, are not the fiction-creating capacities of the early Christians on display in Matt 27:51–53, in the tall tale about the tombs being opened and the bodies of saints exiting to promenade around Jerusalem?[426] Alfred Loisy argued: "The soldiers removed the body from the cross before dark and threw it in some common grave, where they cast the bodies of the criminals.... The conditions of the burial were such that at the end of a few days it would have been impossible to recognize the mortal remains of the saviour, had anyone been looking for them.... Nobody would contest that Jesus had died on the cross. Nobody could prove that he had not been resurrected."[427]

---

423. See further below, 326–31. According to Nauck, "Bedeutung," 260, the empty tomb served not missionary preaching but belonged to discourse aimed at the faithful community. This, he affirms, explains its presence in the Gospels, written for the faithful, and its absence from the kerygma, intended for public consumption.

424. This is a very common judgment; e.g., see Lampe, "Easter," 57–58; and above, 204–7.

425. Herbert Jennings Rose, "Herakles and the Gospels," *HTR* 31 (1938): 140.

426. It is puzzling that Wright, *Resurrection*, 632–36, wants to leave the historicity of this episode open: "Some stories are so odd that they may just have happened. This may be one of them, but in historical terms there is no way of finding out" (636). Contrast Craig A. Evans, *Jesus and the Ossuaries* (Waco: Baylor University Press, 2003), 16–17.

427. Alfred Loisy, *Les évangiles synoptiques* (Ceffonds: Loisy, 1907), 1:223–24.

Unlike the first five arguments, this one has force, even if it is suggestive rather than demonstrative. We must, without doubt, give due credit
to the human ability to create a religious fiction in face of the facts, and
early Christian literature contains abundant illustration. Whether, however, the precise sequence of thought reconstructed by Rose, a sequence
that fails to consider precisely why Jesus' survival of death was conceptualized as a bodily resurrection instead of an ascent or triumph of his
soul, reveals the way in which early Christian minds moved, is an issue
to which we must return below.[428]

7. One can compile a host of obviously legendary stories about empty
tombs or disappearing bodies. Jewish and Christian legends tell us about
Enoch's rapture (Gen 5:24; Heb 11:5), Moses' mysterious disappearance
(Josephus, *Ant.* 9.28),[429] Elijah's ascent to heaven (2 Kgs 2:11–12, 15–
18), the vain search for the remains of Job's children (*T. Job* 39:1–40:6),
the assumptions of Ezra and Baruch (4 Ezra 14:48 Syr; *2 Bar.* 76:1–5),
the resurrection of the two witnesses in Rev 11, the failure to find the
body of John the Baptist's father (*Prot. Jas.* 24:3), the disappearance of
the corpse of the thief who asked Jesus to remember him in his kingdom (*Narratio Jos. Arim.* 4:1), the missing remains of John the Beloved
(*Acts John* 115 Cod. R and V [ed. Bonnet; 215]), the bodily ascension
of Mary the mother of Jesus,[430] the coming forth from their graves of
the dead apostles so that they might travel by cloud to Jerusalem to witness Mary's departure,[431] the empty grave of Symeon of Salos (Leontius
Neapolitanus, *Vit. Sym.* 11.62 [PG 93:1745A–B]), and the light-filled
but otherwise vacant burial cave of Sabbatai Sevi and his occultation.[432]
Graeco-Roman analogies, as Justin Martyr already recognized,[433] also
exist: the missing bones of Heracles (Diodorus Siculus 4.38.4–5), the

---

428. See below, 321–26.

429. On this see Christopher Begg, " 'Josephus's Portrayal of the Disappearance of Enoch,
Elijah, and Moses': Some Observations," *JBL* 109 (1990): 691–93.

430. Simon Claude Mimouni, *Dormition et assomption de Marie: Histoire des traditions
anciennes* (ThH 98; Paris: Beauchesne, 1995); Stephen J. Shoemaker, *Ancient Traditions of the
Virgin Mary's Dormition and Assumption* (Oxford: Oxford University Press, 2002).

431. See, e.g., *Apocrypha Syriaca: The Protevangelium Jacobi and Transitus Mariae* (ed.
and trans. Agnes Smith Lewis; StSin 11; London: C. J. Clay & Sons, 1902), 17–32: Andrew,
Philip, Luke, and Simon the Zealot are raised.

432. Gershom Scholem, *Sabbatai Sevi: The Mystical Messiah* (Bollingen Series 93; Princeton: Princeton University Press, 1973), 919–25. For additional, later Christian reports of
resurrections, see Brewer, *Dictionary of Miracles*, 78–87.

433. Justin, *1 Apol.* 21.1 (ed. Marcovich; PTS 38:63); *Dial.* 69.1–3 (ed. Marcovich; PTS
47:189–90).

rapture of Troas lord of the Trojans (Homer, *Il.* 20.234–235), the failure to find Aeneas's body (Dionysius of Halicarnassus, *Ant. rom.* 1.64), the disappearance of Romulus (Ovid, *Metam.* 14.805–851; Plutarch, *Rom.* 27.7–28.3), the miraculous exit of Empedocles (Diogenes Laertius 8.67–69), the departure of Aristeas of Proconnesus (Herodotus, *Hist.* 4.14–15), the translation of Cleomedes of Astypalaea (Pausanias, *Descr.* 6.9.6–9), and the various rumors about Apollonius of Tyana (Philostratus, *Vit. Apoll.* 8.30; cf. 8.31: no one can say where Apollonius is buried).[434] There were, as Plutarch said, "many such fables" (*Rom.* 28.6).[435] Faced with this certain fact, one recalls the forceful words of Celsus' Jew: "Do you think that the stories of these others are indeed legends, as they seem to be, and yet that the ending of your tragedy is to be regarded as noble and convincing?" (Origen, *Cels.* 2.55 [ed. Marcovich; 127]).

One might counter such a list by observing that several of these legends (e.g., those about the good thief and Mary's ascension) are clearly modeled upon Jesus' resurrection while some (e.g., those about Job's children, John the Beloved, and Aristeas) are dissimilar to the New Testament accounts in that they probably originated not decades but centuries after the supposed facts recorded. Still others concern those who never died and so had no grave (Enoch, Elijah, Cleomedes, Empedocles, Aristeas, Apollonius) or are about old mythological or legendary figures — Heracles, Romulus, Aeneas. I have, however, happened upon at least one old story about a missing corpse that is not based upon the story of Jesus and is not about someone from the distant past. Gregory the Great (540–604) tells the following tale:

> There is another incident which took place here in Rome to which the dyers of the city will bear me witness. The most outstanding craftsman among them died, and his wife had him buried in the Church of St. Januarius the Martyr, near the gate of St. Lawrence. The next night the sacristan heard his spirit shouting from the

---

434. For discussion and additional texts, see Collins, "Apotheosis," 88–100; Pesch, *Markusevangelium*, 2:522–27; Arthur Stanley Pease, "Some Aspects of Invisibility," *HSCP* 53 (1942): 1–36; and Daniel Alan Smith, "The Post-Mortem Vindication of Jesus in the Sayings Gospel Q" (PhD diss., University of Toronto, 2001), 85–174; also the survey and cautious conclusions of Alsup, *Post-Resurrection Stories*, 214–39.

435. Cf. Hyginus, *Fab.* 151, listing sixteen people "who, by permission of the Parcae, returned from the lower world."

burial place, "I burn! I burn!" When the shouting continued, the sacristan informed the dead man's wife, who immediately sent fellow craftsmen to examine the grave and find out the reason for the shouting. On opening it, they found all his clothes there untouched (and they have been kept in the church ever since as a witness to this event), but there was no trace of his body. Seeing that not even his body was allowed to rest in church, we can judge to what punishment his soul was condemned.[436]

This account is so relevant because Gregory, a man of some education, presents this yarn as worthy of belief.[437] He knows people who will corroborate his testimony; he is absolutely concrete about the location of the events; and he indicates that there are relics from the event: anyone with sufficient curiosity can go and see the evidence. Clearly, it is possible to concoct a tale about the missing body of someone not long dead.

I have also run across a modern account in which a corpse miraculously disappears. A modern Tibetan tells this story:

We had been told the story of a very saintly man who had died there [Manikengo] the previous year [1953]. . . . Just before his death the old man said, "When I die you must not move my body for a week; this is all that I desire."

They wrapped his dead body in old clothes and called in lamas and monks to recite and chant. The body was carried into a small room, little bigger than a cupboard and it was noted that though the old man had been tall the body appeared to have become smaller; at the same time a rainbow was seen over the house. On the sixth day on looking into the room the family saw that it had grown still smaller. A funeral service was arranged for the morning of the eighth day and men came to take the body to the cemetery; when they undid the coverings there was nothing inside except nails and hair. The villagers were astounded, for it would have been impossible for anyone to have come into the room, the door was always kept locked and the window of the little resting place was much too small.

---

436. Gregory the Great, *Dial.* 4.56 (ed. Vogüé and Antin; SC 265:182, 184).

437. We need not doubt that *Dial.* 4 comes from Gregory himself; see Paul Meyvaert, "The Enigma of Gregory the Great's *Dialogues*: A Response to Francis Clark," *JEH* 39 (1988): 335–81.

The family reported the event to the authorities and also went to ask Chentze Rinpoche about the meaning of it. He told them that such a happening had been reported several times in the past and that the body of the saintly man had been absorbed into the Light. They showed me the nails and the hair and the small room where they had kept the body. We had heard of such things happening, but never at first hand, so we went round the village to ask for further information. Everyone had seen the rainbow and knew that the body had disappeared. This village was on the main route from China to Lhasa and the people told me that the previous year when the Chinese heard about it they were furious and said the story must not be talked about.[438]

I leave it to readers to make what they will of this story.[439]

Of the seven arguments just introduced, the first five are, like Jesus' tomb in the Gospels, empty. But the sixth cannot be dismissed without a guilty conscience: early Christians did have the imaginative ability to fabricate a fiction on the basis of theological convictions. Similarly, the final argument is formidable and should give its proponents some assurance: people have indeed constructed legends about missing bodies. This is an undeniable fact that merits much pondering. Its force is all the greater when we add that Christians were quite capable not just of making up stories about Jesus but also of making up stories about his resurrection. Surely, for instance, the guard of Matt 27:62–66 and the earthquake of Matt 28:2 are sheer fiction.[440]

But that is not the end of the matter. To show that there is nothing far-fetched about the followers of Jesus conjuring up the idea, against the facts, that his tomb was empty, is not the same as showing that this indeed happened; and there are certain considerations that, according to many,

---

438. Chögyam Trungpa, *Born in Tibet* (London: George Allen & Unwin, 1966), 95–96.

439. Gary R. Habermas, "Resurrection Claims in Non-Christian Religions," *RelS* 25 (1989): 167–77, in discussing some of the parallels I have cited, argues that they are all poorly attested historically. He may well be right, yet one fails to see why this result favors his implicitly apologetical program; for all he has demonstrated if his conclusion is correct is that people can without justification make up stories about the dead overcoming death. One wants to ask: "If others, why not the early Christians?"

440. On the fictional nature of the guard, see already at great length (and for the first time?) Peter Annet, *The Resurrection of Jesus in Answer to the Tryal of the Witnesses* (London: M. Cooper, 1744), with arguments still mostly convincing. Contrast William L. Craig, "The Guard at the Tomb," *NTS* 30 (1984): 273–81; and the implied conviction of Wright, *Resurrection*, 636–40.

show us that Mark 16:1–8 and its parallels are not, after all, unadulterated legend. These considerations I now consider. I review them in their evidential pecking order, starting with the weakest and ending with the strongest.

1. According to Matt 28:11–15, the Jewish authorities put out the rumor that the disciples robbed the tomb.[441] From this we learn, or so it is often said, that anti-Christian propaganda concurred that the tomb was empty. The disagreement concerned only who or what emptied it.[442]

The problem with this pretended, oft-repeated proof is that the age of the refutation in Matt 28:11–15 is unknown. Some have, to be sure, surmised that the verses bear "the mark of fairly protracted controversy."[443] Yet why this should be so escapes me, and the passage, which can hardly be history as it stands, is alone in the New Testament: nowhere else do we hear hostile Jews making the accusation that Jesus' disciples stole his body. So we do not know when this polemic was first formulated, or where it was first formulated, or who first formulated it. Without such knowledge, we cannot safely move from Matt 28:11–15 to the very beginnings of Christianity in Jerusalem. Who can say what Caiaphas, for example, thought about Jesus' empty tomb, if he knew or thought about it at all? For all we know, the view combated in Matt 28:11–15 arose sometime between Mark and Matthew, not in the days or weeks or months immediately after the crucifixion.[444]

2. According to Murray J. Harris, "In the light of Jewish veneration for the burial places of prophets and other holy persons such as

---

441. Cf. Justin, *Dial.* 108.2 (ed. Marcovich; PTS 47:255); *Gos. Nic.* 1:13; Tatian, *Diatessaron* 53:28; Tertullian, *Spect.* 30 (ed. Reifferscheid and Wissowa; CSEL 20:29).

442. So William Lane Craig, "The Empty Tomb of Jesus," in *Gospel Perspectives: Studies of History and Tradition in the Four Gospels* (ed. R. T. France and David Wenham; Sheffield: JSOT, 1981), 2:193; Dunn, *Jesus Remembered*, 836–37; Jacob Kremer, "Zur Diskussion über 'das leere Grab,'" in *Resurrexit: Actes du Symposium international sur la résurrection de Jésus, Rome 1970* (ed. Édouard Dhanis; Vatican: Libreria editrice vaticana, 1974), 157; Gerald O'Collins, *Christology: A Biblical, Historical, and Systematic Study of Jesus* (Oxford: Oxford University Press, 1995), 94; Pannenberg, *Jesus*, 101; Kurt Schubert, "'Auferstehung Jesu' im Lichte der Religionsgeschichte des Judentums," in Dhanis, *Resurrexit*, 218; Ethelbert Stauffer, *Jesus and His Story* (New York: Alfred A. Knopf, 1970), 144–45; Winden, *Osterglauben*, 39–40; and many others. For the idiosyncratic view that Matt 28:15 is not aimed at real Jewish polemic but instead is a way for Matthew to articulate his own views, see Wim J. C. Weren, "'His Disciples stole Him away' (Mt 28,13): A Rival Interpretation of Jesus' Resurrection," in Bieringer, Koperski, and Lataire, *Resurrection*, 147–63.

443. E. L. Allen, "The Lost Kerygma," *NTS* 3 (1957): 351. Cf. Hengel, "Begräbnis," 179.

444. Contrast Raymund Schwager, "Die heutige Theologie und das leere Grab Jesu," *ZKT* 115 (1993): 438, who thinks that later Jewish polemic, if independent of old anti-Christian tradition, would have preferred simply to deny that the tomb was empty. I do not see how we can be confident of this.

righteous martyrs (Matt. 23.29), it is remarkable that the early Christians gave no particular attention to the tomb of Jesus. Remarkable, that is, unless his tomb were empty."[445] Several troubles beset this assertion, which others have forwarded from time to time.[446] While no one has proved that Christians from an early period conducted religious services involving Jesus' grave, no one has proven that they did not, and a few scholars have found hints that they did.[447] While their conclusions admittedly remain speculative,[448] another possibility, equally at odds with Harris's contention, has more support within the academy: there is a real chance that the Church of the Holy Sepulchre stands on the site of Jesus' burial.[449] If that church does stand there, this implies a living memory, implies that Christians passed on knowledge of the site, which in turn makes one wonder about Harris's assertion that "no particular attention" was paid to it. There is yet another difficulty. If Christians knew the location of Jesus' tomb and yet, as Harris implies, did not venerate the place or conduct religious services there, the cause might simply have been because the setting was an unwholesome dump for criminals. Belief in Jesus' resurrection is not the only imaginable reason people might have had for staying away.

The fragility of Harris's logic appears from the circumstance that it can effortlessly be turned inside out. It is almost amusing that Lüdemann, starting from the same alleged fact as Harris — the failure to venerate Jesus' tomb — comes to exactly the opposite conclusion: "Given the significance of the tombs of saints at the time of Jesus it can be presupposed that had Jesus' tomb been known, the early Christians would have venerated it and traditions about it would have been preserved."[450] Clearly

---

445. Murray J. Harris, *Raised Immortal: Resurrection and Immortality in the New Testament* (Grand Rapids, MI: Eerdmans, 1983), 40.

446. Cf. Craig, *New Testament Evidence*, 372–73; Dunn, *Jesus Remembered*, 837–38; and Rigaux, *Dieu l'a Ressuscité*, 301. Contrast Wedderburn, *Resurrection*, 63–65.

447. G. Schille, "Das Leiden des Herrn: Die evangelische Passionstradition und ihr Sitz im Leben," *ZTK* 52 (1955): 161–205; Nauck, "Bedeutung," 260–62; Delorme, "Résurrection," 105–49; L. Schenke, *Auferstehungsverkündigung*.

448. Criticism in Bode, *Easter Morning*, 130–32.

449. See Joan E. Taylor, "Golgotha: A Reconsideration of the Evidence for the Sites of Jesus' Crucifixion and Burial," *NTS* 44 (1998): 180–203; and Rainer Riesner, "Auferstehung, Archäologie und Religionsgeschichte," *TBei* 25 (1994): 319–26.

450. Lüdemann, *Resurrection*, 45. Martin Karrer, *Jesus Christus im Neuen Testament* (GNT 11; Göttingen: Vandenhoeck & Ruprecht, 1998), 44, can regard the story of the empty tomb as an etiology explaining the lack of a cult at Jesus' tomb.

Harris's inference is not required; this is not a pillar of resurrection faith but rather a twig easily snapped.[451]

3. Paul's language in 1 Cor 15 may, some have urged, assume an empty tomb.[452] The sequence is burial followed by resurrection. If this creates any image in the mind's eye, surely it is of a tomb first being filled and then being emptied. It is indeed difficult to know what else one might envision. Resurrection immediately follows the burial, so it naturally includes the body — and all the more because, to judge from 1 Cor 6:12–20; 15:51–54; and 1 Thess 4:17, Paul believed in "some sort of continuity between the present physical body and the totally transformed resurrection body — in spite of all discontinuity."[453] We would, furthermore, not expect anything less, for Paul's Jewish tradition knew not only of bodies being taken up into heaven (e.g., Enoch in Gen 5:24 and Elijah in 2 Kgs 2:11) but also included many texts regarding resurrection that typically make one think about bones and graves, dust and earth. Examples are Isa 26:19 ("Their corpses shall rise"); Ezek 37:5–6 ("Thus says the Lord GOD to these bones: '... I will lay sinews on you, and will cause flesh to come upon you, and cover you with skin'"); 37:13 ("When I open your graves, and bring you up from your graves");[454] Dan 12:2 ("Many of those who sleep in the dust of the earth shall awake"); *Sib. Or.* 4:181–182 ("God himself will again fashion the bones and ashes of people and he will raise up mortals again as they were before"); Matt 27:53 ("They came out of the tombs"); 4 Ezra 7:32 ("The earth shall

---

451. See further Jeffrey Jay Lowder, "Historical Evidence and the Empty Tomb Story: A Reply to William Lane Craig," *Journal of Higher Criticism* 8, no. 2 (Fall 2001): 288–89 (also online: http://www.infidels.org/library/modern/jeff_lowder/empty.html). Although I am unsure how this bears on the issue, it is perhaps worth noting that the particular places where the risen Jesus appeared do not seem to have generated much interest in early times. We have no ancient evidence of any place being venerated precisely because it was where a resurrection appearance was said to have taken place.

452. In addition to what follows, see Ronald J. Sider, "St. Paul's Understanding of the Nature and Significance of 1 Cor. XV 1–19," *NovT* 19 (1977): 134–36; and esp. Craig, *New Testament Evidence*, 85–159, 358–60; idem, "The Bodily Resurrection of Jesus," in *Gospel Perspectives: Studies of History and Tradition in the Four Gospels* (ed. R. T. France and David Wenham; Sheffield: JSOT Press, 1980), 1:47–74.

453. Peter Lampe, "Paul's Concept of a Spiritual Body," in *Resurrection: Theological and Scientific Assessments* (ed. Ted Peters, Robert John Russell, and Michael Welker; Grand Rapids: Eerdmans, 2002), 113. See further Ronald J. Sider, "The Pauline Conception of the Resurrection Body in 1 Corinthians XV. 35–54," *NTS* 21 (1975): 428–39.

454. Whatever the original meaning of the text, later readers — Origen being the exception — took it to be a picture of the eschatological resurrection: 4Q385; Matt 27:51–53; *Liv. Pro., Ezek.* 12; Irenaeus, *Haer.* 5.15.1 (ed. Rousseau; SC 153:196–202); Ambrose, *Exc.* 2.75 (ed. Faller; CSEL 73.7:290–91); the north wall of the Dura-Europos synagogue; etc.

give up those who are asleep in it"); *2 Bar.* 50:2 ("The earth will surely give back the dead at that time; it receives them now in order to keep them, not changing anything in their form").

Here then it seems, at least initially, that the apologists have a point. Why did Paul say that Jesus was raised if he did not mean that he was raised? Why not just: "He was buried and he appeared to Cephas"? Robert Gundry, who reminds us that Paul was a Pharisee, and that Pharisees believed in physical resurrection,[455] has made the point well enough: "*Resurrection* means 'standing up' (*anastasis*) in consequence of being 'raised' (*egeirō* in the passive). Normally, dead bodies are buried in a supine position; so in conjunction with the mention of Jesus' burial the further mention of his having been raised must refer to the raising of a formerly supine corpse to the standing posture of a live body.... There was no need for Paul or the tradition he cites to mention the emptiness of Jesus' tomb. They were not narrating a story; they were listing events. It was enough to mention dying, being buried, being raised and being seen."[456]

One cannot object to this that Paul goes on, in 1 Corinthians, to promote belief in a spiritual body, as though this might have nothing to do with bones and tombs. The apostle, in Lake's words, believed "in a kind of transubstantiation of the body from flesh and blood into spirit, and in this sense he not merely held the doctrine of the resurrection of the body, as distinguished from the resurrection of the flesh, but in so far as the flesh was changed into spirit, he may even be said to have held the doctrine of the resurrection of the flesh, if 'resurrection' be taken to include this process of change."[457] While it may go too far to say that Paul believed that the physical bodies of the saints would be "used up in

---

455. Robert H. Gundry, "The Essential Physicality of Jesus' Resurrection according to the New Testament," in *Jesus of Nazareth: Lord and Christ: Essays on the Historical Jesus and New Testament Christology* (ed. Joel B. Green and Max Turner; Grand Rapids: Eerdmans, 1994), 206–7, observes that, according to Josephus, *J. W.* 2.163, the Pharisees held that a good soul will pass into another body, from which Gundry infers: "The Pharisees ... must have held to physical resurrection for him to have attributed to them a Hellenistically phrased position that ran counter to his purpose in writing."

456. Robert H. Gundry, "Trimming the Debate," in Copan and Tacelli, *Jesus' Resurrection*, 118. Cf. Jindřich Mánek, "The Apostle Paul and the Empty Tomb," *NovT* 2 (1958): 276–80. Contrast Marxsen, *Resurrection*, 70: For Paul "the empty tomb would even be an inconvenience."

457. Lake, *Resurrection*, 21. Cf. 129: "It is almost as certain as anything can be that St. Paul's doctrine of the transubstantiation of flesh and spirit implied a belief in an empty tomb."

the resurrection,"[458] it would be even more misleading to assert that the resurrection would not, for him, involve a transformation of corpses.

Yet, having conceded all this, it is not clear exactly how much if anything follows for our purposes. Paul could have believed in an empty tomb without knowing a tradition about its discovery.[459] The fact remains that the apostle, even if his words assume that Jesus' tomb was empty, fails to say so. So what if anything he knew about Jesus' tomb remains forever beyond recovery. The prudent verdict, then, is that while Paul should not be considered a witness against the tradition of an empty tomb as found in the Gospels, he equally cannot be called upon to support any of the narrative specifics of that tradition or even its pre-Markan existence.

4. Many have insisted that the early Christians could not have preached Jesus' resurrection in Jerusalem unless his tomb were known to be opened and empty.[460] Would opponents have let the troublesome sectarians get away with their outrageous and offensive claim, a claim that had God overturning the verdict of the religious authorities, if it could readily have been falsified? Surely enemies of the faith would have displayed the body if it could have been found.[461] This is exactly what later Jewish polemic makes them do in the *Toledot Jesu*.[462] Paul Althaus insisted that the resurrection was proclaimed "soon after Jesus' death in Jerusalem, in the place where he was executed and buried.... This proclamation signified for all, for those who preached and for all who

---

458. The phrase is from C. F. D. Moule, "St. Paul and Dualism: The Pauline Concept of Resurrection," *NTS* 13 (1965–66): 122n1.

459. See esp. Lorenz Oberlinner, "Die Verkündigung der Auferweckung Jesu im geöffneten und leeren Grab: Zu einem vernachlässigten Aspekt in der Diskussion um das Grab Jesu," *ZNW* 73 (1982): 163–68. Cf. Lüdemann, *Resurrection*, 46: "On the one hand Paul knows no witness to the empty tomb, but on the other he imagines the resurrection of Jesus in bodily form, which seems to require the emergence of the body of Jesus from the empty tomb."

460. See, e.g., Bode, *Easter Morning*, 162–63; Craig, "Empty Tomb," 193–94; Michael Dummett, "Biblical Exegesis and the Resurrection," *NBf* 58 (1977): 66–68; Hengel, "Begräbnis," 180–81; Jacob Kremer, "Die Auferstehung Jesu Christi," in *Handbuch der Fundamental-Theologie*, vol. 2, *Traktat Offenbarung* (ed. Walter Kern et al.; Freiburg: Herder, 1985), 188; Harris, *Raised Immortal*, 38–39; Lohfink, "Auferstehung," 44–45; Nauck, "Bedeutung," 264; Robert H. Stein, "Was the Tomb Really Empty?" *JETS* 20 (1977): 23–29. Over the years Pannenberg has consistently made this point in defending the resurrection; e.g., see *Jesus*, 100. Paley, *Evidences*, 378–79, already laid great weight upon this argument.

461. So George Cook, *An Illustration of the Gospel Evidence Establishing the Reality of Christ's Resurrection* (Edinburgh: Peter Hill, 1808), 15; Cranfield, "Resurrection," 170; Morris, "Resurrection," 319–21; James Orr, *The Resurrection of Jesus* (Cincinnati: Jennings & Graham, [1909?]), 213–14; and many others.

462. Schlichting, *Ein jüdisches Leben Jesu*, 154–62.

heard, that the grave was empty. This could not have been maintained in Jerusalem for a single day, for a single hour, if the emptiness of the tomb had not been established as a fact for all concerned.... In Jerusalem, one could not think of the grave as empty without being certain, without there being testimony, that it had been found empty."[463]

To this one might retort that people just did not know where the body was, as must have happened often with treasonous criminals, who customarily endured the final act of disgrace by being thrown into piles as food for carrion.[464] This possibility requires that the burial by Joseph of Arimathea (Matt 27:57–61; Mark 15:42–47; Luke 23:50–56; John 19:38–42) be a legend. As argued at length in "Excursus 2: Joseph of Arimathea" (below), however, it is likely enough that a member of the Sanhedrin buried Jesus, and that the location was known to any party interested in knowing.

Another way around the inference from the proclamation of the resurrection in Jerusalem is to posit that the earliest Christians did not believe in a physical resurrection of Jesus' body, that they held a more spiritual view of resurrection, akin to what Paul allegedly develops in 1 Cor 15. On such a view, if the location of Jesus' tomb was known, it was irrelevant.[465] The problem with this response is that, despite some scholarly opinion to the contrary, there is just no good evidence for belief in a nonphysical resurrection in Paul, much less within the primitive Jerusalem community.[466] As urged above, even Paul, in 1 Cor 15, when defending the notion of a "spiritual body," teaches — like *2 Bar.* 51:10 — the transformation of corpses, not their abandonment.[467]

There is yet another retort, also less than persuasive: Even if Joseph of Arimathea buried Jesus, it is conceivable that, by the time interested individuals got around to caring and so investigating the spot, it was too late. Any body would have undergone decomposition between Passover and Pentecost, or whenever Christians first began publicly proclaiming

---

463. Paul Althaus, *Die Wahrheit des kirchlichen Osterglaubens: Einspruch gegen Emanuel Hirsch* (BFCT 42.2; Gütersloh: C. Bertelsmann, 1940), 22–23; cf. 25.

464. See John Dominic Crossan, *Who Killed Jesus? Exposing the Roots of Anti-Semitism in the Gospel Story of the Death of Jesus* (San Francisco: HarperSanFrancisco, 1996), 160–77.

465. Bousset, *Kyrios Christos*, 105, implies this possibility.

466. Cf. Gundry, "Essential Physicality," 204–19.

467. See above, 314–16. This is sometimes denied; e.g., see William R. Farmer, "The Resurrection of Jesus Christ," *Religion in Life* 39 (1970): 365–70; and S. MacLean Gilmour, "The Evidence for Easter," *ANQ* 5 (1965): 12–13: "Even if Paul had heard the story of the empty tomb, I do not believe he could have accepted it."

the resurrection. If Peter and his fellow believers did not become active missionaries until several weeks after the crucifixion, maybe empirical inquiry would by then have been unprofitable. In Lake's words, "The emptiness of the grave only became a matter of controversy at a period when investigation could not have been decisive."[468]

This is not the potent argument that it at first appears to be. On the one hand, if Jesus was, as the Gospels have it, buried alone, then all that would have mattered was the place. One could have checked the cave for its one corpse no matter what the condition of that corpse. On the other hand, if Jesus was buried with others, *m. Sanh.* 6:5–6 is evidence that his body would still have been identifiable. The rabbinic text presupposes that, even if a criminal had been buried dishonorably, it was yet possible for relatives to claim the skeleton after some time had passed: "When the flesh had wasted away they gathered together the bones and buried them in their own place." If relatives could collect the bones of an executed criminal after the flesh had fallen off, then those bones were not in a jumbled pile of corpses but must have been deposited in such a way as to allow for later identification. Now, because burial customs tend to be conserved over long stretches of time, it is reasonable to suppose that, already in Jesus' day, the corpses of criminals buried by Jews were somehow separated and identifiable. Even if it were sometimes otherwise, in the case of Jesus probably "all that would have been necessary would have been for Joseph [of Arimathea] or his assistant to say, 'We put the body there, and a body is still there.' "[469]

There remain, however, other defeaters of inferring an empty tomb from the preaching of the resurrection in Jerusalem, and these are harder to nullify. Maybe the first Christians were so convinced of their own beliefs that they never bothered to visit the gravesite. After all, most historians have the disciples, without knowledge of the empty tomb, coming to faith because of resurrection appearances in Galilee; so if they had come to believe without such knowledge, why did they need it

---

468. Lake, *Resurrection*, 196. Cf. Keim, *Jesus*, 6:299; Lowder, "Empty Tomb," 283–84; Macan, *Resurrection*, 106; Strauss, *Jesus*, 743; Thrall, "Resurrection Traditions," 201. It remains theoretically possible that Joseph of Arimathea buried Jesus but kept the fact to himself for some time. Cf. Robert H. Gundry, "Trimming the Debate," 108: "To the extent that in burying Jesus, Joseph of Arimathea acted on his own, or only in partnership with Nicodemus, Lüdemann might say that the rest of the council did not know who had buried Jesus or where he had been buried, and that Joseph feared to incur their wrath by telling them of his service to Jesus' corpse."

469. Morris, "Resurrection," 321.

when they returned to Jerusalem? Perhaps, contrary to the impression that Luke 24:12 and John 20:3–9 leave, their religious enthusiasm was greater than their investigative impulses or their native curiosity. Perhaps their assumption that Jesus was gone to heaven canceled the common human sentiment to visit a loved-one's grave, or perhaps they did visit and the stone was still in place and they saw no compelling reason to move it.[470] Stranger things have happened, and what we would have done as a matter of course is no sure indicator of what early Christians really did as a matter of course. Guignebert remarked, "The very idea of verifying presupposes doubt, and there is no ordinary connexion between the exaltation of the vision and the uninspired business of verification."[471] The Vatican does not appear to have been in any hurry to subject the Shroud of Turin to carbon dating, and surely early Christian converts accepted the proclamation of the resurrection, like the reports of Jesus' miracles, without seeking out and interviewing the principal witnesses or otherwise playing detective. Do we know that the first disciples were of a wholly different character?

What then of the Jewish authorities? Would they not have conducted an inspection? Maybe not. Maybe the focus of the first Christian proclamation was not the resurrection but the Parousia.[472] Or maybe the authorities just did not care because they did not take the business very seriously or regarded it as nothing more than a minor, transient nuisance.[473] Or maybe opponents accepted the testimony of the disciples and did not bother because they knew that more than one explanation would be possible for whatever they found, so what would be the point of on-site research?

---

470. Lindars, "Resurrection," 128–29, argues that the first Christians "were able to get reliable information from friends in Jerusalem about the burial-place, including perhaps the part played by Joseph, but visits to the tomb did not entail removing the stone and looking inside"; it "would be exceptional to open up a tomb unless there were very special circumstances."

471. Guignebert, *Jesus*, 518. Cf. Grass, *Osterbericht*, 184.

472. Cf. Pesch, "Entstehung," 207. Pesch finds support in Q, which has no Easter kerygma but much to say about the returning Son of Man.

473. Cf. Lowder, "Empty Tomb," 282; Oberlinner, "Auferweckung Jesu," 169–75. There is also the possibility that Joseph buried Jesus but that the Christians did not know where; cf. Wolfgang Reinbold, *Der älteste Bericht über den Tod Jesu: Literarische Analyse und historische Kritik der Passionsdarstellungen der Evangelien* (BZNW 69; Berlin: de Gruyter, 1994), 279–80. This supposition must reckon as secondary the watching of the women (in Mark 15:47 the women see not how Jesus is buried but where, ποῦ). Contrast Samuel Byrskog, *Story as History, History as Story: The Gospel Tradition in the Context of Ancient Oral History* (WUNT 123; Tübingen: Mohr Siebeck, 2000), 73–82, who regards the women as genuine eyewitnesses known to the Christian community. Cf. L. Schenke, *Auferstehungsverkündigung*, 98.

It is all but impossible to rate the probability of the various proposals in the previous two paragraphs. None of them, however, beggars belief. In fact, one might imagine them strengthened by the fact, not often remarked upon, that early Christian tradition nowhere records that Jewish leaders went out to the tomb and found it empty. If such a thing did happen, the story, one imagines, would have been told with relish, at least if it became known.[474] So maybe it did not happen. My judgment, then, is that, even though I reckon the burial by Joseph of Arimathea to be historical, I greatly hesitate to conclude from this and from the early proclamation of Jesus' resurrection in Jerusalem that the tomb was certainly known to be vacant rather than being presumed or hoped to be vacant. Here is a case in which the arguments yea are fairly well met by the arguments nay.

5. Leslie Houlden has written, "We can analyse the [resurrection] narratives in the Gospels, pointing to theological features and literary connections, and the more they strike us, the less assurance we are likely to have that they represent history directly."[475] This seems to be acceptable common sense. What then are we to make of W. Nauck's observation that Mark 16:1–8 betrays little if any scriptural intertextuality (a fact all the more striking considering how heavily the preceding passion narrative alludes to the Bible);[476] that the narrative fails to remark on Jesus' resurrection being the dawning of a new age or inaugurating the general resurrection; that it says nothing at all about Jesus' descent to the underworld or his ascent to heaven; that it fails to recount the resurrection itself or inform us about the nature of Jesus' risen body; and that the narrative lacks christological titles and themes? Jesus is not here said to be Lord or Messiah or Son of Man or Son of God. According to Nauck, the only christological motif is that the crucified is risen.[477]

Mark 16:1–8, which Bultmann called "extremely reserved,"[478] is quiescent in a number of surprising ways, and it does not offer us clear theological reflections on the resurrection of Jesus.[479] It also does not

---

474. Contrast Morris, "Resurrection," 321: "It is as certain as anything of this sort can be that an investigation *was* made, and that the preaching of the Resurrection was not discredited simply because the tomb was found empty."

475. Houlden, *Connections*, 143.

476. Wright, *Resurrection*, 599–602, makes much of this.

477. Nauck, "Bedeutung," 249–50, 263.

478. Bultmann, *History*, 286.

479. Cf. Kremer, "Leere Grab," 153: "Every theological reflection concerning the meaning of the resurrection fails."

explicitly defend itself: apologetical interests, if present, remain undisclosed. Mark addresses none of the questions that later defenders of the faith sought to answer. Why were there no eyewitnesses to the resurrection itself? Why were the only eyewitnesses to the opened tomb biased and so not wholly credible? Why were there no spectacular or miraculous demonstrations? Matthew, Luke, John, and the Gospel of Peter, by contrast, are more theological and more apologetically conscious. This does not imply that Mark's narrative lacks its own literary or theological artistry. Still, returning to Houlden, one wonders whether his comment should be turned upside down. Maybe the odd paucity of clear theological and apologetical features in Mark's text is a hint — not strong evidence but a hint, a fragment of a clue — that there is some history behind it, that it was not simply the product of the Christian imagination. "It might be reasonable to expect that in a freely composed mythical narrative the church would maximize the theological depth structure of the tradition."[480] But Mark 16:1–8 is not so maximized. Rather, in the canonical Gospels "it is typical that the discovery of the empty grave remains practically without effect. The report of it only subsequently wins importance as an indication of the reality of the resurrection of Jesus when the resurrection is proven by the appearances."[481]

6. Tom Wright has written: "Neither the empty tomb by itself... nor the appearances by themselves, could have generated the early Christian belief. The empty tomb alone would be a puzzle and a tragedy. Sightings of an apparently alive Jesus, by themselves, would have been classified as visions or hallucinations, which were well enough known in the ancient world."[482]

It is easy to think that these words misread the facts. "Sightings of an apparently alive Jesus" were, even without the empty tomb, never "by themselves." Rather did they come to people whose religious convictions had been thoroughly molded by Jesus over the course of his public ministry, and that means molded by certain concrete eschatological

---

480. Barry W. Henaut, "Empty Tomb or Empty Argument: A Failure of Nerve in Recent Studies of Mark 16?" *SR* 15 (1986): 181. Cf. Rigaux, *Dieu l'a Ressuscité*, 300. Henaut seeks to drain his own statement of force but without good argument.

481. Gustav Stählin, " 'On the Third Day': The Easter Traditions of the Primitive Church," *Int* 10 (1956): 286.

482. Wright, *Resurrection*, 686. See also his article, "Jesus and Resurrection," in *Jesus Then and Now: Images in History and Christology* (ed. Marvin Meyer and Charles Hughes; Harrisburg, PA: Trinity, 2001), 54–71. Cf. Seeberg, *Dogmatik*, 2:209.

expectations. Jesus himself had spoken of the new age with its prefatory resurrection as near, and how could this fact not have contributed to, or even been decisive in, the interpretation of reputed postmortem encounters with Jesus?[483] Even when expectations do not match the facts, religious enthusiasm can absorb the shocks of external reality, carry on, and reinterpret its language in creative ways, so that the formerly literal now gives way to the nonliteral. Illustrations of "secondary exegesis"[484] in the face of cognitive dissonance[485] are abundant.[486]

Given that the creative revision of eschatological belief is well known to students of millenarian movements, one might think it no stretch to envision some followers of Jesus, under the spell of his eschatological expectations, coming to belief in his resurrection, even if the whereabouts of his body were unknown.[487] If they were expecting the eschatological consummation, as Luke 19:11 has it, and if, after Jesus' death, they saw him alive again, might they not have put two and two together?

But here is the problem, and the reason why Wright is probably, despite what I have just said, on to something.[488] Reinterpretation of eschatological expectations stems from dissonance bred by the distance

---

483. John Muddimann, "I Believe in the Resurrection of the Body," in Barton and Stanton, *Resurrection,* 133–34, recognizes that the disciples started from some experience which they then interpreted "in the light of Jewish apocalyptic and perhaps also Jesus' own teaching about the death and resurrection of the Son of Man, and then in turn started to reinterpret the eschatology in the light of their experience." "Perhaps" should be dropped from this sentence. Similarly, although Bockmuehl, "Resurrection," 118, rightly speaks of the proclamation of Jesus' resurrection as "rooted in his own teaching," earlier, on 112–13, he focuses instead on the setting within Judaism in general: resurrection "in the context of first-century Pharisaic and apocalyptic Judaism" was "the only suitable terminology to name an astonishing reality." Yet surely our focus should be on the particular beliefs of the pre-Easter Jesus movement, not the general eschatological beliefs of Palestinian Jews. Despite my disagreement with Ulrich B. Müller, *Die Entstehung des Glaubens an die Auferstehung Jesu: Historische Aspekte und Bedingungen* (SBS 172; Stuttgart: Katholisches Bibelwerk, 1998), about many things, there is much to commend in his attempt, following Pesch and others, to understand the proclamation of Jesus' resurrection against the background of Jesus' teaching and expectation.

484. The phrase is that of Yonina Talmon, "Pursuit of the Millennium: The Relation between Religious and Social Change," *Archives européenes de sociologie* 3 (1962): 133.

485. The classic work on cognitive dissonance within a millenarian group is Leon Festinger, Henry W. Riecken, and Stanley Schachter, *When Prophecy Fails: A Social and Psychological Study of a Modern Group That Predicted the Destruction of the World* (New York: Harper & Row, 1964); see esp. the introduction on 3–32. Although Wright, *Resurrection,* 697–701, scores some points against Festinger, it remains true that the Millerites and Jehovah's Witnesses clearly reveal how eschatological expectation can overwhelm and rewrite historical experience.

486. Allison, *End of the Ages,* 142–46; idem, *Jesus,* 167–69.

487. See esp. Müller, *Entstehung,* one of the more interesting and important of the recent books on the resurrection.

488. What follows repeats points I made earlier in *End of the Ages,* 164–65. Wright's argument at this juncture goes another way.

between prophecy and event, and — despite widespread scholarly assumption to the contrary — before belief in Jesus' resurrection, no such cause for dissonance existed.[489] The disciples had, it appears, unaccountably suffered a moral collapse, for they scattered when their master was arrested: surely there is memory behind Mark 14:27, 50 and John 16:32. And Peter, although he had dared to follow the crowd that had taken Jesus, did not have the courage to confess his allegiance to the Nazarene (Mark 14:54–72; John 18:15–18, 25–27). And yet the disciples' demoralization and their teacher's heinous execution did not directly confute the eschatological teachings of Jesus; for he had foreseen, for himself and for others, suffering and perhaps even death in the eschatological tribulation, understood as near.[490] So when he met his end, the disciples would have been down but not out — that is, emotionally down but not theologically out.[491]

Social psychology leads us to expect that those followers of Jesus who felt obliged to continue the cause despite the crucifixion and despite their failings and initial leaderless confusion would likely have done their best to match event to expectation. That would have meant (a) interpreting his death as part of the end-time chaos; (b) anticipating for themselves suffering and violent ends in the near future; and (c) keeping their hopes firmly fixed upon the coming consummation, when the dead, including Jesus, would be resurrected. There was nothing in the crucifixion itself to undo the basic structure of anybody's eschatological expectations, nothing to extinguish hope, which after all can survive despair. From what we can tell, a martyr's fate agreed nicely with what Jesus had predicted. Deuteronomy 21:23 would not, admittedly, have made things easy, but Gal 3:13, where Paul puts Deut 21:23 to good use, reminds us that one can always do what one wills with Scripture. That is especially so in this

---

489. Hugh Jackson, "The Resurrection Belief of the Earliest Church: A Response to the Failure of Prophecy?" *JR* 55 (1975): 415–25, is flawed precisely in that it turns the crucifixion itself into a cause of theological dissonance.

490. Allison, *End of the Ages*, 115–41; idem, *Jesus*, 145–47; idem, "Q 12:51–53 and Mk 9:11–13 and the Messianic Woes," in *Authenticating the Words of Jesus* (ed. Bruce Chilton and Craig A. Evans; NTTS 28.1; Leiden: Brill), 289–310. See also now Brant Pitre, "The Historical Jesus, the Great Tribulation, and the End of the Exile: Restoration Eschatology and the Origin of the Atonement" (PhD diss., University of Notre Dame, 2004).

491. See further Müller, *Entstehung*, esp. 7–11; also Weiss, *Earliest Christianity*, 1:19–23. Contrast Zorab, *Opstandingsverhaal*, 73–90, and the many who have argued that the disciples were so emotionally distraught and empty after Easter that only a miracle could explain the continuance of Jesus' cause.

case, for the faithful certainly believed that Jesus had suffered a miscarriage of justice, not a divine curse, and Jews knew of unjust crucifixions (Philo, *Flacc.* 83; *T. Mos.* 6:9; 8:1).[492] Christianity soon enough turned the scandal, shame, and horror of crucifixion into a badge of honor. One recalls that Sabbatai Sevi's apostasy to Islam did not utterly destroy his movement.[493]

Unlike Jesus' martyrdom, the resurrection did not conform to anyone's expectations. Not only did the resurrection stand in tension with the collective character of both Jewish expectations and Jesus' prophecies, but it implied two acts of vindication — the resurrection of Jesus and the coming of the Son of Man — and thereby split into two the one eschatological act of redemption that Jesus' words had held together.[494] However surprising the result, it was belief in the resurrection of Jesus, not knowledge of his crucifixion, that would have forced the disciples to reinterpret their expectations in drastic fashion. Far from being the straightforward product of dissonance, then, Easter faith must have been, if anything, the cause of dissonance.[495] Perhaps, after all, the notices of doubt in Matt 28:17; Ps.-Mark 16:14; Luke 24:25, 38; and John 20:24–25 are more than a literary motif.[496]

What does all this have to do with the empty tomb? Simply this: Jesus' expectation of resurrection, and so the expectation of his disciples, was, in accord with the belief abroad in their day, of solid bodies coming back to life (cf. Matt 27:51–53; John 5:28–29; Acts 2:31).[497] And if there was no reason to believe that his solid body had returned to life,

---

492. Cf. Müller, *Entstehung*, 10–11.

493. Scholem, *Sabbatai Sevi*, 687–929.

494. See further Allison, *End of Ages*, 160–62. Although his understanding of Jesus' eschatology is quite different from mine, in this particular I concur with the reconstruction of C. H. Dodd, *The Parables of the Kingdom* (rev. ed.; New York: C. Scribner's Sons, 1961), 73–77.

495. Cf. Gerd Theissen, *The Religion of the Earliest Churches: Creating a Symbolic World* (Minneapolis: Fortress, 1999), 333: "Dissonance was further heightened by the Easter experiences."

496. Those who think that the motif is not purely literary but reflects a memory include Guignebert, *Jesus*, 511; MacGregor, "Growth," 282; and Howard M. Teeple, "The Historical Evidence of the Resurrection Faith," in *Studies in New Testament and Early Christian Literature: Essays in Honor of Allen Wikgren* (ed. David Edward Aune; Leiden: Brill, 1972), 113.

497. On Jewish expectations see Hengel, "Begräbnis," 150–72; Wright, *Resurrection*. Goulder, "Baseless Fabric," 56, is plainly wrong in holding that "the norm" among Jews was a "spiritual resurrection" rather than a "physical resurrection." Within Judaism was a variety of eschatological beliefs and so no "norm"; but when Jews in the Holy Land spoke of resurrection, they were, from everything we know, thinking about corpses and bones, graves and ossuaries; cf. 314–15 above. I also beg to differ with Elliott, "First Easter," 219, who asserts

no one would have thought him, against expectation, resurrected from the dead. Certainly visions of or perceived encounters with a postmortem Jesus would not, by themselves, have supplied such reason. For there was more than one way for Jews to speak about postmortem vindication and to interpret the presence of one dead. Given the widespread dualism of the time,[498] we would expect Jesus' disciples to think in terms of the triumph of his soul or spirit and to imagine his resurrection, like that of everyone else dead and buried, as still belonging to the immediate future.[499]

The ascent of a soul to heaven and its vindication were not the same as resurrection from the dead.[500] As already observed, the *Testament of Job* relates that its hero's soul was taken to heaven immediately after his death, while his body was being prepared for burial (52:10–12). The story of Moses' end in *Deut. Rab.* 11:10 is similar,[501] and in later church history we find that when people see the souls of saints, they speak of ascension, not resurrection.[502] The first Christians, to the contrary, did something else. They proclaimed that an individual had already been raised from the dead, that the general resurrection had begun (1 Cor 15:23). Why? One good answer to the riddle is that they believed his tomb was empty. If there is another good answer, I have yet to stumble across it. We seem then to be stuck with the view, associated in recent times especially with von Campenhausen, that before the disciples

---

that "resurrection was the natural first century Jewish way of describing" an individual's continuing influence. I know of no evidence for this point of view, and Elliott fails to provide any beyond his own assertion.

498. Robert H. Gundry, *Sōma in Biblical Theology, with Emphasis upon Pauline Anthropology* (SBLMS 29; Cambridge: Cambridge University Press, 1976).

499. Cf. Brown, *Virginal Conception*, 75–76; Catchpole, *Resurrection*, 195, 209; Gundry, *Mark*, 994; Lohfink, "Auferstehung," 49–50. See further Gerhard Friedrich, "Die Auferweckung Jesu, eine Tat Gottes oder ein Interpretament der Jünger?" *KD* 17 (1971): 153–87, who shows how strange it was, given the religious world in which they lived, that many Christians from the beginning used the language of resurrection for Jesus' vindication. Friedrich concurs that visions of Jesus after his death would not in themselves have led anyone to think him resurrected. Müller, *Entstehung*, 30–35, is aware of the issue, but he suggests, without sufficient warrant, that Christians, in Jesus' case, combined the traditional notion of the heavenly vindication of the suffering righteous one with eschatological resurrection.

500. *Jub.* 23:30–31, if it speaks of souls being exalted to heaven as a rising up (interpretation of the text is uncertain and cannot be resolved), would be the only exception known to me.

501. Cf. Clement of Alexandria, *Strom.* 6.15.132 (ed. Descourtieux; SC 446:322–24).

502. E.g., Athanasius, *Vit. Ant.* 60 (ed. Bartelink; SC 400:294–98); and Jerome, *Vit. Paul.* 14 (PL 23:27A).

encountered the postmortem Jesus in Galilee or at least before they declared him risen from the dead, they already knew about the empty tomb. Otherwise, they would probably have offered a different interpretation of their experiences.

One possible retort to this conclusion is that, according to Mark 6:14–16, some said that John the Baptist had risen from the dead, and yet we have no evidence of belief in his empty tomb.[503] But this objection will not do. Apart from the fact that we have no evidence one way or the other about what the few purveyors of this ill-informed piece of superstition thought about John's tomb, if anything,[504] the decisive point is this. If some really did regard Jesus of Nazareth as John risen from the dead, then they were identifying the Baptist with a body that was out and about in the real world: the wonder-working Jesus was not a disembodied spirit. The risen John, identified with Jesus, was walking flesh and bones, and precisely that circumstance may have encouraged the terminology of resurrection.

7. Again and again scholars have observed that the discovery of the empty tomb is, in the canonical Gospels, made by women.[505] This, they claim, is not "the kind of detail anyone would have thought or wished to invent." "That it should be these devoted but humble and relatively insignificant followers who are given the credit for the discovery in every gospel is historically impressive."[506] This is perhaps the most popular

---

503. Cf. Macan, *Resurrection*, 106. See also Mark 8:27–30, and the observation of C. A. Evans, *Ossuaries*, 13–14, that if Mark's story is true, John's head was still in the possession of Herod's family!

504. Catchpole, *Resurrection*, 189–90, regards the relevant texts as Markan redaction, so on his view there were no such purveyors at all. Contrast Müller, *Entstehung*, 52–53; and Knut Backhaus, *Die "Jüngerkreise" des Täufers Johannes: Eine Studie zu den religionsgeschichtlichen Ursprüngen des Christentums* (Paderborner Theologische Studien 19; Paderborn: F. Schöningh, 1991), 89–95.

505. Matt 28:1: Mary Magdalene, "the other Mary"
Mark 16:1: Mary Magdalene, Mary mother of James, Salome
Luke 24:10: Mary Magdalene, Joanna, Mary mother of James, other women
John 20:1–2: Mary Magdalene alone, yet using first-person plural ("we")

506. Baker, *Foolishness of God*, 261. Cf. Catchpole, *Resurrection*, 199–202; Dunn, *Jesus Remembered*, 832–34; Birger Gerhardsson, "Mark and the Female Witnesses," in *Dumu-e2-dub-ba-A: Studies in Honor of Åke W. Sjöberg* (ed. Hermann Behrens, Darlene Loding, and Martha T. Roth; Occasional Publications of the Samuel Noah Kramer Fund 11; Philadelphia: University Museum, 1989), 217–26; Lohfink, "Auferstehung," 45; C. F. D. Moule, "Introduction" to *The Significance of the Message of the Resurrection for Faith in Jesus* Christ (ed. C. F. D. Moule; SBT 2.8; London: SCM, 1968), 9; von Campenhausen, *Tradition*, 75–76; Wright, *Resurrection*, 607–8; etc. Contrast Lowder, "Empty Tomb," 274–77. Note the confession of Placher, *Jesus*, 169: "For a good many years, I thought the whole empty tomb tradition was just a story that had grown up later among Christians. . . . If someone had invented the

argument for the empty tomb in recent decades. (Who first formulated it I do not know, but it may well have been a relatively modern scholar or apologist, for I do not recall finding this line of reasoning in works written before the last century or so.)

There are actually three issues here. The first concerns the three women named in Mark 16:1: Mary Magdalene, Mary the mother of James, Salome. Why are precisely these individuals named? One is fairly confident that they were real people, like Simon of Cyrene[507] and most if not all of Mark's named characters.[508] But why is a story built around them in particular? Why name them at all? Setting aside later legend, we know next to nothing about any of these women. One might then contend that memory has here played its part.

Although one sees the point, it really cannot be given much weight, for historical names can be used in unhistorical ways. One recalls that later Christian apocrypha are full of obscure, named people and places with little if any attachment to historical reality. So while the names of Mary Magdalene, Mary the mother of James, and Salome may well be — I myself think they are — reminiscence, other considerations will have to establish the origin of the story in which they appear.

The second issue regarding the women is the question of potential embarrassment. Celsus was able to turn their role in the story into ridicule. According to Origen, *Cels.* 2.59 (ed. Marcovich; 131), the pagan polemicist derided the testimony to the empty tomb as deriving from "a half-frantic woman." Even Luke 24:22–23 ("Some women of our group astounded us. . . . When they did not find his body there, they came back and told us that they had indeed seen a vision of angels who said that he was alive") reflects the reluctance to believe the testimony of women. Nothing similar is said about refusal to believe what the male disciples say, although it is no less unbelievable.[509] Perhaps this explains the

---

story, however, I can think of no reason why women would have been cited as the witnesses. As a result I've come to think that there probably was an empty tomb."

507. Mark 15:21 speaks of Simon of Cyrene, father of Alexander and Rufus, and an ossuary from the Kidron Valley, discovered in 1941, may have contained Alexander's remains; see C. A. Evans, *Ossuaries*, 94–96.

508. See further Bauckham, "Women," 257–310, and L. Schenke, *Auferstehungsverkündigung*, 94–98. Bauckham is particularly helpful regarding the reasons why the names undergo some change in Matthew and Luke.

509. See further Richard Bauckham, "Woman," 268–77. At 276n40 he cites the parallel in *Gos. Mary* 17:16–22 (cf. n. 214, above). Also helpful here is Claudia Setzer, "Excellent Women: Female Witness to the Resurrection," *JBL* 116 (1997): 259–72. For modern examples

women's absence from the old formula in 1 Cor 15:3–8.[510] The text comes from a world in which, sadly, Christian writers could confidently speak of "old wives' tales" (1 Tim 4:7) and "silly women, overwhelmed by their sins and swayed by all kinds of desires, who are always being instructed and can never arrive at a knowledge of the truth" (2 Tim 3:6–7). So, the reasoning runs, it is precisely the testimony of women, once suspect, that for us confirms the truth of the story.

Lüdemann rejects this argument. Like some before him, he asserts: "There is no universal ancient view that women are incompetent witnesses. (That women were not allowed to give testimony was the case only in ancient Judaism)."[511] This misses the mark. Surely the story of the empty tomb arose in Jewish-Christian circles. Mark 16:1–8 speaks of the Sabbath and alludes to the Decalogue's injunction against doing business then (vv. 1–2). It seems to refer to the sort of round stone used to close some tombs around Jerusalem (vv. 3–4; see n. 641). It reflects the Jewish tradition of imagining angels to be young (v. 5; see n. 540). It designates Jesus as "the Nazarene" (Ναζαρηνόν, v. 6). It shows an interest in Galilee (v. 7). And it uses the language of resurrection for his vindication: "He is risen" (ἠγέρθη, v. 6).

Given all this, it is specifically the status of women within Judaism that is the relevant point, and this in turn means that we must come to terms with Josephus, *Ant.* 4.219: "From women let no evidence be accepted, because of the levity and temerity of their sex."[512] Although Josephus's comment is about the court room, the implications are broader, for the justification for the ruling — women are victims of levity and temerity — expresses an attitude many first-century Jewish males presumably held (cf. Philo, *QG* 4.15). It is instructive that, as Richard Bauckham has observed, Luke 24:22–23 has parallels in the first-century *LAB* 9:10 ("When Miriam reported her dream, her parents did not believe her")

---

of the prejudice against women, which would no longer be politically correct, compare Woolston, *Sixth Discourse*, 30 ("womanish Fables"); Anonymous, *Ecce Homo!* 266 (Jesus appeared to women who had "weak minds and ardent imaginations, disposed to form phantoms and chimeras"); and Sherlock, *Tryal of the Witnesses*, 81 (we can believe in the resurrection despite the "silly" women: "the Evidence of the Men surely is not the worse because some Women happen'd to see the same thing which they saw"). The same prejudice has often made itself felt in the critical evaluation of female Catholic visionaries; cf. William Christian Jr., *Apparitions in Late Medieval and Renaissance Spain* (Princeton: Princeton University Press, 1981), 197–99.

510. So many, including Hengel, "Begräbnis," 135.

511. Lüdemann, *Resurrection*, 158.

512. Cf. *m. Šebu.* 4.1; *m. Roš. Haš.* 1.8; *b. B. Qam.* 88a; *b. Šabb.* 30a; also 2 Tim 3:6–7.

and 42:5 ("Manoah did not believe his wife"). In both cases a woman's testimony to divine revelation is doubted.[513] Surely adherents of Jesus were not helping themselves when they admitted that women were the only firsthand human witnesses to some of the events of Easter morning. When Christian storytellers did get around to buoying their apologetics, they constructed narratives featuring male disciples. In Wilckens's words: "Later tradition shows a clear tendency to have the disciples at least confirm the women's discovery afterwards (Luke 24:12, 24; John 20:2f.), and later tradition also has the disciples present on Easter Day in Jerusalem (Luke and John [20] as compared with Matthew and John 21). Accordingly, it must be accepted that the core of the narrative is indeed that the women found Jesus's tomb empty in the early morning of the first day of the week."[514] I agree.

The third issue involving the women is that their appearance coincides with the disappearance of the male disciples, who are otherwise major actors in the drama of Jesus.[515] Why is it not Peter and his male companions who are at the tomb first thing Easter morning?

Many have argued that the unexpected presence of women does not tell in favor of a historical genesis because "the flight of the male disciples was an established fact."[516] In other words, the tradition held that the disciples had fled when Jesus was arrested and so had not witnessed the crucifixion and burial, at which only some female followers were present. When time came to make up the story of the empty tomb, the only characters at hand were the women.

This response is inadequate. It is the hallmark of legends to sin against established facts. Why should Mark 16:1–8 be more conscientious? That

---

513. Bauckham, *Gospel Women*, 271–75.
514. Cf. Wilckens, *Resurrection*, 116–17.
515. Cf. Charles Masson, "Le tombeau vide: Essai sur la formation d'une tradition," *RTP* 32 (1944): 166–69, 173. For patristic texts that view the discovery by women instead of apostles as a problem or topic for discussion, see Rosemarie Nüremberg, "Apostolae Apostolorum: Die Frauen am Grab als erste Zeuginnen der Auferstehung in der Väterexegese," in *Stimuli: Exegese und ihre Hermeneutik in Antike und Christentum: Festschrift für Ernst Dassmann* (ed. Georg Schöllgen and Clemens Scholten; JAC 23; Münster: Aschendorff, 1996), 228–42.
516. Lüdemann, *Resurrection*, 118. Bultmann, *History*, 274, already suggested this. Cf. John Barclay, "The Resurrection in Contemporary New Testament Scholarship," in d'Costa, *Resurrection Reconsidered*, 23: "If Mark was working from a source which had only women as witnesses of the burial of Jesus, only they could be responsible for discovering the empty tomb." Müller, *Entstehung*, 45, offers this argument as well as another possibility: the women are there because it was, in Judaism, the custom of women to visit the tombs of the newly deceased in order to check for premature burial.

is, why not bring Peter and the others onstage despite what really happened? Luke and John reveal that Christian tradition did not need to interpret the flight of the disciples as an immediate exit from Jerusalem which excluded their participation in the discovery of the empty tomb. Indeed, Luke 23:49 ("All his acquaintances . . . stood at a distance") and John 19:26–27 ("the disciple whom he [Jesus] loved standing beside her") place disciples at the crucifixion. And even if pre-Markan tradition believed that the disciples were not around on Easter morn, one fails to see why Christian legend would have created a story with Mary Magdalene at the tomb instead of a story in which the disciples, if gone to Galilee, immediately return, perhaps right after the appearance to Peter, to find the tomb empty in Jerusalem. Or why not a story in which Joseph of Arimathea or, as the *Gospel of Peter* (10:38–11:45) has it, important Jewish officials return to the tomb or see Jesus and so learn the truth?[517]

Aside from all this, the idea that the male disciples fled to Galilee before Easter Sunday and had been there "between Good Friday and the beginning of their activity in Jerusalem,"[518] although commonly asserted, is a feeble construct, a pure postulate without basis in the evidence.[519] Luke and John explicitly assert that the disciples were still in the capital after the crucifixion (so too *Gos. Pet.* 14:58–59), while Mark 16:7 ("Tell his disciples and Peter that he is going ahead of you to Galilee") and its parallels in Matt 28:7 and 10 presume the same circumstance, that Jesus' companions have yet to leave the neighborhood and go north: otherwise, the women, who are in Jerusalem, could not communicate with them before they set out for Galilee.[520] In other words, all four canonical Gospels as well as the *Gospel of Peter* have the disciples in Jerusalem on Sunday. What is more, Gardner-Smith observed that the Gospels say only

---

517. Cf. *Acts Pil.* 15:6 and the Georgian aprocryphon on Joseph of Arimathea discussed by Adolf Harnack, "Ein in georgischer Sprache überliefertes Apokryphon des Joseph von Arimathia," *SPAW* 39 (1901): 920–31.

518. So Schweizer, "Resurrection," 148.

519. Cf. von Campenhausen, *Tradition*, 78–79; Wedderburn, *Resurrection*, 53–57, 59–60.

520. Cf. the sequence in the *Gospel of Peter*. Matt 28:11–15 might also be thought relevant: the accusation that the disciples stole the body assumes their presence in Jerusalem. As an aside one wonders whether the disciples would in fact have abandoned the women who had gone to Jerusalem with them. Would they, even if afraid, have left them without escort?

that the disciples deserted Jesus and scattered among the crowds in Jerusalem. On the day before the feast the most conspicuous thing they could have done would have been to leave Jerusalem, and journey in a direction opposite to the stream of traffic. Probably travelling sixty miles during the feast would have been a difficult if not an impossible undertaking. Why should they try it? A man who wishes to hide himself generally chooses a crowded city, and it must have been easy for a dozen Galileans to escape notice among the enormous population of Jerusalem at the Passover season.[521]

Although there is every reason to believe that the first appearances to Peter and the Twelve took place in Galilee, there is no cause at all to suppose that Jesus' closest followers sped for home directly after the arrest or traveled on a Sabbath.[522] (Incidentally, those who imagine differently will need to wonder how Jesus' followers came to learn that his arrest led to his execution.[523]) Their absence from Mark 16:1-8, then, remains a decent argument for some real memory here — especially when one keeps in mind that "the resurrection narrative is the only place in the whole Bible where women are sent by the angels of Yahweh to pronounce his message to men."[524]

•

Looking back over the debate regarding the empty tomb, there is no iron logic on either side. There is a decent case for it, and there is a respectable case against it. Both sides, moreover, have their faults and suffer from a scarcity of proof: neither exorcizes all our doubts. I am nonetheless not moved to declare a stalemate, for pro and con are not quite here equal. Rather, of our two options — that a tomb was in fact unoccupied or that belief in the resurrection imagined it unoccupied —

---

521. Gardner-Smith, *Resurrection*, 144. Cf. Wedderburn, *Resurrection*, 54.

522. See further Wedderburn, *Resurrection*, 58–60. Contrast Herman Hendrickx, *The Resurrection Narratives of the Synoptic Gospels* (London: Geoffrey Chapman, 1978), 15: "The men left for Galilee after the tragedy of the day of Preparation, and there is no indication that they left with any knowledge of an empty tomb." Although this is a common judgment, my own conclusions call it into question. We must reckon with the possibility that if some women thought they had discovered an empty tomb, they may well have shared their story with Peter and his companions while they were all returning together to Galilee.

523. Cf. Arthur S. Peake, *Christianity: Its Nature and Its Truth* (New York: George H. Doran, 1908), 201.

524. Tibor Horvath, "The Early Markan Resurrection Tradition (Mark 16,1-8)," *RUO* 43 (1973): 446.

the former, as I read the evidence, is the slightly stronger possibility, the latter the slightly weaker. The best two arguments against the tradition — the ability of early Christians to create fictions and the existence of numerous legends about missing bodies — while certainly weighty, remain nonetheless hypothetical and suggestive, whereas the best two arguments for the tradition are concrete and evidential: (a) Visions of Jesus, without belief in his empty tomb, would probably have led only to faith in Jesus' vindication and assumption to heaven, not to belief in his resurrection from the dead. (b) The discovery of the empty tomb by Mary Magdalene and other women commends itself as likely nonfiction. I agree, then, with Jacques Schlosser: "Indications are not lacking which permit the historian to conclude that the tradition of the discovery of the open and empty tomb is historically likely, but one will do so with great hesitation."[525] "Indications are not lacking" and "with great hesitation" seem to me to be just right. A judgment in favor of the empty tomb, which will forever be haunted by legendary stories of disappearing and raised bodies, must remain, if accepted, tentative.

Even so, and although Mark 16:1–8 is undoubtedly stylized drama in the service of Christian theology, that drama and that theology can in my judgment enshrine a real event. "Even narratives of faith contain historical elements."[526] Just as the Romans crucified Jesus and Christian haggadah embroidered the fact, so too was Jesus probably laid in a tomb, which some of his female followers later found empty, a fact that Christian imagination put into a narrative and elaborated.

The details may remain foggy, but my own conjectures come to this. While death in all societies summons certain fixed, ritualistic responses involving corpses and graves, the dedicated followers of Jesus still in Jerusalem after his crucifixion would have been unable to engage in their tradition's ritualistic responses on either Friday afternoon or on the Sabbath. Further, public acts of mourning for a convicted criminal may well have been forbidden altogether.[527] But personal, private lamentation was

---

525. Jacques Schlosser, *Jésus de Nazareth* (Paris: Agnès Viénot Éditions, 1999), 331.

526. Lüdemann, *Resurrection*, 23.

527. Cf. the ruling in *Sem.* 2:6: "For those executed by the court, no rites whatsoever should be observed. Their brothers and relatives should come and greet the witnesses and the judges, as if to say, We bear you no ill will, for you have rendered a true judgment." Perhaps this ruling or the custom behind it was already known and heeded in Jesus' day; see the texts in the next note.

inevitable.[528] And it would have been wholly natural for Jesus' followers to indulge their grief close to the corpse — near which the soul was thought to remain for several days[529] — as soon as there was opportunity, which would have been late Saturday evening or early Sunday morning.[530] It is human nature not to let go of the dead.[531]

Given then that certain women went up to Jerusalem with Jesus, and given further, to quote Kathleen Corley, "the tenacity of women's lament traditions, as well as the overall interest in family retrieval of executed family members, we can at the least assume that the women, and perhaps even some of the men, would have tried to watch the crucifixion proceedings, and would have tried to find Jesus' body after he died in spite of the risks that would entail."[532] Corley goes on to judge that those who sought Jesus' grave did not find it. I am rather inclined to think, in light of the preceding pages, that the evidence nudges us to the contrary conclusion.[533]

---

528. Cf. *Sem.* 2:6 again: "They may not mourn but may grieve, the latter signifying grieving in silence." Similar is *m. Sanh.* 6:6: "They used not to make [public] lamentation but they went mourning, for mourning has place in the heart alone." See further Josef Blinzler, "Die Grablegung Jesu in historischer Sicht," in Dhanis, *Resurrexit*, 100–101; also Josephus, *Ant.* 17.206; *J.W.* 4.331-32; and Suetonius, *Tib.* 61.

529. Cf. Saul Lieberman, "Some Aspects of After Life in Early Rabbinic Literature," in *Harry Austryn Wolfson Jubilee Volume on the Occasion of His Seventy-Fifth Birthday* (Jerusalem: American Academy for Jewish Research, 1965), 2:506. For communicating with the dead near their tombs, see *b. Ber.* 18b. The desire to be physically near the dead lives on in our society with visits to cemeteries and requests to be buried next to loved ones.

530. My best guess is that the tradition was of a discovery on Sunday morning; I am aware, however, of the problem that Matt 28:1 presents to this view; see Daniel Boyarin, "'After the Sabbath' (Matt. 28:1) — Once More into the Crux," *JTS* 52 (1901): 678–88; and J. Michael Winger, "When Did the Women Visit the Tomb? Sources for Some Temporal Clauses in the Synoptic Gospels," *NTS* 40 (1994): 284–88.

531. Cf. *Ep. Apos.* 9–10; and Schwager, "Heutige Theologie," 437, 449, who sees no reason to think that the interest in the empty tomb shown by the four canonical evangelists and later Christians would have been foreign to the people who themselves knew Jesus. On Mark's remark that the women went to perfume the body, see n. 533. Perhaps there was more than one motive. *Sem.* 8:1 v. l. records the habit of visiting graves "until the third day" in order to prevent premature burial. We should also not forget that people soon after a death often wish simply to be near the buried loved one. No one thinks Jesus' desire to visit Lazarus out of the ordinary until he asks for the stone to be removed from the cave mouth.

532. Kathleen E. Corley, *Women and the Historical Jesus* (Santa Rosa, CA: Polebridge, 2002), 138. The entire chapter on 107–39 is quite instructive and justifies the words I have quoted.

533. Many are confident that, because of rapid putrefaction, Mark must be wrong in saying that the women sought to anoint on early Sunday morning a body buried on late Friday evening. Bousset, *Kyrios Christos*, 105, thought this "utterly inconceivable." Cf. Elliott, "First Easter," 211–12. Although the motive imparted to the women may well be Mark's guesswork (Matthew offers different motives for the visit), so that it does not necessarily bear on the origin of the story, one wonders whether the usual objection is decisive. See Gundry, *Mark*, 997. To his observations I add two. (1) *T. Job.* 53:5–7 and *T. Abr.* (rec. long) 20:11 have people remaining

The judgment that some women found a vacated tomb does not, it hardly needs underlining, tell us why this happened. We have here rather an historical dead end. It is always possible to imagine that someone, for reasons unknown, removed the body, as Mary Magdalene first supposes in John 20:13–15.[534] Perhaps the Jewish authorities filched it to prevent veneration of Jesus' remains, and things soon got out of hand. Having dumped the body unceremoniously, they were unable or unmotivated to recover it later. Or maybe Mary went to the wrong tomb and the rumors started. Or maybe necromancers wanted the powerful corpse of an executed holy man.[535] Or maybe Joseph of Arimathea placed Jesus in a temporary tomb[536] — perhaps the permanent grave for Jewish criminals where Jesus ended up was not near the Roman site of the crucifixion — and after the Sabbath, this representative of the Sanhedrin moved the corpse to its final resting place. Having done this, perhaps Joseph died soon thereafter and so never told anyone, or maybe he kept quiet for reasons we can never guess; or perhaps he did speak out, Christians disbelieved him, and the sources understandably preferred to forget his protest. Or perhaps Joseph, knowing the truth, yet was nonetheless happy to see the cause of Jesus continue.

We have no reason to endorse any of these speculations, for which there is not a shred of evidence. They must all be deemed unlikely. Yet they are not impossible. How for instance could one ever demonstrate that Joseph, whatever his motivations, did not move the body before the women showed up?[537] So, given that the return to life of a man truly dead must also be deemed, in the abstract, even more unlikely than Joseph moving Jesus' body, it is not immediately apparent why the traditional Christian interpretation should be, as it is for so many, instinctively

---

around dead bodies for three days. (2) According to *m. Šabb.* 23.5, which surely enshrines old practice (cf. John 5:10), one cannot move a body for burial on the Sabbath. So if a person died right before a Sabbath, the body would have to sit around for a day before burial, even if it was the middle of summer. Assuming for the sake of argument and in accord with Mark that (a) Jesus died in the late afternoon, (b) he was buried soon thereafter, (c) his burial place was in a cave (caves tend to be cool), and (d) it was not summer (John 18:18 has people warming themselves around a fire), then the time between his placement in a cool tomb and the women's visit would have been only twelve hours or so more than the time between the death of someone who died right before the Sabbath and was not placed in a tomb until twenty-four hours or more later.

534. See esp. Carrier, "Guarded Tomb."

535. See above, 202–3. Craig, *New Testament Evidence*, 376–77, fails to rebut this possibility. How could one ever do so?

536. References to such appear in *Sem.* 10:8 and 13:5.

537. See further Lowder, "Empty Tomb," 259–64.

deemed more plausible than a conjecture involving wholly mundane postulates.[538] Many others, understandably, "are prepared to admit almost any conceivable concurrence of natural improbabilities rather than resort to the hypothesis of supernatural interference."[539]

Before passing on to the next stage of the argument, I should like to make one final observation about the empty tomb, or rather the story about it. There is an angel in Mark 16:5[540] and Matt 28:2, and there are two angels in Luke 24:4 and John 20:12. Modern scholars typically affirm that these angels are purely literary constructs. This is Raymond Brown: "Christian readers of the Bible have understood too literally much of biblical angelology.... Most angelic interpreters were no more than mouthpieces for revelation, without any personality. If we pay attention to the freedom with which the evangelists handled the details of the angelic appearance at the empty tomb (especially as to the number and position of the angels), we recognize their awareness that here they were not dealing with controllable historical facts but with imaginative descriptions."[541]

My bet is that Brown is right: his view fits my supposition that Mark's angelophany is a transmuted christophany. Further, John 20:1–10 might reflect a tradition about Jesus' tomb that lacked an angelic interpreter.[542]

---

538. Or more plausible than seeking refuge in ignorance; cf. Shelley's take on the resurrection in his *Notes to Queen Mab*: "All that we have a right to infer from our ignorance of the cause of any event is that we do not know it" (*The Complete Works of Percy Bysshe Shelley* [ed. Roger Ingpen and Walter E. Peck; London: Ernest Benn, 1927], 155).

539. William Edward Hartpole Lecky, *History of the Rise and Influence of Rationalism in Europe* (London: Longmans, Green, 1910), 1:144. Cf. Annet, *Resurrection*, 75–77; and see further Michael Martin, "Why the Resurrection Is Initially Improbable," *Philo* 1 (1998): 63–73.

540. The young man of Mark 16:5 is clearly "an angel in human guise" (Gundry, "Trimming the Debate," 106). Cf. Bode, *Easter Morning*, 26–27. Not only is this how Matthew and Luke (see 24:23) interpret the text, but angels were thought of as young (as always on later icons): Tob 5:5–10 v. 1.; 2 Macc 3:26, 33; Acts 1:10; Josephus, *Ant.* 5.277; *Gos. Pet.* 13.55; Herm. *Vis.* 3.1.6, 8; 3.2.5; 3.4.1; etc. Later texts call Metatron "the youth" (3 *En.* 2:1–2; 3:2; 4:1, 10; *b. Yebam.* 16b). Because in *T. Abr.* (rec. long) 2:5 the archangel Michael is young, it may be of interest that *Ascen. Isa.* 3:15–16 identifies Michael as one of the two angels who appeared at Jesus' tomb. Also favoring the identification of Mark's "young man" with an angel is his white robe; that angels are bright or white is a commonplace; see Dan 10:6; 4Q547 frg. 1.5; 2 Macc 11:8; *LAE* 9:1; Acts 1:10; 2 Cor 11:14; Rev 4:4; 19:14; *Liv. Pro.*, Elijah 2; *Gos. Pet.* 9:36; *Pap. Chester Beatty* XVI 25a v.; *Sepher Ha-Razim* 2.93; etc.

541. Brown, *Virginal Conception*, 122–23. Cf. Bode, *Easter Morning*, 166. L. Schenke, *Auferstehungsverkündigung*, 86, thinks that the appearance of the angel is sufficient reason to label the story a legend. There are many concurring voices; but see Craig, *New Testament Evidence*, 222–30.

542. Behind John one might divine a tradition or memory in which the empty tomb brought only panic, and one could find something closely related to this behind Mark 16:1–5a + 8.

Yet I confess to having a slight qualm that is perhaps worth recording. The immediate appeal of Brown's words is that so many of us in the contemporary academy do not believe overmuch if at all in angels. One needs to remember, however, that firsthand reports of visions of other-worldly beings, often luminous or dressed in white, are a dime a dozen throughout world religious literature and indeed are commonly reported in our own contemporary world.[543] Whatever one makes of this fact, it is a fact: people have sincerely reported seeing such beings, and in Jewish and Christian tradition they have called them angels. So although I reject the historicity of the content of the angel's message because it "reflects the kerygmatic preaching of resurrection and thus requires an understanding of the significance of the empty tomb gained from the appearance tradition,"[544] it escapes me why the report of a vision of angels should be doubted, as it is by some, for no other reason than that it is the report of a vision of angels. It certainly makes no sense, for example, to assert bluntly: "If angels do not exist, then the Markan story of the angelic appearance at the tomb cannot be historical."[545] Even if the premise is sound, the conclusion does not follow: people can and do see things that do not exist. One might as well vainly urge that, because Mary the mother of Jesus died long ago, accounts claiming that many have seen her since then must be wholly fictitious, which is nonsense. Whatever the explanation, some people have experiences that they interpret as encounters with Mary. Likewise, some people have experiences that they interpret as encounters with angels.

Brown's reading is not found in the commentaries written before modern times, which might make one wonder about the sophistication, if that is the right word, he attributes to the Gospel writers. Perhaps we are dealing here with a modern prejudice, rooted in our reluctance to acknowledge the phenomenology of human religious experience when it is foreign to us. This is not to say that I believe Mary had an angelic vision near Jesus' tomb. I am simply unable to share the self-assurance

---

Subtracting the angel from Mark's story admittedly leaves a less than meaningful story (cf. C. F. Evans, *Resurrection*, 76–77; Fischer, *Ostergeschenen*, 59); perhaps then Mark 16:5b–7 has displaced earlier matter.

543. Cf. the argument in Origen, *Cels.* 5.57 (ed. Marcovich; 368–69). The angel books so popular in the late 1980s and early 1990s in North America are full of firsthand accounts of sightings of angelic-like beings.

544. Perkins, *Resurrection*, 94. Cf. Bode, *Easter Morning*, 127–30.

545. Lowder, "Empty Tomb," 273.

with which so many commentators assume, without argument, that she did not. Why do so many find it easier to believe that the disciples had visionary experiences that they construed as appearances of the risen Jesus than that the women had a visionary experience that they construed as an angelic revelation?

PROBLEMS AND PRESUPPOSITIONS

Having now canvassed the evidence, if only in a perfunctory way, where does it lead? While we should not say with Henry Ford that history is bunk, I think we should say that, for better or for worse, history does not give some of us what we want or think we need. We ask, but we often do not receive; we knock, but the door is not always opened. History keeps its secrets better than many historians care to admit. Most of the past — surely far more than 99 percent, if we could quantify it — is irretrievably lost; it cannot be recovered. This should instill some modesty in us.

Consider the weeks following the crucifixion. We have only minuscule fragments of what actually transpired. What, for instance, do we really know about the resurrection experience of James? First Corinthians 15:7 says that he saw the risen Jesus. And that is it. What Jesus looked like, what he said, if anything, where the encounter took place, when precisely it happened, how James responded, what state of mind he was in, how the experience began, how it ended — all of this has failed to enter the record. Almost every question that we might ask goes unanswered.

It is not really different with events for which we ostensibly have something more than just passing allusion. Matthew ends by telling us that the eleven disciples went to Galilee, to a mountain "to which Jesus had directed them," and that they saw him there and worshipped him, although some doubted (28:16–17). These dramatic and unforgettable sentences follow: "All authority in heaven and on earth has been given to me. Go therefore and make disciples of all nations, baptizing them in the name of the Father and of the Son and of the Holy Spirit, and teaching them to obey everything that I have commanded you. And remember, I am with you always, to the end of the age" (28:16–20). One could, if so inclined, pose a dozen questions to this brief narrative. How many doubted? What were their names? Why did they doubt? Was their doubt ever resolved? If so, when and why? Upon what particular mountain did this episode transpire? Do we have here all that Jesus said upon that occasion, or did he impart more? And did the disciples say anything in reply? What did they say to themselves afterward? Did Jesus, at some point, just blink out and disappear, or did he, as in Acts 1:9, ascend into heaven?

I personally reckon these to be bad questions, theologically and exegetically, and attempting to answer them would, even if one wrongly took Matt 28:16–20 to be sober, rock-solid history, issue only in wearisome and idle speculation. Yet they are the sorts of questions historians often ask of old texts. The fact that we cannot begin to answer them shows how emaciated historically — as opposed to theologically — the Gospel narratives really are.[546] Even if we naively think them to be historically accurate down to the minutest detail, we are still left with precious little. The accounts of the resurrection, like the past in general, come to us as phantoms. Most of the reality is gone.[547]

It is the fragmentary and imperfect nature of the evidence as well as the limitations of our historical-critical tools that move us to confess, if we are conscientious, how hard it is to recover the past. That something happened does not entail our ability to show that it happened,[548] and that something did not happen does not entail our ability to show that it did not happen. I emphasize this assertion, obvious and trite, because both skeptical New Testament scholars and their conservative counterparts often have too much faith in their own abilities. Too infrequently do they confess, "This may or may not have happened," or "That is plausible but uncertain," or "That is unlikely but still possible," or "We just do not know." Sometimes, when ruminating on my own area of study, I recall what Mark Twain said about another discipline: "One gets such wholesale returns of conjecture out of such a trifling investment of fact."

---

546. As explanation for this unwelcome circumstance, Gerhardsson, "Evidence," 91, regards the Gospel stories as being, no less than 1 Cor 15:3–8, "substratum texts, textual undergarments so to speak: passages with a fundamental content but from the very beginning presupposing exposition, elucidation, and complement." While this makes some sense, and while it may well be true, it hardly helps us, for the exposition, elucidation, and complement have fallen into the cracks of history.

547. For the interesting theological argument that the silence and gaps in the Matthean and Markan narratives belong necessarily to the resurrection as a mysterious, unimaginable divine act that cannot be narrated, see Francis Watson, " 'He is not here': Towards a Theology of the Empty Tomb," in Barton and Stanton, *Resurrection*, 95–107. For a similar view, although it comes with explicit belief in an empty tomb, see Rowan Williams, *Christian Theology* (London: Blackwell, 2000), 183–96. Williams suggestively sets the image of Jesus' empty tomb beside the emptiness of the space between the cherubim in the holy of holies.

548. Gorham, *First Easter*, xii, commented on the Easter narratives: "True they may be; verifiable they are not."

Detractors of the faith, such as Anthony Flew, are often motivated to deny the resurrection. They confidently bend the flexible indicia and then instruct us that there was no empty tomb, the visions were subjective or legendary, and the resurrection stories and the faith behind them are unfounded fantasies. Apologists, of whom Gary Habermas is a good representative, strive vigorously, to the contrary, to verify their faith, and they convince themselves that robust probability is indeed on their side.[549] Both those actuated by dogmatic doubt and those commending orthodoxy to reason go through the motions and then announce, "I told you so!" They thus validate each other with their common presupposition that proof one way or the other should be in the offing — although one wonders how often they in fact make converts.

Contrary to the gung-ho apologist, it is possible in theory that Jesus awakened from death, that the tomb was empty, that he appeared to some of his followers, and that historians cannot prove any of this to anyone. And contrary to the evangelistic skeptic, it is equally possible, again in theory, that when Jesus died he died for good, that the appearances were altogether illusory, that his tomb remained forever full, and that historians cannot establish any of this.

Even if history served us much better than it does, it would still not take us to the promised land of theological certainty. Let us say, although it cannot be done, that someone has somehow convinced us, beyond all doubt, that the tomb was empty and that people saw Jesus because he indeed came to life again. Even this would not of itself prove that God raised him from the dead.[550] One can draw any number of curves through a finite set of points to create a thousand different pictures.[551] Likewise, and as we often learn at murder trials, one can more often than not offer competing narratives for the same facts. It is not different with the resurrection of Jesus. Someone could, if so inclined, conjecture that aliens, ever since discovering our planet long ago, have followed our play of hopes and fears with great curiosity. Intrigued by human psychology, and

---

549. For the views of Flew and Habermas, see the record of their debate: *Did Jesus Rise from the Dead? The Resurrection Debate* (ed. Terry L. Miethe; San Francisco: Harper & Row, 1987).

550. Here I endorse Wright, *Resurrection*, 720–23, who observes that one can interpret the literal resurrection of Jesus from several points of view: "There seems to be no necessary compulsion, either for those who believe in Jesus' resurrection or for those who disbelieve it, to interpret it within the framework of thought employed by the early Christians themselves."

551. Cf. Quine's famous reflections on the underdetermination of theories.

learning, in 30 CE or thereabouts, of an extraordinary character, Jesus of Nazareth, and of the religious expectations surrounding him, they then designed an experiment. Upon his death, they reanimated his corpse or transplanted his brain into a new and better body (which would explain why Mary Magdalene and others had trouble recognizing him). Then they convinced him that he had conquered death by divine intervention, set him before the disciples, and sat back to take notes.

While there is not a sliver of evidence for such a fantastic state of affairs, it cannot be dismissed as inconceivable, only wholly unlikely for utter lack of evidence (although one can find reconstructions like it in the offbeat literature[552]). The hypothetical scenario goes to show that proof of the Christian confession can never be achieved because possible alternatives can always be imagined. It also raises the question, which must be faced in all seriousness, of how Christians have come to the view that invoking space aliens beggars belief whereas crediting God with a resurrection is sensible.[553] Science fiction — Philip José Farmer's well-known Riverworld series comes to mind — has certainly not hesitated to give aliens the power to raise human beings from the dead, so at least we find the notion intelligible.

We inevitably evaluate matters by means of our presuppositions. If one approaches the New Testament with the sure and certain conviction that there is no God, or that the Creator has an inviolate respect for the regularities of nature or for some other reason is not in the business of old-fashioned miracles, then surely, even if one is not a devotee of Erich von Däniken and his ilk, intervention by space aliens will seem more plausible than the divinely wrought resurrection as traditionally understood.[554] Probability is in the eye of the beholder. It depends upon one's worldview, into which the resurrection fits or, alternatively, does not fit.

Arguments about Jesus' literal resurrection cannot establish one's Weltanschauung. While orthodox Christians may regard the resurrection as the historical and theological foundation of their faith, it cannot

---

552. For example, R. L. Dione, *God Drives a Flying Saucer* (New York: Bantam, 1973).

553. See further Robert Greg Cavin, "Is There Sufficient Historical Evidence to Establish the Resurrection of Jesus?" *Faith and Philosophy* 12 (1995): 361–79.

554. Cf. the candid statement of Goulder, "Baseless Fabric," 48: "We will follow the general principle that it has proved sensible to trust this-worldly explanations rather than ones with ghosts, demons, etc." Again, on 52 is this: "Even if speculative, a natural explanation is to be preferred." This, given Goulder's worldview, makes perfect sense.

be their epistemological foundation. The resurrection of Jesus instead belongs to the Christian web of belief, within which alone it has its sensible place.[555] Outside that web, it must be rejected or radically reinterpreted. This is why, as B. H. Streeter remarked, "The possibility of a naturalistic explanation of some kind or other would doubtless be assumed as a matter of course were the story [of the resurrection] told of any ordinary person."[556] In like fashion, I understand why Richard Swinburne, in his recent defense of the resurrection, commences by first seeking to establish the existence of a certain sort of God and the likelihood of such a God communicating with and redeeming the human race.[557] "Modern logic," in the words of F. C. S. Schiller, "has made it plain that single facts can never be 'proved' except by their coherence in a system."[558] It accords with this that evaluation of the resurrection cannot be isolated from one's other fundamental beliefs, including what Swinburne calls "background evidence."[559] Such evaluation is rather what has been termed a configural judgment, where the interpretation of one item depends upon the interpretation of others. That is, the resurrection is a part that cannot be evaluated apart from the whole to which it belongs. Alvin Plantinga, an orthodox Christian, can admit that, "on sheerly historical grounds," the resurrection seems less than likely, or that its probability, "given all the controversy among the experts," must be reckoned "inscrutable."[560] Obviously, if Plantinga did not have more than "sheerly

---

555. See further A. E. Taylor, *Does God Exist?* (London: Macmillan, 1948), 123–60; also Francis Watson, " 'Historical Evidence' and the Resurrection of Jesus," *Theology* 90 (1987): 372.

556. B. H. Streeter, "The Historic Christ," in *Foundations: A Statement of Christian Belief in Terms of Modern Thought: By Seven Oxford Men*, by B. H. Streeter et al. (London: Macmillan, 1913), 134.

557. Swinburne, *Resurrection*. Cf. Catchpole, *Resurrection*, 187–88; and Sherlock, *Tryal of the Witnesses*, 59: "To what Purpose is it to vindicate the particular Evidence of the Resurrection of Christ, so long as this general Prejudice, that a Resurrection is incapable of being prov'd, remains unremov'd?" Pannenberg, *Systematic Theology*, 1:56; 2:351, 362, concedes that his case for the resurrection presupposes the twin possibilities of an active God and resurrection — hardly universal presuppositions. Stephen T. Davis, *Risen Indeed: Making Sense of the Resurrection* (Grand Rapids: Eerdmans, 1993), regards his defense of the resurrection as "soft apologetics" because he recognizes that nothing he says could convert a "naturalist." Cf. his article, which is more levelheaded than most rationalistic *apologia* for the resurrection: "Is It Possible to Know That Jesus Was Raised from the Dead?" *Faith and Philosophy* 1 (1984): 147–59.

558. F. C. S. Schiller, in *Proceedings of the Society for Psychical Research* 18 (1891): 419.

559. See further Paul Gwynne, "Why Some Still Doubt That Jesus' Body Was Raised," in Kendall and Davis, *Convergence*, 355–67.

560. Alvin Plantinga, *Warranted Christian Belief* (New York: Oxford University Press, 2000), 276. Cf. Placher, *Jesus*, 170: "We do not have enough evidence for a confident answer of

historical grounds" for his beliefs, he would not have his beliefs. But he thinks, and I agree with him, that he does have more. Religious or theological warrant need not be empirical warrant or strictly historical warrant.[561] Kant claimed God to be a postulate of practical as opposed to pure or theoretical reason. Analogously, pure historical reasoning is not going to show us that God raised Jesus from the dead. That conviction is rather a postulate of what one might call practical Christian reasoning.

The resurrection is not a topic unto itself, and we cannot evaluate it independently of our evaluation of Christianity and the nature of the world. Easter faith sits in the middle of "a controversy concerning the nature of reality at large."[562] As William James said in another connection, "The juices of metaphysical assumptions leak in at every joint." Just as a particular moral judgment cannot be made without reference to a larger moral vision, so a verdict about the resurrection of Jesus cannot be made without reference to a larger theological vision or lack thereof. When we look, our eyes are somewhere.

It is our worldview that interprets the textual data, not the textual data that determines our worldview. One who disbelieves in all so-called miracles can, with good conscience, remain disbelieving in the literal resurrection of Jesus after an examination of the evidence,[563] just as a traditional Christian can, without intellectual guilt, retain belief after surveying the pertinent particulars. No doubt both things have happened. One can hardly fault the judgment that "the evidence really is inconclusive."[564] As Bonhoeffer put it, when writing on the historical questions

---

any kind based purely on historical evidence.... Looking at these matters in terms of historical evidence generates only agnosticism."

561. Cf. Philip D. Clayton, *God and Contemporary Science* (Grand Rapids: Eerdmans, 1997), 259: "If a theological belief involves claims that never could be empirically tested, then we cannot fault the belief for not providing empirical warrant."

562. Wolfhart Pannenberg, "History and the Reality of the Resurrection," in D'Costa, *Resurrection*, 64. From an agnostic point of view but here in agreement with Pannenberg, compare Donald Wayne Viney, "Grave Doubts about the Resurrection," *Enc* 50 (1989): 125–40.

563. Cf. Watson, " 'He is not here,' " 105: "The Christian proclamation of the risen Lord is...open to the possibility of a disbelief that can justify itself in terms that are entirely reasonable within their own frame of reference."

564. Donald Wayne Viney, review of Davis, *Risen Indeed*, in *International Journal for Philosophy of Religion* 37 (1995): 122. Cf. Karl Barth, *Church Dogmatics* (1956), 4/1:341. This has been recognized for a long time; cf. Lake, *Resurrection*, 253; and already Weisse, *Geschichte*, 2:426–38: historical criticism cannot judge the extraordinary experiences of the disciples to be true or false, or attribute them either to the Spirit of God or to psychology. Weisse therefore goes on to speak of faith and to discuss its nature. See also the minimalistic conclusions of Vögtle, "Wie kam es zum Osterglauben?" 127–31.

surrounding Jesus' empty tomb: "Even as the Risen One, he does not break through his incognito."[565] The historical data are, at least regarding the present issue, sufficiently pliable, sufficiently submissive to our wills, to be construed in more than one way. It is not just that, if we want, we can torture the data until they confess what we want to hear: it is that even if we try to be impartial and listen, we may be unsure of what they are saying.

The facts in this matter are exceedingly hard for the careful historian to work out. There is certainly no evidence so overwhelming that we are compelled, against our interests, whatever they may be, to accept it.[566] Typically, and even when we seek to be as conscientious as possible, we often no doubt end up seeing what we want and expect to see. Maybe we suffer something analogous to the conflict of interest on display when scientists who are funded by the tobacco industry discover that smoking is less harmful than formerly supposed. My guess is that, as a matter of psychological fact, investigation of the primary texts and relevant secondary literature has less often led to conversions than it has either strengthened an already-existing disbelief or confirmed an already-existing faith. So it is not merely a question of what the historical arguments are, but of what beliefs and predispositions we bring to those arguments. The truth one discerns behind the texts is largely determined by desires, expectations, and religious and philosophical convictions already to hand. We cannot eschew ourselves.

If this is the right conclusion, then we need to scrutinize not just the texts but also ourselves. When I do this, I find that I am neither an atheist nor an agnostic. I do not share the modern fashion of disbelief but rather have a strong distrust of secular pieties. I indeed believe, as best I can, in the God of Western theism, or rather, in the God of Israel. I also believe that materialistic explanations and this-worldly causalities encompass only part of reality, that death is not extinction, and that the dead sometimes communicate with the living. So my view of things allows me to believe that the crucified Jesus triumphed over death and made this known to his followers, and my personal religious history and

---

565. Dietrich Bonhoeffer, *Christology* (London: Collins, 1966), 117.

566. Contrast Samuel McComb, *The Future Life in the Light of Modern Inquiry* (New York: Dodd, Mead, 1919), 123: "Any open and candid mind, prepossessed with no dogmatic assumptions against the survival of the soul after death, can convince itself that Christ emerged from the realm of the dead, and manifested Himself on the material plane to certain witnesses." This is just inane.

current social location — I am a mainstream Protestant who teaches at a Presbyterian seminary — make such a belief congenial. As for the story of the empty tomb, I remain theologically in permanent irresolution. Although I think it more likely to be history than legend, that remains a tentative judgment. Further, although its truth would be, for reasons recounted earlier, welcome, my personal philosophy, rightly or wrongly, has no pressing need for an empty tomb. I do not believe that our life in the world to come in any way depends upon the recovery of our current flesh and bones; and if not for us, why for Jesus?[567] I share neither the philosophic materialism of the naturalist nor the eschatological materialism of many of my fellow Christians.[568]

THE MOST REASONABLE EXPLANATION?

There was a time when an educated Christian apologist could in all solemnity write:

> We hold, then, without the slightest hesitation, that the resurrection of the Lord Jesus Christ, the great central fact of Christianity, is established beyond the possibility of a reasonable doubt. No man who believes that human testimony can establish any fact at all, is at liberty to cast doubt or discredit on that fact, without at the same time, and far more reasonably, doubting every fact that history has ever recorded, — nay, every fact that he himself has not witnessed, — and limiting his belief within the very narrow boundaries of his own sentient perceptions. Can he stop there? No; for the scepticism which has deprived him of the evidence of testimony, will not long leave him in possession of the evidence of his bodily senses.[569]

---

567. For additional discussion of this matter, see esp. Ingolf U. Dalferth, "Volles Grab, leerer Glaube? Zum Streit um die Auferweckung des Gekreuzigten," *ZTK* 95 (1998): 379–409.

568. It is precisely because, unlike me, he finds existence apart from a material body "impossible" that Pannenberg has so much invested in the empty tomb; cf. his *Jesus*, 87.

569. William M. Hetherington, *The Apologetics of the Christian Faith* (Edinburgh: T & T Clark, 1867), 312. From an earlier time, compare Humphry Ditton, *A Discourse concerning the Resurrection of Jesus Christ* (London: T. Cox, 1740), 321: "There is such an evidence for the Resurrection of Jesus Christ, as actually induces an obligation in all men, to whom that evidence is fairly proposed, and who are capable of arguing upon it after a due and regular manner, to give their assent to it as a certain truth"; 322: the evidence lays "an indispensable obligation on rational Creatures to give their assent to it [the resurrection] as real truth."

These silly and arrogant words, which ultimately descend from the Christian rationalism of the late seventeenth century, are as strikingly foreign to us as the outdated claim that "there is no book in the world whose author can be more plainly demonstrated than that of the Pentateuch."[570] Rarely any more does one run across sentences implying that unbelievers in Jesus' resurrection must be either morons or victims of ignorance. Such sentences belong to the past; they are buried in books that have lost their readers and are now crumbling to dust. Historical-critical work has reduced Christian self-assurance on this matter, or at least much of its rhetorical excesses.[571] Nevertheless, one can still land upon a new book or article with the assertion that "the alternative theories that have been proposed are not only weaker but far weaker at explaining the available historical evidence than the claim that God raised Jesus from the dead. That is, there is a patch of first-century history that makes sense from a Christian perspective but not from a naturalist's perspective."[572]

Today's most prominent advocate of the view that all interpretations other than the orthodox one are really untethered to the data is Tom Wright. He has written that, "though mathematical-style proof is impossible," the literal resurrection of Jesus "provides far and away the best explanation" for the preponderance of the data.[573] This conviction, that "inference to the best explanation" equals belief in Jesus' literal resurrection,[574] is one Wright, with his usual splendid vigor, enjoys repeating:

- "The best historical explanation...is that Jesus was indeed bodily raised from the dead."[575]

---

570. Josiah King, *Mr. Blount's Oracles of Reason, Examined and Answered* (Exon: S. Darker for Ch. Yeo, J. Pearce and Philip Bishop, 1698), 31.

571. Yet I observe that the distinguished chemist, Henry F. Schaefer III, in his go at Christian apologetics, has made this incredible claim: "That Jesus rose from the dead...is one of the best attested facts of ancient history"; see his book, *Science or Christianity: Conflict or Coherence?* (Watkinsville, GA: Apollos Trust, 2003), 165.

572. Stephen T. Davis, "Is Belief in the Resurrection Rational? A Response to Michael Martin," *Philo* 2, no. 1 (1999): 58. Cf. Pokorný, *Christology*, 126: "There are no historically more credible alternatives for" the Christian alternative, so that while "the declaration of the Easter faith cannot be verified in any objective way...neither is it irrational"; and Richard Swinburne, "Evidence for the Resurrection," in Davis, Kendall, and O'Collins, *Resurrection*, 201: "Alternative hypotheses have always seemed to me to give far less satisfactory accounts of the historical evidence than does the traditional account."

573. Wright, *Resurrection*, 720.

574. Ibid., 718.

575. Ibid., 8.

- "I shall argue that the best *historical* explanation is the one which inevitably raises all kinds of theological questions: the tomb was indeed empty, and Jesus was indeed seen alive, because he was truly raised from the dead."[576]

- "The other explanations sometimes offered for the emergence of belief do not possess the same explanatory power."[577]

- "The explanation of the data which the early Christians themselves gave, that Jesus really was risen from the dead, 'explains the aggregate' of the evidence better than . . . sophisticated skepticisms."[578]

- "The proposal that Jesus was bodily raised from the dead possesses unrivalled power to explain the historical data at the heart of early Christianity."[579]

While recognizing that there is no neutral standpoint, that how we construe the data depends upon our worldview,[580] Wright nevertheless urges that the evidence for the literal resurrection of Jesus by Israel's God is so strong that it suffices not only to "lure skeptics forward"[581] but actually constitutes "a historical challenge for other explanations, other worldviews."[582] He seems to imply, à la Pannenberg, that once all the arguments come in, Christian believers of a certain stripe are more rational than others. Jesus' tomb was known to be empty, and the disciples saw him alive after the crucifixion. These are facts. They are sufficient to explain Easter faith. They are also necessary: nothing else really accounts for the data. The one postulate that makes sense of everything is Jesus' bodily resurrection, even if this challenges one's *Weltanschauung*.

What should we say to this? Although I am bound to respect Wright's informed judgment, although I think that the tomb was probably empty, although I am sure that the disciples saw Jesus after his death, and

---

576. Ibid., 10.
577. Ibid., 686.
578. Ibid., 717.
579. Ibid., 718.
580. Ibid., 27, 717. See also the concession on 694: "The matter lies beyond strict historical proof. It will always be possible for ingenious historians to propose yet more variations on the theme of how the early Christian belief could have arisen, and taken the shape it did, without either an empty tomb or appearances of Jesus."
581. Ibid., 715.
582. Ibid., 717.

although I would be personally delighted to espy dramatic divine intervention in the world, I remain unconvinced — not that Wright's belief in Jesus' literal resurrection must be wrong, but that his apologetical moves really amount to evidence that demands the verdict he so relentlessly summons us to return. His argument, which puts more faith in historical reason than I can summon, does not and cannot raze all the arguments of those with a different view. Ostensible encounters with the newly departed are, as we have seen, and as Wright admits, not uncommon, however one explains them. Further, although Wright does not register the fact, people often perceive apparitions not as ghostly shades but as solid, as wholly real. So what prevents the unorthodox — who justifiably have a bit less confidence than Wright in the historicity of the biblical reports — from regarding the resurrection appearances, "transphysicality" and all, as instances of a wider phenomenon? Mix in a little Jewish eschatology and the pre-Easter expectations of the disciples and, one might claim, there it is.

What then of the empty tomb? It too does not demand divine intervention.[583] Those who confidently reject every miracle and all supernaturalism will naturally find it easier to think that someone moved or stole Jesus' remains than that Jesus came back to life. Why there is anything here to challenge a worldview escapes me. Given presuppositions other than Wright's, a mundane if necessarily speculative postulate is not unreasonable; indeed, it is inevitable. From where, other than inside his own particular worldview, can Wright assert that nonsupernatural accounts have less explanatory power than his own baptized opinion?

Someone defending Wright might here brandish Ockham's razor: the literal bodily resurrection is the simplest thesis because it has the greatest explanatory scope.[584] It explains at a single stroke both the empty tomb and the postmortem appearances. Human removal of the body, by contrast, is one thing, visions of a departed friend another. This unorthodox alternative posits two unrelated first causes of resurrection faith.

If I may swap metaphors, however, Occam's razor is not the skeleton key to everything. Historical events typically have multiple, complex causes — the fall of the Roman Empire, the Reformation, World War I.

---

583. Wright's attempt, ibid., 706–10, to dismiss naturalistic explanations is too brief for my tastes, although more pages would still fall short: one just cannot decisively eliminate all the unorthodox alternatives.

584. Cf. Craig, "Closing Response," 188–89.

Why should Jesus' resurrection be different? Mormons insist that acceptance of the one foundational fact, that Joseph Smith was a prophet of God, has unrivaled explanatory power. It explains how an unlettered man could produce the Book of Mormon, how several witnesses could swear to having seen plates of gold, how a persecuted religious minority could thrive despite the odds, and so on. The only counter to this is to summon several independent and controverted assertions: Joseph Smith copied much of the Book of Mormon from an unpublished romance novel stolen from a Pittsburgh printing shop; the witnesses to the golden plates were of dubious character; sociological parallels show well enough how persecution can grow a sectarian movement; and so on. Although this retort is not Occam's razor, those of us who do not live in the Mormon mental universe will find such a scattershot approach a perfectly adequate and rational way to proceed, and we will remain secure in our non-Mormon worldview.

If Wright claims too much, how much should we claim? James Anthony Froude, the nineteenth-century essayist and historian, got it just right: "Of evidence for the resurrection in the common sense of the word, there may be enough to show that something extraordinary occurred; but not enough . . . to produce any absolute and unhesitating conviction; and inasmuch as the resurrection is the keystone of Christianity, the belief in it must be something far different from that suspended judgment in which history alone would leave us."[585]

One final comment on Wright's apologetical proof. He outlines his central contention this way:

1. Jewish conceptions of resurrection could not of themselves have generated belief in Jesus' resurrection.

2. Neither the empty tomb by itself nor the appearances by themselves could have given rise to that belief.

3. But the empty tomb and the appearances together would have effected that belief.

4. Christians would not have proclaimed Jesus' resurrection without knowing of his empty tomb and without knowing people who claimed to have seen him alive again.

---

585. James Anthony Froude, *Short Studies on Great Subjects* (New York: Dutton, 1964), 211–12.

5. Explanations other than that offered by the early Christians are not compelling.

6. It is highly probable that the tomb was empty and that the disciples actually encountered Jesus as alive after death.

7. "God raised Jesus from the dead" best accounts for all the facts.[586]

Surprisingly missing from this line of reasoning is any evaluation, even implicit, of the historical Jesus — all the more surprising because Wright's book on the resurrection is volume 3 in a series whose second volume is all about the historical Jesus. Now of course volume 3 presupposes volume 2; but exactly how the central argument in volume 3 depends upon conclusions reached in volume 2 remains mostly for readers to guess. The lacuna is not exactly a defect in Wright's inductive logic, but it is nonetheless an unexpected puzzle. What if volume 2 had produced another Jesus — say the Jesus of Dom Crossan, or my own millenarian Jesus? What would have happened if volume 2 had concluded that we know very little about Jesus, or if the critical reconstruction there had showed him to be a profoundly ambiguous character? Would this have made any difference for the reasoning in volume 3? Would volume 3 work no matter what the character or teaching of Jesus, for example, turned out to be in volume 2?

The way Wright sets up his argument, as though it were a problem in legal evidence, one cannot see that opinions about the pre-Easter Jesus should make much difference. But as a matter of psychological fact, that just cannot be. We all know that Jesus is raised in volume 3 because Wright likes the Jesus of volume 2. How could it be otherwise? Wright's reasoning is conducted with the implicit, large, and controverted assumption that Jesus is someone who *should* have been raised from the dead. Does this circumstance not need to be somehow reflected in the outline of his argument?

In this connection I recall an observation of Graham Stanton: "Early objections to the resurrection hardly ever seem to have been made in isolation from negative assessments of the teaching and the actions of Jesus. Opponents and followers alike saw that claims about the resurrection of Jesus raised the same issues as his actions and his teaching: for opponents, the whole story was riddled with trickery and deceit; for

---

586. Wright, *Resurrection*, 686–87.

followers, the story was God's story."[587] In conformity with this, Peter saw the risen Jesus while Caiaphas (we presume) did not: disputes over the resurrection continued pre-Easter disputes about Jesus. Not much has changed since then. Surely most polemicists reject the resurrection because they have no desire to see Jesus, as they understand him, vindicated by the Deity, if there is a Deity, whereas apologists energetically defend the resurrection because they sincerely wish Jesus to be triumphant over death and to be endorsed and authorized by the Supreme Being in which they believe. Which is to say, if judgment about the resurrection cannot be isolated from one's worldview, it equally cannot be isolated from one's estimation of the pre-Easter Jesus — and yet Wright, who would no doubt agree, executes his argument with this fact in the background rather than the foreground. The reason is unclear.[588]

CODA

In my youth I naively thought of modern critical history as a never-ending success story whose scope seemed almost unlimited. Surely it could take in everything; surely the truth would come to me served on an historical-critical platter. I have since grown up, put aside my narcissistic conceit, and learned that historians are not the keepers of the truth, or at least not its sole keepers. They must share this office with others. A hammer works well for some jobs, not all; and the historical-critical method works well for some jobs, not all. We need the right tool for the right job, and sometimes more than one tool.

If historians alone could cross the last frontiers of understanding with regard to the resurrection, then we would not need the assistance of laborers in other disciplines. This is not the case. When the mundane historical work is done, the results are disappointingly scanty, severely circumscribed. Most of the important questions have eluded our capture,

587. Graham N. Stanton, "Early Objections to the Resurrection of Jesus," in Barton and Stanton, *Resurrection*, 91.
588. Another possible issue for Wright comes from Leander Keck, in his response to Wright's *Resurrection* given to the Evangelical Theological Society in Atlanta, Nov. 22, 2003. According to Keck, Wright's appeal to "any historian of any persuasion" (21) is a sort of self-denial: "For the epistemology of historical explanations, it appears not to matter whether or not the resurrection happened or the New Age appeared." Whatever Wright's answer to this criticism might be, one is surprised, given his theological outlook, that he fails to discuss the so-called "spiritual senses," a topic recently made prominent by Hans Urs von Balthasar, *The Glory of the Lord: A Theological Aesthetics* (7 vols.; San Francisco: Ignatius, 1983–89).

and harder tasks remain. At this point, then, the discussion has to be handed over to the philosophers and theologians, among whose lofty company I am not privileged to dwell. They, not me, are the ones who can address the heart of the matter, the problem of justifying — if such a thing is possible — a worldview, the thing that makes the resurrection of Jesus welcome or unwelcome, plausible or implausible, important or unimportant.

Perhaps, however, I may be permitted to observe here at the end that the frustrating failure of historical investigation to hand us theological conclusions has an analogue of sorts in the Gospel accounts of the resurrection. Those who behold Jesus with their own eyes do not always know him for who he is. There is doubt among those who worship the risen Jesus in Matt 28:17. The pilgrims on the Emmaus road do not, in Luke 24:30-31, recognize Jesus until he has gone from their midst. In John 20:11–18 it takes Mary a while to understand that the man before her is Jesus. And in Acts 9:7 only Paul sees Jesus: his companions do not (and presumably they do not convert or we would hear about it). These stories, in which people see but do not see, distinguish ordinary perception — to which historical-critical knowledge is mostly confined — from the experience or discernment of religious truth. Such discernment, it seems to be implied, has a moral or spiritual dimension independent of historical reason. Although Paul, as a persecutor of Christians, must have known many of the Easter claims and traditions, he did not believe for himself until something overwhelming happened to him. Sight is not insight; knowledge is a function of being; and religious knowledge must be a function of religious being. As the beatitude has it, "Blessed are the pure in heart, for they will see God."[589] This last is an epistemological statement, and it implies that we require more than history if we are to find the truth of things.[590]

---

589. See further Aldous Huxley, *The Perennial Philosophy* (New York: Harper & Row, 1945), vii–xi; also Paul Helm, *Faith with Reason* (Clarendon: Oxford, 2000), 84–101.

590. See further Diogenes Allen, "Resurrection Appearances as Evidence," *ThTo* 30 (1973): 6–13, who argues that contemporary reasons for belief in the resurrection need not coincide with reasons the disciples may have had. Also valuable is Sarah Coakley, "The Resurrection and the 'Spiritual Senses,'" in her *Powers and Submissions: Spirituality, Philosophy and Gender* (Oxford: Blackwell, 2002), 130–52. One issue Coakley does not address is that the failure to recognize Jesus has its parallels in reports of apparitions: one or more individuals may see what others do not (see n. 322 on 280). Whether Coakley would admit the parallel, and if so, what she would make of it, I do not know.

Maybe then it is not so surprising that most who believe in Jesus' resurrection, however exactly they understand it, have as little need for modern historical criticism as birds have for ornithology. When Christians, on Easter Sunday, greet each other with the acclamation, "Christ is risen," the expected answer, "Christ is risen, indeed!" is not a statement about investigative results. Harvey Cox once rightly protested against a "detective-novel approach" to and understanding of the resurrection.[591] Although ignorance should not be the mother of devotion, true religion nevertheless involves realms of human experience and conviction that cannot depend upon or be undone by the sorts of historical doubts, probabilities, and conjectures with which the previous pages have been concerned. For myself, all I have to do is look up at the night sky or look into the face of my neighbor, and then I know that there is more to life and faith than this.

Excursus 2
JOSEPH OF ARIMATHEA

Whether or not one believes that "the historicity of the empty tomb story is dependent to large extent on the historicity of the burial story,"[592] the latter always plays some role in discussion of the former, as it has in the preceding pages, so a treatment of the issue, however cursory, seems required.

According to Bishop Spong, in a popular book, "There is a strong probability that the story of Joseph of Arimathea was developed to cover the apostles' pain at the memory of Jesus' having had no one to claim his body and of his demise as a common criminal. His body was probably dumped unceremoniously into a common grave, the location of which has never been known."[593] Spong also believes that behind the story of the empty tomb is the fact that Mary Magdalene did go to find the place of Jesus' burial. But "she discovered not the empty tomb but the

---

591. Harvey Cox, "A Dialogue on Christ's Resurrection," *Christianity Today* 12, no. 14 (April 12, 1968): 680.

592. So Barclay, "Resurrection," 23. Cf. the argument of Schenke, *Auferstehungs-verkündigung*, 98–102, who thinks that belief in the historicity of the burial story entails belief in the historicity of the empty tomb.

593. Spong, *Resurrection*, 225. Cf. Goguel, *Birth*, 30–37.

reality of his common grave. No one could identify the place." In time, "when Peter reconstituted the disciples in Galilee and they returned to Jerusalem, Mary's story of not being able to find where they had buried Jesus was...incorporated into the resurrection tradition."[594]

Dom Crossan, with more critical resources than Spong, is another who believes that the first Christians did not know what happened to Jesus' body.[595] On the basis of Deut 21:22–23,[596] they inferred that, out of piety, Jesus was buried by Jews (cf. Acts 8:2). Later, Mark turned burial by enemies into burial by someone less hostile and invented Joseph of Arimathea. As for what really happened, Crossan observes that the bodies of crucifixion victims were often left hanging to decompose or become food for scavengers.[597] Under Roman law, executed criminals were also commonly denied burial and instead thrown into a collective pile.[598] We can guess that one of these two fates befell Jesus: "His body [was] left on the cross or in a shallow grave barely covered with dirt and stones"; in either case "the dogs were waiting."[599]

Should we side with Crossan and Spong? I think not.

1. According to the primitive confession in 1 Cor 15:4, Jesus was "buried," ἐτάφη.[600] The verb θάπτω means "bury" and would hardly be used of the unceremonious dumping of a criminal into an unmarked trench as dog food: that was not burial but its denial. Now whether or

---

594. Spong, *Resurrection*, 229.

595. John Dominic Crossan, *The Historical Jesus: The Life of a Mediterranean Jewish Peasant* (San Francisco: HarperSanFrancisco, 1991), 391–94; idem, *Who Killed Jesus?* 160–77; also the more cautious and nuanced argument in idem, *Birth*, 550–55; and his "Historical Jesus as Risen Lord," in John Dominic Crossan, Luke Timothy Johnson, and Werner H. Kelber, *The Jesus Controversy: Perspectives in Conflict* (Harrisburg, PA: Trinity, 1999), 1–47.

596. "When someone is convicted of a crime punishable by death and is executed, and you hang him on a tree, his corpse must not remain all night upon the tree; you shall bury him the same day, for anyone hung on a tree is under God's curse. You must not defile the land that the Lord your God is giving you for an inheritance." Cf. 11QTemple 64:9–13.

597. Horace, *Ep.* 1.16.46–48; Petronius, *Sat.* 111–112; Artemidorus, *Onir.* 2.53; Eusebius, *Hist. eccl.* 5.1.61–62 (ed. Bardy; SC 41:22–23). This presumably happened in Palestine during the civil unrest in 4 BCE and in 66 and 70 CE. See Josephus, *Ant.* 17.295; *J.W.* 2.306–307; 5.450; and the comments of McCane, *Roll Back the Stone*, 91.

598. Pertinent texts include Diodorus Siculus 18.47.3; 16.25.2; Plutarch, *Mor.* 307C; Dio Chrysostom 31.85; Tacitus, *Ann.* 6.29 ("People sentenced to death forfeited their property and were forbidden burial"); Suetonius, *Aug.* 13; *Tib.* 61. Cf. Plato, *Leg.* 909C. Not to be buried horrified the ancients; cf. Homer, *Il.* 22 (Hector's body); Jer 7:33; 8:1–2; Ezek 29:5; Josephus, *J.W.* 4.360.

599. Crossan, *Revolutionary Biography*, 154. The position is an old one; see the discussion of Albert Réville in F. Godet, *Lectures in Defence of the Christian Faith* (Edinburgh: T & T Clark, 1881), 106.

600. I see no reason to follow Myllykoski, "Body of Jesus," 66–67, in imagining that ὅτι ἐτάφη did not belong to pre-Pauline tradition.

not 1 Cor 15:4 summarizes an early form of the story about Joseph of Arimathea, "it would be strange," as Barnabas Lindars observed, "to include this detail in the statement if the burial of Jesus was in fact unknown."[601] One should also observe that Paul elsewhere assumes in passing that Jesus was buried (Rom 6:4: συνετάφημεν οὖν αὐτῷ; cf. Col 2:12: συνταφέντες αὐτῷ).

Beyond Paul's early witness, not only do all four canonical Gospels tell a story about Jesus' burial, but each contains additional traditions presupposing that Jesus was not thrown onto a pile for criminals but rather interred (Matt 27:62–66; 28:11–15; Mark 14:8; 16:1–8; Luke 24:13–35; John 20:1–10, 11–18). Clearly, then, Jesus' burial is well attested, so much so that John A. T. Robinson felt justified in claiming that the burial "must be accepted as one of the most firmly grounded facts of Jesus' life."[602]

To this one could retort that the imaginations of Jesus' adherents transferred Jesus from a criminal's pile to a tomb in order to spare him dishonor. But if so, such a move must have been taken quite early indeed, before the tradition in 1 Cor 15:4, and the suggestion misses a blindingly obvious point. Christians did not save Jesus from the fact of crucifixion but rather redeemed the cursed cross. In their own way they even gloried in it. People capable of that incredible and unprecedented theological move could surely have redeemed burial in a trench or a corpse on a cross if circumstances had presented them that lesser challenge. Are we to believe that Christians who acknowledged the humiliation of crucifixion were somehow unable to allow that Jesus was denied a decent burial, as though the latter were so more dreadful than the former?

2. To depict a member of the Sanhedrin doing a kindness to Jesus, as the canonical burial stories do, goes against the tendency of the passion traditions.[603] This is precisely why Mark and the other evangelists,

---

601. Lindars, "Resurrection," 128.

602. John A. T. Robinson, "Resurrection in the New Testament," *IDB* (1962), 4:45. Contrast Myllykoski, "Body of Jesus," 46, who thinks there are "surprisingly few traces of this major evidence."

603. Against Crossan, *Birth*, 554, I do not think that Mark is ambiguous about whether Joseph was a member of the Sanhedrin that crucified Jesus. Cf. Raymond E. Brown, *The Death of the Messiah: From Gethsemane to the Grave: A Commentary on the Passion Narratives in the Four Gospels* (New York: Doubleday, 1992), 2:1213–14.

probably tendentiously, stress that Joseph was exceptional — he was discipled to Jesus, or looking for the kingdom of God, or disagreed with the Sanhedrin's verdict, or secretly believed.[604]

3. Although Crossan considers Joseph of Arimathea "to be a total Markan creation in name, in place, and in function,"[605] fictional names do not seem to be standard fare either in Mark or his tradition. Surely most of the named characters must on any reading be historical persons, and Joseph of Arimathea is, apart from late legend, known only as the one who buried Jesus.[606] The person and place are both obscure, occurring outside the four canonical gospels only in late, apocryphal sources, and they have no obvious biblical or theological or apologetical significance. So one might suppose that "Joseph of Arimathea" is historical memory, like other names in Mark, such as John the Baptist, Peter, Andrew, James, John, Judas, James the brother of Jesus, Mary the mother of Jesus, Herod Antipas, Pilate.[607]

Historical names do not, assuredly, guarantee the historicity of the narratives in which they occur. One need only recall Matthew's haggadic infancy narrative, starring Herod the king and Joseph the father of Jesus.

---

604. Matt 27:57; Mark 15:43; Luke 23:50–51; John 19:38. The sanctifying of Joseph grew as the time passed; in *Acts Pil.* 15:6 the resurrected Jesus appears to him. See further Brown, *Death of the Messiah*, 2:1233–34.

605. Crossan, *Who Killed Jesus?* 172. He also regards Barabbas and Simon of Cyrene as fictional creations. But on this view of things, surely the qualification of Simon as the father of Alexander and Rufus is unexpected. Robert Funk, *Honest to Jesus* (San Francisco: HarperSanFrancisco, 1996), 228, also believes that "Joseph of Arimathea is probably a Markan creation." Alfred E. Loisy, *The Birth of the Christian Religion* (London: G. Allen & Unwin, 1948), 90–91, already regarded Joseph as pure legend.

Crossan's judgments about Joseph of Arimathea have changed a bit in recent years. In his *Birth*, 550–55, he admits that Mark's story *could* be true but still thinks the evidence is against this; cf. the critical response of William John Lyons, "On the Life and Death of Joseph of Arimathea," *JSHJ* 2 (2004): 29–53.

606. Ingo Broer, "Der Glaube an die Auferstehung Jesu und das geschichtliche Verständnis des Glaubens der Neuzeit," in *Osterglaube ohne Auferstehung? Diskussion mit Gerd Lüdemann* (ed. Hanjürgen Verweyen; QD 155; Freiburg: Herder, 1995), 62, labels Joseph's name "einen erratischen Block."

607. See above all Ingo Broer, *Die Urgemeinde und das Grab Jesu: Eine Analyse der Grablegungsgeschichte im Neuen Testament* (SANT 31; Munich: Kösel, 1972), 280–94. One nonetheless could conjecture that although Joseph was a historical individual known to Christians, he did not bury Jesus. Williams, "Trouble," 232, as his own "piece of speculation," suggests that Joseph of Arimathea offered "his own unused tomb [to early Christians] as a meeting place for symbolic celebration, at Easter, or possibly more regularly on the first day of the week, very early." Pokorný, *Christology*, 154–55, conjectures that several years after the crucifixion "Christians discovered a tomb that had formerly belonged to a certain Joseph of Arimathea, and because it was an opened tomb they identified it with Jesus' tomb. We just do not know whether it really was Jesus' tomb. The women who knew the burial place could no longer confirm it." Such unsubstantiated conjectures are potentially endless.

Nonetheless, Joseph shows up in Matthew 1–2 because he was indeed the husband of Mary and Jesus' father, and Herod is there because Jesus was born during his reign. But why is Joseph of Arimathea at Jesus' burial? One levelheaded explanation is that he was remembered as having been there.[608]

4. Mark's story of Joseph, which contains neither fantastic elements nor Christian motifs and so "creates no impression of being a legend,"[609] does not appear to be an example of what Crossan has called "prophecy historicized." The only element in Mark's adaptation that might plausibly be traced to Scripture is burial before sunset.[610] One could argue that this comes from Deut 21:22–23 (cf. Josh 8:29; 10:26–27) — although given that Jews in reality tried to heed the Mosaic prescription (see below), one can just as easily imagine that here history obediently followed the pentateuchal text. For the rest, Mark's story of Joseph does not accommodate Isa 53:9 ("They made his grave with the wicked"), and the details show no obvious scriptural intertextuality. One wonders whether J. Spencer Kennard was not right: "If Christianity had fashioned the entombment on the basis of prophecy it would have left the body," because of Isa 53:9, "with the corpses of other criminals."[611]

5. Some have supposed that Acts 13:29 ("They [the residents of Jerusalem and their leaders] took him down from the tree and laid him in a tomb") might be evidence for disposal by hostile powers (Jewish rather than Roman[612]) and so show Mark's story of the burial to be a secondary

---

608. Cf. Catchpole, *Resurrection*, 199: "It is extremely difficult to believe that the recollection of his [Joseph's] name would persist in connection with something he had done, while at the same time the location where he had done it remained unknown. It is easier to associate a known agent of burial with a known place of burial, and therefore to be open to the possibility that there was indeed a specific tomb available for visiting shortly after Jesus' death."

609. Bultmann, *History*, 274 (unpersuasively adding: "apart from the women who appear again as witnesses in v. 47, and vv. 44, 45"). Cf. Günther Bornkamm, *Jesus of Nazareth* (New York: Harper & Row, 1960), 168: "The report of Jesus' funeral is concise, unemotional and without any bias." Schenke, *Auferstehungsverkündigung*, 99, quotes Bornkamm with approval and adds that the story is matter-of-fact and "tendenzlose."

610. Matt 27:57, which makes Joseph a rich man, adds another, for this probably echoes Isa 53:9 ("his tomb with the rich").

611. J. Spencer Kennard, "The Burial of Jesus," *JBL* 74 (1955): 230.

612. For dishonorable burial among Jews see 1 Kgs 13:22 (denial of burial in the ancestral tomb); 2 Kgs 9:10 ("the dogs shall eat Jezebel . . . and no one shall bury her"; cf. vv. 36–37); Jer 22:18–19; 26:23 (burial in the place of "the common people"; cf. 2 Kgs 23:6); Jer 19:6 LXX ("the burial place of slaughter"); Ezek 39:11, 15 (burial of Gog in the Valley of Hamon-gog); *1 En.* 98:13 ("No grave will be dug for you"); *Ps. Sol.* 4:19 ("May . . . the bones of criminals [lie] dishonored out in the sun"); *T. Job* 40:13 ("She was not even considered worthy of a decent burial"); Josephus, *Ant.* 4.202 ("buried ignominiously"); 5.44 ("the ignominious burial proper to the condemned"); 13.380 (cf. *J.W.* 1.97); *J.W.* 4.382 (The Zealots "left the dead

development. The verse in Acts, however, just might be redactional.[613] Whether or not that is so, Luke evidently did not observe its tension with the burial tradition about Joseph, which he hands on (23:50–56); and the passing notice in Acts, which accords with the Gospels in that it implies burial by Jews, not Romans, at most excludes only the positive interpretation of Joseph's action, not the core of Mark 15:42–46.[614] Burial by enemies, perhaps in a place for criminals (cf. *m. Sanh.* 6:5; *t. Sanh.* 9:8), does not contradict Mark's basic content, which is that a member of the Sanhedrin interred Jesus.[615] Observe also that the plurals of Acts 13:29 ("*they* took him down [καθελόντες]...and [*they*] laid [ἔθηκαν] him in a tomb") match the plural of Mark 16:6: "the place where *they* laid [ἔθηκαν] him." Mark too seems to imply that Joseph did not act alone (cf. also John 19:31, 39–42).

6. In addition to Acts 13:29, some have appealed to *Gos. Pet.* 6:21 as an argument for the secondary character of Mark's burial story: "And then they drew the nails from the hands of the Lord and laid him on the earth. And the whole earth shook and there was great fear."[616] This, according to Crossan, "presumes that those who crucified Jesus are responsible, from Deuteronomy 21:22–23 [cited in *Gos. Pet.* 2:5], for taking his body off the cross and burying it before sunset."[617] In other words, the story "takes it for granted that Jesus was crucified, removed from the cross, and buried by his enemies."[618] Since Crossan assigns *Gos. Pet.* 6:21 to a hypothetical pre-Markan source that he dubs "The Cross Gospel," he finds here early evidence of a view a bit different from and prior to Mark's account.

---

putrefying in the sun"); Rev 11:9 ("refuse to let them be placed in a tomb"); *Liv. Pro., Mic.* 2 (burial apart from ancestors); *Mart. Pol.* 17 (Jews oppose giving the body of a Christian martyr over to Christians); *t. Sanh.* 9:8; *m. Sanh.* 6:5 (burial places for criminals); *b. Sanh.* 47b ("shameful burial"); *Midr. Qoh.* 1:15:1 ("People did not put you in a coffin but dragged you to the grave with ropes"). Discussion in Hugues Cousin, "Sépulture criminelle et sepulture prophétique," *RB* 81 (1974): 375–93.

613. Lüdemann, *Acts*, 152–58, does not seem to posit pre-Lukan tradition — although contrast his judgment in *Resurrection*, 43. Catchpole, *Resurrection*, believes that Luke here just draws out what he found in Mark. Cf. Broer, *Urgemeinde*, 250–63.

614. Relevant here is McCane, *Roll Back the Stone*, 89–108, who finds behind Mark a shameful burial. So also Raymond E. Brown, "The Burial of Jesus (Mark 15:42–47)," *CBQ* 50 (1988): 233–45; and Snape, "After the Crucifixion."

615. Cf. Schenke, *Auferstehungsverkündigung*, 100–101.

616. Crossan, *Who Killed Jesus?* 169–71. Crossan has discussed his views about the *Gospel of Peter* in several publications; see recently "The Gospel of Peter and the Canonical Gospels: Independence, Dependence, or Both?," *Forum* (NS) 1 (1998): 7–51.

617. Crossan, *Who Killed Jesus?* 170.

618. Ibid., 170.

The case is not compelling. Although the *Gospel of Peter* probably contains some tradition not derived from the canonical Gospels, Crossan's reconstruction of "The Cross Gospel" has scarcely won the day: many of us remain unpersuaded.[619] Even apart from that formidable difficulty, there is an exegetical issue. *Gospel of Peter* 6:21 says nothing about Jesus' burial;[620] that comes only two verses later: "[21] And then they drew the nails from the hands of the Lord and laid him on the earth. And the whole earth shook and there was great fear. [22] Then the sun shone and it was found to be the ninth hour. [23] And the Jews rejoiced and gave his body to Joseph that he might bury it since he had seen all the good deeds that he [Jesus] had done." The unspecified "they" of verse 21 — either the Roman soldiers or "the Jews" (cf. Mark 15:46) — place Jesus' body on the ground (ἔθηκαν αὐτὸν ἐπὶ τῆς γῆς). This is not a reference to burial, only to removal from the cross and a temporary lull in the proceedings. What then happens to the body? In the *Gospel of Peter* as it stands, it is given to Joseph of Arimathea (v. 23). Crossan thinks this circumstance is due to later editorial activity under the influence of Mark: *Gos. Pet.* 6:23–24 interrupts the original sequence, 6:22 + 7:25 + 8:28ff. Only such surgery allows Crossan to find a non-Markan, pre-Markan view of the burial. Yet not only does one fail to see any real justification for the surgery, but the outcome is not credible. If one heeds Crossan and accepts 6:22 + 7:25 + 8:28ff. as the pristine sequence, then we pass, if we are following Jesus' body, from "they drew the nails from the hands of the Lord and laid him on the earth" (6:21) to the Jewish elders asking Pilate, "Give us soldiers that we may watch his sepulchre for three days, lest his disciples come and steal him away" (8:30). In other words, the body has somehow moved from the foot of the cross to a sepulchre that has not heretofore been introduced. Not only does this fail to commend itself as a plausible sequence, but the interment, if *Gos. Pet.* 6:23–24 is a secondary insertion,

---

619. For criticism, see Raymond E. Brown, "The Gospel of Peter and Canonical Gospel Priority," *NTS* 33 (1987): 321–43; Alan Kirk, "Examining Priorities: Another Look at the *Gospel of Peter*'s Relationship to the New Testament Gospels," *NTS* 40 (1994): 572–95; idem, "The Johannine Jesus in the Gospel of Peter: A Social Memory Approach," in *Jesus in Johannine Tradition* (ed. Robert T. Fortna and Tom Thatcher; Louisville: Westminster John Knox, 2001), 313–21.

620. Nor does the earlier 5:15, which cites Deut 21:22–23: this simply records anxiety over whether Jesus' body will stay up past sunset.

is simply bypassed and not narrated at all.[621] How then one can one find here a view different from Mark's?

7. To my knowledge, the assertion that Jesus might have been left upon the cross or denied any real burial at all is found nowhere in the ancient sources, with one dubious exception. That exception is the *Apocryphon of James* from Nag Hammadi. At one point Jesus, addressing James and Peter, says to them, "Or do you not know that you have yet to be abused and to be accused unjustly; and have yet to be shut up in prison, and condemned unlawfully, and crucified without reason, and buried in the sand (ⲍ̄ⲛ̄ⲛ ⲟⲩϣⲟⲩ), as I was myself, by the evil one?" (5:9–21). One hesitates to make much of this, however. Not only is the reading of the text uncertain,[622] but "the date for the original composition is usually put at [the] third century."[623] The text presupposes the martyrdom of James, and it seems to know the canonical Gospels, so it is hardly a safe place to be mining for old, pre-Markan tradition.[624] The interpretation is also unclear. If the illustrations of abuse and unjust accusation — being shut up in prison, condemned unlawfully, crucified without reason, buried in the sand[625] — not only prophesy the future of James and Peter but are also supposed to come from the life of Jesus, then we have here the notion that Jesus was shut up in prison, for which there is otherwise no evidence. It seems more likely that the concluding qualification, "as I was myself," covers not the details of the sentence but its general import, that is, it communicates only that Jesus was abused and unjustly accused, not that he was shut up in prison and buried in the sand.

8. In *Gos. Pet.* 2:5, Herod says to Pilate, "Even if no one had asked for him, we should bury (ἐθάπτομεν) him since the Sabbath is drawing

---

621. Gundry, *Mark*, 983, also observes this.

622. See Francis E. Williams, "The Apocryphon of James," in *Nag Hammadi Codex I (The Jung Codex): Notes* (ed. Harold W. Attridge; NHS 23; Leiden: Brill, 1985), 15–16. Williams accepts H.-M. Schenke's emendation of ⲟⲩϣⲟⲩ to ⲟⲩϣⲱⲥ ("shamefully") and notes further the suggestion of R. Kasser, ⲟⲩϣⲟⲟⲩ = "perfume" (which Louise Roy adopts).

623. J. K. Elliott, *The Apocryphal New Testament: A Collection of Apocryphal Christian Literature in an English Translation* (Oxford: Clarendon, 1993), 673. See further J. van der Vliet, "Spirit and Prophecy in the Epistula Iacobi Apocrypha (NHC I,2)," *VC* 44 (1990): 25–53. For an earlier date for an earlier form of the work, see Helmut Koester, *Ancient Christian Gospels: Their History and Development* (Philadelphia: Trinity, 1990), 187–200.

624. C. M. Tuckett, *Nag Hammadi and the Gospel Tradition: Synoptic Tradition in the Nag Hammadi Library* (Edinburgh: T & T Clark, 1986), 87–97, sees dependence upon Matthew and Luke as well as use of independent traditions. See further B. Dehandschutter, "L'epistula Jacobi apocrypha de Nag Hammadi (CG I,2) comme apocryphe néotestamentiare," *ANRW* 2.25.6:4547–50.

625. Should one compare 2 *Apoc. Jas.* 62:7–12, where James is stoned in a ditch?

on. For so it stands written in the law: The sun should not set on one that has been put to death." This assumes that pious Jews, heeding Deut 21:22–23, did not want bodies left overnight on crosses or wish executed criminals to be thrown into a ditch but rather desired that they be given some sort of burial, and further that the Roman authorities might (if it were not a time of war) acquiesce to this desire.[626] There is every reason to suppose the *Gospel of Peter* correct in this and so every reason to suppose that Jesus was treated accordingly. Not only do 11QTemple 64:10–13 and Philo, *Spec.* 3:151–152, regard Deut 21:22–23 as the law of the land, but according to Josephus, *J.W.* 4.317, "The Jews are so careful about funeral rites that even malefactors who have been sentenced to crucifixion are taken down and buried before sunset" (cf. 3.377; also *Ant.* 4.265: "Let burial be given even to your enemies"). All this accords with the legislation in *m. Sanh.* 6:5–6, which quotes Deut 21:23 as authoritative and speaks of two burial places for victims of capital punishment.[627] One may also appeal to Philo, *Flacc.* 83–85, which knows of instances when victims of crucifixion were buried by their relatives, as well as to Tobit, which depicts its hero burying the bodies of those executed by the government (1:17–18). And then there is *Sem.* 2:11, which says that the days of mourning were counted "from the time that [the relatives of a victim executed by the government] despaired in their appeal [to obtain the body from the authorities for burial] but [had] not [given up hope] of stealing it." This ruling, whose content is consistent with an origin in the early Roman period,[628] implies that the relatives of executed criminals were accustomed to ask for the remains of a loved one. Although the text speaks of refusal, it implies that sometimes the authorities complied: otherwise, there would not have been any custom of appealing. As for what might have happened in the case of Jesus, Eric Meyers has judged that the Romans would probably not

---

626. Cf. *b. Sanh.* 46b. For Pilate bowing to Jewish religious sentiment despite his own traditions, see Philo, *Legat.* 299–305 = Josephus, *J.W.* 2.169–77, and *Ant.* 18.55–62 (the episode with the Roman standards in Jerusalem). Cf. Cicero, *Verr.* 2.5.45, which tells of an official in Sicily releasing a victim of crucifixion to the family. Later Roman law allowed release of crucifixion victims to those who wanted to bury them: Justinian, *Digesta* 48.24.1–3.

627. "Two burial places were kept in readiness by the court, one for them that were beheaded or strangled, and one for them that were stoned or burnt."

628. Dov Zlotnick, *The Tractate "Mourning" (Šĕmḥot)* (New Haven: Yale, 1966), 1–9, dates *Semaḥot* to the third century. Eric Meyers, "The Use of Archaeology in Understanding Rabbinic Materials," in *Texts and Responses: Studies Presented to Nathan N. Glatzer on the Occasion of His Seventieth Birthday by His Students* (ed. Michael A. Fishbane and Paul R. Flohr; Leiden: Brill, 1975), 39–41, shows that it contains even older material.

have forbade his burial simply because he was beloved by so many.[629] With Jesus executed, there was no reason to compound public upset by keeping his body up on its cross and so offending either his followers or those anxious about the observance of Deut 21:22–23. Lüdemann observed: "The release of Jesus' body and its removal from the cross might also have suited Pilate, because this would a priori avoid unrest among the large number of visitors for the festival."[630]

9. The skeletal remains of the crucified man fortuitously discovered at Giv'at ha-Mivtar were buried in a family tomb, which confirms the testimony of Philo, Josephus, and *Sem.* 2:11: Jews buried the victims of crucifixion.[631] Those remains are, admittedly, the only remains of such a victim yet found, a fact that Crossan has stressed: "With all those thousands of people crucified around Jerusalem in the first century alone, we have so far found only a single crucified skeleton, and that, of course, preserved in an ossuary. Was burial, then, the exception rather than the rule, the extraordinary rather than the ordinary?"[632] Yet many victims were surely tied up rather than nailed, so we would not recognize them as having been crucified.[633] More importantly, the nails used in crucifixion — which were prized as powerful amulets[634] — were pulled out at the site of execution (cf. *Gos. Pet.* 6:21) and so not buried with the bodies. The only reason we know that Yehohanan, the man in the ossuary from Giv'at ha-Mivtar, was crucified is that a nail in his right heel bone could not be removed from the wood: it was stuck in a knot. As McCane

---

629. Eric M. Meyers, *Jewish Ossuaries: Rebirth and Reburial* (BO 24; Rome: Biblical Institute, 1971), 90.

630. Lüdemann, *Resurrection*, 44.

631. See Joseph Zias and James H. Charlesworth, "Crucifixion: Archaeology, Jesus, and the Dead Sea Scrolls," in *Jesus and the Dead Sea Scrolls* (ed. James H. Charlesworth; ABRL; New York: Doubleday, 1992), 273–89; and Joseph Zias and Eliezer Sekeles, "The Crucified Man from Giv'at ha-Mivtar: A Reappraisal," *IEJ* 35 (1985): 22–27.

632. Crossan, *Who Killed Jesus?* 168. Cf. Myllykoski, "Body of Jesus," 81.

633. See Joe Zias, "Crucifixion in Antiquity," online at CenturyOne Foundation: http://www.centuryone.org/crucifixion2.html; also the earlier study of Joseph William Hewitt, "The Use of Nails in the Crucifixion," *HTR* 25 (1932): 29–45 — although Hewitt's argument that feet were not nailed is specious.

634. In the name of R. Meir, *m. Šabb.* 6:10 refers to the belief that the nails of crucifixion are "a means of healing." This superstition was presumably taken over from pagans (the Sages, in ibid., brand the practice as "following in the ways of the Amorite," meaning the heathen). Lucan 6.547 depicts a Thessalonian witch collecting, for her magical practices, "nails that pierced the hands." Pliny the Elder, *Nat.* 28.46 (11), speaks of those who "wrap up in wool and tie round the neck of quartan patients a piece of a nail taken from a cross, or else a cord taken from a crucifixion." *Mart. Pionius* 13 (ed. Musurillo; 152) refers to Jesus performing necromancy and spirit-divination with the cross.

observes, "If there had not been a knot strategically located in the wood of Yehohanan's cross, the soldiers would have easily pulled the nail out of the cross. It never would have been buried with Yehohanan, and we would never have known that he had been crucified. It is not surprising, in other words, that we have found the remains of only one crucifixion victim: it is surprising that we have identified even one."[635]

10. There is, finally, a general presumption that probably favors Mark's tradition about Joseph of Arimathea. Crucifixions were public events. Intended as deterrents, they were set up to call attention to themselves.[636] Surely it was not otherwise with Jesus: he was publicly displayed as crucified in order "to deter resistance or revolt."[637] When one adds that Jesus was surely some sort of religious sensation whose fate would have been of interest not just to sympathizers, that his torture would even have been of entertainment value to some, it is hard to imagine that there was no cloud of witnesses. That the Gospels say there were passersby is no reason to think that there were not. It is instead quite likely that people, friendly, hostile, and indifferent, witnessed Jesus' end and its immediate aftermath, and that his crucifixion and burial became immediately the stuff of street gossip, so that anyone who wanted to learn what happened could just have asked around.[638] Crossan says that those who knew did not care and that those who cared did not know.[639] My guess is that most everyone knew whether they cared or not.

All in all, then, it seems highly likely that a certain Joseph of Arimathea, probably acting on behalf of the Sanhedrin, which typically tried to observe Deut 21:22–23, sought and obtained permission from the Roman authorities to make arrangements for Jesus' hurried and dishonorable burial. This accords with Jewish custom, with John 19:31 ("The Jews did not want the bodies left on the cross during the sabbath, ... so they asked Pilate ... to have the bodies removed"), and with Acts

---

635. McCane, *Roll Back the Stone*, 107. Cf. C. A. Evans, *Mark 8:27–16:20*, 517.

636. Martin Hengel, *Crucifixion: In the Ancient World and the Folly of the Cross* (Philadelphia: Fortress, 1977), 50.

637. The quoted words are from Crossan, *Revolutionary Biography*, 127.

638. This commonsense observation has sometimes shown up in the apologetical literature; e.g., see Joseph Agar Beet, *The Credentials of the Gospel: A Statement of the Reason of the Christian Hope* (New York: Hunt & Eaton, 1891), 124: "The burial-place of so famous a man, adored by some, hated by others, would almost certainly be known."

639. Crossan, *Historical Jesus*, 394. Cf. Lüdemann, *Resurrection*, 44: "As neither the disciples nor Jesus' next of kin bothered about Jesus' body, it is hardly conceivable that they could have been informed about the resting place of the corpse."

13:27–29 ("the residents of Jerusalem and their leaders...laid him in a tomb").[640] If, in agreement with Matt 27:60, the place was Joseph's family's tomb, there is no reason to suppose that its location would have been a secret.[641] If, against Matt 27:60, Joseph laid Jesus in one of the burial caves set aside for criminals, close to the place of their execution, then its location would have been public knowledge.

11. One final point. According to Lüdemann, burial in a Jewish cemetery for criminals is "almost impossible, as Jesus was not executed by the Jewish authorities."[642] This remark is injudicious. (a) Even though the Romans crucified Jesus, there is evidence that they did so with the approval of some Jewish leaders, who would surely have followed the legal proceedings and execution with interest. (b) Given the Jewish tradition of burying even criminals, nothing prohibits us from imagining that, if the political situation allowed, some religious authorities would have asked the Romans for the body of a crucified Jew (see pp. 359–61), which is precisely what Mark's story of Joseph of Arimathea presumes happened. (c) If those requesting a body from the Romans regarded the victim as a criminal, as presumably most of the Sanhedrin regarded Jesus, where else but in a criminal's grave would they have placed him?[643]

---

640. See also Mark 12:8 ("threw him out of the vineyard"), which may presuppose a shameful burial. On the possibility of a non-Synoptic source behind John 19:31, see Peder Borgen, *Logos Was the True Light and Other Essays on the Gospel of John* (Tronheim: Tapir, 1983), 68–70.

641. One might think it in favor of Matthew's version that the Synoptics seemingly have the tomb closed with a round stone (προσκυλίω in Matt 27:60; Mark 15:46; ἀποκυλίω in Matt 28:2; Mark 16:3; Luke 24:2). Before 70 CE, 98 percent of tombs in and around Jerusalem were closed with square blocking stones. Rounded stones, which became popular only in the late Roman and Byzantine periods, were rare, being found only with elaborate tombs for the rich. See Amos Kloner, "Did a Rolling Stone Close Jesus' Tomb?" *BAR* 22 (1999): 23–29, 26. So if there was a round stone, one could think that the tomb belonged to Joseph and that he was rich (cf. Matt 27:57). But there are two other options here. (1) Kloner suggests that προσκυλίω and ἀποκυλίω could refer to rolling or moving an unrounded object. This seems plausible; cf. Josh 10:18 LXX; 2 Kgs 9:33 LXX; Diodorus Siculus 17.68.2. (2) The tradition of a rounded block (not in John; cf. 20:1) could be legendary and reflect a desire to dramatize Jesus' burial.

642. Lüdemann, *Resurrection*, 44.

643. I remain with two unanswered questions. (1) What is the meaning of Mark's τολμήσας ("dared," 15:43)? Does it reflect the fact (or is it rather Mark's guess?) that because Jesus was executed for high treason the Romans would be expected to deny him burial altogether? (2) Did Joseph, despite the silence of our sources, also bury the two criminals crucified with Jesus? If so, why did the church not introduce Isa 53:9 ("made his grave with the wicked") into the story? If not, why did Joseph bury only Jesus? Was he sympathetic after all — criminals were probably not buried in caves — or were three different members of the Sanhedrin responsible for three different burials?

Excursus 3
THE DISCIPLES AND BEREAVEMENT

I have, in discussing the resurrection, observed certain points of similitude between reports of postmortem encounters with Jesus and visions of the recently departed. Such comparison is perhaps only part of a larger picture, for there are additional possible parallels between the experiences of the disciples after the crucifixion and the typical experiences of people after the loss of a loved one. This is a topic that, to my knowledge, few in the guild, other than Lüdemann, have thought much about.[644] The only extended treatment known to me is that of Nicholas Peter Harvey, *Death's Gift: Chapters on Resurrection and Bereavement*.[645] This, however, is a theological and even devotional contribution, not an historian's reconstruction.[646] So in this brief excursus I should like to suggest tentatively and with due caution that the recent literature on bereavement may offer some new ways of conceptualizing certain aspects of Christian origins.

Here at the outset, however, I must address two obvious objections. The first is that it is inappropriate to compare the situation of ordinary people in bereavement with the situation of Jesus' disciples, whose "mourning and weeping" (Ps.-Mark 16:10) were so soon turned into joy. The disciples saw the risen Jesus, they knew his abiding presence, and their sadness became thanksgiving. How then can we suppose them in any way akin to average people suffering the loss of a close friend or family member?

The problem with this protest is that it misapprehends the nature of the disciples' situation. The joy brought by belief in the resurrection did not obliterate the memory that Jesus had been publicly humiliated and

---

644. See Lüdemann, *Resurrection*, esp. 97–100. (Kari Syreeni, "In Memory of Jesus: Grief Work in the Gospels," *BibInt* 12 (2004): 175–97, appeared too late for me to consider herein.)

645. Nicholas Peter Harvey, *Death's Gift: Chapters on Resurrection and Bereavement* (London: Epworth, 1985).

646. A more academic presentation is Harvey's article, "Frames of Reference for the Resurrection," *SJT* 42 (1989): 335–39. On 338 he argues for placing "the origin of resurrection faith squarely in the setting of the disciples' bereavement"; but the thought remains undeveloped in this article. Samuel Vollenweider, "Ostern — der denkwürdige Ausgang einer Krisenerfahrung," *TZ* 49 (1993): 34–53, also has some preliminary reflections on our subject. The epilogue on "The Death of Jesus and the Grief of the Disciples (John 16)" in Yorick Spiegel, *The Grief Process: Analysis and Counseling* (Nashville: Abingdon, 1977), 343–48, offers an interpretation of John 16, not a reconstruction of what really happened after Good Friday.

tortured to death.[647] Nor did the appearances, whatever view we take of their nature, restore things to the way they were before. Jesus, although perceived to be present in a new way, remained absent in the old way. A profound deprivation remained. His followers had to make decisions without his counsel. They had to fashion new roles for themselves in a world that was different without him. And they had to undergo a process of internalization, had to learn how to transform an external relationship into an internal image and memory. So when Jesus died, some things died for good with him and never came back. In all this, as also in their need to find meaning in his tragic end, the disciples were not so different from others who have had to come to terms with the premature or painful death of a respected and loved companion. Surely, then, we might expect them to have had some of the same thoughts, to have exhibited some of the same behavior, and to have suffered some of the same stress as other people in not wholly dissimilar situations.

A second possible protest against thinking about the disciples in terms of common bereavement as analyzed by modern psychologists is that we cannot compare first-century Mediterranean Jews with modern Western individuals, as though human nature were static, impervious to cultural influence. In response, I admit that my points of comparison are inevitably based upon data gathered from the contemporary world. Yet the few generalizations I have to make can hardly be regarded as culturally specific. While it is true enough that mourning behaviors differ from place to place and time to time,[648] "intercultural and intracultural differences appear to be more related to bereavement rituals and practices rather than to basic human emotional responses";[649] and the five points that I wish to focus on — sensing an invisible presence, suffering guilt, feeling anger, idealizing the dead, and recollecting one recently deceased — are scarcely restricted to the modern Western world but are

---

647. Relevant here is Harvey, *Death's Gift*, 67: "Joy is not an alternative to grief as a response to bereavement. There is an interaction between the two which does not conform to any neat pattern of joy succeeding sorrow as the end-point of a process."

648. See Kathy Charmaz, Glennys Howarth, and Allan Kellehear, eds., *The Unknown Country: Death in Australia, Britain and the USA* (Houndmills, Basingstoke, Hampshire: Macmillan, 1997); and Donald Irish, Kathleen F. Lundquist, and Vivian Jenkins Nelsen, *Ethnic Variation in Dying, Death, and Grief: Diversity in Universality* (Washington, DC: Taylor & Francis, 1993).

649. Susan Klein and David A. Alexander, "Good Grief: A Medical Challenge," *Trauma* 5 (2003): 266.

rather cross-cultural phenomena.[650] With this in mind, then, I make the following exploratory suggestions:

1. Early Christians conceptualized part of their religious experience as the presence of Jesus. In Matt 18:20, Jesus says that, "Where two or three are gathered in my name, I am there among them"; and in 28:20 he promises, "I am with you always, to the end of the age." In Gal 2:20, Paul writes, "Christ... lives in me," and in Rom 8:10 he appears to say the same of his readers: "Christ is in you." For the first Christians, Jesus was, despite the crucifixion, not absent but present.

My guess is that this theologoumenon of Jesus' abiding presence goes back to the very beginnings of the Palestinian Jesus movement, to the days and weeks after the crucifixion. This is in part because those who have recently suffered the loss of a loved one commonly sense that individual's continued presence. The experience, defined by Rees as "a strong impression of the near presence of the deceased which is not associated with any auditory, visual or tactile hallucination,"[651] is so common that the psychologists now have a standard abbreviation for it: SOP (sense of presence).[652] Here are some representative comments from a few survivors:[653]

- I had a feeling that he was with me and the feeling stayed with me for about a year. It was like having a comfortable shawl around me. Even though I was anxious, I felt he was with me.

- It was like the phantom pain of my limb loss. The limb was still there even though it wasn't. It was the same with Phil.

---

650. On bereavement patterns that are more or less stable across cultures, see Maurice Eisenbruch, "Cross-Cultural Aspects of Bereavement. II: Ethnic and Cultural Variations in the Development of Bereavement Practices," *Culture, Medicine and Psychiatry* 8 (1994): 315–47; Dennis Klass, "Cross-Cultural Models of Grief: The State of the Field," *Omega* 39 (1999): 153–78; and the follow-up articles by Colin Murray Parkes and Dennis Klass in *Omega* 41 (2000): 323–26 and 327–30 respectively; Beverley Raphael, *The Anatomy of Bereavement* (New York: Basic Books, 1983), 63–65; and Paul C. Rosenblatt, R. Patricia Walsh, and Douglas A. Jackson, *Grief and Mourning in Cross-Cultural Perspective* (New Haven: Human Relations Area Files, 1976), esp. their conclusion on 124. Some aspects of bereavement — shock, denial, pining, depression, for instance — even appear to cross species lines; see John Bowlby, "The Process of Mourning," *International Journal of Psychoanalysis* 42 (1961): 328–31.

651. Rees, *Death*, 188.

652. See further S. Zisook and S. R. Shuchter, "Major Depression Associated with Widowhood," *American Journal of Geriatric Psychiatry* 1 (1993): 316–26.

653. The first two quotations are from Carol Staudacher, *Beyond Grief: A Guide for Recovering from the Death of a Loved One* (Oakland, CA: New Harbinger, 1987), 8–9; the next three are from Rees, *Death*, 190–92.

- He's always with me.

- She did come last week. She was there in spirit. I was surprised.

- I feel that no harm can come to me because he is always around me.

- From time to time, since the deaths of both of my grandfathers, I have had the feeling of the sense of their presence in my bedroom just before going to sleep.... I just feel they are near, standing next to the bed. It makes me feel reassured that maybe they're looking after me.[654]

- I always feel the presence of my father in fearful situations. I am more accepting of his death because I know he is around me when I need him.

- I had this feeling that Matt was there in the room. I tried to shrug it off. As I turned to my left to look at Alice and Marie, they were both looking at me, wearing the most unusual expressions. The silence seemed forever until I said, "Do you feel what I feel?" Almost in unison they nodded their heads and said: "Yes." We all felt he was there.

- It was as if the room filled with his presence, a presence almost palpable, as vivid and as real as if he had just physically entered the room, spoken to me, or touched my shoulder.[655]

- All that talk about "feeling that he is closer to us than before" isn't just talk. It's just what it does feel like — I can't put it into words.[656]

- When my father died, I had a feeling of his presence. I knew that he was not dead but alive.[657]

654. This and the next two quotations are from LaGrand, *Communication*, 43–44.
655. Finley, *Whispers*, 168.
656. *Letters of C. S. Lewis* (ed. W. H. Lewis; New York: Harcourt, Brace & World, 1966), 206. For additional reports and discussion, see Gillian Bennett, *Traditions of Belief: Women and the Supernatural* (London: Penguin, 1987), 65–80; Roberta Dew Conant, "Memories of the Death and Life of a Spouse: The Role of Images and Sense of Presence in Grief," in Klass, Silverman, and Nickman, *Continuing Bonds*, 179–96; S. Datson and S. J. Marwit, "Personality Constructs and Perceived Presence of Deceased Loved Ones," *Death Studies* 21 (1997): 131–46; Devers, "Experiencing the Deceased," 23–24, 59–60; Torill Christine Lindström, "Experiencing the Presence of the Dead: Discrepancies in 'the Sensing Experience' and their Psychological Concomitants," *Omega* 31 (1995): 11–21; Green and McCreery, *Apparitions*, 118–22; Ira O. Glick, Robert S. Weiss, and Colin Murray Parkes, *The First Year of Bereavement* (New York: John Wiley, 1974), 146–49; William James, *The Varieties of Religious Experience* (New York: Mentor, 1958), 61–65; C. S. Lewis, *A Grief Observed* (New York: Seabury, 1961), 57–58; Marris, *Widows*, 15, 2–22, 24.
657. From an interview in L. Eugene Thomas, "Reflections on Death by Spiritually Mature Elders," *Omega* 29 (1994): 182. The speaker continues: "So I don't question the resurrection,

As with visions of the newly departed, the explanation of these experiences is the subject of debate.[658] But all that matters for our immediate purpose is that the experience itself is both real and common, and this may go some way toward supplying a plausible experiential setting for the early Christian understanding of Jesus as a sort of ubiquitous presence in which one dwells.[659] Did this not in part grow out of and/or gain confirmation from the concrete sense of Jesus' presence soon after his death? He was known to be gone yet felt to be present. His disciples experienced him as "still caring for them, watching out for their welfare, and protecting them."[660]

2. Jesus' end likely fostered guilt as well as sadness. The disciples had forsaken their master, who had died without them. Peter had added verbal insult to cowardly injury by denying that he knew his companion and leader. If Jesus ever declared that whoever denied him would be denied before the angels of God, the avowal must have hung heavily over those who had gone up with him from Galilee and Jerusalem, only to abandon him in his hour of crisis. Belief in his resurrection would not, moreover, in and of itself have erased the unpleasant facts. On the contrary, Jesus' resurrection would have underscored his followers' failure: they had forsaken the one whom God had vindicated. To the public dishonor of having a friend and teacher crucified, the disciples had heaped shame upon themselves by their failure of nerve. The week of Passover, even after Easter, or maybe even especially after Easter, likely left them not only confused but also bearing a measure of guilt, left them mulling over what might have been and uncertain about what might be.[661]

All this matters for us because bereavement is more often than not the occasion for regret and so guilt. When the dead leave us, we are left with ourselves, and we typically end up asking what we could have done to make things better, or regretting what we did to hurt the one

---

since I have experienced a form of resurrection with him. I think this is the nature of the resurrection in the New Testament. No one saw the raised body; they felt Jesus' presence, and this changed their lives."

658. For discussion and a conjectured neurological etiology, see Michael A. Persinger, "The Sensed Presence within Experimental Settings: Implications for the Male and Female Concept of Self," *Journal of Psychology* 137, no. 1 (2003): 5–16.

659. On the conception itself, see C. F. D. Moule, *The Origin of Christology* (Cambridge: Cambridge University Press, 1977), 47–96.

660. The quotation is from Miriam S. Moss and Sidney Z. Moss, "Some Aspects of the Elderly Widow(er)'s Persistent Tie with the Deceased Spouse," *Omega* 15 (1984–85): 200.

661. Cf. Harvey, *Death's Gift*, 99.

we loved.[662] Sentences that begin with "I should have" or "If only" can be recurrent. "The unfinished work, the unspoken farewell, the guilt of not being with the deceased or of being in some way responsible" for his or her death "can cause deep distress."[663] The upshot, in Harvey's words, is that, in bereavement, "characteristic forms of what might be called symptomatic guilt" appear — "a sense of hopeless unworthiness in relation to the dead person, a sense of having somehow hastened or caused the death, and a guilty reaction to one's own resentment at being abandoned by the person who has died."[664]

The first weeks and months of bereavement, then, frequently become a time of self-reproach. Surveys show that, at least in the modern world, up to half of the grieving wrestle with serious guilt in one way or another — and all the more so when great pain or tragedy is involved, as was the case with Jesus.[665] Psychologists indeed speak of something called "survivor guilt," which emanates from "the belief that one death has somehow been exchanged for another, that one person was allowed to live at the cost of another's life."[666] A parent will say, "I wish I'd died instead of my son."[667]

This psychological syndrome becomes intriguing for the study of early Christianity when one recalls the emphasis upon the forgiveness of sins in early church tradition. Even if Jesus attended to this subject in the Lord's Prayer and some of his parables, there seems to have been a singular interest in the subject this side of Easter (cf. John 11:51; Acts 2:38; 3:19; Rom 5:8; 1 Cor 15:3; 1 Pet 3:18; etc.). One finds a natural

---

662. See, e.g., N. S. Hogan and L. DeSantis, "Adolescent Sibling Bereavement: An Ongoing Attachment," *Qualitative Health Research* 2 (1992): 159–77; and Colin Murray Parkes, *Bereavement: Studies of Grief in Adult Life* (New York: International Universities Press, 1972), 78–88. See also the examples in Marris, *Widows*, 18, 22, 25; and the moving words of Nicholas Wolterstorff, *Lament for a Son* (Grand Rapids: Eerdmans, 1987), 64–65.

663. The quoted words are from Marion Gibson, *Order from Chaos: Responding to Traumatic Events* (Birmingham, England: 1998), 63.

664. Harvey, *Death's Gift*, 104. On 51 he writes: "The bereaved person comes to see himself as in his degree a crucifier of the beloved who has died. . . . The picture of the departed one as a victim of the spirit of this world comes to occupy a central place in the bereaved's consciousness."

665. Stephen R. Shuchter, *Dimensions of Grief: Adjusting to the Death of a Spouse* (San Francisco: Jossey-Bass, 1986), 34–42. According to Staudacher, *Beyond Grief*, 20, "Those who have no guilt about the death of a loved one are in the minority."

666. Staudacher, *Beyond Grief*, 24.

667. Klein and Alexander, "Good Grief," 264. Cf. Judith Lewis Herman, *Trauma and Recovery* (New York: Basic Books, 1992), 54: "To be spared oneself, in the knowledge that others have met a worse fate, creates a severe burden of conscience. Survivors of disaster and war are haunted by images of the dying whom they could not rescue."

genesis for this keen interest among the companions of Jesus, among those who had known him and followed him, but not to the bitter end. We may assume on their parts a preoccupation with regret and guilt, with self-recrimination, so that their perceived need for forgiveness was considerable.[668] We may also assume that at the same time they had a preoccupation with the question of why, which is the human response to all tragedy: "Why did Jesus die?" or rather, "Why was he crucified?" People search for meaning in the face of death, and they especially try to make sense of tragedy. They seek to find benefit and purpose in unnatural, unexpected, and violent death.[669] It is no surprise at all, then, that some early Christians not only addressed the topic of the forgiveness of sins but also did so in a way that found meaning in the crucifixion. At least some of Jesus' followers were able to address the problem of guilt and the problem of the meaning of a violent end by relating them to each other. A death that somehow won forgiveness accomplished two things at once: it found sense in Jesus' sickening execution, and it freed his followers from the guilt of their failure.[670]

3.2 There is little need to document that early Christians idealized Jesus. Not only did they think of him as a moral model embodying virtue,[671] but 2 Cor 5:21; Heb 4:15; 7:26; and 1 Pet 2:22 make him out to be without sin (cf. Matt 3:14–15). It is an interesting question to what extent this idealization of Jesus had already begun in the pre-Easter period. I doubt that we can return much of an informed answer. But one thing we do know is that there is a strong impulse to idealize the dead.[672] Death summons recollections and at the same time rewrites

---

668. In this respect I am in partial sympathy with Lüdemann's analysis of Peter's psychological state after the crucifixion; see his *Resurrection*, 95–100.

669. Chris G. Davis, S. Nolen-Hoeksema, and J. Larson, "Making Sense of Loss and Benefiting from the Experience: Two Construals of Meaning," *Journal of Personality and Social Psychology* 59 (1998): 561–74; Robert A. Neimeyer and Adam Anderson, "Meaning Reconstruction Theory," in *Loss and Grief: A Guide for Human Services Practitioners* (ed. Neil Thompson; New York: Palgrave, 2002), 45–64; C. L. Park and Susan Folkman, "Meaning in the Context of Stress and Coping," *Review of General Psychology* 2 (1997): 115–44; Spiegel, *Grief*, 243–56.

670. I reject the argument that the understanding of Jesus' death as an atonement or substitution cannot go back to the earliest Palestinian community; see Davies and Allison, *Matthew*, 3:97–99.

671. See my article, "Structure, Biographical Impulse, and the *Imitatio Christi*," in *Studies in Matthew: Interpretation Past and Present* (Grand Rapids: Baker Academic, 2005).

672. See esp. Helna Znaniecka Lopata, "Widowhood and Husband Sanctification," in Klass, Silverman, and Nickman, *Continuing Bonds*, 149–62. Cf. Stephen R. Shuchter and Sidney Zisook, "Widowhood: The Continuing Relationship with the Dead Spouse," *Bulletin of the Menninger Clinic* 52 (1988): 275–76.

them, and distance often brings a perspective that exalts. The following comes from an interview with a man who had lost his wife:

Bereaved husband: Looking back over the past — what a perfect woman she was.

Interviewer: Flaws?

Husband: No, as a matter of fact, we were married for thirty-five years and never had a bad argument.... I'd get mad sometimes at something she might do, you know, or something she had done. And she'd always smooth my ruffled feathers and I'd be ashamed of myself.

Interviewer: She didn't have any faults?

Husband: I never knew of any.[673]

Although this humorous example is extreme, it well illustrates a very human tendency, and there is no need to doubt that, whatever our own estimation of Jesus, his tragic death and the remembrance that followed in its wake must have augmented the disciples' idealization of their master. Such idealization on their part clearly led, as it has with others, to a desire to incorporate his virtues, heed his speech, and follow his example. Modern studies have shown how a deceased loved one regularly becomes an "internal referee,"[674] a role model, a source of guidance, and a measure of value.[675]

4. If death can turn an accusing finger inward and so foster guilt, it can also, above all in cases in which mourners have been highly dependent upon the deceased, turn an accusing finger outward and so foster anger.[676] There may even be biological changes that inhibit impulse

---

673. Shuchter, *Dimensions of Grief*, 156–58.

674. John Bowlby and Colin Murray Parkes, "Separation and Loss within the Family," in *The Child within the Family* (ed. E. J. Anthony and C. Koupernik; New York: John Wiley, 1970), 213.

675. Claude L. Normand, Phyllis R. Silverman, and Steven L. Nickman, "Bereaved Children's Changing Relationship with the Deceased," in Klass, Silverman, and Nickman, *Continuing Bonds*, 87–111; Samuel J. Marwit and Dennis Klass, "Grief and the Role of the Inner Representation of the Deceased," in Klass, Silverman, and Nickman, *Continuing Bonds*, 297–309.

676. Cf. Klein and Alexander, "Good Grief," 264; and the discussion in Rosenblatt, Walsh, and Jackson, *Grief and Mourning*, 28–47. The analysis of Elisabeth Kübler-Ross, in *On Death and Dying* (New York: Simon & Schuster, 1969), of the various stages through which

control.[677] Loss of a loved one in any event may make one feel the unfairness of the world, or it may move one to blame God or others, above all if the passing away comes before old age.[678] Whoever is blamed, people can find themselves saying, "I feel angry that it happened."[679]

What does all this have to do with early Christianity? There is no sign of anger in the short, stereotyped narratives of Easter that have come down to us. The disciples, however, would not have been human if they had not felt anger and resentment toward those they held responsible for crucifying the man to whom they were devoted. "Love your enemies" (Matt 5:44) and "Whoever is angry will be liable to judgment" (cf. 5:22) may have echoed in their minds, but such words surely did not suffice to eradicate all their feelings of ill will and hostility.

This circumstance may matter because scholars have tended to hypothesize two different settings in life for the polemical material in the Gospels: either it reflects pre-Easter conflicts between Jesus and Jewish teachers, or it reflects conflict between church and synagogue from a much later period. What I should like to suggest, by way of partial correction, is that the earliest Jesus tradition could not have been devoid of all bitterness toward those thought responsible for Jesus' end, bitterness toward certain Jewish and Roman authorities — the former probably more than the latter[680] — and anyone who could be associated with them.[681] Perhaps indeed the most intense feelings of hostility welled up right after the crucifixion, not days or weeks before or years or decades after. The torture of a friend and revered leader, and all the more one thought vindicated by the Deity, is no recipe for equanimity. Surely, then, the earliest post-Easter Jesus movement was strongly inclined to

---

those informed of their own deaths typically pass, prominently features anger, and many have recognized the resemblances between her proposals and aspects of bereavement.

677. B. van der Kolk and J. Saporta, "The Biological Response to Psychic Trauma: Mechanisms and Treatment of Intrusion and Numbing," *Anxiety Research* 4 (1991): 199–212.

678. See Staudacher, *Beyond Grief*, 10–16; and the section on "search for the guilty" in Spiegel, *Grief*, 243–56.

679. This quotation is from Louis A. Gamino, Nancy S. Hogan, and Kenneth W. Sewell, "Feeling the Absence: A Content Analysis from the Scott and White Grief Study," *Death Studies* 26 (2002): 805. See further James R. Averill, "Grief: Its Nature and Significance," *Psychological Bulletin* 70 (1968): 737–38.

680. Cf. Spiegel, *Grief*, 247: "Interviews during the bombing attacks on England in World War II revealed that the English people were filled with reproaches against their own authorities much more than against the Germans."

681. For related thoughts see Kalman J. Kaplan, "The Death of Jesus, Christian Salvation, and Easter-Week Atrocities against Jews: A Suicidological Approach," *Omega* 36 (1997–98): 63–75.

remember incidents in which Jesus bests his opponents and to create stories in which they appear in a very bad light. Perhaps some of the controversy stories and certain unpleasant portions of the passion narrative were first composed within the context of an enmity that, despite belief in the resurrection, must nonetheless have followed in the wake of Jesus' horrific end.

5. In their desire for continued communion, those who have lost a loved one typically respond by seeking out others who knew the deceased so that stories can be shared. Bereavement brings "remembering, not forgetting."[682] It elicits eulogies, memorials, epitaphs. Further, shortly after a death, memories and imaginations often converge upon a life's end, upon "the events leading up to the loss."[683] This is especially true when death has been unexpected, premature, or violent.[684] As one woman survivor put it, "I go through that last week in the hospital again and again; it seems photographed on my mind."[685] The newly bereaved commonly "recall in infinite detail the actions taken by them or by the dead person in the days and hours before the death."[686]

We can here supplement the secondary literature[687] with our own experience, for most of us can recall how, after the death of a loved one

---

682. G. E. Valliant, "Loss as a Metaphor for Attachment," *American Journal of Psychoanalysis* 45 (1985): 63.

683. Parkes, *Bereavement*, 40.

684. Cf. Jane Littlewood, *Aspects of Grief: Bereavement in Adult Life* (London: Tavistock, 1992), 46: "Events leading up to the death may be obsessively reviewed in an increasingly desperate attempt to understand what has happened." Also see Edward K. Rynearson, *Retelling Violent Death* (Philadelphia: Brunner-Routledge, 2001), xiv: "The continued retelling of a violent death is fundamental to anyone who loved the deceased."

685. Parkes, *Bereavement*, 74. Cf. Conant, "Memories," 185; and Moss and Moss, "Persistent Tie," 197: "Recurring memories of the ravages of illness and death of a spouse, especially the last moments spent together, are indelible. These may stand in the way of more fond and cherished recollections of the deceased when he or she was happy and in good health."

686. Gibson, *Order from Chaos*, 63.

687. See Colin Murray Parkes, " 'Seeking' and 'Finding' a Lost Object: Evidence from Recent Studies of the Reaction to Bereavement," *Social Science and Medicine* 4 (1970): 190: preoccupation with thoughts of the lost person and the events leading up to the loss is the rule; and esp. Tony Walter, "A New Model of Grief: Bereavement and Biography," *Mortality* 1 (1996): 7–25; also the response of Margaret Stroebe, "From Mourning and Melancholia to Bereavement and Biography: An Assessment of Walter's New Model of Grief," *Mortality* 2 (1997): 255–62; and Walter's response, "Letting Go and Keeping Hold: A Reply to Stroebe," *Mortality* 2 (1997): 263–66. In the first article, Walter argues that the purpose of grief is "the construction of a durable biography that enables the living to integrate the memory of the dead into their ongoing lives" (7), and that "the biographical imperative — the need to make sense of self and others in a continuing narrative — is the motor that drives bereavement behavior" (20).

who was an important member of a larger community, people got together in the days and weeks that followed and shared their recollections
of the departed, including the final days. There was a preoccupation with
memory and new memory construction. Stories were told and sayings
repeated. Attachment lingered. There was a need to put the remembered
fragments together and to construct some sort of overview that brought
to light the meaning of the life in its entirety.[688] Without tributes, the
funeral would certainly have been incomplete or even offensive. Unless
one has left an autobiography, it is the survivors, not the deceased, who
put together the memoirs.

It was, we may imagine, not otherwise with the disciples, a circumstance that may well give us the initial *Sitz im Leben* for the construction
of a post-Easter Jesus tradition. When Jesus' followers were bereft of
their friend's physical presence, they would naturally, when together,
have remembered him. Anything else would have been abnormal. Such
recollection, furthermore, was almost certainly one of their collective
preoccupations; and it would have included above all the things that
Jesus said and did toward the end of his life, or what they imagined
that he then said and did.[689] For not only does a tragic, violent death
typically draw attention to itself in powerfully emotional ways and so
both stimulate imaginations and create commanding memories. It also is
a healthy human instinct to come to terms with the horrific by creatively
reclaiming it. Reliving past trauma can be life-enhancing.[690] Surely, then,
it is no coincidence that all four of the canonical Gospels concentrate
on the last few days of Jesus — I suggest that this focus goes back to
the birth of the post-Easter Jesus tradition — and that the first extended
narrative about him was probably a pre-Markan passion narrative.[691]
After violent death "the story of the dying may become preoccupying,"
so that it "eclipses the retelling of their living — the way they died takes
precedence over the way they lived"; only later is the rest of the life

---

688. Cf. Parkes, *Bereavement*, 70.

689. See Rynearson, *Violent Death*, for how people will imagine a violent death at which
they were not present.

690. Cf. Harvey, *Death's Gift*, 101; also J. W. Pennebaker, "Putting Stress into Words:
Health, Linguistic, and Therapeutic Implications," *Behavioral Research and Therapy* 31
(1993): 539–48.

691. See esp. Gerd Theissen, "A Major Unit (the Passion Story) and the Jerusalem Community in the Years 40–50 C.E.," in his *The Gospels in Context: Social and Political History
in the Synoptic Tradition* (Minneapolis: Fortress, 1991), 166–99.

remembered.[692] All this is to say that the evolution of the Jesus tradition — as reconstructed by many modern scholars, according to which large portions grew backward from the telling of his end — matches a pattern, a process of memorialization, commonly found in bereavement.

Before closing, I add that remembering Jesus was not just a normal psychological reflex to his death: it was also a theological necessity occasioned by the resurrection. The proclamation "God raised Jesus from the dead" could not have meant anything to anybody unless Jesus were a known entity. Those who proclaimed the resurrection were saying nothing unless they were remembering who Jesus was before he died, and those who heard their proclamation could not have understood it unless they too remembered the man or were informed about him. The resurrection was not a statement about a blank cipher. It was inevitably a statement about a particular, historical individual and so inevitably an invitation to remember him and his cause. To understand the point, all one has to do is substitute another name. If the first Christians had gone around saying, "God raised Fred from the dead," the only sensible response, the only possible response, would have been, "Who the heck is Fred?"

•

Shortly after his death, the followers of Jesus saw him again, sensed his invisible presence, overcame their guilt by finding sense in his tragic end, idealized and internalized their teacher, and remembered his words and deeds. Given that similar circumstances often attend the bereaved in general, it may be that, to some extent, Christian theology and experience were summoned forth and shaped not just by the pre-Easter Jesus and belief in his postmortem vindication, but also by the psychological process that trailed his disciples' loss. Indeed, it may be no exaggeration to say that the Christian church is in some ways the *Wirkungsgeschichte* of what the disciples' bereavement wrought.

---

692. See esp. Rynearson, *Violent Death*; the quotations are from ix and x respectively.

INDEX OF SCRIPTURE

INDEX OF MODERN NAMES

389

Batdorf, Irwin W., 18 n.72
Bauckham, Richard, 62 n.29, 90 n.112, 114 n.7, 236 n.141, 243 n.178, 251 n.210, 253 n.229, 262 n.266, 304, 327 n.508 n.509, 328, 329 n.513
Bauer, J. B., 232 n.129
Baumann, Eberhard, 180 n.137
Baumbach, G., 26
Baxter, Richard, 95
Beardsworth, Timothy, 278 n.317
Becker, Jürgen, 36 n.35, 41 n.49, 42 n.50, 74, 168, 186 n.153 n.155, 215 n.66
Beet, Joseph Agar, 362 n.638
Begg, Christopher, 308 n.429
Behrens, Hermann, 326 n.506
Bellarmine, Robert, 79 n.69
Beloff, John, 225 n.101
Bennett, Ernest, 240 n.157, 297 n.390
Bennett, Gillian, 274 n.306, 367 n.656
Bennett, Kate Mary, 274 n.306
Bennetts, H. J. T., 274 n.307, 280 n.325
Benoit, J.-D., 28 n.5, 79 n.70, 155 n.22, 158 n.46
Benoit, Pierre, 248 n.202
Benson, D. F., 266 n.280
Bentall, Richard, 242 n.173
Berdyayev, Nicolas, 98
Berger, Klaus, 209, 210 n.49
Berger, Peter, 93 n.123
Bernstein, Alan E., 63 n.32
Bertram, Georg, 9 n.33
Betz, Hans Dieter, 203 n.16
Betz, Otto, 25, 172 n.103, 248 n.199
Beza, Theodore, 227 n.110
Bickermann, Elias, 301 n.401
Bidez, Joseph, 115 n.8
Bieringer, R., 210 n.49, 242 n.172, 252 n.216, 312 n.442
Bingham, Alfred J., 124 n.47
Black, J. Sutherland, 204 n.21
Blake, William, 16
Blanc, Cécile, 204 n.22
Blank, J., 26
Blinzler, Josef, 41, 44 n.56, 333 n.528
Bliss, Shepherd, 281 n.326
Blomberg, Craig, 255 n.239
Blondel, C., 115 n.8
Blunden, Cathy, 273 n.306
Blunt, A. W. F., 131 n.81
Bockmuehl, Markus, 126, 170, 171 n.96 n.97, 245, 322 n.483
Bode, E. L., 231 n.126, 303 n.411, 313 n.448, 316 n.460, 335 n.540 n.541, 336 n.544
Boggs, James, 222 n.91
Boissard, Edmond, 91 n.115

Boismard, Marie-Emile, 286 n.344
Bolingbroke, Lord, 12, 124 n.47
Bolt, Peter G., 301 n.401
Bonhoeffer, Dietrich, 342–43
Bonnard, E., 115 n.8
Booth, Edwin Prince, 4 n.15
Booth, Roger, 176 n.116, 284
Borg, Marcus, 1 n.1, 11, 13, 18 n.70, 63 n.32, 78
Borgen, Peder, 300 n.399, 363 n.640
Borges, Jorge Luis, 35, 36, 56
Bornkamm, Günther, 25, 41 n.49, 356 n.609
Borse, U., 253 n.226
Bostock, D. Gerald, 202 n.10
Bourne, Henry, 295 n.380
Bousset, W., 81, 112 n.2, 210 n.49, 232 n.132, 317 n.465, 333 n.533
Bovon, François, 251 n.210
Bowker, J. 26
Bowlby, John, 366 n.650, 371 n.674
Bowman, John Wick, 18 n.72, 25, 128
Box, G. H., 69
Boyarin, Daniel, 333 n.530
Boyd, Gregory A., 2 n.8
Boyd, W. J., 63 n.32
Braaten, C. E., 1 n.1
Bradley, James V., 136 n.99
Brandon, S. G. F., 26
Branscomb, B. H., 24
Braud, William, 295 n.379
Braude, Stephen E., 225 n.101
Braun, F.-M., 24, 25
Braun, Herbert, 26, 175 n.110
Brewer, E. Cobham, 279 n.320, 308 n.432
Broad, C. D., 200, 218 n.78, 226, 270 n.292 n.293
Brock, Ann Graham, 251, 252
Brock, Sebastin, 61 n.21, 88 n.104, 94 n.134
Broer, Ingo, 207 n.35, 210 n.49, 303 n.412, 355 n.606 n.607, 357 n.613
Brooke, George J., 254 n.229
Brown, Colin, 14, 16, 115 n.9
Brown, Raymond E., 74 n.55, 191 n.171, 228 n.119, 245 n.186, 256 n.241, 257 n.245 n.246, 258, 262 n.264, 325 n.499, 335, 336, 354 n.603, 355 n.604, 357 n.614, 358 n.619
Brown, Warren S., 219 n.81
Brownlee, W. H., 181 n.143
Brox, Norbert, 54 n.75
Brucker, Ralph, 12 n.51, 40 n.45, 51 n.70, 75 n.59, 178 n.125
Brunner, Emil, 81 n.79, 91 n.117, 287 n.348
Buchanan, George Wesley, 79 n.69, 169 n.85
Budge, E. A. Wallis, 61 n.21